The Divorce Revolution

The Divorce Revolution

The Unexpected
Social and Economic Consequences
for Women and Children in America

LENORE J. WEITZMAN

THE FREE PRESS
A Division of Macmillan, Inc.
NEW YORK

Collier Macmillan Publishers
LONDON

The Free Press
A Division of Macmillan, Inc.
866 Third Avenue, New York, N.Y. 10022

Collier Macmillan Canada, Inc.

First Free Press Paperback Edition 1987

Printed in the United States of America

printing number hardcover

   2   3   4   5   6   7   8   9   10

printing number paperback

   2   3   4   5   6   7   8   9   10

Library of Congress Cataloging in Publication Data

Weitzman, Lenore J.
   The divorce revolution.

   1. Divorce—Law and legislation—United States.
2. Custody of children—United States. 3. Divorced
women—United States—Social conditions. 4. Divorced
women—United States—Economic conditions. I. Title.
KF535.W43   1985   346.7301′66   85-6868
ISBN 0-02-934710-6   347.306166
ISBN 0-02-934711-4 pbk.

For my mother,
Ethel Goldberg Weitzman,
with love

Contents

Introduction

WHEN I BEGAN THIS RESEARCH, California had just instituted the first no-fault divorce law in the United States. Never suspecting that the entire landscape of American family law would be transformed in a mere decade, I set out to study the impact of the new law on the legal process of divorce. My original aim was to analyze court records and to interview judges, lawyers, and divorced men and women to see whether a change in the legal process of divorce could, in the words of the reformers, reduce the acrimony, hostility, and bitterness in the divorce process.

As the research unfolded it became evident that the no-fault law had done much else besides that. Without fault-based grounds for divorce, and without the need to prove adultery or mental cruelty, the reformers had not only recast the *psychological* context of divorce (and had in fact reduced some of the hostility and acrimony it generated); they had also transformed the *economic consequences* of divorce and, in the process, redefined the rights and responsibilities of husbands and wives in legal marriage.

Ends may influence beginnings. In a society where one-half of all new marriages are expected to end in divorce, a radical change in the rules for ending marriage inevitably affects the rules for marriage itself and the intentions and expectations of those who enter it. Thus instead of a narrow study of changes in the legal process of divorce, this became a broad study of divorce law reform within the larger context of fundamental alterations in both the legal and social structure of marriage.

California's no-fault divorce law launched a legal revolution. Before 1970 every state required fault-based grounds for a divorce. One party had to be judged guilty of some marital fault, such as adultery or cruelty, before a divorce could be granted. When California rejected this traditional system in 1970, it instituted the first no-fault divorce law in the Western world. The new law permitted either party to divorce when "irreconcilable differences caused the breakdown of their marriage." With this seemingly simple move, California pioneered sweeping reforms that quickly spread to other states. While not all states adopted the California model of totally abolishing fault, nevertheless, within a single decade, every state but South Dakota and Illinois had adopted some form of no-fault divorce law.[1]

These no-fault divorce laws have shifted the focus of the legal process from moral questions of fault and responsibility to economic issues of ability to pay and financial need. Today fewer husbands and wives fight about who-did-what-to-whom; they are more likely to argue about the value of marital property, what she can earn, and what he can pay.

The increased importance of these economic issues suggests the need for more complete information on the economic aspects of divorce. Although we know that legal decisions about property and support inevitably shape the future of divorcing couples and their children, we know very little about how these economic decisions are made and even less about their subsequent social and economic effects.

This book seeks to fill that gap. It examines the economic decisions that are made at the point of divorce—decisions about property, alimony, and child support—and traces the impact of these decisions on the postdivorce lives of men, women, and children.

No-fault's standards for alimony and property awards have shaped radically different futures for divorced men on the one hand, and for divorced women and their children on the other. Women, and the minor children in their households, typically experience a sharp decline in their standard of living after divorce. Men, in contrast, are usually much better off and have a higher standard of living as a result of divorce.

The Unexpected Consequences

How could a simple change in the rules for divorce have such far-reaching effects? Why would a legal reform designed to create more equitable settlements end up impoverishing divorced women and their children?

When I initiated this research I assumed, in the optimistic spirit of the reformers, that the "California experiment" with no-fault divorce could only have positive results. It would not only eliminate the sham testimony and restore dignity to the courts; it would also facilitate fair and equitable economic settlements. The reduced hostility and acrimony that the new law sought would, I believed, also facilitate the parties' ability to cooperate in postdivorce parenting. In addition, the law's aim of legal equality for men and women promised to eliminate the anachronistic legal assumptions about women's subordinate roles and to recognize wives as full equals in the marital partnership.

Yet these modern and enlightened reforms have had unanticipated, unintended, and unfortunate consequences. In the pages that follow we shall see how gender-neutral rules—rules designed to treat men and women "equally" have in practice served to deprive divorced women (especially older homemakers and mothers of young children) of the legal and financial protections that the old law provided. Instead of recognition for their contributions as homemakers and mothers, and instead of compensation for the years of lost opportunities and impaired earning capacities, these women now face a divorce law that treats them "equally" and expects them to be equally capable of supporting themselves after divorce.

Since a woman's ability to support herself is likely to be impaired during marriage, especially if she is a full-time homemaker and mother, she may not be "equal to" her former husband at the point of divorce. Rules that treat her as if she is equal simply serve to deprive her of the financial support she needs. In addition, rules that require an equal division of marital property often force the sale of the family home, and compound the financial dislocation and impoverishment of women and children.

When the legal system treats men and women "equally" at divorce, it ignores the very real economic inequalities that marriage creates. It also ignores the economic inequalities between men and women in the larger society.

In fact, it is marriage that itself that typically creates the different structural opportunities that men and women face at divorce. While most married women give priority to their family roles, most married men give priority to their careers. Even if both of them are in the labor force it is more likely that she will forego further education and training while he gains additional education and on-the-job experience. As a result her earning capacity is likely to be impaired while his is enhanced. Even in two-career families most married couples give priority to the husband's career.

If the divorce rules do not give her a share of his enhanced earning capacity (through alimony and child support awards), and if divorce rules expect her to enter the labor market as she is, with few skills, outdated experience, no seniority, and no time for retraining, and if she continues to have the major burden of caring for young children after divorce, it is easy to understand why the divorced woman is likely to be much worse off than her former husband. Faced with expectations that she will be "equally" responsible for the financial support of their children and herself, she has been unequally disadvantaged by marriage and has fewer resources to meet these expectations.

The result is often hardship, impoverishment, and disillusionment for divorced women (and their children). This research shows that, on the average, divorced women and the minor children in their households experience a 73 percent decline in their standard of living in the first year after divorce. Their former husbands, in contrast, experience a 42 percent rise in their standard of living.

The divorced man generally finds himself much better off financially after divorce because his work and income continue uninterrupted. The courts do not typically require him to share his salary with his former wife, nor do they typically require him to contribute equally to support their children. He is therefore left with a much larger proportion of his income and a higher standard of living than he had during marriage.

Another unintended consequence of the new principle of equality results from its application to the division of marital property. Although an equal division of marital property sounds fair, when the family home is the family's only recognized asset, judges usually order it sold so that the property can be divided equally. (The traditional practice was to award it to the wife, especially if she had minor children.) The loss of the family home, and the subsequent residential moves it necessitates, disrupt children's school, neighborhood, and friendship ties, and create additional dislocations for children (and mothers) at the very point at which they most need continuity and stability.

The rules for dividing marital property often lead to another inequity: the courts systematically omit new forms of property from the pool of family assets to be divided upon divorce. Today the most valuable assets that most couples acquire during marriage are career assets—the major wage earner's salary, pension, medical insurance, education, license, the goodwill value of a business or profession, entitlements to company goods and services, and future earning power. Although there is considerable variation in the extent to which states recognize the assets (see Chapter 5), most states exclude some or all of them from the pool of property to be divided upon divorce. They thereby allow the major wage earner, typically the husband, to keep the family's most valuable assets. Thus the courts *are not,* in fact, *dividing property equally* or equitably. Rather, the current system of dividing marital property makes a mockery of the "equal" division rule.

Nor are the courts recognizing wives and mothers as equal partners in the marital partnership in alimony or spousal support awards. Even women who have been housewives and mothers in marriages of long duration, and who are fifty years old at the time of the divorce, are routinely denied the support they were promised. Although this research finds that both men and women in marriages of long duration assumed that they were forming a partnership, and both assumed that they would share equally in the fruits of their joint endeavors, when it comes to divorce *the courts are redefining* the terms of their "contract": they are treating the husband's income as "his" rather than as "theirs," and are telling her that she must find a job so that she can support herself.

The older homemaker typically feels betrayed by the new laws. She was promised, by both her husband and our society—her contract, if you prefer, both implied and expressed—that their marriage was a partnership and that he would share his income with her. Instead the courts have changed the rules in the middle of the game—after she has fulfilled her share of the bargain. (Actually, it is the last quarter of the game because she can never recapture the years that she devoted to her family and she has passed the point where she can choose another life course.)

Mothers of young children also experience great hardships as a result of the new rules. Courts award inadequate amounts of child support which leave the primary custodial parent, who is the mother in 90 percent of the divorce cases, with the major burden of supporting the children after divorce. Yet even these minimal child support awards go unpaid. Enforcement is lax and less than half of the fathers fully comply with court orders to pay child support. This research shows that men who earn between $30,000 and $50,000 a year are just as likely to fail to pay child support as those who earn less than $20,000 a year.

The net effect of the present rules for property, alimony, and child support is severe financial hardships for most divorced women and their children. They invariably experience a dramatic decline in income and a drastic decline in their standard of living. Even women who enjoyed comfortable middle- and upper-middle-class standards of living during marriage experience sharp downward mobility after divorce.*

The major economic result of the divorce law revolution is the systematic impoverishment of divorced women and their children. They have become the new poor.

While recent years have brought increased awareness of the feminization of poverty and the growth in single-parent female-headed households, what appears to be relatively unknown—or unacknowledged—is the direct link between divorce, the economic consequences of divorce, and the rise in female poverty. The high divorce rate has vastly multiplied the numbers of divorced women who are left alone to support themselves and their minor children, and the present rules for divorce settlements, leave most of these women without adequate economic resources to maintain their standard of living.

The result, in a society that expects close to 60 percent of all children born in the United States today to experience a disruption of their parents' marriage before they reach age eighteen,[2] is that we are sentencing a significant portion of the next generation of American children to periods of financial hardship.

These results are not inevitable. Nor do the findings of this research require a return to the old laws. Rather, reforms based on fairness, equity, and equality-of-results are proposed in the final chapter of this book.

The unintended economic consequences of no-fault divorce provide the first major theme of this book. The second major theme traces the effects of no-fault divorce on the institution of marriage.

---

* In fact, it is the women from families with predivorce incomes of $40,000 a year or more (and, in general, older women) who experience the greatest relative deprivation when their postdivorce standard of living is compared to that of their former husbands. (See Table 28, p. 333.)

The Transformation of Marriage

No-fault divorce has redefined the legal rights and responsibilities of husbands and wives, has altered the obligations of the marriage contract, and, as a result, is creating new norms and new expectations for marriage and family commitments in our society.

A divorce provides an important opportunity for a society to enforce marital boundaries by rewarding the marital behavior it approves, and punishing that which violates its norms. It does this by handing out legal rewards and punishments, and by ordering people to pay for their transgressions in dollars and cents. For example, if a divorce court awards alimony to a fifty-year-old woman who has spent twenty years as a homemaker and mother, it is rewarding the woman's devotion to her family and reinforcing the value of a woman's domestic activities. (It may also be punishing the husband for abandoning his wife in middle age.) But if, by contrast, the divorce court denies the housewife alimony, and tells her that she must instead get a job and support herself, the court is not only releasing the husband from his traditional responsibility for her support; it is also enforcing new expectations for husbands and wives. Although these are articulated in a divorce decree, they necessarily suggest new expectations for marriage as well.

When we change the rules for divorce—that is, when we change the rules about what is expected of husbands and wives upon divorce—we also change the rules for legal marriage: we implicitly create and "institutionalize" new norms for marriage.

Marital rules and boundaries are enforced through divorce laws in a second realm as well. Not only does divorce provide a societal forum for defining and sanctioning marital *behavior*: it also provides a societal forum for defining and allocating family wealth and *property*. As Kevin Gray, the English legal scholar, observed:

> The law regulating the spouses' property relations is fundamentally an index of social relations between the sexes. It affords a peculiar wealth of commentary on such matters as the prevailing ideology of marriage, the cultural definition of the marital roles, the social status of the married woman and the role of the state vis-à-vis the family.[3]

Rules that decide what property is his or hers or theirs implicitly define the financial provisions of the marriage contract and the relative worth being attributed to the contributions of the husband and wife. For example, divorce laws that allow a husband to keep most of the property acquired during marriage suggest that his work and his income were most important in building the family's wealth. In contrast, laws that give the housewife one-half of the marital property upon divorce suggest that her contributions to the acquisition of family assets are of equal worth.

Rules that regulate property acquired during marriage also reveal an underlying philosophy of marriage as either a temporary alliance of two separate individuals, or as a unified partnership in which the parties' individual interests and individual identities are fully merged.

In the past, and in most other societies, and even today, the transfer of family property has typically occurred at two other junctures in the family-life cycle: marriage and death. Rules governing these transfers, from bride price and dowry to primogeniture and widow's dower, have long been recognized as essential indicators of the way each society structures kinship and marriage and have been the focus of anthropological, historical, and legal scholarship.

Divorce has become an increasingly common third occasion for allocating family property in recent years, but the rules for the allocation, and the principles upon which it should be based, are in a state of flux. While mating and death have always been part of the universal human experience, and the laws and customs that govern the transfers of property which they occasion have grown and developed over centuries, a high divorce rate is a relatively recent phenomenon in our society. We are still uncertain about what rules are fair and we are still unsure about what rules foster the types of family roles and commitments that our society wants to encourage. Neither the makers of laws nor the students of society have yet had time to consider the broader implication of rules for dividing property upon divorce, and the way such rules define, control, and shape the nature of marriage in our society.

This is not to suggest that transfers of family property upon divorce have replaced those made at marriage or death. Marriage is still an important occasion for gifts and property transfers and it creates a legal entitlement to a share of one's spouse's estate. But this is a future-oriented right. In our society, most couples have little property when they first enter marriage and we do not, unlike many other societies, have the betrothed or their families arrange contracts concerning their rights to the property they expect to acquire. In fact, our emphasis on romantic love undermines an awareness of legal rules governing marriage and dissuades couples from writing an explicit agreement to alter the *de facto* legal regime.[4] Thus it is common for couples not to confront our society's legal arrangements concerning their property until a spouse dies or they face a divorce.

Over a million couples in the United States divorce each year and have to face these legal arrangements. In fact, the amount of money being transferred upon divorce now "rivals or exceeds" the amount passed by will or intestate succession in the United States.[5] This is partially a result of the sheer explosion in the divorce rate.

We now have the highest divorce rate in United States history.* Each year close to 1.2 million American marriages end in divorce, disrupting the lives of over three million men, women, and children.[8] In California alone, the courts process more than one hundred thousand divorces each year.[9] In fact, demographers project that at least half of current American marriages will eventually end in divorce.**

This means that for the first time in our history, two people entering marriage are just as likely to be parted by divorce as by death. Equally startling is the projection that by 1990 only 40 percent of the children born in the United States will spend their entire childhood living with both natural parents.[11]

These statistics reflect more than the numerical significance of divorce. They suggest its increasing social and economic impact on American family life. Yet because the increase in divorce has been so rapid and so vast, our society has just begun to face these large social implications.

The soaring divorce rate and the widespread adoption of no-fault divorce laws are two components of the divorce revolution. The third component is the changing social context of divorce which is reflected in both attitudes and behavior. The stigma and social ostracism that were often associated with divorce in the past are now relatively uncommon. Divorce has become recognized as a possibility for most American couples, and divorced men and women are no longer considered exceptional or deviant in most social circles.[12]

The increased acceptability of divorce would in itself encourage divorce; this effect is intensified by several other shifts in attitudes. Both men and women now have higher expectations for marital happiness—they demand more from marriage—and this makes it more difficult for them to feel that their own marriage is good enough. In addi-

---

* Except for a brief period after World War II, the divorce rate in the United States increased only gradually from 1860 to the early 1960s.[6] Then came two decades of sustained and rapid growth. In the twelve years between 1963 and 1975 the divorce rate increased 100 percent, and in each successive year until 1981 the divorce rate surpassed all previous records for this country. The actual number of annual divorces climbed to a record high of 1.21 million in 1981.[7]

** Demographer Kingsley Davis projected that 49.2 percent of marriages would end in divorce according to 1976–77 age-specific divorce rates.[10]

tion, because people believe that personal fulfillment is possible in marriage, it is more difficult to justify remaining in an unsatisfactory marriage. Divorce has become the acceptable "solution" to an unhappy marriage.

A related attitudinal shift is a result of women's rising labor force participation. Since a much higher percentage of married women now have jobs, more women (and more men) have come to believe—against some solid evidence to the contrary—that divorced women can earn an equal living on their own. This has not only given women the "freedom" to leave an unsatisfactory marriage; it has also given men the "freedom" to leave, because men are no longer seen as solely responsible for the support of their wives. In fact, the rise in divorce in middle age may be at least partially attributed to the increase in employed wives and liberalized divorce laws *that give men the opportunity* to obtain a divorce without the heavy financial (and psychological) burden they faced in the past.

A final change in the social climate is the increased number of alternatives to the continuation of a present marriage. These include both the greater ease of finding new marriage partners and the growing acceptability of living outside of marriage.

Thus the divorce revolution is the culmination of three trends: more people are getting divorced, divorce has become more socially acceptable than ever before, and more states have no-fault divorce laws. Each of these trends intensifies the effect of the others. Together, they have transformed both the perception and the reality of divorce in our society.

THE RESEARCH

The research presented in this book is based on five types of data: systematic random samples of 2,500 court dockets over a ten-year period; systematic in-depth interviews with 169 family law attorneys; similar interviews with 44 family law judges; a comparative sample of English legal experts; and systematic in-depth interviews with 228 divorced men and women. (A detailed description of the research methods is provided in Appendix A.) After ten years of data collection and analysis there is a vast range of material to provide an integrated portrait of the law and its effects.

This research design is unusual because it utilizes a variety of sources instead of relying solely on judges or lawyers (as legal scholars tend to do) or solely on divorced men and women (as sociologists and psychologists tend to do). It also has the advantage of a systematic data base in the random samples of divorce decrees drawn from court records.

Although most of the data were collected in California, the findings are relevant to the entire United States because the major features of the California law have been adopted by other states (see Chapter 2 which reviews legal trends throughout the fifty states).

A brief description of the major sources of data follows, while a more detailed description of each sample and the research methods is provided in Appendix A. I owe a great debt to Professor Ruth B. Dixon for being my partner in the collection of these data.

Court Records

Approximately 2,500 divorce cases were drawn from court records between 1968 and 1977. Two samples were drawn in 1968, which was two years before the no-fault law was instituted. One systematic random sample of about 500 divorce decrees was drawn from San Francisco County court records. A second systematic sample of about 500 divorce cases was drawn from greater Los Angeles County, giving us a total of about 1,000 divorce cases in 1968.

The same procedure was used to draw two samples of divorce cases in 1972, two years after the no-fault law was instituted. Here again, systematic random samples of about 500 San Francisco cases and 500 Los Angeles cases were drawn.

A third sample of divorce cases was drawn from court dockets in 1977 to examine the extent of the change seven years after no-fault was instituted. Since few significant differences were found between divorce cases in San Francisco and Los Angeles in 1968 and 1972, the 1977 sample was limited to 500 cases from the greater Los Angeles area (where one-third of all California divorces are granted).

Judges

Structured face-to-face interviews with virtually all of the judges who were hearing family law cases in San Francisco and Los Angeles counties, forty-four judges and commissioners, were conducted in 1974 and 1975. These interviews, which enjoyed response rates of 90 and 96 percent of the judges in each county, averaged three hours each.

More informal interviews were obtained at local and statewide

judicial conferences and judicial education courses between 1980 and
1985 in the course of my presenting and discussing the preliminary
results of this research. In addition twenty-six completed written questionnaires were obtained at a statewide conference of family court
judges in 1981.

Attorneys

In-depth face-to-face interviews with 169 matrimonial attorneys were
conducted in the San Francisco Bay Area and in the greater Los Angeles
area in 1974 and 1975. The 77 attorneys from the San Francisco Bay
Area comprised most of the family law bar in the San Francisco-
Oakland-Berkeley area.

In Los Angeles County, where more than 1,400 attorneys identified
themselves as matrimonial attorneys, the potential interview sample
was restricted to a subsample of 92 "experts": those who had held
an office in the Family Law Bar Association or who had been identified
as one of the three most knowledgeable or most effective attorneys
by their peers in the first group.

Although the 115 page interview schedule took an average of 4
hours to complete, there was an extraordinarily high response rate
in both cities: 97 and 100 percent.

These structured interviews were supplemented by informal interviews at local, state, and national bar association meetings between 1980 and 1985 where I presented the preliminary results of this
research.

Divorced Men and Women

Structured in-depth interviews with 228 recently divorced men and
women (114 men and 114 women) were conducted approximately one
year after the respondents' legal divorce. A stratified random sampling
procedure was used to obtain respondents of all socioeconomic groups
and all lengths of marital duration.

The interviews with divorced men and women lasted an average
of nearly six hours. Here too we benefited from a high response rate
(83 percent of the respondents located agreed to be interviewed) and
extraordinary cooperation. The respondents were willing to share vast

amounts of personal information with us and attached great importance to the research. (See Appendix A.)

These face-to-face interviews were conducted in the greater Los Angeles area in 1978. The 148 page structured interview schedule provided us with more information than can be analyzed in a single book. Since these interviews also provided complete information on the occupations, incomes, and employment experience of divorced women and men—information that was often missing in the court records—the data reported in this book rely heavily on these interviews.

In order to obtain enough longer-married couples and couples with property, the interview sample was stratified by length of marriage and socioeconomic status. (See Appendix A for details.) Since most divorcing couples are relatively young and do not have much property to divide, we oversampled couples in longer marriages and couples with property so that we would have enough couples in these groups for analysis. Because this book seeks to present a portrait of the entire population of divorced persons, I have weighted the interview responses to reflect the proportion of each group of respondents in a normal sample of divorced persons—such as our 1977 docket sample.

A Comparative Case: English Solicitors, Barristers, and Judges

One way of discovering the assumptions of our own society is to look at the way the same problems are approached in another society. In 1980 and 1981 I was fortunate to have the opportunity to interview twenty-six legal experts in England—solicitors, barristers, law professors, registrars, and judges—who were dealing with many of the same basic issues following their country's divorce law reform in 1973. Their responses provide an illuminating contrast to the California data and are especially useful in Chapter 4 on property and Chapter 7 on alimony.

The Hypothetical Divorce Cases

One of the unique features of the interviews with lawyers, judges, and divorced persons was the use of a series of hypothetical divorce cases. Four of these cases were used in each of the interview samples and are referred to throughout this book. The text of these cases is provided in Appendix B.

The Legal Appendix

A legal appendix, Appendix C, provides charts with state-by-state listings of the major features of the current divorce laws: the grounds for divorce, the criteria for alimony awards and property awards, recognition of spousal contributions to professional degrees, conversion of insurance at divorce, joint custody statutes, and provisions for the enforcement of child support.

ACKNOWLEDGMENTS

This research began as an interdisciplinary collaborative effort with Professors Ruth B. Dixon and Herma Hill Kay. I am greatly indebted to my co-investigators for all their efforts on the California Divorce Law Research Project and for their continuing advice and inspiration. Professor Dixon co-authored earlier versions of Chapter 6 on alimony[13] and Chapter 8 on child custody[14] and Professor Kay wrote an extensive background paper on no-fault's legislative history discussed in Chapter 2.[15]

Because this research has consumed a decade of my life I have benefited from the support and suggestions of a large number of colleagues. My earliest debts are to those colleagues at the Law and Society Center at the University of California at Berkeley—Jerome Skolnick, Phillip Selznick, Sheldon Messinger, Caleb Foote, and Phillipe Nonet, and to the members of the advisory committee for the California Divorce Law Research Project: attorney Kathryn Gehrels, John McCabe, of the National Conference on Uniform State Laws, sociologists Peter Rossi, Richard Schwartz, and William J. Goode, and psychiatrist Andrew Watson.

At Stanford University I have been aided by discussions with law professors Michael Wald and Robert Mnookin; sociologists Kingsley Davis and Sanford Dornbusch; and economist Myra Strober.

As a visiting fellow at Oxford University in 1980 and 1981, I was fortunate to have John Eekelaar, Mavis McClain, Ruth Deech, Sandra Burman and Barry Supple as mentors, and to enjoy the counsel of Stephen M. Cretny, Michael Freeman, Colin Gibson and Kevin Gray on the English Law. My colleagues on the Executive Council of the International Society on Family Law, especially Professor Anders Agell of Sweden and the Honorable Inger Margaret Pederson and Henrik

Andrup of Denmark, have helped to put the American experience into a broader perspective.

During this past year the members and fellows of the Institute for Advanced Study in Princeton provided a fountain of ideas and suggestions that extend far beyond the scope of this manuscript.

I am also grateful for the research support provided by the National Institute of Mental Health, Grant MH-27617; the National Science Foundation, Grant GI-39218; and for the research support, office space, and colleagueship provided by the Center for the Study of Law and Society at the University of California, Berkeley; and the Youth Development Center, the Center for Research on Women, and the Hoover Institution at Stanford University.

This work was greatly aided by a Guggenheim Fellowship this past year and by earlier fellowships from the Ford Foundation, the German Marshall Fund of the United States, the Rockefeller Foundation Center, Bellagio, Italy, and by Nuffield College and the Centre for Socio-Legal Studies, Wolfson College of Oxford University. Finally, I owe a very special debt to the Institute for Advanced Study in Princeton, and to its Director Harry Woolf, for the privilege of a very special year and the precious gift of time and assistance when they were most needed.

The Executive Committee of the Family Law Bar of the State of California, and its chair, Diana Richmond, provided timely advice and practical suggestions as did the California Law Revision Commission and the many attorneys who responded to preliminary results of this research at state and local bar association meetings, Continuing Education of the Bar courses, and at national meetings of the American Bar Association.

Similar assistance was provided by the judges who responded to my preliminary results at the National Judicial College, the National College for Juvenile and Family Court Judges, and in judicial education seminars in California and other states.

This research would not have been possible without the cooperation of our respondents and a superb staff of interviewers, coders, research assistants, supervisors, and typists who are too numerous to acknowledge individually. But a special note of thanks for help well beyond the call of a job to Joyce A. Bird, Joseph Barberri, Barbara Barer, Carol R. Dixon, Vie Dorfman, Susan Feller, Eve Fielder, Michelle Gambone, Patti Gumport, Moira Kinney, Jennifer King, Esther Kovari, Lorainne Lahr, Cassie Leavitt, David Lineweber, Neil McGinn, Starling Pullum, Fran Stancavage, Natalie Tripp, Holly Wunder, and Gina Zadra.

For the transformation of the research into a manuscript and the manuscript into a book, I am indebted to Erwin Glikes, for his vision; to Carole Norton and Joyce Seltzer for inspired editorial guidance; to Eileen DeWald, Betty Hucheon, and Holly Wunder for trying to save me from countless errors; and to Paula Davidson, Linda Emery, Peg Clarke, and Gloria Parks for good humor and endurance in retyping the numerous revisions of the manuscript.

I have learned a great deal from the colleagues and friends who took the time to read parts of the manuscript and to give me specific suggestions and advice: Ruth B. Dixon, Carole Joffee, Bernard Lewis, Frances Leonard, Nancy Polikoff, Lillian B. Rubin, Joanne Schulman, Arlene Skolnick, and Michael Wald.

There are many others who have helped in many ways, both directly and indirectly, who also deserve a special note of thanks: Angela Aidala, Michael Ballachey, Ava Baron, Joseph Carens, Alan C. Freeland, Julie Fulton, Mary Ann Glendon, Rose K. Goldsen, Meredith Gould, Joan Herrick, Albert Hirschman, Sara Hirschman, Morton Hunt, Bernice Hunt, Herbert Jacobs, Jane Menken, Iris Mitgang, Jenny Nedelsky, Susan Westerberg Prager, Cora Sadowsky, Pepper Schwartz, Roz Schram, Austin Serat, Peggy Thoits, Sheila Tobias, Michael Walzer, Elsie Washington, Marshall Weinberg, Jacqueline P. Wiseman, and Pat Woolf.

Finally, I want to express my profound debt to Professor William J. Goode, for his pioneering study of the experiences of women in divorce, *After Divorce*,[16] which set high standards for all subsequent scholarship in this field; for his mentorship and inspiration in guiding the path of this research; for his critical reading of each successive draft of this manuscript; and for his endless wisdom and emotional support.

CHAPTER 1

The Legal Tradition

THE COMMON LAW ORIGINS of American family law may be traced to the rising power of Christianity in Britain which enabled the Church to make its rules the law of the land.[1] Traditional legal marriage was grounded in the Christian conception of marriage as a sacrament, a holy union between a man and woman, a commitment to join together for life: "to take each other to love and to cherish, in sickness and in health, for better, for worse, until death do us part."

The nature of the marital relationship and the legal obligations of husbands and wives were specified in various forms of law—common law, case law, and statute. Laws governing divorce reinforced these responsibilities, rewarding spouses who fulfilled their marital obligations and punishing those who did not.

The radical innovations of contemporary no-fault laws are highlighted by this historical context. While a thorough analysis of traditional legal marriage is obviously beyond the scope of this book,[2] its basic characteristics, as expressed in the five central principles described below, reflect the legal, social, and economic assumptions embedded in the law.

1

TRADITIONAL LEGAL MARRIAGE

Gender-based Roles and Responsibilities

The traditional law defined the basic rights and obligations of husbands and wives on the basis of gender, creating a sex-based division of family roles and responsibilities. The woman was to devote herself to being a wife, homemaker, and mother in return for her husband's promise of lifelong support. As Professor Homer Clark, the noted authority on U.S. family law, wrote in 1968:

> The courts say that the husband has a duty to support his wife, that she has a duty to render services in the home, and that these duties are reciprocal. . . . A reading of contemporary judicial opinions leaves the impression that these roles have not changed over the last two hundred years.[3]

All states in the United States, even those with community property systems, placed the burden of the family support on the husband; he was legally responsible for providing necessities for his wife and children. Similarly, all states made the wife responsible for the care of her home, her husband, and her children; she was legally required to provide domestic service, companionship, and child care.

The same division of family responsibilities applied to child care. The wife was legally responsible for the children's care, and the husband was obliged to support them financially.

While no one would claim that the law was responsible for the traditional division of labor in the family, it did serve to sanction and reinforce traditional family roles. The law's influence worked through prescriptions and proscriptions, incentives and disincentives. For example, by promising housewives lifelong support, the law created disincentives for women to develop their economic capacity and to work in the paid labor force. In addition, by making them responsible for domestic services and child care, it reinforced the primacy of these activities in their lives, leaving them with neither the time nor the motivation to develop careers outside the home.

The law similarly reinforced the traditional male role by directing the husband away from domestic activities and child care. It encouraged his single-minded dedication to work by making it clear that his family's economic welfare was his primary responsibility.

A Patriarchal Family Structure

Legal marriage designated the husband as the head of the family, with his wife and children subordinate to him. The husband's authority was based on the common law doctrine of coverture, the legal fiction that a husband and wife took a single legal identity upon marriage—the identity of the husband. Upon marriage the wife became a *femme covert* (sic), a legal nonperson, living under her husband's arm, protection, and cover.[4]

In the United States, most of the disabilities of coverture were removed by the Married Women's Property Acts in the nineteenth century. However, the common law assumption that the husband was the head of the family remained firmly embodied in statutory and case law until the last decade.[5] The married woman's subordination was reflected in rules permitting women to marry at a younger age (because they were presumably already prepared for their life's work), the wife's loss of an independent identity by assuming her husband's surname, the husband's power to determine the family domicile, the husband's right to his wife's sexual services,* and the gender-based standards in grounds for loss of consortium (only the husband was entitled to sue anyone who deprived him of his wife's love and sexual services).[8] For example, a married woman who did not assume her husband's identity by taking his name or domicile as her own might encounter difficulties in registering to vote, obtaining a driver's license, running for office, having her estate probated, obtaining a tuition exemption in a state-supported college in her home state, or suing for divorce.[9]

---

* Twenty-seven states still do not allow a husband to be prosecuted for raping his wife. In 1984 women's groups challenged a New York law exempting married men who commit forcible marital rape from criminal penalties, arguing that the law perpetuated "the inferior legal status and stereotypical role of women in marriage" and was "a remnant of a bygone era that regarded women as little more than legal appendages of their husbands."[6] (The marital exemption dates to seventeenth-century England, a time when the law viewed women as the property of their husbands. It had been part of the criiminal law of New York since colonial days.)

In overturning the rule, Judge Sol Wachtler of New York's highest court said married women are no longer considered the property of their husbands, without separate identities:

A marriage license should not be viewed as a license for a husband to forcibly rape his wife with impunity, . . . Rape is a degrading, violent act which violates the bodily integrity of the victim, whether married or single. . . . Marriage does not constitute a woman's irrevocable implied consent to sexual intercourse. A married woman has the same right to control her own body as does an unmarried woman.[7]

A Moral Framework

Marriage was both a moral and legal commitment to another human being. Husbands and wives were bound by moral vows and were expected to remain sexually faithful to each other. Because adultery was considered such a clear violation of both moral and legal norms, it provided one of the earliest grounds for divorce.

A Lifelong Commitment

As noted earlier, the notion of an indissoluble union reflects the Christian influence on civil laws in England as well as the Church's long-standing jurisdiction over matrimonial causes.[10] The Church enforced its view of marriage as a sacrament that could not be dissolved by mere mortals.* Marriage was permanent: a joining together, for better or worse, "until death do us part."

Although the absolute prohibitions of the traditional law gradually gave way to statutes that permitted divorce, it was always regarded as a violation of the norm. This perspective is reflected in the long-standing common law rules for allocating family property upon the death of a spouse (e.g., dower and widow's share) in contrast to the traditional paucity of provisions for dividing property upon divorce.

The lifelong obligations created by legal marriage were also evident in the persistence of marital obligations even if the spouses separated. A divorce did not end the obligations of the marriage contract; a husband remained financially responsible for a former wife for the rest of her life (unless she remarried and became the responsibility of another man).

Marital Partnership

Traditional legal marriage created a unity that transcended the parties' individual interests. While the marital partnership was certainly not egalitarian (it was based on different and unequal roles for men and women), it nevertheless assumed that the spouses were engaged in a joint enterprise, were responsible for each other, and would share the

---

* The conception of marriage under Jewish law is quite different: it is a contract between two parties, not a sacramental fusion of flesh and blood.

fruits of their united endeavors. Thus, even though the housewife did not typically acquire income and property of her own, her contributions to her husband's farm, business, or home were recognized as contributions to the marital partnership and, in return, the law guaranteed her right to share "his" estate.

The forty-two common law states in the United States fostered the partnership concept of marriage by guaranteeing a widow the right to inherit a fixed share of her husband's estate; to elect against his will; to receive benefits related to his employment, such as health, dependent, and survivor's insurance; and to receive Social Security, retirement, and pension benefits as his widow. Since marriage was a lifelong commitment, it was assumed that the only time a widow was financially vulnerable was when her husband died. She, and her children, would then be protected by the provisions enumerated above and by laws that assured their inheritance of his estate.* Recently, as divorce has become more common, most common law states have adopted rules to give the wife an "equitable" share of the property upon divorce as well.

While most states were influenced by the common law of the English tradition, a minority of eight states were influenced by the Spanish-Catholic tradition of community property (Arizona, California, Idaho, Louisiana, Nevada, New Mexico, Texas, and Washington). These community property states recognized the wife's contribution to the marital partnership by giving her ownership of one-half of the income and property that her husband (and she) acquired during marriage.

The rationale for the community property system is that both spouses have contributed equally to the economic assets of the marriage, whether by earning income or by household maintenance, and that both are entitled to an equal share of the results: "While one spouse's earnings may be the immediate source of the couple's income and acquisitions, the labor, efforts and industry of both spouses contribute to the acquisition of property during marriage."[11] Stated more colloquially, community property principles recognize that "yours" and "mine" are "ours." As one writer expressed it: "Whatever I have achieved is at least one half due to her liberation of me for my work

---

* While historical research reminds us of the extent to which the nuclear family and its property were embedded in larger kinship groups that owned and controlled "family" property, in the past half-century nuclear families have gained more control over extended-family property and, in general, the rights of surviving wives have superseded those of the extended family.

and her inspiration and loving kindness and patience and labor and sympathy. All that I have is as much hers as mine."[12]

Since husbands traditionally had the legal right to manage and control the community property during the marriage, the wife's one-half ownership of the community property was of more symbolic than practical value during marriage, although that symbolism was important. In addition, when their husbands died, wives in community property states were guaranteed one-half of the marital assets, and this share typically exceeded the one-third guarantee of many common law states.

Nevertheless, even though the ideal of equal sharing may have been better realized in the community property states, both systems of legal marriage were based on partnership ideals and guaranteed wives a share of the partnership's assets.

TRADITIONAL DIVORCE LAW

Our divorce laws are also rooted in the English common law. Not surprisingly, however, they were relative latecomers. "Divorce, in the modern sense of a judicial decree dissolving a valid marriage, and allowing one or both partners to remarry during the life of the other, did not exist in England until 1857."[13] Since marriage was regarded as an indissoluble union, it could be ended only by the death of one of the parties. A rare exception, originating in the late seventeenth century, allowed divorce (on the sole ground of adultery) by special act of Parliament. As a practical matter, however, few of these divorces were granted.[14] The Church also permitted divorce *a mensa et thoro*, or a divorce from bed and board, which allowed the parties to live apart. But this legal separation left most of the spouses' marital obligations in force.

The underlying premise of divorce law, which remained into the twentieth century, was that marriage was a permanent and cherished union which the Church—and then the state—had to protect and preserve. It was assumed that the best way to protect the bond of matrimony was to restrict access to divorce. As legal scholar Homer Clark observed in his comprehensive review of American law:

> [It is assumed] that marital happiness is best secured by making marriage indissoluble except for very few causes. When the parties know that they are bound together for life, the argument runs, they will resolve their

differences and disagreements and make an effort to get along with each other. If they are able to separate legally upon less serious grounds, they will make no such effort, and immorality will result.[15]

Divorce laws in the United States were heavily influenced by the English tradition. Although there was some variation in the early divorce laws in northern and southern states, by 1900 most states had adopted what I shall refer to as the four major elements of traditional divorce laws: fault-based grounds, one party's guilt, the continuation of gender-based marital responsibilities after divorce, and the linkage of financial awards to findings of fault.

Restrictive Law: Fault-based Grounds Required for Divorce

Since the aim of the law was to preserve marriage as a lifelong union, divorce was restricted to situations in which one party committed a serious marital offense such as adultery, cruelty, or desertion, giving the other party the legal basis or *ground* for the divorce.[16]

The court required evidence to prove that one party had sufficient grounds for divorce, and that evidence typically had to be corroborated by witnesses. In New York, for example, the only ground for divorce was adultery. Private detectives were often hired to follow an errant spouse and to return with photographs or other evidence from the adulterous scene. Since there was no adultery in many cases, the evidence had to be "manufactured" to satisfy the court's requirements. Lawyers would arrange for a detective to "catch" the "philandering husband" at a predesignated hotel to obtain appropriate evidence for the trial.

Even in cases of mental cruelty, the most commonly used ground for divorce, witnesses and evidence were necessary. As one California attorney we interviewed described it:

> I remember this horrible grind we went through to prepare cases under the old law . . . four, five witnesses in the office here and grinding out the list of fault. He beat me, he swore at her, the children were mistreated, he ran out, he was never home—all these complaints back and forth. She didn't take care of the house, it was dirty. She had six kids to watch over, but the house was dirty. That kind of thing.
>
> And lining up all these witnesses, . . . spending the days in court just going into this kind of evidence, which was a terrible waste of time. And it was important because at that time the law provided that if the divorce was granted on the grounds of cruelty or adultery, the innocent party got more than half of the property, so there was a double pressure,

not only personal vindication, but a pressure to get as much of the community assets as one could. Then too there was a feeling, and the old cases so stated, that the award of alimony was a punishment. So again it was necessary to get the dirt on one party or the other.

Another attorney wondered, in retrospect, why attorneys and judges participated in "the charade":

> You would have had to have heard some of the nonsense that went on before. Now I look back and say, "How stupid we were, how idiotic, how much time we wasted. How could the taxpayers have stood for that sort of thing?" Why should these people be allowed to spend 43 days or 48 days or 15 days in a courtroom putting on evidence of who went to a motel with whom, and pictures of this one with that one, and he hit me this time, and he didn't like the soup and he threw it on the table. You know what it costs to run a courtroom? It was idiotic! It was a total charade.

The standards for judging appropriate grounds reflected the gender-typed expectations of traditional legal marriage. While the almost ritualistic "evidence" of misbehavior varied from state to state, husbands charged with cruelty, the most commonly cited ground, were often alleged to have caused their wives bodily harm, while wives charged with cruelty were more typically accused of neglecting their husbands, homes, or wifely duties.[17] Along the same lines, allegations of a wife's desertion were typically supported by evidence of a wife's withdrawal of affection, refusal to do housework, or attention to outside interests, but the same behavior would not be considered as desertion by the husband unless he also stopped supporting his wife financially.

Over time, in actual practice, many divorcing couples privately agreed to an uncontested divorce whereby one party, usually the wife, would take the *pro forma* role of the innocent plaintiff. Supported by witnesses, she would attest to her husband's cruel conduct and he would not challenge her allegations. But even if the testimony was staged, it nevertheless reflected what the courts considered "appropriate violations" of the marriage contract—and thus reinforced what were seen as the sex-appropriate obligations of marriage itself. The husband, obliged to support and protect his wife, was punished for nonsupport and physical abuse. The wife, responsible for the care of her home and husband, was punished for neglecting her domestic responsibilities.

Requiring grounds for divorce had two important consequences. First, it gave the "innocent" party a great deal of power. Since a divorce could only be granted to the innocent or injured party, she (but some-times he) had the *de facto* power to shape the nature of the divorce suit and, even more important, to prevent it. A "guilty" spouse who wanted a divorce had to persuade his "innocent" partner to cooperate, and that could be difficult, emotionally trying, and expensive—espe-cially if the "innocent" spouse genuinely wanted to stay married.

The grounds requirement had a second effect: it created practical, psychological, and moral barriers to divorce and thus made divorce more difficult. On the practical level, as we just noted, the spouse who wanted the divorce had to obtain his partner's cooperation—either through persuasion or through financial incentives.

On the psychological level, the need for grounds meant that one had to face allegations of one's adultery, desertion, or cruelty in court. Divorce hearings could be embarrassing, sometimes even humiliating, with public revelations of adultery, battering, sexual inadequacy, per-sonal failures, or bad moral character. Every divorce required some evidence of spousal misconduct. So even those couples who wanted to separate amicably had to participate in the ritual of proving one partner's fault. And, if one party was having an affair, he or she would have to face the prospect of private detectives, witnesses, and photo-graphs revealing the details of that relationship. The threat of these revelations, even if they were not used in court, could have a chilling effect. As attorney Raoul Felder advised:

> Let us consider for the moment when it may prove advantageous to hire a private detective. . . . as a general rule, it never hurts as long as you can afford it. . . . A detective's report also gives a psychological advantage at bargaining time. . . . You can drop hints as to what the detective uncov-ered. Even if it is not damaging, your spouse never really knows how much more you have.
> . . . You never know what a surveillance will turn up.[18]

Threats of releasing the stories to local newspapers were used to persuade culpable spouses to agree to a financial settlement rather than face a contested hearing. Thus many divorcing couples privately agreed to grounds in an uncontested divorce. However, if an accusatory spouse wanted to be difficult or to embarrass the other spouse, the divorce court provided a forum and the press provided a public arena for malicious allegations. Divorce lawyer Felder observes:

> [Executives are often] pathetically vulnerable to publicity, scandal and rumors, even though the fear may be absolutely unfounded. This is the

reason why their cases are settled quickly. They simply cannot stand the heat. . . . When I say vulnerable, I am not talking about blackmail. If it comes to a fight, it's the lawyer's function, using all ethical, legal and moral means, to bring his adversary to his knees as fast as possible. Naturally, within this framework, a lawyer must go for the soft spots.[19]

Finally, the testimony required in order to prove grounds was morally offensive to many participants and created an ethical barrier for some. In order to prove grounds for a divorce, one spouse might have to commit perjury and provide false testimony about the other spouse's conduct. Many participants felt that was distasteful, demeaning, and morally offensive.

A Moral Framework: Guilt and Innocence

A closely related feature of traditional divorce law was that it framed divorce in a moral context of guilt and innocence. Since a divorce could only be granted to an "innocent party" who was harmed by his or her spouse's violations of the marriage contract, the law required that one party be "guilty," the other "innocent." As the Tennessee Supreme Court stated, "divorce is conceived as a remedy for the innocent against the guilty."[20]

In many states "the party seeking the divorce had to be without reproach: if both parties were at fault, neither could obtain a divorce."*[21] This rule was known as the doctrine of recrimination. The rationale for refusing to grant a divorce if both parties were at fault was that the law should not reward those who come into court with "dirty hands." To get around this rule couples who had decided to divorce would typically conceal the fact that both parties had grounds. Technically their concealment constituted collusion or fraud, but it was nevertheless common practice.[23]

However, even proof of fault did not guarantee that a divorce would be granted. An unwilling spouse might raise a defense to prevent the divorce. The most commonly raised defense, condonation, is explained by Michael Wheeler:

> . . . If a man discovers that his wife has committed adultery but continues to live with her, he may be barred from using her adultery as a ground

---

* "The illogicality of thus forcing an obviously doomed union to continue was recognized and mercifully eliminated" by the 1952 California Supreme Court ruling, in *De Burgh*.[22] But a showing of fault continued to be a prerequisite to divorce until 1970.

for divorce. Condonation reflects the notion that the "innocent" husband in this case should not be able to have it both ways: either his wife's adultery so offended him that it broke up their marriage or it did not. He should not be allowed to continue to live with her while holding the threat of divorce over her head.

. . . Arthur Fox, a Virginia attorney, has noted that the "practical effect of the rule of condonation is to impose a 'do-or-die' decision upon the innocent spouse in the hour of crisis. Confronted suddenly with the knowledge of his partner's infidelity, he must decide promptly whether to pack his suitcase and leave what may have been and could be a very happy home, or to continue marital relations thereby forfeiting the right to dissolve the marriage if it should subsequently cease to be viable.[24]

The need to have a guilty party in order to get a divorce had two consequences. First, it required adversary proceedings. The plaintiff's success in obtaining a divorce depended on his or her ability to prove the defendant's fault. Second, the law imposed moral labels on the parties. One party had to be designated as guilty or responsible for the divorce; the other party was labeled an "innocent victim."

Perpetuation of Gender-based Roles and Responsibilities

Traditional divorce law perpetuated the sex-based division of roles and responsibilities enshrined in traditional legal marriage: the wife's domestic responsibilities and the husband's obligation to provide support. Although traditional family law assumed that the husband's support would be provided in a lifelong marriage, if the marriage did not endure and if the wife was virtuous, she was nevertheless promised alimony—a means of continued support. Alimony thus perpetuated the husband's responsibilities for economic support and the wife's right to be supported in return for her domestic services. It therefore maintained at least part of the basic *reciprocity* in the legal marriage contract.

Traditional divorce laws also reaffirmed the sex-based division of roles with respect to children: the husband remained responsible for their economic support, the wife for their care. All states, by statute or by case law, gave preference to the wife as the appropriate custodial parent after the divorce, and all states gave the husband the primary responsibility for his children's economic support.

Financial Awards Linked to Fault

Finally, traditional divorce law linked the financial terms of the divorce to the determination of fault. Being found "guilty" or "innocent" in a divorce action had important financial consequences.

Alimony, for example, could be awarded only to the *innocent* spouse "as a judgment *against* the guilty spouse."[25] Thus when the court found a woman guilty of adultery, she was typically barred from receiving alimony. And if the husband was found guilty of adultery or cruelty, he might have to pay for his transgressions with alimony. As Eli Bronstein, a New York matrimonial lawyer, justified these rules, "If a woman has been a tramp, why reward her? By the same token, if the man is alley-catting around town, shouldn't his wife get all the benefits she had as a married woman?"[26]

California attorneys reported that both husbands and wives tried to use alimony to punish each other under the old law. As one attorney we interviewed put it: "Of course she would try to use the evidence to get more alimony. . . . It's the screwing he gets for the screwing he got."

The law also linked property awards to fault. In California judges were required to award more than half of the property to the innocent spouse. Since these awards were, in theory, directly linked to the degree of fault, the law created strong financial incentives for parties to exaggerate the transgressions of their spouses. Consider, for example, the ruling of a 1946 California appellate court, holding that an innocent wife was entitled to substantially more than half of the property because of her husband's "heinous behavior":

> The rule drawn from the cases hereinafter cited is that the greater the offense the larger the proportion of the community property that must be awarded to the innocent spouse, where the acts of cruelty are of a flagrant character and have extended over a long period of time the portion of the community property awarded to the non-offending party should be greater than if the acts were more trivial yet sufficient to warrant the granting of a divorce. It obviously follows that where the divorce is granted on the more heinous grounds of adultery as well as for extreme cruelty the amount awarded to the innocent party should be greater than if granted on the ground of cruelty alone.
>
> The acts of cruelty committed by respondent were many and had continued over a period of years. He was intoxicated on frequent occasions both at home and when he attended social gatherings with his wife; his amorous and indecent advances to other women caused embarrassment

to her; he used profane language in the presence of their daughter as well as when they were alone; he confessed to his wife and freely admitted on the witness stand that he had committed adultery with the co-respondent on numerous occasions over a period of approximately two years. . . .[27]

The lure of substantial property awards encouraged heated charges and countercharges between spouses.[28] Proving the other's guilt might not only make one feel morally superior, but might also pay off in a better property settlement. In most separate property states, the courts also had the power to award property held by either spouse upon divorce and could therefore use property as a reward for virtue and a punishment for sin.*

Linking financial awards to fault had four important consequences. The first, just noted, was that it provided financial incentives for spouses to accuse each other of being responsible for the divorce. *The legal requirements thus fostered an adversarial climate of escalating accusations, acrimony, and hostility because successful accusations were rewarded with money and property.*

Second, the legal structure encouraged the parties to seek *monetary awards for personal vindication.* Victory was measured in dollars, whether by the husband who "didn't want to give her a dime" or by the wife who "wanted to take him for everything he had."[30] One Los Angeles attorney recalled how clients saw monetary awards as symbolic of their emotional loss or gain:

> Even when there wasn't any substantial amount of money involved, money became the method for parlaying feelings about who was fair and who wasn't fair in the course of the marriage. . . . People really did relate to financial issues as a vehicle for their emotional concerns.

The third effect of linking financial awards to fault was that it gave the "innocent party" a decided economic advantage. Since both the granting of the divorce and the financial settlements were linked to fault, the "innocent party" had a powerful lever to use in property and alimony negotiations. Indeed, in California the law required that the innocent party get more than half of the property.

The fourth consequence of the linkage of financial awards and

---

* By 1976 only fourteen states retained common law title rules that allowed both parties to keep the property in their names as their own. By 1985, virtually all states had adopted some form of "equitable" distribution of property upon divorce.[28] (See Chapter 2, p. 47 and Table C–4 in the Legal Appendix, Appendix C.)

fault was that *it discouraged divorce by making it costly* for men.
Since it was most commonly the man who wanted the divorce, in practice men, especially middle- and upper-class men, often "bought" their
divorces by agreeing to give their wives more property (such as the
family home), or alimony, or child support, or all of these. As we will
see, alimony awards were less common than is generally assumed.*
But whether or not alimony was awarded the innocent wife typically
received a larger share of the property, especially if her husband's
adultery or cruelty was flagrant or if the only family asset was the
home. Thus a man contemplating divorce faced the expensive prospect
of providing alimony for his ex-wife, providing child support until his
children reached twenty-one, and losing his home and some of his
other assets.

CONCLUSION

Traditional divorce law helped sanction the spouses' conventional roles
and responsibilities in marriage—by both punishment and reward. On
the punishment side, if a wife was found guilty of adultery, cruelty,
or desertion, she would have to pay for her wrongdoings by being
denied alimony (and sometimes custody and property as well). And
if the husband was at fault, he would be punished through awards
of property, alimony, and child support to his ex-wife.

On the reward side, traditional divorce law promised "justice"
for those who fulfilled their marital obligations. It guaranteed support
for the wife who devoted herself to her family, thus reinforcing the
desirability and legitimacy of the wife's role as homemaker and the
husband's role as supporter. And the law assured the husband that
he would not have to support a wife who betrayed or failed him. Justice
in this system was the assurance that the marriage contract would
be honored. If not, the "bad" spouse would be punished, the "good"
spouse rewarded, and the husband's obligation to support his wife
(if she was good) enforced.

When California rejected this traditional system, in 1970, it
launched a legal revolution. Within just a single decade, American
family law was transformed.

---

* In fact, most men did not pay alimony, but most men *believed* they would have
to pay alimony if they divorced, and this belief affected their decisions about divorce.

CHAPTER 2

The Divorce Law Revolution
No-Fault in America

IN 1970, CALIFORNIA instituted the first law in the Western world to abolish completely any requirement of fault as the basis for marital dissolution. The no-fault law provided for a divorce upon *one* party's assertion that "irreconcilable differences have caused the irremediable breakdown of the marriage." In establishing the new standards, the California state legislature sought to eliminate the adversarial nature of divorce and thereby to reduce the hostility, acrimony, and trauma characteristic of fault-oriented divorce.

No-fault divorce reformed each of the basic elements in the traditional divorce law. As exemplified by the California statute, the new legislation reflects six major innovations:*

1. No grounds are needed to obtain a divorce. This permissive standard facilitates divorce and represents a dramatic departure from the restrictive norms of the traditional law.
2. Neither spouse has to prove fault or guilt to obtain a divorce. This too is a radical change signaling a rejection of the moral framework of the old law.

---

* The discussion that follows focuses on the "pure" no-fault divorce law instituted in California. This type of legal regime is in effect in about half of the states. The second half of this chapter reviews the features of divorce laws throughout the United States.

3. One spouse can decide unilaterally to get a divorce without the consent or agreement of the other spouse.
4. Financial awards are no longer linked to fault. The new standards are based on the parties' current financial needs and resources rather than their past behavior, whether guilt or innocence.
5. New standards for alimony and property awards seek to treat men and women "equally," thereby repudiating the sex-based assumptions of the traditional law.
6. New procedures aim at undermining the adversarial process and creating a social psychological climate that fosters amicable divorce.

In retrospect, it may seem surprising to discover that these liberal reforms began, at least in part, as a conservative effort "to stem the rising tide of divorce."[1] The story of how it came about is interesting.

THE HISTORICAL CONTEXT: THE REFORMERS' GOALS[2]

In 1963 a California assemblyman, Pearce Young, concerned about the lack of consistency in judicial decision-making in domestic relations cases, initiated Assembly Judiciary Committee hearings to see what could be done. Many witnesses who testified at those hearings expressed a more general alarm at the high rate of divorce in California and urged a broader reassessment of the adequacy of its divorce laws.[3]

Four major themes emerged from the 1964 hearings and set the agenda for the legislative proposals that followed.[4] The first was the widespread concern about high divorce rates. (In 1960, the ratio of divorces to marriages was 47 percent in California, compared to 26 percent elsewhere in the United States.)[5] Judge Roger Pfaff, who had pioneered in the work of the Los Angeles conciliation court, argued that the "contagious disease of divorce" could be stopped by statewide adoption of premarital and predivorce conciliation procedures patterned after the Los Angeles model.

A second group of witnesses attacked the adversary process citing the hostility, acrimony, and trauma it created. Law professors Herma Hill Kay of The University of California at Berkeley and Aidan Gough of the University of Santa Clara argued for the complete abolition of adversarial divorce.[6] As Professor Kay asserted, the "divorce procedures themselves add to the bitterness and sense of personal failure . . . by requiring that at least one party be found guilty of marital fault." She urged a restructuring of the divorce process so that human beings "who are entitled to divorces can get them with the least possible amount of damage to themselves and to their families."[7] Thus, Professor Kay was the first to assert a link between the legal rules and procedures and the emotional state of divorcing couples. Her suggestion that the abolition of fault would reduce the bitterness and hostility surrounding divorce procedures was ultimately accepted by most of the reformers.

A third theme was the need to recognize the inevitability of divorce for some couples and to try to make the legal process less destructive for them and their children. The establishment of a Family Court was urged by Professors Kay and Gough to help couples divorce with the least possible harm. Court counsellors could assist them in making arrangements for child custody and a financial settlement in a rational and nonpunitive fashion.

A final theme was raised by divorced men who charged that "the divorce law and its practitioners were in league with divorced wives to suck the blood, not to mention the money, of former husbands."[8] Their contention was that the existing law strongly favored women and allowed them to "take their husbands to the cleaners" via alimony and property awards.[9] They urged that the divorce laws be revised to treat men and women "equally."*

The themes that were to shape the new legislation embodied a number of conflicts between "conservatives" who sought to "preserve the family," and "liberals" who wanted to recognize the inevitability of divorce and to make it less emotionally destructive. (Although the terms "conservative" and "liberal" do not adequately capture the complexity of either position, they afford a useful dichotomy for the purposes of this brief historical review.) Even the supporters of the Family Court proposal had different visions of its purpose: the conservatives hoped counseling would help save troubled marriages, while the liberals hoped it would improve the divorce process, structure more equitable financial settlements, and facilitate postdivorce parenting.

As Professor Herma Hill Kay recalls, "to speak of the 'goals' of the drafters of the California law is deceptive: the no-fault divorce law was the product of many different persons whose ideas were as often contradictory as they were complementary:"[11]

> The reform movement did not begin with definite goals and a grand design carefully worked out in advance. Rather, it began inauspiciously in the

---

* The group of divorced men who had been following the legislative hearings, the United States Divorce Reform, Inc., attempted to get an initiative for divorce reform on the November 1966 California ballot. Their failed proposal would have abolished alimony and established Family Arbitration centers to deal with divorce.[10]

California Assembly, moved to a group of experts appointed by the Governor, and returned to the legislature after refinement by the specialists in the bar. At no time did the movement have broad popular involvement or public opposition. In many respects, it was a legal, not social, reform in design. But like other basic legal changes, it has had wide and largely unanticipated social consequences."[12]

Indeed, the apparent contradictions in the law's formulative history probably constituted one of its major strengths so far as public acceptance was concerned: it *"promised" everything*. For example, in 1966, when California Governor Edmund G. Brown appointed his own Commission (on "the Family") to carry on what he termed a "concentrated assault on the high incidence of divorce and its tragic consequences"[13] he too had grandiose hopes for what the legal reform could accomplish. It was to remove the social and economic evils he perceived as flowing from divorce—juvenile delinquency, crime, alcoholism, and the cycle of welfare dependency.[14] The Governor directed his commission to suggest revisions in the divorce laws and to design the means for establishing a Family Court.[15] The Governor's aims for the Family Court encompassed both traditional and liberal goals. It would provide a means of reconciling spouses where a marriage could be saved, as well as a means of facilitating a nonadversarial divorce where it could not.

It was this Governor's Commission that drafted the revolutionary no-fault reforms. Their work was hastened by the gubernatorial election: Governor Brown was being challenged by a screen actor named Ronald Reagan, and the Commission rushed to complete its work before their term expired.[16] (Their report was completed in the Brown administration but their recommendations took two and a half years to enact and were finally implemented under Governor Reagan.)

The lack of opposition to the no-fault reform from such likely foes as the Catholic Church[17] may be explained in part by the reform rhetoric of both the Governor and his commission. No-fault was consistently portrayed as the modern prescription to "preserve the family."

One of the major debates within the Governor's Commission concerned the "moral impetus and deterrent effect" of the traditional fault-based grounds.[18] While no one thought the fault-based grounds represented the real reasons for divorce, some members were concerned that the elimination of all grounds would "give implicit license for the commission of adultery and other marital misconduct."[19] This issue was resolved by the discovery of the report of an English Commission that had struggled with the same issues and had eventually recommended the elimination of all grounds. As Professor Kay reports:

> The Mortimer Commission was appointed by the Archbishop of Canterbury to study changes in the divorce law of England. Its report, entitled *Putting Asunder: A Divorce Law for Contemporary Society*, was published in 1966. It was at once evident that the two groups, so widely separated in distance and orientation, had nevertheless gone through a similar process of analysis and debate. The Mortimer Commission . . . recommended the elimination of all formal grounds for divorce and the substitution of an inquiry into the breakdown of the marriage as the basis for judicial dissolution. The California Commission noted in its minutes that "these expressions of the Church of England Commission constituted the sense of our Commission" and . . . [they proceeded] to draft appropriate language to that end.[20]

In the end, the law that was passed more closely resembled the one that the liberals envisioned. The Family Court was abandoned in a last-minute legislative compromise.[21] It was opposed by some segments of the organized bar, who did not want nonlawyers advising clients, and the judiciary, who saw it as too intrusive. Ultimately the court was seen as too expensive in the legislature. Thus the conservatives who supported the legislation because it promised to save troubled families found themselves without the tool that was designed to meet that need. What were left were the far-reaching no-fault reforms which are discussed below.

Under the new law, fault was eliminated not only from the grounds for divorce but also from the standards for dividing property and awarding alimony. In its place was to be a nonjudgmental criterion—"irreconcilable differences"—for determining whether a marriage had come to an end. Although the conservatives were successful in one respect— the judge could deny divorce if allegations of irreconcilable differences were not substantiated—in practice, this "safeguard" was never used.*

This brief review of the legal background, and the discussion of the legislation in the pages that follow, suggest the bases for some of the surprising findings of this research. The reformers were so preoccupied with the question of fault and its role in both obtaining a divorce and securing a financial settlement, that few of them thought sufficiently about the consequences of the new system to foresee how its fault-neutral rules might come to disadvantage the economically weaker party.**

---

* None of the judges we interviewed had ever denied a petition for divorce.
** This omission is discussed more fully on pp. 24–26 and in Chapter 11.

THE INNOVATIONS OF NO-FAULT

California's no-fault law was immediately greeted as enlightened and historic legislation that would "chart the path for the civilization of domestic relations law throughout the United States."[22] The law did, in fact, launch a nationwide trend toward more permissive divorce laws. Within a single decade, by 1980, all but two states had adopted some form of no-fault law. Let us first consider the major innovations of the California law, and then examine the pattern of change throughout the United States.

Permissive Law: The Abolition of Grounds

The basic premise of the no-fault law "is that the nineteenth century concept of divorce, based only upon a matrimonial offense committed by one or both of the parties, is essentially outmoded and irrelevant, often producing cruel and unworkable results."[23] The new law substitutes "marital breakdown" as the only justification for divorce. In rejecting the restrictive posture of the traditional regime, the reformers argued that fault-based grounds were inappropriate in two respects: first, they were artificial and often bore little relation to the real causes of marital breakdown; second, they fostered perjury, hypocrisy, and collusion and insulted the dignity of the court and the parties involved.

The new law therefore abolished the need for any grounds save "irreconcilable differences" between the parties. Now divorce could begin with a neutral "petition for dissolution," with no further specification of reasons.

The abolition of fault eliminates many of the practical, psychological, and moral divorce disincentives that existed under the old law. At the same time, since "guilt" and "innocence" are no longer at issue, the erstwhile "innocent" or unwilling party no longer has the power to prevent or delay a divorce, or to bargain for financial concessions in return for consent.

Many of the divorced men and women we interviewed said that they were both surprised and disturbed by the freedom the new law gives spouses to simply terminate a marriage. As one woman explained:

> It's just too easy. You shouldn't be able to just walk out on your family. I think there has to be some reason—some real ground for someone to be able to divorce his wife. . . . He made a commitment, and I believe that the vows we took were not empty vows. . . . I think no-fault divorce robs me of my right to my marriage and my right to keep my family.

A man echoed these sentiments:

> I was outraged when I found out that my wife had been having an affair
> and she still had the right to get a divorce without any—and I mean
> any—grounds. That divorce law legalizes adultery.

Another woman complained that the change in the law violated her
marriage contract:

> I thought we had a contract and I lived up to it. . . . For 30 years I was
> a good wife and a good mother. . . . I went to church and I worked in
> the community but my family always came first. . . . Then my husband
> decided he wanted a younger woman and he left me . . . he didn't need
> a reason my lawyer said . . . it didn't matter if I didn't do anything wrong
> . . . it didn't matter that he was the one to commit adultery. He broke
> our contract—the contract we both agreed to when we got married. But
> I'm the one who is being punished.

Many attorneys talked of the need to educate clients to the realities
of the new law. As one said:

> Attorneys today are advising our clients, "Look, you can't go into court
> and do any name-calling." . . . Clients generally come into the office with
> this huge set of facts. You have to make them understand its irrelevant
> now. . . . They can't use it. You can tell your wife today that you're
> going to sleep with Mary Roe tonight and you can tell her where it's
> going to take place, and there isn't a damn thing that she can do about
> it in the courtroom. She can't discuss it at all. All she can get is a dissolu-
> tion, one-half the community property and, under proper circumstances,
> some spousal support. Or the opposite can be true with the husband.
> She can say, "Look, I'm a nymph and I'm going to sleep with three guys
> tonight."
>
> Attorneys tell their clients in advance. Of course we still have this
> problem with the blame syndrome and people are torn to pieces, they
> have this sort of heartache, and we see things happening where the woman
> is either gaining weight or losing weight, or the man is . . . But [now]
> there's less chance to act on this blame factor . . . and it has a curative
> effect . . . because people face up to this reality.

As this attorney suggests, many of the divorcing men and women
responded positively to the "new reality." As one man said

> It's realistic and there's none of that garbage that people in New York
> use. After all, who really knows what went wrong . . . we just grew
> apart . . . and we're better off apart . . . and we're certainly better off
> without an expensive legal hassle to prove it."

Similarly, a woman responded with relief:

> I was so relieved when I found out that it didn't matter why I wanted the divorce, that I didn't have to justify it to anyone. . . . It was my choice. That's the way it should be. It's a private, personal decision.

This attitude was more common among younger men and women. As another man said:

> I think the no-fault law is a great improvement. My brother got divorced under the old law and it was awful. His wife said all these horrible things about him—she had to—and it tore him up. This law is much better. It's the way it should be. No one should bother with why you can't get along with your wife.

Several attorneys noted that the new rules also changed the lawyer's role in the divorce process:

> I think perhaps there's even a difference in selecting lawyers. Prior to the new law a lot of people were going out looking for killer lawyers so they could air all of their frustration and hate . . . there were some lawyers that had that reputation. I don't think that's as much true today. And I think most of the women understand today—unless they're involved in a custody case, which is a different story—that things have changed with the law, as far as no grounds.

While divorcing men and women are sometimes ambivalent about the ease with which a no-fault divorce can be obtained, most of them expressed approval of the new rules.* Even more positive were the attorneys and judges who thought the present system was a vast improvement over the courtroom charades and perjury that were common under the old system. As one attorney put it:

> The old system was degrading for everyone. Today you can practice family law and hold your head up. It's become much more interesting and much more civilized.

No-Fault: Eliminating the Moral Framework

When the new law abolished the concept of fault, it also eliminated the framework of guilt, innocence, and interpersonal justice that had structured court decisions in divorce cases. With this seemingly simple

---

* The percentage of each sex who thought the law was fair varied by how the question was worded, with more affirmative responses to simple yes/no questions. Thus in response to the following question "The California Divorce law provides for a no-fault divorce. That means one person cannot be held responsible for the failure of the marriage. Do you think that is fair?" over 90 percent of the divorced men and women said yes. However, when asked to respond on a five-point scale to the question "Do you think the California divorce law is fair or not?" a lower percentage, although still a majority, rated it very fair or fair (56 percent of the men, and 65 percent of the women).

move, the California legislature not only vanquished the law's moral
condemnation of marital misconduct; it also dramatically altered the
legal definition of the reciprocal obligations of husbands and wives
during marriage.

There were two rationales for rejecting the traditional concept
of fault: it was based on the artificial conception that *one person* was
responsible for the marital breakup, and it was based on the assumption
that the court could determine which person that was. The reformers
argued that even if the court could determine who deserved the greater
blame, which they thought unlikely, this question entailed an inappropriate invasion of marital privacy. The focus of the new law was to
be on the present and the future (i.e., on fashioning an equitable settlement) rather than on the past (i.e., on trying to reconstruct who did
what dreadful thing to whom).

The vision of the reformers is instructive. They hoped to create
a vastly improved system, based firmly in reality, that guaranteed
equitable, workable, and fair awards once the evils of fault were abolished:

> It was unanimously agreed that elimination of the present grounds . . .
> would conform the law to prevailing reality, eliminate the existing evils
> of dissimulation, hypocrisy, and outright perjury, and end the use of con-
> duct not formally alleged as a weapon in obtaining extortionate and fre-
> quently inequitable and unworkable concessions from the defending
> spouse. Under the present system, we in effect . . . determine custody,
> property division, and awards of alimony and support upon the threat
> of disclosure of marital misconduct.[24]

In this respect their vision of the future was correct: our interviews
with California judges and lawyers who handled divorce cases before
and after the legal reform indicate that the abolition of fault has had
a major impact on the legal process. These experts reported that under
the old law the guilt and innocence were important considerations
both in negotiations and in trial outcomes, and they influenced property
and alimony awards. As one attorney remarked, "Fault made a big
difference; if the old man was an S.O.B. or was running around with
a twenty-year-old girl, you knew you were going to clean him out."
Not so under the new law. Neither party's behavior—whether positive
or negative—is relevant today.*

---

* While moral notions of fault have been eliminated, the new law does allow for
adjustments in cases of financial mismanagement. As one attorney explained:

> If the husband expends community funds improperly, he can be surcharged. Say the
> husband has a girl friend who takes a lot of trips, and the wife's lawyer finds out—

Many men and women were distressed to discover that fault no longer matters. The lack of penalties for adultery, for example, and the absence of rewards for "good marital behavior" violated their commonsense understandings of the terms of the marriage contract.

Consider first the question of adultery. Under the old law the adulterous husband or wife typically had to pay for his or her infidelity with a disadvantageous property or alimony award. Today, in contrast, there are no penalties for adultery and no rewards for fidelity. Here is how one divorced woman expressed her outrage at finding out her husband would suffer no financial penalty for betraying her:

> You may want to kill the bastard, humiliate him and make him pay through the nose, but go try and find a lawyer that will help you do it. All they know how to say is, "It's not relevant." "It's not relevant"—I've heard it a hundred times like a broken record. Why the hell isn't it relevant? He screws my best friend and they say "You have to learn to forget it. . . ." What did I get? Not one red cent.

It is evident that this woman believed (as did over 90 percent of the men and women we interviewed) that sexual fidelity was one of the terms of the moral (and legal) contract she had with her husband, and that he should have to "pay" if he violated that term. Although not all our respondents would agree that the payment should be financial (some would have settled for an admission of guilt and an apology; others wanted public humiliation) and some might feel mollified if there were appropriate mitigating circumstances, most of them expressed at least some discomfort with the no-fault norm that no consequences whatsoever—neither financial awards nor the traditional retribution of courtroom embarrassment—are to be imposed on an adulterous spouse.

Along the same lines, many men and women were dismayed to learn that no one cared about who was "responsible" for the divorce. Here again, while most of the men and women we interviewed did *not* feel the responsible party should be "punished," some were nevertheless distressed to find that the legal rules totally ignored the violation of marital vows. As one man said:

> She's the one who left me. She's the one who wanted out. That should count for something.

Along the same lines, a woman complained:

---

takes a deposition, finds out there was a trip to Europe, a trip here, some gifts. I'm talking about the substantial case where the guy has spent $5,000, $10,000, $15,000 on somebody else. It could be a single $500 gift item.

This law legitimizes desertion. It says you do something that is wrong and we won't call it wrong. We'll say it's okay. Well, it's not okay. It is not okay for a man to just walk out on his family when we haven't done anything wrong.

Clearly the no-fault law has obliterated one of the basic functions of the traditional divorce law, discussed in Chapter 1. Under the old law the spousal obligations of the traditional marriage contract were reinforced upon divorce. A party who adhered to his or her marital vows could expect to be rewarded at divorce, and one who strayed could expect to be punished. But today the marriage contract can be broken and the spouse who has abided by its terms is not entitled to any damages or compensation at divorce. Neither the loss of the contract, nor the hardships suffered as a result of that loss, matter under the new law.

Once again, attorneys have to educate their clients to the new legal norms:

Of course they're hurt and want to get back to him or her but I try to use some psychology and cool them out . . . I tell them they are better off without him or her if their ex was such a bastard. Usually I bring them around . . . or I try to get them into counselling.

Other attorneys "allow" their clients to talk about fault, even though it is legally irrelevant, because it helps them to represent their clients in negotiations:

. . . I point out to them that it's not material in court unless we have a custody problem, . . . but I still allow clients to discuss these matters because it's a safety valve, and also, as a lawyer, you get a better picture of the forces that drive your client, so you know how to deal with that.

But not everyone sees his or her marriage in these traditional terms nor does everyone want to discuss these matters with an attorney. As one woman said:

We just didn't get along and we both wanted out. . . . I was glad he (the attorney) didn't try to lay a guilt trip on me.

Similarly, a man said:

My lawyer was a real cool lady and she handled the divorce like a business matter: here's what it's worth and here's your share. . . . I thought that was fine, just fine.

As we noted, most of the divorced men and women we interviewed generally approved of the no-fault concept and thought it was fair "that one person cannot be held responsible for the failure of the marriage."*

The attorneys and judges we interviewed were equally approving of the principles of the no-fault law. Since most of them had practiced under the fault system, they were aware of its abuses, and few of them wanted to return to the sham testimony, mudslinging, and vilification of the old law.

The one source of dissatisfaction with the no-fault regime involves one of its unanticipated side effects; the no-fault rules have eliminated the lever that lawyers used under the old law to get decent economic settlements for wives. As attorney Riane Eisler notes, under the fault system, if a woman made marriage her full-time job, and if a judge thought she had done her job well, and if her husband had the means, she could expect a good settlement. But the elimination of guilt and innocence under the no-fault law took away the weapons lawyers traditionally used to get her that economic settlement.[25] If she isn't innocent, and he isn't guilty, there is no longer any lever to get her more property or spousal support.[26]

No Consent

Perhaps as radical as the elimination of grounds and fault is the new law's abolition of the need to obtain a spouse's agreement to divorce. Under the new law in California all that is needed is *one* party's assertion of marital breakdown. The second party does not have to concur in the assertion, nor agree to the divorce. The no-fault law thereby permits one spouse to decide—unilaterally—to get divorced and there is virtually nothing the other spouse can do to stop it.**

The no-consent standard is entirely different from mutual-consent statutes that allow a no-fault divorce if the parties agree.[27] Mutual-consent rules leave the decision to divorce in the hands of both spouses.

---

* As might be expected, approval varied inversely with marital duration: those married more than 18 years were less likely to approve of no-fault but, still, even in this group, a majority said that both the concept and the law were fair.

** We asked matrimonial attorneys about the following hypothetical situation: Let us say a woman client has come to you for advice. Her husband wants a divorce but she is still in love with him and wants to stay married. What kind of advice would you give her? Is there any legal way in which she could prevent the dissolution?

Not one attorney suggested a way for the woman to stop the divorce. While some attorneys suggested counseling, and others suggested delay tactics, no one said she could do anything to stop the divorce.

But no-consent rules place it in the hands of one spouse. The decision is unilateral: if one party wishes to terminate a marriage he or she can do it regardless of the wishes of the other party.

The no-consent standard reflects the shift from restrictive law to permissive law. The no-fault law took the first step in this direction by placing the decision about the divorce in the hands of the parties involved (in contrast to the state-defined grounds for divorce under the old law.) The no-consent rule carries this reform one step farther: it places the decision in the hands of just one party. In contrast to the old law assumption that one had "a right" to remain married if one adhered to one's marriage contract, the new law elevates one's "right" to divorce by permitting divorce at either party's request.

Obviously, the possibility of unilateral divorce undermines the power of the reluctant spouse, because it eliminates the need for behind-the-scenes negotiations (in fact, the need to communicate at all) to secure his or her consent. Once again, many divorced men and women we interviewed were surprised to learn that their spouse could obtain a divorce without their consent. As two men said,

> I really could not believe it! I felt totally powerless. She didn't ask me what I wanted . . . she didn't even tell me she was going to file. . . . One day I got home from work and found the papers in the mail. . . .

> I couldn't believe it when the lawyer said she was right. I had no choice—she didn't need me to get a divorce.

A major consequence of the no-consent standard has been to shift the power from the spouse who wants to remain married to the spouse who wants to get divorced.

As a result, the no-consent rule encourages—or at least greatly facilitates—divorce. In addition, by empowering the party who seeks the divorce to make a unilateral decision, the new law greatly increases the likelihood that divorce will in fact occur. Finally, the no-consent rule, along with the no-fault rules, removes the other major disincentives to divorce by making divorce less difficult, as we have seen, and less costly, as we will see below.

Once again, the underlying structure of divorce negotiations has been altered. The unanticipated and probably unintended consequences of the no-consent rule have fallen most heavily on the older and economically weaker wife. As attorney Fran Leonard, an attorney for the Older Women's League, notes:

> Under the fault system, if one spouse opposed the divorce, the other had to "bargain" in order to get it. For example, if a man wished a divorce

in order to remarry, either he would have to prove, over her opposing testimony, that his wife was an adulteress, or insane, or some such; or he would "bargain" with her. The bargain often was a property settlement in exchange for her "giving" him the divorce. (She would file, accusing him of one of the traditional grounds, and he would offer no opposition.)

With the advent of no-fault, older wives lost this tool. No longer is there an "innocent" party to be awarded extra property and support. No longer can she unilaterally hang on to the marriage until the terms offered secure her future apart from the marriage.[28]

As Leonard concludes, superficially, this appears fair: few people favor perpetuating dead marriages on something very close to economic blackmail. But the practical result of this apparently fair rule has been a drastically diminished settlement for the economically dependent homemaker.*

Since most of the divorced men and women we interviewed had not experienced a divorce under the old law, they had no standard of comparison for evaluating the no-consent rule. In general, they approved of its underlying principle—the freedom to leave a marriage that was no longer satisfying. For example, in response to the following statement, "No-fault also means that you can't stop your wife/husband from getting a divorce even if you don't want to be divorced. Do you think that is fair?" Over 85 percent of the divorced men and women we interviewed said yes.** In addition, in response to the question, "If one person is responsible for the failure of the marriage do you think he or she should be able to get a divorce if his or her husband or wife doesn't want to be divorced?" Over 85 percent of the interview sample said yes.

No Compensation/No Retribution in Financial Awards

Because the traditional divorce law linked both the granting of divorce and the terms of financial settlement to the determination of fault, it created both moral and financial incentives for spouses to exaggerate and escalate their accusations of fault. Fault-based charges, if substantiated, paid off in financial rewards for the aggrieved or "innocent" spouse.

---

* In the final chapter of this book we suggest some ways to solve this problem without returning to the fault system.

** Here again, those in marriages of more than 18 years were less likely to agree, but even in this subgroup a clear majority agreed with the statement.

Under no-fault, in contrast, there is no punishment for the guilty party and no reward for the innocent because the courts no longer concern themselves with guilt and innocence. The reformers contended that it was outmoded policy to grant alimony and property as a reward for virtue and to withhold them as a punishment for sin. They argued that justice for both parties would be better served by considering their economic situations instead of their guilt or innocence.

Here again attorneys are the critical socialization agents for the no-fault norms: they "educate" their clients about what "counts" (economically) under the current law. The woman who comes in to her attorney's office expecting a generous financial settlement because her husband is a Casanova, and the man who wishes to see his wife cut off without a cent because she ran away with her tennis instructor will both soon learn that they will not find any support for their financial requests in court. Instead, the attorney is likely to counsel both to "forget the past," to "realize you are better off without her/him" and to "build your own life." As hollow as these phrases may sound to many of the newly separated, they accurately reflect the "new economic reality" of no-fault divorce.

The new economic reality also means that there are no financial rewards for "good behavior" during marriage. In most areas of life Americans believe that good conduct and virtue ought to be rewarded. Traditional family law promised these rewards for those who had fulfilled their marital obligations (the housewife who devoted herself to her husband, home, and children, and the husband who devoted himself to providing them with life's necessities), and many of the divorced women and men whom we interviewed felt that was as it should be. Thus the absence of economic rewards for virtue under no-fault often came as a shock.

Most distressed were those who had led their lives according to the traditional norms through long-term marriages. For example, a fifty-five-year-old Los Angeles surgeon, explaining that he never took time off to go to the symphony orchestra or to spend a carefree summer at the beach with his wife and children because he thought his job was to "be there to earn the money so that my kids and wife could have everything they wanted," expressed his feelings of outrage this way:

> Now, *she* walked out on *me*, and what do *I* get? Nothing. Nothing. And what does *she* get? She gets half of my house, half of my pension . . . (etc.). For what, I ask you? For running off with a jerk psychologist. That's my reward?

It is not surprising that many of the older men and women feel that "they've changed the rules in the middle of the game." No-fault laws have changed the rules. And, once again, it is typically the attorneys who must educate the unrewarded "innocent" spouse to the fact that the no-fault law provides neither compensation nor retribution through its financial awards.

The economic messages of the new law are clear: it no longer "pays" to invest in the marital partnership—to be a faithful breadwinner or a devoted homemaker. One's economic "take" from the marriage will be the same no matter what one has done.

The reformers probably did not foresee this result because they were so entrenched in the old framework. Their major concern was the removal of the financial incentives that the old system provided for spouses to blame each other. Their vision extended only as far as the abolition of fault, acrimony, and bitterness and the more realistic financial awards they hoped it would bring.[29]

Consider, for example, the new standards they established for the division of property. To remove the incentives for fault-based accusations, and to remove the possibility of courts considering who did what to whom, the new California law specifies that courts *must* divide the marital property equally: half to the husband, half to the wife. The California reformers favored this fixed rule because it limited judicial discretion. In addition, the equal division standard was seen as fair—and "protective" of wives—because it was based on the community property presumption that marriage is an equal partnership in which the financial and nonfinancial contributions of the two spouses are of equal worth. It guaranteed each spouse one-half of the jointly accumulated property.*

The changes in the rules for dividing property have had a major impact. Before 1970, under the old law, the "innocent" plaintiff, usually the wife, was typically awarded a significantly larger share of the marital assets. In 1968 wives were awarded more than half (60 percent or more) of the property in both San Francisco and Los Angeles cases. Most of these awards allowed the wife to keep the family home and its furnishings, which often constituted the single most valuable family asset.

The no-fault law brought a dramatic shift in property awards: after

* This concept also met with widespread approval among the men and women (and lawyers and judges) we interviewed. For example, when asked, "The California divorce law requires judges to divide equally all the property and possession that a married couple acquires—that is, for each person to get half. Do you think that is fair?" close to 80 percent of the men and women said yes. (There were no differences by marital duration.)

1970 the wife's share of the property declined and "equal" division became the norm. Between 1968 and 1977 the percentage of cases in which the property was divided equally rose from 26 percent to 64 percent of the cases in Los Angeles.

One important result of this shift has been a tremendous increase in the number of family homes being sold upon divorce. The legal tradition was to award the family house to the wife, especially if she had custody of the children and needed the home to maintain a stable environment for them. But today more homes are being sold so that the property can be divided equally. (The number of cases in which there was an explicit court order to sell the home rose from about one in ten in 1968 to about one in three in 1977.)

Surprisingly, the presence of minor children in the home has not deterred judges from ordering it sold: our data reveal that 66 percent of the couples who were ordered to sell their homes had minor children. (The disruptive impact of forced home sales and residential changes on minor children is explored further in Chapters 4 and 8.)

The new standards for alimony were similarly fashioned in the sweeping effort to rid the divorce process of all vestiges of fault and its harmful effects. Surprisingly the Governor's Commission spent little time on the questions of alimony: their major concern was that it be decided without reference to marital fault.[30] At first, the state bar objected to the elimination of fault because, as they pointed out, it would "reward" the adulterous wife:

> Under the Act an adulterous or drinking wife would be as entitled to alimony as one who conducted herself as one would normally expect a wife to act and who was then wilfully abandoned by the husband in favor of a younger woman.[31]

In the end, however, the bar representatives were persuaded that all references to fault had to be eliminated to prevent the acrimony the bill was designed to prevent.*

Gender-neutral Expectations

One of the aims of the divorce law's reformers was to try to effect equal treatment for men and women by abolishing the sex-based assumptions of the traditional law. Thus the new law no longer assumes

---

* Surprisingly, the alimony debate focused on sanctions against the "guilty wife." Since she benefited from the new no-fault rule, the new standards were seen as more protective—rather than as less protective—of potentially vulnerable and dependent wives.

that husbands will be responsible for the financial support of their former wives. Nor does it seek to maintain the dependency of homemakers and mothers after divorce.

In rejecting the traditional assumption of a wife's continued dependency after divorce, the reformers pointed to the changing position of women in general, and to their increased participation in the labor force in particular: they assumed that the new woman would soon be capable of supporting herself after divorce. Thus the new standards for alimony—to be based on the financial needs and circumstances of the parties—instruct judges to "take into account the spouse's ability to engage in gainful employment.[32]

While the reformers recognized that a custodial parent and an older housewife might need support, they did not believe that a young woman, whether a housewife or employed, deserved long-term support; she was a potential "alimony drone" who probably had the ability to be gainfully employed.

Clearly there was an undercurrent of sympathy for the stereotypical divorced man condemned to lifelong alimony payments, and a genuine but naive optimism about the stereotypical divorced woman who would be welcomed with open arms (and a large salary) by an ever-expanding nondiscriminatory labor force.[33]

Surprisingly, it was not until August of 1969, after the no-fault divorce law had been passed (and was waiting for the governor's signature) that someone drew attention to the implicit message in the new rules for alimony. San Francisco Chronicle columnist Charles McCabe observed that "it seemed certain that under the new law, a lot of ladies who usually spend their time at watering places, living off fat settlements, and healthy alimony checks, are going to have to get off their beautiful duffs and go to work."[34] As McCabe predicted, the new law has brought a change in the pattern of alimony awards.

CHANGES IN ALIMONY AWARDS:
THE NEW STANDARD OF SELF-SUFFICIENCY

Since 1970 there have been several changes in the patterns of alimony, or "spousal support" awards, as they are now called. First, in accord with the new law's goal of making the wife self-sufficient after divorce, there has been a shift from permanent awards based on the premise of the wife's continued dependency, to time-limited transitional awards. Between 1968 and 1972 permanent alimony (until death or remarriage), dropped from 62 to 32 percent of the alimony awards in Los Angeles County. By 1972 (and in subsequent years) two-thirds of the spousal support awards were transitional awards for a limited and specified duration. The median duration of these fixed-time awards was twenty-five months, about two years. Thus the average award carries an expectation of a short transition from marriage to self-sufficiency.

Second, the standards of the new law have dictated a greater reliance on the wife's ability to support herself. Economic criteria, such as the wife's occupation and her predivorce income, are therefore more important than under the old standards of fault and innocence. In light of the new criteria, it may seem surprising to find wives with rather low predivorce incomes ($10,000 a year) and wives with rather limited and marginal employment histories, being denied spousal support because the courts presume they are capable of supporting themselves. But that is indeed the case. While a woman's chances of being awarded alimony are also influenced by her age, husband's income, and the length of the marriage, in general the courts are applying minimal and unrealistic standards of self-sufficiency and denying support to most divorced women.

The result of this approach is that the vast majority of divorced women, roughly five out of six divorced, are not awarded alimony. Only 17 percent of the divorced women were awarded alimony in 1978 (these awards averaged $350 a month in 1984 dollars). Although the percentage of alimony awards is less than under the old law, alimony has always been rare because it was awarded only to the wives of middle-class and upper-class men—and these couples have always comprised a small minority of the divorcing population. But the patterns of awards within this group have been drastically altered by no-fault.

Thus the major impact of no-fault divorce on alimony awards is in its *new expectations for middle-class and upper-class women.* Instead of the old law's assumption that these women would remain dependent and therefore need permanent alimony, no-fault has brought an expectation that they *will become independent and self-sufficient after divorce.* Thus, increasingly, middle-class women are either being denied alimony altogether, especially if they have worked or have earned even minimal incomes before divorce, or are awarded small amounts for short periods of time to "ease the transition." However, an award of $350 a month in 1984 dollars for a period of two years conveys a clear message to the middle-class recipient: she must find employment right away to earn enough money to support herself and her children.

It is interesting to note that the new law guarantees, in theory, support for three groups of women who are exempted from the new standards of self-sufficiency: women with custody of young children, women in need of transitional support, and older homemakers incapable of self-sufficiency. However, despite the law's guarantees, the new legal norms are being applied to these women as well. Few of them are awarded support.

Consider first the situation of mothers of preschool children. Alimony awards to mothers of children under six have dropped more than for any other group under the new law. By 1978, only 13 percent of them were awarded spousal support.

Why does the presence of young children appear to have so little effect on alimony awards? In the chapters that follow we will see how the goal of making the wife self-sufficient has taken priority over the goal of supporting the custodial parent. Two-thirds of the Superior Court judges who hear family law cases in Los Angeles espoused this new ideology: it was "good" for a divorced woman to earn money instead of being dependent on her former husband; work was a healthy form of rehabilitation that would help her build a new life, and combining work and motherhood was now normal in our society. Although the sex-neutral standards of the new law give priority to the needs of custodial parents caring for minor children, the judges' responses suggest that they are always balancing the interests of children against the father's interest in keeping his income for himself. When they are able to rationalize work as healthy and good for all newly divorced women, they can conclude that her working is better for "the family as a whole." They thereby solve the problem of the husband's limited financial resources by allowing him to keep most of his income.

Despite judges' reports of how they think they divide the husband's income, empirical analysis of the pattern of awards reveals that the husband is rarely ordered to part with more than one-third of his income to support his wife and children. He is therefore allowed to retain two-thirds for himself while his former wife and children, typically three people, are allowed the remaining one-third. Since living on this amount is usually impossible, the divorced woman must either work or seek other sources of support, such as welfare.

A similar combination of social and economic considerations is used to justify the low level of alimony awards to women in transition. The term "women in transition" refers to women who were employed early in their marriage, or have been employed in irregular or part-time jobs at various times, but who have not worked steadily and need a period of adjustment, retraining, and counseling to reenter the labor force.

As we noted above, women who worked before divorce (even at part-time marginal jobs) and those who earned at least $10,000 a year were typically "presumed" to be capable of supporting themselves after divorce. Thus many who could have benefited from the education and retraining that transitional awards are supposed to provide were denied these opportunities. The small group of women who were awarded transitional support typically got short-term awards—a year or two—which were rarely sufficient in the turmoil and aftermath of a divorce. Nevertheless, judges are clearly reluctant to "require" a husband to "finance" his ex-wife's retraining.

This attitude is exemplified in the judges' responses to the following hypothetical divorce case. A nurse supported her doctor-husband for eight years through college, medical school, an internship, and residency. (See the Rose case in Appendix B, p. 415.) After eleven years of marriage, they decided to divorce. The wife, now twenty-nine years old, wants to go to medical school. Would you, we asked judges, award her four years of support to allow her to do that? Less than one-third (31 percent) of the judges said they would. They did not think it fair to saddle her husband with her "optional" expenses since she was clearly capable of supporting herself. If this is the judicial response to a "strong case" in which a woman had supported her husband for eight years, it is not surprising to learn that few judges seriously support the notion of awards for education and retraining.

The third group of women who were supposed to be exempted from the new law's standards of self-sufficiency are the older women who have been housewives and mothers throughout marriages of long duration. Although many more women in this category are awarded spousal support, one out of three is not. Once again, the judges approach these cases mindful of the husband's need for "his income" and his limited capacity to support two families.

Thus, the empirical consequences of the new standards for alimony awards poignantly illustrate the strength of the new legal norms of gender neutrality and gender equality. No-fault attempts to treat men and women equally—or *as if they were equal*—at the point of divorce. However, it ignores *the structural inequality* between men and women in the larger society. Divorced women and divorced men do not have the same opportunities: the women are more likely to face job and salary discrimination and more likely to be restricted by custodial responsibilities.

A second problem with the reformers' attempt to institute equality at the point of divorce is that women have typically been unequally disadvantaged by marriage itself. If one thinks of the common marital pattern in which a housewife and mother supports her husband's career as a doctor, lawyer, or businessman, it is evident that marriage can vastly alter the employment prospects of the two spouses in different directions. His career prospects may be enhanced, while hers are impaired; his earning capacity may grow, while hers diminishes. Thus marriage itself can be partly responsible for the dramatically different prospects that men and women face after divorce. Their opportunities are not, in fact, equal.

In light of these structural impediments to postdivorce equality for men and women, it is not surprising that this research finds that women and the minor children in their households experience a 73 percent decline in standard of living in the first year after the divorce. In contrast, men experience a 42 percent rise in their standard of living one year after divorce. This vast discrepancy between former husbands and wives is partially a result of the fact that men are typically not ordered to pay alimony and are asked to pay very meager amounts of child support. They do not, in effect, have to share their incomes with their former wives and children after divorce. This leaves them with much more money—absolutely and relatively—to spend on themselves.

Women, on the other hand, who typically earn much less money, often have custody of their children whom they are expected to support with little financial aid from their ex-husbands. As we noted above, it is not just the wage and employment gap between men and women in the larger society, but also the different opportunities and responsibilities that marriage imposes and the way the law reacts—or fails to react—to them that leads to the rapid downward mobility of divorced women (and children) after divorce.

SEX-NEUTRAL RESPONSIBILITIES FOR CHILDREN

The final rejection of traditional marital roles involves the responsibility for children after divorce. The traditional custodial preference for the mother (for children of tender years) was replaced by a sex-neutral standard (the "best interests of the child") and more recently by a joint custody preference. Similarly, the new equality between the spouses is reflected in child support standards: the new law makes both husbands and wives responsible for child support.

In contrast to the clear-cut effects that no-fault law has had on property and alimony awards, the new standards for child custody and child support have not, as yet, resulted in any dramatic changes. In general, most mothers and fathers still prefer maternal custody arrangements as they did under the old law. (But see Chapter 8 for other effects of the new custody law.) Similarly, the pattern of child support awards has not been altered by the no-fault reforms.

Nonadversarial Divorce: The New Social-Psychological Climate

The final but perhaps the most fundamental aim of the no-fault law was to alter the social-psychological climate of divorce by eliminating the adversarial process. As we have seen, the reformers believed that at least some of the acrimony of a fault-based divorce resulted from the legal process itself, rather than from the inherent difficulties of dissolving a marriage. They saw divorcing husbands and wives as potentially "amicable," but the *legal process* forced them to become antagonists. The need to prove fault, and the financial benefits to be gained from exaggerated accusations, were the villains in the process: they encouraged legal wrangling, generated hostility, and exacerbated acrimony.

The reformers hoped that no-fault would create a different climate for divorce. By eliminating fault they sought to eliminate the hypocrisy, perjury, and collusion "required by courtroom practice under the fault system"; to reduce the adversity, acrimony, and bitterness surrounding divorce proceedings; to lessen the personal stigma attached to divorce; and to create conditions for more rational and equitable settlements of property and spousal support.[35] In brief, the new law attempted to bring divorce legislation into line with the social reality of marital breakdown as a more common and more acceptable event in contemporary society.

Although it is difficult to measure hostility and acrimony in the legal process, several indicators suggest that the no-fault law has in fact served to reduce litigiousness. For example, the random samples of divorce cases drawn from court records reveal significant changes after 1970, when the no-fault law went into effect. There was a sharp reduction in legal activity between filing and the interlocutory decree,* and a shorter time between the filing and final decree, both suggesting a less acrimonious process.[36]

---

* The decree that sets out the property, support, and custody awards. The final decree is largely *pro forma.*

A decline in litigiousness is also suggested by the reduction in the number of pages in case files. The percentage of thin files (under twenty pages) increased significantly after the no-fault law was instituted, while the percentage of extremely litigious ones (fifty pages or more) declined. At its minimum, a no-fault California divorce requires only five pages in a court file and approximately two minutes of court time.*

Since few of the divorced men and women we interviewed had obtained a divorce under the old law, they had no basis for comparing their experience with a fault-based system. Although a minority reported that "there was a lot of conflict in my divorce" (28 percent of the men, 31 percent of the women), or that "there was a lot of hostility and bitterness in my divorce" (26 percent of the men, 40 percent of the women), we cannot know how the same respondents might have described their experiences under the old law.

Although it is not a strictly comparable sample, Professor Paul Bohannan, an anthropologist, conducted in-depth interviews with men and women going through the divorce process in California in the mid-1960s, under the old law.[37] After reading through his interviews I have a strong impression of a world of difference. In the 1960s many divorcing men and women seemed preoccupied with making and defending charges of adultery and mental cruelty, with threats of telling the world, or at least the court, of their spouses' personal failures and infidelities. Attorneys encouraged the vilification and stimulated adversarial behavior and animosity. Today, in contrast, with both the financial and legal incentives to exaggerate fault abolished, adversarial spouses are more likely to report being "cooled out" and cut off by their attorneys instead of being encouraged.

The greater antagonism and bitterness under a fault system is also evident in a second "comparative" sample. Sociologists Graham Spanier and Linda Thompson interviewed divorced men and women under a traditional fault law in the state of Pennsylvania in 1977,[38] just one year before our California interviews. They reported that the majority of their respondents expressed a strong dislike of the legal system because it forced them to accuse and blame their partners. Typical comments were: "It was just terrible, all the listing of indignities, and placing blame and fault." and "You have to make him look rotten. I didn't like making him look worse than he really was."[39]

Spanier and Thompson note that the fault-based legal system en-

---

* It is now possible to reduce court time even further and to obtain a divorce without appearing in court. If a couple has no minor children and less than $10,000 in community property they may file for and obtain their divorce by mail.

couraged the parties to become adversaries to a greater degree than they already were, aggravated their already fragile relationship, fostered antagonism between them, and upset and humiliated them by forcing public discussion of their intimate problems. Their respondents reported they were urged to lie about each other and to use "dirty tricks." As one woman stated:

> I just couldn't do the lying, so he did. It really got to me—all the dirty little games you have to play. Having to tell all those twisted half-truths.[40]

As this quote suggests, the Pennsylvania men and women were also disturbed by the dishonesty and perjury in the fault system.

A final complaint of the respondents in the fault system concerned the tactics attorneys used to prolong the divorce, increase fees, and make the parties behave like enemies. As one woman said:

> His lawyer tried to make me crack. I don't know how they live with their conscience. . . . [He] broke me down in stages. I just gave up for peace and serenity. After we started the court case he [husband] wouldn't let me charge anything and would let checks bounce that I wrote. We never finished the case. He told lies. I felt deflated. It was all part of his lawyer's tactics. They work. . . . He [attorney] knew it was tearing me up. I know [it was the lawyer] because other people who have used him told me."[41]

Fortunately the Pennsylvania interviews included several of the same questions we asked in California so that some direct comparisons are possible. Overall, respondents express much less satisfaction with the legal process under the fault system: 55 percent of the Pennsylvania respondents indicated they were dissatisfied with the entire divorce process (including the laws, judges, and lawyers), compared to 18 percent of our California respondents.

Under the fault system in Pennsylvania, respondents were more likely to report that their lawyers advised them to do things that might anger their spouses (29 percent versus 8 percent in California), and were more likely to say that they had to lie or make up statements in order to obtain a divorce (26 percent compared to less than 3 percent in our California sample).[42]

Further, although only a minority of the Pennsylvania respondents were advised by their attorneys to engage in "dirty tricks" such as not paying bills (13 percent) and taking money out of savings (13 percent),[43] even fewer of the California respondents were so advised (respectively 6 percent, 8 percent). Finally, only 6 percent of those under the fault system said that the attorneys *decreased* the conflict and hostility between the spouses,[44] compared to 23 percent of the California men and women.

Overall, these responses reveal that the no-fault system is much less likely to stimulate and encourage antagonistic and hostile divorces.[45]

Interviews with attorneys and judges also suggest that there is less acrimony and hostility under no-fault. One anecdotal example is indicative. When asked how they would "build a case" under the adversarial system, attorneys told of asking clients "What are the most terrible mean things he (or she) ever did?" and encouraging their clients to add to these accusations by asking "What else can you think of?" or "Can you think of anything worse than that?" Under no-fault, in contrast, since the spouse's behavior is irrelevant to both the divorce and the financial settlement, attorneys rarely mention asking their

TABLE 1

Summary of Changes in Divorce Law

TRADITIONAL DIVORCE	NO-FAULT DIVORCE

Restrictive Law
  To protect marriage
	Permissive Law
	  To facilitate divorce

Specific Grounds
  Adultery, cruelty, etc.
	No Grounds
	  Marital breakdown

Moral Framework
  Guilt vs. innocence
	Administrative Framework
	  Neither responsible

Fault
  One party caused divorce
	No fault
	  Cause of divorce irrelevant

Consent of Innocent Spouse Needed
  Innocent spouse has power to prevent or delay the divorce
	No Consent Needed
	  Unilateral divorce
	  No consent or agreement required

Gender-based Responsibilities
  Husband responsible for alimony
  Wife responsible for custody
  Husband responsible for child
    support
	Gender-neutral Responsibilities
	  Both responsible for self-support
	  Both eligible for custody
	  Both responsible for child support

Financial Awards Linked to Fault
  Alimony for "innocent" spouse
  Greater share of property
    to "innocent" spouse
	Financial Awards Based on Equality
	  and need
	  Alimony based on need
	  Property divided equally

Adversarial
  One party guilty, one innocent
  Financial gain in proving fault
	Nonadversarial
	  No guilty or innocent party
	  No financial gain from charges
	  Amicable resolution encouraged

clients "personal questions" about their marriage or their spouses' behavior. Instead they expressed impatience with clients who want to
"waste their time" with these "irrelevant" emotional concerns. One
attorney's technique for handling these clients suggests how different
the no-fault climate is:

> I tell her that I am always willing to listen to her concerns but I'm not
> trained to do counseling. Then I look at my watch and remind her that
> my time is costing her $125 an hour.

A summary of the changes in divorce law that have been reviewed
in this section is provided in Table 1.

LAWS IN THE FIFTY STATES

California's pioneering divorce law reforms spearheaded the transformation of American family law in the 1970s and early 1980s. To what
extent is California's legal regime typical of the divorce laws in other
states? The review that follows[46] indicates the California model has
been extremely influential: many, although not all, of its key provisions
have been widely adopted. In general, the California law represents
the current liberal trends in American family law, and its innovations
are reflected in the laws in the other more progressive states, which
comprise about half of the United States.

One aspect of California's law is, however, unusual: California
is one of only eight community property states and one of the few
states that *require* an equal division of marital property. But here,
too, California may be in the vanguard, as we will see below.

No-Fault Grounds

All American states except South Dakota now have some form of no-
fault divorce. In a 1985 review of family law in the United States,
attorneys Doris Freed and Timothy Walker list eighteen states which
have a "pure" no-fault divorce law:[47] fourteen states, including California, follow the California model and make "marital breakdown" the
only ground for divorce.* (See Table C-1, in the Legal Appendix, Appendix C, on the grounds for divorce in the fifty states.) An additional

---

* Arizona, California, Colorado, Florida, Hawaii, Iowa, Kentucky, Michigan, Minnesota, Missouri, Montana, Nebraska, Oregon, and Washington. The other states with
incompatibility grounds have fault grounds as well.

three states have a similar standard in which incompatibility is the only ground for divorce.*

In contrast to these pure no-fault states, there are twenty-two more conservative jurisdictions that have added the no-fault standard of "marital breakdown" to their traditional fault-based grounds for divorce.** The social structure of divorce in a state with no-fault as an option is significantly different than in states with a pure no-fault system: the option of either a no-fault or a fault-based divorce permits parties to use the threat of fault-based charges in negotiations. That threat gives an unwilling spouse a great deal of leverage: by refusing to agree to a no-fault divorce he or she has the power to increase the cost, time, difficulty, and embarrassment involved in obtaining a divorce. As a result, many of the "no-fault" divorces in these states have been agreed to after behind-the-scenes negotiations involving allegations of fault. Thus these optional no-fault systems retain many of the structural features and consequences of the traditional system.

Some of the no-fault-option states have laws that permit a no-fault divorce for those "living separate and apart" for a specified period of time, while others provide for a judicial separation or separate maintenance agreement to be converted into a divorce after a specified period of time. In these time-based systems a spouse who is anxious to get a divorce may have to engage in negotiations about fault, but one who is willing to wait (and to let financial matters remain unresolved) until the required time has elapsed, may eventually be in a powerful position not unlike that of the leaving spouse in a no-consent state. This is also true if living separate and apart or a judicial separation are the *only* ground for divorce. (If, however, these options are combined with mutual consent grounds, the power of the leaving party is again undermined.)

The obvious multiplicity of options result in a number of states with hybrid systems that defy simple classification. However, among those states that can be easily classified, about half have followed California by adopting a more or less pure no-fault system, while the other half have retained a more traditional system with the addition of a no-fault option.

More recently a few states have extended the already permissive

---

* Kansas, New Mexico, and Oklahoma.

** Alabama, Alaska, Arkansas, Connecticut, Delaware, Georgia, Idaho, Illinois, Indiana, Maine, Maryland, Massachusetts, Mississippi, North Dakota, Ohio, Pennsylvania, Rhode Island, Tennessee, Texas, West Virginia, Wisconsin, and Wyoming.

no-fault system to allow "paper" dissolutions. These dissolutions are typically limited to childless couples with minimal assets. For example, in California, couples do not have to appear in court if they have no minor children and less than $10,000 in community property. They may file for and obtain their divorce through the mail.[48] Florida also has simplified procedures for childless couples who may obtain a divorce without a lawyer.[49]

No Consent

As we noted above, the no-consent rule shifts the power from the party who wants to stay married to the one who wants to get divorced. Consider, for example, a situation in which a husband wants a divorce but his wife is reluctant. Under the traditional law he had the burden of obtaining her agreement and might have to "buy" his freedom (that is, her agreement to file as the innocent party). Similarly, this husband would probably have to pay for his wife's consent under a mutual consent statute. But the no-consent rule shifts the burden to the wife: now she must beg or bargain or pay to preserve the marriage.

Most of the pure no-fault states follow California in allowing one party to make a unilateral decision about the divorce (without the consent or agreement of an unwilling partner). In addition, the three states that permit a no-fault divorce for those living separate and apart, without other requirements, may have a similar effect because they allow the spouse who is determined to divorce to make a unilateral decision if he or she is willing to "wait out" the statutory period. This, then, is still a minority pattern: overall, less than half of the states allow a divorce without the consent of an unwilling spouse.

Separation of Fault and Financial Awards

Although not all states have gone as far as California eliminating all considerations of fault for determining financial awards, the trend throughout the United States "is to minimize the importance of marital misconduct as a factor in settlements."[50]

With respect to alimony awards, most states, like California, now bar marital fault as a consideration. Twelve states explicitly exclude consideration of marital fault in determining whether or not alimony should be awarded (See Table C–2, Legal Appendix, Column A). Even though most other states also exclude fault, they, like California, do so by simply omitting it from the list of factors that should determine alimony. Only a small minority of nine states retain an explicit fault standard and make marital misconduct a bar to alimony (See Table C–2, Legal Appendix, Column B). A few other states retain fault as one of the relevant factors to be considered, and there is a great deal of variation in the extent to which judges explicitly or implicitly consider it.

Ironically, fault is more likely to be a factor in modifying an alimony award *after* divorce: thirteen states modify or terminate alimony if the recipient is cohabiting (see Table C-2, Legal Appendix), while another six make it discretionary. This is an issue that continues to be hotly debated in many states. An emerging consensus in the more liberal states allows modification if the wife's economic circumstances have substantially changed, but does not allow modification on the basis of cohabitation per se. As 1983 decisions in New Hampshire and New Jersey courts put it, the test for modification remains whether the cohabitation relationship has reduced *the financial needs* of the dependent former spouse. The extent of the actual economic dependency, not the status as a cohabitant, must determine the duration of support as well as its amount.[51]

Property awards also are increasingly disassociated from consideration of fault. (Here we are referring to traditional moral notions of fault as distinct from economic misconduct involving the misuse or dissipation of family assets. Most states allow the court to penalize a party who dissipates family property by making an offsetting award to the deprived spouse).

In their 1985 review of family law attorneys Freed and Walker counted sixteen California-like states that specifically exclude all fault-based consideration from property awards (See Table C–3, Legal Appendix.) While this represents a decline from the prevalent influence of marital misconduct in the past, nevertheless, a majority of twenty-two states still consider fault as a relevant factor in dividing property. (In the remaining state the rules are ambiguous or they make no mention of marital fault as a factor to be either considered or omitted from consideration in distributing property.)

Gender Neutrality and Economic Standards for Awards

Most states, following the California model, are gradually eliminating gender-based awards for alimony, property, child custody, and child support. Since each of these matters is discussed in depth in the chapters that follow, this review only highlights a few of the changes to illustrate the trends.

ALIMONY

All states except Texas provide for alimony or maintenance to be awarded upon divorce. As in California, the most important changes in alimony awards involve their new "economic" basis, and the shift from permanent to time-limited transitional awards. Legal changes in many states reflect these "minimalist" aims for alimony.

Even before the 1979 decision of the U.S. Supreme Court in *Orr* v. *Orr*[52] (which held gender-based alimony statutes unconstitutional), most states had "de-sexed alimony and authorized its award, under appropriate circumstances, to either spouse."[53]

Consider first the new economic criteria for alimony awards. Most states still have a long list of factors for the court to consider in awarding alimony. These typically include the length of marriage, the standard of living established during marriage, the parties' age, health, needs, and earning capacities (including the time and expense necessary to acquire sufficient education or training to find appropriate employment), custodial responsibilities, homemaker contributions to the career or career potential of the other party, and tax consequences.

In practice, however, courts are paying less attention to the standard of living of the marriage and more attention to each spouse's earning capacity and (especially the wife's) ability to be self-sufficient. The words of a 1983 Colorado decision are indicative: in distinguishing between "alimony" under the prior fault-based law, and "maintenance" under the new law, the court said "maintenance, unlike its predecessor, alimony, is primarily concerned with insuring that, after dissolution, the basic (economic) needs of a disadvantaged spouse are met."[54] The new terminology is highly significant: increasingly states have redefined alimony as maintenance, and have made maintenance directly contingent upon the recipient's earning capacity and economic need. Among the more extreme statutes is the Indiana law which provides for court-ordered alimony *"only* to physically or mentally handicapped spouses."[55]

The shift from permanent to time-limited alimony awards is also evident throughout the United States. In theory, the duration of these time-limited awards is to be set to allow "the time deemed necessary by the court for the party seeking alimony to gain sufficient education or training to enable the party to find suitable employment."[56] If, however, the California experience is typical, most of these awards are being limited to a few years at most. (They are often referred to by the insulting term "rehabilitative alimony," which suggests that the homemaker has not been engaged in productive or socially useful work during marriage.)

Several states now set a fixed time limit on all alimony awards. For example, New Hampshire limits alimony awards to three years (if there are no minor children), Delaware to two years (unless the recipient is mentally ill or the marriage lasted for twenty years), and Kansas, to an initial award of twelve months. While the awards in New Hampshire and Kansas may be extended, the burden of proof is heavily on the recipient.

Just a few years ago it seemed as if the trends towards short-term awards, based on a minimal concept of economic need, were unidirectional. However, in recent years appellate courts have chastised trial courts for punitive awards to older wives who could not easily become self sufficient.[57] Equally important, recent decisions have reintroduced sharing principles and norms of "equity," which were central to traditional concepts of alimony, and these principles broaden the narrow economic-need definition of alimony to encompass awards based on compensation, reimbursement, shared investments, equalized standards of living, and equity.[58] These issues are discussed at length in Chapters 6 and 7 on alimony,[59] and in Chapter 5 on the new property.[60]

PROPERTY

Two dimensions of California's law are reflected in reforms throughout the United States. The first concerns the pool of property available for the courts to divide at divorce. The second concerns the rules governing the division.

Consider first the pool of property to be divided at divorce. In Chapter 3 we discuss the two systems of property ownership in the United States, the community property system and the separate property system (also referred to as the common law system). Here it is relevant only to note that the distinctions between the two have eroded and a large number of separate property states have adopted community property-type rules, similar to those in California, for defining the marital property available for the courts to divide at divorce. This change represents a major departure from the traditional rule in most separate property states, where "title" controlled and the divorce court had no jurisdiction over property that was held in the name of one spouse. Thus, for example, if the house was in the husband's name, it belonged to him alone and could not be divided by a court upon divorce. Now, however, only one separate property state, Mississippi, retains strict title rules. (See Table C-4 in the Legal Appendix, Column B.)

By 1985 most separate property jurisdictions had adopted equitable distribution rules: in fifteen of these states the court may consider *all* property owned by either spouse as potentially available for division at divorce. In another twenty-seven states the court may divide only the marital property, i.e., the property acquired during the marriage. (See Table C-4, Legal Appendix.)

In most of these states, the definition of marital property excludes inherited property, which remains the separate property of the owner spouse. (However, five of the twenty-seven states—Delaware, Georgia, Missouri, New Hampshire, and North Dakota—allow the courts to divide inherited property as well.)

A related issue in defining marital property concerns the treatment of nontraditional forms of property such as pensions and educational degrees. Are these recognized as property and as part of the marital assets to be divided upon divorce? Again, recent years have brought significant changes in this area of the law, and a majority of states now regard pensions and retirement benefits as marital assets. Fewer states consider a professional degree, goodwill, insurance benefits, and other career assets as marital property. (Each of these assets is discussed at length in Chapter 5; see also Table C-5, Legal Appendix.)

Consider next the question of how the marital property is divided. As noted above, the one feature of California's divorce law that is *not* widely accepted in other states is its equal division rule—the rule that requires judges to divide the marital property equally between the two spouses. Only eight states require a 50/50 division of marital assets.*

In most states with equitable distribution standards the courts have the discretion to divide property "as justice requires." Since equitable distribution standards give judges considerable latitude, there is typically more variation in awards under these rules.

Despite the apparent deviant quality of the California rule, there

---

* Arizona, Arkansas, California, Idaho, Louisiana, Nevada, North Carolina, New Mexico, and Wisconsin. However, as noted below, a number of other states have a *de facto* equal division norm.

are several reasons to believe that equal division rules—or norms for a roughly equal division—are likely to be much more common in the future. The first is the tendency for judges in some equitable distribution states, such as Hawaii, to start with the presumption that a 50/50 division is "equitable." In these states the burden of proof shifts to the judge to justify an unequal award.

The second impetus toward equal division rules springs from a widespread dissatisfaction with the uncertainty, arbitrariness, and high attorney fees occasioned by equitable distribution.[61] For example, in 1983, attorney Emily Jane Goodman (now a judge) wrote of the soaring legal costs after New York instituted an equitable distribution law, and of the disproportionate burden this placed on women. Even wives of well-to-do men often did not have immediate access to cash to pay for lawyers' retainers and the expensive discovery necessary to uncover and document their husband's assets.[62]

A third pressure for equal division rules comes from those who have observed the results of equitable distribution rules in states with a common law tradition of awarding the wife one-third of the marital property. Since many common law or separate property states traditionally used a one-third rule of thumb to divide marital property (i.e., one third to the wife and two-thirds to the husband), judges in these states are still likely to define one-third as an "equitable share" for the wife.* With this as the basis of comparison, the California guarantee of one-half of the marital property for the wife has attracted considerable support among feminists and other reformers who seek greater recognition for the housewife's contribution to marital property.

A final impetus for equal division standards comes from the proposed Uniform Marital Property Act,[63] which would create a California-type system of community property, during marriage, in separate property states. Although the Uniform Act defers to state law at divorce, it is evident that states that define marital property as the property of both spouses during marriage will increasingly be pressed to define it as belonging to both of them at divorce. Thus the Uniform Act should create additional pressures for states to view an equal division as normative.[64]

For all these reasons, California's experience with an equal division rule is of great interest to reformers in other states. In the pages that follow we will see how this apparently fair and equal rule has not, in practice, provided the "equality of results" that it promised (see especially Chapters 4 and 5). Nevertheless, it may still be preferable

---

* A comparison of the property awards under California's "equal" rule and New York and New Jersey's "equitable" standards is discussed in Chapter 4, pp. 106–108.

to equitable distribution and, with minor modifications (see Chapter 11), it probably offers the best route to fair and equitable property awards at divorce.

CHILD CUSTODY

Two shifts in the legal standards for child custody awards throughout the United States reflect the new norm of gender neutrality: the removal of the mother presumption, and the increase in joint custody statutes.

The maternal preference, the traditional rule that favored the mother as the custodial parent after divorce, has lost ground throughout the United States. The more limited "tender-years" doctrine, which created a maternal presumption for custody of young (i.e., preschool) children, has also been increasingly rejected. It remains a "tiebreaker" when all other factors are equal.[65] Today men and women have a statutory equal right to custody in virtually all states.

In a 1984 review of custody standards, Freed and Foster concluded that almost all states now base custody awards on the "best interests of the child"—a sex-neutral standard that allows the court to consider whatever it deems relevant—and that most states have adopted guidelines for "best interest" from the Uniform Dissolution of Marriage Act.[66]

Although the legal rules now give fathers an equal legal right to child custody after divorce, custody is still awarded to the mother in the vast majority of the cases—close to 90 percent—throughout the United States. The major reason for this is that maternal custody remains the preferred pattern for most mothers and fathers. Because most custody decisions are made by the parents, and because most parents decide that the children would be better off with their mother, and because most courts "approve" these parental decisions, the removal of the legal presumption favoring the mother has not, as yet, had a major impact on the actual pattern of custody awards.

This does not mean that the shift in legal norms has not had any effect. It has affected both the bargaining process and the court awards in contested cases. As we will see in Chapter 8, the new legal standards have significantly altered the outcomes of contested custody cases, have increased the proportion of men who are awarded custody when they request it, and have changed the bargaining process and the relative power of men and women in custody negotiations.

The spread of gender-neutral rules for child custody has also led to the proliferation of joint custody statutes. As of January 1985, thirty states had adopted some form of joint custody law,* but there is a great deal of variation in these laws. Most merely authorize the courts to award joint custody, where appropriate. A few go farther and, like California, make joint custody the preferred pattern. These statutes are discussed in Chapter 8.

Although these new statutes are likely to increase the number of joint custody awards, it is not yet clear what effect they will have on the actual pattern of children's living arrangements after divorce. In 1982–83, Stanford University professors Robert Mnookin and Eleanor Maccoby examined custody awards in Santa Clara County for a pilot study of the effects of California's new joint custody legislation. Although they found an increase in joint *legal custody* awards—awards that give both parents the right to make decisions (such as authorizing medical treatment) about the child—most children continue to live with one parent after divorce, and in the vast majority of cases that parent is the mother. In addition, although there had been a small increase in joint *physical custody* awards, in many cases this has simply meant a different label for arrangements that would have been called "liberal visitation" under the old law (such as a child living with the mother during the week and with the father on weekends). No research has found a substantial proportion of couples choosing to equally share physical custody after divorce.

One of the most important developments in child custody law is the adoption—by all states and the District of Columbia—of the Uniform Child Custody Jurisdiction act.[68] The Act seeks to discourage continued controversies over child custody and to deter the abduction of children across state lines. To this end, a number of states have also enacted (or strengthened) laws that make it a criminal offense for a noncustodial parent to abduct a child.[69]

In the past, when a noncustodial parent kidnapped a child and then initiated proceedings for a custody change in a new residence state, the petition was often successful. Judges in the new state were likely to favor the resident parent, and the original custodian faced an uphill and expensive fight in the "foreign" jurisdiction. In some cases the kidnapping parent and child or children disappeared, and the custodial parent was presented with a *fait accompli* once the children resurfaced adjusted and "stable" in their new home.

---

* Alaska, California, Colorado, Connecticut, Florida, Hawaii, Idaho, Illinois, Indiana, Iowa, Kansas, Kentucky, Louisiana, Maine, Massachusetts, Michigan, Minnesota, Mississippi, Missouri, Montana, Nebraska, Nevada, New Hampshire, New Mexico, North Carolina, Ohio, Oklahoma, Oregon, Pennsylvania, Texas, Wisconsin.[67] See Table C–7, Legal Appendix, for details.

Today, however, states that have adopted the Uniform Act cannot begin a custody determination *de novo:* they must return the case to— and defer to—the state of original jurisdiction. In addition, a number of states provide for actual and punitive damages to be assessed against a parent who tries to circumvent a custody decree.

CONCLUSION

The divorce law reforms that swept the United States in the 1970s and early 1980s were embraced with a pioneering zeal. California led the wave of enthusiastic reformers who believed that these modern liberal laws were the wave of the future. The abolition of grounds, fault, and consent were to rid the divorce process of its anachronistic moral elements and reduce the acrimony, hostility, perjury, and hypocrisy that pervaded the divorce process under the old law. The gender-neutral standards of "financial need" and "ability to pay," which replaced the fault-linked alimony and property awards of the old law, were welcomed as enlightened reforms that recognized and supported the emerging equality of men and women. The realistic economic standards of the new laws were to bring justice, equity, and equality to the process of legal divorce.

Legal trends in the fifty states show a growing acceptance of the principles of no-fault, no grounds, gender neutrality, and the separation of fault and financial awards. The new laws' rapid proliferation throughout the United States suggest that these principles have widespread appeal.

But what are the consequences of these new laws? How have they worked in practice? Have they fulfilled the reformers' goals of bringing justice, equity, and equality to the divorce process?

In the following chapters we examine the empirical effects of the divorce law reforms. We will see that they have, in fact, revolutionized the divorce process and have substantially altered the pattern of property, alimony, and custody awards. However, these laws have also had unanticipated, unintended, and unfortunate consequences.

CHAPTER 3

The Nature
of Marital Property

THREE QUESTIONS about marital property are important at divorce: What type of property do married couples have, how much is it worth, and how should it be divided?

Although these may appear to be relatively straightforward questions, the answers to them are not. Courts throughout the United States are wrestling with the complexities of defining, valuing, and dividing marital property.

The precise definition of marital property varies from state to state. It has traditionally included wage and salary income, interest, dividends, returns on investments, and all other income that a husband or wife earns during marriage, as well as the property purchased with that income—homes, cars, stereo systems, and so forth.

The major definitional problem is whether new forms of property—pensions, professional degrees, and other career assets—should be recognized as marital property and divided upon divorce. If these assets are considered marital property, their monetary value has to be ascertained to ensure an equal or fair division.

Calculating the value of these assets presents a second set of problems. While courts have always found it relatively easy to calculate the value of traditional forms of property, such as a home or a business, because some forms of "new property" are intangible and contingent, they raise unique and difficult problems of valuation.

The third issue concerns the division of property: What standards should courts use to divide property fairly? Conclusions about the fairness of the property division must ultimately rest on how marital property is defined—for if significant assets are excluded from the pool of property to be divided, the division of property is not likely to be fair.

We begin our examination with a survey of the nature of marital property. This chapter looks at the types of assets that divorcing couples own. We then turn to the division of these assets in Chapter 4. A discussion of the new property follows in Chapter 5.

The major findings of this chapter foretell the importance of the "new property" because they reveal the relatively modest value of the tangible assets that most couples own. The average divorcing couple has less than $20,000 in net worth. When this property is compared with their yearly income, it becomes clear that new forms of property—career assets and earning capacity—are worth much more than the tangible assets of the marriage. If these assets are excluded from the pool of property to be divided upon divorce, the courts are dividing only a fraction of the couple's total assets—and are allowing one spouse, typically the husband, to keep the family's most valuable assets for himself.

COMMUNITY PROPERTY VS. SEPARATE PROPERTY

Historically, there have been two distinct legal systems governing the property of married couples in the United States. Forty-two states have a separate property system, based on the English common law, which segregates the assets of the husband and wife into two categories, "his" and "hers." Eight states have a community property system (Arizona, California, Idaho, Louisiana, Nevada, New Mexico, Texas, and Washington) based on the Spanish and French traditions, which merges the assets of the husband and wife into a unified "community"—it is all "theirs."

In a community property system, the earnings of each party, together with all other property acquired (other than by inheritance or gift) during the marriage, become "community property." Each spouse owns one-half of this community property—and thus one-half of any property or income the other spouse acquires or earns during the marriage. The community property system assumes that both spouses have contributed equally to the economic assets of their marriage, whether by homemaking or by earning a salary, and that each is entitled to an equal share of the total assets. Thus, the married woman who is a full-time housewife is much better off in a community property state.

In the forty-two separate property states, in contrast, each spouse retains all the property he or she earns or inherits during the course of the marriage. Traditionally the other spouse has had no right to or interest in that property: since each is the sole owner of his or her earnings, each has the sole right to contract with regard to those earnings, to obtain credit based on them, and to manage and control them. Thus, in a traditional separate property system, a wife who is a full-time homemaker has no right to her husband's income—or to any of the property he acquired.

This stark contrast between community property states and separate property states (also called common law property states) has blurred in recent years because of two legal developments. First, many common law states have adopted state equal rights amendments, which have been interpreted to give housewives access to the property that their husbands acquire during marriage.[1] Second, most common law states have adopted equitable distribution rules for dividing property upon divorce.[2] As we saw in Chapter 2, these rules allow the courts to distribute property that was previously regarded as the property of one spouse.

Nevertheless, there is still a critical difference in the way that the two systems approach the division of property upon divorce. In separate property states, the starting point for an "equitable distribution" is typically one-third of the property to the wife, two-thirds to the husband. The underlying assumption is that the property really belongs to the husband because he was the one who earned it. The court then has to decide what would be an equitable share of "his property" for the wife.

In the community property states, in contrast, the basic premise is that all property acquired during marriage was "earned" by the joint efforts of the two spouses regardless of who received the paycheck. The starting point for an "equitable distribution" is therefore a 50/50 award—one-half to the wife and one-half to the husband.

THE VALUE OF MARITAL PROPERTY

Marital property, or what is labeled community property in California, refers to the income and property acquired by either husband or wife during marriage other than by gift or inheritance.[3] Since California is a community property state, this property is owned jointly and equally by both spouses during marriage, and it is divided equally upon divorce.[4]

The first and perhaps most important fact that this research reveals about marital property is that the average divorcing couple has relatively few assets, and those assets are typically of relatively low value. This is evident in all five random samples of court dockets examined over the decade of this research and in the property reported by men and women in the personal interviews. For example, the 1977 random sample of Los Angeles divorce decrees indicates that less than half of the divorcing couples had *any* major assets, such as a community property house, business, or pension.[5]

Most divorcing couples have household furnishings (89 percent), cars (71 percent), and some savings in the form of money in bank accounts, stocks, or bonds (61 percent). Almost half (46 percent) of the couples own or are buying a family home, which is likely to be a couple's most valuable asset. Only a small proportion of divorcing couples have a pension (24 percent), a business (11 percent), or other real estate (11 percent).

Because most divorcing couples are relatively young and in the lower income groups, their lack of assets should not be surprising. Nevertheless, one may wonder whether many couples had property that they divided privately, out of court, without referring to such property in their divorce papers. We investigated this possibility by comparing the property that divorcing couples enumerated in the in-depth interviews with the property listed on the court records. Indeed, those couples who had only a few assets—such as household furnishings and a car—were in fact less likely to list them in the court records. However, in most cases where there were substantial assets, the couples (or their attorneys) specified the nature of their property and the terms of its division in the interlocutory decree of divorce.[6] Thus the limited amount of property listed in court records appears to be an accurate reflection of what most divorcing couples own.

In addition, most divorcing men and women do not have any separate property assets (i.e., property acquired before marriage, or by gift or inheritance, that is kept separate throughout the marriage).[7] Less than 14 percent of the 1977 sample of divorce decrees included a listing or confirmation of separate property assets. In the 1978 interview sample, the median value of separate property claimed by the husband was $10,000. The median value of separate property claimed by the wife was $2,000.

The lack of substantial assets among divorcing couples is illustrated by the data in Table 2. The table shows the value of the community property (in 1977–1978 dollars) owned by couples in the 1978 interview sample (weighted to represent the total population of divorcing couples in California in that year). These statistics include the equity couples had in their home (i.e., the market value of the home minus the amount of the mortgage).

The first two columns of Table 2, listing the *net* value of the community property, show the percentages of divorced couples who own property at various levels of value when debts are subtracted from assets. The third and fourth columns, listing the *gross* value of the property, show the percentages when the community debts are not subtracted from the value of the assets.

The data in Table 2 underscore the relatively low value of the property owned by most divorcing couples.[8] Nine percent of the divorc-

TABLE 2

Total Value of Property
Owned by Divorcing Couples

PROPERTY VALUE	NET WORTH OF ASSETS (INCLUDING DEBTS)		GROSS VALUE OF ASSETS (NOT INCLUDING DEBTS)	
	Percentage	*Cumulative Percentage*	*Percentage*	*Cumulative Percentage*
Negative value	9%	9%	—	—
Less than $5,000	30	39	28%	28%
$5,000–9,999	8	47	11	39
$10,000–19,999	11	58	11	50
$20,000–29,999	5	63	9	59
$30,000–49,999	16	79	17	76
$50,000–99,999	9	88	12	88
$100,000–249,999	8	96	9	97
$250,000+	3	99	3	100
Median* $10,900			Median* $14,700	
Mean** $42,800			Mean** $45,900	

* The median is the value above which and below which lie one-half of the values.
** The mean is the arithmetic average of all the values.

This table is based on weighted data from interviews with divorced men and women, Los Angeles County, California, 1978.

ing couples have a negative net worth because their debts exceed their assets. Another 39 percent have less than $10,000 net worth. As the second column indicates, when these two groups are combined, we find that close to 50 percent of the divorcing couples have less than $10,000 net worth, and close to 60 percent have less than $20,000 net worth. In practical terms, this means that if the property is divided equally, each spouse receives less than $10,000 worth of assets.

Translated into 1984 dollars, this means that close to 60 percent of the divorcing couples have less than $32,200 net worth and, if that were divided equally, each spouse would receive less than $16,100 worth of assets.

Even if we exclude community debts and focus on the gross value of assets, shown in the right-hand side of Table 2, we find that half of the divorcing couples in 1978 had assets worth less than $20,000. Forty-one percent had assets of $30,000 or more, while only 12 percent had assets of $100,000 or more.

Overall, the median net worth of divorcing families was $11,000 in 1978.[9] (This is roughly $18,000 in 1984 dollars.) The median value, which is the value in the middle of the distribution, so that half of the divorcing couples have a higher net worth and half have less, is probably a better index of the amount of property owned by the "average" divorcing couple than the arithmetic mean because the mean is strongly influenced by a few very high values such as the 3 percent of families with assets of more than $250,000 in 1978. Thus the 1978 $10,900 median net worth is more "typical" than the $42,800 mean.

How do these data compare to those from other states? Unfortunately, no comparable research has been done in any other state.[10] However, it is possible to piece together data from other studies and, on the whole, these data support the finding that divorcing couples have relatively little property to divide.

The first report of the scarcity of marital property at divorce is found in sociologist William J. Goode's classic study of divorce in Detroit, Michigan, in 1948.[11] In interviews with 425 divorced mothers, Goode found that 40 percent of the families had "no property" to divide (i.e., had only a few household items.)[12] Only 18 percent of the families had property worth $4,000 or more.[13] More recent is a 1978 survey of court records in Cuyahoga County (Cleveland), Ohio.[14] Although the researchers did not ascertain the monetary value of the property that divorcing couples owned, they reported that only "a small portion of all cases have a house and other property."[15]

Attorneys and judges who specialize in family law in other states also corroborate that most couples have relatively little property to divide at divorce[16]—although this fact is often overlooked when policy-makers design remedies for the "typical" divorcing family.[17]

A further indication that the California data are typical of divorcing couples in the United States[18] is provided by the U.S. Census Bureau. A 1978 survey conducted by the Census Bureau found that less than half of the divorced women reported having any marital property to divide upon divorce.[19] In fact, if there is any discrepancy between the California data and the data collected by the Census Bureau, it is that the Californians appear to have slightly *more* property than the national average.* In the 1978 census study, the divorced women who reported having received any property got an average (median) award of $4,648.[20] Since most of these awards were in separate property states, it is likely that these women received less than half of the marital property. If so, then the total amount of marital property might be estimated at two to three times the amount of their award, or between $9,000 and $14,000. Even the latter figure is slightly less than the California median of $15,000 when couples with no property are excluded from the sample, as they were in the census study.[21]

As might be expected, the amount and value of community property increase with marital duration. This relationship is shown in Table 3.

TABLE 3

Value of Property by Marital Duration

LENGTH OF MARRIAGE	NET VALUE OF ASSETS* (INCLUDING DEBTS)	GROSS VALUE OF ASSETS* (EXCLUDING DEBTS)
Less than 5 years	$ 3,000	$ 4,600
5–9 years	14,200	21,800
10–17 years	46,100	47,000
18 years or more	49,900	62,600

* Median value, rounded to nearest $100.

This table is based on weighted data from interviews with divorced men and women, Los Angeles County, California, 1978.

* One should be extremely cautious about generalizing from the census data because they do not control for number of years since divorce. They therefore include property awards made at different points in time which have not been adjusted for inflation or converted into 1978 dollars.[22]

Couples married less than five years had, on the average, about $3,000 net worth. This increased to an average of almost $50,000 net worth among couples married eighteen years or more.

Along the same lines, the value of community property increases with family income, as shown in Table 4. Couples with family incomes of between $10,000 and $20,000 a year had, on the average, community property with a net worth of less than $5,000. This increased to nearly $22,000 among couples with family incomes between $20,000 to $30,000, and to more than $85,000 among couples with yearly incomes of $50,000 or more.

Table 4 shows two important relationships between income and property. The first is the expected correlation between the two: income and property increase together so that higher-income families have more property. The second relationship is more surprising. It concerns the relative value of income compared with property, and is one of the major findings of this research.

The data in Table 4 reveal the relatively low value of property compared with family income. This is true for couples at all income levels. Consider, for example, a couple earning between $10,000 and $20,000 a year. If this couple has accumulated about $4,000 worth of property and has a median yearly income of $16,000, it would take them only one-quarter of a year to earn $4,000—the value of their total community property. Similarly, a couple in the next higher income

TABLE 4

Value of Property by Family Income

		VALUE OF PROPERTY	
FAMILY INCOME (YEARLY)	MEDIAN INCOME* (IN GROUP)	NET VALUE OF ASSETS* (INCLUDING DEBTS)	GROSS VALUE OF ASSETS* (EXCLUDING DEBTS)
Less than $10,000	$ 5,000	$ 300	$ 1,000
$10,000–19,999	16,000	4,100	6,800
$20,000–29,999	23,000	21,800	24,600
$30,000–49,999	35,000	61,500	62,700
$50,000 or more	55,000	85,600	115,300

* Median value, rounded to nearest $100.

This table is based on weighted data from interviews with divorced men and women, Los Angeles County, California, 1978.

bracket, with a median yearly income of $23,000, would take less than a year to earn the value of the property they accumulated during marriage.

Thus in just one year, the average divorcing couple can earn more money than the value of their total assets. The median family income for the weighted sample of divorcing couples is $20,000 a year (not shown). It would take this median family between six and seven months to earn as much as the median value of community property (which is $10,900, reported in Table 2, p. 56). This suggests that *the spouses' earning capacity is typically worth much more than the tangible assets of the marriage.*

It is only in families with incomes over $30,000 that community property values are greater than family income. And yet, even there, it takes the average family less than two years to earn as much as their property is worth. Since property is divided once, but earning capacity continues to produce income year after year, the latter is clearly of greater cumulative value.

A similar analysis reveals the relatively greater value of the *husband's earning capacity* when compared with the tangible assets acquired during the marriage. It takes the average divorced man about ten months to earn as much as the community's net worth.

Policy Implications

The data in Table 4, showing that the major wealth of most families is in their ability to earn income in the future, have important policy implications. If one partner builds his or her earning capacity during marriage, while the other is a homemaker and parent, the partner with the earning capacity has acquired the major asset of the marriage. If that earning power—or the income it produces—is not divided upon divorce, the two spouses are left with very unequal shares of their family assets. Thus one policy implication is that courts seeking to divide marital property equally may be defeating that purpose by allowing one spouse to retain the largest assets of the marriage.

A second and related implication is that support awards (i.e., awards of alimony and child support) tend to be more valuable in the long run than property awards. This is because support awards redistribute future income, and, as just demonstrated, this is where the real wealth of most families lies. In addition, since property can be divided only once, but income continues to be earned every year, the cumulative value of support awards is likely to be much greater. *This suggests that support awards that divide income, especially future income, are the most valuable entitlements awarded at divorce.*

The idea of relying on support rather than property awards to achieve equity will sound startling to many, especially to lawyers who have spent the last decade arguing about appropriate rules for dividing property. Most states with an "equitable distribution" standard are embroiled in debates about "what is an equitable share for a wife?" As noted earlier, since the rule of thumb in many separate property states has been to give a divorced wife one-third of the marital assets, the California standard of one-half has often been held up as a feminist ideal. The data just examined suggest, however, that the difference between one-half and one-third of a very small pie is not going to provide the average divorced woman with very much property with which to start a new life. The division of future income, in contrast, may.

This is not meant to imply that all of the concern with property has been misplaced. But it does argue for the necessity of examining what the courts are in fact dividing when they say they are dividing the "marital property." Current legal definitions of marital property accept the traditional view of property; they focus on fixed assets like homes and cars. But, as we have just seen, the nature of property in our society is changing so that the family wealth now resides in new forms of property such as "career assets"—a term that I use to include the benefits of employment, such as pensions and health insurance coverage, as well as the capacity to earn future income. If courts would include career assets in the marital property to be divided at divorce, then property might well be the pivotal issue in the financial settlement.

The rationale for recognizing career assets as marital property is discussed at greater length in Chapter 5 on the new property. In the discussion that follows, we use the current definition of marital property and examine the distribution of traditional assets among divorcing couples.

OWNERSHIP AND VALUE OF SPECIFIC ASSETS

The assets owned by divorcing couples in the 1978 interview sample are shown in Table 5, along with the average (median and mean) values for each asset.[23] A quick review of these assets suggests that the family home is the major community asset for almost half (46 percent) of the divorcing couples. The median equity in the family home was close to $33,000 in 1978 dollars (about $53,100 in 1984 dollars.) The 11 percent of the couples who own a business or the 11 percent who own other real estate also have assets of considerable value. Surprisingly, only 24 percent of the husbands and 11 percent of the wives have pensions at the time of divorce.

The data in Table 5 also affirm the relatively low monetary value of most community property assets. While most divorcing couples own household furnishings (89 percent) and automobiles (71 percent), the mean monetary value of these assets is $5,100 and $3,500, respectively (less than $14,000 together in 1984 dollars). Similarly, even though most (61 percent) of the divorcing couples have some savings in the form of money in bank accounts, stocks, or bonds, these assets have a mean value of $9,300 and a median value of only $1,800 (in other words, half of the couples have less than $1,800 in savings).

The type of assets that divorcing couples owned remained quite

TABLE 5

Ownership and Value of Assets and Debts

TYPE OF PROPERTY	PERCENTAGE OF COUPLES OWNING EACH TYPE OF ASSET	MEDIAN* VALUE	MEAN** VALUE
Assets			
Household furnishings	89%	$ 3,000	$ 5,100
Cars or other vehicles	71	3,000	3,500
Money (bank accounts, stocks, bonds)	61	1,800	9,300
Family home	46	32,900	37,300
Other real estate	11	49,900	61,400
Husband's pension	24	3,000	8,500
Wife's pension	11	5,000	7,000
Business	11	29,900	70,900
Other assets	17	3,000	7,500
Debts			
Community debts	44	3,000	5,600

* The median is the value above which and below which lie one-half of the values.
** The mean is the arithmetic average of all the values.

This table is based on weighted data from interviews with divorced men and women, Los Angeles County, California, 1978.

stable over the decade of this research. Table 6 presents the percentages of Los Angeles divorcing couples who listed various types of community property on their divorce petitions in 1968, 1972, and 1977.

Although the percentages from court records are generally lower than those yielded by the more complete information from the personal interviews, the patterns of ownership are fairly consistent over the ten-year period. A few shifts in the percentages are, however, worthy of note. First, the court records show a decline in the percentage of couples who itemized household furnishings and cars between 1968, under the old law, and 1977, under the new law. Since the interviews revealed that most of the couples owned such property, the change probably reflects an increase in private settlements, especially among less well-to-do couples, rather than a real decline in property ownership.

Support for this interpretation is provided by the rise of do-it-yourself divorces between 1968 and 1977. The percentage of petitioners filing *in pro per* (*in propria persona,* or "on their own behalf") rose from less than 1 percent in 1968 under the old law, to 5 percent in 1972, and to 30 percent in 1977 under the new law. Couples who filed

TABLE 6

Property Itemized on Divorce Records,
1968–1977

TYPE OF PROPERTY LISTED	PERCENTAGE OF PETITIONERS LISTING PROPERTY BY YEAR OF FINAL DECREE		
	1968	1972	1977
(*Number of Cases*)	(*507*)	(*468*)	(*500*)
Household furnishings	56%	42%	39%
Cars or other vehicles	50	42	38
Money, stock or bonds	21	21	21
Family home	26	25	32
Real estate other than residence	8	8	10
Pensions	5	8	17
Business	5	5	7
Other property	13	11	17
Community debts	15	9	26

This table is based on random samples of court dockets, Los Angeles County, California.

in pro per usually had relatively few assets and were likely to divide them without listing them on the divorce petitions.

Thus one effect of the equal division rule is to facilitate private settlements. It does this by enabling couples (and their attorneys) to predict what property division a court would order.

The increase in private settlements under the new law is also reflected in another datum from the court dockets: a rise in the percentage of marital agreements (i.e. out-of-court settlements and written agreements that are attached to the interlocutory decree). In 1968, 19 percent of the cases in the court docket samples contained separate marital agreements. By 1972, such agreements were found in 22 percent of the cases, and by 1977 in 26 percent. Thus by 1977, almost one out of four settlements reviewed in court had already been agreed to in writing by the parties. (The financial provisions of these agreements are typically incorporated into court orders.)

These data indicate that clear-cut rules like the equal division requirement encourage and facilitate "private ordering"—a term that is often used to refer to out-of-court settlements. Such rules can save considerable court time (and court costs), as well as litigants' time and legal fees. Attorneys, however, may prefer rules that allow more judicial discretion because clients then need attorneys to assert their claims. In fact, law professor Mary Ann Glendon has argued that the organized bar has supported rules that require property be divided "equitably" rather than "equally" because the "equitable" standard, which permits judicial discretion, fosters greater reliance on attorneys, raises the probability of litigation, and is thus likely to increase legal fees.[24]

The second and most dramatic change in the type of property listed over the decade is the rise in divorcing couples listing pensions—which grew from 5 percent of the couples in 1968 to 8 percent in 1972, to 17 percent in 1977. The dramatic increase between 1972 and 1977 probably reflects the California Supreme Court's 1976 ruling in *In re Marriage of Brown*,[25] which recognized nonvested pensions as community property. Before *Brown*, the courts considered only vested pensions (i.e. those which the parties were already entitled to claim) as community property. After *Brown*, all pensions, whether or not the parties could claim them at the time of the divorce, were considered community property.

A final shift in the assets listed in Table 6 is the increase in community property homes (from 26 percent in 1968 to 32 percent in 1977). This probably represents a real increase in home ownership rather than a change in what is listed in court records.[26] In fact, as noted earlier, the in-depth interviews indicated that home ownership is even more widespread than Table 6 suggests: 46 percent of the couples in the weighted interview sample reported having some equity in a family home (see Table 5).

Patterns of Home Ownership

As might be expected, home ownership is closely associated with length of marriage and income level. This relationship is dramatically illustrated in Table 7.

We can quickly see the effects of marital duration on home ownership by holding income constant. If we look at the second column of Table 7, showing families with incomes between $20,000 and $29,999 a year, we see that 30 percent of those married less than five years owned or were purchasing a home, compared to 57 percent of those married five to ten years, 65 percent of those married eleven to seventeen years, and 93 percent of those married eighteen years or more.

Similarly, we can see the effects of income on home ownership by holding the marital duration constant. If we look at couples married five to ten years, we see that home ownership rises from 21 percent of those with yearly incomes under $20,000, to 57 percent of those earning between $20,000 and $29,999 a year, to 85 percent of those with yearly incomes of $30,000 and over.

TABLE 7

Home Ownership by Marital Duration and Family Income

	PERCENTAGE OF COUPLES OWNING HOMES BY YEARLY FAMILY INCOME		
LENGTH OF MARRIAGE	Less than $20,000	$20,000–29,999	$30,000 and over
Less than 5 years	11%	30%	30%
(Number of cases)	(27)	(10)	(20)
5–10 years	21%	57%	85%
(Number of cases)	(14)	(14)	(20)
11–17 years	56%	65%	96%
(Number of cases)	(9)	(17)	(26)
18 years or more	67%	93%	92%
(Number of cases)	(12)	(14)	(38)

This table is based on weighted data from interviews with divorced men and women, Los Angeles County, California, 1978.

These data indicate that whereas home ownership is virtually uni-versal among long-married or high-income couples in California, most couples in short marriages, especially those with lower incomes, have not acquired homes. The implications are obvious: neither a home nor any other tangible asset of major value is usually available to cushion the financial impact of divorce for the typical lower-income couple who divorce after six or seven years.* For this couple, the primary financial issues are likely to be those of spousal and child support.

The family home also has limited importance for wealthy families who divorce, but for very different reasons. Although home ownership is virtually universal among wealthy families, the home accounts for a *smaller proportion* of their *total* property: they often have a variety of other assets that equal or exceed the value of the home. For example, this research shows that equity in the family home accounts for an average (median) of 47 percent of the net value of the community prop-erty among families with yearly incomes of $50,000 or more, in contrast to 75 percent of the property among families earning less than $20,000 a year.

Although this statistic is for couples married between eleven and seventeen years, the pattern holds for all marital durations. For exam-ple, among couples married eighteen years or more, home equity ac-counts for 42 percent of the property in families with yearly incomes of $50,000 or more, compared to 62 percent in families with yearly incomes of less than $20,000.

Thus, while low-income couples may not own homes, and high-income couples may have other assets to balance the equity in their home, for middle-income couples the family home is likely to be the most valuable—and often the only—tangible asset they own. It is there-fore middle-income couples (who make up about half of the divorcing population) who are most significantly affected by the disposition of the family home at divorce.

Patterns of Pension Ownership

There is a significant difference between husbands and wives with regard to the acquisition of pensions and retirement funds. Husbands

---

* These comments are not meant to suggest that being awarded a home and its equity *will* necessarily provide a sufficient financial cushion for those couples who do have homes. As Table 5 indicates, the average equity in a home in particular, and in community property (as currently defined) in general, is of a relatively low value when compared to wage and salary income.

are much more likely than wives to have acquired pensions during marriage (as shown in Table 5, p. 62), 24 percent of the divorcing men had pensions, compared to 11 percent of the divorcing women. The relationships among pension ownership, length of marriage, and gender are presented in Table 8.

For husbands, the value of the pensions is highly correlated with both income and length of marriage. (Statistically, length of marriage is a surrogate for age and employment experience for men, but this does not hold true for women.) Among men with yearly incomes under $20,000, pension ownership rises from 12 percent of those married ten years or less, to 56 percent of those married eighteen years or more. The same pattern is evident among men earning more than $20,000 a year: pension ownership rises from 30 percent among those in short marriages to 62 percent among those married eighteen years or more.

Married women, by contrast, are much less likely to acquire pensions, irrespective of the length of their marriage or age. Few women with yearly incomes under $20,000 had acquired pensions (an average of 11 percent for all marital durations). It was only women with incomes

TABLE 8

Pension Ownership*

by Gender, Marital Duration, and Individual Income

MARITAL DURATION	PERCENTAGE OF HUSBANDS WITH PENSIONS, BY PREDIVORCE INCOME		PERCENTAGE OF WIVES WITH PENSIONS, BY PREDIVORCE INCOME	
	Under $20,000	*$20,000 or More*	*Under $20,000*	*$20,000 or More*
10 years or less	12%	30%	12%	50%
(Number of cases)	(60)	(44)	(101)	(4)
11–17 years	33%	39%	8%	60%
(Number of cases)	(24)	(28)	(49)	(5)
18 years or more	56%	62%	12%	—
(Number of cases)	(16)	(48)	(64)	(1)
Total	24%	45%	11%	60%
	(100)	(120)	(214)	(10)

* This table refers only to community property pensions. Less than 2% of divorces involved separate property pensions.

This table is based on data from interviews with divorced men and women, Los Angeles County, California, 1978.

of $20,000 or more a year who had a substantial number of pensions—
and only 2 percent of the divorced women earned that much yearly
income.

CONCLUSION

The word "property" evokes an image of substantial assets. When
we think of dividing marital property we often assume that divorcing
couples have such assets and that a share of the property will provide
a cushion for them to weather the expensive process of divorce. However, we have seen that most couples do not have substantial assets:
less than half own or are purchasing a home at the time of the divorce,
and even fewer own a business or pension.

Even more surprising is the low monetary value of the property
they do own. Over 60 percent of the divorcing couples have less than
$20,000 in total assets. This means that if the property is divided equally,
each spouse will receive less than $10,000 worth of assets. That is
hardly a security blanket: it often is not enough for the down payment
on a home.

There are two possible interpretations of these data. One is that
most divorcing couples are very poor and simply do not have much
property to divide upon divorce. The alternative is that most divorcing
couples have invested in something else—something the courts do not
yet label as property—and their real wealth lies in this other type of
investment. In fact, we have seen that most couples do have another
form of wealth: they have invested in their careers and earning capacities. And these assets are much more valuable than their tangible assets. In less than a year, the average couple can earn significantly
more than all the tangible assets they have acquired. In fact, it would
take the average divorcing family only six months to earn as much
as the net value of their assets.

This suggests that the nature of wealth and property has changed
in our society. We no longer invest in family farms—today we invest
in ourselves and in our ability to earn future income. These new forms
of property are our major assets and they need to be included in the
marital property that courts are empowered to divide "equitably" or
"equally" upon divorce.

There is a second policy implication in these data. If current legal
definitions of property continue to prevail, then the redistribution of
postdivorce income (through alimony and child support awards) will

be more important than the division of property for most divorcing families. Because future income is typically of greater value than property (as it is currently defined), the primary financial issues at divorce, particularly for women and children, are those of spousal and child support. An equitable division of family income offers the only possible cushion against the financial hardships that marital dissolution typically creates for divorced mothers and their children.

CHAPTER 4

Dividing the Property
How Equal Is Equal?

ONE AREA IN WHICH the change in the divorce law has had a clear-cut and measurable effect is in the way property is divided at divorce. The equal division rule, which was heralded as a panacea for the fault-based abuses of the old law, has clearly altered the pattern of property awards. It has also had some unanticipated and unfortunate consequences.

THE EQUAL DIVISION RULE

Before 1970, under California's traditional divorce law, the "innocent party" had to receive more than half of the community property. This was typically the wife, both because her husband was more likely to want a divorce and because of prevailing norms of chivalry, in which he would let her file for the divorce.

The no-fault law, in contrast, instructs the court to divide the community assets and liabilities *equally*.[1] A husband and wife may agree to a nonequal division, either in writing or orally in court, but a judge is bound to award each spouse half of the total community assets. The court may make an unequal division only if the total of the community property is under $5,000 and one spouse's whereabouts are unknown, or if the debts exceed the assets.² (The judge may also adjust property in the unusual event of deliberate concealment or misappropriation of community property by one party.)

The drafters of the 1970 California legislation had three justifications for the equal division rule. First, the target of their reform was the fault-based divorce law, and one major aim was to rid the legal process of the "economic blackmail" of property awards based on fault:

> If we eliminate fault as a major basis for divorce action, then we would also eliminate finances as a major weapon either for "bargaining" or for the punishment of the apparently "guilty" party. Instead, alimony and property settlement would be based on equitive judgment as to what is available and how it can be divided.³

Professor Herma Hill Kay, an influential member of the Governor's Commission that proposed the no-fault legislation, reports that because the division of property was specifically tied to fault under the old law, the reformers were eager to ensure the separation of the two under the new law. To do this they needed a strict rule, such as the equal division requirement. They were so convinced of the benefits to be gained from the elimination of fault that they wanted an absolute standard that could not be swayed by a party's behavior—even if it meant allowing a hypothetical "rat-fink" to retain his full half share of the property:

> . . . the separation of the property award from marital fault was a sensitive policy issue for the Commission. Ultimately, however, it was decided that even where the divorce was awarded at the behest of a "rat-fink" (in a spontaneous hypothetical case, the Commission's rat-fink was seen to be a male medical student who allowed his nurse-wife to support him through his expensive training, only to divorce her and marry the Dean's daughter after his residency was completed), division of property would remain equal. *Punishment as well as fault was to be abolished;* the Commission's minutes propose that inequities in the rat-fink hypothetical case should be resolved by the alimony award.⁴

Thus consistent with their general effort to abolish the influence of both real and fabricated marital fault, the reformers proposed a hard and fast rule for marital property: that it always be divided equally upon divorce.

A second reason for the equal division rule was the reformers' belief that the community property system adequately protected wives. Again, the observations of Professor Kay are instructive.⁵ In comparing the California proposals for divorce law reform to those in New York state (and England), she notes that the separate property system in these jurisdictions made it necessary for them to consider creating a community property system upon divorce "as a protection for wives."[6]

The fact that California already had a community property system, and already regarded the wife as an equal economic partner, played a part in "reassuring those scrutinizing the proposed change" that dependent wives were adequately protected in California.[7] Both the community property system, and the equal division rule, were seen as an affirmation of the presumption that marriage was an equal partnership in which the financial and nonfinancial contributions of the two spouses were of equal worth. Each therefore deserved, and would receive, half of the couple's jointly accumulated property.

The third rationale for the equal division requirement was to limit judicial discretion. When the equal division rule was first proposed, the State Bar opposed it.[8] Instead they recommended that judges be allowed to divide the property unequally (but not punitively) "where the court finds an exception (to equal division) is warranted . . . in such proportions as it deems just."[9] When the members of the State Bar realized, however, that their language would unduly broaden judges' discretion—and might reintroduce the very same fault-based considerations that the new law sought to abolish—they withdrew their proposal.*

In summary, the drafters of the California legislation believed that an equal division standard, by limiting judicial discretion and assuring each partner an equal share of their jointly accumulated property, was more fair than the vague standard of an "equitable" division of property. The equitable standard, which is now used in most of the separate property states,[10] not only gives judges the power "to do justice" by dividing the marital property according to need, it also allows judges to use their own subjective standards of equity (and therefore results in a greater diversity of awards).

Equal vs. Equitable Distribution

The debate over "equal" versus "equitable" rules for the division of marital property is a continuing one. In both New York and Wisconsin,

---

* The California reformers seemed more concerned about the prospect of awards based on fault than with judicial discretion per se. They were so preoccupied with the elimination of property awards based on fault that they did not seriously consider the consequences of the equal division rule.

for example, the standards for property division were hotly contested in recent years.[11] In Wisconsin feminists successfully pressed for the California rule, arguing that without a guarantee of an equal share of the property most wives in separate property states received no more than a third of the family property.[12]

In New York the organized bar won the day and passed an equitable distribution law. They asserted that women would be better off under an *equitable* standard that allowed judges to "do justice"* according to the circumstances of the parties[13] and, where appropriate, to award women more than half of the property by allowing them to keep the family home.[14]

Which set of assertions is correct? How do the two sexes fare under equal versus equitable rules? Although the state bar convinced the New York legislature to adopt an equitable division law in 1980, and the feminists convinced the Wisconsin legislature to adopt an equal division law in 1977, neither decision was based on empirical data.**

This chapter provides the data that will enable us to compare the results of the two types of legal regimes. It begins by examining the effects of the equal division rule in California and then looks at some comparative results.

OVERALL DIVISION OF COMMUNITY PROPERTY

Table 9 shows dramatic changes in the distribution of marital property in California since the no-fault law was instituted. In 1968, under the old law, the wife, as the "innocent" plaintiff, was typically awarded the lion's share of the property. She received more than half (i.e., 60 percent or more) in four out of five divorce cases in San Francisco, and in three out of five cases in Los Angeles. Many of these unequal

---

* A more cynical interpretation of the New York bar's position, suggested by law professor Mary Ann Glendon, is that lawyers profit from the increased litigation that is encouraged by vague "equitable" rules. In support of this assertion, Glendon cites an increase in legal costs following the introduction of New York's equitable division law.[15]

** In fact, the debate over the empirical reality has taken place within the feminist community as well. Since no one has had the empirical data (until now), it was possible for women's groups in New York to argue for an equal rule while women's groups in the neighboring state of Pennsylvania, which reformed its divorce law at the same time as the New York reform, argued for equitable rules. In Pennsylvania the women's groups thought women would get *more than half* of the property under equitable rules. There the men's rights groups wanted an equal division rule to guarantee them 50 percent of the marital property.

awards involved the family home and furnishings. In 1968 the property was divided equally in only 12 percent of the cases in San Francisco, and 26 percent of the cases in Los Angeles.

Under the no-fault law, the percentage of cases in which the property was divided equally increased from 12 to 59 percent in San Francisco between 1968 and 1972, and from 26 to 64 percent in Los Angeles. By 1977 equal division was the norm.

The new law brought a corresponding drop in the percentage of wives who were awarded most of the community property, as Table 9 shows. In addition, the wife's share of the property dropped under no-fault. For example, in Los Angeles county, wives who were awarded close to 80 percent of the property under the old fault law were awarded closer to half (54 percent) under no-fault.

Thus the adverse economic effects of the changing pattern of property awards has fallen on women. Under the old law, women were typically awarded most of the marital property, and this tended to cushion the economic impact of the divorce. Today, under the equal division rule, they receive much less. The clearest result of this change is the increase in court orders for the matrimonial home to be sold upon divorce so that the property can be divided equally. The disruptive effects of this pattern are discussed below.

TABLE 9

Division of Property
under Fault and No-Fault Laws

	SAN FRANCISCO		LOS ANGELES		
	Fault (1968)	No-fault (1972)	Fault (1968)	No-fault (1972)	No-fault (1977)
Majority to husband*	2%	7%	6%	21%	10%
Approximately equal division**	12	59	26	44	64
Majority to wife*	86	34	58	35	26
Mean percentage to wife	91%	62%	78%	54%	—***

   * Majority = over 60%.
   ** Approximately equal = between 40 and 60%.
   *** 1977 information not specified in detail sufficient to permit precise percentages.
This table is based on random samples of court dockets, San Francisco County and Los Angeles County, California.

These results parallel those reported by Dr. Karen Seal for San Diego County.[16] Seal compared a random sample of 300 divorce cases in 1968, under the adversary system, with 300 divorce cases in 1976, under the no-fault law. She too found a significant decline in the assets awarded exclusively to the wife.[17*]

One of the justifications for the equal division rule was the reformers' belief that property was usually divided in roughly equal proportions under the old law. (A 51/49 percent division of the property was in technical compliance with the rule that "more than one-half" of the assets be awarded to the injured party.) An equal division rule, the reformers asserted, would merely codify the common practice of roughly equal property splits.

The data strongly contradict those assertions. They indicate that property was not being divided equally under the old law, and certainly not in 51/49 percent ratios. Rather, three-quarters of the 1968 cases involved a *substantially unequal division*. Thus, these findings challenge the widespread misbelief that the no-fault divorce law merely codified existing practice. They indicate instead that the new law has dramatically altered the way property is divided upon divorce.

One might ask how it is possible, under a strict equal division rule, to still have a minority of cases in which property is not divided equally. Since property may be divided unequally only if both parties agree, the question is why one party would agree to accept less than half of the property. The answer probably lies in a property-support tradeoff in which, for example, a wife receives more than 60 percent of the tangible property in exchange for a lower support award. Because property settlements are nonmodifiable, whereas spousal support awards are vulnerable to later modification and to enforcement difficulties, attorneys may advise their female clients to settle for an advantageous property settlement, knowing it to be a "sure thing," instead of seeking a high spousal support award. The low percentage of spousal support orders, discussed in Chapter 6, makes this interpretation appear likely.

In fact, a small proportion of the cases contained a specific reference to a nonmodifiable integrated settlement of property and support. That is, the property award was explicitly linked to spousal support, indicating that the wife or husband received more of one in exchange

---

* Seal does not report the percentages but she states that there was a statistically significant decline in the family assets granted exclusively to the wife. In addition, she reports a significant increase in wives being required to assume a share of the family debts.[18]

for less of the other. These were found in 7 percent of the files in the 1968 sample, 9 percent in 1972, and 19 percent in 1977).*

It is important to keep in mind the average value of the community property when thinking about the practical implications of the trend toward an equal division of marital property. Since close to 60 percent of the divorcing couples in the 1978 interview sample have less than $20,000 in net worth (see Table 2 in Chapter 3), most spouses could expect to be awarded about $10,000 worth of property—assuming the property was divided equally. Or, to put it another way, only two out of five divorced spouses could expect a property award of more than $10,000.

THE ABSENCE OF FAULT

The reformers were, in fact, successful in removing fault as a basis for awarding property. As one attorney said:

> I've seen men get away with the most outrageous conduct and they still get half of the property. . . . I've seen instances where women have literally been driven to psychiatrists and psychologists; they are extremely emotionally upset and disturbed by their husbands' wrongful conduct. He flaunts it to her, knowing that it will have no effect upon the required equal division of the community property.

Under the old law, when fault affected the division of property, the identity of the petitioner, or "innocent party," made a considerable difference in the property distribution. In the 1968 cases in which the wife was the plaintiff, wives received an average of 89 percent of the community property. When the husband was the plaintiff, wives received only 60 percent of the property.** Corresponding awards to wives were 60 and 56 percent under the new law (in 1972), an insignificant difference that suggests fault has become irrelevant.

One example of the role of fault in property awards is provided by a hypothetical case we presented to the attorneys and judges we interviewed. A forty-one-year-old auto mechanic and a thirty-six-year-

---

* Another reason for the apparent inequality in awards may be that the court records are not always complete.[19] However, despite the problem of missing information, the court records are the only source of data on change over time.

** Debts were similarly affected by fault under the old law: wives were ordered to pay a lower proportion of the community liabilities if they, rather than their husbands, were the petitioners.

old typist with two children, ages five and eight, were getting a divorce. Their major asset was the family home. In one version of the case, the husband was "at fault" (he had been openly having affairs with other women). Virtually all of the respondents—98 percent—predicted that the wife would be awarded the family home.

In another version of this case the wife was at fault (she had been openly having affairs with other men). Here the majority of the legal experts, 63 percent, predicted that the husband would be awarded most of the property including the family home. (Less than a quarter said the property would be divided equally, and still fewer, 14 percent, said the wife would retain the home for the children.)

These responses illustrate the role that fault played under the old law. The first scenario was the more common one. A wife who would successfully accuse her husband of adultery or mental cruelty would be granted the divorce and most of the property. But the property consequences were equally predictable if the wife had been at fault. If she was found guilty of adultery or mental cruelty she too would be punished and lose her home.

Under the no-fault law both of these scenarios would have the same outcome. Even though each of the judges and attorneys we interviewed had heard one of the earlier versions of this case, and therefore knew that one of the parties was, or at least might be, responsible for the dissolution, they were unlikely to be influenced by that fact in predicting the case outcome under the no-fault law. Rather, no matter which version they had read first, they were likely to predict that the family home would be sold under the present law, and that the equity would be divided equally between the two spouses.

DISPOSITION OF SPECIFIC TYPES OF PROPERTY

The most common items of property divided in 1968 and 1977 were homes, household furnishings, money, cars, pensions, businesses, and debts. The new law has increased the percentage of cases in which each of these assets is divided equally. Nevertheless, there is some evidence of continued sex typing of various types of property. For example, wives remain more likely to be awarded the family home and household furnishings, while husbands are usually granted the other real estate, the business, and the family car. In both cases these awards are typically offset by awards of other assets of equal value.

Disposition of the Family Home

The home is typically the family's major asset. The legal tradition was to award the family home to the wife upon divorce, both because it was assumed to be hers—in the sense that she organized, decorated, and maintained it—and because she was usually the "innocent" party and therefore entitled to a larger share of the community property. In addition, if she had custody of the children, she needed the home to maintain a stable environment for them.*

With the absence of fault and the trend toward equal division, it is not surprising to find an increase in the number of homes being divided equally: from less than a quarter (23 percent) of the homes in 1968 to more than a third (35 percent) in 1977. There has been a corresponding decline in cases where the majority of equity in the home is awarded to the wife, from 61 percent in 1968 to 46 percent in 1977. These data are shown in Table 10.

"Equal division" of a house can mean either that the two parties maintain joint ownership after the divorce, or that the house is sold and the proceeds divided equally. The number of cases in which there was an explicit order to sell the home rose from about one in ten in 1968, to about *one in three* in 1977. By that year, an equal division of the home typically meant that the house was ordered sold.

TABLE 10

Disposition of Family Home
under Fault and No-Fault Laws

DIVISION OF HOME (OR EQUITY)	FAULT LAW	NO-FAULT LAW	
	1968	1972	1977
Majority to husband*	16%	24%	19%
Approximately equal division**	23	25	35
Majority to wife	61	51	46

* Majority = over 60%.
** Approximately equal = between 40 and 59%.

This table is based on random samples of court dockets, Los Angeles County, California.

* In the weighted interview sample, we found that couples with minor children were more likely to own homes than were childless couples. This holds true even when we control for marital duration and family income. Overall, our data show that 65 percent of the couples with minor children own homes, compared to 33 percent of the couples with no minor children.

In her review of divorce cases in San Diego County, Dr. Karen Seal found a similar trend.[20] In 1968 wives in San Diego were awarded the house in 66 percent of the cases. By 1977 that percentage dropped to 42 percent.[21] As Seal notes, the minority of women who were able to keep the family home under no-fault "paid" for their husbands' share: either the wife agreed to buy out her husband's half of the equity, or she relinquished her claim to some other comparable asset, such as his pension plan.[22]

Surprisingly, the presence of minor children did not increase the likelihood that the wife would be awarded the family home. Our data reveal that 66 percent of the couples who were forced to sell their homes had minor children.*

Although the overwhelming majority of the attorneys and judges we interviewed said they thought the equal division rule was basically fair (and preferable to the fault-based standards of the old law), many expressed concern about a forced sale of the family home, especially in families with minor children. Close to 40 percent of the attorneys thought judges should be allowed more discretion in dividing property so that they would not be bound by an equal division rule for families with minor children. As one attorney stated:

> So often the only asset of any consequence is the family residence. When the couple divorces, it is ordered sold and the children are deprived of their home. . . . There should be a way to keep the home intact for the children.

One way of maintaining the family home for the children is to award the home to the custodial spouse,** and to award an asset of equal value, such as the husband's retirement pension or a vacation home, to him. Indeed this solution has been approved by several courts[25] and was often the way the women we interviewed managed to keep the home. But such tradeoffs are possible only for the minority of families that have other assets to offset the award of the home,

---

* In the random sample of 1977 court dockets, the presence of minor children in the mother's custody made no difference in her chances of being awarded the home. In the weighted interview sample, custodial mothers were slightly more likely than childless mothers to be awarded the home, but couples with minor children were also more likely than childless couples to be ordered to sell the home and divide the proceeds.

** The 1984 Tax Reform Act facilitates the transfer of the house to the wife upon divorce.[23] Prior to that act, the transfer of property between divorcing spouses was treated as a "capital transaction" and could be taxed as a capital gain. This meant a wife who was awarded the house might be liable for a capital gains tax. The 1984 act allows property transfers between spouses (that are part of a divorce decree) with *no immediate tax effect.*[24]

and, as we already know, most families cannot utilize this "solution:" Less than a quarter of the divorcing couples have a pension, and only one in nine has a business or other real estate. (See the data in Table 5, Chapter 3).

Another possibility for the custodial mother who is determined to maintain the home for her children is to "trade" whatever she has for the option, and the only thing she may have left to trade is a support award. Several attorneys said that they recommended this solution to women whose husbands were "difficult" because of the problems they anticipated in collecting support. While bemoaning the situation— "It's tough," said one attorney, "because she has to forgo her support to pay him off"—the attorneys saw no other solution than to change the legal rules.

Since a large number of divorcing women do not have either of these options—that is, there is no pension or other property to "trade" for the home, and they cannot afford to "trade" their support because they cannot live without it—they are forced to sell the home. Consider, for example, the story of one thirty-eight-year-old woman we interviewed. She pleaded with her attorney, and then with the court, to work out some arrangement to allow her to stay in the family home. She had lived there for 15 years. Her fourteen-year-old son was living with her and was experiencing "a lot of emotional turmoil" as a result of the divorce. He needed the security of a stable home. The mortgage payments were $280 a month, which she could manage on her $600 a month alimony and child support award. But alternative housing in her neighborhood was much more expensive and vastly inferior: a minimum one-bedroom apartment would cost $500 a month.

This woman had tried to negotiate with her husband. She offered to forgo her interest in his pension plan, valued at approximately $85,000, which would have covered the equity in the house. But her husband would agree to this only if she also agreed to a) forgo alimony and b) accept $100 a month in child support (for less than three years until her son reached age eighteen), a proposal that seemed both unfair and unmanageable to a woman who had been a full-time homemaker with no recent job experience.

Nor was she able to refinance the house to pay off her husband. She thought she would be able to use the $600 in support she was promised to pay the mortgage. However, in her words:

No bank would give me a loan and no one was willing to accept my spousal support as "income." One loan officer said to me, "Spousal support and child support don't count. Most men stop paying them and we have to repossess the house." Another bank officer said he had seen "hundreds of women like me." He was "sympathetic," but said I was too poor a risk to get through the loan committee.

Since the woman could not buy out her husband's share of the house, and since the parties were unable to "agree" on a division of property, the judge ordered the house sold and gave the woman three months to vacate it. As the woman said,

> I begged the judge. . . . All I wanted was enough time for Brian [her son] to adjust to the divorce. . . . I broke down and cried on the stand . . . but the judge refused. He gave me three months to move—three months to move 15 years—right in the middle of the school semester . . . my husband's attorney threatened me with contempt if I wasn't out on time . . . he also warned me not to interfere with the real estate people—in *my* house—he said if I wasn't cooperative in letting them show the house when they wanted to, he'd "haul me into court for contempt." . . . It was a nightmare. . . . The most degrading and unjust experience of my life.

Similar threats were recounted by a fifty-four-year-old woman who was "ordered" to vacate her house so that it could be sold.

> I had lived in that home for 26 years and my three children still considered it their home. But the judge ordered it sold. . . . He said he had to follow the letter of the law. . . . I married at a time when a woman who spent 30 years of her life raising a family was worth something . . . but in the eyes of the court I was merely "unemployed." No one would rent me an apartment because my only income was $700 a month spousal support and landlords said that was "unstable" and "inadequate." Two months later my husband's attorney took me into court for contempt because I hadn't moved. . . . He said I was interfering with the sale of the house. . . . The judge gave me ten days to get out. . . . I am still outraged. It is a total perversion of justice. I was thrown out of my own house.

One solution, which was approved by a minority of forty percent of the attorneys, would be to exempt the home from the required equal division of property (if the total value of community property is limited). As suggested by one attorney who expressed his discomfort with the present system:

> I personally wish that the court would have some leeway in doing something other than an absolute down-the-middle division, especially in the low income bracket. Where there's a couple of hundred thousand dollars it's not so terrible, but where you have a single family residence . . .

and some furniture and car, I think most of us still feel we'd be happier if the wife got it.

Significantly, the California legislature did *not intend* that the family home be sold in order to meet the equal division requirement. Indeed, a 1970 Assembly Committee report specifically states that a temporary award of the home to the spouse who has custody of minor children should be seen as a valid reason to delay the division of property:

> Where an interest in a residence which serves as the home of the family is the major community asset, an order for the immediate sale of the residence in order to comply with the equal division mandate of the law would, certainly, be unnecessarily destructive of the economic and social circumstances of the parties and their children.[26]

Most of the justification for maintaining the family home for the children has focused on the social and psychological disruption they experience in forced moves and changed schools and neighborhoods. There are, however, also sound economic reasons for allowing the wife to retain the family home. As Karen Seal suggests, the home provides the wife with leverage to insure the husband's payment of support:

> When a husband receives his half of the assets immediately upon divorce, it is much easier for him to overlook his responsibilities. If he stood to lose his interest in the family home for nonsupport, however, perhaps he would be more likely to comply. Or at least if he did not comply, the wife should be able to claim a larger share of the ownership of the home as a result of his default. At a minimum, a property interest of this nature should be held as security for compliance with support orders.[27]

Fran Leonard, attorney for The Older Women's League, echoes some of these thoughts in asserting the importance of a similar delay to allow older homemakers to retain their homes:

> Unlike her spouse, she may have no credit history, no income aside from alimony, and almost no prospects of recovering her lost earning capacity. The chances of her ever buying another home are almost nil. Yet all too commonly the court orders the home sold, in order to divide its value. Attorneys frequently favor this, because their fees can be paid out of escrow. . . . Instead, older women should try to keep the family home and, if necessary, leave their husband's name on the deed as a tenant in common: "This will give the husband an investment that is growing, and she effectively has a lien on his spousal support and child support.[28]

Leonard also stresses the critical psychological importance of the home for a woman who has built her world there:

> For the older woman, especially a homemaker [the sale of the family home] is a major cruelty. Upon divorce, she loses her husband and her occupation—then all too often, her home. This nearly comprises her universe.[29]

The California appellate courts have upheld the rationale for maintaining the family home for minor children when a sale would have an adverse economic, emotional, or social impact on them. Consider, for example, the 1973 case of *In re Marriage of Boseman*.[30] The family home was the only asset the parties had. The wife was awarded custody of the three minor children, ages thirteen, eleven, and three. The trial court issued an order for the house to remain in joint ownership, but gave the wife possession of the house for the "use and benefit" of the minor children until the youngest child reached majority. Thereupon, the house was to be sold and the proceeds divided. The award of the home to the wife was upheld on appeal.

Similarly, in the case *In re Marriage of Herrmann*,[31] the trial court awarded Mrs. Herrmann the house and, to satisfy the equal division rule, ordered her to deliver to Mr. Herrmann a promissory note for half of the value of the house at the date of the dissolution, bearing 7 percent interest per year and payable upon the sale of the residence. The house was ordered sold either when the Herrmann's child reached fifteen, the child or the mother died, the mother remarried or began living with a man, or the mother and child moved away for more than sixty days, or upon the agreement of the parties. The court of appeals approved of the goal of maintaining the home for the children but disapproved of the promissory note. Instead, it recommended the *Boseman* formula of awarding each party a half-interest in the house.

The rationale for maintaining the home for the children is clearly articulated in the case *In re Marriage of Duke*. There, the trial court refused to defer the sale of the home, but the appellate court reversed that decision, stating:

> Where adverse economic, emotional and social impacts on minor children and the custodial parent which would result from an immediate loss of a long established family home are not outweighed by economic detriment to the noncustodial party, the court shall, upon request, reserve jurisdiction and defer sale on appropriate conditions.
>
> The value of a family home to its occupants cannot be measured solely by its value in the marketplace. The longer the occupancy, the more important these noneconomic factors become and the more traumatic and disruptive a move to a new environment is to children whose roots have become firmly entwined in the school and social milieu of their neighborhood.[32]

But despite the legislative and judicial authority for exempting the home from the immediate equal division of community property, the judges we interviewed in 1974–1975, 1981, and 1983 attested to the prevailing pattern of ordering the home sold and the proceeds divided upon divorce. While some judges were willing to leave the home in joint ownership for "a few years," very few were willing to let it remain unsold until small children attained majority. Even fewer were willing to make an exception for an older woman who, they asserted, didn't "need" the home anymore (even if her college age children considered it their home as well).

There is considerable dissatisfaction with the current judicial practice of interpreting the equal division rule to "require" the forced sale of the family home. One alternative is to exempt the home from the equal division rule and to award it to the custodial parent or older homemaker as was done under the old law. This would not require a return to fault: rather these awards would be based solely on the no-fault criteria of greater economic need. A second alternative is to award the use and possession of the home to the needy party.* Since both of these alternatives are used in England, it is useful to compare their legal system with ours. (We return to specific recommendations for the home in the final chapter, Chapter 11.)

THE TREATMENT OF THE FAMILY HOME IN ENGLAND AND CALIFORNIA: A COMPARATIVE EXAMINATION

In England the welfare of the children is the court's primary concern. This leads the English courts to adopt a very different approach to the treatment of the family home at divorce. As a prelude to our examination of the results of the two systems, a brief note on the English law is in order.[34]

The Two Legal Systems

One fundamental difference between the English and California divorce laws is that England retains fault-based grounds for divorce,[35] as well as a no-fault ground. Under the Matrimonial Causes Act of 1973, a

---

* 1984 legislation, which was partially influenced by the findings of this research, reaffirms judicial discretion to make "family home awards" but creates a presumption that the award will terminate upon remarriage.[33]

fault-based divorce is still permitted if one party is guilty of marital misconduct. In addition, if a spouse is innocent of marital misconduct and does not consent to the divorce, he or she may prevent a divorce until the parties have lived separately for five years.[36]

While there is some disagreement about the role that fault actually plays in English divorce settlements, the possibility of fault-based accusations allows for something that the California law precludes: pre-divorce negotiations concerning the grounds and timing of a legal divorce. In this respect, the English law gives the "innocent" and/or unwilling spouse the power to delay or deny a divorce—and to use this power as a lever in negotiating property and maintenance awards. In California, by contrast, an unwilling or "innocent" spouse has no extra bargaining power in negotiating a property settlement.

Another major difference between the English and California laws relates to "marital breakdown" as a ground for divorce. Whereas the parties' agreement to dissolve their marriage is regarded as a sufficient justification for divorce in California, the English law requires two years of living separately as "evidence" of the breakdown.[37]

A third major difference between the two legal regimes is found in their rules governing the ownership and division of property. Before 1970, England had a separate property or title system in which each spouse owned the property he or she held title to or earned in marriage. Since most income was (and still is) earned by husbands, the practical result of this rule was that the husband typically owned most of the property acquired during marriage. Before 1970, if the title to property was in the husband's name, the courts had virtually no power to transfer "his assets" to his wife upon divorce.[38]

Under the English reforms of 1970 and 1973,[39] the courts were empowered to go beyond title and to award whatever property or lump-sum awards they deemed "reasonable" and required to do "justice." The rule of thumb has been to award a wife *one-third* of "the husband's assets" (in addition to maintenance) upon divorce.

Thus the two systems start with different premises about what is an equitable property award for a divorced wife: one-half of the marital assets in California, and one-third in England. Nevertheless, the English legal experts report that the "one-third rule" is no more than a rough starting point, a report that is substantiated by the discussion that follows.

The following two cases examine a common situation in both societies: families who have most of their net worth in the family home. In both the United States and England, about half of the divorcing couples own (or are purchasing) a family home at the time of the divorce.[40]

In 1980 and 1981 a sample of English judges, attorneys (i.e., barristers and solicitors), and law professors were asked to predict the outcome of the same series of hypothetical divorce cases that were discussed with California lawyers and judges in 1975 and 1981. (The English sample and research methods are described in Appendix A, pp. 411–412.)

In both settings, the legal experts were asked to *predict* the outcome of the hypothetical cases. After that they were asked for their *personal opinion* of the predicted outcome and why they thought the result was or was not fair.

Case 1: A Young Couple with Two Young Children

In the first hypothetical case the marital property consists of a car and a home. During their short marriage, the Byrds have had two young children. Ted Byrd is an accountant, while Pat Byrd has been a full-time housewife and mother during their seven-year marriage. (The complete text of the Byrd case is found in Appendix B, p. 414.)

In the English version of the case, the title and deed to the family home are held in Ted's name. In both versions, the house is worth $40,000. Half of that, $20,000, is equity. There is a mortgage for the remaining $20,000.

What Happens to the Home?

As might be expected, the two sets of respondents approached this case from different perspectives. In California, the experts' first concern was the required equal division of the community property. Since the major community asset was the family home, most of the California respondents (close to two-thirds) said that the home would have to be sold so that the proceeds could be divided equally between the two spouses. As one judge put it:

> The court would be prone to order the house sold and the proceeds divided, especially under the new law where you don't want to saddle him with a note.... So the court would compel the sale of that house and encourage the woman to get a job. In fact, that's the only way this thing could work out.

Most of the remaining Californians (one-third) favored allowing the wife to retain the house but giving the husband a note for his half of its equity value. As one attorney explained, he didn't see how the wife could make it without the house:

> . . . the wife couldn't make it if she had to go out and rent a place. The court will say, "All right, give the wife the house," but she has to give him a note for his half of the equity so that if she sells the house in a certain number of years when the kids are a little older, she has to pay him off.

The first priority for the English experts, in contrast, was the preservation of the family home for the children. Most of them (87 percent) predicted that the wife and children would continue to live in the family home with the husband's support. For example, one barrister (a specialized lawyer who appears before judges) explained the way the court would approach this case:

> First let's make sure the children are looked after. . . . the children have always lived in that house. . . . you want to finish a child's schooling.

Similarly, a solicitor (an attorney who deals with clients) predicted:

> The wife would get the house because she has to make a home for the children, and the children come first—you don't want their home to be disrupted. You want to stabilize the situation for them.

The underlying principle in the English approach is "children first."[41] This principle also emerges from an analysis of the reported decisions under the Matrimonial Causes Act conducted by John Eekelaar of Oxford University.[42] Eekelaar notes that even though it is not explicit in the statutes, the major principle in the English case law is that "adequate provision must be made to ensure the support and accommodation of children of the marriage."[43] This principle is also echoed in the English Law Commissions statement that "the welfare of the children . . . should take precedence over the adjustment of financial rights and duties of former spouses to each other."[44]

While the English children and their needs are given first priority, the benefits accorded their custodians are more limited. Note that the English experts predicted that the mother and her children would be given the *right to continue living in the home*. (Close to 70 percent of the English experts predicted that she would be entitled *to occupy* the home until her children were grown.) But they did not predict that she would become the sole owner of the home. As one law professor predicted:

> The house will be held in trust for the children so they can live in it until the youngest finishes school or training—but only if she [the wife] doesn't remarry or no other man is living in the house.

As this quotation suggests, two limitations were typically placed on the wife's (and children's) right to continue living in the family home. Two-thirds of the experts who said the wife would remain in the home noted that she would have to sell it when her children were eighteen or finished their education, and a (somewhat overlapping) third said that the home would be sold before that if she remarried or cohabited with another man.

Consider the implications of each of these restrictions. The restriction that requires the sale of the family home if the wife cohabits or remarries may appear reasonable at first—if it is assumed that any male will immediately be able to (or be willing to) provide a divorced woman and her children with alternative housing. However, the "remarriage or cohabitation" standard is *not a means-related standard*, which suggests that "moral" rather than financial criteria are involved.

The implication seems to be that as long as the wife remains "faithful" to her former husband she can retain her entitlement to the family home. It seems odd to expect a wife to remain faithful to her ex-husband—and odder still to have the children's security in the family home jeopardized by this requirement.

The second restriction, which requires the sale of the home when the children reach age eighteen, is also problematic. If the major rationale for maintaining the wife and children in the family home is to provide stability and security for the children, it may similarly seem reasonable at first to plan to sell the house when the children are grown. Indeed, orders for a wife to sell the house when the youngest child reached eighteen were fairly common in England in the early 1970's. But in recent years there has been increased concern about the middle-aged housewife who, though no better off than she was at the time of divorce, is suddenly forced to sell her home and move. She also loses most of the equity, as we will see below, is left with little or no security for her later years, and cannot afford to buy another home. This is why a significant minority of English experts—one out of five—explicitly *rejected* the possibility of a delayed sale and instead awarded the wife the home (i.e., all of the equity in the home) outright.*

Delaying the sale of the family home until the children reach majority is increasingly common in a number of separate property states in the United States as well.[45] Here too, however, matrimonial attorneys are becoming disenchanted with maintaining the house in joint owner-

---

* This latter solution also suggests that the custodial parent may be entitled to a greater share of the family property as compensation for the services she performs for the children. But no English expert mentioned compensation as a rationale for the award of the family home to the wife; need was their sole explicit rationale.

ship. For example, New York Attorney Joanne Schulman, of the National Center for Women and Family Law, points to the pitfalls in three equitable distribution states—New York, New Jersey, and Connecticut: "It only delays the women's impoverishment and forecloses her chances of buying another home when real estate values have risen further."[46] In addition, the arrangement means that

> she is performing unpaid work for her husband. She is maintaining the home, and caring for their children. When the house is eventually sold, her husband cashes in on her maintenance and improvements when he "cashes out" his share of the equity. But she has been doing all the work.[47]

Instead, Schulman argues, the wife should be entitled to keep the home as compensation for the child-care services she performs. Other attorneys in the tri-state area point to the ongoing conflicts over home repairs, maintenance, and whether new cohabitants should be allowed to live in the house, and advise one partner to buy out the other's share of the house with other assets.[48] As we noted, however, this solution will not help the average divorcing couple whose home equity is their only major asset.

Thus the practical alternatives in most cases are these: first, the family home could be awarded to the custodial parent because that parent has a greater need for family resources, or because, as attorney Schulman suggests, that would recognize and reward custodial care. Second, use and possession of the home could be awarded to the custodial parent with a note for a share of the equity to the other parent.* Third, the home could remain in joint ownership. A final alternative would be for legislatures to adopt a policy that puts the interests of the children first and allocates a share of the family's property directly to them.[49]

HOW IS THE EQUITY IN THE HOME DIVIDED?

An English order that awards the house to the wife until the children are grown typically specifies in advance how the equity in the

---

* Often the court fixes the dollar value of the husband's share of the equity at the time of the divorce. This permits the wife to benefit from the home's increased value, if any, under her tenancy. But courts vary considerably on the details of these arrangements. In some states the wife pays the husband interest on his half of the equity, sometimes at the market rate and sometimes at a "token rate." In some states she pays the mortgage and maintenance costs, and in others these are split. Still other states require her to pay rent. In many states she and the children live in the home without any costs as a form of child support. (Under the 1984 child support enforcement law the home may be used as security for child support payments.)

house will be divided when it is sold. The English experts predicted that Pat Byrd would, on average, receive one-third of the equity from a postponed sale while her husband would receive two-thirds. This might leave the woman who has invested her life in raising children and maintaining her home with no home, little equity, and, therefore, limited security for her middle and older years.

The California solution for the Byrd case was to order an immediate sale of the family home so that the equity could be divided equally. Close to 70 percent of the experts predicted that the Byrds' home would be sold. They offered two justifications for this solution: it permitted a "clean break" between the parties, and it did not unduly hamper the husband by tying up his equity in the house. The California judges and lawyers stressed the husband's "right" to "his half" of the family property. Since the only substantial family property in this case, as in many divorce cases, is the home, its sale was seen as necessary to give the husband the money he would need to start a new life. As one California attorney said:

> You have to be fair to the husband. If you award a house to a woman when it is the only asset, you are then faced with the man who asks, "Why am I not entitled to the present enjoyment of the community asset that we have? Why should I stand still for deferred enjoyment?" He wants to start a new life. He doesn't want to hang around waiting for his equity. And, by law, he has a right to that equity.

Similarly, another attorney explained that it would be unfair to leave the husband with nothing:

> There is nothing else to do but sell the house. They have all their savings in that. Otherwise, the wife gets all the savings and the husband gets nothing. That isn't quite fair. It isn't just.

In contrast the English emphasis on the children's welfare as the court's first priority, the "interests" of children were rarely mentioned by the California experts. Marital property was defined solely in terms of the relative rights of the husband and wife, and it was divided between the two of them.

A minority of the California experts (slightly more than a third) predicted that the sale of the home would be postponed to allow the wife and children to continue living in it (in contrast to the 87 percent of English respondents who predicted that outcome). Those Californians who projected a delayed sale typically said that the wife and children would be allowed to live there for only three or four years, enough to provide "a cushion" during the transitional years.[50] As one judge said:

> I would be more inclined to give the house to the wife, because she has two infant children of tender years . . . and give the husband a note and a deed of trust for his share. It would be payable six months after her remarriage . . . or upon the elapse of a specific number of years, whichever occurs first.
> [Q: You said a specific number of years. How long do you think she would be allowed to keep the house in this case if none of those other things happen?] The kids are four and six. Oh, I would say anywhere from three to five years.
> [Q: And then?] She would either have to pay off the note or sell the house.

This solution simply postpones the disruptive effects of the home sale and ignores the question of where the woman and her children will live in three to five years.

As we noted above, even though the California law clearly gives judges *the discretion* to delay the sale of the home when the pressing needs of minor children are at stake, nevertheless, the responses of the judges we interviewed reveal that many of them do not consider it "fair" to issue these orders. For example, in informal interviews about the Byrd case in 1983, several California judges said that the children were so young that it would be unfair to "tie up" the husband's equity in the house for the fourteen years until the younger child reached eighteen. Although a few, when pressed, said they might delay the sale for a year or two, they saw no ultimate advantage in that because the children would "have to" move eventually. As one judge said:

> After all, there is a limit to how long you can make him wait . . . and fourteen years is too long. . . . But after five years the kids will be adjusted to the divorce, and everyone in this country moves every five years anyway.

One very basic and important difference between the responses of the experts in California and England is that the English awards show much more variation. Thus while the California wife can be certain that she will receive half of the assets accumulated during the marriage, the English wife, who is subject to the registrar's or judge's concept of fairness, may receive anywhere from 0 to 100 percent. In the Byrd case, for example, the English experts' estimates of the share of the equity that the wife would receive varied from 0 to 50 percent when they predicted a delayed sale of the house, and from 50 to 100 percent when they predicted an award upon divorce.* The most common English prediction was that she would eventually get a third of the equity, after being allowed to live in the house while she has dependent children.

One may be tempted to conclude that English wives with minor children are better off after divorce than those in California—if they own or are purchasing a family home. Almost all of them are allowed to live in the family home while raising their children, and about a third of them are awarded the entire equity at the time of the divorce. Even those who are not awarded the home outright, but who are nevertheless allowed to live there with their children, have been awarded an "entitlement" to preferred housing, which is an entitlement of considerable financial value. These advantages, however, are reduced somewhat by the restrictions on the English wife's personal life (i.e., on her cohabitation or remarriage) and by her typically lower share of one-third of the equity when the house is sold.

The advantages of the English system are more pronounced for the older homemaker, as the next case shows.

Case 2: A Long Marriage, Wealth, and an Older Housewife

A second hypothetical case involves a twenty-seven-year marriage between a corporate executive and a homemaker and mother who raised their three children through college. The Thompsons have the following property: a $90,000 home and furnishings (£50,000 in the English version), two cars (worth $5,000 and $2,000), and $10,000 worth of stocks and bonds. (The complete text of the Thompson case is found in Appendix B, p. 414.)

Once again, a comparison of what the experts predicted about the division of property in the Thompson case reveals a basic difference in orientation. The California judges approach the problem as a mathematical calculation: they add up the net value of the assets and divide the total into two equal shares. As one California attorney said:

> In 1968, under the old law, she'd get the family home and the stocks. But today, the court would divide the assets equally. She'd get $45,000 for her half of the house.

---

* The 13 percent of the English respondents who predicted that the family home would be sold immediately upon divorce typically gave the wife a large share of the equity (a median share of three-quarters) to enable her to buy a smaller house for herself and her children.

[Q: Are you saying the house would have to be sold?] In this case it looks as if it would have to be sold to divide the community [property] equally. But if she made a strong indication to the judge that they'd lived in the home for years, and that she can get a new mortgage and make the installments (and that they would be no greater than she would have to pay in rent if she moved elsewhere, into an apartment, for example), I think the court might allow her to live in the house and pay the husband off. After all, so long as the husband got the dollar amount that he wanted, or was entitled to receive, there would be no reason to reject her offer in that respect.

Here again, California experts are concerned with a solution that allows the husband to get his equity out of the house. In contrast, the English respondents begin by trying to provide the wife with an adequate home. For example:

[A family court judge]
He will have to provide his wife with an income and a home. She is fifty-three years old and isn't earning, so she cannot get a mortgage. . . . So, she'll have to buy herself a flat and provide herself with an income. . . .

[A solicitor]
This is a wife who's got to have a decent home for the rest of her life. He'll have to buy her a home or a flat [outright; i.e., she won't have to pay a mortgage].
[Q: How much would that cost?] Well, it depends where she is living. But she could probably buy a nice flat or a smaller house for £45,000 or £50,000. Mind you, she'd get £60,000 or so if that was what was needed.
. . . [Q: But that is more than half. What about the one-third rule?] The one-third rule is only a starting point. First, he has to house her. If you only give her one-third of the home, that isn't really fair. But there is too much equity in the house, so they won't let her keep the whole thing.

[A law professor]
Husband will argue house is too big for her, but she'd probably get at least half of the £100,000 in capital available. So she will have £50,000 for housing and can easily buy a smaller house for herself for that.

[A high court judge]
If she wants to stay in the house and he agrees—fine. If not, I'd sell the house and give her half to buy a new house. You can't expect her to live in anything of less value than £45,000. . . . But she'd do all right for that and she'll own it free and clear [i.e., no mortgage].

As these quotes suggest, the first priority in England is to provide a comparable home for the older housewife. This leads to more variety in the English awards. Almost 60 percent of the English experts predict that the wife would receive between £45,000 and £50,000, which is roughly half of the £90,000 home, or half of the £90,000 home plus the £10,000 of stocks and shares. However, these awards seem to be based on a notion of equity in housing rather than the concept of an equal division. Most of the remaining English experts (30 percent) predicted that the wife would receive two-thirds of the value of the home so that she could buy a new house—a rationale that clearly differs from the concept of an equal division. (In California, by contrast, where virtually *all* of the experts predicted that the property would be divided equally, the awards to the wife ranged from 49 percent to 51 percent of the total property.)

Another major difference in legal philosophy is the English law's assumption that after a long marriage a husband has a responsibility to provide for his ex-wife for *the rest of her life*. To ensure that this responsibility is met, the English courts typically require an older (and well-to-do) husband to purchase an insurance policy or annuity to compensate his wife for the widow's benefits she forfeits by getting divorced. As one solicitor explained:

> He has an obligation to take out an annuity to provide her with the same benefit she would have received on his death. Otherwise, the divorce would cause her grave hardship.

This type of provision, which assures the older housewife financial security, is virtually unheard of in California. (Even though California, like England, recognizes the divorced wife's entitlement to share her husband's pension, this may be illusory security because wives may be forced to trade their pension rights in order to keep the family home.

Summary: The Two Perspectives Compared

Before summarizing the differences between the two systems, a cautionary note about generalizations is in order. Clearly the results of any divorce case will depend not only on the legal system, but also on the socioeconomic status and life circumstances of the divorcing parties. While the legal rules can enlarge the pool of available assets to be divided—by including, for example, the right to live in publicly owned council housing in England, or the right to a pension or medical insurance in the United States—the scope of any property settlement is necessarily limited by the amount of family property that is available.

Thus whatever the legal rules, men and women of the upper class will, on the average, be better off after divorce than working class men and women. These class factors are as critical in determining divorce settlements and postdivorce consequences as the legal rules. They set the parameters within which the legal system can act.

Not withstanding this important caveat, several fundamental differences between the two systems are evident. The first is the relative emphasis placed on children's needs and the *child's entitlement* to share the family's wealth and property. While both legal systems pay lip service to the lifelong responsibility of parents for their children, this responsibility seems to be taken more seriously in England. The English experts were more likely to emphasize the importance of children and their social and financial "rights" to both property and maintenance after divorce. Almost all of the English respondents emphasized the child's independent "right" to the matrimonial home and the child's "interest" in remaining in a stable home environment. In California, by contrast, both property and maintenance are perceived as issues for the two adults. Marital property is divided between the husband and wife. Not one California respondent mentioned the possibility of a child's entitlement to share the marital assets.

A second important difference between the two systems lies in the *amount of judicial discretion* they permit. California judges have relatively little discretion in dividing community property—they must divide it equally between husband and wife. English judges, however, are free to allocate property as "justice" requires. Their greater discretion, as we have seen, results in a wider range of property awards. Thus, even when faced with the *same* case, the English jurists' predictions for Pat Byrd's share of the home equity ranged from 0 to 100 percent.

One advantage of having greater discretion is that judges can tailor their awards to the unique circumstances and needs of individual couples. On the other hand, since judicial discretion permits variation among judges, it stimulates "forum shopping"—shopping for the most sympathetic judge—and thereby encourages litigation and appeals. This, in turn, increases legal costs and *favors the spouse with more power or resources*. Thus, if one spouse has more money than the other, and therefore has access to better attorneys or can afford more extensive litigation, he or she is in a better position to take advantage of the discretionary rules and to obtain a more favorable settlement.

A third, and perhaps the most important, difference between the legal systems in England and California is that they rely on different *conceptions of justice and equity*. In England, justice is typically seen as requiring provisions that assure the future security of a dependent housewife (and any minor children in her custody) after divorce. The

English system tries to divide the family resources so as to provide roughly *equal standards of living* for husbands and wives after divorce. Justice in this system means that a mother with young children will typically remain in the family home, and an older woman who has been a housewife and mother will be taken care of, with housing and financial support for the rest of her life. Although the security and protection that a wife receives will always be dependent on her husband's resources, and will therefore be limited for many divorced wives, the English system's vision of justice is one that assures a woman that her husband will remain responsible, insofar as his means permit, for her welfare and support. Since it is assumed that he will be there to "provide for her," the law does not guarantee her any fixed share of the family property.

In California by contrast, the underlying assumption is that justice is best assured by severing the financial ties of the marriage, awarding both the husband and the wife one-half of the family assets, and giving each of them the "freedom" to build a new life. Justice in this system means that the family home will often be sold, so that each spouse can be assured of an equal amount of the proceeds with which to "start over."* Both the young mother and the older housewife are assured the same amount of property as their former husbands—and both are encouraged to build new lives.**

While the California woman is assured a fixed share of one-half of the family property, more than her English counterpart would typically receive, she is also expected to bear the economic consequences of the divorce without help from her former husband. Thus the California vision of justice, which relies heavily on the assumption of a new equality between the sexes, may be based on an erroneous assumption about the equality that actually exists between men and women in the larger society. Women have typically been economically disadvantaged by marriage, in that they are more likely to have dropped out of the labor force or worked part-time or forgone career opportunities because of their family and child care responsibilities. In addition, because women are typically going to continue to bear the lion's share of the family responsibilities after divorce if they have minor children, "equal" treatment means, in practice, that divorced women in California will be left alone to shoulder the economic disadvantages they face because of their family contributions during marriage.

* This is so even if there are minor children who would benefit more from continuity and stability than from a "fresh start" of changing schools, neighborhoods, and friends.

** But divorced women are rarely given the resources to do this. (See Chapter 7 on alimony awards and Chapter 9 on child support.)

DISPOSITION OF OTHER MARITAL ASSETS

There is a clear trend between 1968 (under the old law) and 1972 and 1977 (under the new law) toward an equal division of community assets and debts. This is shown in Table 11.

Although the pattern is evident for each of the assets listed, some sex typing of awards still persists. For example, wives continued to be awarded more homes and household furnishings than were husbands (when there were sufficient assets to offset these awards with items of comparable value for the husband). Similarly, husbands continued to be more likely to be awarded the family business and the single family car. (In families with two or more cars (not shown), an equal division was more common with each spouse keeping one car.)

The pattern of dividing each of the major family assets—the family business, pensions, money, and debts—is discussed below.

Disposition of a Business

It has traditionally been assumed that a business belongs to the husband, even in cases where it is legally part of a couple's community property. In the past, the easy property settlement in this regard was one in which the divorcing parties owned both a home and a business: the wife could be awarded the home, the husband could be awarded the business, and the two assets were assumed to balance each other out. Since an equal division was not required under the old law, identifying the exact values of the two assets was not considered necessary.

Table 11 reveals that husbands were almost always awarded the business (91 percent of all cases) in 1968 under the old law. This pattern remained strong under the new law in both 1972 and 1977, with businesses awarded to the husband about 80 percent of the time. (These awards were typically offset by notes, with interest, payable over time or by awards of comparable value to the wife.)

These data reveal an interesting paradox: while the courts are anxious to sell the matrimonial home to effect an equal division of property, they do not seem to feel any similar pressure when it comes to a business. Instead, the courts go to great length to keep the business intact (and typically in the hands of the husband) and utilize the same procedures that they find unworkable when discussing the delayed sale of the home.

The courts face three questions in dealing with a community-property business at divorce: How much is it worth? How should the equity be divided? And, who should retain possession and control?

TABLE 11

Division of Assets and Debts
under Fault and No-Fault Laws

DIVISION OF ASSETS	FAULT LAW (1968)	NO-FAULT LAW	
		(1972)	(1977)
Family Home			
Majority to husband*	16%	24%	19%
Approximately equal division**	23	25	35
Majority to wife	61	51	46
Household furnishings			
Majority to husband*	6	8	7
Approximately equal division**	3	5	42
Majority to wife	91	87	51
Single family car			
Majority to husband*	62%	59%	54%
Approximately equal division**	—	—	—
Majority to wife	39	42	44
Money, stocks, and bonds			
Majority to husband*	27%	38%	24%
Approximately equal division**	29	27	50
Majority to wife	44	35	26
Family business			
Majority to husband*	91%	78%	81%
Approximately equal division**	0	13	14
Majority to wife	10	9	6
Community-property debts			
Majority to husband*	88%	85%	58%
Approximately equal division**	6	7	29
Majority to wife	7	8	13

* Majority = over 60%.
** Approximately equal = between 40 and 59%.

This table is based on random samples of court dockets, Los Angeles County, California, 1968, 1972, and 1977.

The task of determining the worth of a business has become much more critical since the equal division rule was instituted. Attorneys report that they now have to be more careful and thorough in establishing its value. In fact, in response to the question, "What has been the main impact of the new law on the way you prepare a case?" the most common reply was that there is more time spent on the financial aspects of the case and the valuation of property and businesses.

Similarly, when asked, "Is there any change in the skills you need as a lawyer?" 69 percent of the attorneys mentioned an increased emphasis on finance-related skills such as projecting the tax consequences of awards, reading financial statements, evaluating appraisals of businesses and pensions, and working with accountants and other expert witnesses. As one lawyer put it, "You spend less time investigating dirt and more time on business ledgers."

We were surprised to discover that, despite the need for more precise valuation spurred by the new equal division requirement, the old-law practice of valuing a business as equal to the price of the house was still fairly common. As one attorney said:

> I think since property does have to be divided equally, the courts are much more inclined, assuming that the husband is running the family business, to find a substantial value [to the business] that offsets the house. I tried a case last week and surprise, surprise, the court found a $40,000 value for the business and by an amazing coincidence the equity in the family home was $40,000.

Many attorneys pointed out that this method of division tends to favor the husband. For example, one attorney said:

> I think there's a tendency on the part of the judges to give the wife less than one-half of the business, even under the new law, and it works this way: You take a going business which the husband is usually awarded. In evaluating that business, the judge has wide discretion. The wife will put on the stand an expert who will value the business at, let us say, $300,000, and the husband will put on an expert who values the business at $100,000. If the judge wants to lean in the direction of the husband, and many of the judges are obviously husband-oriented, he'll take the lesser value and award [the business] to the husband. This is especially easy for him to do if the house is worth $100,000 or $150,000. He sets the business as equal to the house, and the husband picks up an extra $75,000 or $100,000. I find that happening all the time.

Another attorney pointed out that the husband generally has the advantage of controlling business profits and losses and can manipulate its balance sheet to a certain extent. In addition, since he controls expenditures, he can charge both living expenses and luxuries to the business. As one attorney suggested, the possibilities are endless:

> The husbands always get the break. They have the business acumen, so they get the biggest piece. The skill of the wife's lawyer determines how close to one-half she gets. In a family business, if she takes her share in stock, she never gets a dividend. He keeps the profits for himself by buying cars, a boat, etc., for the business. Even if the wife gets one-half of the business, the husband still has control. He can threaten not to work and he can appoint a receiver and put the business up for sale. Meanwhile, he can start a new corporation. No one will buy the old business, as the husband probably won't sign a convenant not to open a competitive business. The wife always has the uphill battle.

Other attorneys, while agreeing that granting control of the business to the husband may give him more than half the property, argue that this measure is necessary:

> In an ongoing business, the owner always gets the biggest piece because much of the value cannot be proven. The wife usually gets less than half of the true value. But you've got to be realistic. You don't want to kill the entrepreneur goose.
>
> Under the old law, if the judge really felt strongly about giving the husband the business, they'd find enough fault on her side to give it to him without very much offset. Now they have to give her what they regard as a fair value. While the values are generally low, nevertheless they are better than they used to be, because the courts are forced to place a value on the business.
>
> But the reason they're low is not because the judges are necessarily sympathetic to businessmen, but because the question is, "Where's the money going to come from to buy her out?" Then you've got to look at the kind of cash flow he's got. You deduct his taxes, because he's going to have to pay his federal income taxes and so on, and look at the net dollars he has available to him. Then you've got to pay for the asset, child support, and the alimony from the same net dollars. And you've got to leave him enough so that he has an incentive to go on, which has to be more than half.

While many judges echoed these sentiments and asserted that *the husband needed the business,* or that the husband could not afford to buy out his wife's share of the business, few of them used the same logic to argue that *the wife (or the children) needed the family home.*

The results of these attitudes are reflected in Table 11 above, as the husband is awarded most of the family business in 81 percent of the cases. In addition, if a business remains in joint ownership, possession and control is invariably awarded to the husband (88 percent of the time according to the attorneys), because judges say it is unfair and unrealistic to expect him to share control with his wife. As one judge said, "you can't run a business by majority rule."

Disposition of Pensions

Pensions (not shown in Table 11) are typically awarded to the worker, with an offsetting monetary award to the other spouse. Male and female workers are equally likely to be awarded their own pensions in a divorce settlement.[51] However, since men are more likely than women to hold jobs that allow them to acquire pensions, they are more likely to be awarded the pension at divorce (especially if there is a family home of similar value for a home/pension tradeoff). Several methods for apportioning pension benefits between husbands and wives are discussed in Chapter 5.

Disposition of Savings, Stocks, and Bonds

Money stocks and bonds are most amenable to an equal division and their disposition reflects the equalization trend observed for all community assets. It is not surprising, however, to find only about a quarter of these assets awarded to one or the other spouse because these assets are commonly used to offset other awards and to equalize the overall division of property.

Disposition of Community Property Debts

The court records reveal a rising percentage of divorcing couples with debts, from 15 percent in 1968, to 26 percent in 1977 (see Table 6, Chapter 3).

Under the old law, the husband was typically ordered to pay the community debts because it was assumed that he was the wage earner with the income to pay them. Eighty percent of the Los Angeles judges said they generally "awarded" the debts to the husband under the old law. Only 8 percent said they typically split the debts, while another

8 percent said they tried to "award" the debts to the spouse who kept the property.

Here again, the data from court records show a steady increase in the percentage of debts that are divided equally. Nevertheless, the husband continues to be ordered to pay the community debts in more than half of the cases—58 percent in 1977, compared to 80 percent in 1972 and 88 percent in 1968. The share of debts to be paid by wives has increased under the new law. Yet even in 1977, only 29 percent of the debts were divided equally (see Table 11 above).

The attorneys in our study reported that the major difference in the way debts are handled under no-fault is that while the husband is still required to pay them off, he now is given a "credit" for the obligation by being awarded an asset of equivalent value. As one attorney explained:

> The husband still pays them, but he now gets a credit on the total community property. It's a relief.
> [Q: So then really the debts are split 50/50?]
> Yes, that's right, they are split 50/50. The husband gets more property if he pays more debts.

Seal found a more pronounced trend toward equal responsibility for debts in San Diego County, where joint responsibility for debts rose from 30 percent of the old law cases in 1968 to 58 percent of the new law cases in 1976.[52] She also notes an increase in joint responsibility for attorney's fees (from 12 percent in 1968 to 44 percent in 1976) a trend which is also evident in both San Francisco and Los Angeles counties.[53]

In the early years of the no-fault law, there was uncertainty about whether the equal division rule applied to debts. By 1975, most (58 percent) of the Los Angeles judges we interviewed reported that they were dividing the debts equally (or using community funds to pay them off before the remaining property was divided equally). However, a minority of judges (31 percent) said that they usually made the husband responsible for most of the debts.

In recent years case law developments have clarified the rule for the disposition of community debts. In general, debts are to be considered along with assets, and the total net worth is to be divided equally between the two spouses.[54] If, however, there are only debts at the time of divorce, or if the debts exceed the assets so that the community has a *negative net worth,* the judge has the discretion to dispose of the debts in an equitable manner depending on the earning capacities of the two spouses and other relevant factors.[55] In addition, there is a statutory exception for debts incurred for educational purposes: they may be awarded to the student spouse who benefited from the educational loan.[56]

ATTITUDES TOWARD EQUAL DIVISION

The overwhelming majority of the attorneys and judges we interviewed (over 80 percent) said they thought the equal division rule was basically fair and preferable to the fault-based standards of the old law. As one attorney observed:

> I think the equal division requirement is fair. I don't have any complaints about it. And people seem to accept it. I have found very little—even representing mostly husbands—very little client resistance to that concept. I won't say none at all. But they accept it. That was their idea of community property—it all belonged to both of them.

Further, only 20 percent of the attorneys and judges thought that property awards should be clearly linked to the spouse's behavior during the marriage, as they were under the old law.

However, despite their generally favorable view of equal division, close to 40 percent of the attorneys thought judges should be allowed more discretion in dividing the community property. Their reservations about the strict equal division rule typically focused on the forced sale of the family home. Many thought a wife and minor children needed the home and should be awarded more than half of the property if the home was the only family asset. As one attorney explained:

> Where the children are involved, a greater proportion of the couple's assets should be allocated to the wife. If the husband has a business, he can always build a new estate, but she can end up with nothing. If she needs financial help to raise the kids, she should be awarded the lion's share of the assets.

Other commonly mentioned situations in which more discretion— and unequal awards—were seen as desirable were those involving long marriages, few assets, or a combination of these factors. Several attorneys focused on the problems of older women in long marriages and the loss of their homes (or the doublebind they face if they have to choose between the loss of their home or the loss of a share of their husbands' pension to keep the home). Others noted their difficulties when the husband retains control of the family business:

> Generally we find that in most cases of businesses, the husband is in control of all of the community property, all of the assets, and that control

of course gives him a big edge. When you bring about an equal division and leave the business to the husband, because it may be his only source of income, the wife has a real hard go at it. His business can increase, he can handle his books the way he wants to, he can show losses that don't really exist and bring about surpluses. In a long marriage, particularly where the husband has been the sole provider, equal division is not really fair to the wife.

CONCLUSION: IS EQUAL MORE EQUITABLE?

Is marital property being divided "equally" upon divorce? Has the equal division rule brought more equitable results?

On the one hand, the data presented in this chapter show that the divorce law reforms have brought a dramatic change in the way property is divided. On the whole, property (as the term is presently defined) is being divided more equally in accord with the explicit directives of the new law.

On the other hand, the word "equality" suggests fairness and equity for all parties involved. In this light, the results of the legal reform are less clear. The required equal division of property has brought more forced sales of family assets, especially the family home, so that the proceeds can be divided between the two spouses. The result is increased dislocation and disruption in the lives of minor children (in contrast to the old law pattern in which the wife with custody of minor children was typically awarded the family home). This does not seem fair, in that the needs and interests of the children are not considered. It is as if the family consisted of two people—a husband and a wife— rather than the average four people. Under the equal division rule, "equality" means that three people (the wife and, on average, two children) share one-half of the marital assets while one person (the husband) is entitled to the other half for himself.

One obvious solution to this inequity is to allow an exception to—or a delay of—the equal division rule to accommodate the interests of minor children. This would recognize that the parent who cares for children both needs and is entitled to a larger share of the family's resources.

In a sense, it is ironic to label this an exception, since most divorcing couples have children.[57] It might be wiser to begin to formulate policy for this average case and then worry about the exceptions when there are no children. The solution offered by the English sample of judges and lawyers suggests the more equitable outcomes of a rule that places the interests of the children first.

The English data also illuminate another implicit finding: one effect of the American rule is to "disenfranchise" the children of divorce. In England they are seen as entitled to a share of the family property, or at least to have their interests considered in the distribution of that property. They have no such rights in the United States.

A second problem of "equality" emerges from these data: a 50/50 division of family property may not produce equality of results—or equality of standards of living after divorce—if the two spouses are unequally situated at the point of the divorce. This is most evident in the situation of the older housewife under the new law. In contrast to the traditional pattern of awarding a larger share of the community assets to the wife, ostensibly because she was "innocent" but in practice because her greater need was recognized, the new rules require that she be treated "equally." Yet after a marital life devoted to homemaking, she is typically without substantial skills and experience in the labor force and typically needs a greater share of the property to cushion the income loss she suffers at divorce. She is, simply put, not in an equal economic position at divorce. The traditional law took her special needs into consideration and gave her more than half of the family property because she needed more than half. Today, with only half of the tangible assets and with a lesser capacity to earn a reasonable income after divorce, she is severely disadvantaged by the so-called "equal" division of property.

One solution to this inequity is to allow a second exception to—or to require a delay in applying—the equal division rule for women who have been housewives and mothers in marriages of long duration. If these women are at a clear disadvantage in their ability to earn a comparable income after divorce, and if the detriment is a result of their family responsibilities during marriage—both of which are likely conditions in such cases—then they should be awarded a larger share of the property to achieve the goal of "equality of results," i.e., equality in the postdivorce standards of living of the two spouses. Here again, it seems ironic to label the remedy for this common situation an exception. In fact, a substantial majority of divorced women have either raised children or are currently raising children, and these responsibilities are directly related to their disadvantaged earning capacity at divorce. These "average" divorced women ought to be awarded more property in recognition of their greater need.*

A third issue is suggested by the question of whether the equal division rule has brought more equitable results: what is the basis

---

* One law review writer has suggested a judicial presumption of an award of 75 percent of the marital property to a dependent spouse.[58]

for comparison? In California, the implicit comparison is with the traditional law, under which wives typically received more than half of the property (especially if the family's major asset was the home). But this does not mean all wives benefited under the old rules, or that awards based on fault produced more equitable results. As we have seen, a woman who was labeled guilty under the old law was barred from a larger share of property even if she had minor children. This was so even if she had been a homemaker for 30 years. Thus the fault system created its own inequities, and there are few incentives to return to it in order to provide the average "innocent" wife with the property award she needs. Rather, the time has come to fashion rules that overcome the inequities of both systems. What we need is a new standard based on equality of results for the two spouses. (This is discussed further in the final chapter, Chapter 11.)

The question of whether the equal division rule produces more equitable results invites another comparison: How fair are the results of this rule when compared with the results of the "equitable distribution" standard used in most other states? While there has been no comparable empirical research on property awards in common law states, two recent studies, which rely on testimonies at hearings and reported cases, are suggestive.

The first is a 1983 report by a judicial task force in New Jersey on women in the courts. After conducting hearings throughout the state, the task force concluded that their state's equitable distribution standard typically resulted in awards to wives that were significantly *less than half* (i.e., 35 to 40 percent) of the family property. As the judicial report states:

> Attorneys from all parts of the State observed that there appears to be an unofficial standard that the wife will receive no more than 35 percent to 40 percent of the net marital assets in equitable distribution, . . . even when there are small children in the custody of the wife.[59]

They concluded that "women suffer inequitable long range outcomes with respect to property division."[60]

A second review of property awards in an equitable distribution state, New York, similarly concludes that wives are awarded *less than half* of the marital property in the vast majority of cases. Attorneys Harriet Cohen and Adria Hillman analyzed the 70 reported decisions during the first four years of New York's Equitable Distribution Law and concluded that "the courts are not treating the wife as an equal partner in the marriage."[61] As they summarize their findings:

. . . judicial dispositions of marital property upon the dissolution of a marriage reflect that property is not being distributed equally to the marital partners. Except in rare instances, such as where a husband attempted to murder a wife and was in prison, where a wife was dying of cancer, or where a wife had had sufficient foresight to take back promissory notes for the invaluable medical school education she had afforded her physician husband during the marriage, . . . *dependent wives whether they worked in the home or in the paid market place . . . were relegated to less than a 50 percent overall share of marital property; . . . de minimis* shares of business and professional practices which, in addition, the courts undervalued; . . . and inadequate or no counsel fee awards. These findings demonstrate that the marriage partners' contributions to each other and to the marriage itself are not being viewed as of equal value.[62]

Cohen and Hillman also reveal that the wife in the separate property state of New York has much more difficulty than her California counterpart in asserting a claim to a share of her husband's business. As they state:

A reading of all cases reveals threshhold problems: The burden of proof on the homemaker spouse is heavy; if she fails to adduce proof sufficient to untangle and adequately evaluate the husband's business or professional practice (generally possible only through the testimony of experts), she is precluded from any interest in the business.

And even if she succeeds in showing a husband's financial chicanery and an "unexplainable" economic shortfall, she is not awarded a share of the marital property commensurate with its true extent or value.[63]

The attorneys conclude that the equitable distribution law has proved to be a perversion of its intent. The law was adopted with promises that marriage would be viewed not only as a social partnership but also as an "economic partnership:" "The decisions, however, reflect that the principle of "economic partnership" is routinely being applied to deprive the wife of rights, rather than to benefit her."[64]

These conclusions are supported by attorney Lester Wallman, who chaired the Legislative Committee of the Family Law Section of the New York State Bar Association.[65] Although Wallman originally supported the "equitable" division law in New York, by 1982 he called for its revision and chastized the courts for failing to carry out the law's goal of treating wives as full economic equals:

It was the intention of this bill that women were to share on an equitable basis in the distribution of the marital assets. But recent court decisions have held that medical and legal practices and certain family businesses were to be excluded from distribution to wives. More discouraging is that the yardstick for distribution of assets is being disregarded by the courts, inasmuch as women are not getting equitable distribution but seem to be averaging only twenty-five to thirty-five percent of the total marital estate.[66]

These studies indicate that wives are likely to be awarded less than half of the tangible property in equitable distribution states. Although some legal scholars, and some practicing attorneys, continue to assert the contrary—and to claim that wives are better off under these discretionary rules because judges can award them *more than half* of the property in case of obvious need[67]—there is simply *no empirical evidence* to suggest that this is what typically happens.* Perhaps in cases in which the sole family asset is a home, the judge may be favorably disposed to award it to a young mother or older housewife. But the data reveal that this occurs in a minority of the cases: it is the exception, not the rule.

What, then, of our question about whether "equal" or "equitable" rules are preferable? Clearly, equitable distribution standards are not more favorable to wives. Wives are, in fact, likely to fare better under rules that guarantee them an equal share of the marital property. Thus, rather than abandon the equal division rule, the best route to reform seems to be to delay its application in cases in which the family home is the only significant asset.

As we noted above, judges already have the authority to delay the sale of any asset, and they routinely use this authority to delay the sale of a business. But since they do not see the same compelling need when it comes to delaying the sale of the home for minor children or an older housewife, a clear judicial directive may be necessary. (This is discussed further in the final chapter, Chapter 11.)

A final question about equality as a result of the equal division rule relates to the pool of assets considered for division by the courts.

---

* The disparity in claims about the empirical reality can be enormous. For example, when New York attorneys Henry Foster and Doris Freed argued for the equitable distribution law in New York, they claimed it would allow courts to award women more than half of the property as they did in Connecticut where, they asserted, it was not uncommon for 85 percent of the marital property to be awarded to the wife if she had been out of the labor market for years.[68] However, a blue ribbon Connecticut task force on marital dissolution, which surveyed divorced men and women in that state, found that most women were disadvantaged by the property awards in Connecticut courts. Instead of the mythical 85 percent they received *less than half* of the marital property at divorce.[69] The task force concluded that the division of property at divorce "did not reflect the assumption that marriage was an equal economic partnership."[70] Rather, the pattern of property allocation had "a more adverse impact on women, particularly homemakers whose primary contributions to the marriage have been non-monetary."[71]

Recall the data in Chapter 3 comparing the value of the family's tangible property at divorce with their yearly income: there we saw that income, and the ability to earn future income, are usually worth much more than the tangible assets acquired during marriage. If only the tangible assets are divided at divorce, while earning capacity and other forms of "new property" are excluded, it is rather like saying we are going to divide the family jewels by first giving the husband the diamonds, and then allocating the semiprecious stones in two equal parts.

This leads directly to the subject of the next chapter, which examines that "diamond" of marital property, career assets, and its relation to divorce settlements.

CHAPTER 5

The New Property
Pensions, Education, and Other Career Assets

"CAREER ASSETS" are tangible and intangible assets that are acquired as a part of either spouse's career or career potential.[1] The term *career assets* includes a large array of specific assets such as pension and retirement benefits, a license to practice a profession or trade, medical and hospital insurance, the goodwill of a business, and entitlements to company goods and services.

In this chapter we examine the legal status of several of these new forms of property and argue that *if they have been acquired in the course of a marriage they should be included in the pool of marital or community property to be divided upon divorce.* This conclusion is based on two assertions. The first is that career assets are joint property. As we will see below, most married couples have accumulated career assets during marriage in much the same manner that they have accumulated the other property that the courts currently recognize as marital (or community) property.

The second assertion is that it is impossible to have an equal or equitable division of marital property if these assets are excluded. This is because, as we saw in Chapter 3, the major wealth of most divorcing families lies in these assets. To exclude them from the pool of marital property is to skew the apportionment in favor of the primary working spouse, and to assure an inequitable and unfair division of marital property.

THE RATIONALE FOR RECOGNIZING
CAREER ASSETS AS MARITAL PROPERTY

The definition of community property in California, and of marital property in other states, has traditionally been limited to tangible assets. Most married couples, however, acquire "career assets" in much the same manner as they acquire tangible assets. To illustrate this point, consider first the family in which the husband is the sole wage earner. Such a family typically devotes a great deal of time, energy, and money to building the husband's career. The wife may abandon or postpone her own education to put him through school or help him get established; she may quit her job to move with him; or she may use her own job skills—skills that would command a salary if she were working for someone else—to help advance his career. Whether she types his papers, entertains his clients, writes the payroll checks for his employees, or keeps the children from disturbing him, she is performing services that contribute to his career. This couple has invested its joint resources in the "human capital" of the breadwinning spouse.

Sociologist Hannah Papaneck has suggested that most single-income families have what should be conceptualized as a "two-person career," the product of a cooperative effort by the partners.[2] The ambassador's wife, the military wife, and the corporate executive's wife are obvious examples of women who are "required" to be on call for their husbands' jobs, but the concept holds true for many other single-career families as well.

As a result of the couple's united efforts, the husband may obtain a valuable education or training, a license to practice a trade or profession, or perhaps membership in a trade union or professional association that assures steady work, income, and an array of benefits. His career assets may include his education; his job experience; his seniority at a particular company; a network of professional contacts; a track record or reputation that commands a good salary; life, health, hospitals, and disability insurance; the right to unemployment and social security benefits; entitlements to discounted or free goods and services; the goodwill value of a professional practice or business; the right to paid sick leave and vacation benefits; and the right to a pension or other retirement benefits. Many of these assets are like wages in that they are part of what a worker earns, even though they may not be paid directly to the worker or be used immediately.

While some of these assets, such as pensions and goodwill, are currently recognized as part of the community property in California, others, such as insurance and professional degrees, are not. Yet the distinction between the two sets of assets is arbitrary. If career assets have been built with joint resources during marriage, it seems arbitrary not to recognize them as joint assets, especially because they usually have much greater monetary value than the physical property most couples acquire.

The issue is often no less significant in two-income families. Even though both spouses may have worked during the marriage, they have probably chosen to give priority to one spouse's career in the expectation that both will share the benefits of that decision.[3]* A career that is developed in the course of a marriage is just like the income that is earned or the real property that is accumulated during marriage. It is a product of the couple's joint efforts and resources.

If a spouse enters a marriage with a preestablished career, there is justification for regarding that person's career assets as his or her separate property. But if a career is partially or wholly built in marriage, it seems reasonable to view that career (and the assets that are attached to it) as a product of the marital partnership. If only part of a career is developed during marriage, courts could acknowledge that there are both separate and community property interests, just as they do with real property, and apportion them appropriately at divorce.

Recent years have brought more social awareness of the joint efforts that go into building a career. Case law developments in both community property and separate property states suggest at least some hopeful prospects for their increased legal recognition as well.

In the pages that follow, we will look at recent developments with respect to four types of career assets: pension and other retirement benefits, the goodwill value of a business or profession, a professional education or license, and life and health insurance benefits.

While most jobs include some of these assets—such as medical insurance, goodwill, and pensions—the range of assets varies considerably with the occupation. For example, doctors and members of their families receive "professional courtesy" from other doctors and are

---

* Even dual-career professional couples seem to follow this pattern. For example, in one study of 107 dual-career couples with Ph.D.'s in psychology, the couple most typically moved to advance the husband's career despite their strong commitment to an egalitarian ideology.[4]

not charged for medical treatment; airline employees and their families are entitled to free and discounted travel; members of the U.S. armed services have access to the PX and commissary privileges; corporate officers may benefit from company planes, apartments, expense accounts, meals, and vacations; professors are entitled to reduced tuition for their children and to sabbatical benefits for themselves; writers receive royalties for books and articles they have written that continue, hopefully, for years to come; and the employees of some companies are given discounts on company products, and are entitled to use company goods, services, and facilities that range from cafeterias and day care to executive dining rooms and villas in Europe. Thus even though this chapter focuses on the most common career assets, the concept of new forms of property in employment-related assets extends far beyond the scope of this discussion.

Let us consider, first, the objections that have been raised to the recognition of career assets as marital property. Some courts have objected to the contingent nature of career assets. They note that if a worker is killed or dies he or she may never receive the benefits of his or her education or retirement plan. Such contingencies, they reason, make career assets "theoretical but not real." A second objection to career assets focuses on the difficulty of calculating their value. Since many career assets involve future benefits, calculating their value requires actuarial projections. In the pages that follow we will see how the courts have answered each of these objections and have developed procedures to value future benefits and contingent career assets.

We are now on the brink of a critical expansion in the definition of property in our society. The future is likely to bring increased awareness of the importance of career assets and more widespread recognition of the fact that they are marital property.

PENSION AND OTHER RETIREMENT BENEFITS

Pensions are like wages in that they are part of what workers earn during marriage. However, they are deferred compensation because they are paid in the future rather than the present.

Pensions are increasingly being recognized as part of the joint property acquired during marriage and as part of the assets to be divided upon divorce. Practically all of the community property states and a majority of the separate property states now allow courts to divide pensions at divorce.[5]

Pension and retirement benefits that are earned during marriage are potentially of great value and, in a longer marriage, they may be the most valuable asset a couple owns. (As we saw in Chapter 3, husbands are much more likely to "have" pensions than wives.) As the 1983 Minnesota Supreme Court stated, to exclude pensions from the marital property to be divided at divorce is to violate the partnership presumption in marriage:

> The pension was one of the major assets of the marriage, and only the house ranked with equal stature. To award one party this asset would ignore the [statutory] presumption that each spouse contributed to the acquisition of property while they lived together as husband and wife.[6]

Types of Pensions: Vested and Nonvested

Courts have traditionally distinguished between two types of pensions. A *vested* pension is one that is secure. If an employee's interest in a pension or retirement plan has vested, the employee is entitled to collect the pension even if he or she leaves the job (or is fired) before retirement age. A *nonvested* pension is not secure; it is a contingent right that is subject to forfeiture if the employee relationship terminates before retirement.[7]

The major trend in divorce law in recent years has been the recognition of nonvested—as well as vested—pensions as marital property. California was the first state to recognize nonvested pensions as property to be divided upon divorce, and its rationale is instructive.

The traditional California rule was similar to the traditional law in many states: nonvested pensions were not considered marital assets because they were "mere expectancies" and not "truly property." (California courts did, however, recognize vested pensions as marital property.) The traditional rule was changed by a 1976 California Supreme Court decision in the case of *In re Marriage of Brown*.[8] The court held that the right to future benefits, even though those rights are not guaranteed, is *a property right* nevertheless. If these assets had been acquired with community funds (and community efforts), they were now to be recognized as part of the community property.

A major justification for the *Brown* decision was the clear inequity that resulted from allowing the working spouse, who was typically the husband, to retain all of the pension and retirement benefits for himself. As the California Supreme court noted, the old rule compelled "*an inequitable division* of rights acquired through community effort."[9]

The court also explicitly acknowledged that the exclusion of nonvested pensions from marital property *skewed the division of property toward the working spouse* and did not accomplish "that equal division of property contemplated by the Civil Code."[10*]

Other states have followed California's lead and recognized nonvested pensions as valuable marital assets. Minnesota, North Dakota, and Pennsylvania were the first separate property states to do so.[11] As the 1983 Pennsylvania court said, a pension earned during marriage is divisible marital property: it makes no difference whether a pension plan is vested or not vested since "we find that *any pension plan* is a marital asset to the extent that it was acquired during marriage."[12]

Similarly, in 1983 the Oklahoma Supreme Court reversed prior rulings and held that a spouse's pension acquired during marriage should be considered jointly acquired marital property. The court said that whether the pension is "vested," in the sense that it is now due and owing, is not significant:

> It is a valuable right, purchased through joint efforts of the spouses to the extent that it was enhanced during the marriage; and as such, it should be regarded as having been jointly acquired during the marriage. The pension should be divided between the parties "as may appear just and reasonable," by a division of the property in kind, or by setting the same apart to one of the parties and requiring the other . . . to pay such sum as may be just and proper to effect a fair and just division thereof.[13]

Private Pensions

The Retirement Equity Act of 1984[14] facilitates the distribution of private pension benefits after divorce by requiring private pension plans, such as company and union plans, to comply with court orders in a divorce decree. Under the act, if a "qualified domestic relations order"[15] (e. g., a divorce decree) requires it, "all or part of a participant's benefits under a profit-sharing, or stock bonus, or pension plan" may be made to an alternative payee.[16] California courts, for example, issue orders for the private pension plan to mail monthly checks directly to the spouse (as well as to the employee) and can order the plan to pay benefits to the spouse on the death of the employee.

---

* It is evident that a parallel argument could be made for all career assets: the major inequality in property awards in California today is that the primary wage earner, who is more often the husband, is allowed to retain the future benefits of the career and earning capacity (that was built during marriage) for himself.

The importance attached to pension benefits—and the monetary value of these benefits—is illustrated by a now famous California case in which a wife successfully sued her divorce attorney for malpractice because he neglected her interest in her husband's pension.[17] In *Smith v. Lewis,* the California Supreme Court affirmed a malpractice judgment of $100,000 against an attorney who represented the wife in a 1967 divorce for failing to assert her claim to a share of her husband's federal and state military retirement benefits.[18]

Military Pensions

Military pensions have received a great deal of attention in recent years because of the publicity and outrage that followed a 1981 U.S. Supreme Court decision in the case of *McCarty v. McCarty.* [19]

McCarty was brought by a California doctor entitled to military retirement benefits. The California court treated his pension as part of the community property and awarded his wife an interest in the pension when they divorced.[20] Dr. McCarty appealed that decision, arguing that a federal pension was not community property. He cited a 1979 Supreme Court ruling that federal pensions for railroad employees could not be divided as community property upon divorce.[21] The Supreme Court agreed with Dr. McCarty. It found that the treatment of military pensions as community property "threatened grave harm" to two substantial federal interests: providing for retired military members, and meeting personnel needs (by frustrating efforts to attract enlistment).[22]

The outrage that followed the McCarty decision led to the formation of EXPOSE (Ex-Partners of Servicemen for Equality) to lobby for federal legislation that would guarantee divorced wives an equitable share in the assets accrued during a military marriage.[23] Doris Mozley, the wife of a military doctor, and the founder of EXPOSE, argued that military wives served their country along with their husbands and were entitled to share their military pensions:

> [We need legislation] to redress the unfairness of a system that says that a wife who served our country for years earned nothing in her own right. . . . The law should recognize the special sacrifices of the military spouse and the lack of security which former spouses of service members face as they approach retirement years. . . . What the military wife must have in order to serve best is the security of knowing that if her marriage ends, the country will reward her service by giving her what she has earned. . . . What military wives want is the same type of law to protect

us that Congress has already passed for the Foreign Service wife, and that is a presumption that the long-term military wife is entitled to a pro rata share of the pension. . . .[24]

EXPOSE members picketed military facilities to protest the "throw-away military wife system" with signs saying, "I served my country 20 years with my military husband."[25] Newspaper articles chronicled their heart-rending stories:

> Sue was married thirty years ago when women were raised to believe that marriage was forever. She followed her air force officer husband, raised three children, entertained other officers, and kept the home stable and steady despite the constant moving Earl's transfers required. (The family moved 20 times during the 30-year marriage.) . . . "We used to be called the perfect couple."
> Her domestic duties kept her so busy that she had little time for an outside job, although she did plenty of volunteer work. Even if she'd had more time to work, jobs were hard to find. "When you move to a town that's a big base town, the first thing an employer asks is, 'Are you military?' And if the answer's yes, they won't fool with you as a clerk or a secretary or anything, "cause they know you're not gonna be there long."
>
> Many military wives are like Sue: they don't know how much their husband earns, and they develop no career of their own as they regularly uproot themselves to follow a husband to a new assignment. They can't work in one place long enough to build up a pension of their own and—like Sue—they assume they don't need to, that their husband's pension will always be there to fall back on.
>
> What they want is a federal law that guarantees the woman a pro rata share of the pension for the rest of her life—not his life. . . . Many women, like Sue, feel they have already waited too long. "Damn it, I am *tired* of having to beg for what I feel is morally and ethically mine."[26]

These efforts led to the 1982 Uniformed Services Former Spouse's Protection Act.[27] Although the act did not provide the 50 percent guarantee (i.e., half of the pension after 20 years of marriage) that EXPOSE lobbied for, it did overturn the *McCarty* decision by explicitly permitting state courts to treat retirement pay as community property if the court has jurisdiction over the service member (i.e., if the member lives in the state for a reason other than military assignment). The court can award up to, but not more than, 50 percent of the disposable retirement pay. (The legislation also provides limited medical care and commissary privileges for some former spouses.)[28] Unfortunately, this leaves many military wives subject to state laws and does not assure them the pro-rated share of their husband's pension that is now provided for wives of foreign service officers (see below).

Other Federal Retirement Benefits: Foreign-Service, Civil-Service, and Social Security Pensions

Recent legislation has enabled the divorced wives of other federal workers to share their ex-husbands' retirement and survivor's benefits.

The pioneering legislation for federal employees, introduced by democratic Congresswoman Pat Schroeder, was the Foreign Service Act of 1980.[29] While the foreign service retirement system covers only a few thousand workers and their spouses, it provided the first formula for pension sharing at divorce and has been the model for proposed changes in other federal pension systems.[30] The 1980 act entitles the divorced wives of Foreign Service Officers to a share of their ex-husband's retirement benefits if they were married ten or more years. The wife's share is pro-rated according to the years of the marriage and is 50 percent after a 20-year marriage. It is also possible for a divorced wife to receive her share of the pension directly from the government.[31]

Wives of federal civil service workers have also been granted greater access to a share of their husbands' pension, but their "right" is contingent upon state courts. The Civil Service Reform Act authorizes state courts to award civil service retirement benefits as part of a property settlement in a divorce, annulment, or legal separation.[32] Thus the act permits, but does not require, states to treat these pensions as marital property and to divide them upon divorce.[33] Once a share of the pension is awarded, however, the court may order the government to pay the wife's share directly to her.

The Social Security system allows a divorced spouse to receive social security benefits from the earnings of a working spouse if their marriage lasted for more than ten years.[34] (A spouse is not entitled to any benefit if the marriage ends before the ten-year threshold.) Under the present system, a divorced woman is entitled to half of her ex-husband's benefit, which is based on his earnings record, unless she would get more on the basis of her individual earnings.*

---

* Working women who are married often get little or no return on the social security tax they pay, according to a 1984 study of social security benefits.[35] That is because they typically earn lower wages and are entitled to lower benefits than they can claim as the wife of their higher paid husbands. In many cases their benefits are about the same as if they have never worked outside the home.[36]

Most divorced wives would be eligible for higher benefits under
the proposed "shared-earnings" system of computing social security
benefits.[37] Under this system each spouse would be credited with half
of the couples' total earnings in each year of the marriage. This means
that the earnings of a husband and wife would be split equally for
the purpose of computing benefits. For example, if a married woman
left the paid labor force to care for their children, she would get credit
for one-half of her husband's earnings. If both spouses worked, their
combined earnings would be split 50/50. These credits would be added
to any wages the individuals earned before or after the marriage.[38]
(This earnings sharing system is still being studied.)

Who Controls Pension Options

A divorced person who has been awarded a share of his or her spouse's
pension may still face problems in collecting the benefit. One problem occurs if the worker elects to forego survivor's coverage. Under
most pension plans, a worker can opt for a reduced pension, to provide a survivor's benefit for his widow, or can opt for full monthly
checks during his lifetime.[39] Many workers elect to "opt out" or
waive survivor's coverage, and the choice has typically been theirs
alone.[40]

As of 1979, more than 64 percent of the federal civil service, 31
percent of the foreign service and 95 percent of the military had opted
out of survivor's benefits.[41] As a result, millions of older women, most
of whom were married, but some of whom were divorced, learn for
the first time upon their husbands' death, that they had been "elected
out" of any interest in future pension benefits."[42]

This problem is dealt with by the Retirement Equity Act of 1984.[43]
This law prevents workers from opting out of survivor's benefits without
the knowledge or agreement of their spouses. Now workers must obtain
the written consent of their spouses (or ex-spouses, in the event of a
court-ordered pension split at divorce) before they can waive survivor's
benefits.[44]

A recipient spouse may face other difficulties in collecting court-
awarded pension benefits. If the employee spouse dies before retirement age, his equity in the pension may be lost. As Sylvia Porter notes,
"there is a provision called the "widow's blackout" in most pensions
that denies a survivor's benefit to the spouse of a worker who dies
before "early retirement age," usually 55. What the husband intended
and expected for his widow simply doesn't count."[45]

The Retirement Equity Act of 1984 eliminates this problem by guaranteeing the pension rights of spouses of workers who die before retirement age.

Another barrier may arise if the worker chooses to delay retirement—and thereby delays both his and his former spouse's benefits. In many states there is nothing a dependent spouse can do: she must simply wait until the worker decides to retire before she can collect her share of the pension.[46] But in some states, like California, the nonemployed spouse may elect to begin receiving benefits at any time after the employed spouse becomes eligible to retire.[47] Similarly, on a national level as of 1985, a divorced spouse may collect social security benefits even if her former husband has not applied for them for himself (as long as the husband is eligible to collect social security and as long as the wife is entitled to benefits as a spouse of ten or more years.[48]

Ways of Dividing Pensions at Divorce

Throughout the United States courts are struggling with the practical problems of how to value and divide pensions. There are two main schools of thought. One approach is to "buy-out" or "cash-out" the interest of the nonemployee spouse by awarding her (or him) a lump sum settlement—or a marital asset of equivalent value, such as the home—at the time of the divorce. The second approach is to delay the division until the pension benefits are paid. At that time each spouse is awarded a percentage of the monetary benefit.

The preferred method depends on the age of the parties, the extent of their assets, and each spouse's alternative prospects for retirement income. Most of the California attorneys we interviewed favored the buy-out method for younger couples with other assets. The cash value of the pension (which is typically its future value discounted to today's value)[49] is included in the total community property to be divided at divorce. The pension is invariably awarded to the worker while the spouse is given an offsetting asset (such as the house, or stocks and bonds) of equal value.* A major aim of this approach is to achieve a "clean break" at the time of the divorce.

---

* The California courts have explicitly rejected the use of spousal support to offset a pension award. As the *Brown* court asserted, the "spouse should not be dependent on the discretion of the court . . . to provide her with the equivalent of what should be hers as a matter of right."[50]

The second approach, referred to here as the "future-share" method, was often favored for older and longer-married couples, especially if they have few assets or no other source of retirement income. It focuses on the *percentage* of the pension owned by the marital partnership. Each spouse is awarded a pro-rated share of the community's percentage when (and if) the pension is paid.[51] This method was adopted by Congress in the Foreign Service Act of 1980.

To calculate the percentage of the pension that is considered community property, the courts have typically used a simple "time rule." For example, let us say a man who has worked for twenty years is entitled to a pension of $1,000 a month. Assume he was married for fifteen of the twenty years. Three-fourths of his twenty-year pension, or $750 a month, would then be community property.[52] Half of the community's share, or $375 a month, would be awarded to his spouse. The worker would also be entitled to $375 for his half of the community property plus $250 for the nonmarital share of the pension which is his separate property.*

A number of courts have adopted the future-share approach in order to sidestep the valuation problem at the time of the divorce. They simply retain jurisdiction until the worker retires. The *Brown* court followed this approach, candidly stating, "This method of dividing the community interest in the pension renders it unnecessary for the court to compute the present value of the pension rights. . . ."[54]

GOODWILL VALUE OF BUSINESS OR PROFESSION

An ongoing business or profession typically has two types of assets: tangible assets such as the property, equipment, inventory and accounts receivable, and an intangible asset known as goodwill. The goodwill value of a business or profession is the "expected future income or opportunity for income that results from the owner's past efforts."[55] Despite the intangible nature of goodwill, California courts have long recognized that it is a valuable community asset to be included in the divisible community property upon divorce.

* A second method for arriving at the community property's share involves calculating the *percentage of the funds* contributed to the pension fund during marriage. This method favors a working spouse who is divorcing before retirement if he (or she) expects a salary increase after the divorce because it allows the worker to claim a larger percentage of the pension as separate property. It is not widely used, and at least one state court has held that if a worker continues to work a spouse is entitled to share any increase in pension benefits and salary that is provided after divorce.[53]

California appellate courts have found goodwill to be community property in a dental laboratory business,[56] a medical practice,[57] a law practice,[58] a private investigation service,[59] and a horse slaughter and horse auction business.[60]

The Los Angeles judges we interviewed reported that they had found goodwill in the professional practices of an accountant, architect, banker, consultant, dentist, doctor, engineer, insurance agent, lawyer, pharmacist, professor, sales representative, social worker, and in a wide range of small and large businesses including a barber shop, hardware store, restaurant, indoor sign business, and beauty salon chain. The value of the goodwill ranged from $100 to $720,000.

Recently, two separate property states, New Jersey and Oregon, also concluded that professional goodwill must be considered marital property in a dissolution action.[61]

Unfortunately, current definitions of goodwill have a strong social-class bias. While the good reputation of a professional or a business owner is recognized as an asset that can produce future income, no court has yet recognized that a career asset like goodwill exists for salaried employees. This is surprising because the courts have recognized a goodwill type of career asset in other kinds of cases—most notably in personal injury and workers' compensation litigation where the value of seniority, union membership, or a steady job has been taken into account to predict future income. Thus the principles for recognizing the goodwill that salaried employees acquire have already been established.

Ways of Valuing Goodwill

There are no rigid rules for determining the value of goodwill. A court may use "any legitimate method of evaluation that . . . takes into account some past result."[62] The preferred formula or rule of thumb for valuation varies with both the industry and the appraiser. The Los Angeles judges we interviewed said they had relied on one or more of the following standards: evidence of the goodwill's *market value* (established by the sale price of a comparable business or by a buy-out agreement among partners or shareholders)[63]; one year's gross income (multiplied by a factor that varies with the business); an excess earnings formula (when compared to the average person in the field) and, quite frankly, reliance on "whichever accountant or appraiser presents the most convincing testimony in court." In appellate cases several courts have explicitly refused to rely on a formula and have instead enumerated a number of factors to be considered in valuing goodwill.[64]

Perhaps most straightforward (and honest) were the judges we interviewed who admitted that they often set the goodwill value to equal the equity in the family home. As three judges said,

> . . . goodwill . . . allows you to give the wife the home. . . . You feel that you've been fair, and the parties do too.

> [Goodwill gives] the wife some compensation after a long marriage.

> [Goodwill lets] you give the wife the community property she deserves.

Despite the fact that some judges found goodwill useful to compensate for the inequities between husbands and wives, most of the judges we interviewed adopted a very conservative approach to valuing goodwill: they were reluctant to recognize it and even more reluctant to put a high value on it. Thus, in spite of the extensive testimony of accountants, appraisers, and other experts in valuing the good name and reputation of a business or profession, the judges rarely found large amounts of goodwill. In one case, for example, the judge cut the purchase price of a year-old fast-food franchise in half (even though the price was a well-established method of valuing goodwill.) The judge held that the husband had unanticipated start-up costs "so the franchise wasn't worth as much as he paid for it." In addition, several judges expressed annoyance and impatience at having to listen to testimony about goodwill. As one judge said:

> To tell you the truth, I think goodwill is a lot of b.s. There's nothing there. And it burns me up to have to sit there for hour after hour listening to b.s. from accountants. They invent the formulas on the spot. . . . They think they are putting one over because they bring in color charts and graphs . . . . Well I don't buy any of it.

A similar skepticism about goodwill was evident among the attorneys we interviewed, who were more blunt in stating that they simply "do not believe in good will." It was, they asserted, "too speculative," or it "put too much of a financial burden on the operating spouse," or it "couldn't be sold."

The attitudes of both attorneys and judges resulted in attorneys' less than vigorous efforts to seriously assert the goodwill claims of their clients. This is one subtle way in which the claims of the nonprofessional and nonproprietor spouse, who is likely to be the wife, do not get adequately represented, despite the law on the books.

PROFESSIONAL EDUCATION AND LICENSE

A third career asset is the marital partnership's interest in one spouse's professional degree and license. The issue arises when one person, usually the wife, supports the other's professional education and training with the expectation that she will share in the fruits of her investment through her husband's enhanced earning power. If they divorce soon after the student spouse completes training, the young couple typically has few tangible assets because most of their capital has been used to finance the student's education.

This is a significant problem: one in six husbands in the weighted interview sample, a sample that represents the population of divorced couples, had acquired some education during their married years.

Kentucky was the first state to provide recompense for a wife who supported her husband's education. In the 1979 case of *Inman v. Inman*,[65] the wife paid her husband's way through dental school. At the time of the divorce the couple had no traditional assets. Despite some reservations, the court ordered the husband to reimburse his wife for the cost of the education, allowing for interest and inflation, stating "that there are certain instances in which treating a professional license as marital property is the only way in which a court can achieve an equitable result."[66] The holding was limited, however, to situations in which there were few or no traditional assets, and the award was restricted to the cost of the education.

New Jersey expanded on this holding in 1980 in *Lynn v. Lynn*.[67] There, the husband and wife met while both were premed students. The wife went to work as a biologist to finance her husband's medical education, with the understanding that after his degree was completed she would return to finish hers. However, the couple separated after his first year of residency. At the time, the wife's earnings were approximately twice those of her husband. The court held that the medical school degree and license to practice medicine, obtained by the plaintiff during marriage, were both "property" and were to be considered assets subject to equitable distribution. To establish the value of the husband's medical education, the court accepted the assessment provided by a financial analyst who testified to the capitalized, discounted value of the differential in earning capacity between a man with a four-year college degree and a specialist in internal medicine. The court valued the education at $306,000 and awarded the wife 20 percent of this amount over a five-year period, in addition to alimony.*

In a 1985 review of case law developments, attorneys Doris Freed and Timothy Walker reported that the "medical student syndrome"— the classic case of the wife who puts her husband through medical school only to be handed a divorce summons when the diploma is handed to her husband—is no longer a disease related solely to medical education: the contagion has spread to other occupations and professions—such as law and dentistry—and to spouses receiving a Ph.D. or M.B.A.[68]** Thus a 1981 Massachusetts court granted a wife who had supported her husband through dental and postgraduate training a share of the value of his orthodontic license,[70] and a 1983 Michigan court awarded a working wife an interest in her husband's law degree.[71]

In the 1983 Michigan case, *Woodworth,* the State Court of Appeals extended its 1978 ruling in which it said merely that "gross inequity" would result if the wife "was left by the roadside before the fruits of that education could be harvested," and returned her $15,000 contribution to her husband's medical education.[72] By 1983 the Michigan court envisioned a greater return, noting that the law degree was a "family investment" and mere reimbursement was not enough to provide the nondegree holder with the "realization of her expectation of economic benefit from the career for which the education laid the foundation."[73] It went on to state that the critical issue was the compensation of the nondegree spouse in the most equitable manner:

> . . . whether or not an advanced degree can physically or metaphysically be defined as "property" is beside the point . . . . Courts must instead focus on the most equitable solution in dividing among the spouses what they have.[74]

Along the same lines, a 1982 court in the state of Washington ruled that a spouse's license to practice dentistry, obtained during the marriage, was community property subject to division upon divorce.[75] The court found the contributions of the wife substantial, and that it was not "fair" for the husband to leave the marriage with an extremely

---

* In 1982 the New Jersey Supreme Court overruled *Lynn* by creating a new remedy, reimbursement alimony, which is discussed on pages 128–129.

** Although Freed and Walker state that "it may now be the husband who puts a student-wife through graduate school,"[69] every one of the fifty-five cases (from 23 states) that they discuss involved a claim from a wife who financed her husband's education.

valuable asset without regard for the wife's interest. Justice demanded that she be "accorded some share of that future economic benefit," the court said, and it ordered the husband to pay her one-fourth of his net income each year for five years.[76] This principle was later affirmed in a 1984 Washington decision on a veterinarian's degree.[77]

As of 1985, six states* had case law precedents that recognized a property interest in a professional degree, while eight states had statutes requiring consideration of property interests.**

On the other hand, in six states the courts have heard similar cases and refused to recognize a professional degree or license as marital property.† For example, a 1981 Illinois court found that a husband's medical degree was not divisible marital property because his earning potential could not be determined and the court therefore refused to engage in speculation about his future income.[78]

Similarly, the Indiana Appellate Court held that future earning capacity lacks the attributes ordinarily associated with property and is purely speculative. It therefore held that a professional degree or license is not property subject to distribution.[79] A 1983 New Hampshire Supreme Court decision echoed this finding in a case involving a graduate degree acquired during marriage.[80]

Finally, Texas decided that an education is not property in a typical medical-degree case in which all of the marital income came from the wife's earnings while the husband was in school.[81] Due to the husband's work record, there was no substantial accumulation of a community estate. The wife argued that the husband's education was property and should be divided. The opinion held, however, that since education was not property, it did not have to be divided at divorce.

A midway position adopted by a number of states, such as Florida, is to reimburse the contributing spouse for the costs of a professional education if the divorce occurs soon after the degree is obtained. If, however, the parties stay married long after the attainment of the degree, it is assumed that the supporter has received some "return on her investment."[82] The theory behind this position is that the supporting spouse invests in the student spouse with the reasonable expectation that she or he will be rewarded for such efforts by sharing a higher standard of living. If, however, the student spouse walks away with the enhanced earning capacity for himself (or herself) alone, there is

---

* Colorado, Kentucky, Massachusetts, Michigan, Washington, and Wisconsin.

** Indiana, Iowa, Nebraska, New York, North Carolina, Pennsylvania, Utah, Wisconsin.

† Illinois, Indiana, Kansas, New Hampshire, Texas, and Wyoming.

unjust enrichment of the student spouse, an inequity that needs to be remedied.*[83]

California has adopted a similar position after a six-year struggle with the *Sullivan* case.[84] Mark Sullivan entered medical school a year after he married Janet in 1967. He completed his residency in 1977 and a year later the couple filed for divorce. During the 11 years the couple was married Janet worked to support the family. At the time of the divorce the Sullivans had a daughter and few tangible assets. Janet was awarded some used furniture, her car and half the couple's savings—$500 in cash.[85] Since she held a job as a systems analyst, she did not "need" alimony. (She was, however, awarded $250 a month in child support.) Janet claimed Mark's medical education was community property which she was entitled to share. Arguing that the degree had been attained through joint efforts and joint sacrifices, her attorney said it constituted the greatest asset of the marriage.[86]

At one point it appeared as if Janet's cause would prevail. The court noted the long-standing rule in California that "if community ability, activity, or capacity" is used to increase the separate property of one spouse, then the increase is considered "the property of the community." The court saw little distinction between the enhancement of separate assets in a business, which had always been recognized, and that of "an expensive education, degree and license to practice a profession." The court decided that, at a minimum, "the community should be reimbursed for the amount of any community funds that were expended to acquire the education, degree, and license if the community has not received any economic benefit from that training."[87]

After two Appellate hearings, a hearing and rehearing, the Fourth Division Court of Appeals finally decided that "medical education is not property and cannot be divided upon divorce."[88]

While the case was pending before the California Supreme Court,** California legislators began to fashion their own remedy for Sullivan type cases. They enacted a law providing for reimbursement, with interest, "for contributions to the education or training of a party that

* One issue which the courts have not yet addressed, is that of an education that does not result directly in enhanced earning capacity. In some relationships, a husband and wife may jointly agree that one of them should return to school for personal enrichment. In these cases, the couples' intent may be to share more intangible benefits such as one of the spouses becoming a happier, more fulfilled person.

** On December 31, 1984 the Supreme Court sent the case back to the trial court to be reheard in light of California's new reimbursement law which took effect January 1, 1985.

'substantially enhances' the earning capacity" of that party.[89] The reimbursement is limited by a rebuttable presumption: if the divorce occurs ten or more years after the contribution was made, it is assumed that the contributing spouse has benefited from the enhanced earnings (by way of acquired community property and increased standard of living) and no further reimbursement is necessary.

The California law suggests another midway position—that of using alimony awards to compensate for contributions to an education or degree. The new law states that courts must consider the extent to which the party seeking spousal support has contributed to the education, training, or attainment of a license by the other party.[90]

This approach has a long tradition in the state of Ohio. Back in 1961, in the *Daniels* case, an Ohio court decided that "the right to practice medicine . . . constitutes property . . . which the trial court had a right to consider in making the award of alimony."[91] The court awarded the wife $24,000 in periodic payments. In this particular case, the wife's father had paid most of the couple's living expenses during marriage, and the award may have been seen as compensation for the father-in-law's support. However, in 1980, the Ohio Appellate Court upheld the principle explicit in *Daniels*, i.e., that a spouse's contribution to a medical practice should be considered in determining alimony.[92]

Another state that relies on alimony rather than property as the vehicle for redressing imbalances in earning capacity is Oklahoma. In a 1983 case, *Adair v. Adair,* a woman supported her husband while he studied for his degree in dentistry.[93] The court used her $32,000 contribution to his expenses as the basis for its award. It then added $10,000 for inflation, plus interest at 10 percent, for a total award of $55,573 which the court called alimony.

The New Jersey courts also have decided that equitable remedies and alimony awards were the preferred vehicle for achieving justice. In a 1982 case, *Mahoney,*[94] the New Jersey Supreme Court coined the concept of *reimbursement alimony* for a wife who financed her husband's M.B.A. degree stating:

> a primary purpose of alimony . . . is "to permit the wife, who contributed during marriage to the accumulation of the marital assets, to share therein."
>
> Where a spouse has received from his or her partner financial contributions used in obtaining a professional degree or license with the expectation of deriving material benefits for both marriage partners, *that spouse may be called upon to reimburse the supporting spouse for the amount of contributions received.*
>
> In the present case, the defendant's financial support helped her hus-

band to obtain his M.B.A. degree, which assistance was undertaken with the expectation of deriving material benefits for both spouses. . . . We are remanding the case so the trial court can determine whether *reimbursement alimony* should be awarded in this case and if so, what amount is appropriate.[95]

How does this all add up? In a Winter 1985 review of statutes and case law development regarding spousal contributions to professional degrees, attorneys Doris Freed and Timothy Walker provide the following information on how the states line up. With regard to the statutory law, two states (North Carolina and Utah) require consideration of a spouse's contributions to a professional degree in property awards; three states (California, Florida, and Georgia) require that they be considered in support awards; and another six states (Indiana, Iowa, Nebraska, New York, Pennsylvania, and Wisconsin) require consideration in both property and support awards. (See Table C-6, Appendix C, pp. 426–427).

These statutes are, of course, in addition to the case law decisions we have just reviewed. If we tally the statutory provisions and the case law rulings together, we find that a total of 22 states allow for some form of compensation for the spouse who has contributed to the professional education, degree, or license of her or his student spouse, whether the remedy is through an award of property, or by means of alimony or reimbursement or "equity."* (See Table C-6, Appendix C, pp. 426–427.) Only seven states have totally rejected such claims: six to share property and one, Delaware, to alimony.

ATTORNEYS' AND JUDGES' ATTITUDES

One of the hypothetical cases presented to the attorneys and judges we interviewed dealt with this situation: Sheila Rose, a twenty-nine-year-old registered nurse, supported her husband Barry for ten years until he became a doctor. Their divorce occurred after Barry's first year of practice, when they had neither a home nor any significant tangible assets. Barry's current net income of $24,000 a year is expected to rise steadily. (The Rose case is detailed in Appendix B, p. 415.)

Most of the experts predicted that the doctor-husband would be

---

* Although Freed and Walker unequivocally state that the majority view is that a degree is not property, their own data show that the situation is less clear-cut: 14 states support some form of property claim, while 16 states reject property claims.[96]

awarded the family car, his medical equipment, and the debts for his equipment. The nurse-wife would receive her personal belongings and some furniture—not much to show for ten years of investment in her husband's education.

While most of the California lawyers and judges (70 percent) predicted that Sheila Rose would be awarded some support, their estimates averaged only $338 a month for an average of three years (the support would then be terminated). This award (a total of $12,168 over the three-year period) pales in comparison to what a wife would be entitled to as a co-owner of the husband's professional degree, no matter what method might be used to calculate its value. Even just the eight years of the husband's tuition expenses, with simple interest added, would be valued at several times as much as the $12,168.

Sheila Rose's fate would be quite different if the courts accepted Professor Joan Krauskopf's rationale for treating Barry's education as community property.[97] Krauskopf argues that a community-property marriage is based on equal-partnership principles comparable to those in a business partnership. To achieve maximum utility of resources in a business, it is sometimes necessary to make sacrifices for the good of the whole. In the case of the wife's supporting her husband's education, the wife is making an investment in his "human capital"— his skills and knowledge acquired through schooling. She expects her investment to improve the status of the partnership as a whole, and expects to share in those improvements as any business partner would.

Consider, for example, the costs that the Rose marriage has paid for Barry's education (and his enhanced human capital). If we follow Krauskopf's analysis, we first note that the Roses have lived without the wages Barry would have earned if he had been employed instead of studying. Thus, one "opportunity" cost of Barry's education has been the lower standard of living Barry and Sheila have had for ten of the eleven years of their marriage.[98]

In a 1982 Wisconsin case, for example, the court heard testimony from an economist who calculated a doctor's forgone earnings (i.e., what he would have made if he had not gone to medical school) at the rate of the average earnings of white males with a college education over the eight-year period of his medical education.[99] (This case, *In re Marriage of Lundberg*, will be discussed in more detail shortly.)

A second set of costs involves the drain on community-property funds and labor to finance Barry's education: the money that Sheila earned was spent on Barry's tuition, books, meals, and other living expenses.

A third set of costs are the "opportunity" costs of the additional education or training that Sheila had forgone while she was supporting Barry. Sheila might have taken specialized courses to improve her own earning capacity—or decided to get a medical degree herself. Since Sheila (and Barry) assumed that her investments in Barry's human capital were investments in partnership assets that they would share, the couple together bore the costs of forgoing alternative investments in Sheila's human capital.

Ways of Valuing an Education

Courts have typically used two approaches to calculate the value of a professional education: one focuses on the costs incurred, the second on the gains received (in future earning capacity). A third approach seeks to achieve equity or parity between the parties through either an alimony award, or by providing the nonprofessional spouse with an equivalent opportunity for educational advancement.

COST INCURRED: THE REIMBURSEMENT APPROACH

The approach that focuses on the cost of an education is evident in many of the cases discussed above. This method calculates the financial cost of the education at the time it was acquired. Simple estimates focus on the direct, out-of-pocket costs of the education—such as tuition, lab fees, bank loans, and living expenses—plus whatever interest that money would have earned if it had instead been invested. More complex calculations include indirect costs such as forgone opportunities.

BENEFITS GAINED: ENHANCED EARNING CAPACITY

A second approach involves ascertaining the capacity of the professional education to produce a future stream of income; once such a value is established, the total sum can be divided, or a percentage awarded to each spouse over time. Professor Krauskopf suggests first calculating the present value of the post-education earning capacity, and then subtracting the present value of the pre-education earning capacity and the present value of the costs of the education.[100] The difference is the return on the investment, which the nonstudent spouse would share.

A report of this type of calculation is found in a 1982 case reviewed by the Supreme Court of Wisconsin, *In Re Marriage of Lundberg.*[101] At the trial, the wife, Judy, called upon an economist to establish the value of her investment in the medical degree obtained by her husband, David. The economist established two methods of valuing her investment. The first method compared the average earnings of family practitioners with the average earnings of white males with five or more years of college education. The difference between these two figures was $24,976 per year. Over an assumed twenty-five-year working period, the difference amounted to $624,400. This amount was then reduced to present value, using both a 10 percent and a 12 percent discount rate.

David's forgone earnings—that is, what he could have made if he had worked instead of going to medical school—were deducted from each figure, along with the additional taxes he would owe as a result of his increased income. From these rather complex calculations, the economist found the net present value of David's additional income that he will earn as a result of his degree to be between $110,837 and $132,402, depending on which discount rate was used. The trial court found that these present-value figures were established by credible economic evidence.

The second method used by the economist to value Judy's investment in her husband's education was based on the amounts she spent to support him. Here, the economist accepted Judy's account that she spend $25,000, and he added the interest she would have realized on that money.

This suggests the great variations in monetary value that can result from different methods of evaluation. In this case, the economist calculated the value of the enhanced earning capacity as at least $110,831, while the costs incurred for the degree were only $25,000 (plus interest). Surprisingly, Judy finally asked the court to award her only $25,000, which she thought represented the value of her support. Her husband said her contribution was worth $20,207.39 and was willing to pay her that amount. The trial court granted Judy's request and awarded her $25,000, stating: ". . . the amount of this award is fair. In fact, much more could be justified. Any less would be inequitable to Judy Lundberg." This award was later upheld by the Wisconsin Supreme Court.[102] The court's language indicates that it recognized the husband's medical degree as the major asset of the marriage: "Both parties sacrificed so that David could become a doctor. In a sense, his medical degree is the most significant asset of the marriage. It is only fair that

Judy be compensated for her costs and foregone opportunities resulting from her support of David while he was in school."[103]

EQUITY AND PARITY: ALIMONY OR AN EQUIVALENT OPPORTUNITY

A third approach to effecting a fair resolution of the problem is through an alimony award. This might be set with an eye toward awarding the lesser-educated spouse the funds necessary for an equivalent educational opportunity. Although this remedy may be largely limited to younger and highly motivated career-oriented spouses, it could provide equity through a reimbursement-in-kind approach. A New York court fashioned this type of remedy in the 1975 case of *Morgan v. Morgan*, in which a wife who put her husband through college and law school asked the court to award her support so that she could attend medical school.[104]

The Morgans met in college, during her sophomore year and his junior year. Recognizing that they could not both simultaneously continue their education and be self-supporting, they agreed it would be preferable for him to finish his undergraduate and law school education while she worked. She worked full-time until the day before her son was born and then continued to work part-time to support the family and pay for her husband's college and law school education. Her husband was a Wall Street attorney at the time of the divorce, earning $27,500 a year in 1975 with prospects for significant increments in the future.

After the parties separated, Mrs. Morgan returned to college, enrolled in a premedical program, and excelled. (The judge noted that she had received an A in organic chemistry and had a 3.83 grade-point average, out of a maximum of 4.0.) She wanted to go on to medical school and asked the court to award her enough support to complete her medical training. The case presented a difficult issue because Mrs. Morgan was a skilled executive secretary capable of earning $10,000 a year and thus had "the ability to be self-supporting." As the judge evaluated her earning capacity:

> Mrs. Morgan has become very proficient at shorthand and typing and also worked as a data analyst. I am satisfied that she is very skilled and, as an executive secretary or technician, could probably command an annual salary of at least $10,000 in a normal economy and, very possibly, even in the present [difficult] employment market.[105]

He nevertheless concluded that "self-supporting" does not imply that the wife shall be compelled to take any position that will be available when her obvious potential in life would be greatly inhibited. Further, the judge recognized that "any possible short-term economic benefit which would result from the wife's returning to a position similar to the one she held over two years ago, is far outweighed by the potential benefit, economic, emotional and otherwise, of her pursuing her education." The issue, he concluded, was whether she should be compelled to work as a secretary to earn $10,000 a year in order to finance her medical school education or whether, on the basis of her potential, she should have an opportunity to achieve a professional education comparable to the one her husband received as a result of her assistance by working during their marriage.[106]

The judge's answer was that under these circumstances, the wife is entitled to equal treatment and a "break," and should not be "automatically relegated to a life of being a well-paid, skilled technician laboring with a life-long frustration as to what her future might have been as a doctor, but for her marriage and motherhood." He therefore awarded her enough support to complete medical school, concluding:

> I am impressed by the fact that the plaintiff does not assume the posture that she wants to be an alimony drone or seek permanent alimony. Rather she had indicated that she only wants support for herself until she finishes medical school in 5½ years (1½ years more in college and 4 years in medical school) and will try to work when possible.[107]

Although Mrs. Morgan requested alimony instead of asserting a property claim, the case is relevant here because the remedy (e.g., being helped to acquire an asset of equivalent value to her husband's law degree) is one that is appropriate to both types of claims. In addition, and perhaps of equal practical importance, many states do not distinguish between property and alimony awards but rather approach the package as a whole and decide what would be equitable.

The *Morgan* case fits into this general framework of providing equity in divorce. The difficulty of successfully asserting a claim to an equivalent educational opportunity is suggested by the fact that *Morgan* was reversed on appeal. The higher New York court focused on Mrs. Morgan's ability to be self-supporting and concluded that "although the wife's ambition is most commendable, the court below was in error for including in the alimony award monies for the achievement of that goal."[108] Nevertheless, the lower court's opinion sparked considerable interest and undoubtedly will inspire other similar suits.

MEDICAL, LIFE, AND OTHER INSURANCE BENEFITS

A fourth type of career asset involves the benefits that workers receive in the form of health, accident, and life insurance. During a marriage in which only one spouse is employed outside the home, the members of the employee's family are covered as his or her dependents and share in the benefits for doctors' fees, medicine, hospital care, and other health and accident protection. Upon divorce, the nonemployee (typically the wife) and minor children generally lose this coverage because of the traditional assumption that the rights to insurance belong only to the worker.

Increased awareness of the value of these entitlements, and an influential article by Yale Law School Professor Charles Reich, arguing that the "new property" in our society is the property of entitlements—i.e., the right to government and private benefits such as medical insurance[109]—led to claims that this new property should be divided upon divorce. There are really two issues here, and they parallel those for pensions and educational degrees: whether insurance rights are "assets" or "property," and whether they should be—and can be—divided upon divorce. The slow but steady trend is to answer both questions affirmatively.

The assertion that insurance rights are a form of property is most convincingly put forth by those who experience the results of losing these rights at divorce. For example, consider the story told by one fifty-two-year-old woman in our interview sample:

> Since I had always been covered by Bill's policy at Lockheed I never thought about insurance, and no one mentioned it when we drew up the settlement. We agreed to have Bill keep the kids on his policy, but since he was going to remarry I couldn't be covered as his wife. About two years before the divorce, I [had] found a lump in my breast and they removed it and said it was benign.
>
> After the divorce, when I applied for individual Blue Cross they wrote in a cancer exclusion because of my history. There was nothing I could do—it was take it or leave it . . . . Then, when I discovered the other lump about eight months later, I went into a total panic. I had to have a radical [mastectomy] and chemotherapy, and there was no way I could

possibly afford it. I just wanted to die . . . I did think of suicide—but I couldn't leave the kids.

A similar experience led Tish Sommers, president and founder of the Older Women's League (OWL), to successful advocacy of insurance conversion laws.[110] These laws permit a divorced woman who was once covered by a group or family policy to be able to convert to an individual policy without new proof of eligibility. When Sommers was divorced at the age of fifty-seven, she lost her health insurance under her husband's policy and was subsequently refused coverage "by one carrier after another" because she had a history of cancer. Then, six months before she became eligible for Medicare, she suffered a recurrence of cancer and faced expensive radiation treatments with no medical or hospital insurance whatsoever.

"In today's medical economy, health coverage is a must," argues Frances Leonard, legal counsel for the Older Women's League. "It is no longer possible for an individual to pay his or her own medical expenses."[111] Yet access to medical care is almost entirely through employment-related health plans. Since women are often covered as dependents of employees, they are especially vulnerable at divorce when they may lose their dependency status and their insurance coverage. Women between the ages of forty-five and sixty-five are most severely affected because they are often unable to secure individual coverage if they lose their group coverage. They are too young for Medicare, and they are too old to be "good risks" for private coverage.*

As of January 1985, twenty-two states had statutes providing for the conversion of insurance upon divorce (see Table C-7, Legal Appendix, Appendix C). In some states, the statutes provide that accident and health insurance policies which terminate upon divorce *must* contain a conversion privilege for divorced spouses without proof of insurability. This means that the insurer must offer a conversion policy to a dependent spouse without regard to whether he or she would normally qualify, and must bypass the physical examination and doctor's report normally required to obtain coverage.

Even these laws may not go far enough in providing divorced wives with adequate medical and hospital insurance. Many of the conversion policies afford far less coverage than the original policy and require

---

* About four million American women between the ages of forty-five and sixty-five, which one Older Women's League member called that "no-woman's land between menopause and Medicare," are not covered by health insurance.[112]

the beneficiary to pay costly premiums to maintain them. For example, one of the women we interviewed found, to her dismay, that her conversion policy cost over $3,000 a year:

> They said there would be no problem about my medical insurance because I would get a conversion policy to cover me and my son. No one mentioned cost. I assumed the company paid just as they pay for his. I was shocked to find out that I would have to pay $265 a month for the same insurance the company provides free for all employees. That's over $3,000 a year, and I've been told that figure will increase annually as my age increases.

Dental insurance is another valuable asset that is often lost at divorce, as one fifty-three-year-old woman we interviewed discovered:

> It was always my dental health that could wait. . . . There is a yearly ceiling on each family's bill under the company dental insurance plan, so Andy and the kids went first. . . . I never intended to do without it, but it was always to be next year . . . and then next year. . . . Last year, my turn finally came—after the divorce—and it cost me $6,000. His teeth, of course, were paid for, as a community expense.

The inferior coverage and inflated cost of conversion policies and individual insurance have led the Older Women's League to press for legislation requiring the insurer to maintain the divorced wife as a member of the group plan and/or to provide her with an equivalent policy in terms of both benefits and price.[113] Along these lines the wives of retired military officers have argued that they deserve the same military health insurance and hospital benefits that their husbands receive when they retire after twenty years of service. As one military wife put it:

> I earned those military health benefits through very hard work. . . . I served my country for twenty years with my husband . . . . These are not privileges we're asking for. These are *rights*—we've earned them."[114]

Long-term military wives particularly object to the unfairness of a system that would take a long-term wife off the military health care rolls in order to make room for a new wife who never shared the duties and responsibilities of wives of men in active service.

One tragic example of this problem is fifty-eight-year-old Elizabeth Meyers, who was divorced against her wishes (in Virginia), and lost the privileges she had enjoyed while her Navy captain husband rose through the ranks and they raised five sons.[115] After a thirty-five-year marriage, her husband, who knew he was terminally ill, divorced her and remarried so that his benefits—the medical care and widow's annuity—went to his second wife, even though their marriage lasted only thirty-nine days. (At that time, in 1984, a widow's annuity for the surviving spouse of someone on active duty with thirty-five years of service was $1,700 a month. The value of medical benefits, varied with need but averaged $1,000 a year.) Meyers and other military wives argued that military personnel move so often that they do not acquire other forms of property. These medical benefits and pensions are often their only assets.[116]

The principle behind the military wives' claim is the same one that OWL invokes when it asserts that long-married wives have earned the right to remain a member of their husband's group plan for medical insurance. A bill to accomplish that objective, jointly sponsored by OWL and the representatives of the insurance industry, was introduced in California in 1985.[117]

The same principle was used by fifty-five-year-old Edith Curtis who applied for state unemployment compensation after her thirty-year marriage to a college professor ended in divorce.[118] Although Curtis had never been employed, and had not contributed to the unemployment insurance fund, she claimed that all of the fringe benefits and assets of her husband's career were community property in Idaho, and that she was entitled to share them.[119] The story of the couple's "shared career" is typical of families who married in the 1950s:

> While her husband attended school, she kept house, raised babies and taught art to children at home to make a few dollars. When her husband rose to a faculty post, Edith Curtis graduated to faculty wife. "You were expected to serve on graduation committees, bake cookies, and help graduate students," she recalls. "The dean's wife said my husband's promotions depended on these little things." His career flourished, but their marriage didn't. After three decades and four children, Miss Curtis says, "I was replaced by a 25-year-younger model." . . .
>
> She job hunted for two years, yet her 75 applications proved fruitless to "a shopworn and obsolete" housewife, as she called herself. Her 30-year-old B.A. degree in English and a lack of salable skills didn't help. In a desperate charge at the bureaucracy, Edith Curtis filed for state unemployment compensation. . . .
>
> Wearing a lawyerly black suit, she argued her own case before the Idaho Supreme Court in October of 1984. She lost. Idaho's justices branded her case "frivolous" and ordered her to pay the court costs.[120]

Although Edith Curtis lost her suit, the case for an expanded definition of career assets as marital property, including unemployment benefits, is certainly not closed.*

Finally, in some states, life and disability insurance policies, whether privately owned or company financed, are treated as marital assets to be divided at divorce. Even if a policy has no cash surrender value, the court may order the wage earner to maintain payments on the policy and to keep his children or former wife listed as the beneficiary. (This provides some protection against the loss of support payments if the wage earner dies or is killed in an accident.)[122]

PRECEDENTS FOR THE VALUATION OF CAREER ASSETS AND ENHANCED EARNING CAPACITY

The examples discussed above suggest that courts are beginning to recognize a variety of career assets as marital property and, when they do, are finding ways to estimate the assets' value. The one career asset that the courts have been most reluctant to value is enhanced earning capacity, especially when it is linked to a salaried employee rather than to the holder of a professional degree.

Precedents for calculating future earning capacity have, however, been established in other areas of law. Although court decisions in these other areas have not yet been utilized by courts dealing with divorce, these decisions have established important precedents. The lessons learned from such cases have vital implications for the career-asset issues confronting divorce courts today.

Precedents for calculating future earning capacity, have been established in litigation involving workers' compensation,[123] personal injury,[124] and wrongful death.[125] Courts have consistently held that earning capacity—what an employee could have earned had he or she not been killed or injured—should guide juries and administrative bodies in determining the size of awards in these cases.

In personal injury cases the courts have been able to deal with the problem raised most frequently by opponents to the inclusion of career assets in divorce settlements—the difficulty of predicting future income for a person who has low current earnings because he or she has not yet completed an education or training. For example, in *Rodri-*

---

* Some claims to unconventional assets have fared better. For example, some courts have been willing to consider claims for a share of personal injury awards as marital property if they were compensation for lost earnings or medical expenses borne by the marital community.[121]

guez v. *McDonnell Douglas Corporation,* a twenty-two-year-old sprinkler fitter was severely injured at a construction site when a large
piece of metal pipe fell and hit him on the head.[126] A three-month
jury trial resulted in a substantial award to the injured worker based
on his projected future earning capacity.

The appellate court upheld the award, noting that even though
the injured worker was an apprentice at the time of the accident "without an economic track record of any consequence,"[127] he was a member
of the union, and the union contract guaranteed annual wage increases
for sprinkler fitters from 1970 onward. The court also approved of testimony by an expert witness who included expected fringe benefits in
calculating the plaintiff's lifetime earning capacity at $1,440,114.

The court stated that the California rule for determining damages
in this sort of case was "not what the plaintiff would have earned,
but what he could have earned." As a result, the court estimated his
lifetime earning capacity at over a million dollars.

Similarly, the earning capacity of a UCLA student who was working toward a teaching credential was calculated at the rate of a full-
time teacher, not the rate of the part-time recreational job she held
when she was injured. The court held:

> The fact that the injured employee is a student working part-time because
> of the necessity to complete her educational goal in order to obtain a
> full-time position in the future is a special circumstance which should
> be considered in predicting earning potential. . . . The petitioner's earning
> "potential" during the term of her temporary disability included the salary
> paid to a teacher as of September 1967.[128]

These decisions show that the courts already acknowledge the
value of the career assets that salaried employees accrue. The *Rodriguez* court explicitly acknowledged the value of the sprinkler fitter's
career assets—his apprenticeship, union membership, and fringe benefits—and relied on them in determining his future earning capacity.

Since California courts have long recognized the ability of juries
and administrative bodies to consider career assets such as an education, union membership, and entitlement to fringe benefits in determining the size of awards in personal injury cases, it appears logical for
them to consider the value of such assets in determining the value of
a divorcing couple's community property.

Family court judges could draw on the body of expertise developed
in these areas to calculate the value of such career assets as a professional education, possession of a secure job (especially in a high-

unemployment economy); work experience and seniority rights; a professional license; union membership, or certification in a trade; job-related benefits such as health, accident, and life insurance; fringe benefits such as access to discounted goods and services, paid vacations, and other industry-specific privileges; goodwill in a company job, business or profession; and disability, Social Security, and other pension and retirement benefits.

CONCLUSION

What does this discussion of the new property reveal? How does it affect our conclusions about the extent to which property is being divided equally or equitably upon divorce?

We have seen that the career assets analyzed in this chapter are typically acquired during marriage in the same manner that other marital property is acquired. These assets are, along with the family home, often the most valuable assets a couple owns at the time of the divorce. If courts do not recognize some or all of these assets as marital property, they are excluding a major portion of a couple's property from the pool of property to be divided upon divorce. In addition, if the courts treat these assets as the property of only the major wage earner, they are in most cases allowing the husband to keep the family's most valuable assets.

Obviously, any conclusions made about the *de facto* equality or inequality of current divisions of property will rest on whether career assets are defined as "marital property."

If we accept the current limited definition of property used by the California courts, we are led to two (erroneous) conclusions: first, that the property of most divorcing couples in California today is relatively modest, and second, that their property is being divided equally.

On the other hand, if we adopt an expanded definition of property that includes the intangible assets of a marriage, such as the career assets discussed in this chapter, we are led to two very different conclusions: first, that most divorcing couples have accumulated property of considerable value, and second, that the husband typically leaves the marriage with most of their assets.

As the second set of conclusions gains acceptance, we see a growing dissatisfaction with the current laws and a rise in claims from women for their share of the new property. Increasingly, divorce courts are being asked to recognize and divide pensions, professional degrees, goodwill, medical insurance, and a range of other career assets. This is one of the most innovative and rapidly changing areas of family law, and the changes are visible in both legislative and case law developments throughout the United States.

Legal decisions about the new property that will be made in the next decade will have profound long-term consequences, and be critical in defining and redefining the nature of the marital partnership in our time.

CHAPTER 6

Redefining Alimony
How Awards Have Changed

ALIMONY EXEMPLIFIES, more than any other aspect of the law, the transformation in the position of women under the new divorce laws. The traditional law encouraged women to devote themselves to their husbands, homes, and children by promising them that their husbands would support and take care of them. Even if they divorced, their support was assured, at least in theory, because they would receive alimony.

Under the new divorce laws, however, women have no such assurance. In fact, the present legal system makes it clear that instead of expecting to be supported, a woman is now expected to become self-sufficient (and, in many cases, to support her children as well). These new standards for alimony not only create new expectations for women at divorce, they also redefine the expectations for women in marriage. For a legal system that expects a woman to be self-sufficient after divorce can no longer logically expect her to be solely a housewife and mother during marriage.

THE ALIMONY MYTH[1]

Until recently, folk wisdom in the United States led one to assume that nearly every divorced woman was awarded alimony.[2] Newspapers sensationalized stories of seemingly exorbitant awards, while books and magazines warned men of the financial burdens they would endure following divorce.[3] Women assumed that their husbands would continue to support them following a divorce, and men anticipated being saddled with heavy monthly payments.

This alimony myth—the belief that both sexes shared in the reality of alimony awards—undoubtedly shaped their perceptions of the feasibility and desirability of divorce. As a woman in a Doonesbury comic strip put it, "If Morris didn't have the threat of alimony hanging over him, he'd probably walk right out of here."[4] An assumption of the inevitability of alimony might deter a man from dissolving his marriage or enable a woman to feel secure in the knowledge that she would be taken care of even if she were forced to divorce. Thus, whether it was viewed as restrictive from the male point of view or facilitative from the female point of view, alimony was central to the structure of social control through which the law shaped individual behavior.

In the past, lawyers helped to perpetuate the alimony myth in the popular press by publicizing high alimony awards they had won for their clients. This contributed to the widespread belief that ex-wives were often freed from worldly cares while their former husbands struggled to support them in the style to which they had become accustomed. Judges similarly gave credence to the prevalence of long-term alimony. As Judge Samuel Hofstadter complained:

> Alimony was never intended to assure a perpetual state of secured indolence. It should not be allowed to convert a host of physically and mentally competent young women into an army of alimony drones who neither toil nor spin and become a drain on society and a menace to themselves.[5]

In fact, like the general public, the lawyers and judges who specialized in family law seemed genuinely to believe that most divorced women were awarded alimony. For example, in 1975 the Los Angeles matrimonial attorneys estimated, on the average, that two-thirds of all currently divorcing women got alimony. Similarly, the judges hearing family law cases in the greater Los Angeles area estimated that alimony was awarded to more than half of the divorced women.

In reality, however, alimony has always been awarded to a relatively small percentage of divorced women. In 1968, for example, under the traditional divorce law, our research shows that less than 20 percent of the divorced wives in California were awarded alimony.[6] Nor does California appear to be unique: only 14 percent of the divorced wives in a census survey said they were awarded alimony.[7]

The amounts of alimony actually awarded similarly contradicted the stereotype. The average award was quite modest: a 1968 median of $98 a month, or about $300 a month in 1984 dollars. Such meager awards could hardly have been adequate to free ex-wives from wordly cares or assure them "a perpetual state of secured indolence," since they were barely as much as welfare or Social Security payments.

The discrepancy between the myth and the reality of alimony awards raises a number of questions. But first let us consider the rationale for alimony and the pattern of awards. Perhaps then we can explain the persistence of the myth.

THE TRADITIONAL RATIONALES FOR ALIMONY

Alimony, from the Latin for nourishment or sustenance, was the traditional allotment for a wife's support fashioned by the English ecclesiastical courts before 1857, when divorce was still prohibited.[8] The courts allowed the parties to live separately, but the husband remained responsible for his wife's economic welfare. Since the husband automatically gained control of his wife's property and income with marriage,[9] he retained this control if they separated, and with it came his continuing financial responsibility for her. Because employment opportunities for the separated wife were virtually nonexistent, alimony often provided her only means of financial survival. This then was the first basis for alimony—*it enforced the husband's continuing obligation to provide for his wife's needs.* (It also prevented dependent women and children from becoming a public charge.)

In theory, even after divorce was permitted, the husband's responsibility for his wife's support was a lifelong obligation: alimony was awarded "until death or remarriage," that is, until he or she died or until she remarried (and became another man's responsibility). Although many divorced women did remarry, those who did not were assured—again in theory—of lifelong support. And while the lower courts were often sympathetic to a long-divorced man and might reduce his alimony payments, and while a larger number of divorced men did not bother to ask the courts' permission but simply stopped paying or reduced their payments themselves, the appellate courts vigorously upheld the letter of the law.[10] The divorced man was responsible for his ex-wife's support, even if he had to support her for twenty years after they divorced. That was the law.

A second rationale for alimony in the United States is based on the moral orientation of the English system, which linked both the granting of a divorce and the awarding of alimony to findings of fault.[11] In virtually all states, only an innocent spouse could obtain a divorce, and only an innocent wife could receive alimony[12] (a wife found guilty of adultery was typically barred from receiving alimony). Thus the second legal purpose of alimony was to *reward virtue and punish wrongdoing*. These first two rationales for alimony were rooted in the state's interest in supporting family commitments by providing justice for those who fulfilled their marital obligations.[13]

Professor Judith Areen identifies a third rationale for alimony: the *status principle*, rooted in "the windfall view of marriage—if you marry a millionaire, you are entitled to live like one even after the marriage ends."[14] Although this principle is often implicit in statutes that direct judges to consider the standard of living during marriage, few judicial decisions have openly based alimony on status.[15] However, in *Casper* v. *Casper*, the Supreme Court of Kentucky interpreted a need standard as related to the family's lifestyle during marriage, noting that "what might be ample for a scullery maid is not necessarily sufficient for one accustomed to the life of a duchess."[16]

There is disagreement as to whether traditional alimony had a fourth purpose, that of *compensating the wife for her labor* during marriage. Professor Herma Hill Kay argues that the English common law regarded the wife as a nonproductive dependent and ignored her important contribution toward building the family assets.[17] However, Professor Homer Clark suggests that the contribution of the full-time homemaker and mother was implicitly recognized by statutes that instructed judges to consider the length of the marriage in awarding alimony,[18] as they allowed judges to compensate the woman for her years of service to the family.[19]

A fifth and final rationale for alimony was to reinforce sharing, pooling, and partnership in marriage. Alimony was a means for adjusting equities and for providing the wife with a share of the fruits of the marriage. This was especially critical in separate property title states (where the wife had no legal right to a share of the property to which the husband held title in his own name).[20] Her only right to share the marital assets was a right to share his future income through alimony.

Attorney Riane Eisler describes the way California's alimony law operated in practice, using the legal fictions of guilt and innocence:

> Under pre-1970 California law, alimony could be awarded across the board to the "innocent spouse," "for his or her life, or for such shorter period as the court may deem just," so that a wife who was found guilty of marital misconduct could be cut off with no support at all while a man

who was found guilty could be "punished" with an order to continue to support his wife.

Everyone knew that innocence and guilt were legal fictions. Still, these were the instructions of the statute. . . . [B]y social convention, the vast majority of divorces were filed by women. Usually the wife was the plaintiff and the husband was the defendant. The wife's complaint had to accuse the husband of some wrongful behavior. Even if in 90 percent of the cases the ground for the divorce was the catch-all "cruelty,". . . In entering its decree the court had to find the husband guilty, or there was no statutory authorization to award the wife anything or even to grant a divorce. Although this procedure was a convention, and very often a farce, it still tended to affect the size of the [alimony] award husbands were ordered to pay.[21]

Gradually, as Eisler notes, it became increasingly difficult for judges and attorneys to continue to deal with these legal fictions: "If a man was not really guilty of anything, and if he and his wife were simply getting a divorce because they were not compatible, why then should he be punished [by having to pay alimony]?"[22]

This type of thinking guided the no-fault reforms. The new California law eliminated the words "innocent spouse" from the alimony statute. It also eliminated the phrase for "his or her life." These two simple changes had a radical effect.

RATIONALES FOR ALIMONY UNDER NO-FAULT DIVORCE

As of 1985, forty-nine states retained statutory provisions for alimony, variously referred to as maintenance, allowance, support, recovery payment, separate maintenance, rehabilitative alimony, and spousal support.[23] For convenience, we will continue to refer to all postdivorce support as alimony, but as the variety of names suggests, the concept of alimony and the justifications for granting it have undergone considerable change. Much of the impetus for change comes from the shift to no-fault divorce and the changing position of women in society. While this chapter focuses on the impact of no-fault, it is important to note that societal changes and the generalized pressure for sex-neutral laws, as illustrated by the 1979 U.S. Supreme Court's rejection of sex-based alimony rules in *Orr v. Orr,*[24] have had a parallel influence on the trends discussed below.

As we just saw, the changes in the language of California's alimony statutes were actually quite simple. The no-fault divorce law eliminated the traditional rule that courts were to award alimony to the "innocent spouse" for "his or her life" and set forth two new bases for alimony awards: the wife's employability and the duration of marriage. The new statute directed judges to consider "the circumstances of the respective parties, including the duration of the marriage, and *the ability of the supported spouse to engage in gainful employment* without interfering with the interests of the children of the parties in the custody of each spouse."[25]

The new language, in and of itself, was not startling, because courts were already considering the duration of marriage and the wife's ability to support herself—along with a long list of other factors such as "the wife's needs and accustomed standard of living, her health, and her contribution to the marriage."[26] However, because these other factors were not specifically mentioned in the new law, attorneys for husbands began to argue that they should be given less weight—now decisions should be based primarily on the wife's ability to become gainfully employed. The result, in the perceptive words of Los Angeles attorney Riane Eisler, was that *"the burden of proof shifted to the wife to show that she could not find a job."*[27]

In establishing the new alimony statute, the proponents of no-fault divorce transformed the traditional rationales for alimony.[28] First, they rejected the presumption of the wife's dependency. Pointing to the changing position of women in general, and to their increased participation in the labor force in particular, the reformers revised the alimony law to "recognize" the growing ability of women to be self-supporting.[29] Instead of a presumption of dependency, alimony would now be reserved for women who truly "needed" it.

Second, the no-fault reformers rejected the notion of using alimony as a punishment. They argued that justice would be better served if alimony were based on the financial circumstances of the parties, rather than on their guilt or innocence.*

Third, and most vehemently, the status rationale was rejected. A wife would no longer have an automatic "right to support" just because she had been married to a well-to-do man. The new concept of fairness was an award based on her future potential rather than her prior status.

The reformers did not, however categorically rule out the last two justifications for alimony. While they did not explicitly endorse either

---

* As we noted in Chapter 2, in the eyes of the reformers the critical question here was whether a "guilty" wife should be permitted to receive alimony. When they finally decided that she should, against the opposition and warnings of those who feared that would encourage immorality and adultery, they saw the reform as freeing her from the outdated morality of the past. They did not forsee (or simply did not discuss) the flip side of the reform—the effect of the elimination of fault on "innocent" wives and their husbands.

the concept of compensation or the concept of sharing, both of these may be inferred from the marital duration standard. In fact, the specific inclusion of the duration of marriage as a criterion for alimony awards suggests that some different assumptions—such as notions of compensation and sharing—might be deemed appropriate in longer marriages.* (In addition, the legislative history indicates that the framers of the law intended that alimony would continue to protect older housewives.) Parenting, which was another basis for compensation, was also recognized as a justification for alimony awards under the new law.

In summary, the new alimony awards were to be pragmatic economic decisions. While traditional alimony sought to deliver *moral* justice based on *past* behavior of the parties, the new alimony was to deliver *economic* justice based on the financial *needs* of the parties.

Since it was the wife who typically had to prove need, the task of justifying an award henceforth would fall on her. She would have to show that she was unable to support herself (and her children). At the same time, the practical economic approach of the new law explicitly recognized three groups of women who (temporarily or permanently) had compelling financial needs:

1. those with custodial responsibility for children;
2. those who require transitional support to become self-supporting;
3. and those who are incapable of becoming, or are too old to become, self-supporting.

The first purpose of the new alimony is to provide *custodial support* for the parent of a child or children (as distinguished from direct support for the child). Professor Homer Clark notes that alimony has served this function for many years, even though the function was seldom explicitly referred to by the courts.[30] It is, however, explicit in the Uniform Marriage and Divorce Act which followed the example set by the California law.[31]

Second, under the new norms, alimony is justified for women needing *transitional support* in order to adjust to their new life situation and become self-supporting. The term "transitional support" incorporates what other states have called, variously, "rehabilitative alimony,"

---

* The deliberations about property also suggest that the law's formulators saw alimony as a flexible vehicle that could be employed in adjusting equities. Recall the hypothetical rat-fink who was assured his half of the community property (see page 71). Presumably, the equities or inequities in that case were to be adjusted through alimony.

"retraining support," "transitional support," and "support for displaced homemakers." Underlying these labels is an assumption that homemaking is like any other job or career. When one loses a job or one's marriage, one needs a period of adjustment and retraining.

Some judges carry this analogy still further and assume that since unemployed people spend the transitional period trying to locate a new job, the divorced woman simply needs time to locate a new husband. As one Los Angeles judge stated, "I would think she is entitled to some severance pay . . . that's probably not the right terminology but something to give her an opportunity to have a year or two where she's not hurting and maybe she'll find some other doctor to marry her and/or get a chance to try to get herself reoriented to her new status." The focus is increasingly on helping the divorcée to acquire new skills or update old ones so that she can become self-sufficient.

The third justification for the new alimony—to provide support for a woman divorced after a long marriage if she is incapable of self-support and too old to be retrained—recognizes that a housewife's *earning capacity is impaired* by periods of "unemployment" while she devotes herself to homemaking and child care. In this case alimony is somewhat like a disability pension in that it provides support for one who has incurred *earning disabilities* as a result of a marriage of long duration.

As noted above, it is not clear to what extent the new alimony was to be used to adjust inequities between the spouses. While judges were prohibited from using it to compensate for fault, or to circumvent the equal division rule, the judicial instruction—to "consider the circumstances of the respective parties"—was sufficiently broad to permit considerable latitude. As we will see, however, judges choose not to use that latitude and instead interpret the law to mean that equity requires nothing more than the most minimal economic need.

ATTITUDES TOWARD ALIMONY

In general, the law's ideals are seen as fair, not only by judges and lawyers, but by divorcing men and women as well. In response to the question "Can you tell me if you agree or disagree with the following statements about alimony?" the divorced men and women we interviewed expressed considerable support for the standards of the new law. As Table 12 indicates, they endorsed four justifications for alimony: to support the long-married housewife with impaired earning capacity, to support the transitional woman through education and retraining, to support mothers of young children, and to allow the wife to share the wealth that she helped her husband acquire.

The most widely accepted justification for alimony is to provide *support for the older housewife* with an "earning disability": "if she is disabled and can't support herself" (approved of by 94 percent of the women and 87 percent of the men) and "if she's been married a long time and is too old to get a good job" (supported by 87 percent of the women and 66 percent of the men).

Most of the interviewees also endorsed the new-law standards of *providing transitional support* ("to go back to school or to be retrained so that she can get a good job to support herself," approved by 73 percent of the women and 52 percent of the men) and of providing support for *mothers of young children* ("if she has young children and wants to stay home to care for them," supported by 67 percent of the women and 63 percent of the men).

These first three standards are embodied in the California law. The fourth rationale for alimony, approved by a majority of both men and women, is *sharing of partnership assets* ("if she has helped her husband get ahead because they are really partners in his work," endorsed by 68 percent of the women and 54 percent of the men). Although this rationale is not explicit in the new statutes, it reflects a long-standing function of alimony and may be subsumed, but only in part, under the required consideration of marital duration. (If, however, the present law—or the way it is interpreted—ignores this factor in alimony awards, it may not be perceived as fair or just.)

While women are generally more likely to see alimony as justified than are men, the two sexes are fairly consistent in their rank ordering of the standards for awarding alimony. The largest disparity between them is in their responses to the statement, "A woman does not deserve alimony if she can go to work and support herself." Eighty-five percent of the men agreed, compared to 65 percent of the women.*

Overall support for the no-fault ethic is also reflected in the fact that most divorced men and women *reject* the fault-based standards of traditional divorce law. Less than half of the respondents thought it appropriate to punish a woman for adultery ("if she had an affair and was unfaithful to her husband") or a man for leaving his wife ("if her husband left her for another woman"). In both cases, however,

---

* The remaining 35 percent of the women indicated that other factors, such as the level of self-support possible, the disparity between the wife's and husband's incomes, the presence of children, and the history of the marriage, should all be taken into account.

TABLE 12

Attitudes Toward Alimony

	PERCENTAGE WHO AGREE (WEIGHTED SAMPLE)	
	Women (n = 111)*	Men (n = 112)
	(Percentage)	
A. A woman deserves alimony if she has helped her husband get ahead because they are really *partners* in his work	68	54
B. A woman does not deserve alimony if she had an *affair* and was unfaithful to her husband .	23	40
C. A woman deserves alimony for at least a year or two so she can *adjust* to the divorce	31	21
D. A woman deserves alimony if she wants to go back to school or to be *retrained* so that she can get a good job to support herself	73	52
E. A woman deserves alimony if she's been married a long time and is *too old* to get a good job..	87	66
F. A woman deserves alimony if she has young *children* and wants to stay home to care for them	67	63
G. A woman does not deserve alimony if she can go to work and support herself	65	85
H. A woman deserves alimony if her husband left her for another woman	29	39
I. A woman deserves alimony if she is *disabled and can't support herself*	94	87
J. A woman deserves alimony because when she got married her *husband promised* to support her for the rest of her life	9	3
K. A woman deserves alimony because her husband should *pay her back* for her years of work as a homemaker and/or mother	25	19
L. A woman deserves alimony because she can never recapture the years she has given to her marriage and the *opportunities* she *missed* to have a career of her own	20	4

* n refers to the number of cases (i.e., interviews) on which the percentages are based.

This table is based on weighted data from interviews with divorced men and women, Los Angeles County, California, 1978.

men were more likely to approve of fault-based standards than were women. Similarly, less than 10 percent of the men and women subscribed to the traditional law's notion that the husband is obligated to support his former wife because he undertook this commitment upon marriage ("when she got married her husband promised to support her for the rest of her life").

The one anomaly in these responses is the somewhat contradictory attitudes expressed in response to questions about partnership, compensation, and lost opportunities. While the majority of both sexes supported the partnership concept of marriage by indicating that alimony should be provided for a woman "who has helped her husband get ahead because they are partners in his work," they were not inclined to "pay her back for her years of work as a homemaker and/or mother" or for "the years she has given to her marriage and the opportunities she missed to have a career of her own." The interviewees seemed to feel that a wife should share in the *positive contribution* she made to her husband's career[32]—which, the statement suggests, is viewed as a partnership asset—but they do not think she should be compensated for her own *losses* (or opportunity costs).

PERSONAL REACTIONS: "ALIMONY IN MY CASE . . ."

The attitudes discussed above relate to alimony awards in general. Let us consider next how divorced men and women feel about alimony (or the lack of alimony) in their own cases. Did men expect to pay alimony? Were they willing to pay it? Did women expect to receive alimony? Did they think they needed or deserved it?

Need (and Sharing)

As might be expected, the single most important criterion for deciding if alimony was appropriate—among both men and women—was need. Thus, men who expressed willingness to pay alimony most often said their wives needed it:

> [Q: Did you expect to pay alimony?] Yes. [Q: Can you tell me why?] She hadn't really worked much. She had no profession. I owed it to her.

Similarly, wives who felt they deserved alimony most often focused on need:

> [Q: Did you expect to get alimony?] Yes. [Q: Can you tell me why?] I have been married seventeen years and hadn't worked all that time. I

had briefly taught school many years before. I had no means of support
and no way to go back to teaching. I had no idea of how much I would
need. I didn't know of any available jobs and I had no credentials. Most
important of all, I have two children who I felt truly needed my presence
in the home.

Likewise, men and women who said they did *not* expect to pay or
receive alimony often focused on need. As one woman said:

I'm perfectly capable of supporting myself. If you're capable of working,
you shouldn't sponge off your ex-husband.

Men, too, said they didn't feel they should support women whose financial assets or earning capacity was equal to theirs:

She was quite capable of taking care of herself. She made a good salary
and she wanted to prove her independence. Part of being her own person.
And I left her in a position with dollars in the bank and minimal monthly
obligations.

There is a direct parallel between the law's definition of need
and the categories of women who saw themselves (and were seen
by their husbands) as "in need" of alimony.* Three of the four most
commonly mentioned bases of need were those of older women who
would not be able to get jobs, women with custodial responsibilities,
and women who had to further their education and training. The fourth
definition of need that emerges from the interviews is closer to the
concepts of sharing and compensation, as we will see below.

OLDER WOMEN/LONGER MARRIAGE

One group of women who were seen as unquestionably deserving
of support, by both men and women respondents, were housewives
who had been married for many years. As two women explained:

Because I was a housewife and mother for fifteen years and not used to
working . . . when he first left, he wanted me to have $1,000 a month
because he knew I needed it. I had no other income.

I deserved it because I wasted the best years of my life raising children
and being married, and I needed the money so that I could get back in
the working world again, so that my children would be cared for. . . .

I needed it . . . . I was being thrown out of my own home after 26 years
. . . . I never had a job.

* Obviously our respondents had also been "educated" about the legal rules in
the process of obtaining their own divorces.

Men leaving marriages of long duration also felt an obligation to continue to support their wives:

> She had it coming. She gave up the best years of her life to being a housewife.

For many older women, the concept of "need" is inextricably linked to notions of "compensation" and "sharing." Although it is possible to distinguish these rationales in theory, in practice they are often intertwined. Consider, for example, the response of one fifty-four-year-old woman:

> I was married for thirty years and I did whatever it took to keep my husband and family going. . . . When we married I gave up my lucrative secretarial business to move with him. . . . Six years and two children later, he was laid off and I went back to work and provided our only income while he finished his MBA. I was the personal secretary for the president of the company, but he got a job offer in Chicago, so we moved again. . . . I then raised three children, entertained for his very social company, where he was now "on the rise," and invested our savings in real estate. I turned our $10,000 into $100,000. . . .
>
> We moved back to California when he was made Vice-President, and my social obligations increased: dinner parties, benefit committees, the junior league . . . . I had lots of energy and everyone said I was his greatest asset. I put everything into his career—wives were really important to the company then—and I loved it! I loved setting an elegant table and cutting the fresh flowers and choosing the wine and orchestrating a lovely meal. . . .
>
> Twice I was offered jobs, but he wouldn't hear of it—he wouldn't let *his* wife work. *He said I was his partner in his career. . . .*
>
> Why do I think I should get alimony? . . . For all of that . . . for all the years I devoted myself to him and his career . . . for my contribution to what he is and what he earns today . . . because I have not held a job for twenty-two years . . . and because I have no money of my own and even if I get half the property all I will have is a house, while he'll go on earning over $100,000 a year. . . . He took the best years of my life and left me with nothing. . . .

As this quote suggests, for many women, the basis for feeling that they deserved alimony represents the natural intertwining of motives that are evident in any partnership. It is clear, however, that compensation is at least one critical element in their views. As another woman said:

> I was one of those totally devoted, perfect wives. My whole life was
> my family and my home. . . . I was the mom who was always available
> for the car pool, who made chocolate chip cookies for the kids after school,
> who cooked a hot, nourishing meal every night. I sewed their costumes
> for Halloween and their prom dresses. . . . And I was always there for
> Keith—the perfect hostess, the perfect dinner parties, the thoughtful thank-
> you note. . . . I took care of everything.

Others saw it as compensation for being abandoned:

> I needed it and, in my case—the long marriage and all—I don't think I
> should have to get a job when I'm not responsible for the breakup of
> the marriage. . . . My husband said he was sorry about what happened
> and sorry about leaving me but that I would never want for money. . . .
> He wanted me to be well cared for. . . . And he had the money. He
> had no complaint about alimony.

MOTHERS WITH CUSTODIAL RESPONSIBILITIES

A second justification offered for alimony, again by both men and
women, was to provide support for a full-time or part-time mother:

> I knew he would want to give me what I needed for the sake of the
> children. . . . he was willing to pay because we had children in common
> and he had to take care of them since I had custody.
> [Q: How much was he willing to pay?] $175 per month because I wasn't
> self-supporting and would need support until I was.
>
> He realized that his children were involved and that's the only reason
> he was willing to pay.

Although some men made a sharp distinction between alimony and
child support, others treated the distinction as meaningless and saw
alimony as part of their obligation as fathers:

> It was my way of making sure the kids were O.K. and had what they
> needed. . . . Also, there was a tax advantage in calling more of it alimony
> because alimony is tax deductible.
> [Q: Are you saying that you thought of it all as child support?] No, it
> was partially for the kids and partially for her so she could take care of
> them—so she could work half time and have the afternoons to ferry them
> around. They're involved in a million activities.

As this last respondent noted, there were tax advantages to calling
"child support" alimony, but they have been altered by the 1984 federal
tax reforms.

EDUCATION AND TRAINING

Men and women alike considered alimony an appropriate means of providing money for the wife's education or retraining. As one woman said:

> I knew I could support myself—and he agreed to help me financially until I got my master's. . . . He's generous and he gives me money whenever I want it. He offered to support me until I could get my degree.

Similarly, a husband talked about his willingness to support his wife through training.

> She said she hadn't worked at a regular job since 1963 (15 years) when she'd been a legal secretary—and therefore she'd lost her skills. I was willing to pay alimony for a period of time until she was able to regain her skills as a legal secretary—at least for as long as it took for her to go back to school and get back into the job market. . . . I was willing to let a *judge* decide how long a reasonable time *was*.

The women quoted below echo the sentiments of many other women who felt that the support they were awarded was not a "gift," but rather something they had earned. In several cases it was not the woman herself but her parents who had contributed to the man's education. For example, one woman said,

> Especially because my parents had paid for my ex-husband to go to law school, and paid for a lot of our family support at that time, he saw the fairness of it. My parents helped him . . . and I hadn't been earning money because I was home with our children. . . . It was my share of the partnership from the marriage.

Many of these women had supported their husbands in the past or had given up career opportunities for marriage:

> I supported him through medical school, and I was entitled to equal time. [Q: How much did you think you should get per month?] $2,000 child support plus alimony, and I'd work for free in his office for two years. . . . He was willing to pay but angry. He said once something's over, you don't keep feeding a dead horse.

> It cost a hell of a lot more for him going to U.S.C. [University of Southern California] than for me to go to nursing school. . . . Anyway, he felt he

owed it to me. . . . We'd planned it that way since we were first married—
or before. It was our contract.

I felt I was entitled to it—because I had worked to put my husband through
school, kept house, and took care of the children, while he had an opportunity to develop his career.

Several men similarly viewed alimony as compensation for the support
they had received in the past. As one husband said:

She put me through school. Women have it tough. I can always afford a
house and make a living. She could never earn enough to buy a house.
My thought—let's face it—she's thirty-four years old and not too attractive.

I knew she had sacrificed her career for me and the kids. . . . She dropped
out of law school when we moved so I could teach at UCLA. . . . Now
she's lost ten years, has two kids, and is going to be the oldest student
in her class. If she's willing to juggle all that, I have to help her out.

Contribution and Sharing

All of the women who sought alimony for education or training had
concrete career plans: they wanted support for a specific period of
time so they could attain a degree or occupational goal. Another segment of women have no such career objectives. They are either unsure
about what they want to do next or they already have jobs or careers.
Yet they too feel they deserve alimony, and they base their assertions
on concepts of contribution and sharing. As one woman said:

I deserve it because I spent the last seven years of my life doing everything
I could to help him get tenure . . . and deferring all of my own needs
and goals. . . . I edited his papers, worked as his unpaid research assistant
and his all-around go-fer. . . . I spent two vacations reading galleys instead
of the trips to Europe he promised—and there are three hundred examples
like that. Every day, every week, every year we put off something for
us in order to do something for his career. . . . Well, now that he has
tenure I think I should share the results of my work. I earned it.

The case of this woman is enlightening because, like many others
in our survey, she had never earned money or provided financial support for her husband during her marriage. She had worked as a social
worker before marriage but encountered difficulty finding a job after
they moved, and "he discouraged my job search because there was
always some project he wanted me to do first." Her claim, and the

claim of many others, is that she invested in him because they were partners in his career, and she "earned" the right to share the fruits of that career. Although she noted that her own career had been put "on hold," her claim to a share of his salary was because she *contributed* to it.

As might be predicted, this woman was denied alimony because she did not "need it." She, and many other women in similar situations, thought the denial unfair and unjust. This is one area in which the law—or at least the way law is being applied—clearly diverges from the commonsense perception that justice requires "sharing" and compensation for the contribution one spouse makes to the other's career. (These attitudes are reflected in the attitudinal data reported at the beginning of this chapter as well.)

A second type of sharing claim that is widely perceived as just, without reference to a spouse's career contributions, surfaces in the case of a long marriage. This claim, however, *is* covered by the alimony criteria of the new law.

Fault

One criterion for alimony that was repeatedly mentioned by the divorced men and women we interviewed is intentionally *not* embodied in the new law: fault—that is, feelings of guilt and responsibility or a desire for retribution. Many of our respondents linked money to questions of who left whom, who wanted the divorce, who was abandoned, who suffered, and so on. For example, several men who initiated the divorce felt guilty and were therefore more willing to pay alimony. As one man said:

> I felt guilty.
> [Q: Why?] I don't know—I just did. I was the one to bring up the divorce. Also, while we were married she had less career advancement than if she had stayed single.

Similarly, some of the wives of men who had left felt that "since he was responsible, he should have to pay for it:"

> At the time, in my heart I believed him to be more at fault than myself and therefore that he should be punished. . . . I had mistaken impressions of what the law would award me as alimony. . . . I was under the impression that most women got alimony and thought I deserved it.

The strongest sentiments, however, were expressed about women who initiated the divorce. In many of these cases, the husband refused

to pay alimony because he felt the woman had abdicated her claim
to it. Consider these statements from men:

> Why should I reward her with alimony? She was the one that broke up
> the marriage. No-fault is bullshit. She got as much use of my earnings
> during our married life as I did, so why should I pay her now? An ex-
> wife is not a relationship.

> I believe a marriage relationship is much like an employer and em-
> ployee relationship—each has set duties. I am an employee; if I fuck up
> my job, I don't do my work, I get fired, and the boss isn't going to continue
> my salary. Same if I quit. So if a wife fucks up or if she quits her job,
> she doesn't get paid. That's just what happened to my wife.

Wives who encountered this type of attitude typically did not press
their claim to alimony:

> He didn't feel he should have to support me, because he didn't want a
> divorce. I just took a cash settlement—I didn't want it—but I couldn't
> hassle him for it.

> I guess I felt guilty about leaving him. . . . God knows I needed it . . .
> but I considered poverty the price I had to pay for my freedom.

In the same vein, many other women seemed to assume that they
had to "pay for their freedom." Even if they did not "initiate" the
divorce, and even if it meant a lower standard of living, they did not,
as they put it, want to be dependent on their former husbands.

> It was part of being my own person; I didn't *want* to need his money. I
> wanted to make it on my own.

> I was so fed up I loathed the idea of having him support me. I wanted
> to be as independent as possible.

> The less we had to do with each other the better. Some women go out
> for *blood!* I'll settle for a Pepsi.

MEN WHO REFUSE TO PAY

In addition to fault and independence, a factor in actual alimony
awards that is not explicit in the law is the absolute opposition of
some men to the very idea of alimony. Many women reported that
they had not asked for alimony because they knew their husbands
would not pay it, "no matter what." As three women reported:

He doesn't believe women should collect alimony; they have two hands and feet and can get off their ass . . . . He felt that a woman can make money like a man, just go out and get a job. That's it, that's how he felt, so there was no point in asking for it.

He doesn't believe in the alimony laws. I could support myself, that was his feeling—either by working or public assistance. . . . He didn't care. It wasn't his problem.

He is so afraid of being taken advantage of . . . he is adamant about marriage not being a meal ticket for a woman.

Other women said they had wanted or expected alimony until they encountered their husband's refusal:

He just refused.
[Q: Why?] Why should he? That was his reaction—why should he pay me? Out with the old, in with the new.

He honestly felt he owed me absolutely nothing. He felt no obligation towards me unless I was his wife. . . . If I wasn't sleeping with him, he didn't owe me anything.

Several women whose husbands were strongly opposed to alimony nevertheless asked for and were awarded it—but they were never able to collect it:*

He wasn't willing to give me anything. The judge felt I needed it and ordered him to pay, but he never did.

I really needed the money because I wasn't working, and our income and debt structure was such that I needed it . . . but he does not make the payments. . . . He just refuses.

Some men refused to give their wives any money whatsoever even before the divorce decree was final. This tactic, known among lawyers as the "starve-them-out" technique, puts the woman who has no income of her own at a great disadvantage and exerts additional pressure on her to agree to her husband's terms for a settlement.

He wouldn't give me any money at all, and I literally had no money to buy food or pay the utility bill. . . . I was terrified. . . . I'd never been

---

* The difficulty of collecting alimony was a recurrent theme: In fact, within six months of the divorce decree, one out of six men owed an average of $1,000 in unpaid spousal support. Collection problems are discussed further in Chapter 9 on child support, pp. 285–295 and 298–309.

in that situation before. . . . I never worried about money before in my life. . . . I got so upset I couldn't think straight. . . . [Q: What did you do?] I borrowed from everyone—it was mortifying, but I had no choice— and then my parents helped me. They gave me the money for the retainer so I could pay the lawyer. He wouldn't take my case without it.

THE ROLE OF ATTORNEYS

One may wonder what women's attorneys do in cases where, during negotiations about divorce, it becomes clear that the husband will refuse to pay alimony. Some women said that their attorneys had tried to get them more property when it became obvious that the husband's resistance made compliance with an alimony order unlikely:

> My attorney said the man is a flake, take whatever you can—house, negotiable equity—but do not depend on him as far as money goes. . . . So I ended up giving up my claim to his medical practice for two years' support and the home.

> The lawyer said that if alimony was going to be an issue, give it up for property because in the long run it was cheaper.

Other attorneys pressed their female clients to assert their right to alimony. As one woman reported:

> My attorney was great. He said "You can't let him push you around like that. You gave him thirty years of your life and you deserve it." . . . at that point I didn't know what I was doing I was so upset and hurt. . . . I was willing to agree to anything. But my lawyer insisted . . . and we got it in the agreement . . .

In rare cases the attorney might try to talk to the husband. For example, one male respondent had originally planned to "share" an attorney with his wife, but then decided he did not like the attorney's advice:

> The attorney said alimony was not required under the law if the wife works, as long as she is physically able to support herself. . . . But he told me that if I paid alimony we wouldn't have to sell the house so she could survive. I told him to go to hell. . . . That's when I went to get my own attorney.

The most common attorneys' response was to counsel female clients to "forget it" and get on with building their new lives.

> [My lawyer] said it wasn't worth the effort or the money to even try for alimony. He said I'd be better off forgetting about him and his money. . . .

> My lawyer said that some men get that way, and there is nothing you can do. . . . Since my husband was a lawyer, he could build up my legal costs and wear us down. It wasn't worth fighting him. . . . He said I should accept it and cut my losses.

> My lawyer said it would cost me more to get him to pay than I would ever collect. . . . He said I should put my energy into my new life. . . . He was a real chauvinist and told me I'd have no trouble finding a new husband. . . . I knew he was selling me short, and did not want to fight to get me the support I needed. . . . But I also realized he was right in telling me I couldn't fight it. I would crack up if I spent my energy trying to make Bob pay . . . the whole system was stacked against me. . . . It still makes me angry when I think about how I got screwed.

As this last quotation suggests, if some of these women sound like victims in accepting their husband's refusal to pay alimony instead of fighting for their right to it, it should be noted that they (and their attorneys) were also making a realistic prediction about how the legal process operates. In divorce negotiations as in many other areas of the law, the party who is more insistent and more intransigent is likely to prevail. The other party must be willing to go to extreme lengths (and to spend a lot of money) to pursue his (or her) own cause. Not surprisingly, when faced with a husband's adamant refusal to pay and the choice of "accepting" this refusal or spending vast amounts of time, dollars, and psychic energy in litigation, most women decided to "accept" their husband's decision. In the present legal system a woman's options to "choose" to fight for alimony are severely constrained.

The empirical data on alimony awards, to which we now turn, reflect this underlying reality.

NO-FAULT'S IMPACT ON ALIMONY AWARDS

The changing pattern of alimony awards adds up to a success story, of sorts, for the legal reformers. The data reveal five changes in alimony, now called "spousal support," under no-fault. There has been a shift from "permanent" to short-term "transitional" awards, so that even those relatively few women who are awarded alimony receive it for short periods of time with the expectation that they will rapidly become self-sufficient. The new law has also brought a reduction in the percentage of settlements involving alimony awards, the virtual elimination of alimony after short-term marriages, and the abolition of fault as a basis for awards. Finally, wives considered "employable" and capable of supporting themselves are now rarely awarded support. Each of these changes is discussed below.

But the implementation of the new law is not an unqualified success story. As we have seen, the reformers singled out three groups of women for special treatment and assured support: those who were housewives and mothers in lengthy marriages, those with full-time responsibility for young children, and those needing transitional support to become self-supporting. Many of these women are not being awarded the support they were promised. These data are discussed in greater depth in Chapter 7.

Although the sex-neutral wording of the law permits alimony for a dependent spouse of either sex, since women were much more likely to be in that position during the years covered by this research, I refer to the dependent spouse as the "wife" or "divorced woman" in the discussion that follows.

A Shift from Permanent to Transitional Awards

The most important change in the pattern of alimony awards following the introduction of no-fault divorce law has been the change in the duration of the awards. Before 1970 most alimony awards were labeled as permanent, or open-ended. This reflected the old law's assumption that the wife would remain dependent on her former husband for an indefinite period of time—"his or her life." Under the new law, in contrast, the assumption is that the wife can and should become self-sufficient after divorce (after receiving some education and training if necessary), and this has led to time-limited alimony awards.

The data clearly reveal a shift from permanent to transitional alimony awards after the institution of the no-fault law in 1970. Between 1968 and 1972 open-ended alimony awards—those labeled "permanent," "until death," "until remarriage," "until further order of the court," or some combination of these—dropped from 62 to 32 percent of the alimony awards in Los Angeles County.[33]

Thus, by 1972, only a minority of the divorced women who were granted alimony were awarded anything resembling "permanent" alimony. The pattern has remained stable since 1972. In 1977, a similar one-third of the alimony awards were open-ended or permanent, while two-thirds were for a limited duration.

Of course, even those awards that are labeled "permanent" do not necessarily last because the court retains jurisdiction and may later modify or terminate the support award. Since in most cases support may be reduced if there is a change in circumstances, these awards are vulnerable to downward modifications if the husband's job or income changes, or if he remarries.* (While the awards are also potentially open to upward modifications, increases in support were virtually nonexistent in our sample.)

In addition to the potential reduction or elimination of these spousal support awards in court, there is always the possibility that husbands will simply stop paying them (without permission from the court), or will reduce the amount they pay, or will pay sporadically. The burden of collecting these awards is on the recipient.

Along with the decrease in permanent alimony awards, the 1970 no-fault law brought a rise in transitional, or fixed-duration, awards. This increase is most evident between 1968 and 1972, when transitional awards doubled, from one-third of all the Los Angeles awards, to two-thirds. (There were no further changes after 1972 and 1977. Roughly two-thirds of the awards remained fixed-duration awards.)

These figures do not include lump-sum alimony awards, which would make the percentage of short-term awards even greater. Nor do they include token awards of $1 a year, which simply allow the court to retain jurisdiction over the case.

The trend toward transitional awards was also reported in the interviews with attorneys and judges. When asked if the nature of alimony awards had changed under the new law, both types of experts most frequently mentioned the shift toward limited-duration awards.

By 1977 the median duration of transitional awards was twenty-five months, or about two years,[34] suggesting that the courts assumed the transition to self-sufficiency could and should be accomplished quickly. Since one of the aims of the new alimony was to provide transitional support for the woman who needed education and retraining, one cannot but question how this could be accomplished in the relatively short period of two years. No doubt awards of such short duration provide a strong incentive for the supported spouse to find a job, but they also seem to overestimate the ease with which a divorced

---

* Alimony can not be changed if the attorneys have arranged a nonmodifiable integrated agreement in which a higher support award has been traded for less property, or vice versa.

woman who has been a housewife can find an adequate job and become self-sufficient. This problem is examined more fully in Chapter 7.

The judges' and lawyers' views of "what constitutes an appropriate alimony award" clearly reflect the trend toward short-term transitional awards. Recall, for example, the case of Sheila Rose, the twenty-nine-year-old registered nurse who supported her husband through medical school. (The Rose case is described on p. 415 of Appendix B.) At the time of the divorce, Sheila was earning $650 net (after taxes) per month. Her husband Barry earned $2,000 net per month in his first year of private practice as a physician, and his earnings were expected to rise steadily. We asked the attorneys what, if anything, they predicted Mrs. Rose would be awarded in alimony, and for how long.

Under the old law, 81 percent of the attorneys predicted that Sheila Rose would be awarded alimony (attorneys tend to overestimate the percentage of women who are awarded alimony because they are more likely to deal with upper-income clients, among whom alimony is more common). Approximately one-third predicted an open-ended award (typically until her remarriage), while the remaining two-thirds predicted a limited-duration award averaging about four years.

In a later section of the interview, the attorneys were asked to predict the outcome of the same case in 1975, under the no-fault law. While 70 percent predicted that she would be awarded some alimony, only 10 percent predicted an open-ended award; the remaining 90 percent predicted a fixed-duration award averaging less than three years.

The different predictions for Sheila Rose not only reflect the trend toward shorter-term and fixed-term awards; they also reveal a decline in the average amount of money that is awarded in support. The average (mean) monetary award the attorneys predicted for Sheila Rose in 1968, under the old law, was $400 per month. By 1975 that had dropped to $338 per month. In constant 1968 dollars, the value of the award dropped from $400 per month to $220.

Although the major rationale for transitional awards is to permit a woman time for the education and training she needs to become self-sufficient, it is not clear whether the time allowed is actually long enough to permit retraining. For example, recall the attorneys' and judges' responses to Sheila Rose's request for support to attend medical school. Less than a third of the respondents (31 percent of the judges and 27 percent of the lawyers) said that she would be awarded support for the four years of medical school, even though she had supported her husband through eight years of his medical education.

These shifts in alimony awards are part of a nationwide trend to define alimony as a short-term, stop-gap support or what is often called "rehabilitative alimony."[35] (I have avoided the use of the term rehabilitative alimony because it suggests that the housewife and mother has not been economically productive when she has worked at home and/or that her contribution has been deficient.) These meager awards create severe pressure on the newly divorced woman and may be counter-productive. They thrust her into the job market without affording her the time and financial resources to gain the education, career counseling, and training she needs to improve her long-term job prospects.

A Decline in Alimony Awards

With the removal of the traditional legal assumption that a husband had an obligation to continue to support his ex-wife, it was reasonable to expect a decline in the percentage of women awarded alimony after no-fault was instituted.

The overall frequency of alimony awards did drop significantly after 1970, when the no-fault law went into effect. Thus, between 1968 and 1972, the percentage of wives awarded alimony dropped from 20 to 15 percent of the divorce cases, a statistically significant difference, in both Los Angeles and San Francisco counties.[36]

These awards include a few cases in which alimony was to be paid in a few lump-sum payments rather than in monthly amounts. If these lump-sum cases are excluded (as they are in the tables that follow), on the assumption that they are actually part of the division of property, then the percentage of women awarded monthly payments dropped from 19 to 13 percent between 1968 and 1972.

Neither of these figures includes token awards of $1, which allow the court to retain jurisdiction. Such token awards also declined after no-fault was instituted in 1970: from 19 to 11 percent in Los Angeles County, and from 17 to 11 percent in San Francisco County.[37]

By 1977 the percentage of token awards dropped to 6 percent while 17 percent of the divorced women were awarded some monthly alimony. (This apparent rise in non-token awards is a result of a slightly greater proportion of older women in the 1977 sample and does not represent a real increase over the 1972 awards.) Thus, overall, there was a small but significant decline in alimony awards after the no-fault law was instituted, and a leveling off after that.

Karen Seal reports a parallel decline in the percentage of alimony awards in San Diego County following the introduction of no-fault. In San Diego, the percentage of women who were awarded alimony dropped 50 percent between 1968 and 1976.*

The small percentage of California women who were awarded alimony is in line with national data reported by the U.S. Census Bureau: in 1978, 14 percent of the divorced women in the United States had been awarded alimony.[39]

While these data indicate that the courts are applying a new minimalist standard of alimony, it should be stressed that most divorced women were not awarded alimony even before the law changed. *Under both legal systems, the reality of alimony awards has diverged sharply from the legal ideal.* Nor is this a recent phenomenon: even earlier in the century, when married women were far less likely to be employed, historian Elaine May found that alimony was awarded to only 32 percent of the women in a sample of 346 divorce complaints filed in Los Angeles County in 1919.[40]

The Elimination of Alimony Awards After Short Marriages

Since the law directs judges to consider the length of the marriage in making alimony awards, there should be larger differences between awards to women in long and short marriages after no-fault was instituted. The economic standards of the new law would also lead one to predict a decline in alimony awards to women in short marriages because it is more likely that they will now be considered capable of supporting themselves. Women in longer marriages, however, should be clear candidates for the economically based new alimony.

The data in Table 13 support these expectations about the results of no-fault. In this and in subsequent tables only the Los Angeles data are reported, but significant differences between the data from the two cities, which are rare, are noted.

We see that alimony awards have been significantly linked to the duration of marriage throughout the decade, but marital duration has become even more important since 1970 under the new law. In 1968 women in longer marriages (15 years or more) were three times as likely to be awarded alimony as those in short marriages (less than

---

* Because Seal includes token awards of $1 a month as "alimony awards," she reports a much higher percentage of San Diego wives were awarded alimony both before and after no-fault: 66 percent in 1968 and 30 percent in 1976.[38] She does not specify what percentage of these awards were token awards.

TABLE 13

Percentages of Wives Awarded Alimony by Length of Marriage

LENGTH OF MARRIAGE	FAULT LAW 1968	(n)*	NO-FAULT LAW 1972	(n)	1977	(n)	DIFFERENCE BETWEEN 1968 AND 1977
Under 1 year	10.3	(58)	1.5	(68)	0.0	(58)	−10.3
1 to 4 years	13.7	(183)	5.8	(189)	5.0	(179)	−8.7
5 to 9 years	14.7	(102)	12.2	(90)	14.8	(115)	+0.1
10 to 14 years	20.3	(69)	29.4	(51)	27.6	(58)	+7.3
15 and over	38.8	(85)	31.0	(74)	45.5	(88)	+6.7
TOTAL SAMPLE	18.8	(497)	12.9	(472)	16.5	(498)	−2.3

* n refers to the number of cases on which the percentages are based.
This table is based on random samples of court records, Los Angeles County, 1968, 1972, and 1977.

5 years). By 1977, they were nine times as likely to be awarded support.

As predicted, alimony awards to wives in short marriages were virtually eliminated under the no-fault law: by 1977 only 5 percent of the women married less than five years were awarded monthly alimony. Awards to wives in marriages of medium duration (five to nine years) remained close to 15 percent over the 1968–1977 period. Awards to wives in longer marriages (ten years or more) showed more fluctuations, but by 1977 a higher percentage of women in this group were awarded alimony. Yet even though women married 15 years or more were more likely to be awarded alimony than any other group of women, they were still more likely to have alimony denied than to have it awarded (54 percent were not awarded alimony, while 46 percent were).

The fluctuating awards for longer-married women tell an interesting story. When no-fault was first instituted, judges imposed a stringent standard of self-sufficiency on all divorced women, which is reflected in the 1972 data. But the harshness of this standard was criticized in a 1972 appellate court decision, *In re Marriage of Rosan.*[41]

The *Rosan* case involved a 17-year marriage. There were two children one of whom was experiencing "emotional problems." The husband's income, after taxes, averaged approximately $25,000 per year and the parties enjoyed a high standard of living. Mr. Rosan was a sales manager for two jewelry stores. In addition to his income, he earned commission and bonuses and had an expense account of $150 per month. Mrs. Rosan was a housewife and mother during the marriage. She held only one job, in a department store, for less than a year, but had to quit because of the emotional problems of her child.

At the trial Mrs. Rosan was awarded only three years of spousal support: $400 per month for the first year, $300 a month for the next, and $200 for the third year. (She was also awarded half the equity in the family home, which amounted to $6,790 after the home was sold, and half of some other family assets.)

The California District Court of Appeals ruled that the trial court had abused its discretion, both by awarding the wife an inadequate amount of spousal support, and by not retaining jurisdiction over support past the three-year period of the award.[42] The higher court found that the trial court erred in terminating Mrs. Rosan's alimony because her earning capacity and future income were totally unknown: the order was based on "mere hopes and speculative expectations" rather than the evidence.[43]

The *Rosan* decision sent a clear message to trial court judges: they should not expect housewives in marriages of long duration to become self-sufficient too rapidly.[44] As the court stated:

> We find nothing in the Family Law Act indicating any legislative intent that a wife of a marriage of long standing whose attentions have been devoted during the marriage to wifely and parental duties and whose earning capacity has therefore not been developed should be, at a time when the husband is reaching his peak of earning capacity, relegated to a standard of living substantially below that enjoyed by the parties during the marriage or to subsistence from public welfare.[45]

These were powerful words. The appellate court found trial courts misinterpreting the law. Following *Rosan,* the percentage of awards to women in longer marriages increased, as the 1977 data indicate.

Nevertheless, even after *Rosan,* the data suggest that trial court judges—or at least a fair number of trial court judges—did not follow the appellate court's instructions: five years later over half of the women in longer marriages were still being denied alimony altogether (see Table 13). Professor Herma Kay suggests that judges were affected by the feminist movement in the early 1970s, and were using women's demands for equality as a justification for denying and terminating alimony.[46] Along the same lines, attorney Riane Eisler quotes a California judge who described his colleagues' attitudes as "What they [divorcing women] need is to go to work, so they can get themselves liberated."[47]

This tension between trial court judges' rulings and appellate court instructions continued throughout the 1970s and early 1980s. In a series of cases that have been appealed the trial courts have been admonished for being too harsh on older women. (See Chapter 7, pp. 193–194.)[48]

The same concern has also inspired legislative changes. As of 1980 the California Civil Code instructs judges to consider "the earning capacity of each spouse taking into account the extent to which the supported spouse's present and future earning capacity is impaired by periods of unemployment that were incurred during the marriage to permit the supported spouse to devote time to domestic duties."[49]

In summary, while the percentage of alimony awards to women in short marriages has declined under the new law, the percentage of awards to women in longer marriages has not declined. Nevertheless, the majority of the women married for fifteen years or more still were not awarded alimony in 1977. In light of the language in the law, and the explicit directives of the higher courts, it is, in fact, hard to explain why more than half of the women married more than fifteen years are awarded no alimony at all.

The Amount of Alimony Awarded

For the minority of divorced women who are awarded spousal support of over $1, the typical award is quite modest—a median of $210 per month in 1977, or about $2,500 a year (about $4,400 a year in 1984 dollars). The mean award is slightly higher, an average of $333 a month, or $3,996 a year (roughly $6,900 in 1984 dollars). In this case the median award, the award in the middle of the distribution, is probably a better indicator of the "average" than the statistical mean, which is influenced by a few high awards.

These amounts are roughly comparable to those reported in national surveys conducted by the U.S. Census Bureau. In 1978 the mean alimony for all divorced women in the United States was $3,162 a year, compared with the $3,996 mean in California.* Obviously, the average alimony award is hardly sufficient to provide economic support for a dependent spouse—even if it is paid in full.

The duration of marriage also affects the *amount* of alimony awarded. Table 14 shows that the average (median) monthly alimony

---

* The Census figure is for alimony received, because the Bureau does not report alimony awarded. In 1981 the mean alimony received in the Census study was $3,000 a year, a decline of about 25 percent from the 1978 level after adjusting for inflation.[50]

TABLE 14

Median Monthly Alimony Awards*
by Length of Marriage

Length of Marriage	Median Monthly Award* (n)**	
Under 1 year	none	(58)
1 to 4 years	$100	(5)
5 to 9 years	$149	(16)
10 to 14 years	$200	(16)
15 years and over	$299	(38)
Total Sample	$209	(133)

* Excluding no award and awards of $1 per month
or per year.
** n refers to the number of cases in each group.
This table is based on a random sample of court records, Los Angeles County, 1977.

award in 1977 increased directly with the length of the marriage, from
$100 for marriages under five years to $299 for marriages over fifteen
years. Since these figures are based on a random sample of all divorced
persons, a population that is heavily weighted toward lower-income
families, these median awards may appear low. In 1984 dollars they
are equivalent to $173 per month in marriages under five years and
$517 per month in those over fifteen years.

The generally low amount of alimony awards has been a subject
of considerable concern. Above we noted the California appellate
court's warning that wives in marriages of long standing should not
be forced to live on substantially less than their husbands or to subsist
on the level of public welfare. Yet it is obvious that these low alimony
awards must leave many women at precisely that level.

Among those women who were in fact awarded alimony, there
was almost universal dissatisfaction with *the amount* of the award.
Many felt that judges were treating them like "second-class citizens"
or "charity cases" and did not award them enough for their basic needs.
On the other hand, they saw their husbands being allowed to keep
more money than they "needed" for themselves.

Interestingly, the same charges of judicial sexism came from
women at both ends of the income spectrum. Consider first a woman
who was awarded $400 a month (in alimony and child support) from
her husband's $1,200 net salary.

> It's an insult . . . but I can't live and feed my son on my pride, so I
> take it. . . . Why am I and my son worth so much less than he is? . . .
> It's because the judge looks at him and thinks he needs it—but I can
> get by. . . . He gets a company car and the privilege of eating out whenever
> he wants to—I have the privilege of food stamps. . . . I've never lived
> like this before in my life . . . it's degrading and it's not fair.

Similarly, at the other end of the income range, after a twenty-five-year marriage, the wife of a corporate executive earning $60,000 a year (net) salary, complained that the court awarded 80 percent of her husband's income to him. Although the judge awarded her $20,000 a year in alimony, she alone was supporting their eighteen-year-old son and the judge "overlooked" a major part of her husband's income:

> The judge just looked at his salary, and said he'd award me one-third,
> but he knew my husband had a much larger income than his salary. . . .
> He receives an annual bonus of $10,000 and up, an annual contribution
> to his deferred savings plan, free medical and dental insurance, and most
> important his expense account. In an average month he receives $1,500
> to $2,000 for meals and utilities, phone, and household expenses. That's
> in addition to his free car and gasoline. We've often lived "free" on his
> expense account. I calculated that he has an extra $40,000 in income a
> year that the judge ignored—so he gave him 80 percent and gave me
> and my son 20 percent and that's not fair. . . . I've lost everything . . .
> my house . . . everything . . . the judge thought I could live on less but
> *he needed* the house. . . . It's okay to ruin my lifestyle and to deprive
> me of everything I worked for—and counted on—but he's untouched. . . .
> It's just sexism, that's what it is. He counts and I don't. But I was just
> as important in building his career as he was, and I'm entitled to it. Why
> should he live on $80,000 while my son and I have to scrimp and do
> without on $20,000?

Another woman spoke for many when she said her alimony award was "an insult":

> I figured it out. After ten years of marriage I got $200 a month for five
> years. That comes out $1,100 for each year of marriage. That means I
> was his 60-hour-a-week servant for $100 a month. Just about slave labor
> . . . housekeeper, nurse, chauffeur, mother. And prostitute—that's what
> I felt like. . . . It's an insult.

One woman summed it up this way:

> It's horrible when you have to face how little you are worth—what a
> low value the society places on all those years of your life. . . . Or maybe
> it's just the judges who have no common decency, who don't care if a
> fifty-year-old woman's life is ruined.

The Elimination of Fault as a Basis for Awards

In Chapter 2 we noted the nationwide trend to eliminate fault as a basis for alimony awards. Before these reforms, judges were more likely to award alimony to an "innocent" wife. In California, in 1968, under the adversary system, over three-quarters of the plaintiffs—those who initiated the legal divorce proceedings—were wives filing charges against "guilty" husbands.[51] Judges awarded alimony to 20 percent of the Los Angeles wives who were plaintiffs, compared with only 10 percent of those who were defendants. Corresponding figures for San Francisco were 20 percent and 13 percent.

These differences have disappeared under the new law. Since innocence is no longer a consideration, the petitioner is not more likely to be awarded alimony. Thus there is no difference in the percentage of alimony awards to "petitioners" vs. "respondents," the terms for plaintiffs and defendants, after the 1970 reforms. In 1972 judges ordered alimony to 12 percent of the Los Angeles wives who were petitioners, compared with 14 percent who were respondents; in 1977 the comparable percentages were 16 and 18 percent. (These differences are the reverse of what might be expected, but too small to be significant.)

When asked whether the no-fault law had brought any changes in alimony awards, the second most common response among judges and attorneys was the diminished role of fault in determining alimony awards.* (The first response was the shorter duration of awards.) One index of this change is provided by the attorneys' responses to a series of hypothetical divorce cases. When asked to predict the outcomes of these cases under the old law, their predictions about alimony awards were clearly influenced by considerations of fault. For example, in one case in which the wife was portrayed as strongly at fault ("she was promiscuous and openly having affairs"), only 18 percent of the experts predicted she would receive alimony under the old law (in 1968). When asked about the identical case in 1975, under the new law, 70 percent predicted she would be awarded alimony.

---

* Fault-based evidence about the character of the parties is admissible only if custody is at issue. Some attorneys however try to introduce it to persuade the judge that their client is really the "good guy." They can do this indirectly by various means, including requests for restraining orders (for example, to prevent a husband from hitting his wife, or a wife from harassing her husband at work), or by asking for spousal support to cover the wife's psychiatric treatment (showing the emotional anguish caused by her husband's mistreatment).

Here again, the attorneys consistently overestimate the percentage of alimony awards. Thus what is important here is the *difference* in their predictions under fault and no-fault systems rather than the absolute numbers.

Under the old law, plaintiffs bargaining for alimony or property not only could accuse each other of wrongdoing, but also could try to escalate the *degree* of fault alleged, frequently taking up considerable court time with charges and countercharges.[52] Although valid indicators of the degree of fault obviously cannot be obtained from court records, we varied the degree of fault in a second series of hypothetical cases. Each judge or attorney was given a set of ten unique divorce cases, which had been randomly generated by computer so that the total sample would cover a wide range of possible situations.[53] In response to the 1968 (old law) cases, the experts estimated that the wife would receive alimony in 19 percent of the cases in which she was pictured as strongly at fault ("the wife was guilty of extreme cruelty, she was openly having an affair with another man"). In contrast, when milder fault was involved ("the wife was tired of the marriage and willing to be at fault"—that is, she was willing to be the guilty party), 30 percent predicted that she would be awarded alimony. (Once again, the attorneys' predictions are high, since a woman found guilty of adultery was barred by law from receiving alimony.)

The degree of the husband's fault, however, made little difference. On the average, the experts predicted that the husband would be ordered to pay alimony in 84 percent of the sample cases in which he was strongly or mildly at fault under the old law.

In the aggregate opinion of the experts, then, under the old law guilty husbands would be punished almost automatically by being ordered to *pay* alimony, whereas the extent to which guilty wives were punished by being *denied* alimony depended on the degree of their fault.

Self-sufficiency as a Basis for Awards

The standards of the new law dictate a strong reliance on economic criteria in general, and on the wife's ability to support herself in particular. It thus seemed reasonable to predict that after 1972 a wife's occupation and income would become more important factors in alimony awards.

HOUSEWIVES VS. WIVES WITH OCCUPATIONS

Since the new law specifically directs judges to consider the "ability of the supported spouse to engage in gainful employment," we examined the relationship between wife's occupation and alimony awards. Unfortunately, the California court forms contain an ambiguous question about the wife's occupation. At the time of filing, the divorce petitioner is asked to list the wife's "present or last occupation." This allows petitioners to list the wife's "last occupation" even if she has not been employed for a number of years.

In the absence of other data, the occupation listed on court forms is used here as a rough indicator of the wife's employment potential, although this measure probably overestimates many women's marketable skills. The reverse error—that a woman listed as a housewife has been employed—is unlikely because only 18 percent of Los Angeles wives in 1968 were listed as housewives. This percentage is similar to the 16 percent who reported being housewives throughout their marriage in the weighted interview sample, where we asked extensive questions about the wife's labor force experience throughout the marriage (see page 205, Chapter 7).

Table 15 compares alimony awards to housewives with those to wives who listed occupations. It controls for length of marriage because, as noted earlier, marital duration has a significant independent effect on alimony awards.

The table shows that a greater percentage of Los Angeles women identified as housewives were awarded alimony than were wives identified as having some occupation. This is in line with the law's goal of paying more attention to occupational self-sufficiency as a basis for awards but it still does not fulfill the law's goal of providing support for dependent housewives because three-fourths of the housewives were still not awarded support.

The real changes that occurred during this period have to do with duration of marriage, which had an important independent effect on the awards. In marriages of less than 10 years, the difference between the two groups of women declined. By 1977 *neither* housewives *nor* wives listing occupations were awarded alimony (i.e., less than 8 percent in the 1977 column of Table 15) if they had been married less than ten years. In contrast, in longer marriages the difference between housewives and wives with occupations increased. By 1977 housewives were more than twice as likely to be awarded alimony (64 versus 29 percent) than wives with occupations, if they had been married more than ten years. (See Table 15, 1977 column.)

TABLE 15

Percentage of Wives Awarded Alimony,
by Occupation and Length of Marriage

LENGTH OF MARRIAGE	FAULT LAW 1968 (n = 423)*	NO-FAULT LAW 1972 (n = 441)	1977 (n = 500)	DIFFERENCE BETWEEN 1968 AND 1977
All marriages (all lengths)				
Housewife	24.7%	18.0%	26.1%	+ 1.4%
(n)*	(77)	(100)	(119)	
Other occupation	15.0%	10.3%	13.4%	− 1.6%
(n)	(346)	(341)	(381)	
Marriages under 10 years				
Housewife	16.7%	10.3%	7.6%	− 9.1%
(n)	(54)	(68)	(79)	
Other occupation	10.3%	5.9%	7.3%	− 3.0%
(n)	(243)	(256)	(273)	
Marriages over 10 years				
Housewife	43.5%	34.4%	64.1%	+20.6%
(n)	(23)	(32)	(39)	
Other occupation	26.2%	23.2%	29.0%	+ 2.8%
(n)	(103)	(85)	(107)	

* n refers to the number of cases on which the percentages are based.
This table is based on random samples of court records, Los Angeles County, 1968, 1972, and 1977.

Overall, then, being a housewife increases one's chances of alimony only after a marriage of ten years. Thus while 64 percent of the longer-married housewives were awarded alimony, only 8 percent of the housewives in shorter marriages were by 1977. In that year, the longer-married housewives were almost eight times as likely to be awarded alimony as housewives in shorter marriages (64 percent vs. 8 percent). Thus, irrespective of the woman's occupational training, if she had not been married long she was expected to be—or to become—self-supporting.

Because the court dockets do not provide clear, complete information on wives' occupations and incomes, we turn to two other sources of data to examine the effects of these factors on alimony awards: interviews with attorneys and judges, and interviews with divorced men and women themselves. We begin with the legal experts.

When faced with a large array of computer-generated hypothetical cases, the judges and lawyers' aggregate predictions ranked employed women less likely to be awarded alimony than housewives, and women in high-prestige occupations less likely to win support than those with lower occupational prestige. In addition, they predicted that women working full time would be less likely to be awarded alimony than those who worked part time or intermittently; that higher-income wives would receive less alimony than lower-income wives; and that the wife's income would have a greater effect on alimony awards under the new law than under the old. These predictions suggest that few of the women whom judges perceive as capable of self-support can expect to receive even temporary alimony, regardless of the length of the marriage.

The Effects of a Wife's Income

Most of these predictions by attorneys and judges are supported by the information obtained in 1978 interviews with recently divorced California men and women. Before these data are presented, however, a note of caution about the interview sample is necessary.

The interview sample was stratified by length of marriage and socioeconomic status to enable a systematic examination of the effects of marital duration and income on the terms of the divorce settlement. Since most divorcing couples are young and have little property at the time of divorce, we intentionally oversampled longer-married and high-property couples. This overrepresentation of long-married, high-income families leads to a higher percentage of alimony awards in the interview sample, when compared to a random sample of divorced couples such as our 1977 docket sample. Nevertheless, because we were able to obtain complete information on the occupations, incomes, and employment experience of women and men in this sample—information that was generally unavailable in the court records—the sample is especially useful for examining the effect of the wife's income on alimony. In addition, if we control for both income and length of marriage, as we do in all of the tables in this book, we eliminate the sample bias.

Analysis of the data from the interview sample reveals that two factors are more important than the wife's occupation and income in determining alimony awards: the husband's income, and the duration of marriage. Since we have already looked at the effect of marital duration, we now turn to the husband's income. Table 16 shows that the husband's income is a powerful determinant of alimony awards. We see that the wives of men with a yearly income of $30,000 and over were more than four times as likely to be awarded alimony as those whose husbands earned less than $20,000 (62 versus 15 percent).

Turning next to the effects of the wife's income, we find, as expected, an inverse relationship: wives who earn the highest salaries are the least likely to be awarded spousal support. But what is surprising is the low level of income that seems to qualify a woman as "self-sufficient"—$10,000 a year is the significant juncture. Once a divorced woman earns $10,000, her chances of being awarded alimony decline precipitously.

Table 16 shows that women with their own predivorce incomes of less than $10,000 are, on the whole, about twice as likely to be awarded alimony as those with predivorce incomes of over $10,000 a year—if, and this is a big if—their husbands earn more than $20,000 a year. If a woman's husband earns *less* than $20,000 a year, he is rarely asked to pay alimony regardless of her earning capacity.

This does not mean that *all* women who earn less than $10,000 are awarded alimony if their husbands do earn $20,000 a year or more. A husband's income of $20,000 or more merely increases a wife's chance of alimony if she has low earnings. It does not assure her an award.

Although a wife's income of $10,000 may not seem like self-suffi-

TABLE 16

Percentage of Wives Awarded Alimony,
by Annual Predivorce Income of Husband and Wife

| | PERCENTAGE OF WIVES AWARDED ALIMONY* | | |
| HUSBAND'S PREDIVORCE INCOME | WIVES BY PREDIVORCE INCOME | | ALL WIVES |
	Under $10,000	*Over $10,000*	
Under $20,000	14%	16%	15%
(n)**	(77)	(24)	(101)
$20–29,999	49%	9%	33%
(n)	(35)	(22)	(57)
$30,000 and over	67%	36%	62%
(n)	(49)	(22)	(60)

* Because this table does not control for marital duration, these data are influenced by the overrepresentation of long marriages in the interview sample.
** n refers to the number of cases on which the percentages are based.
This table is based on data from interviews with divorced men and women, Los Angeles County, 1978.

ciency for a woman who has been married to a man with an income exceeding $20,000 or $30,000 a year (especially not if she has minor children to support) the courts apparently consider it appropriate to apply this "minimal" standard of self-sufficiency.*

Overall, the data indicate that under the new law, alimony is likely to be based on the wife's employability and capacity for (rather minimal) self-sufficiency, but that these factors are less important in determining alimony than are the husband's income and the duration of marriage.

The one anomaly in these data appears in the relationship between the wife's occupational prestige and alimony awards. Surprisingly, in families with incomes of over $30,000 a year, wives with higher-prestige occupations were *more* likely to be awarded alimony. This finding cannot be explained by the presence of children, the wives' work histories, their current employment status, their full- versus part-time work experience, or the discrepancy between the wives' and husbands' incomes. Professor Michael Wald suggests that wives in higher-prestige occupations are more likely to get better divorce settlements simply because they are more assertive themselves and hire better, more assertive attorneys to represent them.[54]

EXPLAINING THE PERSISTENCE OF THE ALIMONY MYTH

The discrepancy between the myth and the reality of alimony awards is puzzling. How can we explain the persistent belief that most divorced women get alimony in light of our findings that such a small percentage of California divorcées have been awarded alimony under both the old divorce law and the no-fault law?

One possibility might be historical lag: perhaps the experts and the public are not aware of recent changes in the pattern of awards. Although the available historical evidence is limited, it appears to negate this hypothesis. There is no evidence that alimony has ever been awarded in more than a relatively small minority of divorces. The U.S. Census Bureau collected national data on alimony awards between 1887 and 1922 and found that only 9.3 percent of divorces between 1887 and 1906 included provisions for permanent alimony, as did 15.4 percent of those in 1916, and 14.6 percent of those in 1922.[55] The limited

---

* This finding helps to explain the large discrepancy between men and women's standard of living after divorce. Wives are expected to live on only a fraction of the postdivorce incomes of their former husbands. See Chapter 10.

historical data from single states point to the same conclusion: alimony was awarded in 31 percent of the divorce cases in Los Angeles in 1919;[56] in 6.6 percent of 3,000 Maryland cases in 1929; and in 16.5 percent of 6,800 Ohio cases in 1930.[57] Although the information is scarce, it appears that the reality of alimony has always diverged from both the legal ideal and the popular myth.

A second possibility is that alimony is being confused with child support and perceived simply as "money that divorced men have to pay." When we consider that about half of the 1977 divorcing couples had minor children, and that child support was ordered to the wife in about 85 percent of these cases, then it becomes evident that many divorced women are awarded some monthly support. These payments might be misconstrued as "alimony."

A third—and more likely—explanation for the persistence of the myth may rest in the differential visibility of those who receive alimony and those who do not. Those few wives who are awarded significant alimony are more likely to be visible—both to the public and the legal community of judges and lawyers—because, first, they are likely to have been married to wealthy men, and second, their awards receive publicity; when Johnny Carson's wife asks for $220,000 a month in alimony it makes headlines. In addition, upper-income families are more salient in the legal system and may therefore have a greater influence on judges' and lawyers' conceptions of "normal" alimony awards. These families hire the most experienced attorneys, and their cases are more likely to be contested and appealed, thus consuming more court time and judicial attention. Since these men and women are *indeed likely to pay and receive alimony,* their disproportionate visibility gives credence to the alimony myth.

The data in Table 16 on the relationship between husband's income and alimony awards among the interview sample support this conjecture. Only 15 percent of the men who earned less than $20,000 a year were ordered to pay alimony, in contrast to 62 percent of the husbands who earned $30,000 or more. Obviously the alimony "myth" is not a myth for upper-middle-class families. But it is a myth for the families of *most* divorced men—men who earn less than $20,000 a year. Since only 17 percent of the divorced men in the 1977 random sample of divorce decrees reported gross incomes of over $20,000 a year, it is the other 83 percent of the men—those who are, in fact, the typical divorced men—whom judges view as incapable of supporting two households, and therefore unable to pay alimony.

Thus alimony is typically not awarded because judges do not perceive it as "possible" in those families that constitute the vast majority of the divorcing population. As one judge remarked during a contempt hearing, "You can't squeeze blood from a stone."

Whether or not the judges' perception of the impossibility of supporting two households is appropriate, and whether or not it imposes an unfair or disproportionate burden on the ex-wife, it is clear that most judges are not willing to impose the financial burden of alimony on most divorced men. In addition, if faced with a choice between alimony and child support, a judge is likely to order a lower-income man to support his children first, no matter how acute his wife's financial need or how long the marriage has lasted.*

In contrast, higher-income husbands are seen as capable of paying alimony and are typically ordered to do so. Although these men constitute a relatively small percentage of all divorcing men, they figure disproportionately in contested cases as well as in appellate cases and thus influence legal norms and judicial standards.

In summary, then, the persistence of the alimony myth appears to be largely attributable to the visibility and salience of the divorces of middle- and high-income families where alimony is awarded. It is *their* divorce cases which make case law, generate publicity, and form the basis for the folk wisdom about alimony and divorce.

Even this brief excursion into the differential impact of the law on the rich and poor suggests the existence of a deeply rooted dual system of family law.[58] There is one set of legal rules for the highly visible upper-middle-class and upper-class minority, for whom the achievement of the law's stated goals is at least feasible, and another for the less visible lower-income majority, for whom the new law's goals of equity—when they are filtered through judges' and lawyers' assumptions about economic possibilities—are as irrelevant as the fault-based standards of the old law.

CONCLUSION

The public policy question most often asked about the impact of no-fault divorce is whether the housewife who has devoted her life to

---

* Among couples with children, data from the 1977 docket sample reveal a clear judicial preference for child support over alimony for lower-income men: 80 percent of the men with gross incomes under $10,000 were ordered to pay only child support in contrast to 32 percent of the men with gross incomes over $20,000. In the higher-income group, 47 percent of the men were ordered to pay both alimony and child support, while another 11 percent were ordered to pay only alimony, presumably for the tax advantages alimony conferred.

her family is being treated justly.[59] Have the new divorce laws deprived these women of support? Are older women now being forced to support themselves, even though they have little training and few marketable skills?

The data reviewed in this chapter show that many older housewives, more than half, are being denied alimony under the new law. But this chapter also shows that such questions are themselves based on a persistent misconception about alimony awards in the past: many people assume that most older housewives were "justly rewarded" with alimony under the traditional divorce law. Clearly they were not. The minority who were, however, were not threatened with being cut off after three or four years or pressured to find a job. In addition, under the old law wives were indisputably rewarded with a much larger share of the community property, which the no-fault law denies in its insistence on an equal property division.

In the end, under both legal systems, alimony is awarded according to judges' (and lawyers') conceptions of what the husband can afford, and this in turn is largely determined by his income level. Judges who express great sympathy for the plight of divorced men regard most men's income as too low to support two households adequately, too low to even provide half of the support for the husbands' children who are in the custody of their former wives. They therefore decide that it is often "better" to leave most of the family's postdivorce income with the husband—viewing it as his rather than theirs. Even when judges feel that a husband can afford to support his former wife and children, they rarely require him to help them sustain a standard of living half as good as his own. Most judges appear to view the law's goal of equality as a mandate to place an equal burden of support on men and women without regard to the fact that the parties' capacities to support that burden are clearly unequal by virtue of their differing experiences during marriage.

CHAPTER 7

Where the Law Fails
Young Mothers,
Older Housewives,
and Women in Transition

THE NEW CRITERIA for alimony explicitly recognize three groups of women who are not expected to meet the new standards of self-sufficiency: women with full-time responsibility for minor children, older homemakers in marriages of long duration, and women in transition. Formulators of the new law recognized that women in each of these groups had special needs that required their continued support. In all three cases, however, the data reveal that these women are often denied alimony and are left without the support they were promised.

This chapter first examines the data on actual alimony awards. It then looks at the experiences of two families to compare the practical effects of the California law with the effects of the more traditional system in England. The contrast allows us to place the California data in perspective by illuminating the different assumptions about "justice" and about "marriage" embodied in the two legal systems.

CALIFORNIA ALIMONY AWARDS

Women with Children

The new California law explicitly directs judges to consider the special needs of custodial parents in setting alimony awards: "The court must consider . . . the ability of the supported spouse to engage in gainful employment *without interfering with the interest of dependent children in his or her care.*[1] In light of this concern, one would expect to find support awarded to most women who have custody of minor children. Instead we find that most mothers are not awarded any alimony at all. Although women with minor children are more likely to be awarded alimony than women who do not have children under eighteen (22 percent vs. 11 percent), the difference between these two groups is not as large as one might expect because *most mothers are denied alimony.* Evidently the new norm of self-sufficiency is being applied whether or not a woman has custodial responsibilities for minor children.

One might also expect women with preschool children to be awarded alimony more frequently than women with school-age children.* Surprisingly, the data show that the rate of alimony awards to mothers of preschool children experienced the sharpest decline in awards of any group of women under the new law. As Table 17 indicates, in 1977 only 13 percent of the mothers of preschool children were awarded spousal support (a decline from 20 percent in 1968). Mothers of older children are more likely to be awarded alimony than those with preschool children. This is a result, at least in part, of the effects of marital duration. Since women with children between ages six and seventeen have been married longer than those with pre-school children, and since women in longer marriages are more likely to be awarded alimony, awards to these women must be seen as a product of the joint effects of marital duration and the presence of minor children.

The group of mothers most likely to be awarded alimony were those whose youngest child was between six and seventeen; after an initial downswing between 1968 and 1972, awards to these women increased significantly to 31 percent in 1977. These data are shown in Table 17.

If we control for marital duration (not shown here), we can separate the effects of the two variables. We find that within each childbearing category, wives in marriages of 10 years or longer are more likely to be awarded support than those in shorter marriages. Thus it is the *mothers of young children* who divorce after *short* marriages who

---

* Although the primary rationale for alimony in these cases is to enable the custodial parent to be a caretaker, it is evident that her time with the children also makes it more difficult for her to work full time and to earn income. One study estimated that a mother staying out of the labor force until her child reached 14 would forgo, on the average, $100,000 in earnings.[2]

TABLE 17

Percentage of Wives Awarded Alimony
by Age of Youngest Child

	Fault Law		No-Fault Law				Difference between
	1968	(n)*	1972	(n)	1977	(n)	1968 and 1977
Presence of children:							
No minor children	12.8	(187)	10.1	(237)	10.9	(248)	−1.9
Any child under 18	22.3	(309)	15.4	(233)	21.8	(252)	− .5
Age of youngest child:							
Child under 6	19.7	(188)	11.9	(134)	12.8	(125)	−6.9
Child 6 to 17	26.4	(121)	20.2	(99)	30.7	(127)	+4.3
Total	18.7	(496)	12.8	(470)	16.4	(500)	−2.3

* n refers to the number of cases on which the percentages are based.
   This table is based on random samples of court records, Los Angeles County,
California, 1968, 1972, and 1977.

experienced the most dramatic decline in spousal support after the
new law went into effect.

Why does the presence of young children appear to have so little
effect on alimony awards? One possible explanation is that "wife support" is being included in a child support award instead of an alimony
award. This is unlikely for two reasons. First, tax incentives encourage
a husband to refer to "child support" as "alimony" rather than vice
versa, because the latter is tax-deductible.

Since attorneys and judges are mindful of these tax considerations
in establishing awards, it is unlikely that alimony is being subsumed
under child support; rather, it is more likely that the alimony figures
are *inflated* by awards actually intended for child support.

A second reason for rejecting the possibility of alimony being included in child support is that child support awards are too low to
include anything extra for wife support. Our data indicate that child
support awards are typically insufficient to cover even *half* of the costs
of raising children. (The median child support award in 1977 in Los
Angeles was $125 per month per child.)

A better explanation for the decline in awards to mothers of young
children lies in the priority that judges give to the goal of making divorced women self-sufficient over the goal of supporting the custodial
parent. When asked whether they expected "mothers of preschool children to stay home with the children, or to go back to work to earn
money," only a third of the Superior Court judges who hear family

law cases in Los Angeles said they preferred to have her stay home to care for her children. The two-thirds majority who preferred that she work explained their reasons as follows. First, the judges felt it was good for a divorced woman to earn money instead of being dependent on her former husband. Second, work was seen as healthy—a form of rehabilitation that would help her build a new life. Third, the combination of work and motherhood was viewed as normal and thus a reasonable expectation of a divorced mother. The fourth and most frequently mentioned reason, however, was pure economic necessity: judges assumed that most divorced women would have to work because their former husbands could not earn enough to support them.

In sum, the law's stated aim of supporting a full-time custodial parent seems to give way to the goal of making the divorced woman self-sufficient.

Older Housewives

The number of divorces involving longer marriages has increased in recent years. Just 25 years ago only 4 percent of the divorces involved couples married more than 15 years.[3] Today, 20 percent of the divorces dissolve marriages of 15 years or more.

The law explicitly recognizes marital duration as an important factor in setting support because a woman's earning capacity is usually impaired during the period in which she devotes herself to her home and children. Yet today, more than half of the women married 15 years or longer *are not* awarded support. (Table 13, page 169, shows that 46 percent of the women in 15 year marriages are awarded alimony. The remaining 54 percent are not.)

One possible explanation for the low percentage of women awarded support after long marriages is that some of them have worked part time or full time at some point during their marriage and that judges therefore assume they can get a job and do not need support. Although the divorced women's employment histories are discussed in more detail later in this chapter, here it is useful to note that the data show only a third of the divorced women were employed throughout the marriage (and those so employed were likely to be younger women). A much larger proportion of women were not employed, or not employed regularly during marriage. However, that simple statement encompasses a vast array of short-term, erratic, irregular employment histories.

These irregular work records leave a lot of room for judicial discretion in deciding whether any individual woman is "capable of engaging in gainful employment at the time of the divorce." A judge may conclude that a woman who was employed during the first three years of her marriage but has not worked in the last sixteen years is immediately capable of self-sufficiency. Similarly, a judge may decide that because a woman has done volunteer work at a hospital she can now obtain a paid job there, or that because a woman has spent three months a year in an accounting office during the tax season she is now capable of earning an equivalent salary twelve months a year.

Since few women in longer marriages have held full-time, long-term jobs, their "employment histories" tend to be ambiguous. As an example of how judges tend to gloss over the ambiguities in assessing a woman's ability to get a job and be self-sufficient, consider the following two statements from judges we interviewed:

> [Referring to a case just presented in court] The best thing for her is to get right out and get a job—earn her own money—and make her own life.
> [Q: What kind of job do you think she can get?] Oh, anything. She can get a job in a store selling . . . clothes . . . or whatever. . . . There are lots of jobs out there, just read the want ads.
> [Q: What about that woman? What kind of job do you think she might find?] She said she used to work as . . . a . . . oh, what did she say? In an office as something—a bookkeeper or something like that. Well, that's a good job. She could probably get good hours, too . . . and be able to pick up her kids after school, as she was worried about that.
>
> [Referring to a woman who testified that she had not taught for twenty years and did not have California teaching credentials.] Just because she's been married twenty years doesn't mean she can be a sponge for the rest of her life. If she was once a teacher, she can always get a job teaching. Maybe she'll have to work as a substitute for a while, or at a not so fancy school, but just because she hasn't taught for twenty years doesn't mean she can't teach. She is a teacher.

In both of these cases the women had not been employed since the early years of marriage, and in both cases they had spent most of their married years raising children. Both still had children at home and both were now in their late forties. The first woman had no formal training as a bookkeeper, but had worked as one ten years earlier. The second woman had not held a paid teaching job for twenty years—of a twenty-two year marriage (which the judge apparently misheard as twenty years)—but had taught on a volunteer basis in the adult education program at her church. Both cases suggest how easily judges can read evidence of employability in a diversity of situations and conclude that a woman does not need support.

The one group of women for whom such assumptions would be difficult are those who have been full-time homemakers throughout marriages of long duration. One might assume that these women would certainly be awarded support. Yet here too there is a gap between the written law and the law in practice. One out of three longer-married, *full-time housewives* is not awarded support. (Table 15, p. 177, shows that 64 percent of the full-time housewives are awarded alimony: the remaining 36 percent are not.) Thus, despite the law's stated concern and rhetoric of protection, one-third of the "displaced homemakers" were not awarded any alimony.

The interview data permit further analysis of the cases of these displaced homemakers. For this analysis we have restricted our attention to women who were married eighteen years or more and who were full-time housewives throughout marriage.* What happens to women who have been housewives throughout a long marriage?

Our analysis reveals that those displaced homemakers who had been married to *upper-income* men stood a good chance of being awarded the support that the new law promised them. But those who had been married to *lower-income* men did not.

These conclusions emerge from an analysis of the patterns of alimony awards to women who have been housewives, controlling for both husbands' income and length of marriage (not shown). Overall, alimony awards to homemakers are directly correlated with their husbands' income: 64 percent of the housewives married to men earning over $30,000 a year were awarded alimony, compared to 57 percent of the housewives married to men earning $20,000–$29,000, and to 17 percent of housewives married to men earning under $20,000.

When the length of marriage as well as the husband's income is taken into account, we find that length of marriage has no effect on the likelihood of alimony for housewives married to *upper*-income men (not shown). A fair majority of the wives of men who earned over $30,000 a year are awarded alimony irrespective of the length of marriage. But among housewives whose husbands earned $20,000–$29,000 a year, alimony is assured only for those married eighteen

---

* As might be expected, a relatively larger percentage of women who were full-time housewives are to be found among women married more than eighteen years. In the 1978 Los Angeles interview sample, 26 percent of these longer-married women had been full-time housewives. (The percentage of full-time housewives in the total population of divorcing couples is about 18 percent.)

years or more (four out of five wives in the long-duration group are awarded some alimony).

Finally, when we turn to housewives married to men who earn less than $20,000 a year (not shown), the percentage of alimony awards drops sharply. Only half of the women in this group are awarded alimony even though they have all been full-time housewives and married more than eighteen years.

In summary, then, despite the legal standards and despite the ideals of no-fault divorce law, the displaced homemaker from a long-duration marriage has a good chance of receiving alimony only if her ex-husband has a substantial income. But if her husband earns less than $20,000 a year, her chances are no better than 50/50.

It is not surprising to find that the women who feel most betrayed by the legal system of divorce are those older homemakers who are denied alimony. As one woman said:

> You can't tell me there's justice if someone uses you for twenty-five years and then just dumps you and walks out scot-free. . . . It's not fair. It's not justice. It's a scandal . . . and those judges should be ashamed of themselves sitting up there in their black robes like God and hurting poor people like me.

What about the older homemakers who *are* awarded alimony? How much money are they awarded? Is it enough to provide an adequate standard of living? How does it compare with their husbands' postdivorce incomes?

When we compare the postdivorce incomes of long-married husbands and wives, we find that wives are expected to live on much smaller amounts of money, and are economically much worse off, than their former husbands. For example, wives married eighteen years or more with predivorce family incomes of $20,000–$30,000 a year had, on the average, a median income of $6,300 a year after the divorce. Their husbands, in contrast, had a median income of $20,000 a year— even if we assume that they actually paid the support awards. (These data are presented in Chapter 10 where they are discussed in more detail.) The result is that the postdivorce income of these wives is 24 percent of the previous family income, whereas the average post-divorce income for their husbands is 87 percent of that standard.*

---

* The 24 percent and 87 percent add up to more than 100 percent because the combined income of the two spouses had typically increased in the year that elapsed between the divorce and our interviews. Most of this additional income comes from men's salary increases and bonuses during the year. In addition, some women began or returned to work, or increased their working hours or received raises. Others received supplementary income or aid from the government.

The pattern is similar in all income groups: the postdivorce income of men married eighteen years or more is substantially higher than that of their former wives. On the average, these divorced men are allowed to retain twice as much income as the court allows the women who shared their career-building years.

Yet these figures probably *underestimate* the economic differences between men and women, because they assume that the postdivorce households of the two ex-spouses are of equal size. Women, however, are more likely to have dependent children in their households, and their disposable income is usually shared with these children. We can adjust for the number of people in each spouse's new household by comparing *per capita incomes* in the two households. (This figure is calculated by dividing each spouse's postdivorce adjusted income by the number of people in his or her household.*)

These *per capita* comparisons reveal an even *larger difference* between the postdivorce circumstances of former husbands and wives. On the whole, men married more than eighteen years have a much higher per capita income—that is, they have much more money to spend on themselves—than their former wives at every level of predivorce family income.

Where the discrepancy is smallest—namely, in lower-income families—the husband and every member of his postdivorce family each have about *twice* as much money as his former wife and every member of her postdivorce family (i.e., typically, his children). Where the discrepancy is greatest—in higher-income families—it is enormous: among families with predivorce incomes of $40,000 or more a year, the wife is expected to live at 42 percent of her former per capita standard of living, while her husband is allowed 142 percent of his former per capita level. (See Table 28, Chapter 10.) In addition, each person in the husband's new household—a new wife, or cohabitor, or possibly a child—has three times as much disposable income as those living with his former wife. Inasmuch as the other members of his former wife's household are almost always his own children, the discrepancy between the two standards of living is especially striking.

In summary, when the total postdivorce resources are divided— or not divided—between the two new households of the former spouses

* For example, per capita income for the wife's family is calculated by adding the wife's total income from alimony, child support, wages, and welfare, and dividing the total by the number of people in her household, including any children in her custody. Similarly, for husbands we subtract the amount of money the husband is ordered to pay in alimony and child support from his total income, and divide the remaining money by the number of people in his postdivorce household, including, if applicable, a new wife and any children in his custody.

through alimony (and child support awards), the husband is typically permitted to retain two-thirds to three-quarters of that total, while the wife (and children) are typically left with no more than one-third.

Before continuing, it is important to note that, so far, all of these calculations are based on the assumption there is full compliance with all alimony and child support awards. But if alimony or child support is not paid, or if it is not paid in full, the husband's income will be even greater than we have calculated, and the wife's income less.

The issue of noncompliance is not inconsequential. Men often fail to pay the full amount of alimony and child support the court has ordered. Noncompliance with child support orders is now so common that it has reached the level of a national scandal: less than half of the noncustodial fathers comply with court orders (see Chapter 9).

On the whole, compliance with alimony awards is better (but recall the relative rarity of alimony awards to begin with). Nevertheless, we found that within six months of the divorce decree, one out of six men was already in arrears on alimony payments, owing, on the average, over $1,000.*

The discrepancy between the postdivorce standards of living for former spouses leads to feelings of injustice among many long-married divorced women. Since most of these women assumed for many years that they had formed a lifelong partnership, they believed their efforts to build the husband's career (and earning power) were investments in a future that the two were going to share. But, as these data indicate, when the marriage dissolves, the husband's income is treated as "his" rather than "theirs," and he alone reaps most of the monetary benefits of the partnership that she helped to build. The disillusionment of these women is aptly described by Tish Sommers and Laurie Shields, founders of the first center for displaced homemakers: "It just doesn't seem fair to let him go on living so well when she has to struggle to make ends meet. She's spent her life—twenty, thirty, or forty years—raising a family and helping her husband, and all she gets is a cruel shock when she learns that the law encourages the discarding of older wives."[4]

Consider, for example, the case of one veteran of a thirty-year marriage to a college professor:

---

* It may be easier to enforce alimony awards now that they have become part of the states' enforcement mandate under the 1984 child support enforcement legislation. The federal law requires state agencies to collect alimony when collecting child support if a spousal support order is already established and the child is living in the household of the parent entitled to support.

We married at 21, with no money. . . . When he was a graduate student I worked as a secretary and then typed papers at night to make extra money. When he became an assistant professor I "retired" to raise our children but I never stopped working for him—typing, editing, working on his books. . . . My college English degree was very useful for translating his brilliant ideas into comprehensible sentences. . . . My name never appeared on the title page as his co-author, where it belonged, only in the dedication or thank you's. . . . There's more, lots more—the hours mothering his graduate students, hosting department parties, finding homes for visiting professors. . . . I was always available to help. . . . I got $700 a month for three years. The judge said, I was "smart and healthy enough to get a job." I am to "report back like a school girl" in 3 years. Never mind that I am 51. . . . Never mind that I *had* a job and did it well and am old enough to be entitled to a pension. . . . It's not that I regret my life or didn't enjoy what I did. But it was supposed to be a partnership—a fifty-fifty split. It isn't fair that he gets to keep it. It isn't fair for the court to treat it as his. . . . I earned it just much as he did.

It was no doubt in response to such concerns about the injustice of alimony awards to older housewives, that the California Court of Appeals admonished a lower court for using the alimony statute "as a handy vehicle for the summary disposal of old and used wives."[5] The case, *In re Marriage of Brantner,* involved a twenty-five year marriage. The forty-five year-old husband had a gross income of $1,578 per month. The forty-four-year-old wife had arthritis and suffered serious eye problems which posed a threat of eventual blindness. She had been a homemaker during the marriage and raised two daughters, who were fourteen and sixteen at the time of the divorce. The trial court assigned custody of the children to the wife and ordered child support for $100 per child per month. Spousal support was ordered on a declining schedule: $200 a month for the first two years, $150 for the next two years, $100 for the next two years, $50 for the next two years, and $1 for the last four years, with termination of all support at that point.

The appellate court found that the trial court abused its discretion in forming the declining schedule for support payments and in terminating all support at the end of twelve years. Although the amounts of the original support order were not appealed, Appeals Court Judge Robert Gardner characterized them as "niggardly" and a "mere pittance." As he declared:

In those cases in which it is the decision of the parties that the woman becomes the homemaker, the marriage is of substantial duration, and at separation the wife is to all intents and purposes unemployable, the hus-

band simply has to face up to the fact that his support responsibilities
are going to be of extended duration—perhaps for life. This has nothing
to do with feminism, sexism, male chauvinism, or any other trendy social ideology. *It is ordinary common sense, basic decency and simple
justice.* . . .

[No-fault divorce] has been heralded as a bill of rights for harried
former husbands who have been suffering under prolonged and unreasonable alimony awards. However, *the act may not be used as a handy vehicle
for the summary disposal of old and used wives. A woman is not a breeding
cow to be nurtured during her years of fecundity, then conveniently and
economically converted to cheap steaks when past her prime.*[6]

Both the *Brantner* case and the data presented in this chapter
suggest that the courts may have been overzealous in applying the
self-sufficiency norms of the new law—while failing to heed the equally
important goal of providing support for the longer-married homemaker
whose earning capacity has been impaired. Although the new law does
not assure her of compensation for her lost earning potential, it does,
in theory, assure her that she will share in the partnership's achieve-
ments and will not be abandoned without support. And yet our data
indicate this "simple justice" (in the words of Judge Gardner) is being
denied to many of these housewives—especially those who were married to lower- and middle-income men.

TWO FAMILIES: ALIMONY IN CALIFORNIA AND ENGLAND

The vision of justice in California is illuminated by the contrast in
the way alimony is awarded in England. The English law seeks to
maintain the standard of living that prevailed during the marriage
and, insofar as practicable, to place the parties in the financial position
in which they would have been had their marriage not broken down.[7]
This standard is based on a conception of *marriage as a lifelong union*
in which the husband has an ongoing obligation to "maintain" his former wife. (Thus support is called "maintenance" in England.)

In California, by contrast, postdivorce support is based, in theory,
solely on economic factors such as the needs and resources of the
spouses. As distinct from English assumption that a divorced man has
a continuing responsibility to support his former wife, the California
standard assumes that the divorced man should be freed of his burden
as soon as possible, and that a divorced woman can be—and should
be—financially self-sufficient.

Thus the California standard seeks *to sever* the financial bonds of marriage as soon as possible, while the English standard is based on the assumption of *continuing* financial obligations between formerly married spouses. The English rules for maintenance are congruent with the property rules discussed in Chapter 4: they seek to provide some protection and financial security for the divorced woman and her children.

Even this cursory summary of the two legal systems suggests two very different visions of marriage. The English law envisions marriage as, ideally, a lifelong commitment that is harder to break: it is more difficult to obtain a divorce in the first place, and it is more difficult to sever the financial obligations of matrimony in the second. In California, marriage is treated as a more voluntaristic commitment. California law therefore makes it easier for the spouses to dissolve the commitment and easier for the parties to sever their economic ties.

How are these principles applied in practice? Once again we use the vehicle of the hypothetical Byrd and Thompson cases which were presented both to the California judges and lawyers and to a sample of English legal experts (judges, law professors, barristers, and solicitors). For both cases the experts were asked to predict how the case would be decided and what they themselves thought was fair.

The Byrd Family: A Short Marriage and Two Young Children

We begin with Mr. and Mrs. Byrd who are divorcing after a five-year marriage. At the time of the divorce, Ted Byrd is an accountant with a net income of $1,000 per month. Pat Byrd has been a full-time housewife and mother throughout the marriage, caring for their two preschool children. She does not want to take a job, because it would interfere with her time for her children. (See Appendix B, p. 414, for the complete case.)

The Los Angeles judges predicted an average (median) award of $200 per month in spousal support for Pat Byrd, for an average duration of slightly less than two years.* The judges also predicted an average (median) of $250 in child support.

Because tax incentives in the United States and England lead to the differential labeling of maintenance awards as "wife support," "child support," and sometimes even "mortgage payments" (in En-

---

* The Los Angeles attorneys predicted Pat Byrd would get even less: a median award of $150 per month.

gland), I have added all maintenance awards together to facilitate comparisons.

Overall, the total amount of maintenance was slightly greater in England. On the average, the experts said that the English wife and children would be awarded 51 percent of the husband's salary, in contrast to the average of 45 percent predicted in California. The difference can be partially explained by the greater priority given to the needs of the children under the English law. As one English solicitor explained:

> There is so little to go around [that] the emphasis of the court must be on the wife and children. Why should they be relegated to a lower standard of living than the husband?

In California, by contrast, greater concern was expressed for the husband. The California experts stressed the importance of maintaining *his* standard of living and *his* incentive to earn. As two California judges explained the awards they would have made:

> You have to have enough money for him to be satisfied, to give him an incentive to keep earning and improving in his profession.

> He can't live on less than $7,000 a year and exist. So I have to leave him with $7,000. That leaves $5,000 of his net income for her.

Thus the California husband with a dependent wife and two small children would typically be allowed to retain more of his salary than would his English counterpart.

A second and perhaps more critical difference between the two societies lies in the assumed purpose of maintenance, and in its intended duration. The husband's *lifelong* responsibility for his wife and children's support—and their dependence on him—remain basic tenets of the English law.[8] It is therefore taken for granted that the husband's responsibility for support continues after divorce—as does his ex-wife's dependency on him.

In the United States, in contrast, the husband's postdivorce responsibilities are more circumscribed—and so is the system's tolerance for a dependent wife. Thus maintenance after divorce is viewed as a *temporary* solution in California—a means of assisting the wife *until* she becomes self-sufficient.

These differing legal philosophies give rise to the most striking difference between the responses of the U.S. and English experts concerning alimony: in California, slightly more than half of the experts predicted that Pat Byrd's spousal support award would be reviewed by the court and/or terminated in an average of two years. (Most of the remaining California experts assumed that she could become self-sufficient within five years.) However, *none* of the English respondents put a time limit on her maintenance award.

The California assumption of a *transition to self-sufficiency* was clearly reflected in the experts' attitudes about the possibility of Pat's working in the paid labor force. Consider these comments from California judges:

> She has to go to work . . . but she will need time—about two or three years—to get into the job market and earn decent wages.

> She will have to be retrained and enter the labor market. I would expect her to become self-supporting in five years. So I would maintain jurisdiction for five years and terminate her support then, unless she can demonstrate a continued need for support. I'd put the burden on her to show need at that time.

> You have to encourage her to work and use her education. I'd give her $3,000 the first year and reduce it to $2,000 the second year to give her an incentive to find a job soon.

In contrast, none of the English respondents said that Pat Byrd would *have* to work. Although a number of them did discuss the possibility, the tone they characteristically used underscores the English presumption of continued dependence. The following comments by a London solicitor summarize the English attitude toward this case:

> Now what on earth are we going to do for this poor woman? She doesn't want to work and why should she? She has two small children. Mind you, if she wants to work she'd be better off . . . and I'd tell her that, because if she worked, she'd increase the family income. But you say she doesn't want to—so fair enough—she won't.

> Now, if we gave her one-third of the income . . . that isn't enough. So she's got to have more to provide a home for the children. It's hard cheese on the husband, but she'll probably get about £6,000 a year for herself and £1,250 a year for the two children. So he'll pay out more than half of his income to her. But he'd get tax relief on it so it won't be so bad.

While one can discern some seeds of change in the solicitor's remark that Pat Byrd would "be better off" if she got a job, the presumption is that most divorced mothers in England still have the *choice* of whether to work—while most divorced mothers in California do not. The different assumptions under the two systems can be explained, in part, by the legal experts' perceptions—perhaps accurate—of more limited employment opportunities for English women and the restricted options for day care in England. In California, judges and lawyers assume that divorced women can (and should) find jobs and that day care "will not be a problem." (Of course, it often is.)

The Thompson Family: A Long Marriage, Wealth, and an Older Housewife

The differences between the English and American views of appropriate women's roles are equally pronounced for older housewives. The Thompson case involves a twenty-seven-year marriage between an IBM executive and a traditional housewife. At the time of the divorce, fifty-five-year-old Victor Thompson is earning a net (after tax) income of $72,000 per year, or $6,000 net per month. His wife Ann has been a housewife and mother. The couple's three children are now in college. (See Appendix B, p. 414, for the complete case.)

In the English view, Ann Thompson is entitled to a home, financial security, and lifelong support. There is an unquestioned assumption that she "has earned" the right to continued support and "deserves" to be taken care of with a comfortable standard of living. Consider the following comments from English experts:

[A law professor] The emphasis in this case is on providing a home for her and being sure she has security. The exact amount of money doesn't matter that much.

[A high court judge] She's an older wife, and that has to be considered. He has to protect her—he has to house her and give her a portion of his income and security for the future. She's entitled to the total assets a wife should get: she's been married twenty-seven years and had three children. She's done everything a wife can do except keep him amused.

[A solicitor] First thing the court would do is provide the wife with a house at their standard of living. After twenty-seven years of marriage and bringing up three children with the husband entirely at fault,* the court would be most sympathetic to the wife. . . . She'd get a third of his income and half of the house.

[A family court judge] He will have to provide his wife with an income and a home. She is 53 years old and isn't earning, so she cannot get a

---

* Both sets of experts were given an identical case which included this sentence: "Victor was bored with the marriage and had recently fallen in love with a younger woman." Since fault is still relevant in England, this fact was (sometimes) mentioned there. It was generally ignored in California.

mortgage . . . So, he'll have to buy her a flat and provide her with an income. Or he can buy an annuity to assure her of an income of £15–£20,000 a year for the rest of her life.

Interestingly in the debate on divorce law reform in England there has been great concern about the potential effects of the new reforms on older housewives. Fear that a more liberal divorce law would give men a "Casanova's charter"—a license to "dump" their dependent, middle-aged wives—resulted in a special provision of the English law: if the "innocent" spouse does not consent to the divorce, a five-year waiting period is required, and the divorce may still be denied if "the dissolution of the marriage will result in grave financial or other hardship."[9] The British Parliament adopted this provision primarily to protect older housewives from financial abandonment by their ex-husbands.

So far from expecting Ann Thompson to get a job, none of the English respondents seemed to think she need even consider supporting herself; the responsibility for her financial support was seen as lying squarely on her husband. As two English solicitors explained:

> She is comparatively late in life and she has not worked and is not used to working. She wouldn't (and shouldn't) have to work.

> The court would not expect this wife to go out and work. She'd get the house outright, and if I was advising her I'd be after a capital sum as well [and would let her invest it]. . . . I'd also advise her to hang on and not get divorced—after five years, she'd show financial hardship. He'd have to buy some sort of insurance for her to get half of his pension after death.

When pressed about the possibility of work for the fifty-three-year-old Ann Thompson, most of the English respondents said it *might* be considered in *unusual circumstances*. As one London registrar (i.e., judge) commented:

> I wouldn't expect the wife to work at this age, although if the issue was raised, I'd have to listen to it. Five years ago, no one would even have raised the question of if she should work. To do it now is like changing the rules in the middle of the game.

The California respondents were more divided about the appropriateness of "changing the rules in the middle of the game" for older women. The majority of the California judges (about 63 percent) agreed with the English respondents and predicted that an older housewife like Ann Thompson would be supported, without question, for the rest of her life. But a significant minority, slightly more than a third, predicted that the courts would put some pressure on her to find work and *share* the responsibility for her support. As one judge remarked:

> The wife should be entitled to support for a substantial time due to the lengthy marriage. On the other hand, she should also *become prepared* to support herself.

The California judges who sought to "encourage" Ann Thompson to become self-sufficient talked of her getting counseling and retraining to secure employment. Some judges spoke of "lecturing her on the importance of finding a job and starting a new life" and "explaining to her that *she* will benefit." Others said that they would require that "she set herself a training schedule," while still others would require a progress report from her in a few years. For example:

> I'd set a hearing two to three years away to review the wife's need and her progress towards self-sufficiency.

> I'd set up a schedule for her to train for employment. Depending on her education, I'd allow her maybe one, two, or three, or more years. Then I'd want to review the case for a stepdown [decrease in maintenance] after she has a job. She should be able to have a job in a few years.

While all of the California respondents felt that Victor Thompson had a continuing responsibility to support his former wife after a marriage of twenty-seven years, those judges who encouraged Ann Thompson to work envisioned a better future for both of them if she created a "new life" for herself and began "sharing" some of *his* responsibility by earning some income on her own. As one judge summarized this attitude:

> Ann's standard of living during the relationship should be recognized and maintained. But Ann should be encouraged to become self-supporting to the maximum extent possible. They will both benefit.

None of the California respondents predicted that the court would *require* Ann Thompson to become self-sufficient. All of them predicted that she would be awarded spousal support, with an average award of $2,000 per month. Since her children are all over eighteen and living away from home, she would not be entitled to any child support.

Comparing the maintenance awards in this case is complicated by the fact that the first ten English questionnaires omitted the word "net" before Victor Thompson's income. Since all ten respondents assumed this was a gross income figure, the word gross was inserted in the remaining questionnaires given to English respondents. As a result, the California judges based their awards on a net income figure, the English respondents on a gross income figure. When this difference is compounded by the differential impact of the two tax systems, a direct comparison between the two samples is virtually impossible. The median maintenance award for Ann Thompson among English respondents was £20,000 a year, or 28 percent of gross income of £72,000. In California, as noted above, the awards averaged $24,000 a year, or 33 percent of a net income of $72,000. Despite the difficulties of making comparisons, it clearly appears that the English wife would be better taken care of if one considers the total package of alimony and property that she receives.

The discussion on property in Chapter 4 indicates that most of the English experts considered the provision of an adequate home for Ann Thompson their first priority. In addition, because of the English assumption that the husband has a responsibility to provide for his ex-wife for the rest of her life, the English courts have typically required an older (and well-to-do) husband to purchase an insurance policy or annuity to compensate his wife for the widow's benefits she might forfeit by getting divorced. As one solicitor explained:

> He has an obligation to take out an annuity to provide her with the same benefit she would have received on his death.

All the English respondents assumed that Ann Thompson's maintenance would continue for the lives of the parties. While this was also the most common response in California, a minority of the Californians discussed the possibility of a reduced award if Ann Thompson entered the labor force—which this minority thought she should be encouraged to do. In both societies, however, postdivorce maintenance would automatically terminate if Ann remarried.

Underlying Differences: Two Visions of Justice

This rather brief review of two typical divorce cases suggests several differences in the attitudes toward divorced women (and thus toward married women as well) in England and California. A more protective and paternalistic attitude is discernible in England. The English respondents are more likely to describe divorced women as both *needing maintenance* (i.e., as being financially dependent on their husbands for support) and as *deserving maintenance* (i.e., of having a moral entitlement to maintenance). They are also more likely to emphasize the *husband's responsibility* "to protect, support and look after" his former wife. In California, as we have seen, the new norm of self-sufficiency means that support is being increasingly restricted to a *transitional* period.

This difference is reflected in the attitudes toward working mothers. In England it is assumed that a divorced woman with young children should be supported so that she can provide the children with the care and attention they need. In California, by contrast, it is assumed first and foremost that the divorced mother should work and become self-sufficient—whether or not she has child-care responsibilities.

It is not clear whether the English wife is better off than her American counterpart. On the one hand, she obviously benefits from a greater maintenance award, and because of the English assumption that she has a right to stay at home to care for her children, she more often has a choice concerning whether she will work for pay to support herself. However, as we observed in Chapter 4, the benefits she enjoys are not without their costs. While the English ex-wife is "taken care of" by her former husband, her right to continue living in the family home with her children may be contingent on her not cohabiting or remarrying. In addition, the English wife typically receives a smaller share of the family property than the California divorcée. While all California wives are guaranteed one-half of the family property, the English wife is typically awarded only one-third.

The contrast becomes sharper, however, when we consider the situation of older women, especially those who have been housewives and mothers in long marriages. For these women, there can be little doubt of the advantages of the English system. The older housewife in England is assured of her husband's continued responsibility for her support and, if he can afford it, of being able to continue living comfortably, with dignity. In California, the rules have been changed "in the middle of the game" for many older housewives. They are increasingly faced with pressure to retrain and become employed at fifty or even at fifty-five—at an age when they are almost certain to encounter job discrimination, in addition to problems created by their lack of work experience, self-doubts, and fears. The same woman in England is provided with the security of a home, a reasonable maintenance award, and an annuity in the event of her husband's death.

A second and fundamental difference between the two legal systems involves their conceptions of the marital bond. As mentioned earlier, in England it is still assumed that marriage is a lifelong bond (although the appropriateness of this assumption has recently been questioned).[10] This assumption results in postdivorce continuation of more of the rights and obligations of marriage in England. In California, marriage is seen as less permanent: it lasts only as long as it is "good" for both spouses. This has the advantage of allowing each spouse to obtain a divorce more easily, but it also allows a husband to free himself from his marital responsibility for the support of his former wife. The result is less postdivorce protection for a dependent home-maker and mother.

Finally, the two legal systems rely on different conceptions of justice and equity. The English vision of justice is to provide security (in the form of housing and maintenance) for a dependent housewife and for any minor children in her custody. In apportioning the family's property upon divorce, the English system places the welfare and secu-rity of the children first. It then tries to divide the remaining family resources to provide roughly equal standards of living for husbands and wives. Although the security that a wife receives will always be dependent on her husband's resources, and will therefore be limited for many divorced wives, the English system's vision of justice is one that emphasizes the husband's continued responsibility for her support. Since he will be there to "provide for her," the law does not guarantee her any fixed share of the family property.

The California vision of justice, in contrast, is to award each spouse one-half of the family assets and the "freedom" to build a new life. The division of family property is exclusively between the husband and wife, with no mention of the potential interests of children (other than their right to be supported by their parents after divorce). Justice in this system means that the family home will often be sold, so that the husband can be assured of his half of its value. Equity in this system is the assurance that each spouse will leave the marriage with an equal amount of the proceeds with which to "start over." Both the young mother and the older housewife are assured the same amount of property as their former husbands—and both are encouraged to build new lives. Both are also expected to make their own way thereaf-ter with little or no reliance on their former husbands.

The California vision of justice relies heavily on the assumption of a new equality between men and women, but sad to say, economic equality between the sexes simply does not exist in the larger society. How reasonable, then, is it for judges to assume that either Pat Byrd, our young mother, or Ann Thompson, the fifty-three-year-old housewife, will be able to become fully self-sufficient? How likely is it that either of them will remarry? Let us examine the two major alternatives to postdivorce support from a former husband: remarriage and work.

Remarriage

The Los Angeles judges often referred to remarriage as an alternative for the woman who could not support herself and, in some cases, as a preferable solution to "saddling" her former husband with the responsibility for her support. However, the data on remarriage suggest that it is erroneous for judges to assume that most divorced women will remarry. The likelihood of a woman's remarriage is largely a function of her age at the time of divorce.[11] If she is under thirty, she has a 75 percent chance of remarrying. But her chances diminish significantly as she grows older: between thirty and forty, the proportion is closer to 50 percent, and if she is forty or older, she has only a 28 percent chance of remarriage.

Thus it is often inappropriate to base alimony awards on the notion of remarriage. If a woman is between thirty and forty she is just as likely to remain single—or, more typically, a single parent—as she is likely to remarry. And if a woman is over forty, it is more probable that she will not remarry. Thus the assumption of remarriage is clearly inappropriate for all divorced women over thiry. Furthermore, many of these women will first spend a good number of years alone (or as single parents) before that happens, an average of five years.[12] So whether or not a woman eventually remarries, she is likely to spend a number of years as a single parent first.

It therefore makes sense to assume that most divorced women will be single heads of households after divorce, and to structure financial awards based on that assumption. (If they remarry alimony award becomes irrelevant, since it typically terminates upon remarriage.)

Since few divorced women remarry immediately, and since few are awarded alimony, a fair number of newly divorced women are forced to turn to the state for support. Close to 14 percent of the divorced women in the weighted interview sample were supported by welfare in the first year after the divorce.

Women's Employment and Job Opportunities

Our interviews indicate that most California judges view employment as the major alternative to postdivorce support. So, let us examine the employment prospects for divorced women.

This research reveals that about a third of the divorced women had been employed *throughout* their marriage: only 32 percent of the women in the weighted interview sample were employed full-time throughout marriage; another 3 percent were employed part-time throughout marriage. Another small minority of divorced women, 9 percent in the weighted interview sample, returned to work shortly before the divorce (within two years). Although many of these women could benefit from education or retraining, they are not of major concern to us here.

Our focus here is rather on the other two-thirds of the divorced women, women like Pat Byrd and Ann Thompson who were not employed during marriage and who were faced with strong pressures to find a job immediately upon divorce. While only 18 percent of the women in the court docket sample and only 16 percent of the women in the weighted interview sample were full-time housewives throughout the marriage and had *never held a paying job*, another 46 percent had been employed only sporadically: they had worked at some point during the marriage but had not worked steadily at either a part-time or a full-time job.

This latter group of women, the most prevalent group in both samples, presented a tremendous array of employment histories—ranging from one who worked during the first year of marriage and stayed home for the sixteen ensuing years; to one who regularly took a part-time job as a sales clerk for the six-week Christmas season; to one who worked for one year before the first child, 18 months between the first and second child, and thereafter only to help out in emergencies; to several who put in many hours every week as volunteers in responsible but unpaid positions. Such diversified and irregular "careers" defy easy categorization. In fact, it is this type of career history that makes it so hard for many women to compete in the job market against applicants with "normal" work histories. The same factor, as we noted earlier, also contributes to the "ambiguity" of a woman's employment potential and allows unsympathetic or uninformed judges to assume she can easily secure a job that will enable her to become self-sufficient.

Thus our concern here is the woman who has been underemployed or employed part-time or never employed because she has given priority to family commitments. The alimony laws, as they are currently interpreted, seem to assume that most of these women can fairly easily find well-paid, full-time jobs and become fully self-supporting. Are these assumptions appropriate? How "employable" is a woman like Pat Byrd or Ann Thomson?

Both Pat Byrd and Ann Thompson will be affected by the persistent second-class status of women in our society with respect to both occupational level and income. Most working women are clustered in a limited number of low-status, low-paying jobs. As Robert Smith notes:

> One-third work in clerical occupations. Another quarter work in the fields of health care (not including physicians), education (not including higher education), domestic service, and food service. The extreme form of occupational segregation in which a woman remained at home may have ended years ago, but the majority are still doing "women's work."[13]

Thus, the first and biggest problem facing women in the labor market today, is, in Smith's words, "the occupational and industrial concentration of female workers in a few women's jobs."

The second problem, which is a consequence of this sex segregation of occupations, is that women's wages are low: "the median annual earnings of women working full time, year round, were only 60 percent of those of men."[14] (Nor is the situation improving. In fact Stanford economist Victor Fuchs has shown that women's wages have actually declined, relative to men's, between 1959 and 1979.[15]) Further, if a woman has minor children at home she is likely to work only part time, and this too diminishes her potential wage income.[16]

The literature on women's participation in the labor force is vast and for the most part beyond the scope of this book. What is relevant here is that in addition to the general problems besetting women who seek entry into the job market, divorced women often face special problems. One set of problems is created by the time pressure: they are often expected to find a job and become immediately self-sufficient. In this respect the support awards play a critical role in shaping the women's future. The presence or absence of alimony can make the difference between having the time to do a job search (or to get counseling or retraining) and having to take the first job one is offered.

From this perspective it is evident how an alimony award at the time of the divorce can significantly affect a woman's subsequent career. Although it may seem that her "earning capacity" is more or less established at the time of the divorce—that is, either she has employment skills and experience or she does not—*the nature of her alimony award can in fact critically affect her future earning capacity.* If she is awarded no alimony or only a minimal amount for a short period of time, she is likely to sell herself short in the job market— to forgo retraining and take a low-paying job that offers few opportunities for advancement—simply to assure herself a steady paycheck.

One of the clearest themes in our interviews with recently divorced women was their lack of self-confidence and their panic about finances. Even well-educated, attractive, and articulate women confessed the anxiety they experienced at the prospect of having to support themselves on a drastically reduced income, and of not having enough money to make ends meet.

Consider, for example, Pat Byrd. She was an English major in college. She may not only lack salable skills, she is also likely to lack information on opportunities to acquire new or relearned job skills. The process of finding jobs is often inefficient and costly. Having the time and resources to obtain counseling and assistance is critical to one's long-range job prospects.

Without that time, and without a support award to see them through the process, *the financial pressures impel many women* to take the first job they are offered, no matter how low the salary. Even women who have worked part-time during marriage, or who worked before their children were born, typically feel forced to sell themselves short when faced with the prospect of a drastically reduced budget and the possibility of real impoverishment.

This is not to suggest that only women experience insecurity, pressure, and loss of self-confidence after a divorce. Any divorce is likely to be emotionally trying for both husband and wife. But even though many men may have severe difficulties in other areas in beginning a new life, they usually have some degree of security in their jobs and can rely on the continuity of receiving their paychecks.

IMPLICATIONS FOR SPOUSAL SUPPORT AWARDS

How might a different type of spousal support award better serve the needs of women like Pat Byrd? For example, as the former wife of an accountant Pat may have acquired a reservoir of financial insights and interests. If so, a counselor could guide her to commercial courses or urge her to invest two years in an accounting or business administration degree. Similarly, as the wife of a corporate executive, Ann Thompson may have transferable skills for a career in finance or public relations.

These possibilities suggest four important considerations for judges setting alimony or spousal support awards: first, evaluating the divorced woman's salable skills and interests; second, assessing the state of the job market for those skills; third, considering what training she would need in order to develop those skills or to learn an entirely new career; and fourth, recognizing the potential long-term payoff of investments in her training. Part of the challenge of this ap; roach lies in the need to educate all of the parties—the woman, her attorney, her husband, and her husband's attorney—about the long-term advantages of investing in her future career.*

Providing the alimony that will enable a divorced woman the time and money to invest in her future career, instead of requiring her to find immediate employment, should pay off in real dollars not only for the divorced woman and her children, but eventually for her former husband as well, as it will ultimately lighten his burden of financial support for the children. The success of centers for training "displaced homemakers" provides an affirmation of this prediction.[18]

In fact, research from Ohio State University shows that women who enrolled in a training program, rather than taking a job in the first year after divorce, were more successful in terms of both job level and annual earnings in the long run.[19] Professor Frank Mott followed a group of married women over five years from 1968 to 1973. A subsample of this group got divorced during the study period, and Professor Mott compared the postdivorce experiences of women who began working immediately after the divorce with those who obtained job counseling, enrolled in a training program, and delayed entry into the labor force for a year or more.[20] He found that both young and mature women who enrolled in a training program were more successful than their counterparts who received no training in "finding a job after the transition and in obtaining higher annual earnings during that year." Mott concluded:

> It is suggested that, while the new transition family obviously needs income support to carry it through the often-difficult marital disruption period, it probably needs as much job-related assistance. While many mature women who become household heads ultimately acquire new or relearned job skills, as well as an understanding of how to seek and find jobs, the process is often inefficient and costly. Many social and economic traumas could be avoided by timely assistance at this crucial point in the life cycle.[21]

The policy implications of Mott's findings and our own research are worthy of note. They provide clear empirical evidence of the practical advantages of generous support awards in the first few years after

---

* Several states now require the court to consider the time necessary for retraining when it sets support awards. For example, in both New York and Georgia the court must consider "the time and training needed for the supported spouse to become self supporting."[17]

divorce.* Early "balloon payments" would allow the newly divorced woman to take advantage of educational and training opportunities that will maximize her long-term earning potential and thus maximize the long-run payoffs for both herself and her former husband.

But whatever solutions we fashion for Pat Byrd, we cannot assume that they will be equally appropriate for older women like Ann Thompson. Sound public policy must distinguish between short- and long-term marriages and between women in their twenties and women in their fifties. What is realistic and fair for one group may be totally unrealistic and unfair for the other.

Women, like Ann Thompson, who have been housewives throughout lengthy marriages face far greater difficulties trying to find jobs. Fran Leonard, legal counsel for the Older Women's League, notes that judges and lawyers have been "utterly oblivious to the desperate unemployment plight of the career homemaker."[22] Employers do not recognize homemaking skills as having a market value. They only recognize "recent paid work experience" and even with such experience, older women are unwanted in today's labor market. Consider the difficulties some of the older women we interviewed faced:

I've been turned down for hundreds of jobs . . . it's been the most frustrating and degrading experience of my life.

There is no way I can make up for twenty-five years out of the labor force. . . . No one wants to make me president of the company just because I was president of the PTA.

An older woman is a pariah. . . . One employer told me I was too old to learn the job, another seemed to think I'd bankrupt his medical insurance plan. . . .

I could get a job as a "salesgirl" at Magnin's because I still look like the upper middle class woman I was, but it would be too humiliating.

It's so hard to start at the bottom when you've been a respected member of the community for years. . . . I just never realized that the respect and admiration and civic work doesn't count for anything in the job market . . . and it certainly doesn't help pay my rent.

My master's degree was twenty-five years old and I had never had a job. I'd done counseling all my life (without pay, of course) but no one would take a chance on hiring me instead of someone fresh out of school.

* The 1984 tax law may further discourage short awards because it requires six years of payments for alimony to be deductible to the payor.

The judge told me to go for job training—but no training can recapture twenty-seven years of my life. I'm too old to start from the beginning and I shouldn't have to. I deserve better.

No wonder that women over forty-five make up a large number of discouraged workers—people who want jobs but are not looking for them because they believe no work is available, or that they can not find work; or that they lack the education and skills; or that they are too old.[23] Obviously, the problem is not limited to California. Recall the case of Edith Curtis, the fifty-five-year-old Idaho woman who applied for State unemployment compensation after her divorce from a college professor. Edith Curtis' two-year job search and seventy-five applications proved "'fruitless to a shopworn and obsolete housewife . . . with a thirty-year-old B.A. in English and a lack of salable skills.'"[24] She was finally offered and accepted a job as a fast-food cashier, part time, at the minimum wage.[25]

As these examples suggest, the middle-aged woman who has few marketable skills can not make up for twenty or twenty-five years out of the job market. Most end up in low-paying jobs, living in greatly reduced circumstances, often on the edge of poverty[26].

"The harsh reality," as Eleanor Smeal, the former President of the National Organization for Women, described it,

> is that women in midlife find that their opportunities for employment and economic security are severely limited, and their futures precarious and uncertain. They face an economy that treats women as a marginal, surplus labor supply. As middle-aged women, they must compete with younger workers for low-paying, dead-end jobs. Women working in the labor force earn only 58 percent of what men earn, and account for more than 80 percent of the workers in eight of the lowest paying occupations.
>
> If they have been homemakers, midlife women discover the actual value society places on homemaking and motherhood when employers refuse to consider their years in the home as work expreience, and when Social Security records show "zero" for each year they've invested in nurturing and serving the family. They discover the false security of marriage: they can be fired from their job at a moment's notice, with no unemployment compensation, nor retirement benefits, no profit-sharing.
>
> For many of these women, society's promise that women will be taken care of in marriage is a cruel joke. They have fulfilled traditional expectations of "always being there," to care for the children and husband, only to find themselves in midlife with no rewards, no recoginition, and no financial security."[27]

The cruel joke is that both these women and their husbands never assumed that she would have to work. Rather, they assumed they had a contract; he would support her and she would care for him and their children. The problem, once again, is that society has changed the rules on her—and those new rules are most evident and most vigorously applied at the point of divorce.

This point is illustrated by a divorce case that received a fair amount of publicity in California, because the husband was the man who authored and introduced California's no-fault divorce law, James Hayes.[28] Janne Hayes married before she was twenty, after one year of college. She raised four children in their twenty-five-year marriage and was a full-time homemaker, mother, and wife of an ambitious lawyer on the rise. With the exception of a "two-week job in a department store over Christmas vacation . . . Mrs. Hayes never worked outside her home, before or during her marriage."[29]

When James Hayes, who was earning over $3,000 a month, decided he could no longer afford to pay the $650 in alimony he originally agreed to, he argued that his wife should be able to get a job and support herself. (Since their four children were over eighteen she was not entitled to any child support.)

Mrs. Hayes suffered from severe arthritis and asthma and she said it was impossible for her to hold a job. Besides, she had no experience or job training of any kind.

Mr. Hayes argued that the new law mandated a new approach to divorced women and cited the following passage from the Assembly Judiciary Committee (which he chaired):

> When our divorce law was originally drawn, woman's role in society was almost totally that of mother and homemaker. She could not even vote. Today, increasing numbers of married women are employed . . . [and] have long been accorded full civil rights. Their approaching equality with the male should be reflected in the law governing marriage dissolution and in the decisions of courts. . . .[30]

Mrs. Hayes' attorney's answer to his claim is an eloquent defense of his client's continued right to her alimony award:

> Counsel writes of the modern concern for women's equality. With respect to petitioner he is some thirty-three years too late. She was and is a housewife for some thirty years. Her husband provided the income for the family and she took care of that family—a situation which still prevails in most families today. To tell her that she has now attained equality which means that she must now go out and support herself is a

cruel and inhuman joke and a perversion of the equality movement. . . .
    The court should recognize that respondent bears a substantial part
of the blame for petitioner's current predicament. Until the divorce he
was apparently satisfied for petitioner to remain a housewife. During this
time he provided for his own education and experience in the business
world and politics, while she maintained the home.[31]

The judge, however, sided with Mr. Hayes. He ordered Mrs. Hayes'
support to be gradually reduced over the next months from $650 to
$300 a month.
    A year later Mr. Hayes, who felt the burden of supporting her
was still too much of a strain on the high standard of living he "had
to maintain" for his work, went back to court and petitioned to have
the entire alimony terminated. As the *Los Angeles Times* reported:

> James A. Hayes, 53, who earns $40,322 a year but complains that his
> expenses are nearly double his net income, was successful Tuesday in
> his bid to reduce the alimony he pays to his first wife, Mrs. Janne H.
> Hayes, 53. Superior Judge Julius A. Title lowered the payment from $300
> to $200 monthly and told Mrs. Hayes, who complains of asthma and back
> pains, to get a job.[32]

When her alimony was reduced to $200 Janne Hayes applied for
welfare and food stamps. Attorney Riane Eisler, writing about the case
two years later, reported that Mrs. Hayes was still on food stamps.[33]
    One lesson from this harsh reality is that the woman who is di-
vorced after fifteen or twenty or thirty years of marriage *can not* recapture the lost years in the labor force. But an equally important lesson
is this: she should not be expected to because she was promised by
both her husband and her society—her contract, if you prefer, both
implied and expressed—that he would share his income with her. It
simply is not fair to change the rules in the last quarter of the game,
after she has fulfilled her share of the bargain.

CONCLUSION

One of the perplexing themes of this chapter is the way in which the
California law is being applied so that standards of "equality" are
being used to further disadvantage the disadvantaged. Equal treatment
for men and women in divorce has been interpreted to mean, in practice,
that divorced women in California are typically left alone to shoulder
the economic burdens they incurred because of their roles and responsi-

bilities in marriage. In contrast, the responses of the English experts reflect an awareness of economic reality that seems to have been obscured in California's rush to legislate equal treatment for men and women.

What was merely obscured in the law has been almost lost in the courts. The abiding lesson of the California experience is this: to grant equal rights in the absence of equal opportunity is to strengthen the strong and weaken the weak.

When the California legislature established new standards of awarding alimony, it did so in recognition of the fact that these rules were not appropriate in all cases, and it carefully specified that older women, mothers, and women in transition were to be exempted. Nevertheless, in practice the new standards for alimony seem to be applied to all women, irrespective of their age, custodial responsibilities, and life circumstances. As a result thousands of women are *unjustly* subjected to hardship.

These hardships are not confined to California. Consider the report of two attorneys in New York State, who analyzed alimony awards in that state.[34] Harriet Cohen and Adria Hillman concluded that the awards reflected a "prevalent and unfounded judicial assumption that women who have devoted much of their adult lives to the marriage partnership can quickly and readily relocate from the marital home . . . and can find suitable paid employment." They report that:

> After marriages of at least fifteen years wives received no or short-term maintenance after long-term marriages even though their future earning capacities were dubious at best. The decisions evince a judicial preconception that wives, whose own career opportunities were sacrificed and lost as part of a tacit or express marital partnership plan, can easily be recycled into the paid marketplace. The preconception is not grounded in fact. . . . With rare exceptions, the decisions handed down by the Appellate Divisions and the Court of Appeals exacerbated, rather than alleviated, the problems.[35]

Along the same lines Judge Betty Barteau of Indianapolis reports that the situation is even worse in Indiana where there is no alimony, just limited maintenance for a period of two years.[36] She describes the situation as a tragedy:

> [The provisions for maintenance are] pretty drastic. In no-fault if a husband wants a divorce, he gets it. If there aren't any minor children and she's a forty-five-year-old empty-nester who has accumulated no property, she ends up with nothing. It's a tragedy.[37]

Underlying the new rules for alimony—rules that have now been adopted throughout the United States—is an altered vision of the meaning of marriage and marital commitments. By limiting or severing the husband's financial responsibility to support his former wife, the legal system is redefining the traditional legal assumption of lifelong commitment in favor of the assumption that marriage—and marital commitments—are voluntary and temporary. In addition, the law is undermining traditional notions of sharing and partnership by leaving the wife to fend for herself after divorce.

CHAPTER 8

Child Custody
From Maternal Preference to Joint Custody?[1]

MORE THAN TWO MILLION CHILDREN are involved in a parental divorce in the United States each year.[2] Legal decisions about the care, custody, and support of these children have profound and far-reaching effects. These decisions not only influence the life chances and emotional experiences of children after divorce; they also play a critical role in structuring the social and economic well-being of their parents.

The total number of children affected by divorce has more than tripled since 1960. The rise is impressive because it cannot be attributed to an increase in the total number of children in the United States. (Between 1970 and 1980, the total number of children actually declined.) It is a direct result of the rising divorce rate.[3] In fact, it is now projected that *more than half of all the children in the United States* will experience a parental divorce or dissolution before they reach age eighteen.[4]*

---

* Arthur Norton of the U.S. Census Bureau estimated that 59 percent of all children born in the United States in 1983 are likely to live in a single parent family before they are eighteen,[5] while Sandra Hofferth of the National Institute of Child Health and Human Development projects that *two-thirds* of the children born in wedlock in 1980 will experience the disruption of their parents' marriage by age 17.[6] If we add the percentage of children born out of wedlock (18.4 percent of the births in 1980) to Hofferth's projection, it is evident that the census projection is very low, and that a sizable majority of American children will not spend their childhood with both natural parents. Since the

The large number of children affected by divorce has focused increased attention on child custody decisions. The legal rules for determining which parent should have custody of minor children after divorce have evolved from a traditional father's right, based on a view of children as part of their father's property, to a judicially constructed preference for the mother to retain custody of children of "tender years," to a sex-neutral rule that based custody on the child's "best interest," to increased emphasis on shared parenting after divorce and the adoption of new laws that allow or mandate joint custody.

Both the legal rules for determining custody and the social norms for defining "what is best" for children are in a state of flux. They are being rethought and revised in an emotionally laden arena in which there are strong positions but little empirical evidence about what is best for most—or even some—children at divorce. (Nor do we know what arrangements are best for most parents.)

In addition, the trend towards joint custody is still an open question. On the one hand, if we were to measure change by the rapid and widespread proliferation of joint custody laws, we might well conclude that a major social revolution is under way. By 1985, thirty states have adopted some form of joint custody legislation to encourage fathers to share postdivorce parenting.[8]

On the other hand, if we were to measure change by the actual arrangements that most divorced mothers and fathers make for the care and custody of their children, we would receive a very different impression. This investigation reveals that most mothers remain the primary caretakers and custodians of their children after divorce, that most fathers do not want to be involved in equal or shared parenting, and that the legal revolution has had relatively little impact on the day-to-day lives of most children after divorce.

Neither of these portraits is entirely correct. The impression of rapid change given by alterations in the law ignores the deep reservoir of social assumptions about the appropriateness of mother custody in our society. It also neglects the current social reality of child care arrangements in most American families: mothers typically assume the day-to-day responsibility for their children's needs, and since they have always been the primary parent, it is natural for both the husband and the wife to assume that the children will be better off living with

---

out-of-wedlock births are not relevant to the divorce situation, the projected percentage of children who will experience a parental divorce is, according to Hofferth, close to 66 percent.[7]

their mother after divorce. Simply put, the recent changes in the law have not greatly affected these continuing social realities.

However, it would be equally inaccurate to conclude that changes in the law have had no effect. The legal revolution in custody law has had a major impact on contested custody cases, which account for about 10 percent of the divorces involving children. When parents disagree about what is best for their children, the law assumes pivotal importance. It can empower one party and make it more costly (or impossible) for the other party to obtain custody.

For example, the traditional maternal preference custody laws enabled women usually to obtain custody when they wanted it. Most of the recent reforms have made custody determinations sex-neutral and have undermined the preference that mothers traditionally enjoyed. Some of these new laws have gone further and reversed the bargaining positions of the sexes by giving fathers the *de facto* power to determine the nature of the custodial arrangements. (This is a result of a complex set of processes discussed later in this chapter.) These legal presumptions are important when parents disagree because they influence the bargaining power of each party in the negotiations and, if the case is contested, determine its outcome in court.

The law may also affect the outcome of less conflicted cases in which couples are simply unsure about what form of custody would be best for them and their children. If, for example, their attorneys tell them that joint custody is the preferred legal option, and if they know they will have to justify any other arrangement in court, they are more likely to agree to joint custody. Thus, laws that make joint custody *preferred* are more coercive than those that make it *elective* because they put the burden of proof on couples (and judges) to justify any other arrangement.

One ironic result of California's joint custody preference, which creates such pressures, is that more arrangements are called "joint custody" even though the children continue to reside with their mothers. In other states, where joint custody is one of several legal options that are regarded as equally desirable, fewer couples have nominal "joint custody" when the term does not really apply. Thus, other states are likely to report a lower percentage of joint custody awards—but this may not represent any real difference in actual custodial arrangements.

Thus a focus on changes in the law may not provide a true index of custody arrangements because it ignores the *de facto* arrangements and mother custody preferences of most divorcing couples. However, a focus on the actual circumstances of these average couples ignores the minority of couples for whom legal rules are influential if not determinative.

SUMMARY OF THE LEGAL CHANGES IN CALIFORNIA

Between 1970 and 1985, there were three changes in California's custody law. Before 1970, California, like most states, relied on a traditional maternal preference in making child custody awards. The presumption favoring the mother was weakened by the no-fault divorce law in 1970 and was replaced by a sex-neutral "best interest of the child" standard in 1973. The custody laws were again changed in 1980, when California became the first state to adopt a joint custody preference.

Underlying these changes are three fundamental shifts in the legal framework for making custodial decisions. First, the law has moved from an emphasis on parental preferences to an emphasis on the child's welfare.[9] The doctrines of "paternal rights" and "maternal preferences" have given way to statutes that place the child's best interests first.* Second, the law has shifted from rules that help judges choose *one* parent as the child's postdivorce custodian, to rules that try to maintain the child's ties to both parents. Finally, the law has shifted the role that judges and courts play in determining custody awards. Instead of appearing in court and having a judge hear the evidence about each parent's fitness, couples are now encouraged to work out their custody arrangements by themselves or with the assistance of court affiliated mediators and counselors. This increased reliance on "private ordering" has made judicial determinations the last resort.

Let us first consider the legal evolution of custody rules and then look at their effect on the pattern of custody awards.

The Tradition of Maternal Preference

The common law of England recognized the father, not the mother, as the natural guardian of the couple's children: he controlled their

---

* Attorney Joanne Schulman suggests that the current interest in joint custody is couched in terms of the child's interest, but it is really a move back to a parents' rights approach because it aims at giving both parents what they want—i.e., a share of the child—even though the arrangement may not be best for the child. Thus she asserts that "one of the major rationales for joint custody is to give the father a legal status and to make him feel better in the hope that he will stay more involved in the child's life."[10]

education and religious training and had the primary right to his children's services. In return, he was liable for their support and maintenance.[11] Children were viewed as the property of their fathers, so if the parents separated, the father of a legitimate child, not the mother, had the right to and responsibility for child custody.[12] Blackstone, the authority on the English common law, stated the rule: the father had a natural right to the custody of his children. The mother was not entitled to have any control over them; she was entitled only to their reverence and respect.[13]

In the widely cited 1804 case of *King v. De Manneville,* for example, the English Lord Ellenborough ordered a nursing infant returned to its French father, despite the British antagonism toward the French, and despite the fact that the father's cruelty had driven the mother and children from his home, because the father was "entitled by law to custody of his child."[14]

"The common law preference of the father," as attorneys Henry Foster and Doris Freed note, "disintegrated with the advent of the industrial revolution."[15] As fathers moved off the farm into wage labor in factories and offices, women's maternal instincts were "discovered," and mothers became increasingly associated with child care. In 1839 the British Parliament modified the fathers' absolute right to custody by granting the mother the right to be awarded custody of children who were less than seven years old.[16] Thus, the "tender years" presumption in favor of the mother—what we refer to as the traditional presumption—was itself an innovation when it was first introduced into law.[17]*

American courts in the nineteenth century were less likely to apply absolute rules: they were more likely to look at the circumstances and facts of the particular case and to rely on fault as evidence of parental fitness.[19] Since social convention customarily led to the wife's filing for and being awarded the divorce as the "innocent party," the courts' reliance on fault as evidence of parental unfitness led to a larger proportion of maternal custody awards.[20]**

The twentieth century brought the establishment of a new legal

* Although the tender years presumption is considered a maternal presumption, it is important to note that it was restricted to young children. Attorney Nancy Polikoff points out that older children, especially boys in need of education and training, were still considered better off with their fathers.[18]

** This is not to suggest that the fault doctrine always worked in women's favor. If a woman was an "ideal mother" she was favored, but women who violated conventional norms and "didn't behave as proper wives or mothers" could be punished by being denied custody as well as alimony and property.[21]

presumption in the United States—one that *expressly* preferred mothers as the custodians of their children after divorce, particularly if the children were young.[22] This new "legal tradition" was established primarily through case law—that is, by judicial interpretation—rather than by "black letter law" (by statute). While most statutes continued to put the husband on an equal footing with the wife, and instructed the courts to award custody in the best interests of the child, the judicial interpretation of these statutes held that it was in the child's best interests not to be separated from the mother unless the mother was shown to be unfit.[23]

Thus the statutory standards of "the child's best interest" and "parental fitness" evolved into a judicially constructed maternal presumption because it was assumed that the love and nurturance of a fit mother served both the child's and society's best interest. As a 1942 California court stated, the preference for the mother is "not open to question, and indeed it is universally recognized that the mother is the natural custodian of her young. This view proceeds on the well-known fact that there is no satisfactory substitute for a mother's love."[24]

Eventually, the belief that the mother was the natural and proper custodian of her children became so widely accepted that it was rarely discussed and even more rarely challenged. The few rationales that were offered for the maternal preference had the ring of divine right theory.[25] For example, an Idaho court concluded that the preference for the mother "needs no argument to support it because it arises out of the very nature and instincts of motherhood; nature had ordained it."[26] Similarly, a 1958 New Jersey decision referred to the preference as the result of an "inexorable natural force," and a 1972 Maryland decision called it a "primordial" maternal tie."[27] Other courts justified the maternal presumption because it was grounded in "the wisdom of the ages," as a 1973 Pennsylvania appellate court phrased it.[28]

The result was a consistent pattern of decisions that both justified and further reinforced the maternal presumption. This judicially constructed preference appears to have operated as effectively as a statutory directive in upholding the mother's right to the postdivorce custody of her children.

The wisdom of using a maternal presumption in custody cases was also supported by psychologists and child development specialists who emphasized the unique relationship between an infant and its mother.[29] Social science dogma asserted that women were uniquely suited, biologically and psychologically, for the task of rearing children; that an inherent nurturing ability disposed them to be more interested in and able to care for children than men; and that "young children needed a mother in order to develop optimally."[30] For example, the noted psychologist Bruno Bettelheim cautioned against the unnaturalness of fathers raising children—even in cooperation with the mother.[31]

Even those who questioned the social science evidence considered the maternal presumption wise because it avoided the "social costs" of contested cases. For example, in 1968, to assist the drafters of the Uniform Marriage and Divorce Act, attorney Robert Levy and psychologist Phoebe Ellsworth undertook an exhaustive review of the social science research on divorce, broken homes, maternal deprivation, and father absence to learn "what social scientists have discovered about custodial arrangements and their consequences."[32] They found that the research did not lead to any clear conclusions. However, they nevertheless recommended that a maternal presumption be included in the Uniform Marriage and Divorce Act to discourage harmful custody contests:

> Since wives will, under most circumstances, be awarded custody regardless of the statutory standard, and since it seems wise to discourage traumatic custody contests whenever it is possible to do so, the [Uniform Marriage and Divorce] act should discourage those few husbands who might wish to contest by establishing a presumption . . . that the mother is the appropriate custodian—at least for young children, and probably for children of any age. . . . It may well be true that because of the presumption some fathers who would be better custodians than their wives will either fail to seek custody or will be denied custody following a contest, but that disadvantage has a lower "social cost" than the disadvantages of any alternative statutory formulation—more contested cases (with the trauma that contests seem to produce), more risk of a custody award to a father who will be only marginally better than the mother or even much worse.[33]

Thus, whether it was supported by a belief in the mother's inherent nurturing ability, or by an assumption that mother custody was in the best interests of the child, or because it reduced the social costs of contested custody cases, the legal presumption in favor of the mother flourished in U.S. courts into the 1970s.[34]

As recently as 1978, Foster and Freed concluded that the "tender years" doctrine remained "gospel" in fourteen states, and in at least twelve other states there was still a preference for a "fit" mother, other things being equal.[35] Surprisingly, they found that the "tender years" doctrine remained "alive and well" in eight states that had passed equal rights amendments.[36] Courts in these states reasoned that the child's welfare is ordinarily best served by being with the mother.

The Maternal Preference in Practice

When we turn from the law on the books to the law in action, we find strong evidence of a similar preference for the mother as the postdivorce custodian of minor children. Although there has never been a nationwide study of custody awards, and although the historical data are sparse, every study of divorce decrees reveals a predominance of mother custody awards. A review of the studies of child custody awards in individual states and cities between 1875 and 1973 shows that mothers were typically awarded custody of their children after divorce in every jurisdiction.[37] In chronological order of the research, mothers were awarded custody of their children in 76 to 80 percent of the divorces in Hennepin County, Minnesota, between 1875 and 1939; in 81 to 87 percent of the cases in Ohio between 1900 and 1949; in 85 percent of the cases in New Haven County, Connecticut, between 1919 and 1932; in 83 to 87 percent of Kansas divorces between 1927 and 1939; in 68 percent of Maryland cases in 1929; in 86 percent of the Cook County, Illinois, divorces between 1945 and 1948; in 84 percent of Missouri cases in 1948 and 1955; in 95 percent of Michigan divorces in 1948; in 74 percent of New Jersey cases in 1949; in 82 percent of Tennessee divorces in 1949; in 74 percent of the cases in Tippecanoe County, Indiana, in 1956; in 87 percent of the cases in Maine in 1960, and in over 90 percent of the cases in Missouri in 1968 and 1973.[38]

While a fascinating story probably lies behind the variation from state to state and the fluctuations over time, it is nevertheless evident that the great majority of children have been entrusted to the custody of their mothers over the past century.* On the average, mothers have been awarded custody in close to 85 percent of the divorce cases in which children were involved. Fathers were typically awarded custody in about 10 percent of the cases while the remaining awards were to relatives, and/or for shared custody.

The high percentage of mother custody awards does not mean that courts were actively making decisions that favored the mother. Since our culture defines the mother as the appropriate custodian of minor children, and since most parental caretakers during the ongoing marriage were mothers, most divorcing couples simply took these arrangements for granted. Both parents assumed that children were the mother's responsibility. Few couples thought about or questioned the appropriateness of this assumption because it reflected the *de facto*

---

* It is, of course, possible that the mother was awarded custody of young children at divorce but was then required to "return" them to the father when the children, especially boys, were older so that they could be prepared for occupations and "the world."[39]

division of responsibilities during most marriages. So most children stayed with their mother when the couple separated and were therefore living with her at the time of the divorce. These *de facto* arrangements were later translated into custody awards by the courts.

THE CALIFORNIA EXPERIENCE

The traditional legal pattern in California reflected maternal custody norms in both "the law on the books" and "the law in action." The traditional law on the books included a mother preference for young children: "other things being equal, custody should be given to the mother if the child is of tender years."[40] Although the presumption applied only to young children, since 66 percent of the divorced families with children (in the 1968 sample) had at least one child under the age of six, it affected a significant majority of all divorced families with children.

The California law in action similarly reflected a maternal preference. Historian Elaine May examined 500 divorce cases from the Los Angeles County archives in 1919 and found that custody was awarded to wives in 84 percent of the cases.[41] Fathers were awarded custody in 13 percent of the cases, while the remaining 2 percent were awarded to third parties or divided.

Almost fifty years later, in 1968, we found a similar pattern in the court records in Los Angeles County: at that time California still had a tender years rule and mothers were awarded sole physical custody of their children in 88 percent of the cases. Fathers were awarded custody in 9 percent. The remaining 3 percent of the awards were for joint or divided custody or awards to third parties. Thus, for at least half a century, the mother was clearly preferred as the custodial parent in California, as in other states.

THE IMPACT OF NO-FAULT ON CUSTODY

The first change in the legal rules governing custody in California occurred in 1970, with the passage of the no-fault divorce law. Although the no-fault law did not change the rules for custody because it eliminated fault from all other aspects of the divorce process, *it left custody as the only sphere in which fault was still relevant.* As the law stated, "evidence of specific acts of misconduct shall be improper and inadmissible, except where child custody is in issue and such evidence is relevant."[42]

For example, allegations of a wife's promiscuity or adultery, which would be considered irrelevant in a divorce action, could be discussed in court if her fitness as the child's custodian was at issue.[43] Similarly, a husband's physical abuse of his children would normally have no bearing on a no-fault divorce.[*] But it could be used as evidence to deny his request for custody or to counter his claim of his wife's unfitness.

Although the legislature sought to restrict allegations of fault to specific acts of misconduct bearing directly on the custodial competence of the parent (as the *Assembly Journal* states, "It is intended that the court be very strict in exercising its discretion to admit evidence . . ."[47]), there was concern that the loophole would be used by vindictive spouses seeking a forum to air their grievances. Angry husbands and wives might raise child custody claims to embarrass or harass an ex-spouse or simply to vent their anger and feelings of betrayal.[48]

A second concern was that the threat of a custody suit might be used in negotiations over property or support awards. For example, a husband could claim that he wanted custody when his real aim was to pressure his wife to forgo support or accept a smaller share of property. One attorney frankly acknowledged this tactic and discussed the standard "form letter" used for such purposes:

> I could write the blackmail letter by heart (although I haven't written one in a long time), but this is how it goes: "Dear Mrs. Jones's lawyer, I received the proposal you offered on behalf of your client, and my client is willing to agree to everything. Although we would prefer to have custody of the children, he realizes it is probably not in the best interest of the children to contest custody. However, my client is not interested in paying alimony, and if your client is willing to waive alimony, we would be willing to accept the proposal which you suggest; if not, then all the issues will have to be litigated."

Most attorneys we interviewed said they dismissed such threats as "hot air" and "posturing," and predicted that they did not succeed.[**]

---

[*] Many courts in the United States do not consider evidence of spouse abuse—in contrast to child abuse—as relevant to a determination of custody.[44] Joanne Schulmann, staff attorney for the National Center on Women in Family Law, who has chronicled state laws in this area, reports that only a few states have laws that require judges to consider wife abuse in custodial decisions.[45] The state of Florida, however, recently ammended its law to provide that "the court shall consider evidence of spousal abuse as evidence of detriment to the child."[46]

[**] Their answers might well be different today under California's joint custody law, which is discussed later in this chapter, pp. 250–260.

As one attorney reported:

> In one case, the husband said he was going to fight for custody of the kids, so I called his bluff and said, "Okay, take the kids." Boy did he cave in! That scared the hell out of him.

Another attorney said:

> In the typical case, it becomes obvious to any sensible person whether the custody challenge is a viable one. Can you imagine me fooling around saying, "I am going to take the kid"? What we say to each other is, "C'mon, you know you wouldn't let him near the kid with a ten-foot pole."

While attorneys may dismiss these threats, they are often taken seriously by the divorced women we interviewed and can have a chilling effect on the financial claims of mothers who seriously fear they may lose custody. (The effects of custody threats on financial negotiations are discussed in Chapter 9, pp. 310–318.)

At the same time that the new law opened the door to spurious custody suits, it also opened the door to fathers who genuinely wanted to gain custody of their children. In this regard, the passage of the no-fault divorce law coincided with the first stages of the fathers' rights movement and reflected, in part, men's increased interest in parenting both during marriage and after divorce.[49]

The No-Fault Law in Practice

It was assumed that more fathers would *request* custody under no-fault: some would be genuinely interested in gaining custody; others would feel morally wronged or vindictive enough to use custody as a means of intimidating or harassing their ex-wives; and still others would ask for custody as a route to economic gain, especially if they thought that their ex-wives would be willing to take less property or support in order to avoid a custody fight.

These predictions are *not* supported by our empirical results. The no-fault divorce law, by itself, had little impact. Our analysis of custody requests and awards from the 1972 court records, two years after the no-fault law went into effect, show no change in the percentage of fathers who requested custody, or in the percentage of fathers who were awarded custody.

PHYSICAL CUSTODY

Table 18 shows that the no-fault law had no consistent or significant impact on *requests* for physical custody. After no-fault divorce

TABLE 18

Fathers' Requests for Physical Custody
Before and After No-fault Law

	SAN FRANCISCO		LOS ANGELES	
	Before No-fault (1968) (n = 276)*	After No-fault (1972) (n = 241)	Before No-fault (1968) (n = 310)	After No-fault (1972) (n = 245)
Mother (sole physical custody)	85.9%	84.2%	79.7%	86.9%
Father (sole physical custody)	10.5	14.1	18.4	11.1
Children split	0.0	.4	1.3	1.2
Joint physical custody	1.1	.8	.3	.4
Other	2.5	.4	.3	.4
Total	100.0%	99.9%	100.0%	100.0%
Total father's requests (sole, split, and joint)	11.6%	15.3%	20.0%	12.7%

* n refers to the number of families with minor children at the time of the divorce in each sample of approximately 500 divorce cases.

This table is based on the divorcing couples with minor children in random samples of court records, Los Angeles and San Francisco Counties, California, 1968 and 1972.

was instituted in 1970, the percentage of husbands who requested sole physical custody of their children declined in Los Angeles and rose slightly in San Francisco.[50] The percentages of husbands who requested split custody (i.e., that one or some children be awarded to the husband and others to the wife) or requested joint custody (i.e., that physical custody be shared by the husband and wife) also show no significant changes between 1968 and 1972.

Awards to fathers were similarly unaffected by the 1970 no-fault law. Table 19 shows that the percentage of fathers who were awarded sole physical custody declined slightly in Los Angeles between 1968 and 1972, and rose slightly in San Francisco.

Nor was there any significant difference in the *success rate* of fathers who requested physical custody. In Los Angeles 35 percent of the fathers who requested physical custody received it in 1968, as did 37 percent of those who requested it in 1972.*

In summary, the data in Tables 18 and 19 indicate that the no-

* Note that some husbands who did not officially "request" custody (on the divorce petition or response) were awarded it nevertheless. This seemingly improbable situation occurs when there is a private agreement between the parties. If the wife files for a divorce, and stipulates that custody be awarded to the husband, and if he does not participate in the formal legal process, he has not formally requested custody.

TABLE 19

Physical Custody Awards Before and After No-fault Law

	SAN FRANCISCO		LOS ANGELES	
	Before No-fault (1968) $(n = 267)^*$	*After No-fault (1972)* $(n = 228)$	*Before No-fault (1968)* $(n = 310)$	*After No-fault (1972)* $(n = 245)$
Mother (sole physical custody)	88.4%	84.6%	87.7%	88.8%
Father (sole physical custody)	8.6	9.6	9.4	5.8
Children split	1.1	1.8	2.3	2.9
Joint physical custody	.4	2.2	0.0	.8
Other	1.5	1.8	.6	1.7
Total	100.0%	100.0%	100.0%	100.0%
Total to father or partially to father (sole, split, and joint)	10.1%	13.6%	11.7%	9.5%

* refers to the number of cases on which the percentages are based.

This table is based on the divorcing couples with minor children in random samples of court records, Los Angeles and San Francisco Counties, California, 1968 and 1972.

fault law did not lead to an increase in frivolous or punitive custody claims by fathers. While it is difficult to distinguish tactical claims from genuine requests for custody in court records, the fact that there was no change in the percentage of fathers' requests and awards suggests that the no-fault law did not encourage *additional* custody claims that were designed to raise fault-based allegations.

LEGAL CUSTODY

Thus far we have focused on physical custody decisions, which designate the parent with whom the child will live. The court, however, also awards *legal* custody to one or both parents, and it may differ from the physical custody award. The child's legal custodian is responsible for the education and welfare of a child under eighteen; he or she may control the religion the child is or is not taught, and has the power to authorize medical care for the child.[51]

Table 20 shows that the 1970 no-fault law had no consistent or statistically significant effect on legal custody awards: the percentage of husbands receiving legal custody declined slightly between 1968 and 1972 in Los Angeles, and rose slightly in San Francisco.

One puzzling finding is the high rate of joint legal custody awards in San Francisco in both 1968 (10 percent) and 1972 (16 percent, as

TABLE 20

Legal Custody Awards Before and After No-fault Law

	SAN FRANCISCO		LOS ANGELES	
	Before No-fault (1968) (n = 263)*	After No-fault (1972) (n = 221)	Before No-fault (1968) (n = 310)	After No-fault (1972) (n = 245)
Mother (sole legal custody)	80.6%	72.4%	87.7%	87.6%
Father (sole legal custody)	6.8	8.1	8.4	5.4
Children split	1.5	.9	2.3	2.9
Joint legal custody	10.3	16.3	1.0	2.9
Other	.8	2.3	.6	1.2
Total	100.0%	100.0%	100.0%	100.0%
Total to father or partially to father (sole, split, and joint)	18.6%	25.3%	11.8%	11.2%

* n refers to the number of cases on which the percentages were based.

This table is based on the divorcing couples with minor children in random samples of court records, Los Angeles and San Francisco Counties, California, 1968 and 1972.

compared with the rates in Los Angeles in the same years (1 percent and 3 percent respectively). In checking the court dockets we found that in both years only 2 percent of the fathers requested joint legal custody in San Francisco, the same percentage as Los Angeles fathers. Thus the higher percentage of joint legal custody awards in San Francisco is not generated by husbands' requests. It must be initiated by judges: San Francisco judges (or at least a few of them) obviously favored joint legal custody awards and ordered them for couples who had not requested it. This pattern was evident long before the current joint custody law.

In summary, contrary to the prediction of more custody claims and disputes following the no-fault divorce law, there were no significant increases in fathers' requests for physical or legal custody, or in awards of physical or legal custody to fathers.

VISITATION ORDERS

The traditional formula for parenting after divorce is to award legal and physical custody of the children to one parent, and visitation rights to the other. Prior statutory law did not spell out the standards for establishing visitation rights.[52] Consequently, the courts developed standards on a case-by-case basis. The no-fault law, however, attempted to make these vague standards explicit by providing for "reasonable" visitation rights to be awarded to the noncustodial parent except where detrimental to the child's best interests.[53]

Over 90 percent of the visitation orders are for "reasonable" visitation, which still leaves the precise arrangements to the parents to work out. Only 5 percent of the interlocutory decrees either spell out the visitation order in greater detail, or make reference to a marital agreement that specifies the particular dates and times at which visitation is permitted. While some of these agreements include elaborate specifications (for birthdays, Christmas, Chanukah, alternate Saturdays and Sundays, particular afternoons, summer vacations, and other times), they are not the norm.

Disputes over visitation may provide an arena for a continuous battle between the spouses that can persist long after the divorce is finalized. It is easy for parents to disagree about whether the time, location, activities, or parental behavior during visitation has a detrimental effect on the child.[54]

As William Goode observed, ". . . the relationship with children contains one of the most important weapons in the conflict of wills between ex-spouses: both during the divorce conflict and afterwards. This exploitation of the parent/child relationship may, of course, be unconscious, since few parents can admit that they use their children as punitive instruments. Our child centered values argue rather strongly against any such open usage."[55]

It is easy to see how two parents with complex schedules and competing priorities can find themselves in conflict about visitation arrangements: women may find it easier to restrict the husbands' visits, and fathers may find it easier to skip a planned visit than to constantly argue about the plans. Further, a parent may use visitation and the children to get at, or find out about, the other spouse.[56]

Our review of court records indicated many disputes over visitation. Perhaps what is most noticeable is the wide variety of fault-based allegations that were made: charges that physical violence was used against the children, or against the former spouse in the children's presence; claims that abusive language, liquor, or drugs were used in the children's presence; allegations of sexual misconduct (by the father or by the mother's male companions) toward the children; assertions that the children were taken to dangerous or inappropriate places during visits; and so forth.

Nevertheless, visitation privileges were almost never denied or revoked by the court. In fact, both before and after no-fault, fewer than 1 percent of the Los Angeles fathers were legally forbidden to see their children. This was surprising—especially when there were allegations that a father had battered or sexually molested the children. Apparently the courts preferred to set conditions on the exercise of visitation rights rather than to terminate them. About 20 percent of the cases in both 1968 and 1972 included such restrictions. They required that the father notify his ex-wife before visiting the children, or that he confine his visits to the children's home (or, conversely, that he be required to take them to another place), or that he restrict his visitation to times when he is not under the influence of alcohol or drugs.

In the interview sample less than 25 percent of the parents complained about visitation problems. There was no significant difference in the percentage of custodial and noncustodial parents with such complaints. Noncustodial fathers were more likely to complain of mothers making access to the children difficult and inconvenient, or denying them access altogether. Custodial mothers were more likely to complain about fathers' erratic schedules, or changes of plans, or their behavior during visitation (being drunk or on drugs, threats of physical abuse, etc.).

But custodial mothers seemed even more concerned about fathers who *failed* to visit their children. In fact, their spontaneous comments suggest that *they worry most about their children feeling neglected or abandoned by fathers who do not call or see them regularly.*

Since we did not ask mothers a direct question, it is impossible to report the percentage who responded this way, but there were numerous spontaneous comments from mothers who tried to persuade (or beg) the father to pay more attention to and spend more time with his children. Complaints about fathers who failed to call, or missed an important baseball game or school play, or forgot a birthday, or cancelled a trip the children had been anticipating for months, or who simply stopped visiting their children, were reported with great emotional anguish.

In this regard, it is notable that experts have begun to debate whether visitation is a right for the noncustodial spouse to exercise or an *obligation* that must be fulfilled except under unusual circumstances. For example, some feminists who have taken up the claims of fathers' rights groups argue that if the father is so important for the child's development, he should not be allowed the option of *not* visiting them. They propose that visitation be viewed as a *child's right* rather than as a matter of parental choice, and suggest that courts apply some form of negative sanctions to fathers who consistently fail to visit their children.[57]

Increased awareness of the detrimental effects of breaking the child's ties with his or her family has led a number of states to protect grandparent visitation after divorce.[58] These grandparent visitation statutes view "the child's continuing access to grandparents . . . as a right of the child in the child's best interests."[59]

REPEAL OF THE MATERNAL PRESUMPTION: TOWARDS THE BEST INTEREST OF THE CHILD

The second major change in the California custody law occurred in 1973, when the traditional mother preference was replaced by the best interest standard. Judges were now instructed to award custody to either parent "according to the best interests of the child."[60] The law was changed in large part as a result of the pressure from potential custodial fathers who complained that the sex bias in the old law prevented men from even trying to gain custody. The fathers' rights groups in California welcomed the 1973 law as the beginning of a new era of "equal rights for fathers."[61]

At the same time, expectations about women's roles were changing. The women's movement encouraged women to abandon their traditional assumptions about exclusive motherhood and to devote themselves to careers as well as—or instead of—children. These ideas helped to persuade at least some women that they should not accept sole responsibility for their children after divorce.[62] The women's movement also supported a woman's right to choose not to have custody of her children after divorce without feeling guilty or deviant.[63] Thus, quite apart from the custody law itself, the social climate was changing: both mothers and fathers were being encouraged to allow fathers to assume greater parental responsibility after divorce.[64]

Although journalistic predictions of a widespread increase in father custody following the 1973 law seemed exaggerated,[65] one would have expected at least a modest rise in fathers' custody requests and awards.

Once again, however, the change in the law appears to have had no effect on the patterns of custody requests and awards. The relative proportions of mothers and fathers who were awarded custody of their

children remained virtually the same four years after the mother preference was eliminated. Table 21 indicates that there was no significant
increase in the percentage of fathers who were awarded physical custody of their children between 1972 and 1977. In both years, Los Angeles
fathers were awarded sole physical custody in about 6 percent of the
final decrees, while mothers were awarded sole physical custody in
close to 90 percent of the final decrees.

The same pattern is evident in legal custody awards (not shown).
Fathers were awarded sole legal custody in 5.4 percent of the 1972
cases and in 6.1 percent of the 1977 cases in Los Angeles County. In
both years, they were awarded joint legal custody in less than 3 percent
of the cases while mothers were awarded legal custody in about 88
percent of the cases. What is striking about these statistics is the stead-
fast persistence of mother custody awards despite the change in the
law.

The 1977 data do reflect two small and statistically insignificant
changes that are nevertheless worthy of note. First, although the percentages are tiny, there does appear to be a slight increase in joint
physical custody awards in Los Angeles (from 0 percent of the 1968
cases, to less than 1 percent of the 1972 cases, to 2 percent of the

TABLE 21

Physical Custody Awards
Before and After Repeal of the Maternal Presumption

	MATERNAL PREFERENCE (1972) (n = 245)*	BEST INTEREST OF CHILD (1977) (n = 246)
Mother (sole physical custody)	88.8%	90.2%
Father (sole physical custody)	5.8	6.1
Children split	2.9	1.6
Joint physical custody	.8	2.0
Other	1.7	0.0
Total	100.0%	99.9%
Total to father or partially to father (sole, split, and joint)	9.5%	9.7%

* refers to the number of cases on which the percentages were based.

This table is based on the divorcing couples with minor children in random
samples of court records, Los Angeles County, California, 1972 and 1977.

1977 cases), indicating that a very small but growing number of couples are willing to share the day-to-day tasks of raising their children. (This change is too small to be statistically significant.)

A second notable but statistically insignificant change is in the "success rate" of fathers who ask for custody, as shown in Table 22. Although the number of fathers requesting custody is small, among the small number of fathers who requested physical custody, 35 percent were awarded it in 1968, 37 percent in 1972, and 63 percent in 1977. Similarly, the success rate of fathers who requested legal custody rose from 33 percent in 1968, to 35 percent in 1972, to 63 percent in 1977. Thus, by 1977, a surprisingly large proportion—close to two-thirds—of the fathers who requested custody were awarded it.

The cases in which the father obtained custody had several notable characteristics: the fathers who requested and were awarded custody tended to be slightly older, better educated, and have a higher occupational status than most divorcing men.[66] The fathers who asked for custody were also much more likely to be petitioners—that is, they had taken the initiative in the divorce. Furthermore, there was less likelihood of a response being filed in cases in which the father asked for custody, suggesting a *de facto* agreement on the part of the wife.[67] Finally, most cases in which the father was awarded custody did not go to trial, once more indicating an agreement between the two parties.[68]

In fact, the single most important factor in explaining paternal custody awards was the presence of an "agreement" between the parties. More than half of the cases in which the father was awarded custody contained evidence of such an "agreement." Most of these were explicit stipulations, or written agreements, but in some the moth-

TABLE 22

Success Rates of Fathers Who Asked
for Sole Custody

	PHYSICAL CUSTODY	LEGAL CUSTODY
1968	35% (n = 57)	33% (n = 60)
1972	37 (n = 27)	35 (n = 26)
1977	63 (n = 16)	63 (n = 16)

This table is based on the divorcing couples with minor children in random samples of court records, Los Angeles County, California, 1968, 1972, and 1977.

er's acquiescence was suggested by the fact that she had moved out of the family home, leaving the children with the father; or by the fact that she did not participate in the divorce proceedings at all. Thus the husband is most likely to get custody when he takes an active role in initiating the action or when he has his wife's "agreement."

One obvious question about these data concerns the nature of these "agreements." Since we did not interview the men and women involved, we do not know how these agreements were reached. We do know, however, that some of the women in our interview sample who said that they had "agreed" to paternal custody arrangements, had been pressured into these agreements.

For example, one of the women we interviewed had "agreed" to her husband's having custody of her son after months of "incredible harassment including his threats to get the children, no matter what, even if he had to kill me to do it."

Another woman was threatened with an endless legal battle that her husband said "would ruin my reputation and use up every penny I had." Others told of more subtle financial pressures. As one woman said:

> He said if you really loved your children you'd want them to have the best—and that's what they'll have with me. . . . and what will they have with you? The privilege of living in some flea bag graduate student housing?

Although some of these ploys, like the one above, were not successful, others were, and it is impossible to distinguish such agreements from truly voluntary agreements in data from court dockets.

In the 1977 sample of Los Angeles court dockets, only fifteen custody cases were fully contested and went to trial. In this small subsample of cases decided by a judge, custody was awarded to the husband in five cases (33 percent) and to the wife in the remaining ten cases (67 percent). These statistics are remarkably similar to data compiled by the Legal Aid Society in Alameda County, in the San Francisco Bay Area of northern California. Of the thirteen contested custody trials in 1979, there were eight awards (62 percent) to mothers and five (38 percent) to fathers.[69]

It may be significant that men are more successful in obtaining custody in negotiated settlements than in court (63 percent in negotiations versus 33 percent in the Los Angeles trials). If the men who seek custody are as determined as the men who refused to pay alimony, similar structural patterns may work to their advantage in negotiations. Just as the men who adamantly refuse to pay alimony often manage to prevail because their wives cannot afford to litigate the issue, so too the men who are determined to have custody may make it extremely difficult and expensive for their wives to successfully oppose their wishes. As one woman said:

> I finally agreed because it was tearing both me and my son apart. . . . He was threatening to drag me through the mud if we went to court—and in the end I decided it would be better for Chris to be with his father than to be used as a pawn in a court battle.

Such cases must, of course, comprise a very small minority of all cases because the vast majority of all children remain with their mothers after divorce. In fact, it is this persistent pattern that requires some further exploration. How can we explain the continued prominence of maternal custody awards over time?

EXPLAINING THE PERSISTENCE OF MATERNAL CUSTODY

There are three possible explanations for the persistence of custodial arrangements that provide for most children to live with their mothers after divorce. One explanation attributes the responsibility for custody awards to judges, the second views attorneys as the critical decision-makers, while the third assumes that these patterns reflect the choices of divorcing men and women.

Judicial Attitudes Toward Custody

The first explanation for the ongoing pattern of maternal custody awards is that judges are still employing a traditional rule of thumb that favors mother custody. Since most judges were trained and practiced in an era in which it was assumed that mothers were uniquely qualified to raise children, it would not be surprising to find them employing a *de facto* mother presumption.

The judges we interviewed in both San Francisco and Los Angeles did, in fact, express a preference for the mother to have custody of young children: they were reluctant to "take little children away from their mothers" and sincerely believed that maternal custody was usually in the child's best interest. In fact, 81 percent of the Los Angeles judges we interviewed said they thought that there was still presumption in favor of the mother for preschool children, although most of them qualified their responses by noting that the presumption was an attitudinal predisposition rather than "the law." As one judge put it: "Even though the law says there isn't a presumption, *I think mothers make better mothers.*" Similarly, Illinois judges who were primarily responsible for hearing divorce cases revealed an "underlying assumption that the mother would assume custody in a survey of judicial attitudes conducted in 1976."[70]

It is also indicative that many attorneys who specialize in divorce cases perceive this predisposition in judges. For example, even though we interviewed attorneys two years after the maternal presumption was removed from the law, 98 percent of them said that they thought most judges still acted as though there were a maternal presumption in cases where preschool children were involved.

This consensus disappears, however, with regard to older children. Although one-third of the attorneys thought that judges used an implicit maternal presumption in awarding custody of older children, another third reported that neither parent was preferred, while the final one-third said that the outcome depended on the child's preference, age, and sex. (Thus, when asked, "If a child of fifteen has a strong preference, will that be decisive?" 72 percent of the attorneys said yes.)

Even if judges retain a maternal presumption only for preschool children, that would affect a substantial majority of the custodial awards, since 66 percent of the divorcing couples who had children had at least one preschool child, and it is generally considered preferable not to divide the children.

Judges' attitudes alone, however, cannot explain what happens in the vast majority of divorce cases, since only 10 percent of the divorce cases in either Los Angeles or San Francisco go to trial. While one cannot deny the precedent-setting value of the decisions that judges make in those contested cases, nor the influence that judges have in preliminary hearings and temporary orders, it is clear that the forty-four family-law judges and commissioners in Los Angeles cannot directly shape the outcome of the vast majority of the 36,000 divorce cases processed each year.

In addition, as we have already seen, the court records indicate that when fathers do request custody, they have a fairly good chance of obtaining it in both negotiated and contested cases. Two-thirds of the fathers who petitioned for custody obtained it through negotiations or private "agreements," which were then approved by judges, and one-third of the fathers who contested custody in court were awarded it by judges. Thus, the predominance of mother custody awards cannot be attributed to judicial bias. It must be traceable to an earlier stage in the legal process.

Attorneys' Attitudes Toward Custody

A second explanation offered for the low percentage of father custody awards is that lawyers dissuade fathers from asking for custody. Attorneys play a central role in divorce cases: they provide clients with their basic knowledge of the law and the legal process, help them decide what to ask for, and shape their expectations of what they will get. If attorneys think that judges favor the mother for custody of young children, that perception influences their advice about whether it is legally possible for a client to get or lose custody. These expectations then shape what clients strive for—and settle for.

Attorneys also give their clients explicit advice. For example, when asked if he or she had ever tried to talk a client out of attempting to get custody, over 95 percent of the attorneys reported that they had. The most commonly mentioned situations were those in which they thought their clients' legal chances were poor (46 percent), when they thought their client was trying to be vindictive (19 percent), and when they did not think their client would be the better custodial parent (19 percent).[71]

On one hand, the 46 percent of the attorneys who are reluctant to ask for custody for a client whose legal chances "were poor," when read in light of the 98 percent who think an informal maternal presumption is still in effect, suggests that many attorneys do not want to take a custody case they cannot win.*

On the other hand, when we consider the attorneys' explanations for their advice, it may be that they feel the need to justify their advice in terms of legal predictions, but that they are also motivated by what they think is socially and psychologically best for the child (and the client). As one attorney explained:

> I'm not just a hired gun. I have a responsibility to steer my client on the right course and to help him see what is best for his kids.

The California attorneys' guide urges them to utilize such ethical considerations: "the attorney who feels that the parent's goals are contrary to the child's best interests should . . . influence the client to act in

---

* This is the complaint of groups like Equal Rights for Fathers, whose president, Dave Gerfen, charged: "Even the father's lawyer will try to argue him out of trying to win custody of the children, regardless of the mother's fitness to have custody, because he knows it will be an expensive court battle with little chance for success. If the father insists on seeking custody, many attorneys will then refuse to handle his case. . . . The current system creates a 'quiet conspiracy' involving attorneys, judges, probation departments, Conciliation Courts—even the husband's attorney—and is clearly not in the best interests of the child."[72]

a manner beneficial to the child, and to refrain from acting in a manner harmful to the child."[73]

Social responsibility, rather than poor legal prospects, also seems to motivate attorneys to discourage custody claims they think are being used as a threat or punishment. As one lawyer said:

> Generally speaking, a man is asking for custody to punish his spouse. He feels that he can hurt his wife the most by trying to take the kids away from her. . . . It's hard to see how the kids profit from that.

Since clients may not be receptive to this type of guidance, attorneys may explain or justify their advice with dismal predictions or warnings about the expense of a contested case (about $20,000 in 1984 dollars) to assure their clients that they have the clients' interests in mind and want to save their time and money.

Thus, attorneys do, in fact, try to influence custodial decisions, and their advice is based not only on their evaluations of the client's chance of legal success, but also on their opinions of the client and what would be best for the child.

In this regard, note that the attorneys' own attitudes seem to be more supportive of father custody than the attitudes they attribute to judges. These personal preferences must also affect the advice they give to clients. When asked for their personal preferences about the mother presumption for preschool children, only 48 percent of the attorneys said that they favored it, compared to 98 percent who thought most judges did. A significant minority of the attorneys (38 percent) believed that fathers should have an equal right to custody of young children. (The remaining 13 percent were ambivalent).

At the same time, the attorneys clearly believed that things were changing (when interviewed in 1975). For example, 87 percent of the attorneys said they thought it was now easier for fathers to get custody. Among those attorneys, 42 percent attributed the change directly to the change in the law and the presumption of equality for men, while another 46 percent attributed the difference to general societal changes—to men's increased interest in obtaining custody, to the increased general acceptance of male custodians, and to the increased willingness of women to relinquish custody. As one attorney observed:

> The policy of favoring the mother has eroded, and this is the temper of the times. The law no longer presumes [that] a mother's fit—now we talk about the welfare of the kids. . . . There are also more affluent young fathers who are serious about their children and who are not embarrassed to go to a shrink for a psychiatric evaluation of who is the better parent.

They are much more aware and have opened things up. . . . These young fathers really want to keep the children—and they have the ability and financial resources to do it.

As this attorney notes, since the traditional law based maternal custody on the assumption of a fit mother, fathers who wanted custody sought to prove the mother unfit with allegations about her immoral behavior or adultery. Women who strayed from conventional norms risked losing their children. Under the best interests standards, in contrast, the focus shifts from unfitness to a consideration of each parent's relationship with the child. Which parent, the court asks, is best able to care for the child? Since this best interest standard leaves a lot more room for judicial discretion (in contrast to a maternal preference or tender years doctrine), we wondered how judges were deciding what would be best for the child. The attorneys said that the key factor, under the new law, was the quality of the care that each parent can provide for children. As one attorney said:

The major factor is the mother's psychological relationship with the children. If she is nurturant and cares for them, it doesn't matter what she does outside. . . . Conversely, if the mother is gone all the time, doing her thing, even if legitimate, and if her time with the child is minimal, she should not get custody.

What about the divorced woman who works outside the home? Is she considered an unfit mother because her job takes her away from her children? If a woman does not follow the traditional female role of full-time housework and motherhood, is she more likely to be penalized in custody decisions?

Most attorneys said no—her job was irrelevant if she provided care for the children. In response to a hypothetical case in which the mother worked while the children were in day care, most attorneys (75 percent) said her work was not a detriment. As one attorney put it, "There is no evidence of neglect . . . and it's the quality of mothering, not the mere quantity, that counts." Another explained:

He can't complain unless he can support her at home. The court doesn't care what she does—if she's a women's libber or a go-go dancer—as long as she takes care of the kids . . . . She has to work . . . a wife's working would be a plus to most judges.

In fact, in response to the direct question, "Do you think judges are more likely to want a woman with young children to work today?", 77 percent of the attorneys said yes. Thus the attorneys' responses suggest that a mother's employment does not make her a less fit parent, as long as she provides the necessary care for her children.

Other experts disagree. Nancy Polikoff, an attorney who directs the Child Custody Project of the Women's Legal Defense Fund, observes an "undercurrent of punitiveness in the custody decisions involving employed women":

> The mother's employment, even if a matter of absolute financial necessity, is the easiest excuse a judge has to find her the less than adequate parent. . . . Although the best interests of the child standard is not a fault-based standard, the (working) woman . . . is likely to find her behavior punished by judges who disapprove of her independence, even if under an honest "best interests" test she would be better able to provide nurturance to the children.[74]

Polikoff argues that courts fail to recognize the value of women's primary nurturing and regard their employment as evidence of their "diminished capacity" to care for their children. In contrast, a father's employment is taken for granted and not considered as a handicap in his child-rearing ability.

Employed mothers are also victims of a corollary misconception according to Polikoff. Judges usually assume that if both parents work outside the home, they are "equal" in the amount of time and care they can (and do) provide for their children.[75] But, in reality, employed mothers overwhelmingly continue to assume the primary responsibility for child-rearing. In fact, one recent study showed that fathers are less likely to spend time with their children when their wives are employed.[76] This is because fathers are more willing to "relieve" a mother who has been home alone with the children all day. If judges assume two working parents are equal, instead of recognizing that mothers have been providing more care and nurturance, they are overrating the fathers' abilities and, in effect, discriminating in his favor.[77]

Another way in which custodial decisions under a best interest standard may favor the father is by equating the quality of care with financial resources. In the past, in the traditional maternal custody system, it was assumed that the father's economic resources would be transferred to the custodial mother in the form of child support. But under the best interests standard, some courts may consider financial resources in deciding which parent can provide "better" care. Although the attorneys and judges we interviewed typically dismissed family income as "an inappropriate" basis for awarding custody, the issue surfaced in our interviews with divorced men and women. Typically it was fathers who suggested that their superior financial resources should qualify them for custody over their lower earning wives. As one woman reported:

> He said, "I can give them a better standard of living. . . . They'll have summers in Europe and learn French." I said, "I could give them those things just as well if you'd pay child support." "Fat chance," he said, "Fat chance. . . . If you get them, I'll cut you off without a dime. . . . If they live with you, they'll get culture at the public library."

Again, although the attorneys and judges we interviewed said that financial factors do not influence custody decisions, other experts disagree. While there appears to be a consensus that finances *should not* be substituted for the more important considerations of which parent is better able to provide nurturance and care, there is less agreement about what actually happens under best interest standards. Attorney Joanne Schulman, of the National Center on Women and Family Law, surveyed contested custody cases throughout the United States and found that "courts were using economic criteria and awarding custody to the parent with the greater economic resources, who is usually the father:"[78]

> Judges explicitly consider employment prospects, current income, material advantages and other wealth-based criteria. Some concerns about economics are expressed in such questions as who is the more "stable" parent, who can provide the "best" (most expensive) home and child care, and who can afford to continue to maintain the children in the family home. This trend is devastating for women; it discriminates not only against women who, in fulfilling the traditional role of homemaker have not worked outside the home or have worked only part time, but against women who have worked outside the home as well, because they generally have lower earning power than men.[79]

Attorney Schulman asserts that reliance on a financial standard is, in effect, a move away from the "best interests" standard because it devalues the importance of the emotional relationship and the psychological ties between the child and the primary caretaker in the day-to-day care of the child.[80]

Obviously, the use of financial criteria, either explicitly or implicitly, to determine child custody, will almost always work to the father's advantage. As Schulman concludes: "Only rarely can a divorced woman offer her children the material advantages her ex-husband can. Her earning capacity is usually much less than the father's; indeed she is likely to have sacrificed career opportunities in order to care for the children during the marriage, and she faces pervasive job and wage discrimination."[81]

The last way in which the best interest standard may favor the father is by giving priority to his "complete" family if he remarries. This situation typically arises in a request to change the original maternal custody award a year or so after the divorce when the father remarries. Because men are more likely to remarry, and more likely to remarry within the first year after divorce, if the court considers a two-adult family preferable, that standard will favor men.

Since we did not ask the attorneys to compare a single-parent mother with a remarried father, we do not have any data on how attorneys perceive the relative merits of such families. But some of the single-parent mothers we interviewed said that their attorneys' explanation of how the law worked made them worry about convincing a judge that they were providing optimal care for their children if they were compared with a stay-at-home, full-time stepmother.

In fact, in the small minority of disputed cases in the interview sample, none of the primary caretaker mothers lost custody to a remarried father (in the first year after the divorce). Thus these results conform to the legal rule that makes primary caretaking, and the continuity of primary caretaking, the highest priority. (But it is not known whether most judges and attorneys consider such continuity more important than the perceived benefits of a two-adult family.)

Overall, however, what is evident is that one subtle but powerful result of the best interest standard is a shift in the relative bargaining power of fathers and mothers in contested cases. The repeal of the maternal presumption not only signaled a new "equality" between mothers and fathers, it also signaled new standards by which potential custodial parents were to be judged. Instead of the moral categories of the old law, both mothers and fathers were evaluated for "what they could provide for the child." There are some indications that, when faced with a choice between two interested parents, courts have become more skeptical about the mother's ability to care for her children if she has to work outside the home, and more skeptical about the value of her primary care when measured against the father's superior economic resources. It is also possible that her primary care may be considered less valuable when weighed against a remarried father's family, but this research provides no evidence of that.

What this research does show is that mothers are less secure under the best interest standard and worry about potential custody threats based on any of the above claims. Thus beneath the surface of the apparently stable pattern of maternal custody over time, there are increasingly troubled waters. And beneath the surface of the statistically infrequent paternal custody awards is a bargaining climate in which women who are scared or threatened may feel compelled to give up or compromise their financial interests in order to retain custody. As attorney Nancy Polikoff observed:

> The fact that women no longer feel assured of getting custody has had its major impact outside the courtroom. It's significantly changed the bargaining climate in uncontested cases. Women who are scared to death of losing custody will trade away anything else—child support, property, alimony—to keep it from happening. They'll end up bargaining away a substantial amount of their potential financial recovery.[82]

But even if the best interest standard has changed the bargaining climate, it is still somewhat puzzling to note the persistently small percentage of fathers who seek legal custody. Clearly, this must have something to do with how men (and women) view the appropriateness of father custody after divorce.

Divorcing Couples' Attitudes Toward Custody

The interviews with recently divorced men and women in California provide complex, multilayered answers to the question of how men and women feel about being their children's custodian after divorce. Overall fewer fathers than mothers said they wanted custody of their children after divorce: 96 percent of the divorced women in our sample reported that they wanted custody, compared to 57 percent of the divorced men. Nevertheless, the fact that over half of the divorced men reported that they wanted custody is, in and of itself, an astonishing figure.[83]

However, the fathers' expressed interest in custody fluctuates depending on how the question is asked. For example, when asked if they ever told their wives that they wanted custody, the 57 percent drops to 41 percent of the men who said yes. And when queried if they ever asked their lawyer if they had a chance of getting custody, the 57 percent drops to 38 percent of the men who said yes. Finally, only 13 percent of the sample of men we interviewed actually requested custody on the divorce petition.[84]

One way to make sense of this diversity of responses is to assume we have a random sample of 100 divorcing fathers. Forty percent, or two out of five men, would say that they had never thought of having custody of their children after divorce and would, if given the option again, simply reject it. Both they and their wives would assume that the children would stay with her, and would assert that was "natural" and best for the children.

The remaining 60 percent of the men would say that they had positive thoughts about having their children with them after divorce. But when they are "being practical" one out of three (20 percent of the total men) would decide that they do not really want to commit themselves to the full-time job of taking care of their children. Thus although close to 60 percent of the divorcing men could honestly report that they may have wanted custody in the abstract sense of wanting to have their children with them, their reports of their own behavior (talking to their wives or their attorneys) indicate that one out of three in this subsample have not taken any steps to try to obtain it.

That leaves about 40 percent of the divorced men who have seriously considered the idea of obtaining custody. Some of them, however, are dissuaded by their wives, others by their lawyers, and others by their own realization of the difficulty of practical day-to-day arrangements and the financial burdens that custody entails. (The financial costs of custody are substantial, as we will see in the next chapter.) Still others, who may have been discussing custody as a means of harassing their ex-wives or as an economic bargaining device, will drop their claims because they have already achieved their ends. Eventually, only one-third of this subsample of men, about 13 men out of 40, will decide that they want custody enough to pursue the matter in the legal process, either formally or informally.

It is the claims of this minority of about thirteen fathers in a hundred, or one out of every eight fathers, that are processed by the legal system. About three of these men will work out the custodial arrangements with their wives, and will want the court to sanction their agreement. One or two of the others will eventually settle their cases and obtain joint custody or liberal visitation. The remaining eight or nine men will proceed with a fully contested custody battle, and their claims will be heard in court.

These data reveal that the major reason for the low rate of father custody awards lies in the preferences of divorcing men and women: most divorcing fathers are not seriously interested in having custody while most divorcing mothers are.

The Primary Caretaker Presumption

Although California went on to refashion its custody law in one direction (by adopting a joint custody preference discussed below), other states have based their new policies on the *de facto* arrangements and preferences of divorcing couples that are expressed so clearly in the interview data reported above. For example, in 1981 the West Virginia Supreme Court articulated a primary caretaker presumption and instructed courts to award custody to the parent who had assumed the primary responsibility for the care and nurturance of the children during marriage.[85]

This standard, which has gained widespread attention, has the dual advantages of valuing primary caretaking and decreasing ambiguity about the primary criterion for custody awards, so that custody can less easily be used as a bargaining tool. In fact, the "establishment of certainty" was one of the justices' main goals as they sought to prevent the use of custody as "a coercive weapon."[86]

THE JOINT CUSTODY LAWS

In 1980 California became the first state to institute a statute favoring joint custody.[87] The concept of joint custody, with its appealing promise that the children of divorce could "keep both parents," rapidly spread to other states. By 1985, thirty states had adopted some form of joint custody law.[88] (See Table C-7 in the Legal Appendix for a comprehensive state-by-state listing of the provisions of these laws.) Following the typology established by attorney Joanne Schulman,[89] it is useful to distinguish between four types of joint custody legislation as follows:

JOINT CUSTODY AS AN OPTION

The least specific form of joint custody statutes are those that simply allow the court to make custody awards that "may include provisions for the joint custody of the children." (See Table C-7, Legal Appendix.) Since these laws may not establish clear standards for such awards, they allow the possibility of courts ordering joint custody for parents who have not requested it.

JOINT CUSTODY WHEN PARENTS AGREE

The second type of joint custody statute is one that allows the court to award joint custody *only* when both parents are in agreement in requesting it. These laws follow the growing consensus among experts who conclude that the agreement of the parties is a prerequisite to making joint custody work.

Although this is probably the most judicious and widely approved type of joint custody law, it nevertheless allows the possibility of coerced agreement. Assume, for example, that one parent does not want joint custody but is afraid of losing sole custody if a judge learns that she or he was "uncooperative" and refused joint custody. This parent may feel she or he has to agree to joint custody in order to avoid the risk of losing custody altogether.

An unwilling parent is more likely to be coerced into a joint custody "agreement" in states with a "friendly parent" rule. Such rules require courts to consider which parent would be most likely to provide the other parent "with frequent and continuing access to the child" when the court makes a sole custody award. Because of their potential for duress and coercion in arriving at joint custody "agreements,"[90] friendly parent roles have been opposed by several bar associations.

JOINT CUSTODY AT ONE PARTY'S REQUEST

A third type of joint custody legislation allows judges to award joint custody when only *one* of the parents requests it. These statutes, which allow judges to force joint custody on two hostile parents, can have dangerous consequences for the child. They may place the child in the center of parental crossfire and may impede important life decisions: for example, even in a medical emergency the child may have to wait for the court to resolve a parental dispute.

As attorney Joanne Schulman notes, "legal edicts cannot force parents to agree on childrearing questions."[91] When parents cannot agree on the existence of the moon, "much less on the handling of their children, a joint custody order will not change anything."[92]

Attorney Schulman warns of the pernicious effects of these laws when coupled with a "friendly parent" provision: they give the parent who wants joint custody much more power than he or she has in a mutual consent state and provide him or her with "un unconscionable bargaining lever."[93] If the other parent resits joint custody, she or he risks the loss of custody altogether. These laws may thereby empower the party who may be least fit for custody:

> A parent opposed to joint custody might be more willing to risk loss of sole custody if she or he feels that the other parent is capable of providing sufficient care for the child. However, the parent opposed to joint custody cannot, and probably will not, take that risk when an award of custody to the other parent would not provide minimally sufficient care for the

child. Thus, the more "unfit" the parent requesting joint custody, the more bargaining leverage that parent gains under this type of statute.[94]*

JOINT CUSTODY PREFERENCE OR PRESUMPTION

These are the strongest and most coercive forms of joint custody laws. A joint custody *preference* is established by legislation that prioritizes custody options and requires judges to give first preference to joint custody. Even more forceful is a joint custody *presumption*. This is a legal presumption that joint custody is in the child's best interests. In order to overcome this presumption, the party who does not want joint custody has to prove that joint custody would be detrimental to the child.

Both the preference and presumption are attempts to institute new legal and social standards for parenting after divorce—to instill the norm that joint custody is appropriate for all families. Sole custody is treated as an exception to the norm and requires special justification.

Many professionals have challenged the appropriateness of the new legal preference for joint physical custody. They question both the advisability and the feasibility of such arrangements for all families. As attorney Gary Skoloff puts it:

> Joint custody is not a panacea for every case . . . parents should not be compelled to enter into an arrangement that is counterproductive to them and counterproductive to their children's best interests."[96]

Instead, many professionals argue, most children need the security and stability of one home,[97] and there is especially strong opinion about this need for young children.[98]

Since joint custody requires an extraordinary level of cooperation, communication, and goodwill between parents, it is surprising to see courts ask this of parents who may still be antagonistic and who can not—and do not wish to—cooperate on a daily basis. If these couples are pressured into a joint custody agreement, it may turn out to be a prescription for exacerbating and prolonging the tensions of divorce for children.

---

* Schulman offers the following example: Consider the case of a battered wife. Since most courts do not regard violence against *wives* as having any bearing on the child-centered custody issue, she may risk losing her child if she contests joint custody.[95] So she will not risk the safety of her children by opposing a joint custody request from her husband.

The New Legal Ideology

The rapid adoption of some form of joint custody law in two-thirds of the states, and the quick acceptance of joint custody preferences in six states, signal a radical break from legal tradition. Notwithstanding the differences among the statutes we have just discussed, they have four ideological features in common.

First, the laws emphasize the importance of the child's postdivorce relationship with both parents. In contrast to the traditional assumption that the court had to choose one parent as the child's custodian after divorce, the policy objective of these new laws is to "assure minor children of frequent and continuing contact *with both parents* . . . and to encourage parents to share the rights and responsibilities of child-rearing in order to effect this policy."[99]

Second, the new laws reject the traditional legal and psychological assumption that divorcing parents should not be expected to cooperate (and perhaps cannot cooperate) in the care of their children after the divorce. Parents are now pressed to work out a joint custodial agreement for the sake of their children, despite the reluctance or objections of one of the parties. This feature of the new laws is controversial because it compels cooperation between parties who may still be antagonistic and thereby challenges the received wisdom of psychological experts who argue that children will be more stressed in the crossfire of these antagonisms.[100] In fact, psychologists Judith Wallerstein and Joan Kelly found that the children who were most distressed after divorce were those who were caught in the middle of their parents' continuing hostilities.[101]

Third, in contrast to the traditional mode of having judges decide to whom custody should be awarded, the new laws make private ordering—that is, parental agreements about custody—the preferred mode of determining custodial arrangements. Mediation for custodial arrangements has become increasingly popular, and it's now required in some states. In California, for example, as of 1981, the law makes mediation *mandatory* whenever custody is contested.[102] Now parents may not have a judge hear their case until after they have been to mediation.

As must now be obvious, the final thrust of the new joint custody laws is to signal an end of the era of the maternal presumption. By 1984 most states had replaced the "tender years" preference for the mother with laws that make sex-based custody awards impermissible (e.g., the 1979 California law states that the gender of a parent cannot be a basis for a custodial decision).

California's Joint Custody Presumption

California was the first state to adopt a joint custody preference and has one of the strongest pro-joint custody laws in the United States.* The statute allows judges to order joint custody in disputed cases where only one of the parents wants it.[103] (Since the court has discretion, the judge may order joint custody when neither parent wants it if "it is best for the children.") The judge may ask for a custody investigation by court personnel to provide information for the decision.

When the parents themselves agree to joint custody, there is a presumption that joint custody is in the best interests of the child.[103] If the court does not then award joint custody, it must state the reasons on the record.[104] Thus the law puts a burden on judges who do not order joint custody by requiring them to justify any other award in writing. This exerts pressure on judges, as well as on the parties, to settle on a joint custody award.

The stated aim of the law is "to assure children of frequent and continuing contact with both parents . . . and to encourage parents to share the rights and responsibilities of child-rearing in order to effect this policy.[105] To help achieve this result, the California custody statute includes a "friendly parent" provision which creates additional pressure, as noted above, on the parents to agree to joint custody.[106]

A final feature of the California law, added in 1983, defines and distinguishes joint *legal* custody from joint *physical* custody and permits the courts to award one without the other (for example, joint legal custody may be awarded to both parents, with physical custody awarded to the mother). The law now defines joint physical custody as an arrangement whereby both parents share in the day-to-day care of the child. Joint legal custody gives both parents the right to participate in certain important decisions. The latter definition is amplified by the California attorneys' guide to family law practice, which notes that common usage in California defines joint legal custody as the right of the parent without physical custody to be consulted and to help make major decisions about the child's care, control, education, health, and religion. Attorneys are advised to use a checklist presented in the guide to spell out exactly which decisions are to be made jointly and which are to be made by the parent with physical custody.[107]

---

* Since then Florida and Louisiana have enacted even stronger laws that contain an express presumption for joint custody in all cases.

The Joint Custody Law in Practice

Once again, as might be expected, the new custody law was greeted with predictions of a vastly increased paternal role in postdivorce parenting. And once again, it seems that the new law has brought less change than anticipated.

What has been the effect of California's new joint custody law? While it is too soon to answer this question with confidence, the preliminary results of two studies, discussed below, suggest that one result has been a change in labeling: since joint custody is now preferred, arrangements that would have been called "liberal visitation" before 1980, under the old law, are now being called "joint custody." The shift may have important psychological consequences for fathers who can now define themselves as joint parents after divorce, but it has not changed day-to-day arrangements for the care of most children.

This caveat about labels is important in evaluating the extent of the change because preliminary reports indicate considerable variation in the interpretation of the new law. For example, in my efforts to obtain data on the pattern of awards after 1980, I spoke to a court official in one county who reported a major increase in joint *legal* custody awards, because the judges were interpreting the new law as applicable only to *legal* custody awards. In another county I was told there was a significant increase in joint *physical* custody awards, because the judges were interpreting the new law as a mandate for joint physical custody unless there was opposition from both parents. And, in yet another county, I was told that the new law had brought little change because the judges believed they should follow the parties' wishes. Since the predisposition of judges plays such a critical role in how the joint custody law is being applied, one must be cautious in assuming that data on the pattern of awards correspond to actual practice—or that they accurately represent "real changes" in custodial arrangements after divorce.

With this caveat in mind, let us consider the preliminary results of two ongoing studies of the effects of California's joint custody law.

The first study involved a review of 138 randomly selected court records in 1981 from Santa Clara County, in northern California, by Stanford professors Eleanor Maccoby and Robert Mnookin, in preparation for a large interview study of the custodial parents.[108]

The second study is being conducted by Drs. Judith Wallerstein and Dorothy Huntington in Marin County, also in northern California, as part of the community counseling and mediation program offered

by the Center for the Family in Transition.[109] Wallerstein and Huntington interviewed 184 families with minor children soon after they filed
for divorce between 1981 and 1983. Some of these families ended up
in the control group, while others received assistance in working out
their custodial arrangements (as well as continued counseling over a
two-year period). The data reported below are the temporary custodial
arrangements of these 184 couples at the time of their "intake" interview. (Most of these couples were living apart, were already represented by attorneys, and were aware of and influenced by California's
joint custody law.)

Let us consider three types of custody awards: joint physical custody, joint legal custody with physical custody to the mother, and sole
physical custody to the father.

Joint Physical Custody

Both studies report what appears to be an increase in joint physical
custody arrangements. Maccoby and Mnookin found that joint physical
custody was awarded in 13 percent of the divorce cases in Santa Clara
in 1981,[110] and Wallerstein and Huntington report 18 percent of their
Marin families used this option.[111] At first glance, this seems to be a
significant increase over the 2 percent joint custody awards in the
1977 Los Angeles sample (see Table 21). But, as we noted, some of
these "joint custody" arrangements provide for considerably less than
equal sharing of day-to-day responsibility for children, e.g., the child
may live in the mother's home, but visit with the father on weekends.

What then does the increase mean? Is it high or low?

In view of the extent to which the California law actively encourages joint physical custody, it is somewhat surprising to find that there
was not a larger percentage of such arrangements. The fact that less
than one out of five couples elected (or felt pressed to try) joint custody
underscores the pervasive societal attitudes described above. Most
men—and most women—prefer not to share postdivorce parenting.
These arrangements require unusual commitments of time, energy, and
financial resources that most couples simply cannot afford.

When we look at the limited research on couples who have elected
to share physical custody of their children, it becomes evident why
more couples do not elect this option. For example, Susan Steinman
studied twenty-four couples in the San Francisco Bay area who chose
joint physical custody (before California's joint custody law went into

effect). She found both fathers and mothers well educated, with at least average incomes, and strongly committed to their parental responsibilities.[112] They had a reasonably friendly postdivorce relationship, and were willing to endure the strains of complex logistical arrangements to make shared parenting possible. In addition, these arrangements were expensive. These parents had—and were willing to spend—a fairly large amount of money to maintain two complete homes (with two sets of toys, books, etc.). Obviously these divorcing couples were not the norm.

Steinman observed that these arrangements, and the commuting they required, could be anxiety-provoking for children who became confused about where they were actually supposed to be and who was supposed to care for them. Consider the following:

> Nine-year-old Josh, who lived one month with his mother and one month with his father, indicated that he felt many things in his life were in disarray, that he was preoccupied with loss and anxious about his ability to keep track of things. He was not working up to his potential at school, and there was a discrepancy between his considerable abilities and his low self-concept. When Josh was contacted about our interviews, he immediately volunteered that "The big problem with joint custody is that you have to remember where the spoons are." His worry about the spoons reflected all the other worries he had, and an overall sense of instability.[113]

Even if the parents lived reasonably close to each other, the distance might be frightening and disorienting for a child, as the following case indicates:

> Nine-year-old Roy, whose parents lived two miles apart, spent three days a week at his mother's and the remaining days with his father, taking the bus from school to each home. This child, who did not have a clear sense of his schedule or the location of his parents' homes, worried about his personal safety and was frightened of getting lost or going to the wrong house. The distance between homes, as he experienced it psychologically, was of great concern to him. When Roy was asked what he would say to another boy whose parents were getting a divorce, he advised, "Tell him that his mother and father might live close together and then he could go and live with the other person and get to see them. This never happened to me." In reality, Roy did get to see both parents, but rather than feeling that he had access to both—as the adults would hope—Roy experienced a lack of understanding and control over his life.[114]

Steinman's follow-up data indicated that many of the complex logistical arrangements involved in joint physical custody broke down when one parent moved or remarried.[115]

Although many things are magnified in a child's world, the inevitable stress of these arrangements should not be surprising. How many of us, after all, would not be stressed if we had to change homes every three days, or every week throughout the year?

In fact, the stress of joint custody is not confined to the children. Denver sociologists Jessica Pearson and Nancy Thoennes found that 30 percent of the joint custody mothers were dissatisfied with joint custody—compared to only 10 percent of the sole custody mothers they interviewed three years after the divorce.[116]

If these are the experiences of a special group of self-selected couples who are highly motivated and unusually committed to make joint physical custody succeed, it not only seems unrealistic to expect the average divorcing couple to be joint physical custodians, but to mandate it for all couples sounds like a prescription for increasing the trauma of divorce for children.

As Lillian Kozak observed, "After twenty-five years of psychological theorizing that children are better off when homes break up rather than remaining in homes where arguing is the rule, we are now asked to place these children back into a situation worse than that from which we extricated them, via a sort of forced remarriage of hostile parents."[117]

Joint Legal Custody with Maternal Physical Custody

A more common legal arrangement is to award joint *legal* custody to both parents, with *physical* custody to the mother. This arrangement gives fathers the right to participate in major decisions affecting the child.

Bearing in mind our cautions about generalizations, the preliminary results of both studies suggest that the largest change has been in this category of awards. Both studies found that more than a third of the couples had joint legal custody with maternal physical custody.

Since there has not yet been any comprehensive research on couples with this arrangement, we do not know precisely what its ramifications may be. But it is useful to examine the arguments advanced by its proponents and to see whether they are supported by other data.

Three rationales have been offered for joint legal custody. First, it is asserted that children benefit from such an arrangement because the continued postdivorce involvement of both parents is a practical and psychological necessity. If the children perceive that their father and mother share in the decision making and planning of activities involving them, their sense of abandonment lessens and the need to "choose" between one or the other parent diminishes, thus decreasing the harmful impact of the divorce.

There is, in fact, considerable evidence to support the assertion that children of divorce benefit from the postdivorce involvement of their fathers. After a five-year follow-up study of the impact of divorce on children, Drs. Judith Wallerstein and Joan Kelly concluded that children who adjusted best maintained a continuing relationship with both parents during the postdivorce years.[118]

> While no single factor was associated with good outcome . . . *the continuity of relationship with both parents* and the extent to which the conflict between the divorcing partners had subsided all contributed to the well being of the child.[119]

As this summary indicates, there is an important caveat to the advantages of continued contact with both parents: the parents cannot be adversarial. If the two parents are hostile, then continued contact with both parents is not desirable because the children are typically caught in the middle. In fact, Judith Wallerstein, who recently completed a ten-year follow-up of the same families, notes that prolonged hostilities between the parents result in the most destructive outcomes for children.[120] Thus if two hostile parents are forced to interact by a joint legal custody order, it may be extremely detrimental for the children.

There is a second caveat to generalizations from the original Wallerstein-Kelly finding of benefit from continuing contact with both parents. Their conclusions were based on families who had worked out these arrangements voluntarily—and presumably as a result of a good relationship between the parents. Those parents in the Wallerstein-Kelly study who cooperated in making decisions about their children—an arrangement that closely resembles joint legal custody—were those who were able to and chose to cooperate. But what if joint custody is coerced or imposed on the parents? What happens to children in joint legal custody arrangements if the two parents are hostile?

Clearly, a court order cannot force parents to cooperate: the outcome of such orders is likely to be further litigation, conflict, extended and increased harm for the children. While some fathers' rights groups insist that "meaningful contact with both parents is impossible without joint legal custody"[121] the Wallerstein-Kelly research demonstrates that the conventional sole custody-visitation formula permitted meaningful association with both parents.

The second rationale for joint legal custody asserts that it improves the chances that child support will be paid. Support for this argument is drawn from the assumption that fathers who are more involved in parenting via joint legal custody will be more likely to provide emotional and financial support following divorce.

Do fathers who have joint legal custody perform better in meeting their child support obligations than their sole-custody counterparts? Preliminary research conducted by Pearson and Thoennes suggests that they do not. Rather, they found support payments to be "comparable across the custody groups."[122] About half of the mothers with sole custody and half with joint legal/maternal physical custody arrangements reported that they had received the full amount of support eleven or twelve months out of the year. About 30 percent of the mothers with sole custody and about 30 percent of those with joint legal/maternal physical custody reported that they received payments in no more than six months out of the year.[123] Thus whether or not a father has joint legal custody does not seem to affect his compliance with child support orders.*

The third rationale for joint legal custody is that it will eventually reduce the conflict between divorced spouses. If the mother is assured that she is not "giving up" her day-to-day custody of the children and the father is assured that he now has a clear legal right to be involved with them, each parent should be satisfied and the tension between them should be reduced.

Once again, the preliminary findings of the Pearson-Theonnes research seem to refute this claim. These researchers found that many of the couples who settled on an arrangement for joint legal custody with physical custody to the mother had originally disagreed about what custodial arrangement they should have. Typically the preference of one or both of the parents was to have sole custody. The solution of joint legal custody was a compromise. Pearson and Theonnes report that the mothers who are dissatisfied with the arrangement (three years later) felt that they were talked into it, have a poor relationship with their ex-spouse and sense that their children are aware of the conflict and anger between the parents.[124] There is little to suggest that the arrangement has decreased the conflict between the spouses. Rather, the conflict seems to have become more prominent.

Similar conclusions were reached in a Massachusetts study that

* Not only does joint custody do little to improve the dismal performance of many fathers in paying child support, but there is some preliminary indication that it may be used as a device to lower child-support awards to begin with. Fathers who spend more time with their children, even if they have them for just two days a week, argue that they should not have to pay any child support because they are "sharing" the actual costs of the child.

compared the rates of postdivorce litigation among couples with joint legal custody and sole maternal custody.[125] The Massachusetts researchers report that a greater percentage of parents with joint legal custody returned to court (20 percent joint, 12 percent sole) to resolve child-related matters.[126] There were also marked differences in the number of requests for modifications with joint legal custody families "asking for numerically and proportionally more changes in custody, visitation, and in the areas of financial support."[127]

The higher rates of conflict and relitigation among couples with joint legal custody in both Denver and Massachusetts is significant because the couples in both studies had entered these arrangements voluntarily, and that suggests that these couples must have started out with plans to cooperate. If such families end up more conflict-ridden, how can we expect parents who are pressured into joint legal custody to suddenly be able to resolve their conflicts and make joint decisions regarding their children? Joint legal custody requires that parents be able to put aside their differences but that is just what parents in the aftermath of divorce have difficulty doing.

Sole Physical Custody to the Father

It is not clear that there has been any basic change in the percentage of fathers who have been awarded sole physical custody of their children. Wallerstein and Huntington found that 4 percent of the fathers in Marin County assumed sole physical custody of their children. On the other hand, Maccoby and Mnookin report that 14.5 percent of the Santa Clara fathers did. While this higher figure may be a statistical or local artifact, it seems less unusual in the context of the "normal variation" within the past century. For example, 6 percent of the Los Angeles fathers received physical custody in 1977 (Table 21), but before that, in 1968, over 9 percent of the divorced men were awarded physical custody in Los Angeles and San Francisco (Table 19). Similarly, historian Elaine May reported that men received custody in 12 to 13 percent of the Los Angeles cases in 1880 and 1920.[128]

Whether the percentage of children who live with their fathers after divorce is closer to the 4 percent in the Marin sample or the 15 percent in the Santa Clara sample, the more important finding is that mothers continue to have physical custody in the vast majority of cases. That pattern continues to reflect the underlying social reality in which mothers assume the major share of the day-to-day care of their children after divorce, as they do during marriage. It seems unlikely that this pattern will change in any fundamental way in the near future because of the deeply ingrained social patterns that support women's greater investment in their children.

Summary of the Results of the Legal Changes

In summary, then, there were small increases in awards of joint legal custody and joint physical custody, or at least in what people are labeling "joint physical custody," under a statute that presses couples to apply this term to their behavior. As Table 23 indicates, in the large

TABLE 23

Physical Custody Arrangements Under Four Legal Regimes, 1968–1983

	MATERNAL PREFERENCE	MATERNAL PREFERENCE WITH NO-FAULT	BEST INTEREST OF CHILD	JOINT CUSTODY PREFERENCE	
	(1968*) n = 310†	(1972*) n = 245	(1977*) n = 246	(1981**) n = 138	(1981–83***) n = 184
Mother (sole physical custody)	87.7%	88.8%	90.2%	68.1%	67%
Father (sole physical custody)	9.4	5.8	6.1	14.5††	4
Joint (physical custody)	0.0	.8	2.0	13.0	18
Other (children, split, etc.)	2.9	4.6	1.6	4.3	11
Total	100.0%	100.0%	99.9%	99.9%	100%

* Los Angeles County
** Santa Clara County
*** Marin County
† n refers to the number of cases on which the percentages are based.
†† Includes arrangements that would have been called "Liberal visitation" in 1972 or 1977 (see text).

These data are based on systematic random samples of court records in Los Angeles County, California, for 1968, 1972, and 1977 collected by Lenore Weitzman and Ruth Dixon, a sample of Santa Clara County records in 1981 collected by Eleanor Maccoby and Robert Mnookin, and a sample of Marin County families collected by Judith Wallerstein and Dorothy Huntington in 1981–83.

majority of divorced families—between 67 and 85 percent, depending on how one classifies the joint physical custody awards—mothers continue to provide most of the nurturance and day-to-day care of their children. This has remained consistent under all four changes in the law summarized in Table 23.

CUSTODY IN PRACTICE

What is the effect of these custody awards on parental behavior after divorce? On the whole, most families abide by the court-ordered arrangements for child custody. However, one out of five families in our sample changed the arrangement within the first year after divorce.* A parent may get sick, or remarry, or move in order to take a new job; or a child may decide that he or she wants to live with the noncustodial parent. Most couples make these changes without going back to court, so the court records become static and give an inaccurate portrait of actual living patterns soon after the final decree.

In most of the families in our sample, the children lived with the mother. Thirty percent of the fathers saw the children at least once a week, another 33 percent saw them once or twice a month, and the remaining 14 percent of the fathers who exercised visitation rights saw them less than once a month. The other 23 percent of them did not see their children after the divorce.

These percentages are sample averages of the combined responses of men and women. The two sexes, however, report different rates of visitation. When asked how often the noncustodial parent actually sees the children, the median response by men is that they see their children weekly; the women's median response is that the fathers see the children less than once a month.

Over the long run, there is a process of gradual disengagement of noncustodial fathers from active participation in the lives of their children:[130] twenty percent of the men say they are less close to their children since the divorce (compared to less than 2 percent of the women). This loss of closeness is not a casual event. In fact, 77 percent of the fathers in our sample said that "missing the children" is one of the worst results of divorce.

Yet 70 percent of men without custody said they would prefer to see their children *less* often (30 percent said the same amount; and

* In Massachusetts, Barbara Hauser reports that one-third of the couples had changed the custody order.[129]

none said more often). Among women with custody, 43 percent of them agreed and wanted the noncustodial parent to see the kids less often as well. Taken together, these responses show a predisposition for divorced fathers to reduce their visitation over time.

In fact, the men in our sample were more active in postdivorce parenting than reports from national samples.

In a nationally representative sample of children in the United States between ages eleven and sixteen, Frank Furstenberg and his colleagues found that *most* children of divorce have had no contact with their noncustodial fathers within the past year. Only one child in six (16 percent) saw his or her father at least once a week.[131] Another 16 percent saw their fathers at least once a month, and 15 percent saw them at least once a year. *The remaining 52 percent of the children had had no contact with their fathers whatsoever in the past year.* They conclude that "a divorce not only severs the marital bond, but often permanently ruptures the parent-child relationship, especially if the child is living apart from the father."[132]

They also report that the process of the father's estrangement from the child typically begins soon after the marriage breaks up.[133] The rate of frequent contact appears to drop off sharply after about twelve months. The proportion of fathers who had had no contact with their children for at least a year rose to 64 percent among individuals whose marriages had broken up ten or more years ago.[134]

The findings are not affected by either the gender or the age of the child. However, race, educational level, remarriage, and propinquity apparently have some effect.[135] Black fathers, less educated fathers, and remarried fathers typically have less contact with their children. Black fathers are less likely to have seen their children in the past five years than either whites or other minorities. Although 57 percent of the college- and post-college-educated fathers saw their children at least once a *month,* their rates of *weekly* contact were no more regular than among less educated groups.

One factor which is systematically related to parental contact with children is the remarriage of either spouse. Furstenberg found the level of contact between father and child is twice as high if he does not remarry. The differences are even greater when the mother remains single. If both parents remarry, only 11 percent of the children have weekly contact with the father, compared to 49 percent of the children when neither parent has remarried.[136] The relationship between remarriage and lower visitation has been reported by other researchers,[137] and is evident in our sample as well.

A final factor related to contact is residential propinquity. Fursten-berg found that fathers who lived within an hour's drive of their children were twice as likely to see them at least once a week (31 percent, vs. 16 percent if they lived farther away). However, propinquity is no guarantee of regular contact: 42 percent of the fathers who lived within an hour's drive of their children saw them less than once a month.[138]

It is interesting to note that children have more contact with their noncustodial parent when that parent is the mother. In the national sample that Furstenberg et al. studied, 86 percent of the children had seen a noncustodial mother in the past year, as compared with 48 percent of the children who had seen noncustodial fathers. And nearly a third (31 percent) of the children with noncustodial mothers saw their mothers on the average of once a week, as compared to only one in six (16 percent) of the children with noncustodial fathers who saw their fathers.[139]

CONCLUSION

Although there have been major changes in the legal rules for custody awards in California over the past fifteen years, there has been less change. Our findings indicate that despite the major changes in the California divorce law over the past fifteen years, there has been little change in the actual distribution of child custody awards. Yet media reports and common perceptions suggest that a growing number of fathers are seeking and obtaining custody of their children after divorce. There are several possible ways to reconcile our data with this common impression.

One explanation is that even though the *percentage* of fathers who obtain sole custody has remained fairly constant, the total *number* of such fathers has increased dramatically because of the steady rise in the number of divorcing couples each year in the past decade. In Los Angeles County alone, there were over 3,000 divorces each month, and half of them involved minor children. If about 6 percent of the fathers are awarded sole physical custody, and an additional 2 percent are awarded joint physical custody, 120 fathers a month, or close to 1,500 fathers each year, are obtaining sole or joint custody in just Los Angeles County. Simply because there are more fathers who are being awarded custody, more people know "someone" who has custody of his children.

Although one must always be cautious in extrapolating California data to the country as a whole, if these figures were representative, it would mean that among the more than one million divorces each year, there would be 30,000 fathers with sole physical custody of their children nationwide, and another 10,000 with joint physical custody. Thirty to forty thousand new custodial fathers each year constitute a *socially* significant group even if they represent a small minority of all divorced fathers.

A second explanation for the common perception lies in the characteristics of those fathers who are asking for and being awarded custody. They tend to be well educated and to have a relatively high occupational status. Thus they are more visible, and are likely to be seen as trend-setters. They are also more likely to hire the attorneys who have greater access to the media.

But, despite their increasing absolute numbers, and despite their social visibility, fathers who are sole physical custodians of their children remain a distinct minority. Overwhelmingly, it is mothers who continue to be children's primary caretakers after divorce.

There has been considerable debate about the desirability of dual parenting after divorce. Even if there were widespread agreement that this is an appropriate societal goal, it is important to recognize that changing the law will not alone accomplish this result.[140] To overcome the pervasive weight of tradition, we would have to change the material conditions of men's and women's lives, and the costs and benefits of custody for fathers and for mothers.

Until now the vast majority of divorced fathers have not been interested in obtaining custody of their children after divorce, while the vast majority of divorced women have been. But one result of the new joint custody laws—when joined with the major dislocations that the financial aspects of the new divorce laws have brought—may be that these attitudes, and the social patterns upon which they are based, are beginning to change.

In the past, the legal system served primarily as a means of formalizing the caretaking patterns that had existed in most families during marriage, and that parents agreed to continue after divorce.[141] But the new laws provide a clear and powerful stimulus for change.

CHAPTER 9

Child Support
The National Disgrace

DESPITE COURT ORDERS, noncustodial fathers fail to pay $4 billion in child support each year. More than half (53 percent) of the millions of women who are due child support do not receive the court-ordered support.[1] Child support awards that go unpaid and unenforced make a mockery of the judicial system and the value of court orders. They also leave millions of children without the basic necessities of life. If the present system of unenforced child support were to continue unabated, half a generation of American children would suffer years of financial deprivation.

In 1984 Congress unanimously approved legislation to strengthen child support collection through mandatory income withholding and the interception of federal and state tax refund checks to cover past-due support. Margaret Heckler, Secretary of the U.S. Department of Health and Human Services, who lobbied for the congressional action, decried the national disgrace of billions of unpaid dollars owed America's children:

> I . . . feel very strongly the destitution, the desperation, and the simple human suffering of women and children who were not receiving child support payments legally owed them. Frankly it offends my conscience because I believe that a parent's first responsibility is to reasonably pro-

vide for the upbringing and welfare of his or her children. To deny that responsibility is a cowardly act.[2]

Fifteen million children live in homes without their fathers. Only 35 percent of these households receive child support and nearly one-third live in poverty. Children deserve to be supported by both their parents. For the sake of America's children, we must put an end to what has become a national disgrace. Our new federal legislation will help States obtain child support orders quickly and pursue them vigorously.[3]

Witnesses at the congressional hearing echoed the Secretary's charges and testified that the "epidemic of nonsupport" had spread to middle- and upper-class fathers.[4] Willful disregard of court orders, a pattern that people assumed was limited to lower-income men, was now common among fathers of all social classes because, it was asserted, judges failed to enforce the law:

Confronted with overcrowded dockets, judges continue to exhibit a great reluctance to strictly enforce the existing laws. Instead, child support cases are often subjected to broad and inconsistent interpretation, making a mockery of our judicial system. The most pathetic aspect of this entire tragedy is that parents are unnecessarily subjecting their own children to substandard levels of living.

Both the non-paying parents, [and] the legislative and judicial branches [of government] are at fault in this miscarriage of justice.[5]

Key figures in the congressional debates pointed to fathers' flagrant violation of the law: Tennessee Representative Harold Ford bemoaned the ease with which parents were able to escape their legal and moral responsibilities, cheating children out of $4 billion a year.[6] Colorado Representative Patricia Schroeder said it would be a national scandal if you could buy a car, drive it to another state, and not pay for it, but that was what we had allowed nonsupporting fathers to do.[7] She spoke of the tragedy that resulted from the law's tolerance of parents more conscientious about their car payments than their child support.

Noting that single-parent families on public assistance cost the taxpayers $20–30 billion a year, President Ronald Reagan stressed the need to put the responsibility for support back on the absent fathers:

The American people willingly extend help to children in need, including those whose parents are failing to meet their responsibilities. However, it is our obligation to make every effort to place the financial responsibility where it rightly belongs—on the parent who has been legally ordered to support his child.[8]

Secretary Heckler stressed the human costs and hardships when child support checks never come:

> Almost eight million single parents share the frustration, and often real hardship, that can result from the failure of absent parents to meet their child support obligation. The disappointment and bitterness which grows out of these situations may add emotional burdens to the financial load these children and their custodial parents frequently face. What may appear to be just a dollars and cents issue has much more far reaching implications for them.
>
> The scope of this problem has grown to the point where it affects not just these children and those who care for them, but society as a whole.[9]

Those who lobbied for the 1984 legislation promised that it would curb the scandalous behavior of wayward parents: Representative Marge Roukema of New Jersey said the landmark bill put the federal government on record that "child support would no longer be treated as a voluntary commitment," and Margaret Heckler promised "fast track" implementation of the new regulations.[10]

Why do many divorced men feel free to disregard the law and not pay child support? Are they ordered to pay excessive amounts of child support? Or is there something wrong with the system of enforcement? We now turn to these issues.

THE AMOUNT OF CHILD SUPPORT AWARDED

A useful way of examining child support awards is to think about a hypothetical family and see how the courts would apportion its post-divorce income. One of our hypothetical cases, that of Pat and Ted Byrd, involved the question of child support for their two children, a four-year-old daughter and a six-year-old son (see Appendix B). After a seven-year marriage, twenty-seven-year-old Ted Byrd, an accountant, has a net monthly income of $1,000 (after taxes). Pat Byrd has been a housewife and mother throughout the marriage and has no outside income.

In response to the hypothetical Byrd case, the Los Angeles judges proposed a median child support award of $250 for the two children. The attorneys' predictions were similar, averaging $271 a month for the two.*

These predictions are somewhat higher than the average child sup-

---

* The attorneys' predictions for total support awards were not consistently higher than the judges'. For example, the median alimony award in this case was $200 a month among judges and $150 a month among attorneys.

port awards in the sample of court dockets because the hypothetical Ted Byrd's income is above the average income for divorced men. In the 1977 Los Angeles court docket sample, the mean child support order was $126 per month per child. The average child support award in families with two children averaged slightly less per child, presumably due to economies of scale. It was $195 per month per family, or a total of $2,340 a year. (That is about $4,050 a year in 1984 dollars for the support of two children.)

Although these child support awards may seem low, they are comparable with—if not slightly higher than—the national average reported by the U.S. Census Bureau. According to a 1978 census survey, divorced fathers paid an average of $1,951 per year.[11] In 1981 they paid an average of $2,220 per year.[12] These statistics are for the amounts of child support received, because the Census did not report data on the amount of child support awarded to *divorced* women (as distinct from *all* women due child support).

We do know, however, that the amount of child support actually received by divorced women is invariably less than the amount the court orders. The Census Bureau reports on the difference between the two for all women who were supposed to receive child support in 1981: the mean amount of support ordered was $2,460, but the mean amount paid, including those who received nothing, was $1,510.[13] (These amounts are lower than those for divorced women because they include awards to never-married women for whom compliance is even lower.)

Among divorced women, black women fared worst in terms of both child support orders and payments. Child support was awarded by the court to 69 percent of the white women, 44 percent of the Hispanic women, and only 34 percent of the black women in 1981. The level of support payments showed the same pattern: the white mother received $2,180; the Hispanic mother, $2,068; and the black mother, $1,640.[14]

When the Census Bureau compared the 1981 child support payments to those in 1978, it found that child support payments actually decreased by about 16 percent in real dollars between 1978 and 1981.*

Another way of looking at the typical child support award is as a percentage of the husband's income. In Ted Byrd's case, $250 out of a net monthly income of $1,000 is 25 percent of his take-home pay for child support. That was about the average percentage in Los Ange-

---

* However, child support payments as a percentage of average male income remained fairly constant over the years (at 13 percent), since the real income of males declined during this period as well. Average male income was $13,110 in 1978 and $16,520 in 1981.[15]

les, but was slightly below the average in San Francisco, where child support averaged about one-third of the husband's net income. In national data, child support averaged 13 percent of average male income in both 1978 and 1981.[16]

The percentage of a husband's income awarded in child support varies by the husband's income level, with lower-income men typically being required to pay a greater proportion of their incomes in child support. (However, there is a large amount of variation in data based on different samples.) In the random sample of 1977 court dockets, men who earned less than $10,000 a year were, on average, ordered to pay 20 percent of their gross incomes in child support. The percentage dropped to 10 percent of gross income among men earning $30,000 or more. Along the same lines, Professor Judith Cassetty found regressive child support awards in Michigan data in 1975: men who had gross incomes of over $15,000 contributed, on average, only 11 percent of their incomes to child support.[17]

The same inverse relationship is evident among the divorced husbands in our interview sample. Table 24, which uses net income, shows an even larger disparity between low- and high-income men in the percentages of income ordered for child support. On average, men with net incomes of under $10,000 were ordered to pay 37 percent of their net income in child support, while those with net incomes of $50,000 or more were ordered to pay only 5 percent.

One reason for this difference is that higher-income men are more likely to pay alimony as well as child support, so that the child support figures do not necessarily reflect the full extent of the men's support contributions. Thus if we look at the last column of Table 24, which shows the total amount of support (child support plus alimony—or one or the other), there is less difference between high- and low-income husbands.

One important finding in Table 24 is that no matter what his income level, a divorced man is rarely ordered to part with more than *one-third* of his net income. This one-third limit is surprising because the judges and the attorneys we interviewed often referred to a *one-half* limit: they said there was an informal rule that judges should never require a man to pay more than one-half of his net income in support. In light of these frequent references to an award limit of 50 percent of the payor's income, we were surprised to find a much lower one-third "ceiling" operating in practice.*

---

* While most of the Los Angeles judges said they were aware of the informal 50 percent rule, only one-third said they themselves followed it. The other two-thirds said

TABLE 24

Child Support and Alimony Awarded as a Percentage of Husband's
Postdivorce Net Income

Husband's Net Income	PERCENTAGE OF HUSBAND'S NET INCOME AWARDED FOR SUPPORT		
	Child support ordered	*Alimony ordered*	*Total ordered (either or both)*
Under $10,000	37%	—	37%
$10–19,999	25	13%	25
$20–29,999	25	30	32
$30–49,999	10	24	30
$50,000 or more	5	20	19

This table is based on weighted sample of interviews with divorced persons, Los Angeles
County, 1978

In explaining the awards they set, the California judges stress the
need to protect the father's ability to pay by not making the award
too burdensome for him. They want to leave him with "enough" money
to maintain his motivation to earn, and this means setting aside
"enough" income for him. While the judges may not be aware of the
extent to which they are allocating income to the father at the expense
of his children, they are aware of and clearly express their priority
for taking care of his needs first. As one judge said, "you can't touch
the goose that lays the golden egg."

This "father first" principle stands out in contrast to the "child
first" principle subscribed to by the English judges, discussed in Chapter
4. The English perspective first considers the children's needs and sets
aside enough family income to take care of them. It then allocates
the rest of the income to the adults. In California, the procedure is
the reverse: the children (and their caretakers) get what is left after
money is set aside to meet the father's needs. While the California
judges justify their *modus operandi* by saying they need to protect
the father's motivation to earn, the bottom line is that he comes first,
and his "right" to build a new life comes first, even if his new life is
built at the expense of his children and former wife.

The data on the California awards are surprising in another respect:
the amounts of support that were awarded were lower than the amounts
suggested in the judicial guidelines.[18] These guidelines, or schedules

they would award *more* than half of the husband's net income (in combined alimony
and child support) where appropriate. This suggests an even larger discrepancy between
what judges say they do and what they actually do.

as they are typically called, suggest appropriate amounts of support by family income level. While they are intended as a rough norm for temporary orders, close to 60 percent of the judges we interviewed said they consistently relied on them.

Schedules that set uniform award levels have become increasingly popular in recent years, and the 1984 federal child support legislation requires the drafting of optional guidelines throughout the United States. The attorneys we interviewed were generally in favor of such guidelines because they provide predictability and consistency of results, minimize court time necessary to set support awards, facilitate client acceptance of attorney recommendations, and assure that at least minimum standards for support are met.[19] Those who oppose schedules argue that they tend to become rigid rules rather than guidelines, and thereby deprive each case of its uniqueness and opportunity to be heard.

In light of the impetus of the federal law for more widespread use of guidelines in the future, it is disturbing to find that guidelines seem to have the unanticipated effect of depressing award levels because most awards fall into the lower range of the levels set forth in the guidelines. Why is this so? Perhaps the schedules are being read as establishing upper limits, or ceilings, on award levels. Or perhaps attorneys who use the guidelines in negotiations believe that they can never expect to get awards in the upper range of the schedule so they settle for less.

Whatever the reasons, this finding has important policy implications: since the federal legislation of 1984 requires states to draw up child support guidelines, the drafters of these guidelines should be aware that the schedules tend to depress award levels. If a schedule encourages most couples to "settle" for support in the lower and middle ranges specified, drafters might consider setting higher ranges, or using schedules based on a fixed percentage of the payor's gross income, as is done in the schedule used in the state of Wisconsin[20] (discussed later).

The limited data from other states suggests that the amount of child support and alimony awarded in California is roughly comparable to support awards in other states. For example, a 1983 study of the New Jersey courts concluded that there appears to be an unofficial standard that a total support award will be for "no more than 30 percent of the husband's net pay even when there are small children in the custody of the wife."[21] Researchers in the state of Michigan[22] and in Alberta Province, Canada, have also reported a *de facto* norm whereby no more than one-third of the husband's income is awarded to the wife and children.[23] In Cleveland, Ohio, researchers found that divorced fathers typically retained about 80 percent of their predivorce income.[24]

THE ADEQUACY OF CHILD SUPPORT AWARDS

Three standards can be used to evaluate the adequacy of child support awards. The first compares awards with the actual costs of raising children and asks if the awards are enough to cover the costs of raising children. The second assesses the reasonableness of the award in terms of the payor's financial resources: Does the father—over 95 percent of those ordered to pay are fathers—have the ability to pay the award? Both of these standards are embodied in the California law, which specifies that support be set in accordance with *needs* and *ability to pay*.[25]

Recent policy discussions of the standards for child support have referred to the first standard as the "cost approach" and the second as the "income sharing approach," terms that were first suggested by University of Maryland economist Barbara Bergmann.[26] The two approaches reflect the fundamental dilemma that all courts (and policy makers) must resolve in establishing standards for child support. The cost approach assumes that there is a basic cost for raising a child that is appropriate for all families. The income sharing approach is more realistic: it assumes that the cost of raising a child depends on the income level of his or her parents.

The two approaches not only produce different numerical results, they also represent different public policy goals. The cost approach, which establishes uniform costs for all families, typically results in lower amounts and assumes a welfare-like basic-needs approach to raising children. As Judith Cassetty, a pioneer in child support research, notes, the income sharing approach, in contrast, results in higher amounts (in middle- and upper-income families) because it is based on "the belief that children should benefit proportionately from the resources of each parent: this means that children would not inevitably suffer a decline in their standard of living in the event of a parental divorce.[27]

A third standard for evaluating child support is to ask if the awards fairly apportion the responsibility between the father and the mother. Here we can compare the financial contributions of the two parents in absolute terms (i.e., the amounts of money they contribute) and relative terms (what percentage of their respective incomes each contributes).

The Cost of Raising Children [28]

Many different methods have been used to estimate the cost of raising children. Almost all of them involve conservative calculations and produce low estimates. The following analysis relies on one of the most conservative estimates, that of economist Thomas Espenshade. Espenshade estimates that it would cost $85,163 to raise a child to age eighteen in a moderate-income family in 1980. In a low-income family in the United States it would cost $58,238.[29] His calculations include all direct maintenance costs: out-of-pocket expenditures for the child's birth, food, clothing, housing, transportation, medical care, education, and other expenses. A final component included in Espenshade's calculations is the cost of a four-year college education.

Parents magazine used a similar procedure, but included an adjustment for yearly inflation and estimated that the cost of raising a child born in 1980, would run to over $175,000.[30]

Before we proceed with this analysis, it is important to note just how conservative Espenshade's estimates are. First, they do not include any costs for child care *services*. Rather, he assumes that someone is "available" to take care of the children—and that someone is there *cost-free*. Obviously, if one has to pay for child care or day care, the cost of children will be much greater.

Second, a brief look at the costs of individual items suggests that Espenshade's estimates are unrealistically low. Consider, for example, his estimates for the cost of a college education. (We have omitted these costs in our calculations below because they may extend beyond age eighteen.) Espenshade calculates that *four years* of college will cost a total of $10,000.[31] This is only $2,500 per year, or $278 per month (for a nine-month academic year). It is difficult to find a public university in the United States today at which the cost of tuition, books, room, board and other living expenses are so low. Private colleges may cost between $10,000 and $15,000 or more each year, with the total cost of four years running more than $40,000. Espenshade's clothing, food, and laundry estimates are likewise unrealistic.

Bearing in mind that these estimates are very low to begin with, let us now look at how they compare with child support awards.

If we use Espenshade's total budget for a moderate-income family ($85,163), and subtract $10,000 cost of college (since college costs may not be included in child support once the child reaches age 18), we find that it averages $4,200 a year to raise one child at a moderate income level. Because of economies of scale, Espenshade calculates that a second child increases the costs by roughly half as much as the cost of the first child, so that the total child-rearing cost for two minor children would be about $6,300 a year. Similarly, for a low income standard of living, we find the cost close to $3,000 a year for one child ($2,680 to be precise), and over $4,000 for two children.*

Let us assume that our hypothetical Pat Byrd was raising her children at the "moderate" standard of living. We find that her court-ordered child support award of $250 a month (or $3,000 a year) would give her *$3,300 less* a year than the cost of raising her two children. Even at the lower standard, her court-ordered child support is inadequate—$1,020 less than she needs to raise her children at the poverty level.

The inadequacy of court-ordered child support is underscored by another relevant comparison. Pat Byrd's *total* support award—$450 a month for alimony and child support together—is not even as much as she would get from the Aid to Families with Dependent Children (AFDC) program. The California AFDC level of support for a household with two children was $463 per month plus $73 in food stamps, or a total of $536 per month.[32] If this is the amount that the government established as necessary for families at the lowest economic levels, it is evident that Pat Byrd and her children will not be able to live above the poverty level on the child support she was awarded.**

Further, as we have noted, one problem with Espenshade's calculations is that they omit child care expenses, a major cost that Pat Byrd will have to bear. Since Espenshade's calculations are based on two-parent families, he assumes that one parent, typically the mother, is available full time to care for the child. But if the mother in a single-parent family has to work,[34] she typically must pay someone else to take care of her children. And, as sociologist Karen Seal noted, the cost of child care alone typically exceeds the child support award.[35]

In order to determine adequate child support for such single-parent families, these child care costs should be added to Espenshade's estimates.

A 1980 report of the California Advisory Commission on Child Care compiled the average cost of child care in various California communities at that time.[36] In Los Angeles County, the monthly cost

* Since these costs vary between urban and rural areas, and by region, regional consumer price indexes for food, clothing, and housing are available.
** New legislation, which was influenced by an earlier report of the findings of this research, established a minimum for child support awards in California as of July 1985.[33]

for a preschool child averaged $205 in family day care and $195 in a day-care center for an average of $2,400 a year. If Pat Byrd's daughter was under two years of age, instead of four years old, day care for her would cost another $600 a year. If Pat Byrd works a full day, she will also have to pay for after-school care for her six-year-old son. That will cost her an additional $160 a month in family day care, or $116 a month in an after-school center, for an average of $1,600 a year.

Thus if we assume that Pat Byrd will work full time, her child care costs would be about $200 a month for her daughter ($2,400 ÷ 12) and $133 a month for her son ($1,600 ÷ 12). That adds up to $333 a month—considerably more than her entire child support award of $250 a month. (The child care costs are close to $4,000 a year in contrast to her entire child support award of $3,000 a year.) Of course, if she is lucky enough to get the children into a public day-care center with a sliding fee scale, her costs may be lower, but that typically entails a long waiting list and places her under pressure to go to work immediately.

Quite clearly, child support awards are not adequate to meet the cost of raising children. They fall short of every standard we have used: they are less than the average cost of day care alone, which would leave no child support money for food, or clothing, or housing.

These data suggest the importance of educating those who are setting child support awards about the actual costs of raising children. It is not surprising to find that judges and lawyers underestimate these costs[37] because parents themselves do not realize how much they are spending on their children. In fact, in one study, middle-class parents estimated that they were spending 14 percent of their incomes on their children when they were actually spending 40 percent.[38]

The Father's Ability to Pay: The Income Sharing Approach

The second and the preferable approach to establishing a child support award is the income sharing approach. Here the focus is on the family's resources and the father's ability to pay child support.

One frequently hears the complaint that divorced men cannot afford to pay the amount of child support the court has ordered. For example, the president of Fathers' Rights of America portrays the typical divorced man as a conscientious father who is forced to live at the poverty level because he is paying exorbitant child support.[39] Is this claim true? Are most divorced men unable to "afford" the child support award? How do child support awards compare with the fathers' incomes?

There are two standards for evaluating a father's ability to comply with the court order: one examines child support as a percentage of the husband's income; the second evaluates it in relation to standard of living.

Consider first what percentage of the father's income is awarded to child support. If we look back at the far right column of Table 24 (p. 267), we see that it is very rare for any court to order more than 25 percent of a man's income in child support or more than 32 percent of a man's income in combined child support and alimony.* Even though judges *report* that their typical award is closer to one-half of the husband's income, the data from the interviews with divorced persons show that the real proportion is quite different. Instead of a 50/50 division of the husband's income, the typical award is one-third for the wife and two children to two-thirds for the husband. Among upper-income men it is one-fifth to four-fifths: men who earn $50,000 or more a year retain an average of 81 percent of their net incomes for themselves (see Table 24).

The implications of awarding one-third of the family income to the wife and children and leaving two-thirds for the father are immediately apparent when we look at the distribution of family income graphically, as shown in Figure 1.

FIGURE 1   Division of Family Income After Divorce

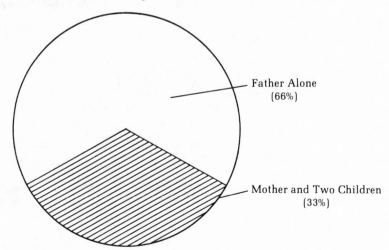

Father Alone (66%)

Mother and Two Children (33%)

* Men whose net incomes are under $10,000 are the only exceptions—their support awards average 37 percent of their incomes.

What happens if men fully comply with the court order: would they have enough left to live on? In a classic study of child support Michigan law, Professor David Chambers found that most fathers would be relatively well off.[40] In fact, 80 percent of the men would live at or above the government's "intermediate" standard budget level if they paid the support the court ordered. Using similar procedures to construct an index of ability to pay, Canadian researchers concluded that 80 percent of the divorced fathers could afford to pay child support and still live comfortably.[41]

Our analysis of the California data also follows Chambers' procedures. The starting point for these computations is the U.S. Department of Labor's standards for a high, intermediate, and lower level budget for an urban family of four for autumn 1977.[42] The basic budgets were devised for a typical family of two adults and two children. (For example, the lower level budget for a family of four was $10,481.) A separate procedure adjusts this budget to other types and sizes of families (depending on family size, age of oldest child, and age of household head).[43] A family of only two persons, for example, with a thirty-five-year old head of the household, would need only 60 percent of the money a family of four would need at a lower level budget. In analyzing the California data,* we found that 73 percent of the divorced men were able to live at or above the lower standard budget. Thus, close to *three-quarters of the California fathers had the "ability to pay" the amount the court ordered without a substantial reduction in their standard of living.* Figure 2 shows that 61 percent of the California fathers would be able to comply fully with the court order and still live above the high standard budget. An additional 12 percent would be living above the lower standard budget. Thus 73 percent of the men could live at a level above the lower standard budget.

Next, Chambers asked what would happen to the men's ex-wives and dependent children if the fathers paid the full amount of child support ordered. Obviously, if the family income stays constant, both the husband and wife cannot maintain the standard of living of the former intact family if they are living in two separate households. In Michigan, Chambers found that 97 percent of the divorced women and

---

* Using this procedure, a higher, intermediate, and lower budget was computed for *each* postdivorce family in our interview sample. For each predivorce family, there were two postdivorce families (the husband's and wife's). Postdivorce families were defined as a divorced person, a new spouse or cohabitee (where applicable), and any children whose custody was assigned to that spouse. The actual income of each postdivorce family was then compared with the three standard budgets and ranked according to the level of need.

children would be living below the poverty line—that is, below the lower standard budget.[44] Similarly, in California, 93 percent of all divorced women would be living below the lower standard budget.

Figure 2 shows the standard of living of California women and children if they had to live on the child support the court ordered. In contrast to the 73 percent of the men who could live comfortably, only 7 percent of the women and children would be living at the same level—even if the support were paid in full. *Almost all of the women and children—fully 93 percent—would be living below the poverty level.*

One of Chambers' conclusions, which is equally applicable to our data, is that "under the levels of child support that are ordered by

FIGURE 2   Standards of Living if Husband Pays Support *

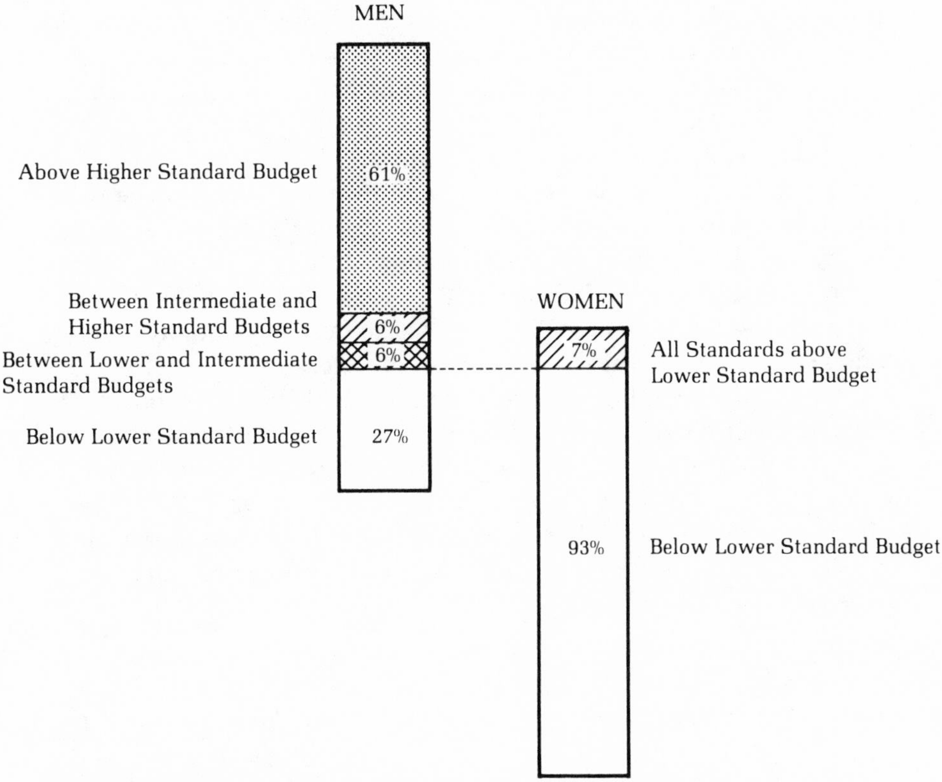

MEN

Above Higher Standard Budget   61%

Between Intermediate and
Higher Standard Budgets   6%   WOMEN

Between Lower and Intermediate   6%   7%   All Standards above
Standard Budgets   Lower Standard Budget

Below Lower Standard Budget   27%

93%   Below Lower Standard Budget

*Income standards of divorced men and women if men pay all support ordered and women live on support

Based on weighted sample of interviews with divorced persons, Los Angeles County, California, 1978 the court . . . *it is only the women and children whose standards of living decline,* even when the father is making payments."[45] Why does this happen? As Chambers explains:

> . . . a mother with two children needs between 75 and 80 percent of the family's former total income to continue to live at the prior standard. The father will have been ordered by the court to pay around 33 percent of his income. There remains a painful gap. On the other hand, the father who pays child support and retains two-thirds of his income still remains better off financially than he was before divorce. Four in five fathers can live at or above the Intermediate Standard Budget.[46]

Clearly, women and children cannot live on these awards even if they are paid in full. They must find other financial resources, such as employment or welfare.

The data in this section answer the question of whether men can afford to pay the amounts of child support ordered by the courts with an unequivocal yes. Whether one considers the percentage of the supporter's income or the standard of living he has after paying, the vast majority of divorced fathers can pay child support and still maintain a relatively comfortable standard of living.

Significantly, both divorced men and divorced women agree with this conclusion. When asked, "Can you (or your ex-husband) afford to pay the child support the court ordered?", fully 80 percent of the women and 90 percent of the men say yes. Thus both men and women see the award as reasonable in terms of the husband's ability to pay. Only a small minority feel the awards are excessive.

Along the same lines, when asked about their satisfaction with the amount of child support awarded in their case, the vast majority (91 percent) of *divorced men see the awards as reasonable* in terms of their income. Only 9 percent of the men say they were dissatisfied. (As might be expected, a larger percentage of the *women,* 36 percent, are dissatisfied with the amount of child support awarded and see it as inadequate.)

The Standard of Equitable Contributions from Husband and Wife

The final standard for evaluating the adequacy of child support awards is whether they equitably apportion the burden between the two parents. One way of apportioning the financial responsibility for child support would be to ask each parent to contribute half of the child's expenses. Another way would be to ask each parent to contribute according to his or her ability to pay. The latter standard, which is codified in the California law, aims at placing a lesser burden on the spouse with the lower earning capacity, who is typically the wife.

How do the child support awards fare when measured against the first standard, a 50/50 division of expenses? Earlier, in the discussion of the Pat Byrd case, we compared the amount of child support the father would typically be ordered to pay ($3,000 per year) with Espenshade's estimates of the actual cost of raising two children at a moderate income level ($6,300). Setting aside our criticism of Espenshade's cost estimates as too low, we might at first conclude that the child support awards provide close to half of his low estimate. But this is so only if we ignore the wife's contribution of time and child care services which Espenshade conveniently assumes are "free." But there are foregone costs when a mother spends time caring for her children. She is relinquishing wages that she could earn at a paid job and she is avoiding the cost of paying someone else to care for her children.

How much are these forgone costs worth? Even if we use a partial estimate of the cost of child care services, the cost of day care, it would mean that the monetary value of the mother's contribution was *more than twice* as much as the father's (i.e., $4,000 plus $3,300 is $7,300 versus his $3,000 child support award). Once the real cost of the wife's custodial services are recognized, it becomes evident that she is not only bearing more than half of the cost of the children, she is probably contributing the vast majority of it.[47]

Thus, California child support awards typically do not meet the first standard of equity, because the noncustodial father is not required to contribute an equal share of the actual costs of raising his children.

This conclusion is strengthened by an additional fact: the data on noncompliance show that men tend to pay far less than the court has ordered.* As a result, the mother is forced to assume an even more disproportionate share of the costs of raising her children after divorce.

The California awards also fall short of the second standard of equity, whereby each parent is expected to contribute according to his or her ability to pay. As we saw earlier, child support is typically set in accordance with the husband's ability to pay while still allowing him to maintain an adequate standard of living. The wife, however,

---

* These data are reviewed on pages 283–284 below.

who usually has far less earning capacity, and thus less ability to pay, typically ends up shouldering a disproportionately larger share of the cost of child support. Thus, rather than finding that child support has been apportioned in accord with the second norm of equity—according to the ability of each parent to pay—we find it has been apportioned in *direct contradiction* to that norm, with the heavier burden falling upon the parent who can *least* afford to pay, the custodial mother. This inevitably results in a drastically reduced standard of living for both the mother and the children.

In summary, the data point to three conclusions. First, the amount of child support ordered is typically quite modest in terms of the father's ability to pay. Second, the amount of child support ordered is typically not enough to cover even half the cost of actually raising the children. Third, the major burden of child support is typically placed on the mother even though she normally has fewer resources and much less "ability to pay."

THE NEW AGE OF MAJORITY FOR CHILD SUPPORT

Another factor that adds to the financial burden of divorced mothers in California is their *de facto* responsibility for the support of their college age children. In 1972 the California legislature reduced the age of majority from twenty-one to eighteen. As a consequence, college age children who are over eighteen are no longer considered minors in need of support, unless otherwise specified.[48]

Thus divorced women suddenly found themselves responsible for child support for children between eighteen and twenty-one in their custody, just when expenses for schooling are likely to be heaviest. In the California cases we studied, *fewer than 5 percent of cases* in any year involved a court order requiring a father to pay for the children's education. A higher percentage of fathers (about 40 percent in Los Angeles, 20 percent in San Francisco) are required to pay their children's medical expenses, but these obligations last only until the child's age of majority. Cumulatively, these data indicate that the major responsibility for older children also falls on the custodial mother.

The financial strain of having to support college age children is particularly devastating for middle-class women. For example, as one woman, whose son was still in high school when his support was terminated, expressed it:

> We mothers get minimal spousal support, or none at all, and then
> have that bled from us in the process of having to assume a disproportion-

ate share of the support of minor children, first, and ultimately, the total support of those of our college age children . . . And the fathers . . . What, pray, did they do when the age of majority was the more realistic twenty-one? . . . Did they kill off those bothersome offspring who dared to aspire to vocational training or a university education while remaining dependents? . . . Do you know what it's like to eke out an existence for 365 days of the year? My son and I do. . . .[49]

Other women complained that their children were denied college financial aid because their ex-husbands had adequate income to support them (even though they were not, in fact, providing them with any support).

This woman is correct in asserting that mothers typically bear the *de facto* responsibility for supporting their college-age children who are no longer legally minors. Even though the divorced mothers of college-age children whom we interviewed invariably had less money than their former husbands, a larger percentage of them voluntarily contributed to their children's support past age eighteen. Independent confirmation of this fact comes from a second survey, although it is a less systematic one than our interviews. Students in my 1983 class at Stanford University undertook a survey of their peers who had experienced (or were experiencing) a parental divorce.[50] The students found that more of their peers considered their mother's home "their own home," and they were more likely to ask their mothers than their fathers for money, even though they realized that her financial resources were more limited.

On the whole, the students felt their father expected them to work and support themselves in college, and were more likely to demand a *quid pro quo* in return for financial assistance. They saw their fathers as more distant, judgmental, and selfish, and often felt psychologically (as well as financially) abandoned by these men who were now pursuing "new lives." Their mothers, in contrast, were more likely in all ways to stay involved in the students' lives (which the students described as both a "burden" and as "helpful and important to me"). Although the mothers had less money and no legal obligation for support, many nevertheless continued to support their children through college.

This is one issue that suggests relatively easy and straightforward policy changes: California could extend parental responsibility for post majority support until children complete their education. This is currently the law in several states.[51] For example, the state of Washington's Dissolution of Marriage Act permits courts to order parental contributions to college education for post-majority children of divorced parents.[52] When faced with a 1978 challenge to this law, the court construed the act as basing the requirement of support on dependency, not minority, which it deemed justified:

> It has long been the law in Washington that a divorced parent may have a duty of support for college education if it works the parent no significant hardship and if the child shows aptitude. This duty is no longer limited by minority. . . . In allowing for divorce, the state undertakes to protect its victims. . . . A number of courts adopt the policy that a child should not suffer because his parents are divorced. The child of divorced parents should be in no worse position than a child from an unbroken home whose parents could be expected to supply a college education. . . . Parents, when deprived of the custody of their children, very often refuse to do for such children what natural instinct would ordinarily prompt them to do. . . . In most cases the father, who is the one who holds the purse strings, and whose earning capacity is greater than that of the mother, is the one who is able to give the minor a proper education. [If we do not take this position then] the court, in providing for the custody of the child, [would be] in the dilemma of knowing that if the child is given to the mother the father would, in very many cases, refuse to give it an education greater than that required under the penalty of the law, and that the mother could not do so.[53]

As the Washington court astutely notes, if the court does not order the financially more able parent to provide support, support may be used as a lever in custody decisions (i.e., fathers may refuse to pay for college costs unless they are awarded custody). Thus the current rule allows a father to use financial leverage to obtain custody (a subject which is discussed further below) and may thereby undermine the child's best interest.

A second negative consequence of the current rule is that it encourages fathers to be less honorable and less responsible than they would be normally. In fact, many of the attorneys we interviewed were disturbed because the law put them in the position of having to choose between compromising their own ethical standards or advising their clients not to support their children. As one attorney said:

> It's tough. . . . If I fully inform him of his legal rights—that he has no obligation to support his children—it exerts an influence, no doubt about it. . . . But if I advise him to agree to support them through college, I could be sued for malpractice.

The current law may also put mothers in a double bind by forcing them to choose between their own financial security and their children's college education. As one attorney said "the problem is convincing my women clients not to sell themselves short to get him to pay for college. I tell them they have to protect *themselves,* but they are in a no-win situation."

The alternative, as suggested above, would be to adopt a law that would encourage fathers to "follow their natural instincts" and to be honorable parents by maintaining their responsibility to support their children through college.

FURTHER EROSION OF CHILD SUPPORT: INFLATION AND NONCOMPLIANCE

Thus far, we have focused primarily on the adequacy of child support orders made by the courts. Let us now consider two critical factors that further erode the value of these awards: inflation, and noncompliance. The disparity in the financial burden placed on mothers and fathers is even greater when one considers how inadequate support orders are further diminished by inflation and noncompliance.

Inflation

Even if support awards are fully complied with, their value may be severely eroded by inflation. Surprisingly, less than 10 percent of the support awards in both the interview and court docket samples included a cost of living escalator or other form of anti-inflationary adjustment. Without such periodic adjustments, the purchasing power of court-ordered support can be drastically reduced by inflation. For example, a child or spousal support order for $500 per month which was awarded in 1978 would have brought only $465 worth of the same goods one year later.[54] The purchasing power of the same order entered ten years ago would be cut nearly in half.

The potential influence of inflation is easily seen in the context of the hypothetical Byrd case. Let us assume a judge awarded Pat Byrd $200 a month in alimony and $250 a month in child support in 1975. One year later, in 1976, her award would have brought only $236 worth of the same goods.[55] Within two years, in 1977, it would have declined to $219, and in five years, in 1980, it would yield a mere $117 in purchasing power. By 1984 it would have dwindled to $13.

This obviously leads us to the question of what it would take to maintain the value of the original award over time.[56] The spousal support award of $200 would have to be increased to $225 in two years, and to $306 in five years. Similarly, to maintain the children's level of support, we would have to increase the $250 child support award to $383 in five years, and to $448 by 1984.

Compounding the inflationary factor in diminishing the effectiveness of a child support order is the increasing cost of supporting a child as he or she grows older. In fact, in an intact marriage, the amount spent in the seventeenth year of a child's life would be almost three and a half times the amount spent at age one.[57]

Forensic economist Philip Eden aptly illustrates the diminished effectiveness of an unmodified support order of $500, awarded a decade ago for three children aged one, three, and five:

> The growth of the children in the last decade increased the amount needed to maintain the original standard [from $500] to $633. The purchasing power of the original amount has been eroded by inflation down to $275. The proportion of the noncustodial spouse's income used for support of the children has dropped from one-third down to one-sixth.
>
> While the original award represented a certain standard of living for these children, their growth and inflation have combined to reduce the buying power of that same $500. For each dollar now needed to purchase that original standard of living, they have only 43 cents.[58]

These statistics point to the importance of including automatic cost-of-living adjustments (known as COLA or escalation clauses) when support awards are first made to protect the awards from the erosive effects of inflation. This is not a new concept: such clauses are common in labor management contracts and are routine in private and public benefit programs such as Social Security. COLA clauses can also help meet the increased cost of raising children as they grow older.

Although some state courts have objected to COLA adjustments because they want to hear evidence of "the change in circumstances" typically required to warrant an increase, it is gradually being recognized that since modification proceedings put the burden on the mother (since it is she who must hire an attorney, lose time from work, and risk possible retaliation by the noncustodial parent) they are rarely used. COLA adjustments merely shift that burden to the payor and therefore "favor" the growing needs of the child. State courts in a number of states have approved the use of automatic increases in child support awards based on the Consumer Price Index (CPI). For example, courts in Colorado, Minnesota, and Washington state have ruled that automatic escalation clauses are enforceable in court,[59] and the Iowa Supreme court held that initial support orders should include adjustments that avoid the need for repeated hearings on predictable modifications.[60] In addition, a 1984 California law, which was shaped in part by an earlier report of the findings of this research, permits a simplified procedure for adjustments in support awards, up to 10 percent a year, without proof of charged circumstances.[61]

NONCOMPLIANCE: THE PROBLEM OF ENFORCEMENT

The widespread lack of compliance with court-ordered child and spousal support has been well documented by previous research in the United States and Canada. For example, a 1981 survey conducted by the U.S. Census Bureau revealed that less than half of the women who were awarded child support received it as ordered; about 30 percent of the women received partial payments, while another quarter never received a single dollar.[62] Similarly, a 1980 survey of maintenance orders in Alberta, Canada, revealed that only a third of the women received the full amount of the court-ordered support.[63] Another third received less than the full amount, while the final third received nothing.

Our California data *under*estimate the extent of noncompliance because both the docket sample and the interviews were limited to events within the *first year* after the divorce. The 1977 court records that we examined contained complaints from 15 percent of the Los Angeles wives who went back to court to complain of noncompliance within twelve months of following their final decree of divorce.[64] The interview data, however, suggest that this figure greatly underestimates the extent of nonpayment, underpayment, and irregular payment. Many wives reported that they did not file a formal complaint about their husband's noncompliance because they lacked the time, knowledge, or monetary resources to do so. In fact, only about *one-third* of our female interviewees reported that they regularly received the full amount of court-ordered child support in the first year of the court order.* A hefty 43 percent of the women reported receiving little or no child support during that first year. The remaining 22 percent reported having problems either in obtaining the full amount of the order, or in obtaining it on time.

Further, since these interviews were conducted just one year after the divorce became final, it is reasonable to assume that for many of

---

* Compliance with alimony orders appeared to be somewhat better, probably because alimony tends to be awarded only in higher-income families. Nevertheless, as noted in Chapters 6 and 7, one out of six men was in arrears on spousal support within just six months of the divorce.

those women noncompliance would become an even greater problem in later years.

There are three consistent findings reported in the research on compliance with child support orders.[65] First, not one study has found a state or county in which even half of the fathers fully comply with court orders.[66] Second, the research suggests that many of the fathers who are ordered to pay support pay it irregularly and are often in arrears. In several studies, the average arrearage is for half or three-quarters of the money owed, and in one study the average reached 89 percent.[67] (While some contribution is certainly preferable to total noncompliance, irregular or infrequent child support payments can create serious hardships for the dependent mother and children.) Third, the research indicates that a very sizable minority of fathers—typically between a quarter and a third—never make a single court-ordered payment.

The problem of noncompliance is particularly serious because child support can make the difference between poverty and nonpoverty for many families. Women who are near the poverty line and receive child support can easily fall below that line if the payments are eliminated. In fact, one U.S. Census Bureau study showed that about a third of the divorced and separated women who did not receive child support fell below the poverty line, compared to only 12 percent of the women who received such support.[68]

Child support payments are also a major determinant of whether or not a woman applies for public assistance. In a 1978 census sample, 38 percent of women who were not receiving child support from the father of their children received public assistance income, compared to only 13 percent of women who had child support income.[69]

The lack of compliance not only causes great economic hardship, it also undermines confidence in the law and in the force of court orders. Our California interviews were replete with complaints about the court's failure to enforce its support orders, the negative or hostile responses of the court officials to requests from nonsupported mothers, and the resulting frustration and disillusionment that women experience when they confront the apparent ease with which a violation of the law is tolerated. As one woman said:

> The whole judicial process is a fraud. You have to hire an expensive lawyer and prepare all these documents for the judge . . . and in the end, all you get is an order that isn't worth the piece of paper it's written on. It's a sham—a charade! I can't believe our whole system of so-called justice is such a fraud.

Testimony at the 1984 congressional hearings on child support echoed these sentiments. Women throughout the United States testified to their frustration with a legal system that often seems to aid and abet nonsupporting fathers. As one divorced mother said:

> My own children, like thousands of others, have been denied their economic birthright by a father who swore he would never pay a dime in child support, and by courts that have failed to enforce their own orders. The truth is that if a father chooses to be uncooperative, there is little a mother can do.[70]

> I went to court five times between 1972 and 1979, traveling to a distant State and paying attorney fees. The last trip in 1979 cost me $1,300. That court in Media, Pennsylvania, raised the support and required that my former husband pay all medical bills plus almost $2,000 in arrears in a lump sum. When my former husband didn't obey that order, I was told to come back into court—again at my own expense—and sue him for contempt of court. I was told that, even if I did this, I had no guarantee that he would be made to pay. I decided that I couldn't afford to collect my support.[71]

Getting Child Support Paid: The Burden on Women

The typical child support order calls for the father to send the mother a check every month or every pay period. It is up to the mother to keep track of the checks and to try to obtain the money when the checks are late or are for less than the full amount ordered. In most jurisdictions, judges have the option of ordering payments through the court so that the court can monitor compliance.[72] *

The judges, however, rarely order men to pay child support through the court. They say it's an "additional bureaucratic impediment for the man" and they do not want to "embarrass" men, especially middle- and upper-class men, by requiring them to send their checks to the court. The lack of court monitoring leaves the burden of collecting support on the mother. As one woman described it:

> It's outrageous. The law gives him full control. He decides if he wants to pay or not. . . . No one monitors him . . . . He has the money but wants to make me call to ask for it. . . . It is his way of keeping power

* As of January 1985, thirty states gave judges discretion to have child support payments made directly to a court officer (see Table C-8, Legal Appendix, pp 436–437) and this option is now required in all states, at the request of either party, under the Child Support Enforcement Amendments of 1984.[73]

over me. . . . If I hadn't needed the money so badly, I wouldn't have put up with it. . . . But it was a choice between that and my children's welfare. . . . The system puts you in this impossible degrading position. If you aren't nice to your ex-husband, he doesn't send the check.

Along the same lines, a woman who had been married to a dentist complained:

My lawyer said, "He's a professional man, the judge won't make him pay through the court. But you don't have to worry, he's going to pay." . . . But he never pays on time. Every month there is a new trick. First he sent checks but "forgot" to sign them. Then he made a mistake in the amount—like writing two instead of two hundred dollars, or putting one amount in writing and another in figures. Then the checks started coming late. I'd call and he would say, "It's in the mail." He has a postage meter at his office. Each time I had to call my lawyer and ask him to call his lawyer. My lawyer wrote letters every month. . . . I never had the money when I needed it!

The wives of other "professional men" told similar stories of their ex-husbands' ability to manipulate the system without a technical violation of the law. For example, at the time of our interviews California required a payor to be sixty days in arrears before a wage attachment could be issued. As the wife of a corporate officer-engineer complained:

My former husband used the sixty-day loophole as a tool to harass me.* He would delay mailing checks so that they would always be late. I had no recourse because the checks were not sixty days late—even though my credit cards and mortgage company made me pay fines for the late payments. Just before Christmas his check was two weeks late and we had no heat (by that time my credit rating had been ruined and I was required to pay cash for everything including heating oil) and no hot showers . . . and no money for gifts to each other or any nice things over the holiday period . . . all we had was beans and anger.

The divorced women we interviewed reported five major problems in securing child support awards: locating the ex-husband, finding an attorney—or getting help from the district attorney—to press their case, the expense of pursuing the case, and the judges' attitudes and practices.

LOCATING THE EX-HUSBAND

The easiest way for a man to evade a child support order is to move to another state. His ex-wife then has to find him before she

---

* As of January 1981, California courts do not have to wait sixty days to order wage assignments.

faces the even more difficult task of trying to get the order enforced in another state. The experiences of three mothers are illustrative:

> He got furious when the judge ordered him to pay $300 a month in child support, so he got himself transferred to their plant in Oregon. . . . I didn't get anything for eight months until they tracked him down and instituted new proceedings there. . . . It was an incredible hassle . . . you can't imagine what it's like not to have money to feed your children. . . . I broke down and applied for AFDC. . . . Then they found him for me.

> I went to the district attorney and they were supposed to find him, but they never did. He moves from county to county. I have to know his exact whereabouts before the papers can be filed. I could never keep up with him. I do not have the emotional or financial resources to do it.

> I don't know where he is and I don't know how to find him. Short of hiring a private detective or paid assassin, there is really nothing a person can do. I've contacted everyone who knows him—at work, his family— and no one will tell me anything.

THE ROLE OF THE ATTORNEY

Instituting new legal proceedings to obtain court-ordered support can be expensive, and many women are distressed when they discover that their divorce attorney does not want to be bothered with their enforcement problems. Those attorneys who are willing to handle enforcement typically require a retainer that adds up to several months of child support payments. A recurrent theme in our interviews with divorced women was their surprise and distress over this situation. As the ex-wife of a doctor reported:

> I had to force him [the lawyer who represented her in the divorce proceedings] to help me collect the support. He didn't want to be involved. He said it was ridiculous to get uptight because my checks were late, because ultimately he would have to pay. When I said I couldn't wait three or four months until we took him to court, my lawyer was very unsympathetic. He just said, "Borrow the money from someone." And I said I had no one to borrow from, that "I need it and I want you to write a letter and get it for me." He would very grudgingly write a letter which would ultimately produce the check even though it would be three weeks or a month late. It would eventually come. But his idea was that I should wait three or four months and then file for contempt.

Despite the fact that 75 percent of the women who complained of compliance problems had been represented by attorneys during their divorce proceedings, the majority of them (61 percent) said their attorneys did not help them in their efforts to secure enforcement of child support orders. As two women expressed it,

> My lawyer said it's out of his hands, once the final decree has been signed. I'm not his case any longer."

> He [lawyer] told me to go to the district attorney's office. He said enforcement was their job, not his.

Several attorneys advised their clients to "reason with their husbands" or "to wait." As the wife of a highly paid engineer reported:

> My lawyer said he's a professional man, when he calms down he'll do right by you. Don't antagonize him by taking him to court.

Only a minority of the women in our sample who had been represented by attorneys reported that these attorneys were willing to help them secure compliance after they were divorced. Thirty-nine percent of the women said that their divorce attorneys had in some way helped them in their efforts to obtain child support payments. When the women were asked what the attorneys had done, the most common responses were "called husband or husband's lawyer" and "wrote husband or husband's lawyer."

> I had the lawyer write a letter and then I got checks that were no good . . . they bounced. My lawyer wrote more letters but it didn't do any good. It cost me more to try to get the money than he owes me.

The women's reports of their attorneys' efforts suggest that most attorneys were simply unwilling to devote their best efforts to secure compliance. Only 18 percent of the attorneys filed contempt charges, forcing the fathers to return to court, and only 15 percent of the attorneys tried to obtain some security such as a bond or trust fund to guarantee the husband's payment. Most surprising is that only 1 percent of the attorneys tried to attach the man's wages.

The inaction and ineffective action on the part of attorneys is revealing. If only one percent of the attorneys use the most effective method of securing compliance—a wage attachment—it is no wonder that men get the message that child support is "voluntary." They are rarely pressed to pay.

A wage attachment (also referred to as a wage assignment) is a court order for part of an employee's wages to be set aside and sent to another party, such as a creditor or a custodial parent. While not all fathers are salaried employees, wage assignments are feasible for a substantial portion of the population and are extremely effective:

in a survey of cases in New York State the payment rate doubled from 40 percent to 80 percent for cases covered by mandatory wage withholding.[74]

GETTING HELP FROM THE DISTRICT ATTORNEY'S OFFICE

One of the women quoted above said her attorney told her to go to the district attorney's office to get help in collecting her child support. This was a common response among attorneys who did not want to be bothered with enforcement.

District attorneys have the responsibility for criminal nonsupport although there is considerable variation in the procedures used by D.A.s in different counties who deal with child support. Most often, it was women who could not afford attorneys who turned to the district attorney's office for help. The experiences of these women are typical:

They do everything they can to avoid you. . . . They rotate attorneys, so it's hard to keep track of what's happening on your case. . . . The receptionist won't let you talk to anyone—she tells you to put it in writing. They don't want to see you, they won't talk to you on the phone, they want everything in writing.

When you finally get an appointment, they tell you how busy and over-worked they are—they make you feel like you are the one who is causing trouble, like it's your fault, not your husband's.

The D.A. said he couldn't deal with anything on the phone—I'd have to put it in writing. . . . I said, "But this is an emergency." He said, "Well then drop off the letter here and don't forget to make it legible, honey."

Before you can ever get to the judge you have to go to the D.A.'s office, but they have such frequent personnel turnover that I had to deal with fifteen different people in two years. . . . As soon as one of them gets wise to my husband's tricks, they switch workers on me and the new one wants to begin by giving him a break.

These reports are echoed throughout the state. As the *Handbook on Divorce for Women in Santa Clara County* states:

The endless red tape, the long waits, the uncooperative civil servants, the confusing forms, and the unsympathetic attitudes that women are confronted with when they attempt to get help from public agencies, has forced many women to simply give up trying to obtain for their children what they legally have coming to them.[75]

Those who do not give up are represented by an attorney from the district attorney's office in court. Once again, however, many women report difficulty in securing the help they need:

> He [district attorney] said that I was so much better off than a lot of people I should be thankful—I had a home and wasn't starving. I said that neither was my husband on his $3,000 a month. He told me not to get angry because I'd alienate the judge.

> He said the judge would probably forgive the arrearage [it was over $5,000], and I was furious. He said it's really not worth getting upset about it. . . . You'll get by without it. I told him it was my kids' summer, my kids' food, maybe my kids' losing their home.

> He told me outright not to bother him about alimony—it wasn't the legislature's intent to fool with alimony.

> Before we went to court, he said, "remember Mrs. R, it's whether the judge likes your looks. . . . he might look at your husband and may like him, and then you won't get your arrearage . . . so don't get angry. Try to be nice."

A common complaint concerned the reluctance of district attorneys to ask for wage assignments.

> I said I wanted an automatic wage attachment. . . . The D.A. said judges don't like that law . . . they won't bother with it.

> They talk about the judges being idiots and not knowing what they are doing. . . . I said "The law says the judge is supposed to order a wage assignment." He [the D.A.] said "Yes, but this judge doesn't know what he's doing."

As these reports suggest, it is often the judge who does not want to issue a wage assignment and the district attorney is simply reflecting that reality. As one woman said:

> The D.A. who tried to help me was very nice but he said it was like banging his head against a brick wall to get the judge to act. . . . When we went before the judge he said my husband had not yet violated *his* order (only the orders of the other two judges). So *he* had to give him a chance to comply with *his* order first.

THE EXPENSE OF PURSUING THE CASE

Even those women who were determined to have their day in court and to make their ex-husbands explain their nonpayment to the judge often found that their case was postponed so many times that they simply could not afford to pursue it.

> Each time I went to court I lost a day's pay, and I had to pay my lawyer for his court rate. We had to wait two hours for the case to be called, and then [my ex-husband] got a postponement to get his papers together. . . . . The next time he was sick. . . . Then he changed attorneys. . . . Each time the judge said he had a right to have his side represented . . . but I couldn't afford it anymore. They let him get away with murder.

> I had to wait until I earned enough money to be able to afford to pursue him. You can't afford to go to court unless you have the money to begin with. It's a catch 22.

Similar experiences were reported by women from other states who testified at the 1984 congressional hearings on child support. As one woman put it, many delinquent fathers "learn the brinksmanship of the process." They know that the first offense or two brings a wrist slapping or suspended sentence. If they are hauled into court again, they make a token partial payment which results in their being given another chance and in further delays. Even states with routinized collection procedures allowed men repeated opportunities which, to the women forced to wait for support, seemed unnecessarily lenient.

> Although my ex-husband did not pay the support or meet the timeline, he was granted two extensions. At one point, when I contacted the court officer to voice my dissatisfaction at the delay, he explained that he was allowing my ex-husband ample time so that he could make an equitable decision and asked if I had considered reconciliation since I was having so much financial difficulty. Another show cause hearing was finally scheduled in April. At that time my ex-husband purposely did not appear in court even though his lawyer and mine were both present, and a writ of body attachment was issued for his arrest. Nevertheless, the writ was never served. . . .[76]

As Elaine Fromm, president of the Organization for the Enforcement of Child Support, testified at the House hearings:

> It has long been common knowledge that a parent who does not wish to pay support does not have to. It is easy for a parent who is in arrears to make a rather lame excuse in front of a lenient judge and be let off with a warning. Some of the more affluent obligors will hire high-priced

lawyers to avoid paying child support and, ironically, will sometimes pay fees in excess of the arrearages. Many non-custodians keep moving one step ahead of the law or flee to more liberal States and continue their luxurious lifestyles while their children exist in poverty.[77]

In her congressional testimony, Secretary Margaret Heckler of Health and Human Services reported the results of an informal survey that showed backlogs of three to six months just to schedule hearing dates:

> For the large urban jurisdictions, such delays could go as long as two years. These may not sound like lengthy delays in the context of normal court proceedings, but let me assure you that for child-support cases, they can mean . . . losing a home or wanting the other basic necessities of life.[78]

JUDICIAL ATTITUDES AND PRACTICES

Those women who went before a judge to secure enforcement were typically unsatisfied with the process. They were likely to feel that the judge was unsympathetic and impatient with their request. As one reported:

> The court didn't want to hear it about all I had been through trying to make him pay. The judge said to me, "Say it concisely." He didn't want to hear how many times I had to go to his house to get the money. He didn't want to hear about my daughter left crying on the street because he didn't pick her up for the school picnic. . . . He was so patronizing . . . and I was so bottled up with anger and frustration I couldn't even talk.

Many others complained of judges' excessive leniency, which put the entire burden of doing without on the woman and her children:

> My husband put on a big act in court saying he wasn't working and had no money . . . but he works at the same plant as my brother-in-law and he has seen him there every day. . . . The judge let him get away with all that sweet talk about how he cared about his children. [Q: What did the judge do?] He told him to come back in a month with his pay stubs . . . then he [the husband] didn't show and we had to start all over again. . . . Meanwhile, how am I supposed to buy food? With his promises?

Two judicial practices—the failure to order wage assignments and the waiving of arrearages—are the subject of widespread dissatisfaction among those who seek better enforcement of support orders.

Wage assignments, as noted above, have proven most effective in securing compliance. Yet the vast majority of the California judges are reluctant to order them. In the 1977 random sample of court records only 5 percent of the cases with a child support award had a wage attachment. (This includes wage attachments established with the award as well as those added within the first year after the divorce.) For alimony orders, the figure was 3 percent.

Senator Paula Hawkins of Florida reported a similar low incidence of wage assignments on the part of Florida judges:

> An alarming discovery was that many of the courts responsible for enforcement were unaware of the variety of enforcement techniques available to them. For example, many of the judges were not aware that Florida State law permitted the courts to impose mandatory wage assignments on non-AFDC as well as AFDC recipients if the absent parent missed two or more payments. Even worse, many judges who were aware of the provision were very reluctant to use it.[79]

Unlike the Florida judges who said they were unaware of the law, the California judges we interviewed were well informed (and were aware that *the law required* wage assignments when support was two months overdue). But they chose not to follow the law. (Their reasons are discussed below in the section on judicial attitudes.)

A second complaint about current judicial practice is that many judges are willing to excuse arrearages (money owed for past-due child support). Most of the judges we interviewed said they would retroactively decrease or "forgive" large arrearages. Their explanations included not wanting to make payments too difficult ("It would be a financial hardship for a man to make back payments in full"); wanting to give the father a break so that he can get on the right track; and trying to look to the future, not the past (after all some judges reasoned, "The children have managed to survive"). The implicit message in the judges' treatment of arrearages is that fathers are rewarded for noncompliance by having their debt reduced or forgiven.

In no other area of the law do judges retroactively adjust court orders and arbitrarily dismiss debts. Although relief from some debts is permitted if a person is bankrupt, child support obligations are not dischargeable in bankruptcy. They have a special status and cannot be forgiven. This is because the law recognizes that they have a *higher* claim and deserve greater respect than other debts. In light of the special status of support obligations, it is unconscionable for family court judges to simply "forgive" them.

In summary, it is clear that the end result of the present legal system is to provide virtually every incentive for fathers not to pay child support.[80]

In the end, many divorced women feel that there is nothing they can do and no one who can help them collect child support. When women we interviewed reported difficulty in collecting support, we asked, "What have you done to try to get him to pay what the court ordered?" Two-thirds of the women said, "Nothing." Their comments are indicative of the sense of hopelessness and resignation they feel:

You feel so helpless—you are totally dependent on his whims.

I have to fight with him over every single medical bill for my daughter. After a while, you just give up. . . . It's not worth the time or the effort.

Last time he stopped paying, I was on the phone every month. I was so upset I was terrified we'd be evicted. . . . This time, I can't afford to take time off from work and track him down. It's worthless. What can you do?

The Catch 22 dilemma of whether it is worth all of this trouble to collect child support awards is captured by the dialogue between two women in the film *Who Remembers Mama*.[81] The first woman argues that you can't let them get away with it, you have to summon up all your energy and fight for your rights:

Sondra: I have a lot of friends that will say, "Well, if he's not man enough to pay it, I'm not going to make him." You know, I could have three seizures at one time, to hear somebody say that. It takes time. It takes effort. It takes sweat. It takes cursing. It takes praying to go down there, number one. And then it takes all of that to go to court. Then you pray a little while longer for the check to come.[82]

The second woman said she just couldn't stand the tension and aggravation it created in her life:

Jean: When I lost custody of my kids, that was the one good thing. Never again did I have to look for that date on the calendar and wring my hands, worrying: Is it coming? Is it going to be a week late this month? Is it going to be two weeks late? Can I pay the rent this month? What can we do this month? How many bounced check charges am I going to get if it's two weeks late? Am I going to get an eviction notice if it's late this month? What's going to happen tomorrow?

And I have told all my kids, . . . if you come back and live with me,

I'll tell you one thing: I don't want any child support. We're going to have to see to it that we can live with never being dependent on that man again for money. I will not give him that control over my life again.[83]

The tragedy behind this statement, as with so many of those quoted in these pages, is that the children are the helpless victims of the present legal system.

Different Perceptions of the Problem: Men vs. Women

It is interesting to note that men and women have radically different perceptions of "the rate" of noncompliance. While two-thirds of the women we interviewed reported that they had difficulty collecting child support, only 11 percent of the men perceived any problem. Although part of this discrepancy may stem from the men's desire to appear honorable or impress an interviewer, the discrepancy might also be explained by the different stakes the two sexes have in the outcome. For the woman, a check that is a week or two weeks late may mean no money to pay the rent and a struggle to find money for food. It also means late charges and fines from creditors which add to the expenses she bears and may destroy her credit rating as well. In addition, the uncertainty of the payment is likely to create anxiety and disrupt her budgeting. Her husband, on the other hand, may perceive the same delay as inconsequential and assume that he has fully complied as long as he sends the check sometime during the month.

WHY DON'T FATHERS PAY?

How can we explain the high rate of noncompliance with support orders? One widespread belief is that fathers simply cannot afford to pay the child support and alimony ordered by the court. However, Chambers' data from Michigan and our data from California indicate that most divorced fathers could comply with the court orders and still live quite well after doing so. Every study of men's ability to pay arrives at the same conclusion: the money is there. Indeed, there is normally enough to permit payment of significantly *higher* awards than are currently being made.

The suggestion that men cannot afford to pay child support is refuted by a second set of data. If lack of ability to pay were the cause of noncompliance, we would expect the highest rates of noncompliance among men with the lowest incomes. But the California data in Table 25 show little relationship between income and noncompliance (for all men earning less than $50,000 a year). Men with incomes of between $30,000 and $50,000 a year are just as likely to avoid child support payments as are men with incomes of under $10,000 a year.

TABLE 25

Compliance with Child-support Orders by Father's Postdivorce Gross Income

FATHER'S YEARLY INCOME	PERCENTAGE IRREGULAR OR NO PAYMENTS
Under $10,000	27%
$10,000–20,000	27
$20,000–30,000	22
$30,000–50,000	29
$50,000 or more	8

This table is based on the combined responses of male and female respondents in the weighted sample of divorced persons, Los Angeles County, 1978.

The Canadian study of support orders found a weak positive relationship between income and compliance, although excellent payers and nonpayers had similar mean incomes.[84] (In that study low income was associated with irregular payment but not with nonpayment.) The Canadian researchers concluded that 80 percent of the fathers could afford to pay.

The one category of men that one might at first assume do not have the ability to pay are those who are unemployed. However, here too compliance is not related to lowered income. For example, one woman reported that her husband's child support payment record improved when "he went on unemployment because they gave him an allowance for child support so he gave it to me . . . first time he paid steady since the divorce." But another woman with an unemployed husband complained:

> Just because he doesn't have a job doesn't mean his kids can stop eating. When we were married he was out of work sometimes and we managed . . . on the benefits . . . in fact I know he is collecting extra because he has kids, but I never see the money.

Since child support awards are based on the husband's ability to pay, they are adjusted for reduced income and unemployment. Thus even men who are unemployed have the ability to pay what the court orders.

Three other explanations have been offered for why men do not pay: they consider the law unreasonable, they are retaliating for visitation problems, or they are responding to ineffective enforcement. Let us briefly consider the evidence.

The assertion that fathers do not pay child support because they consider the law unreasonable is strongly contradicted by the data. The overwhelming majority of divorced men we interviewed feel that they are responsible for the support of their children. They do not consider the law unfair or unjust. Rather there is a strong moral consensus that "men should support their children." (See also the public opinion data discussed below.) In fact, because the law seems to have widespread moral legitimacy, men who do not pay child support need to rationalize their nonpayment by offering excuses or justification for nonpayment. They think all men, and they themselves, *should* pay child support.

The moral consensus about men's responsibility for their children helps us to evaluate the second reason offered for nonpayment—a response to visitation problems. Here again the empirical data directly contradict the assertion: there is no correlation between compliance and complaints about visitation. That means that men with no visitation problems are just as likely not to pay child support as they are likely to pay. It also means that men who comply with child support awards are just as likely as those who do not comply to say they have some visitation problems. Canadian researchers similarly report the lack of a statistically significant relationship between visitation and compliance.[85]

Clearly some men who do not comply use visitation as an excuse because they need to explain why they are failing to do something which they believe is morally right. As a 1984 editorial in the *Washington Post* put it: "Men claim they have stopped supporting their children because they have been denied visitation rights, but that's an excuse not a justification."[86]

It should be noted that most states explicitly forbid the withholding of child support in retribution for the denial of visitation.[87] Child support belongs to the child. There are separate remedies for the denial of visitation, the most severe being a change in custody.*

There is another datum that suggests that visitation problems are

---

* Joanne Schulman, an attorney at the National Center on Women in Family Law, notes that a common tactic of men who are charged with not paying child support is to counter sue for a change of custody. This puts custodial mothers in the difficult position of having to choose between foregoing child support or fighting a custody challenge.[88]

not the cause of noncompliance. A significant portion of women who complained of noncompliance also complained about their ex-husband's *failure* to visit the children. In fact, many of the women we interviewed were as upset about the fathers' lack of parenting (and visitation) as they were about their failure to pay support per se.*

The last—and by far the most convincing—explanation for the lack of compliance lies in the absence of—or the failure of judges to use—effective enforcement procedures.

Strong Enforcement and Increased Compliance

Recent years have brought a dramatic increase in the range of available machinery to enforce child support orders both within and across state lines.** At the time this research was conducted, the California law already contained a wide variety of enforcement mechanisms, but the attorneys and judges we interviewed were reluctant to use them.[89] For example, as noted above, less than 5 percent of the random sample of cases from the court dockets included wage attachments to secure support. (The Canadian research also revealed ineffective enforcement: 40 percent of the cases in one city involved unserved summonses and 14 percent involved unserved warrants.[90])

In his pioneering work on the collection of child support, Professor David Chambers has shown that strong enforcement procedures are essential to an effective system of collection.[91] In an examination of twenty-eight Michigan counties, Chambers found that the counties with the highest rates of compliance shared two characteristics: a self-starting system of collecting child support, and a high incarceration rate. In a self-starting system, child support payments are made directly to the court so that court personnel can keep a careful watch on compliance. As soon as a father is delinquent, action is initiated by the Friend of the Court, a publicly supported collection system that pursues non-supporting fathers whether or not their ex-wives are on welfare. The Friend of the Court does not wait for a complaint from the mother to begin enforcement efforts. It initiates a series of reminders, prodding

---

* Since we did not ask mothers a direct question, it is impossible to report the percentage who responded this way, but there were numerous spontaneous comments from mothers who tried to persuade (or beg) the father to pay more attention to and spend more time with his children. Complaints about fathers who never called or saw their children were common and a source of great concern.

** The 1984 legislation is discussed later in this chapter on pages 307–309.

letters, and warnings, and, if these fail, follows through with mandatory wage assignments, judicial reprimands, probation, and, if necessary, jail.

The second essential component of an effective deterrent system appears to be a high probability of jail for continuously delinquent fathers. When Chambers compared the rate of compliance among different Michigan counties, he found that those counties which most often used jail had the highest rates of compliance.[92] Michigan, which ultimately jails one out of seven divorced fathers who are under court orders to pay child support, collects more child support per case than any other state in the country.[93] Chambers also showed, however, that jail alone does not increase compliance; it must be paired with self-starting enforcement machinery.

In summary, Professor Chambers concludes that no-nonsense enforcement brings compliance:

> The sad finding of our study has been that, in the absence of sanctions, so many fathers fail to pay. . . . [S]wift and certain punishment can reduce the incidence [of noncompliance] so long as potential offenders perceive a clear link between their own behavior and a system that leads to punishment."[94]

Chambers further concludes that the uniformity of the findings "suggests both that there are few identifiable groups so self-motivated toward payment that they pay as well as they are able without threat and, conversely, that there are few groups so unable to pay that the threat of jail does not produce substantial additional benefits."[95]

To reduce the need for incarceration at the end of the process, Chambers recommends the establishment of a system of direct child support deductions from wages when the order is first made. This possibility already exists in California, where a wage assignment can be instituted at the time of the initial order.[96]

Similar results are reported by Judge Rosemary Barkett of West Palm Beach, Florida, who found that the most effective means of securing compliance was to sentence noncomplying fathers to jail, but to delay the incarceration if they paid the arrearage.[97] If Judge Barkett found that a father had the ability to comply but had refused to do so, he was found in contempt and sentenced to jail. If the man paid the arrearage and current court order, his sentence was suspended. In three months, all but two of the men managed to pay and avoid jail.

Another Florida judge who was determined to secure compliance from nonpaying fathers ordered men appearing in his court to empty their wallets and pockets and to leave their money, rings, and watches with the court as security for past-due support. He also ordered cars, boats, and other property attached (and delivered to former wives) to satisfy past-due support orders. His effective collection results were reported in *People* magazine:

> The delinquent father was unapologetic, a mite defiant even. Yes, he told the judge, he owed his former wife $1,070 for the support of their three children. But the $180-a-month payments were beyond him, explained insurance salesman Jesse Metz, because he had a second family to support and payments to make on the car he needed for his job. Judge Charles McClure crisply dismissed the excuses. "These children need support," he declared. "They come before any subsequent children, before any second marriage. They come before any automobile payments." After making that Solomonic declaration, the judge asked a very practical question: "Do you have any money on you?" Surprised, Metz replied, "Eight dollars." The judge instructed him to place the bills on the table, then asked, "Is that a gold ring on your hand?" Metz nodded sadly and tugged the ring from his finger. The judge ordered the confiscated cash and jewelry delivered to Metz's former wife, Versie, as a down payment on the arrears. The judge also directed Metz to sign an authorization for automatic deduction of child support from his paycheck. Metz signed.[98]

Attitudes Toward Enforcement: California Judges, Lawyers, and Divorced Men and Women

Our data indicate that divorced spouses—both the men and women—favor strong enforcement of child support obligations. In fact, the attitudes they expressed were stricter than those of the judges and lawyers we interviewed. Consider, for example, the following case which we presented to all of the attorneys, judges, and divorced men and women:

> Stephen and Beverly have been divorced for three years. Beverly has custody of their three minor children. At the time of the divorce, Stephen was ordered to pay $200 a month in child support ($67 per child). He stopped paying this amount five months ago.
>
> Beverly earns $250 *net* (income after taxes) per month as a waitress. Stephen earns $650 *net* (income after taxes) per month as a delivery truck driver. He has remarried and now has two children with his new wife. He stopped paying child support to Beverly, as he claims he cannot afford to support two families. His new wife is not employed.

We first asked, "Do you think Stephen should be ordered to pay child support to Beverly?" The overwhelming response was yes (over

90 percent of the attorneys, divorced men, and divorced women in Los Angeles County). We then asked how much Stephen should have to pay each month. The respondents were divided between continuing his obligation to pay the $200 the court had ordered and reducing his obligation somewhat. The mean responses were $166 for judges, $175 for attorneys, $150 for men, and $200 for women. While most of the women would maintain the original award, the judges and lawyers, and to an even greater extent the divorced men, would reduce it somewhat.

Next we asked the Los Angeles judges and lawyers if Stephen would be held in contempt of court (i.e., sanctioned for not paying). Most said yes (81 percent of the attorneys and 88 percent of the judges). However, when asked what they would do as a result of the contempt holding, most judges said they would "give him a stern lecture and a warning."

The divorced men and women had stronger reactions to the case and were more activist in their proposed solutions. Many of the men were emphatic about holding Stephen to his responsibility and forcing him to pay. For example:

> I don't know what you can do, but order him to do it! You can attach his wages. He knew he had this obligation before he remarried.

> Threaten to throw his ass in jail!

> I'd order him picked up—so he'd either work and pay—or I'd send him to a camp where he could work and then *they'd* send the child support.

> Public lashing! Tell him he'll go to jail! They should garnish his wages.

The women's responses were similar:

> The money should be sent to the court each month so he can't soft-talk his ex-wife. The judge should hold him in contempt if he fails to pay. I believe in what's fair!

> There's two ways to go about it: Garnish wages, or go to jail. Usually they'll pay before they go to jail. Or make his other wife go to work.

> Put [him] in jail if he doesn't pay. Or put him on county work project to earn the money.

> You can't order his ex-wife to work. His new wife should find some employment at home to help out. . . . Suggest he look for a better paying job.

"Forgiving" the Arrearage

None of the judges we interviewed said they would insist that the arrearage be immediately paid in full. Most would order Stephen to pay off the past-due support by making a minimal monthly payment (which averaged $26 a month). The attorneys' responses were similar, but they predicted average arrearage payments of $37 a month.

These figures suggest that what the judges and lawyers have done is to maintain Stephen's payments of roughly $200 a month by reducing his monthly award so that he can be credited for paying off the arrearage. (For example, his child support award is reduced to $175 a month and $25 a month arrears.) The de facto result, as noted earlier, is to reward the father for noncompliance by reducing his obligation. The message is that the greater the arrearage, and the longer the father manages to stay out of court, the better his chances of getting a judge who will consider his case a hardship and give him "a break" by reducing his support. His children are then left with even less than the minimal award with which they began.

Types of Enforcement

Next we asked about enforcement: "[If you were the judge,] what would you do to get him to pay what the court ordered?" The most common response among judges, attorneys, and divorced persons was to order a wage assignment (65 percent of the judges, 61 percent of the attorneys, 46 percent of the men, and 64 percent of the women).

What is surprising about these responses is that at the time we conducted these interviews, the California law *required* judges to order a wage assignment if the man had not paid support for *two* months.[99] Yet, even though this hypothetical ex-husband was five months in arrears, one-third of the judges said they would *not* order a wage attachment.

Even more telling are the judges' responses to the question, "How many wage assignments have you ordered in the past six months?" The average was only one or two wage assignments per judge over the six-month period, and more than a quarter of the judges said they had *never* ordered a wage assignment. When one considers that there were about 36,000 divorce cases heard in Los Angeles County each year, and that the Los Angeles County judges (and commissioners) are a "specialized bench" assigned to hear only family law cases, it is evident that these judges heard thousands of noncompliance complaints during this six-month period. Yet they ordered wage assignments in only a tiny fraction of the cases—less than one in a hundred.

If, as Dean Pound said, "the life of the law is in its enforcement,"[100] it is clear why the child support laws make a mockery of the legal system. Precisely these sentiments were echoed over and over again by the women we interviewed:

> It literally makes me sick . . . . It is so contrary to everything I was taught about the law, the courts, and justice. I feel totally betrayed. . . . He totally disregards the whole legal system.

In 1979 this issue reached the California appellate court. In *Le Claire v. Le Claire,*[101] a mother filed a petition for a wage assignment because the father was $900 in arrears. He was ordered to pay $75 a month child support for each of his two children ($150 a month total) and had not payed for six months. At the hearing the father opposed the wage assignment saying it would adversely affect his employment and he might be fired. He promised to pay the arrearage without an assignment. As was common, the judge denied the mother's petition, and did not order a wage assignment. The Court of Appeals, however, said the trial court judge erred: he had no discretion because the law specified the two-month arrearage required for a wage assignment.

Apparently California judges were not alone in failing to enforce the law. As noted earlier, Senator Paula Hawkins reported that Florida judges were also unwilling to use the enforcement procedures provided by the law, and Blanche Bernstein, former head of Social Services in New York City, reported the same pattern among family court judges in New York City.[102]

When asked directly about the law that required wage assignments, more than one-third of the California judges said they disapproved of it. Their most common explanations were that it "took away judges' discretion" and "could jeopardize a man's job."* The New York City judges who refused to enforce a similar law argued that it was unconstitutional, a view that was rejected by that state's highest court.[103]

Consider next the attorneys' responses to our hypothetical case. When asked what they would do to secure compliance, attorneys most often mentioned wage attachments (61 percent, as noted earlier). A

---

* The Child Support Enforcement Amendments of 1984 make it illegal for an employer to fire or discipline an employee because the employer is required to withhold wages for child support, even if the withholding orders already exist.

somewhat overlapping one-third said they would try to get voluntary compliance by writing letters and calling the ex-husband's attorney; and another one-third mentioned attaching property.

There are two surprises in these responses. The first is the limited number of means suggested by attorneys to secure compliance. Presumably they would be more imaginative and more assertive—since attorneys usually are—if the financial stakes were higher or they considered the cause more worthy. Clearly, this problem does not evoke normal "lawyerlike" responses.

The second surprise is the apparent discrepancy between the attorneys' responses to the hypothetical case and what they actually do on behalf of their clients. Although some differences are to be expected, because the attorneys we interviewed were not the attorneys who represented the men and women we interviewed, nevertheless the hypothetical case suggests that attorneys know how to be more effective in securing compliance. In actual cases, however, they decide it is not worth the bother. (Recall only 1 percent of the women's attorneys sought wage attachments in contrast with the 61 percent who said this is what *should* be done in response to noncompliance in the hypothetical case.)

The divorced men and women offered other solutions for the hypothetical case. In addition to wage attachments, they would make him pay to or through the court; force him to get a better-paying job; have the first wife go on welfare because nothing can be done; threaten him with jail; and put him in jail. More women suggested forcing the husband to get a better-paying job and putting him in jail, while more men suggested having the court be an intermediary or having the first wife go on welfare. In fact, one of the most noticeable differences between men's and women's responses is that 11 percent of the men suggested that the first wife go on welfare, while only 1 percent of the women recommended this "solution."

MEN'S ATTITUDES TOWARD WAGE ASSIGNMENTS

Although only a small percentage of men had experience with wage assignments, it is useful to report their reactions—especially because they are different from what might be expected.

The men in the interview sample who expressed the most satisfaction with the child support award and payment process were those who had wage assignments or paid through the court. These men offered three reasons for preferring wage assignments as a way of having child support collected. First, wage assignments eliminated the problem of budget decisions: the men didn't have to think about the decision of whether or not to pay.

Second, as one man put it, with a wage assignment "I have what I have." Child support was deducted from his paycheck, just as with withholding taxes and Social Security payments. He knew that he could spend whatever he got in his net paycheck. It made child support payments less painful.

Third, several men said that having the child support deducted from wages eliminated the resistance they encountered from new wives and girlfriends. In some households the woman writes the checks, and some men said they had difficulties getting their "new woman" to write child support checks to their ex-wife. (One man, who was brought into court on a contempt charge before the wage assignment was instituted, swore that his new wife had assured him she had been sending the money. He said he did not know that she had stopped paying it until he received a subpoena to appear in court.)

In other families or cohabiting situations, the men said that even though they made the financial decisions and wrote the checks, they felt they had to justify the child support each month. As one man said, the wage assignment "took the decision out of my hands so she couldn't nag me anymore."

These responses suggest that most men are willing to pay child support but they have a hard time parting with the money if they are given a choice. (After all, how many of us would choose to pay taxes if we were given a choice?) Wage assignments eliminate the choice: when payment is automatic a father does not have to choose between a car payment or dinner at a restaurant and paying child support.

THE THREAT AND USE OF JAIL

In response to the hypothetical case, close to half of the attorneys mentioned the threat of jail. But most of them added that jail would be inappropriate at this point. As one attorney put it, "I frequently threaten it, but I never want to get it. It doesn't serve any useful purpose."

Judges, too, appear to use jail as a threat but are very reluctant actually to sentence a man to jail. As one judge reported:

> We talk a lot . . . we threaten. We are boogeymen. But people in authority should use their position sparingly—threatening produces results.

In fact, a few judges reported that *the threat* of jail did often work:

> I would sentence him to jail for five days for each payment missed—
> suspend the sentence for one year and put him on summary probation
> on the condition that he pay $10 a month in arrears and keep up the
> current payments.

Only two of the Los Angeles County judges we interviewed considered
jail an appropriate sanction. As one of them said, "You don't see the
money until the slammer door opens."

In view of these attitudes, it is not surprising to find that 45 percent
of the Los Angeles County judges said that during the past six months,
they *had never jailed a single father* for noncompliance. The remaining
55 percent said they had sentenced an average of about two men to
jail during that period.

When these practices are read in light of what we now know
about noncompliance rates with child support awards (which must
involve at least 6,000 seriously delinquent cases a year), it is easy to
see why many men believe they can ignore child support orders with
impunity.

Public Opinion About Enforcement

Public opinion supports stricter enforcement of child support obligations than is evident in the attitudes of most judges and lawyers. A
1983 national opinion study conducted by the state of Missouri indicated that most people favored strong-arm types of enforcement (short
of jail), such as wage assignments and work programs (see below) to
collect support. The overwhelming majority of respondents (98 percent)
felt strongly that absent parents have an obligation to provide financially for their children, regardless of their personal situation.[104] They
also believed (90 percent) that absent parents have an obligation to
repay delinquent child support.

When questioned about the obligations of noncustodial parents
who have remarried, 84 percent felt that parents' obligation to support
their children should remain unchanged: they should still be obligated
to make court ordered support payments for their children from previous marriages. Similarly, the loss of a job does not negate the obligation
in the eyes of the public. When questioned about whether a parent
without employment should still be obligated to pay child support,
63 percent responded affirmatively.

When questioned about sanctions for parents who are delinquent in their support obligations, participants in the survey approved of forcing the parent to make payments (90 percent). Three-fourths of the respondents were in favor of "forced labor" (whereby those jailed would be released so they could work to earn funds to meet their support obligations), mandatory wage assignments, and automatic deductions from state and federal tax refunds. About one-third (29 percent) were in favor of jailing the nonpayor.

THE NEW FEDERAL LEGISLATION

Nearly a decade ago, Congress was sufficiently alarmed by the noncompliance problem to pass Title IV-D of the Social Security Act to improve enforcement of child support obligations for families on welfare. While this measure has helped (in 1982, nearly $1.8 billion in child support was collected under the program), full payment of child support obligations is still the exception rather than the rule.[105] Increases in collections are outpaced by the increasing numbers of children in need of support. In fact, the percentage of families receiving full payment *actually declined* from 49 percent to 47 percent between 1978 and 1981.[106]

Child support enforcement on the federal level was strengthened by new legislation in 1982 and 1984. The 1982 law established a federal Parent Locator Service, available to the custodial parents of children on welfare, that has access to various government record-keeping systems. (There are also locator services in each of the states.) Most important is the access to records of the Internal Revenue Service. These facilitate two key aspects of enforcement: the location of absent fathers, especially those who move to another state to avoid paying child support; and the interception of federal income-tax refunds to cover past-due support.

The 1984 legislation, the Child Support Enforcement Amendments of 1984, goes beyond the 1982 law in several respects.[107] First, it allows middle-class families to use the IRS's locator and tax refund intercept services and encourages states to collect unpaid child support for families who are not on welfare (as well as those who are).[108] Thus, one significant feature of the 1984 law is its acknowledgement of the fact that noncompliance is not just a "welfare" problem. As we have seen, middle-class men are just as likely to avoid child support if they can get away with it. Effective enforcement procedures are the key to securing compliance from men of all income levels.

Second, the 1984 legislation provides a mandate for a number of enforcement techniques that have proven successful. The most important is mandatory wage attachments. Under the new regulations, states are required to enact laws requiring that "all child support orders issued or modified in the state include provisions for withholding of wages."[109] Withholding must be triggered when payments are one month in arrears, or when an absent parent voluntarily requests withholding. (A state may establish an earlier time for withholding to be triggered.)[110] In addition, employers now have a greater incentive to comply with court orders for wage attachments because they are liable for any amounts they unlawfully fail to withhold.

State agencies charged with enforcing child support payments also have several new legal mechanisms at their disposal. They are required to establish procedures for expediting the imposition of liens against property and the posting of bonds to guarantee payment of overdue support. Once a lien has been established on real or personal property, the state may take possession of the property to satisfy a judgment of past-due support. Similarly, posting a bond or other form of security is a way of guaranteeing child support payments and is especially useful if a payor is planning to move to another state or country, or if the court has reason to believe he may not comply with the order. The 1984 legislation also extends provisions for bonds and liens against property to out-of-state orders.

One of the most effective means of securing past-due support has been the tax intercept program. The 1984 bill adds to the federal tax intercept program by requiring states to also intercept state tax refunds when support is owed.

Further, states now have added financial incentives to establish programs to collect child support because the federal government will provide the bulk of each state's enforcement budget. (The federal share of the program's cost will be reduced after 1988.) In addition, the states will receive federal incentive payments equal to 6 percent of the state's AFDC collections and 6 percent of their non-AFDC collections. Higher incentives may be paid to programs regarded as very cost-effective. Further savings to the state will result from "cost avoidance" benefits: to the extent that women who obtain child support are able to stay off welfare, the state may save millions of dollars in avoided welfare payments.

In addition to the collection aspects of the 1984 legislation, there are several other components of the bill that deserve mention. States are now *required* to provide information on past-due child support to consumer credit agencies when the amount of the arrearage is in excess of $1,000. States may also impose late-payment penalties of 3 to 6 percent on overdue support payments. Further, state agencies entrusted with the responsibility for child support collections are *required* to seek medical support as part of the child support order whenever health insurance for dependent children is available to the noncustodial parent at a reasonable rate.

Another important feature of the 1984 legislation is that it provides the option of having payments made through a state agency—at the request of *either* parent. The presence of an impersonal buffer that receives and dispenses payments should decrease the potential for parental conflict over child support payments and help to establish regular and stable support for children.

The 1984 legislation also requires states to establish specific guidelines for child support awards through legislative, judicial, or administrative action. Since these guidelines would not be binding on judges, they will not guarantee uniform award levels. But they may be helpful in states that currently have no guidelines at all.

Finally, the 1984 legislation requires states to publicize the availability of their child support enforcement services. Secretary Heckler pledged a nationwide public information campaign "to bring home the message that child support cannot be shirked."[111]

OTHER ALTERNATIVES: SWEDEN, FRANCE, AND THE WISCONSIN EXPERIMENT

The present system in the United States, which relies on an individual judge making a decision in each case, leads to great disparities in award levels. "Nearly every father can find someone who earns more than he does but pays less child support, and nearly every mother knows someone who is receiving more child support even though the father earns less."[112]

There are two approaches to eliminating this unfairness. One is to guarantee a minimal level of support for each child. The second is to require a fixed percentage of fathers' income for child support and eliminate all judicial discretion.

Both Sweden and France have taken the first approach: they have family allowance plans that guarantee a minimum amount of support to all parents with children. After divorce, the custodial parent continues to receive the allowance directly from the state.

In Sweden, the amount of child support to be paid by a noncustodial parent is established by a judicial procedure.[113] The state then advances that amount to the custodial parent each month and assumes the responsibility for collecting the money from the noncustodial parent. This guarantees that the custodial parent's support is not interrupted even if the government is unsuccessful in collecting payment. In addition, Sweden has established a statutory minimum for child support awards to guarantee each child an adequate standard of living. If the court-ordered child support is less than this minimum, the government will make up the difference.

In France, single-parent families receive a 50 percent supplement to their basic family allowance, which is based on the family's income level.[114] As in Sweden, the French government pays the allowance directly to the parent who has custody.

The second approach to eliminating inequities in support awards is to eliminate all judicial discretion by establishing fixed amounts of child support. In 1984 the State of Wisconsin implemented a percentage-of-income formula proposed by Professor Irwin Garfinkel of the University of Wisconsin.[115] The formula establishes a child support "tax," based on the father's income and the number of children to be supported. It requires the payment of 17 percent of the father's gross income for one child, 25 percent for two, 29 percent for three, 31 percent for four, and 35 percent for five or more.[116] The child support "tax" is implemented through wage withholding and is now being tried on an experimental basis to see if it alleviates inequities and increases compliance.

NEGOTIATIONS ABOUT SUPPORT (AND CUSTODY): SOME MALE/FEMALE DIFFERENCES

It is somewhat artificial to treat custody and support awards as separate issues. Although the two decisions are distinct in legal theory, in practice the two issues are often negotiated together and involve implicit or explicit trade-offs. In light of the small percentage of men who actually seek custody,[117] we were surprised to find a significant minority of divorced women—one-third—reporting that their husbands had threatened to ask for custody as a ploy in negotiations. Many of these threats appear to be motivated by financial gains:[118] by threatening to ask for custody men have a lever for getting their wives' agreement to less support or property. In some cases the linkage between the two issues was explicit, as in these reports of outright threats:

He said he wasn't going to give me any money [for support] and if I gave him any legal trouble he'd take the kids away from me.

He said—straight and clear—if you don't agree to $200 a month in child support, I'll go for custody and you won't get a cent. . . .

He had an agreement prepared and told me to sign it. He said, "Trust me, I'll protect you." When I didn't want to sign it, he said, "If you don't sign it, I'll take the kids away."

He threatened me with a custody fight if I insisted on more child support, and my children are worth more than the money.

Most men were more subtle, but for many women even the hint of a custody contest was enough to stifle all determination to seek an equitable support or property arrangement:

One day he told me Steve [a recently divorced friend] told him to take the kids instead of turning all that money over to me. I knew he didn't want them, but it didn't matter. . . . He had me—I wouldn't take any risks—I wanted to get that agreement signed.

The one phrase we heard repeated over and over again was "it's only money." When faced with a choice between less child support (or less alimony, or less property) and the possible loss of their children the women said that for them, there was no choice: the support was "only money" and insignificant in the context of a potential loss of incalculable value—the loss of their children.

Underlying these comments about support and custody negotiations are more fundamental differences in the perspectives of husbands and wives. Because we did not ask about these matters directly in the interviews, we have few quantitative indicators of the differences; nevertheless, the two perspectives emerge rather clearly from the qualitative data.

The first difference is a willingness to consider negotiating about children in negotiations about property and support. Men see custody as part of a total package of divorce issues that are, to some extent, "all up for grabs." Women, by contrast, draw a line when it comes to custody. They are more likely to consider custody on an altogether different level—it is something they simply cannot negotiate about because it is too important—it is worth any price. Since women attach such great importance to their children, they are not only willing to give up financial benefits for custody, they are also willing to lose a great deal just to avoid even the *risk* of losing the children. As one woman said:

> It was like a game for him . . . like trading property in Monopoly . . . but it was life and death to me . . . losing the children would be like losing my life. . . . I couldn't stand back and "negotiate" as my lawyer suggested. I couldn't let them go—no matter what.

Attorney Nancy Polikoff observes that this attitude is common, and it invariably results in a disadvantageous financial settlement for women. As she states it, "the reality is that most women faced with a contested custody hearing are unlikely to turn down a proposed settlement which removes that threat, no matter how low the child support or how disproportionate the property settlement. . . . All women can be intimidated by the threat of losing their children.[119]

New York attorneys Henry Foster and Doris Freed call this pattern of negotiating "custody blackmail" which they describe as follows: a husband proposes a small child support or property settlement and threatens to take the kids away if his wife does not agree to it.[120] Because the threat of losing custody is more terrifying than the threat of losing money, she is likely to agree to his proposal. Moreover, as with other forms of blackmail, the threat may continue to hang over her: he may threaten to take her back to court if she finds a new male companion, or if she works, or if he remarries. And at each point she is likely to "pay him off."[121]

The detrimental effects of custody blackmail influenced a landmark decision of the West Virginia Supreme Court. As Judge Neely stated, "Uncertainty of outcome is very destructive of the position of the primary caretaker parent because he or she will be willing to sacrifice everything else in order to avoid the terrible prospect of losing the child in the unpredictable process of litigation. . . . Moreover, it is likely that the primary caretaker . . . will be unable to sustain the expense of litigation."[122]

These concerns led the West Virginia Court to a primary caretaker presumption in custody cases in order "to prevent the issue of custody from being used in an abusive way as a coercive weapon to affect the level of support payments and the outcome of other issues underlying divorce proceedings. When a custody fight emanates from this reprehensible motive, children inevitably become pawns to be sacrificed. . . ."[123]

As we noted in Chapter 8, clear cut legal rules, such as primary caretaker presumptions, discourage custody threats and the financial coercion associated with them.

A second difference is apparent in the way mothers and fathers approach divorce negotiations: women are more likely to focus on the interpersonal aspects of a decision while men are more likely to focus on its economic aspects. Thus when women think about child support they are likely to focus on how the financial transaction will affect their relationship with their former husband (and, in some cases, his family). Men, in contrast, are more likely to see child support as a purely economic matter or as a purely legal matter: they think about how much it will cost, what a judge is likely to order, and how much money they will have left.

For women the economic issues of divorce are embedded in a social context. But for men—and it is the male perspective that the law reflects—the economic issues stand alone. Consider first the following examples of women's analysis of the economic issues of divorce:

> I wanted to stay on good terms with him, so I didn't want to hassle him about the money. . . . It was more important to have him as my friend and to part amicably.

> I didn't want him (and his parents) to think I only cared about money. . . . They were always talking about women who took advantage of men and just took them for a ride and I didn't want to be seen as that kind of woman. . . . They lived near by and I depended on them. . . . They are my children's grandparents. . . . I wanted them to respect me.

> I was afraid that if I pushed him on child support he'd resent the children and I wanted him to maintain his relationship with them . . . it was more important to me than the money.

These women saw "giving in" on monetary issues as a means of maintaining a relationship with their former husbands, or with his family, or between him and his children. Other women were willing to give in on monetary issues as a means to a very different goal—to extricate themselves from the relationship.

> I wanted him to leave me alone. I didn't want any connection to him (including receiving his checks).

> I figured it wasn't worth getting support and having to put up with his control over me. . . . When we were first separated, before the divorce, he wanted an accounting of every penny—how much I spent for food, why didn't I buy hamburger meat on sale at Safeway, why didn't I buy them new shoes instead of more jeans. . . . He drove me crazy. . . it wasn't worth $125 a month to have to put up with him.

I didn't want to have to beg him for anything. He can take his money and shove it.

I left him, so I didn't feel right taking any money from him.

The thread that links what may at first appear to be contradictory goals—one focused on maintaining a relationship, the other focused on ending a relationship—is that the focus is on the *relationship* rather than the economic issues. Since women seem to care more about the relationship, and appear to emphasize social-emotional needs over financial needs, they are predisposed to give up support (and property) in exchange for good will, control of their own lives, control of their children, and the avoidance of conflict. When they talk about financial issues the discussion often focuses on these issues: how the money will affect their independence of or dependence on their former husbands, whether it will allow them to break or maintain their relationship with him and/or his family, whether it will reduce their exhusbands' good will and respect, and, finally, how it will affect their own feelings and actions (such as whether it will make them feel less guilty about leaving him, or able to stand up to him and insist on what they think is best for the children). As for financial considerations, over and over again these women say, "It's only money."

Not so for men in our sample. The men were more likely to discuss economic decisions as clear cut issues of dollars and cents. They spoke of the "going rate," the cost, the law, and their rights:

My lawyer said that was the going rate for child support so that's what I agreed to pay.

Her lawyer was trying to get me to let them stay in the house but the law says I'm entitled to my equity. . . . Why should I give her my half of the house?

The law does not require me to support them [his children] once they are 18. . . . Then, that's it!

She wanted me to forego interest on the note so she could keep the house. . . . Why should I take that loss? I told her I'd treat it like any other note. I'd charge her whatever the market rate was—no more and no less.

It [child support] was simple. You look at the schedule and see what the judge would order and negotiate from there. Naturally, I tried to get it down as low as possible.

A third underlying difference in the way men and women approach these issues is their willingness to compromise. Women were more likely to talk about compromise and to say they could understand their husbands' perspective.

> I understood how he felt about money and I didn't want him to think I was taking advantage of him. . . . I wanted to ask for something he would consider reasonable.

> I know how upset he'd get if I pressed him . . . he's very emotional and temperamental and if he gets angry he just won't budge. . . . I didn't want to get him angry by pushing him for more support [than he offered].

Men were likely to aim at "getting the best deal" and to treat the settlement as a financial negotiation they wanted to win:

> My attorney told me what was in the ball park . . . and what she was entitled to . . . so we offered about half of that for starters.

> I wanted to protect my business and not get stuck with a big support order hanging over me for the next ten years . . . but it was no big deal. I knew she'd agree if we held out long enough . . . and she did.

It often seemed as if both partners were focused on the husband and what he wanted or offered: while he worried about his checkbook, she worried about how he was feeling, how he would react, and how she might find a solution that would please, or at least satisfy, him.* Because of their greater tendency to empathize, then, women may well agree to solutions that compromise their own interests.

A closely related dimension is a differing tolerance for conflict. Men are likely not only to ask in a forthright and forceful manner for what they want, but to fight for it. Women, by contrast, shy away from negotiation and conflict. When a woman says, "It wasn't worth the fight," she is saying she does not like to fight (and also, perhaps, that she does not *know how* to fight for herself).

Finally, men and women commonly express differing conceptions of their own entitlement to money and property. Women, especially those who have been housewives and mothers throughout marriage, are likely to devalue their entitlement to support, even if it is child support, and their right to share the assets of the marriage.

---

* This may also suggest that mediation of family law disputes may result in further disadvantages for women and children.

Community property laws notwithstanding, many divorcing women still see the money their husbands have earned as "his money," and do not feel entitled to it (especially if she is the one who initiated the divorce). In this way, women discount their own contributions to marriage and the uncompensated services they provide to make it possible for husbands to earn money.

It is easy, of course, to find the roots of these differing perspectives in sex-role socialization; that is, in the differing behavioral expectations that society imposes on males and females. What Carol Gilligan calls "women's different voice"[124] is reflected in women's orientation toward people, their need to please others and gain approval, and in their preoccupation with interpersonal considerations. Men, on the other hand, are likely to be socialized to assert their independence and self-interest, and to have their claims valued and rewarded in our society.

It may appear at first glance that this analysis "blames the victim." That is, if women get inadequate support awards, it is only because they agree to accept those awards. But women do not agree to anything in a social vacuum. The legal process sets the parameters for their expectations and structures their negotiations.[125]

How does the legal system allow—and even foster—inadequate settlements for divorced women (despite the fact that at least half of the attorneys in divorce actions are paid to represent the interests of women)? Surely part of the answer lies in the legal profession itself, still heavily dominated by men, and in the ways that profession represents, or fails to represent, divorcing women. Because women typically have fewer financial resources than their husbands and, therefore, less financial clout, they have greater difficulty obtaining aggressive legal representation. In addition, the legal process rewards those who are willing to accept a certain level of risk to gain their ends, and women in general show greater "risk aversion" than do men. That is, women are more likely to accept an award that is "a sure thing" rather than chance a greater loss if a bid for improved settlement should fail. Instead of counteracting these power differentials between men and women, wives' attorneys tend to play into them by allowing their clients to make "their own" agreements.

In fact, one may look at a woman's agreement to a low support award as a *realistic economic calculus*. The costs of bargaining may in fact be greater than the pay-off she can expect. For example, if her husband is aggressive, persistent, and uncompromising, she can expect to pay dearly in terms of time and energy (and money) for any extra dollar she might obtain. Thus she may realistically calculate that she cannot bear what economists call the *transaction costs* of fighting him. These costs include the direct costs of litigation (such as filing fees, court costs, the cost of taking depositions, hiring expert witnesses, and most important, attorneys' fees), as well as the indirect costs—the costs of not being able to use property and money while the issues are being resolved, and the emotional costs of negotiating, litigating, and living with uncertainty.

Recall the difficulties faced by women whose husbands refused to pay alimony; these women were often advised to cut their losses by avoiding the high cost of litigation (and negotiation).[126] Here, too, the party who cannot afford to bear the transaction costs of litigation is at a great disadvantage. Lawyers who specialize in divorce refer to the "illicit bargaining leverage" used by the more affluent or bread-winning spouse to extract agreement to his financial terms as the "starve out" technique. As New York attorneys Henry Foster and Doris Freed describe it:

> The "starve out" technique is particularly effective where joint bank accounts have been closed, the husband's credit is cut off from the wife, bills are coming in, and the wife has little or no personal income or assets. A variation of the technique may also occur where arrearages pile up and the obligee is forced into repeated court appearances in order to collect some or all that is past due.[127]

If a woman has not been employed during marriage and if she has no income of her own, she may be especially vulnerable. Her financial situation may be so precarious (which is, after all, the aim of the starve-out technique) that she is willing to agree to a ridiculously low award just to have some money on which to live.

A final factor that may contribute to a party's willingness to accept a low support offer is lack of information. In most divorce cases neither party has a great deal of knowledge about what they might gain by going to court. A court battle might result in more litigation (and higher attorneys' fees) and little else. Thus, fighting for one's position might not pay off and most would-be contestants do not have the experience to predict whether it will. What they do know is how their spouse is likely to react to negotiation—and how they can best deal with that reaction. If a divorcing woman believes her husband will insist on his position and fight to the finish, then this perception alone will shape the "real market" in her case. If, in addition, her former husband has more money and power, can hire better lawyers, is better able to endure high transaction costs and withstand risk, it may well be a "rational" decision for her to "agree" to what he offers.

THE IMPACT OF ECONOMIC CHANGES ON CHILDREN

One of the most persuasive indictments of the system that produces radically different economic circumstances for men and women after divorce lies in the detrimental effects of such economic changes on children in general, and on the mother-child and father-child relationships in particular. While there is a large and growing literature on the effects of divorce on children, it tells us little about how property and support awards directly affect the children of divorce.

The research conducted by Drs. Judith Wallerstein and Joan Kelly provides impressive qualitative evidence on these effects.[128] Wallerstein and Kelly interviewed parents and children in sixty divorcing families in Marin County, California, a relatively affluent community, at three points in time: six months, eighteen months, and five years after separation. While no one would contend that this well-to-do community is typical, the findings of this research are all the more impressive because one might expect the economic impact of divorce to be minimized there.

Wallerstein and Kelly confirm the central role that financial awards play in the lives of men, women, and children after divorce: "virtually every parent in our study was preoccupied with the change in family economics created by the divorce. . . . [However,] the women in our study were affected by severe economic changes more substantially and more permanently than were the men."[129]

Although a very high percentage of the men in the Wallerstein-Kelly sample paid child support on a more or less regular basis, three-quarters of the women experienced a notable decline in their standard of living. For a third of the women, the economic change was abrupt and severe; few of the women had made any preparation for the drastically diminished economic circumstances they were forced to confront. These changes affect women at every economic level and the stress is no less acute for middle-class women. As Wallerstein and Kelly note:

> While our own sympathies and concern quite naturally tended to be directed more to those whose standard of living moved toward or plummeted below the poverty level, the sudden reduction in available monies was as deeply affecting to women of middle-class means. While such women

perhaps worried less about feeding their youngsters adequately or having their car repossessed, the stress of adjusting themselves and their children to living on substantially less money was nonetheless real.[130]

The sharp decline in the mothers' standard of living led to a series of very dramatic changes for their children. It forced the mothers into hectic and exhausting schedules that diminished the time and emotional energy they had available for their children. The extreme pressure to earn money left these mothers with little time for career development, child care, household chores, and a new social life.[131] Children were carried to babysitters early in the morning and picked up on the way home—before or after the rush to do the shopping, prepare dinner, and clean the house. Several mothers, working full time outside the home for the first time in their lives, had to regularly work past midnight to complete their household chores.[132] Thus, the children in these one-parent families not only had less of their fathers; they clearly had less of their mothers as well. As Wallerstein and Kelly describe it:

> Within six months of separation, one-quarter of the mothers interviewed judged themselves to be substantially less available to their children due directly to expanded work schedules and/or new educational demands. One of the ironies of the woman's move toward independence, increased self-esteem, and personal growth was that the children did not always share in the benefits, at least not in the first year. Certainly one of the most pressing dilemmas for the single parent is the difficulty in balancing financial and psychological needs of parent and child in the wake of the separation.[133]

The children of these mothers rarely received compensatory care and attention from other family members: few grandmothers (or other extended-family members) or neighbors were available for assistance. In addition, the fathers typically refused to babysit, even if their schedules would have permitted them to do so. As Wallerstein and Kelly note:

> Rather than welcoming the potential time with the child as an opportunity to continue or enrich their relationship, they viewed the mother's request as a manipulative exploitation. Some fathers refused, on principle, to be available for the mother's "convenience," even if, for example, she was taking weekly night classes to improve her career or vocational opportunities.[134]

Thus, child-care responsibilities typically fell on the mother alone.

Another major change was that the diminished income available for the wife and children often led to a residential move, and thus to unfamiliar neighborhoods, friends, and schools for the children. Within the first three years, "almost two-thirds of the youngsters had changed their place of residence, and a substantial number of these had moved three or more times."[135] Many of these moves were directly tied to economic factors—the need for cheaper housing, a better job, or more adequate child-care arrangements.

These residential changes represented more than a change in life-style and standard of living for the children. They typically caused disruptions in the child's education, close friendships, and neighborhood life. Even when teachers or friends were not particularly helpful, the familiar and relatively stable environment of a school had frequently become an importance source of continuity in the child's life.

The effects of these disruptions in the child's home and school environments were heightened because they occurred simultaneously with the child's loss of one parent, and with the onset of greatly reduced care from the other parent. Since many of the mothers had not been employed before divorce, their children felt altogether abandoned when their mothers had to adopt new work schedules.[136] As a result, the children's basic sense of stability was significantly affected.

The researchers concluded that the quality of care that is given by the custodial parent declines precipitously for a period immediately following divorce.[137] This is a result of the increased stress on both the mother and the children, and the mother's inability to spend as much time with the children after divorce as she did before: the cumulative effect simply makes her physically and psychologically less accessible to her children. Probably most children would be able to adjust satisfactorily to any one of these changes, but their rapid and simultaneous occurrence can be overwhelming to almost any child. Thus, the emotional impact of divorce clearly reflects its economic impact.

The economic changes following divorce also have serious detrimental effects on the father-child relationship. Wallerstein and Kelly found that children often compared the economic situation in their mother's and father's households:

> [T]he ambiance of the divorced family is that the economic status of mother and children does not stand alone, but is frequently, and sometimes continually, compared with the standard of living which the family had enjoyed earlier, as well as with the present standard of living of the husband, or the husband's new family.[138]

In cases where the wife and children were experiencing downward mobility and where the father earned very little money, the wife and children were most often compassionate toward the father and protected him. However, when the wife and children experienced downward mobility and the father did not, the discrepancy between the two households was a source of great bitterness. Children in this situation experienced a pervasive sense of deprivation and anger.[139]

Psychologist E. Mavis Hetherington and her colleagues found remarkably similar patterns—downward economic mobility, increased task overload, residential moves, and the disruption of support systems—among white middle class preschool children in Virginia whose parents were divorced.[140]

CONCLUSION

Children are the tragic victims of the present system of inadequate and unpaid child support. Even though the typical child support award provides less than half the cost of raising a child, chances are that the noncustodial father will not pay it, and the legal system will do nothing about it. Current estimates of noncompliance with child support orders range from 60 to 80 percent.[141] These are appalling statistics for a society that purports to place such a high value on the welfare of its children.[142]

This research reveals that a majority of divorced fathers have the ability to pay court-mandated child support without seriously jeopardizing their own standard of living. A majority also believe they *should* pay. Yet two-thirds of the divorced women we interviewed said that they did not regularly receive the child support that had been ordered by the courts.

In large part, men don't pay because enforcement of child support awards is so lax that noncompliance rarely incurs a penalty. Lawyers, judges, and court personnel are reluctant to use the sanctions the law allows against defaulting fathers. The burden for securing payment therefore falls on the custodial mother, who is already disadvantaged by time and monetary constraints. In addition, the present custody rules may create additional pressures on mothers to accept a lower support award in order to secure and retain custody.

In the end the current legal system places the economic responsibility for children on their mothers and allows fathers the "freedom" to choose not to support their children. The result is that children almost always experience a decline in their standard of living after divorce. The dislocation from friends, neighborhoods, and family that many of these children endure, and the bitterness and anger they may harbor against one parent or the other, often translate into a pervasively un-happy, distrustful, and pessimistic view of life. This has profound impli-cations for the future of a society which expects more than half of its children to experience the dissolution of their parents' marital rela-tionship before they reach age eighteen.

Increased public recognition of the national disgrace of unpaid child support has been growing in recent years. As Representative Dan Coats of Indiana said in the 1983 Congressional hearings on child support:

> We see a picture of single mothers struggling to enter and make their way in a marketplace in which many lack the necessary training and experience to successfully compete. The burden for those mothers in pro-viding economic and emotional security for the family is nearly an over-whelming task but even more complicated when they don't receive adequate child support from the fathers.
>
> It is our responsibility to do what we can do to alleviate this shameful child support record. I think ultimately we are faced with a task of reawak-ening our population to the importance of accepting and fulfilling the re-sponsibility of caring for children that are brought into this world. That responsibility does not end upon separation or divorce but continues to an even greater degree. Fathers have both a legal and a moral obligation to provide child support, and we should do what we can to insure that that is done.[143]

But notwithstanding Representative Coats's proscription, and not-withstanding the 1984 federal legislation that seeks to alter the nonpay-ment–nonenforcement cycle, the attitudes and practices of judges and lawyers reviewed in this chapter suggest that many courts are moving in the opposite direction; that is, they are asking fathers to contribute minimally, if at all, to child support and making compliance almost discretionary. We have seen that nonsupporting fathers have the eco-nomic capacity to pay significantly more than they are currently asked to pay, and substantially more than they are actually paying. In addi-tion, we have seen that noncompliance is just as common among men earning $40,000 a year as among those earning $10,000 or $20,000. The question that therefore lies before us is whether we, as a society, will decide that men should indeed share the financial responsibility for the support of their children (and whether we will revise our divorce laws, court procedures, and enforcement efforts to accomplish this end), or whether we will tolerate the persistence of the present system whereby children and former wives are sentenced to bear the economic brunt of divorce.

CHAPTER 10

The Economic Consequences of Divorce

DIVORCE HAS RADICALLY DIFFERENT economic consequences for men and women. While most divorced men find that their standard of living improves after divorce, most divorced women and the minor children in their households find that their standard of living plummets. This chapter shows that when income is compared to needs, divorced men experience an average 42 percent rise in their standard of living in the first year after the divorce, while divorced women (and their children) experience a 73 percent decline.

These apparently simple statistics have far-reaching social and economic consequences. For most women and children, divorce means precipitous downward mobility—both economically and socially. The reduction in income brings residential moves and inferior housing, drastically diminished or nonexistent funds for recreation and leisure, and intense pressures due to inadequate time and money. Financial hardships in turn cause social dislocation and a loss of familiar networks for emotional support and social services, and intensify the psychological stress for women and children alike. On a societal level, divorce increases female and child poverty and creates an ever-widening gap between the economic well-being of divorced men, on the one hand, and their children and former wives on the other.

The data reviewed in this chapter indict the present legal system of divorce: it provides neither economic justice nor economic equality.

The economic consequences of the current system of divorce emerge from two different types of analysis. In the first analysis we focus on income. Here we compare men's and women's *incomes* before and after divorce. The second analysis focuses on *standards of living.* Here we ask how the husbands' postdivorce standards of living compare with that of their former wives. Since it is reasonable to expect postdivorce incomes and standards of living to vary with the length of marriage and the family income level before divorce, these two factors are controlled in the following analyses.

POSTDIVORCE INCOME: RELATIVE DEPRIVATION FOR WOMEN AND CHILDREN

To compare the experiences of men and women after divorce, each spouse's postdivorce income is measured against the "baseline" figure of the family's predivorce income.

In this analysis, we assume full compliance with court-ordered alimony and child support awards. This means the wife's postdivorce income has been "adjusted" by adding the amount of alimony and child support she was awarded to her income from other sources, such as wages or welfare payments. Similarly, the husband's income has been adjusted by deducting the amount of alimony and child support he was ordered to pay from his postdivorce income.

In view of the high rate of noncompliance with support orders, this method of calculation obviously underestimates husbands' incomes and overestimates wives'. (Since many husbands do not comply with court orders for support, husbands will have *more* income than these calculations assume and wives will have *less*—and the real income difference between the two spouses *will be greater* than these figures suggest.) Thus, if there is an error in these calculations it is that the income differences between men and women have been *minimized.*

The data were collected in interviews that took place about a year after the legal divorce. In many cases the year brought additional income for one or both parties—from new jobs, increased working hours, supplementary income or aid from the government, and (among some women and a large number of men) salary raises and cost-of-living increases. Thus the combined postdivorce income of the two former spouses is often greater than the family income at the time of divorce.

Here we compare postdivorce incomes for three groups of couples: those divorced after shorter marriages (under 10 years), after mid-length marriages (11 to 17 years), and after long marriages (18 years or more).

Shorter Marriages

For couples married less than ten years, we found a striking disparity between the postdivorce income levels of former husbands and wives (see Table 26.) One year after the divorce, husbands had postdivorce incomes equivalent to at least three-quarters of the family's total income before the divorce. Most wives, in contrast, lived on a fraction of the family's predivorce income—a half, or a third, or a quarter.

Only wives from low-income families had close to three-quarters (71 percent) of the family's predivorce income—but they too had less income than their former husbands. In middle- and higher-income families, the wives had much less. For example, in families with predivorce incomes between $30,000 and $40,000 a year, the wife's income was reduced to 39 percent of the former family standard, while her husband maintained 75 percent.

The contrast is most pronounced among families with predivorce incomes of $40,000 or more. Relative to other divorced women, these wives appear to be moderately well off: they had mean support awards of close to $8,000 a year and total yearly incomes of $18,000. But compare them to their former husbands: the wives' income is only 29 percent of the former family income, while the husbands' is three-quarters of that standard, or more than twice as much dollar income ($18,000 vs. $46,550 per year).

In short, as family income goes up, divorced wives experience greater "relative deprivation." That is, they are relatively worse off than their former husbands, and they are relatively worse off than they were during marriage. Thus wives in families with incomes of less than $20,000 before divorce had 71 percent of that income after divorce, but this dropped to 56 percent for wives in families with between $20,000 to $30,000 incomes before divorce, to 39 percent for wives in families with incomes of $30,000 to $40,000, and to a mere 29 percent for wives in families with incomes of $40,000 and more before the divorce.

TABLE 26

Postdivorce Incomes of Couples Married Less Than Ten Years

PREDIVORCE YEARLY FAMILY INCOME	MEAN YEARLY SUPPORT AWARDED TO WIFE[1,2]	MEDIAN POSTDIVORCE INCOME		MEDIAN POSTDIVORCE INCOME AS PERCENTAGE OF PREDIVORCE FAMILY INCOME	
		Wife's (Adjusted)[3]	Husband's (Adjusted)[4]	Wife (Adjusted)	Husband (Adjusted)
under $20,000 (n = 41)[5]	$ 550	$ 9,050	$10,750	71%	94%
$20–29,999 (n = 24)	$1,350	$13,000	$18,100	56%	78%
$30–39,999 (n = 19)	$1,750	$15,000	$30,000	39%	75%
$40,000+ (n = 21)	$7,750	$18,000	$46,550	29%	75%

[1] All dollar figures are rounded to nearest $50.

[2] Court-ordered alimony and child support, including zero and one dollar awards.

[3] Wife's adjusted income calculated by adding court-ordered alimony and child support awarded plus income from any other source (such as wages or welfare).

[4] Husband's adjusted income calculated by subtracting court-ordered alimony and child support from husband's total income.

[5] n refers to the number of cases on which the percentages are based.

This table is based on data from interviews with divorced men and women, Los Angeles County, California, 1978.

PER CAPITA INCOME

The foregoing discussion treats the postdivorce households of men and women as if each contained only one person. However, women are more likely than men to have dependent children in their households and more likely to share their postdivorce income with them. One way of building this factor into the analysis is to calculate the *per capita income* in the two households by dividing the adjusted income of each spouse by the number of people in each household.

Before discussing these data, however, it is important to note two methodological decisions that were made. First, we have once again assumed full compliance with alimony and child support orders. Second, although we have included new spouses and permanent cohabitors in calculating the number of persons in each postdivorce household, we have not included the income these adults may bring into the household. (Rather, we have assumed that *none* of these new members is contributing to the family's income.)

Again, both of these decisions are likely to lead us to underestimate the husbands' income after divorce. Not only does noncompliance result in more income being left in the husbands' households, so does remarriage—since men were more likely than women to remarry or cohabit within the first year after divorce and most second spouses and cohabitors were employed. Among couples married less than 10 years, 19 percent of the husbands had remarried within one year of the divorce, in contrast to only 4 percent of their former wives.

Table 27 shows the *per capita* income for the same group of families examined in Table 26. It reveals that the presence of children in the wife's postdivorce household makes a major difference: it diminishes the amount of money available to each member. As a result, the wife and each member of her household have far less *per capita* income than the husband (and each member of his household).

Table 27 highlights three major findings. First, divorced men at every income level who were married less than ten years had a much higher *per capita* income—that is, they have much more money to spend on themselves—than their former wives. Second, the disparity between former husbands and wives is much greater when we compare *per capita* income rather than household income because the *per capita* measure takes into account the additional needs of the children. And third, the children and wives of upper-middle-class men experience the greatest relative deprivation. When we compare *household* income for the average divorcing couple (in Table 26), we see a 22 percent discrepancy between husbands' and wives' postdivorce incomes (78

TABLE 27

Median Postdivorce Per Capita Incomes of Couples Married Less Than Ten Years

PREDIVORCE YEARLY FAMILY INCOME	PREDIVORCE PER CAPITA FAMILY INCOME[1]	POSTDIVORCE PER CAPITA INCOME		POSTDIVORCE PER CAPITA INCOME AS PERCENTAGE OF PREDIVORCE FAMILY PER CAPITA INCOME	
		Wife (Adjusted)[2,4]	Husband (Adjusted)[3,5]	Wife (Adjusted)	Husband (Adjusted)
under $20,000 (n = 41)[5]	$ 6,050	$ 7,000	$10,450	116%	172%
$20–29,999 (n = 24)	$11,000	$ 8,900	$18,050	81%	164%
$30–39,999 (n = 19)	$17,500	$13,050	$27,000	75%	154%
$40,000+ (n = 21)	$23,500	$12,000	$45,700	51%	195%

[1] All dollar figures are rounded to nearest $50.
[2] Wife's postdivorce adjusted per capita family income was calculated by taking the wife's total income (from all sources including alimony and child support) and dividing by the number of people in her postdivorce family (including children in her custody).
[3] Husband's postdivorce adjusted per capita income was calculated by taking the husband's total income, subtracting any alimony and child support awarded to his ex-wife, and dividing the remaining amount by the number of people in his postdivorce family (including any new spouse, permanent cohabitant, or children in his custody).
[4] These figures do not include any additional income provided by the new spouse for the 19% of the divorced men and the 4% of the divorced women in this subsample who had remarried by the time of the interview (approximately one year after the legal divorce), or by a permanent cohabitant.
[5] n refers to the number of cases on which the percentages are based.

This table is based on data from interviews with divorced men and women, Los Angeles County, California, 1978.

328

percent vs. 56 percent), but when we compare *per capita* income, the discrepancy increases to 83 percent (164 percent vs. 81 percent). Similarly, for lower-income couples, a household discrepancy of 23 percent is a *per capita* discrepancy of 56 percent. For the highest income couples, a household discrepancy of 44 percent becomes a *per capita* discrepancy of enormous proportions—144 percent difference between the *per capita* incomes of former husbands and wives.

These comparisons show how the presence of children in the wife's household increases demands on her income. When a mother shares her smaller portion of the pie with the couple's children, both she and the children end up with significantly less money than the father.

It seems somewhat ironic to note that judges often explain their higher awards to the husband by saying that he will soon have to support a second family. Yet these data show that it is more typically women who are supporting other family members. When men do remarry, the court awards allow them to support their new families at a much higher level. In this subsample, for example, the 19 percent of the men who remarried were supporting their new families at per capita levels well above those of their former wives and children.

Paralleling the findings in Table 26 on household income, we find that the discrepancy between the husbands' and wives' postdivorce *per capita* income is smallest among low- and average-income families. In the average-income range, for example, the husband has about *twice* as much money as his former wife and each of his children. In the higher-income range, the ratio is closer to four times as much. Thus among families with predivorce incomes of $40,000 a year or more, the wives and children are left with half of their former *per capita* level, while the husband's *per capita* income is close to 200 percent above his former level.

The result is that most wives experience rapid *downward* mobility after divorce, while most husbands' economic status is substantially improved. Indeed, our interviews reveal that it is the *discrepancy* between the two households, a discrepancy that is largest among middle-class and upper-middle-class couples, that engenders the resentment that so many divorced women express. The injustice, in their eyes, is that she is forced to live so poorly when he is allowed to live so well.

Marriages of Eleven to Seventeen Years

The same discrepancies in postdivorce incomes are evident among couples divorced after marriages of 11 to 17 years. Here the data (tables not shown) follow the patterns in Tables 26 and 27. Again, analysis of postdivorce *household* incomes reveals men to be relatively better off after divorce than their former wives. And again, analysis of *per capita* income intensifies the differences because many wives are still sharing their smaller household incomes with minor children. Since the costs of raising children increase with the age of the child and are highest in the teenage years, the older children in these families fully consume their *per capita* share of the family budget.

As with couples in shorter marriages, the greatest gap between men and women's postdivorce incomes among those married 11 to 17 years occurs in the higher-income groups. In families with predivorce incomes of $40,000 or more, the wife's postdivorce *per capita* income is 64 percent of the family's former standard, while that of the husband is 222 percent.

One implication of these findings is that a man can substantially improve his standard of living by getting a divorce. In addition, the richer he is, the more he has to gain. The parallel implication, of course, is that women have a lot to lose—economically—from divorce, and those married to well-to-do men have the most to lose. Instead of living the life of the mythical alimony drone surrounded by luxury, the wife of fifteen years is more likely to find herself deprived of virtually all the benefits she enjoyed as the wife of a relatively well-to-do man. For this reason, she suffers a much greater financial loss by divorce than does a divorced woman from a lower-income family.

Long-married Couples and Displaced Homemakers

Economically, older and longer-married women suffer the most after divorce. Their situation is much more drastic—and tragic—than that of their younger counterparts because the discrepancy between men's and women's standards of living after divorce is much greater than for younger couples, and few of these women can ever hope to recapture their loss.

Once again, among this group the discrepancy between former husbands and wives is evident at all income levels, and most pronounced—and severe—for those with predivorce family incomes of $40,000 or more a year.

When the courts project the postdivorce prospects for women after shorter marriages, they assume that most of these women will be able to build new lives for themselves.[1] They reason that a woman in her twenties or early thirties is young enough to acquire education or training and thus has the potential to find a satisfying and well-paid job. To be sure, such women will probably have a hard time catching up with their former husbands, but most of them will be able to enter or re-enter the labor force. In setting support for these younger women, the underlying assumption is that they will become self-sufficient. (I am not questioning that assumption. What has been questioned is the court's optimism about the ease and speed of the transition. Younger divorced women need more generous support awards for training and education to maximize their long-run job prospects.[2] But their potential for some level of "self-sufficiency" is not questioned.)

But what about the woman in her forties or fifties—or even sixties at the point of divorce? What are her prospects? Is it reasonable for judges to expect her to become self-sufficient? This woman's problems of job placement, retraining, and self-esteem are likely to be much more severe.[3] Her divorce award is likely to establish her standard of living for the rest of her life.

The hardest case is that of the long-married woman who has devoted her life to raising children who are now grown. Consider, for example, the hypothetical Ann Thompson, age fifty-three, who was formerly married to a wealthy corporate executive. She is much better off after divorce than the vast majority of divorced women her age because her former husband earns $6,000 a month net. The average Los Angeles judge would award Ann Thompson $2,000 a month in spousal support, giving her a total income of $24,000 a year in contrast to her former husband's $48,000 a year (after alimony payments are deducted from his income). Her former husband will be able to maintain his comfortable standard of living on his $48,000 income (which is likely to rise) and the tax benefits he gets from paying alimony. But Ann, with her house sold, no employment prospects, and the loss of her social status and social networks, will not be able to sustain anything near her former standard of living.

Since Ann Thompson's three children are over eighteen, she is not legally entitled to any child support for them.[4] She is likely, however, to be contributing to their college expenses. In addition, one or more of them is likely to still be living with her, and all probably return from time to time for extended visits. Thus she may well be providing as much if not more for their support than their well-to-do father.*

The combined effects of a less than equal income and a greater

---

* When Stanford University students from divorced families were interviewed for a class research project most reported that they first asked their mother for money, even though they knew she had less than their father, because they found her more sympathetic and willing to support them.[5]

than equal share of the children's expenses invariably result in extreme downward mobility for long-married divorced women in California. They are both absolutely and relatively worse off than their former husbands. Although the courts are supposed to aim at balancing the resources of the two postdivorce households, the data reveal that they do not come near this goal.

HOUSEHOLD INCOME

Because the data comparing household income of long-married couples are similar to the patterns in shorter marriages, they are not discussed in the same detail here. They reveal (tables not shown) that the postdivorce income of men in all income groups is substantially higher than that of their former wives. On the average (i.e., considering all predivorce income levels), courts allow long-married divorced men to retain twice as much disposable income as they award to the women with whom these men shared the building years of long marriage.

PER CAPITA INCOME

Data on the *per capita* incomes of ex-husbands and wives after eighteen years or more of marriage are presented in Table 28. These data follow the pattern observed in short marriages (Table 27) and reveal a wider gap between men and women than the comparison of household income reveals. They also show lower incomes and greater deprivation for long-married women when compared with their younger counterparts.

Table 28 indicates that men married more than eighteen years have a much higher *per capita* income—that is, they have much more money to spend on themselves—than their former wives at every level of (predivorce family) income. Even where the discrepancy is smallest, in lower-income families, the husband and every member of this postdivorce family have *twice* as much money as his former wife and his children. In higher-income families, the discrepancy is enormous. The husband and each person in his postdivorce household—his new wife, cohabitor, or child—have three times as much disposable income as his former wife and the members of her postdivorce household. When we realize that the "other members" of the wife's postdivorce household are almost always the husband's children, the discrepancy between the two standards of living seems especially unjust.

Table 28 shows only one group of women who maintain the stan-

TABLE 28

Median Postdivorce Per Capita Incomes of Couples Married Eighteen Years or More

PREDIVORCE YEARLY FAMILY INCOME	PER CAPITA FAMILY INCOME[1]	POSTDIVORCE PER CAPITA INCOME		POSTDIVORCE PER CAPITA INCOME AS PERCENTAGE OF PREDIVORCE FAMILY PER CAPITA INCOME	
		Wife (Adjusted)[2,4]	Husband (Adjusted)[3,4]	Wife (Adjusted)	Husband (Adjusted)
Under $20,000 (n = 12)[5]	$ 5,750	$6,500	$11,950	113%	208%
$20–29,999 (n = 13)	$11,500	$6,100	$11,500	53%	100%
$30–39,999 (n = 16)	$12,306	$9,100	$18,000	74%	146%
$40,000 or more (n = 22)	$20,162	$8,500	$28,640	42%	142%

[1] All dollar figures are rounded to nearest $50.

[2] Wife's postdivorce adjusted per capita family income was calculated by taking the wife's total income (from all sources, including alimony and child support) and dividing by the number of people in her postdivorce family (including children in her custody).

[3] Husband's postdivorce adjusted per capita income was calculated by taking the husband's total income, subtracting any alimony and child support awarded to his ex-wife, and dividing the remaining amount by the number of people in his postdivorce family (including any new spouse, permanent cohabitant or children in his custody).

[4] These figures *do not* include any additional income provided by the new spouse for the 36 percent of the divorced men and the 6 percent of the divorced women who had remarried by the time of the interview (approximately one year after the legal divorce).

[5] n refers to the number of cases on which the percentages are based.

This table is based on data from interviews with divorced men and women, Los Angeles County, California, 1978.

dard of living of their marriage: those with predivorce family incomes of less than $20,000. However, even these women are worse off than their former husbands, who are living on over 200 percent of their former per capita income after they divorce.

Since the contrast between husbands and wives follows the pattern observed above, and increases as we go up the income scale, the wives who experience the most relative deprivation are, here again, those who shared a median family income of over $40,000 a year before divorce. They are expected to live at less than half (42 percent) of their former *per capita* standard, while their former husbands advance to 142 percent.

Although considerable concern has been expressed about the plight of the wife after a lengthy marriage,[6] and California courts have explicitly held that the parties' incomes should *not* be sharply disparate after long marriages,[7] it is nevertheless clear that *the pattern of support and property awards tends to impoverish the long-married woman* while it provides the long-married man with an ongoing comfortable standard of living.

The women in this group are much worse off than their younger counterparts because they not only face a severely diminished income, they also have less potential for supplementing the money they receive from their ex-husbands with money from employment or other sources. They thus remain more dependent on their former husbands, and are more likely than any other group of women to suffer from the courts' unequal allocation of the husband's income at divorce.

In light of these data, it is not surprising to find that the group of divorced women who report the most distress with their financial loss and who express the strongest feelings of outrage and injustice, are the longer-married middle- and upper-middle-class women we interviewed. These relatively well-to-do women—those who shared family incomes of $40,000 or $50,000 or more before the divorce—experience the *greatest downward mobility* after divorce.

Accompanying their loss of income are the secondary effects of downward mobility: the moves to less comfortable housing and poorer neighborhoods, the loss of neighborhood and friendship networks, the need to establish credit and find services in new communities, and the need to help out with the financial problems of children who are legally grown but not financially self-sufficient.

Not inconsiderable among these secondary effects of economic deprivation is the woman's estrangement from established social activities and social networks. Newly restricted income often precludes her participation in activities that her friends take for granted but she can no longer afford. When she declines their invitations they soon stop asking her and she becomes increasingly isolated from both friends and social community.

In addition, when a woman's friendship networks have been built around her husband's job or profession, she usually loses her place after divorce and finds herself on the outside looking in. While most divorced women retain a few married friends who remain supportive, social activities with the old "circle" usually decline. Within a year, the dissociation from marital friends is typically much greater for women than for men.[8]

For the women whose social life has been husband-centered, the postdivorce losses often entail more than friends and social networks. Being the wife of a doctor or corporate executive, for example, can be the anchor of one's identity and the major source of one's self-esteem. It can also be the basis for one's social acceptability, as well as a full-time career in its own right. Many women who have lived through and for their husbands say that the loss of the role of wife is tantamount to "losing a part of myself." As one woman put it, "it was like cutting me out of my life." Many women expressed both terror and anger at the "total and irrevocable loss of status" because their entire lives had been built around and sustained by their involvement in their husbands' work.[9]

Psychologists Judith Wallerstein and Joan Kelly report the experiences of divorced upper-middle-class women in Marin County, California, as one of losing the moorings of their identity:

> The decline in the standard of living was made more troublesome for some women by the way it brought them into a lower socioeconomic class. Women who had been in the highest and most prosperous socioeconomic group, in particular, faced an entirely changed life. For these women, all of them left by their husbands, the moorings of their identification with a certain social class, and with it the core of their self-esteem—formerly exclusively determined by the husband's education, occupation, and income—were shaken loose.[10]

It should not be surprising to find that women feel more socially and psychologically dislocated by divorce than men. In general, women are far more likely than men to define the family not only as the anchor of their identity, but also as the source of their continuity. Work typically fulfills these functions for men. As sociologist Robert Weiss states it, "The occupational role affords a man structure, an opportunity to engage with others socially, and a self-definition to which his marital status is largely irrelevant."[11] Since divorced men maintain their occupational roles after divorce, they are less likely than women to feel a disjuncture between their former and present selves.

In addition to the emotionally jarring effects of lost identity and status, divorce for middle- and upper-class homemakers commonly means an abrupt career cessation. Women who have filled their days with activities that demand considerable competence—whether as volunteer members of hospital boards, or charitable fund-raisers, or more directly as their husbands' advisors, editors, or speech writers—suddenly find their skills unwanted and devalued when no longer enhanced by a husband's prestigious name. Furthermore, skills developed in the course of such a partnership career are usually not transferable to the marketplace because employers consider an employment history legitimate only if it has been *paid* employment.

Inevitably, some of these women feel regret at having relinquished earlier career opportunities. But many more feel that they and their husbands made conscious choices about the type of relationship they would share, and they are proud of the role they played as wives and mothers. Their only regret is the way their contributions have been devalued or ignored entirely at divorce.

In this context, it is significant that both the men and the women who had been married over eighteen years said they believed in partnership and sharing principles. (One hundred percent of the wives and 99 percent of the husbands agreed with the following statement: "I assumed that we would share all of the property and income we would acquire.") But, as the data in Table 28 so clearly show, the divorce courts do not honor their implicit contract.

Instead, the rules have been changed in the middle of the game. And the current rules—or rather the way the current rules are being interpreted—suggest that when the marriage dissolves, the property they have acquired and the income the husband earns are treated as "his" rather than "theirs," and he alone reaps the lion's share of the benefits from the partnership that she helped to build.

No wonder many of these long-married women feel betrayed by a society that encouraged them to believe their husbands would support them for life, and frustrated by discovering the importance of forgone options only when they are past a point where they can easily choose a different course. Betty Friedan has aptly described this kind of disillusionment: "It is growing up and believing that love and *marriage will take care of everything,* and then one day waking up at thirty, forty, fifty, and facing the world alone and facing the responsibility [alone]."[12]

POSTDIVORCE STANDARDS OF LIVING:
IMPOVERISHMENT OF WOMEN AND CHILDREN

The income disparity between men and women after divorce profoundly affects their relative standards of living.

To examine this effect we rely on an index of economic well-being developed by the U.S. government. The model for our analysis was constructed by Michigan researchers who followed a sample of 5,000 American families, weighted to be representative of the U.S. population.[13] Economists Saul Hoffman and John Holmes compared the incomes of men and women who stayed in intact families with the incomes of divorced men and divorced women over a seven-year period.*

A comparison of the married and divorced couples yielded two major findings. First, as might be expected, the dollar income of both divorced men and divorced women declined, while the income of married couples rose. Divorced men lost 19 percent in income while divorced women lost 29 percent.[14] In contrast, married men and women experienced a 22 percent rise in income.[15] These data confirm our commonsense belief that both parties suffer after a divorce. They also confirm that women experience a greater loss than their former husbands.

The second finding of the Michigan research is surprising. To see what the income loss meant in terms of family purchasing power, Hoffman and Holmes constructed an index of family income in relation to family needs.[16] Since this income/need comparison is adjusted for family size, as well as for the each member's age and sex, it provides an individually tailored measure of a family's economic well-being in the context of marital status changes.

The Michigan researchers found that the experiences of divorced men and women were strikingly different when this measure was used. Over the seven-year period, the economic position of divorced men actually improved by 17 percent.[17] In contrast, over the same period divorced women experienced a 29 percent decline in terms of what their income could provide in relation to their needs.[18]

To compare the experiences of divorced men and women in Califor-

---

* Detailed information from the interviews provided the researchers with precise income data, including income from employment, intra-family transfers, welfare, and other government programs. Alimony and/or child support paid by the husband was subtracted from his income and added to the wife's postdivorce income. Finally, to facilitate direct comparisons, all income was calculated in constant 1968 dollars so that changes in real income could be examined without the compounding effect of inflation.

nia to those in Michigan, we devised a similar procedure to calculate the basic needs of each of the families in our interview sample. This procedure used the living standards for urban families constructed by the Bureau of Labor Statistics of the U.S. Department of Labor.[19] First, the standard budget level for each family in the interview sample was calculated in three different ways: once for the predivorce family, once for the wife's postdivorce family, and once for the husband's postdivorce family. Then the income in relation to needs was computed for each family. (Membership in postdivorce families of husbands and wives included any new spouse or cohabitor and any children whose custody was assigned to that spouse.) These data are presented in Figure 3.

FIGURE 3   Change in Standards of Living* of Divorced Men and Women (Approximately one year after divorce)

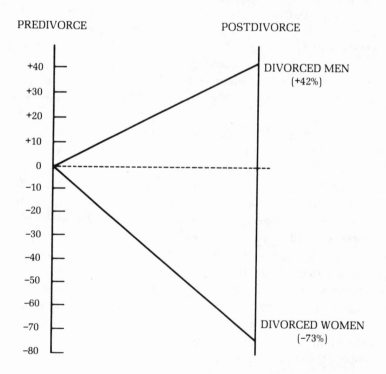

*Income in relation to needs with needs based on U.S. Department of Agriculture's low standard budget.

Based on weighted sample of interviews with divorced persons, Los Angeles County, California, 1978

Figure 3 reveals the radical change in the standards of living to which we alluded earlier. Just one year after legal divorce, *Men experience a 42 percent improvement in their postdivorce standard of living, while women experience a 73 percent decline.*

These data indicate that *divorce is a financial catastrophe for most women:* in just one year they experience a dramatic decline in income and a calamitous drop in their standard of living. It is hard to imagine how they deal with such severe deprivation: every single expenditure that one takes for granted—clothing, food, housing, heat— must be cut to one-half or one-third of what one is accustomed to.

It is difficult to absorb the full implications of these statistics. What does it mean to have a 73 percent decline in one's standard of living? When asked how they coped with this drastic decline in income, many of the divorced women said that they themselves were not sure. It meant "living on the edge" and "living without." As some of them described it:

> We ate macaroni and cheese five nights a week. There was a Safeway special for 39 cents a box. We could eat seven dinners for $3.00 a week. . . . I think that's all we ate for months.

> I applied for welfare. . . . It was the worst experience of my life. . . . I never dreamed that I, a middle class housewife, would ever be in a position like that. It was humiliating . . . they make you feel it. . . . But we were desperate, and I *had* to feed my kids.

> You name it, I tried it—food stamps, soup kitchens, shelters. It just about killed me to have the kids live like that. . . . I finally called my parents and said we were coming . . . we couldn't have survived without them.

Even those who had relatively affluent life-styles before the divorce experienced a sharp reduction in their standard of living and faced hardships they had not anticipated. For example, the wife of a dentist sold her car "because I had no cash at all, and we lived on that money— barely—for close to a year." And an engineer's wife:

> I didn't buy my daughter any clothes for a year—even when she graduated from high school we sewed together two old dresses to make an outfit.

The wife of a policeman told an especially poignant story about "not being able to buy my twelve-year-old son Adidas sneakers." The boy's father had been ordered to pay $100 a month child support but had not been paying. To make up that gap in her already bare-bone budget, she had been using credit cards to buy food and other household necessities. She had exceeded all her credit limits and felt the family just could not afford to pay $25 for a new pair of Adidas sneakers. But, as she said a year later,

> Sometimes when you are so tense about money you go crazy . . . and you forget what it's like to be twelve years old and to think you can't live without Adidas sneakers . . . and to feel the whole world has deserted you along with your father.

Others spoke of cutting out all the nonessentials. For one woman it meant "no movies, no ice cream cones for the kids." For another it meant not replacing tires on her son's bike "because there just wasn't the money." For another woman it meant not using her car—a real handicap in Los Angeles—and waiting for two buses in order to save the money she would have had to spend for gas. In addition to scaled-down budgets for food ("We learned to love chicken backs") and clothing ("At Christmas I splurged at the Salvation Army—the only "new" clothes they got all year"), many spoke of cutting down on their children's school lunches ("I used to plan a nourishing lunch with fruit and juice; now she's lucky if we have a slice of ham for a sandwich") and school supplies and after-school activities ("he had to quit the Little League and get a job as a delivery boy").

Still, some of the women were not able to "make it." Fourteen percent of them moved onto the welfare rolls during the first year after the divorce, and a number of others moved back into their parents' homes when they had "no money left and nowhere to go and three children to feed."

EXPLAINING THE DISPARITY BETWEEN HUSBANDS' AND WIVES' STANDARDS OF LIVING

How can we explain the strikingly different economic consequences of divorce for men and women? How could a law that aimed at fairness create such disparities between divorced men and their former wives and children?

The explanation lies first in the inadequacy of the court's awards, second in the expanded demands on the wife's resources after divorce, and third in the husband's greater earning capacity and ability to supplement his income.

Consider first the court awards for child support (and in rarer cases, alimony). Since judges do not require men to support either their children or their former wives as they did during marriage, they allow the husband to keep most of his income for himself. Since only a few wives are awarded alimony, the only supplementary income they are awarded is child support and the average child support award covers less than half of the cost of raising a child. Thus, the average support award is simply inadequate: even if the husband pays it, it often leaves the wife and children in relative poverty. The custodial mother is expected to somehow make up the deficit alone even though she typically earns much less than her former husband.

In this regard, it is also important to note the role that property awards play in contributing to—rather than alleviating—the financial disparities between divorced women and men. Under the old law, when the wife with minor children was typically awarded the family home, she started her postdivorce life on a more equal footing because the home provided some stability and security and reduced the impact of the income loss suffered at divorce. Today, when the family home is more commonly sold to allow an "equal" division of property, there is no cushion to soften the financial devastations that low support awards create for women and children. Rather, the disruptive costs of moving and establishing a new household further strain their limited income—often to the breaking point.

The second explanation for the disparity between former husbands and wives lies in the greater demands on the wife's household after divorce, and the diminished demands on the husband's. Since the wife typically assumes the responsibility for raising the couple's children, her need for help and services increases as a direct result of her becoming a single parent. Yet at the very time that her need for more income and more financial support is greatest, the courts have drastically reduced her income. Thus the gap between her income and her needs is wider after divorce.

In contrast, the gap between the husband's income and needs narrows. Although he now has fewer absolute dollars, the demands on his income have diminished: he often lives alone and he is no longer financially responsible for the needs of his ex-wife and children. While he loses the benefits of economies of scale, and while he may have to purchase some services (such as laundry and cooking) that he did not have to buy during marriage, he is nevertheless much better off because he has so much more money to spend on himself. Since he has been allowed to retain most of his income for himself, he can afford these extra expenses and still have more surplus income than he enjoyed during marriage.

The final explanation for the large income discrepancy between former husbands and wives lies in the different earning capacities and starting points of the two adults at the time of the divorce. Not only do men in our society command higher salaries to begin with, they also benefit from the common marital pattern that gives priority to their careers. Marriage gives men the opportunity, support, and time to invest in their own careers. Thus marriage itself builds and enhances the husband's earning capacity. For women, in contrast, marriage is more likely to act as a career liability. Even though family roles are changing, and even though married women are increasingly working for pay during marriage, most of them nevertheless subordinate their careers to their husbands' and to their family responsibilities. This is especially true if they have children. Thus women are often doubly disadvantaged at the point of divorce. No only do they face the "normal" 60 percent male/female income gap that affects all working women, they also suffer from the toll the marital years have taken on their earning capacity.

Thus marriage—and then divorce—impose a differential disadvantage on women's employment prospects, and this is especially severe for women who have custody of minor children. The responsibility for children inevitably restricts the mother's job opportunities by limiting her work schedule and location, her availability for overtime, and her freedom to take advantage of special training, travel assignments, and other opportunities for career advancement.

Although the combined income of the former spouses typically increases after divorce, most of the rise is a result of the husband's increased income. Even though women who have not been employed during marriage seek jobs after divorce, and part-time workers take full-time jobs, neither of these factors accounts for as much as the rise in male wages in the first year after divorce.

It is, in fact, surprising to see how many divorced men receive salary increases (and bonuses) immediately after divorce. While some of these are probably routine raises, and others may be the result of more intense work efforts or overtime work, it is also evident that some men manage to delay a bonus or commission or raise until after the divorce is final. This allows them to minimize the income they have to report to the court when child support (or alimony) awards are being made.

While the courts have long been aware of the control that self-employed men can exercise over the amount and timing of the income they receive, our data suggest that many salaried employees may exercise similar control over their income since many of them manage to obtain salary increases soon after their divorces become final. Whether or not this is coincidence, the fact remains that the income of divorced men often increases substantially in the first year after the divorce.

During the same period, the obligations that these men have for alimony and child support typically remain fixed or diminish: some support obligations have been reduced or terminated by terms of the divorce settlement (and others have been reduced or stopped without the courts' permission). The result, once again, is that divorced men have more "surplus income" for themselves.

The discrepancy between divorced men and women has been corroborated by other research. Sociologist Robert Weiss and economist Thomas Espenshade found parallel disparities in the standards of living of former husbands and wives after divorce, and Weiss corroborates the finding that the greatest reduction in postdivorce income is experienced by women who shared higher family incomes before the divorce.[20] Census Bureau data also document the disparities in both income and standards of living of men and women after divorce. In 1979, the median per capita income of divorced women who had not remarried was $4,152, just over half of the $7,886 income of divorced men who had not remarried.[21]

The situation of divorced women with young children is even more grim. The median income in families headed by women with children under six years of age was only 30 percent of the median income for all families whose children were under six.[22] Thus, for the United States as a whole, the "income of families headed by women is at best half that of other families; the income of families headed by women with young children is even less, one-third of that of other families."[23]

SOCIAL CONSEQUENCES: STRESS, ISOLATION, COMPETENCE, AND HEALTH

The economic disparity that divorce creates between former husbands and wives not only brings economic hardships for most divorced women and their children, it is also one of the major causes of economic inequality between men and women in the larger society. But before we move to these larger societal consequences, let us first look at some of the more immediate social effects on the participants themselves.

Financial Pressure and Stress

It is not surprising to find that the financial hardships generated by the present system of divorce create greater pressures on women than on divorced men at all income levels. Many middle-class women who "manage to survive" nonetheless report that they are in a constant state of financial crisis after divorce.[24] More women than men at all class levels in our sample reported that they were "more concerned about money now than when they were married," "more careful about budgeting," and "spending their money on necessities, not extras."

Nor is it surprising to find that 70 percent of the divorced women we interviewed reported being perpetually worried about "making ends meet" and "not being able to pay their bills." They worried about obtaining court-ordered support, terrified of large unexpected expenses, anxious about mounting costs, frustrated by their own inability to earn enough or to find a better job, and overwhelmed by their steadily diminishing standard of living in an inflationary economy. (In contrast, most divorced men say they *never* worry about being able to meet their bills.)

In fact, in a national survey of the quality of American life, divorced women were more likely to report that they feel "frightened," that "life is hard," that they "always feel rushed," "worry about a nervous breakdown," and "worry . . . about bills" than were *any* other group of American men and women.[25]

Since financial worries cannot help affecting their social and emotional lives, it is not surprising that divorced women report more stress and less satisfaction with their lives than any other group of Americans. As the authors of a national survey report:

> Our data demonstrate . . . that divorce has a different meaning to women than to men. We have pointed out the great dissatisfaction divorced women feel with the economic circumstances of their lives, a feeling not shared by divorced men. [There are numerous] other evidences that the life of a divorced woman is more stressful than that of a divorced man. . . . Divorced women report far more stress in answer to these questions than any of the other groups of women. Divorced men, on the contrary, are somewhat *less* likely to report stress than the other groups of men . . . [they] do not find their lives strained or disturbing. The life of divorced women is unrelievedly negative. . . . [T]hey find their lives less satisfying than other women do and marked by much psychological stress.[26]

Social Isolation

Since divorced women tend to be more readily excluded from former social networks, they are likely to become more isolated after divorce. Although most of the women we interviewed maintained one or two close friends, their larger circle of friends gradually dissolved. Divorced men were much more likely to report being invited to dinner by old friends, being included in social activities, and "maintaining most of my old friends after the divorce."

The demands of being a single working parent severely limits the time, energy, and money the divorced woman has to devote to her own life,[27] and many report feeling "locked into the world of their children and obligations" with little time for themselves.[28]

Although sociologists have long known that adults who live alone have generally lower levels of well-being than those who are married, until recently no one considered the single-parent family as a distinct living arrangement. But a 1984 University of Michigan study found major differences in social isolation between "singles" and single parents.[29] They report that single adults who live alone are not socially isolated because most of them "compensate" by establishing many more contacts outside the household (than do people who live with others.) But the women who are single parents turn out to be "true isolates": "even though they have contact with some neighbors and relatives, their lives are severely restricted in terms of opportunities for much social contact with friends."[30] The authors conclude that "these patterns of living appear to have detrimental consequences" and that "these women reveal significantly negative feelings about their life circumstances."[31]

Competence and Self-esteem

One ironic result of the fact that most divorced women begin their postdivorce lives with a long list of negatives—less money, inadequate vocational skills, low self-esteem, heightened anxiety and stress, and great fear about the future—is that they are likely to find their lives after divorce better and more satisfying than they anticipated. Thus most divorced women, along with most divorced men, report a rise in competence and self-esteem at some time during the first year after divorce. The majority of respondents (83 percent of both sexes) reported they were now functioning better than during the marriage. They also felt better about themselves (82 percent of the men, 88 percent of the women) and considered themselves more competent in their work (47 percent of the men, 68 percent of the women), more physically attractive (45 percent of the men, 50 percent of the women), and possessed of better parenting skills (48 percent of the men, 62 percent of the women with minor children).

Thus, in spite of the pervasive economic difficulties that divorce brings, a portrait of resilience and resourcefulness also emerges from these data. While the postdivorce period is obviously one of many contrasts and many possibilities, and while there is obviously a great deal of variation in reactions to divorce among different individuals (and, as we found, within the same individual at different points in time), a surprisingly large percentage of divorced persons of both sexes report that they are functioning better and are more competent than they were during marriage. Although those who are younger, richer, and male tend to report less stress and relatively greater well-being after a divorce, even those who suffer economically report that they have "grown" from the experience of divorce and feel better about themselves.

The implicit comparison, is, of course, a marriage that has failed and the turmoil of the breakup. Since both men and women report their greatest trauma and psychological distress (as well as their greatest physical distress) occurred in the final stages of the marriage, it is not surprising to find that the divorce itself comes as something of a relief.

These positive feelings not only suggest the depressant effect of an unsatisfying marriage; they also reveal underlying expectations about life after divorce. Here it is significant that women often exceed men in their reports of postdivorce competence and self-esteem. This may reflect the fact that women had greater fears about the future and thus took greater pride in coping and surviving.

Thus even the longer-married older housewives who suffer the greatest financial hardships after divorce (and who feel most economically deprived, most angry, and most "cheated" by the divorce settlement) say they are "personally" better off than they were during marriage. They are proud of the skills they used to deal with the crisis, to marshal a support network, to manage their finances, and to take control of their lives. They also report improved self-esteem, more pride in their appearance, and greater competence in all aspects of their lives.

These dramatic reactions expose the extent to which the self-confidence and self-esteem of so many women are stifled during marriage, leaving them with the most minimal expectations for themselves and their lives after divorce. For women who have defined themselves in terms of their husbands and children, this may be the first time in their lives that they have felt free to focus on themselves and develop their own interests. As one woman put it, "I have been there for others all my life. Now I can be for me." Said another: "It's important to have my own identity. When I was a doctor's wife I lost my whole identity, even my name was his—first and last."

It is perhaps significant that many women expressed particular pride in their ability to cope with the economic hardships they had confronted. The double message of pride and economic hardship pervades the interviews. Consider for example the following responses to these two questions: "What has been the best thing about your life since the divorce? What has been the worst?" A fifty-six-year-old divorcee replied,

[The best:] The change in me, I am a whole person. I like myself better. The children like me better. I am happier. I am my own person to make my own mistakes for the first time in my life.

[The worst:] I had absolutely no concept of the legal and financial aspects or expectations of the world. I had to find out about taxes, paying bills, etc., the hard way—no kidding. It scared me. . . . I'm more careful and pinch pennies. I cut down everywhere and cut out all the luxuries in my life. I'm not financially as well off and balancing my checkbook is quite a problem for me.

And a forty-six-year-old woman:

[The best:] I learned how strong I am. I've been through hell and back and I know that I can make it.

[The worst:] I don't have any money. I can't afford a lot of things I need . . . and I probably rely on my kids too much.

And a sixty-two-year-old woman:

[The best:] My children and the friends who were there for me . . . and that I was able to get myself back on my feet after the emotional trauma . . . that I survived and am in control.

[The worst:] I'm still very bitter about losing everything. . . . it still eats at me to hear about my husband's lifestyle and vacations when I have to count every dollar . . . and I worry a lot about my future—about money and medical bills and all that.

Similarly, a thirty-three-year-old woman said:

> [The best:] I feel much better about myself because I'm doing things that
> I want to do, that are making me grow as a person. I've become a lot
> more independent. I've learned how to do things that I depended upon
> other people to do before.

> [The worst:] Before I was divorced I had absolutely no concern with how
> I spent money, where it came from or how much I spent. I spent what I
> wanted and needed, and now I have to be very careful not to spend
> more than I have. I've had to save and cut down on everything. I do
> not spend money on entertainment, do not join my group to go out for
> dinner. I have fewer clothes, have given up [domestic] help, am more
> careful at the market—money is my biggest problem.

The composite portrait that emerges from these data is one of
divorced women who are generally relieved to be rid of the stress of
the end-of-the-marriage tensions and to have the divorce process itself
completed; who are proud of the strength and resourcefulness they
have discovered within themselves; who enjoy their new-found sense
of control over their lives; and who are nevertheless stressed and anxious about their precarious financial situation and the hardships the
divorce has created for their children. Their positive attitudes are thus
qualified by and mitigated by financial tensions in their lives.

While men and women alike perceive the financial disparity in
their postdivorce circumstances, they do not agree on their relative
well-being in all other respects. When asked, "Who do you think is
financially better off since the divorce?" both sexes reported that the
man was. However, when asked, "Who do you think is better off in
nonfinancial terms?" the majority of each sex saw themselves as better
off since the divorce (60 percent of the men and 69 percent of the
women). In fact, a third of the women and a quarter of the men said
that the divorce "helped me realize my true potential."

It is indicative that what women say they miss most about marriage
is the husband's income (and this is especially true of those from higher-
income, longer-married families), while men report that they most miss
having a sexual partner (especially younger men), and having a partner
in life.

In this context, it is important to note one important difference
in the strategies used by men and women to adjust after divorce. Divorced women appear to be much more skilled than their former husbands in calling upon one or two friends or relatives to help them
weather the transition. Thus even though divorced women are more

likely to report that they have lost "a community" of friends through the divorce, they are more likely to have one person they can call on if they have a problem (most typically a mother, a female friend, a male friend, even the ex-spouse). Divorced men in contrast are more likely to say there is "no one" they can call on. While they say they have many friends, they are not as likely to ask them for help.

These findings may reflect male-female differences in willingness to ask for help, or willingness to admit they got help, or both. They certainly also reflect women's greater lifetime reliance on others for support: they do not expect to be able to handle their problems alone, nor does society generally expect them to do so. All the greater the irony, then, that the law now effectively demands that they summon forth self-sufficiency in just one sphere: finances.

Mental and Physical Health

Data from national samples consistently document the disruptive effects of divorce on the mental and physical health of both sexes. This is not surprising, since divorce and marital separation consistently rank second and third in a list of 42 stressful life events; the death of a spouse is the only event considered to require greater readjustment.[32]

The psychological distress engendered by divorce is revealed by the fact that divorced men and women exhibit more symptoms (such as "nervous breakdown" and "inertia"), and in more serious degree, than do persons of other marital statuses.[33] Divorced and separated people have the highest admission rates to psychiatric facilities (compared to married, widowed, and never married people), and this holds true across different age groups, for both sexes, and for blacks and whites alike.[34]

Divorce also takes a toll on the physical well-being of both sexes. Divorced people have more illness, higher mortality rates (in premature deaths), higher suicide rates, and more accidents than those who are married.[35] In fact, the marital status of a person is one of the best predictors of his or her health, disease, and death profile.[36]

While both sexes "share" some of the psychic and physical distress of divorce, women seem to experience the greater stress and their stress seems to take a higher toll. Beyond question, much of the women's stress is attributable to their economic condition. This is to be expected in light of the well-known relationship between low socioeconomic status and both mental and physical illness.

Three decades of research have shown a strong correlation between low income and both stress and psychiatric disability.[37] Having a low socioeconomic status and being a single mother is "additively and cumulatively associated with physical morbidity among mothers."[38]

When present low income is combined with the prospect of continuing low income, stress is intensified. Anticipated income for the coming year is related to both physical and mental health following divorce: the lower the anticipated income, the less favorable the individual's physical and psychological well-being.[39]

Clearly the sex-linked differences in stress and mental health are not a direct or necessary result of divorce itself. Rather, they are created in large measure by the present legal system which, through inadequate property awards and low and poorly enforced support awards, drastically reduces the standard of living of divorced women and their children.

SOCIETAL CONSEQUENCES

The rise in divorce has been the major cause of the increase in female-headed families,[40] and that increase has been the major cause of the feminization of poverty. Sociologist Diana Pearce, who coined the phrase "feminization of poverty," was one of the first to point to the critical link between poverty and divorce for women.[41] It was, she said, the mother's burden for the economic and emotional responsibility for child-rearing that often impoverished her family.

Contrary to popular perception, most female-headed single parent families in the United States are *not* the result of unwed parenthood: they are the result of marital dissolution.[42] Only 18 percent of the nearly ten million female-headed families in the United States are headed by an unwed mother: over 50 percent are headed by divorced mothers and the remaining 31 percent by separated mothers.[43]

When a couple with children divorces, it is probable that the man will become single but the woman will become a single parent. And poverty, for many women, begins with single parenthood. More than half of the poor families in the United States are headed by a single mother.[44]

The National Advisory Council on Economic Opportunity estimates that if current trends continue, the poverty population of the United States will be composed solely of women and children by the year 2000.[45] The Council declares that the "feminization of poverty has become one of the most compelling social facts of the decade."[46]

The Rise in Female Poverty

The well-known growth in the number of single-parent, female-headed households has been amply documented elsewhere. (The 8 percent of all children who lived in mother-child families in 1960, rose to 12 percent by 1970,[47] and to 20 percent by 1981.[48]) Also well-documented is the fact that these mother-headed families are the fastest growing segment of the American poor.[49]

What has not been well documented, and what appears to be relatively unknown—or unacknowledged—is the direct link between divorce, the economic consequences of divorce, and the rise in female poverty. The high divorce rate has vastly multiplied the numbers of women who are left alone to support themselves and their minor children. When the courts deny divorced women the support and property they need to maintain their families, they are relying, they say, on the woman's ability to get a job and support herself. But with women's current disadvantages in the labor market, getting a job cannot be the only answer—because it does not guarantee a woman a way out of poverty.[50] Even with full-time employment, one-third of the women cannot earn enough to enable them and their children to live above the poverty level.[51] The structure of the job market is such that *only half* of all full-time female workers are able to support two children without supplemental income from either the children's fathers or the government.[52]

In recent years there have been many suggestions for combating the feminization of poverty. Most of these have focused on changes in the labor market[53] (such as altering the sex segregation in jobs and professions, eliminating the dual labor market and the disparity between jobs in the primary and secondary sectors, eradicating the discriminatory structure of wages, and providing additional services, such as child care,[54] for working mothers) and on expanding social welfare programs (such as increasing AFDC benefits to levels above the poverty line, augmenting Medicaid, food stamp, and school lunch programs, and making housewives eligible for Social Security and unemployment compensation).[55]

A third possibility, which has not received widespread attention, is to change the way that courts allocate property and income at divorce. If, for example, custodial mothers and their children were allowed to remain in the family home, and if the financial responsibility for children were apportioned according to the means of the two parents, and if court orders for support were enforced, a significant segment

of the population of divorced women and their children would not
be impoverished by divorce.

The Rise in Child Poverty and Economic Hardships
for Middle-class Children of Divorce

Beyond question, the present system of divorce is increasing child poverty in America. From 1970 to 1982, the percentage of American children
living in poverty rose from 14.9 percent to 21.3 percent.[56] According
to demographer Samuel Preston, most of the growth in the number of
children in poverty occurred in the category of female-headed families.[57]

While the vast majority (82 percent) of all children born in the
United States today are born into two-parent families, more than half
of these children are likely to experience the disruption of their parents'
marriage before they reach age eighteen. As noted above, U.S. Census
Bureau data show that close to 60 percent of the children born in
1983 *would not* spend their entire childhood living with both natural
parents,[58] while Sandra Hofferth of the National Institute of Child
Health and Human Development, projected that two-thirds of the children born in wedlock in 1980 would experience a parental divorce
before they reach age seventeen.[59]

Whichever figures we use, the statistics suggest that we are sen-
tencing a significant proportion of the current generation of American
children to lives of financial impoverishment.

Clearly, living in a single-parent family does not have to mean
financial hardship. The economic well-being of many of these children
is in jeopardy only because their mothers bear the whole responsibility
for their support. That jeopardy would end if courts awarded more
alimony, higher amounts of child support, and a division of property
that considered the interests of minor children. It would also be greatly
reduced if the child support awards that the courts have already made
were systematically enforced. Under the present legal system, however,
the financial arrangements of divorce foster the financial deprivation
of millions of children.

Although the deprivation is most severe below the poverty level,
it affects children at every income level. In fact, middle-class children,
like their mothers, experience the greatest relative deprivation. The
economic dislocations of divorce bring about many changes which are
particularly difficult for children: moving to new and less secure neighborhoods, changing schools, losing friends, being excluded from activi-

ties that have become too expensive for the family's budget, and having to work after school or help care for younger siblings.

Not surprisingly, the children of divorce often express anger and resentment when their standard of living is significantly less than that in their father's household.[60] They realize that their lives have been profoundly altered by the loss of "their home" and school and neighborhood and friends, and by the new expectations their mother's reduced income creates for them. It is not difficult to understand their resentment when fathers fly off for a weekend in Hawaii while they are told to forgo summer camp, to get a job, and to earn their allowance. That resentment, according to psychologists Judith Wallerstein and Joan Kelly, is "a festering source of anger":

> When the downward change in the family standard of living followed the divorce and the discrepancy between the father's standard of living and that of the mother and children was striking, this discrepancy was often central to the life of the family and remained as a festering source of anger and bitter preoccupation. The continuation of this discrepancy over the years generated continuing bitterness between the parents. Mother and children were likely to share in their anger at the father and to experience a pervasive sense of deprivation, sometimes depression, accompanied by a feeling that life was unrewarding and unjust.[61]

The middle-class children of divorce may also feel betrayed by their disenfranchisement in their parents' property settlement. Since the law divides family property between the husband and wife and makes no provision for a child's share of the marital assets, many children feel they have been unfairly deprived of "their" home, "their" piano, "their" stereo set, and their college education. The last item is indicative, for children's taken-for-granted expectations about the future are often altered by the divorce. For example, one mother reported that the most upsetting thing about the divorce was her son's loss of the college education he'd been promised. His father, who had always pressed him to follow in his footsteps at Dartmouth, told him that a private college was now out of the question; he would have to stay home and take advantage of the low tuition at the state college. While this father could still "afford" to send his son to Dartmouth, his priorities had changed.

The loss of an education at a private college is symbolic of the changed fortunes of children of divorce at all class levels. Recall the U.S. Census Bureau data on child support which indicated that even though child support awards are quite modest, less than half of all fathers comply fully with court orders for child support. Another quarter make some payment, and close to 30 percent do not pay anything at all.[62]

Inasmuch as about 1.2 million children's parents divorce each year, the 30 percent who receive no support from their fathers adds up to 360,000 new children each year. Over a ten-year period, this amounts to 4 million children. If we add to these the approximately 3 million over the years who receive only part of their child support (or receive it only some of the time), we find a ten-year total of 7 million children deprived of the support to which they are entitled. Remembering that fewer than 4 million children are born each year helps to put all these figures in perspective.[63]

The failure of absent parents to provide child support has taken an especially severe toll in recent years because of sharp cutbacks in public programs benefiting children since 1979. The Children's Defense Fund shows that children's share of Medicaid payments dropped from 14.9 percent in 1979, to 11.9 percent in 1982, despite a rise in the child proportion among the eligible.[64] The Aid to Families with Dependent Children (AFDC) program has also been sharply cut back. In 1979, there were 72 children in AFDC for every 100 children in poverty, but only 52 per 100 in 1982.[65]

It is not surprising to find a strong relationship between the economic and psychological effects of divorce on children. Economic deprivation following divorce has been linked to increased anxiety and stress among American children.[66] Mounting evidence also shows that children of divorce who experience the most psychological stress are those whose postdivorce lives have been impaired by inadequate income. For example, Hodges, Tierney, and Buchsbaum find "income inadequacy" the most important factor in accounting for anxiety and depression among preschool children in divorced families.[67] When family income is adequate, there are no differences in anxiety-depression levels between children in divorced families and those in intact families. However, "children of divorced families with inadequate income had substantially higher levels of anxiety-depression."[68] Hodges, Wechsler, and Ballantine also find significant correlations between income and adjustment for preschool children of divorce (but not, interestingly, for preschool children of intact families).[69]

In summary, the accumulating evidence shows that children in divorced families are likely to suffer a variety of adjustment problems if they experience greater geographic mobility, lower income, and poorer adequacy of income. Unfortunately, these experiences are common to most children of divorce.

CONCLUSION: THE TWO-TIER SOCIETY

The economic consequences of the present system of divorce reverberate throughout our society. Divorce awards not only contribute heavily to the well-documented income disparity between men and women, they also lead to the widespread impoverishment of children and enlarge the ever-widening gap between the economic well-being of men and women in the larger society. Indeed, if current conditions continue unabated we may well arrive at a two-tier society with an underclass of women and children.

Thrust into a spiral of downward mobility by the present system of divorce, a multitude of middle-class women and the children in their charge are increasingly cut off from sharing the income and wealth of former husbands and fathers. Hampered by restricted employment opportunities and sharply diminished income, these divorced women are increasingly expected to shoulder alone the burden of providing for both themselves and their children.

Most of the children of divorce share their mother's financial hardships. Their presence in her household increases the strains on her meager income at the same time that they add to her expenses and restrict her opportunities for economic betterment.

Meanwhile, divorced men increasingly are freed of the major financial responsibility for supporting their children and former wives. Moreover, these men retain more than higher incomes. They experience less day-to-day stress than their ex-wives, they enjoy relatively greater mental, physical, and emotional well-being, and have greater freedom to build new lives and new families after divorce.

The economic disparities between men and women after divorce illuminate the long-standing economic disparities between the incomes of men and women during marriage. In theory, those differences did not matter in marriage, since they were partners in the enterprise and shared the husband's income. As Christopher Jencks observes, "As long as most American men and women married and pooled their economic resources, as they traditionally did, the fact that men received 70 percent of the nation's income had little effect on women's material well being."[70] But with today's high divorce rate, the ranks of unmarried women are vastly increased, and the relative numbers of women who share a man's income are greatly diminished.

The result is that the economic gulf between the sexes in the larger society is increasing. Some of this would have occurred even if the traditional divorce law remained everywhere in force. But the new divorce laws—and the way these laws are being applied—have exacerbated the effects of the high divorce rate by assuring that ever greater numbers of women and children are being shunted out of the economic mainstream.

The data on the increase in female poverty, child poverty, and the comparative deprivation of middle-class women and children suggest that we are moving toward a two-tier society in which the upper economic tier is dominated by men (and the women and children who live with them). The former wives of many of these men, the mothers of their children, and the children themselves are increasingly found in the lower economic tier. Those in the first tier enjoy a comfortable standard of living; those in the lower tier are confined to lives of economic deprivation and hardship.

Obviously the two tiers are not totally segregated by sex: professional women for example, whether married or divorced, are more likely to be found in the first tier, and members of many minority groups, both men and women, are more likely to fall into the second. Yet among these groups, and among all families at the lower income levels, divorce brings a better economic future for men than for their former wives.

The concept of a two-tier society does not imply a static model. There is movement between the two tiers. But the structural conditions of the lives of women in the lower tier make it extremely difficult for them to improve their economic fortunes by hard work or any of the other traditional routes to economic mobility. The divorced women in the lower tier face not merely the sex-segregated job market and the male-female wage gap that confront all women, but also the responsibilities and restrictions that devolve upon heads of one-parent families. For these women, the discrepancy between earnings and need is typically too large to allow them to provide even the bare necessities of life for themselves and their families.

Obviously, membership in the second tier is not necessarily permanent. Some women will find jobs or return to school or obtain training that will enable them to improve their status. Many of those who are under thirty and some of those who are under forty will accomplish the same result by remarrying. But even those women who manage eventually to improve their financial situation will typically spend their early postdivorce years in acute economic hardship. The fact that they are poor only temporarily does not mean that they and their children suffer any the less[71] or that they can ever recapture the losses of those wasted years.

CHAPTER 11

Divorce and the Illusion of Equality

ILLUSION AND REALITY

I began this research in a spirit of great optimism. I expected to discover that California's pioneering divorce law was all its formulators hoped it would be—a law that would bring the divorce process out of the shadows of outmoded tradition into the just light of the twentieth century. The legal reforms, in the words of Professor Herma Hill Kay, could be a triumph of "honesty over perjury, a concern for the individual over legal fictions, and a commitment to understand and deal fairly with the realities of family interaction, rather than to pursue an artificial search for fault, and an unproductive assignment of blame."[1]

Equally important was the law's promise of equality for men and women. Here, finally, was a law that would shed the anachronistic assumptions about women's roles and women's capacities that permeated traditional family law, and would free women from the so-called protections they had enjoyed—protections that in reality served to make them second-class citizens, and perpetuate their dependence on their husbands.[2] The no-fault divorce law promised the abolition of all sexist, gender-based rules that failed to treat wives as equals in the marital partnership.

I assumed the reformers were correct in their belief that only good could come from the reform of the fault-based divorce process. The sham testimony and vilification that were required to prove fault insulted the dignity of the law, the courts, and all the participants. How much better to construct a legal procedure that would eliminate vicious scenes and reduce, rather than increase, the antagonism and hostility between divorcing spouses. How much better to lessen the trauma of divorce for both parents and children. And how much better to end a marriage in a nonadversarial process that would enable the parties to fashion fair and equitable financial arrangements. If I, as a researcher, had a personal or political goal beyond my stated aim of "analyzing the effects of the new law on the social and legal process of divorce," it was to discover what made this law successful so that potential reformers in other states could learn from the California experience.

In the early days of exploratory research, I began to confront cases of upper-middle-class women who had been married for twenty-five years and were being cut off with only a few years of alimony and hardly any property. They were forced to move so their homes could be sold. With little or no job experience, and minimal court-ordered support, it seemed that they were headed for near-poverty. I assumed they were exceptions—women who had incompetent lawyers or who "got the wrong judge."

But as we conducted more interviews, and as the systematic data from the court dockets became computer printouts with statistical results, a disquieting pattern emerged, a pattern that pointed to substantial hardship for women and children. Somehow the elimination of grounds, fault, and consent, and the institution of gender-neutral standards for financial awards were having unanticipated and unfortunate consequences.

It gradually became clear that an ostensibly equal division of property is not in fact equal when women have the responsibility for child care in nine out of ten divorces involving children.[3] To divide the property equally between husband and wife typically means that one-half of the family assets are awarded to one person, the husband, while the other half are left to an average of three people, the wife and two children.[4]

It also became clear that judges were interpreting the equal division rule as requiring the forced sale of many family homes.[5] Accepting the well-intended goal of allowing the parties to make a "clean break" after divorce, many of them probably believed, in those early days, that the wife was "better off" without a home that tied her down to old neighborhoods and children's schools and children's friends, that locked her into the suburbs and restricted her personal, social, and economic options. But it soon became evident how much more hardship the new solution caused: it was much worse for a woman to have no home at all, and to be evicted from her neighborhood and its social supports. If equal division of property meant the sale of the family home, it also meant disruption, dislocation, and distress in the lives of women and children. And it meant they were forced to shoulder a disproportionate share of the financial hardships of divorce.

Nor was it only younger women with children who were suffering from the forced sale of the family home. Some of the most tragic victims were older homemakers who not only lost their residence of twenty-five or thirty-five years, but also lost their whole social structure in a forced move to the other side of town.[6]

As I became more aware of the disparities in the lives of men and women after divorce I realized that the assets and property that they had acquired during marriage were not, if fact, being divided equally. This was partially a result of major changes in the nature of property that had occurred in our society. Husbands and wives were increasingly investing in careers and human capital—most particularly in the husband's education and career. The new property resulting from this kind of investment was often the family's major asset. Yet this property was not being divided equally upon divorce.[7] (Indeed, in many states it was not being divided at all.) If the law allowed men to retain their career assets—their professional licenses, their health insurance, and their earning capacities, then their wives were not in fact being awarded an equal share of the property, despite the equal division rule.

It did not take long to see that many sex-based assumptions that were ridiculed a decade ago—assumptions about women's economic dependence, their greater investment in children, their need for financial support from their ex-husbands—were ironically not so ridiculous after all. Rather, they reflected, even as they reinforced, the unfortunate reality of married women's lives, and they softened the economic devastations of divorce for women and children.

In the early days of the women's movement, and in the rush to embrace equality in all its forms, some feminists thought alimony was a sexist concept that had no place in a society in which men and women were to be treated as equals. Alimony was an insult, a symbolic reflection of the law's assumption that all women were nonproductive dependents. Similarly, some viewed the maternal preference in custody decisions as an encumbrance: it perpetuated a divorced woman's responsibility for children and restricted her opportunities in the world of work and economic mobility.

But it soon became clear that alimony was a critical mechanism for realizing the goal of fairness in divorce. To a woman who had devoted twenty-five years of her life nurturing a family and who at age fifty had no job, no career, no pension, and no health insurance, alimony was not an insult. It was often her lifeline—her sole means for financial survival. As Betty Friedan explained the reversal in feminist thinking:

> The women's movement had just begun when the so-called divorce reform law was passed. At that time, we were so concerned with principle— that equality of right and opportunity had to mean equality of responsibility, and therefore alimony was out—that we did not realize the trap we were falling into. . . . We fell into a trap when we said, 'No alimony!' because housewives who divorced were in terrible straits. We fell into another trap by accepting no-fault divorce without provision for mandatory economic settlements."[8]

Along with this attitude came the realization that most of these women not only needed alimony, they had *earned* it. Alimony is a woman's due, her entitlement, and part of her compensation for her contributions to her husband's and children's welfare. Alimony is an essential part of the reciprocity in the marriage contract: it is the share of the family income that the wife was promised for her contributions to the marital partnership.[9]

These concepts of entitlement, need, compensation, and sharing also applied to the mothers of preschool children. Women who had the full-time job of caring for the couple's children after divorce had taken over many of their husband's family responsibilities and faced greater burdens and greater expenses as single parents. Even if many young mothers wanted to be self-sufficient, their economic reality compelled support from their former husbands. But it was not need alone that justified their support: they had earned it—and continued to earn it as the children's primary caretaker after divorce.

Perhaps the word should not be alimony—perhaps the term should reflect the concepts of entitlement and compensation, but the need for postdivorce support was apparent. Again, consider Betty Friedan's words:

> Alimony? It's a sexist concept, and doesn't belong in a women's movement for equality. But that economic equality we seek is not a reality yet. Half of all women are unpaid housewives still, and the ones who work still

earn barely half what men earn, and are still expected to take the entire responsibility of the kids, as well. Maintenance, reimbursement, severance pay—whatever you want to call it—is a necessity for many divorced women, as is child support.[10]

Another insight that mocked the laudable goals of legal equality for men and women came in the custody arena. It gradually became evident that legal "equality" in custody decisions could backfire in some circumstances and create more hardship than the traditional maternal preference. If the automatic legal assumption that the mother would have custody engendered guilt in some women who wanted to give up or share custody, far greater numbers so feared losing their children that they were willing to give up the money or the property they were due if they were threatened with a custody fight.[11]

Thus, "sex-neutral" custody laws meant women might be forced to bargain for custody to their own financial loss. Fathers with superior legal resources, knowledge, money, and negotiating skills now also had the legal leverage to threaten to deprive mothers of their children unless they agreed to relinquish their claims to alimony or property or child support. Faced with such a threat, most women would choose children over money or property or child support.[12] As they said in our interviews, "It's only money." But the ironic results of these negotiations were even greater economic hardships for the women and their children than would have been the case under the traditional maternal preference laws.

Similarly disillusioning were the consequences of the well-intended experiment with joint custody and its vision of fathers and mothers sharing the care of their children after divorce. Although joint custody laws hold the promise of men assuming equal responsibility for postdivorce parenting, in practice these laws have given men equal authority, but not equal responsibility.[13] Since most children in what the courts label "joint custody" continue to live with their mother,[14] and since fathers are not required to share the day-to-day tasks of child rearing (or to even assume regular visitation), laws that force custodial mothers to consult with and gain the father's approval on all major decisions about their children serve primarily to give fathers more power and control over their former wives. The father's right to veto the mother's decisions gives him the power to veto her lifestyle as well. Joint legal custody laws also give fathers a new justification for reducing their child support: men·can more easily persuade a court that they are sharing the child rearing expenses because they are "sharing" custody.[15]

In sum, this research reveals that the law does not provide an effective mechanism 1) to recognize and accommodate the differences in the structural position of most men and women in our society today; 2) to honor and reward women's work in the home and their contributions to their husbands and children; 3) to offset the impairment of women's earning capacities during marriage, and 4) to recognize that women who are caring for children after divorce need extra support because they do not have equal skills and resources to support themselves and their children. The result is that women are unequally disadvantaged by divorce. Divorce laws that treat women "equally" and assume that all women are equally equipped to survive the breakup of their families without support from their ex-husbands or society, only serve to enlarge the gap between men and women and create even greater inequalities.

Why were these realities not immediately apparent? Why did it take so long for those concerned with social justice to realize that the new laws placed an unequal and unconscionable burden on women?

One reason was simply lack of information. No one knew just how devastating divorce had become for women and children. Few people were aware of the fact that only 17 percent of the divorcing women were awarded alimony,[16] or that more than half of the women were not able to collect the child support they had been awarded.[17] Few knew that the standard of living of divorced women and their children dropped 73 percent in the first year after divorce, while that of divorced men increased 42 percent.[18] Nor was it generally understood that divorcing couples had so little property that an equal division of marital property would mean the forced sale of the family home.[19]

While individual women complained of the hardships they faced, they did not know that they were not alone. Nor did they realize that their plight was not a result of the failure of their lawyers, or the skill of their husbands' lawyers, or the bias of the judge, but rather part of *a systematic pattern* by which women were routinely denied the support and property they and their children needed.

The research reported in this book is the first to examine systematically the effects of the new divorce laws. These data, which took years to collect and analyze, provide the first comprehensive portrait of the results of the new provisions for property, alimony, custody, and child support awards—and of their combined effects. Moreover, it was not until 1978 that the U.S. Census Bureau began to collect national data on alimony and child support and only in the early 1980s that these data were analyzed and published.[20] Thus, the consequences of the divorce law reforms are just coming to light.

A second reason for the slow acknowledgment of the law's effects is that these consequences were largely unanticipated. In retrospect, this seems somewhat surprising. How could the original reformers have been so oblivious to the potential for inequality in the new law?

While a definitive answer to this question is impossible, one explanation lies in the concerns of the coalition of reformers who launched the divorce law revolution in California. They were totally *preoccupied* with the negative aspects of the traditional adversarial system:[21] they wanted to eliminate the perjury and hypocrisy in the traditional divorce process, the hostility and acrimony generated in the course of establishing grounds and fault, and the law's incentives for spouses to exaggerate charges of fault in order to maximize their property or alimony awards. And, most important, they wanted to eliminate the detrimental effects of the adversarial process on spouses and their children.[22]

The reformers assumed that the abolition of fault, grounds, and consent would eliminate the abuses of the old law and bring civility and honor to the divorce court.*

To the extent that they considered the question of equality, they believed that the new law would foster the "emerging equality" of women. Recall their conviction that women were protected by the community property system in California.[24] They truly believed that the elimination of fault as the basis for financial awards would better serve justice and equity. If property were divided equally, it seemed no one would be deprived of a fair share. If alimony awards were based on need and ability to pay, standards reflecting economic reality, the interests of both parties would be protected. If men and women were treated equally, neither spouse would be given an unfair advantage in divorce.

In light of the aims and goals of those who formulated California's no-fault divorce law,[25] it is not surprising that no one focused on the potential economic impact of the legal changes on women and children. Ironically, one might say the reformers were too busy looking backward at the multiple abuses engendered by the old law, and too busy looking forward to the specter of increased acrimony, hostility, and trauma with an ever-rising divorce rate.

Another explanation for the reformers' failure to anticipate the

* In fact, if one examines the impact of the legal reforms from the perspective of the legal profession, it becomes evident that the profession is a major beneficiary of the no-fault reforms: lawyers and judges are no longer required to systematically compromise their professional ideals by assisting parties in collusion and perjury.[23]

results of their reforms was their own *misinformation* about the reality under the old law. Recall the testimony of divorced men before the Assembly Judiciary Committee who contended that it was men who were routinely "taken to the cleaners" by wives who demanded and got exorbitant alimony and property awards.[26] We now understand how this myth was conceived and why it was perpetuated: the very men who were testifying and reforming the law were the ones who were most likely to be paying alimony and to know others who were. These men assumed their own experience was universal. They did not know that less than one-fifth of divorced women were awarded alimony under the old law, because their wives and their friends were among this small minority of women who did receive some alimony.[27]

Nor did they know how little property the average divorcing couple owned so they did not realize that the common practice for dividing property under the old law merely allowed a woman to keep the family home and have a small cushion against postdivorce financial strains.[28] Their assumptions about what was likely to happen in divorce settlements were again based largely on their personal observations of the small percentage of couples who had substantial property; to award more than half of the property to the women in those cases seemed to them an unjust deprivation for the men. Thus the goal of equality—of giving each spouse a one-half share—seemed eminently reasonable.

In light of these erroneous beliefs, it is not surprising that the profession did not foresee how drastic the effects of an equal division rule could be. Nor did they see what a loss their female clients would incur when no-fault took away their legal leverage to bargain as aggrieved parties.[29]

When the California law was being reformulated in the 1960s, there were no organized feminist groups to participate in the debates, which were largely confined to the legal community.[30] The relatively few female attorneys who took part in those discussions believed that the removal of fault-based awards would guarantee fair treatment for all wives, including the "guilty" ones who were severely punished for deviating from traditional morality under the old law. If alimony was based on need, they reasoned, those wives who needed it would receive it. If property was divided equally, they reasoned, women would be guaranteed their half share. Thus the reforms were seen as an assurance that wives would be treated fairly and equally—in accord with more liberal concepts of fairness—rather than be judged (and sometimes punished) by traditional notions of morality.

Although California's no-fault law was passed by an almost all-male legislature, four women (out of 20) were members of the Governor's Commission which proposed the new law.[31] At least one of these women, Professor Herma Hill Kay, was keenly aware of women's concerns and had played a major role in the recent liberalization of the state's abortion law.[32] But all members of the Commission were so deeply convinced of the fairness of the new law that they did not foresee how *de jure* equality might not result in equity in a society lacking *de facto* equality.

It is also possible that the reformers were simply too quick to assume that the "approaching equality" in the larger society would be swift in coming. As they wrote:

> When our divorce law was originally drawn, woman's role in society was almost totally that of mother and homemaker. She could not even vote. Today, increasing numbers of married women are employed, even in the professions. In addition, they have long been accorded full civil rights. Their approaching equality with the male should be reflected in the laws governing marriage dissolution and in the decisions of the courts with respect to matters incident to dissolution.[33]

The concept of equality had a compelling appeal. The new divorce laws held the promise of fulfilling a dream: they projected a vision of a world in which men and women could be truly equal. This shining vision dazzled the reformers' perceptions of the real world in which we live.

A major reason for their miscalculation doubtless lies in the American belief that we can legislate equality. Americans have always believed in equality before the law, and in the late 1960s and early 1970s many reformers assumed that they could create equality by legislation alone—without changing the social realities that promote inequality. The new divorce laws give us a heartbreaking refutation of this belief, for in this case, the legislation of equality actually resulted in a worsened position for women and, by extension, a worsened position for children.

It is now obvious that equality cannot be achieved by legislative fiat in a society in which men and women are differently situated. As long as women are more likely than men to subordinate their careers in marriage, and as long as the structure of economic opportunity favors men, and as long as women contribute to their husband's earning capacities, and as long as women are likely to assume the major responsibilities of child rearing, and as long as we want to encourage the care and rearing of children, we cannot treat men and women as "equals" in divorce settlement. We must find ways to safeguard and protect women, not only to achieve fairness and equity, but also to encourage and reward those who invest in and care for our children and, ultimately, to foster true equality for succeeding generations.

We do not have to abandon the nonadversarial aims of the no-fault reforms to accomplish these goals. Nor do we have to return to the charade of the fault-based traditional system. The reformers correctly diagnosed many of the problems in the traditional system and correctly prescribed remedies to eliminate them. What they failed to do in the process was to address the disjunctures that these changes would create in the *other* parts of the system of divorce—most notably in the terms of the economic settlement. Even though many divorced women were not very well off after divorce under the old law, the levers of fault and consent gave them some power to bargain for a better financial settlement. The reformers did not realize that without these levers women would need alternative provisions in the law to enable them to negotiate adequate financial settlements.

Nor did the reformers anticipate the profound impact of the women's movement on the consciousness of all the participants in the divorce process. Since the California legal reforms came before the forceful organizational efforts of the women's movement in the 1970s, the reformers did not realize that the concept of "equality," and the sex-neutral language of the new law, would be used by some lawyers and judges as a mandate for "equal treatment" with a vengeance, a vengeance that can only be explained as a backlash reaction to women's demands for equality in the larger society. Thus the reformers did not forsee that the equality they had in mind for a childless divorcee of twenty-five would be used to terminate alimony for a fifty-five-year-old housewife who had never held a paying job.

The challenge that now lies before us is that of refashoning the current legal system so that we can retain the positive aspects of the no-fault reforms while we alter its present economic results. To that end, we would do well to stand back and assess the larger issues and implications of these legal changes on the status of marriage in our society. As the twentieth century draws toward its end, we might ask how our laws view that venerable institution, how the present views compare with past perceptions, how these views are reflected in the current divorce laws, and how today's divorce laws are likely to influence our future outlook toward marriage.

THE TRANSFORMATION OF MARRIAGE

The divorce law revolution transformed more than the traditional legal assumptions about divorce. It transformed the legal norms for marriage by articulating, codifying, and legitimating a new understanding of the marital partnership and marital commitment in our society. The new laws reflected, among other things, altered social realities, evolving social norms, and everyday legal practice. Ideally, that is as it should be: if law is to be effective, it must accord with social and practical reality. However, because the present laws do not *adequately* or accurately reflect social reality, they are exacerbating some of the grossest inequities in our society.

Traditional family law established a clear moral framework for both marriage and divorce: marriage was a partnership, a lifelong commitment to join together "forsaking all others," for better or for worse.[34] Husbands and wives were assigned specific roles and responsibilities, and these obligations were reinforced by law: men remained legally obligated to support wives and children, while women remained responsible first and foremost for the care and custody of the children. The moral obligations of marriage were, in theory, reinforced by alimony and property awards so that spouses who lived up to their marriage contract were rewarded, and those who did not were punished.

Of course we now know that the reality of divorce settlements often diverged from this theoretical ideal. Alimony was the exception rather than the rule, and fathers often honored their responsibility for child support in the breach. But the old structure did give the spouse who wanted to remain married considerable bargaining power, and to that extent it reinforced marriage as against the alternative of divorce. The required grounds and the need to prove fault created effective barriers to divorce by making it difficult.[35] In addition, because the old structure linked fault to the terms of the economic settlement, divorce was expensive for men of means. If she was "innocent," the wife of a man with money and property could expect to be awarded a lifetime alimony, the family home, and other property to meet her needs. In addition, her husband would remain responsible for her financial support. (So, too, could the guilty wife expect to be punished and be denied alimony and property.)

The new reforms altered each of the major provisions of the traditional law[36]—and, in the process, redefined the norms of legal marriage. No-fault laws abolished the need for grounds and the need to prove fault in order to obtain a divorce. They abandoned the gender-based assumptions of the traditional law in favor of standards for treating men and women "equally" in alimony and property awards. They negated the traditional role that fault played in financial awards and instead decreed that awards should be based on the divorcing parties' current financial needs and resources. And finally, the new rules shifted the legal criteria for divorce—and thus for viable marriage—from fidelity to the traditional marriage contract to individual standards of personal satisfaction. They thereby redefined marriage as a time-limited, contingent arrangement rather than a lifelong commitment.

From State Protection of Marriage to Facilitation of Divorce

The divorce law reforms reflect an underlying shift in the role of the state from a position of protecting marriage (by restricting marital dissolution) to one of facilitating divorce.

The new divorce laws adopt a laissez-faire attitude toward both marriage and divorce. They leave both the terms of the marriage contract—and the option to terminate it—squarely in the hands of individual parties.[37] The pure no-fault states also eliminate the traditional moral dimension from the divorce: guilt and innocence, fidelity and faithlessness, no longer affect the granting of the decree or its financial consequences.[38]

The individual's right to freely choose to end his or her marriage is further bolstered in some states by no-consent rules which give either party the right to obtain a divorce without the other's agreement.[39] Since pure no-fault no-consent rules allow one spouse to make a unilateral decision to terminate the marriage, they transfer the economic leverage from the spouse who wants to remain married to the spouse who wants to get divorced. This is an important difference. Under the traditional divorce law the party who wanted a divorce might well have to make economic concessions or "buy" a spouse's agreement. But under the no-consent rule it is the one who hopes to preserve the marriage who must do the bargaining. Apart from the economic implications, which are considerable, the outstanding effect of these laws is to empower the party who seeks the divorce, and this increases the likelihood that divorce will in fact occur.

From a Lifetime Contract to an Optional, Time-limited Commitment

The new divorce laws no longer assume that marriage is a lifelong partnership. Rather, it is now seen as a union that remains tenable only so long as it proves satisfying to both partners. In addition, the traditional obligations of marriage, like the institution itself, are increasingly being redefined by the new divorce laws as optional, time-limited, contingent, open to individual definition, and, most important, terminable upon divorce.

In contrast to the traditional marriage contract whereby a husband undertook lifelong responsibility for his wife's support, the new divorce laws suggest that this and other family responsibilities can—and may— be terminated upon divorce, or soon after divorce. Thus we see time limits for alimony, which is now awarded for a limited number of years under the no-fault divorce laws. Throughout the United States alimony has been redefined as short-term, transitional support and the new standards of self-sufficiency define women as "dependents" for shorter and shorter periods of time.[40] (Current awards in California run an average of two years.)[41]

Similar in its effect is the emphasis on a speedy resolution of the spouses' property claims. There are many more forced sales of family homes than in the past, to hasten the day when each spouse can "take his (or her) money and leave."[42] Arrangements that delay the sale of the home so that minor children do not have to move are viewed with disfavor by the courts because they "tie up the father's money." The judges we interviewed asserted that each spouse is entitled to his or her share of the property and should not have to wait for it.[43] This view is also reflected in the tendency to "cash out" other shared long-term investments such as pensions and retirement benefits. Such practices are designed to provide a "clean break" by dividing the family's property completely and finally at the time of the divorce.

The severing of family obligations is also reflected in the lax enforcement of alimony and child support awards. While this is certainly not condoned in the law itself, it is the practical result of the attitudes and behavior we observed among judges and attorneys, and their obvious reluctance "to bother" with enforcement of court-ordered support.[44] (Although the 1984 child support enforcement law suggests a possible improvement in this area, it is important to recall that the wage assignments mandated by the federal law were already required in California at the time of this research, but the judges chose to ignore them.[45])

Even parenting is becoming increasingly optional. Indeed, the *de facto* effect of the current laws is to deprive children of the care, companionship, and support of their fathers. This is implicit in the courts' treatment of postdivorce visitation and parenting. Since national data show that 52 percent of the children of divorce (who are not currently living with their father) had not seen him at all in the past year, it is evident that the majority of divorced fathers are abandoning much of their parental role after divorce and are being allowed to do so without legal sanction.[46]

In fact, one of the strongest supports for the assertion that fathers are legally allowed to abandon their children is the lack of a legal course of action to compel a father to see his children. The implicit message is that joint parenting—and even parenting itself—is an "optional" responsibility for fathers.

This conclusion is also evident in the law's tolerance for fathers who abandon their children financially. It is reflected in the meager amounts of child support the courts award to begin with, thereby allowing fathers to rid themselves of much of their financial responsibility for their children, and by the courts' failure to enforce child support awards once they are made, thereby giving tacit approval to fathers who abandon altogether their financial responsibilities for their children.[47]

Professor Samuel Preston contends that the current "disappearing act of fathers" is part of a larger trend: the conjugal family is gradually divesting itself of care for children in much the same way that it did earlier for the elderly.[48] To date, indications of parental abandonment have focused on fathers. Thus far, most analysts have seen mothers as firmly committed to their children. But as the norms of the new divorce law permeate popular awareness, this picture also may change.

The import of the new custody laws, especially those that remove the maternal presumption and institute a joint custody preference, is to undermine women's incentives to invest in their children.[49] As women increasingly recognize that they will be treated "equally" in child custody decisions, that caretaking and nurturance of children find no protection in the law and are punished by the job market, and that joint custody awards may push them into difficult, restrictive, and unrewarding postdivorce custodial arrangements, they may increasingly take to heart the new laws' implied warning that they not become so invested in their children.

It is evident that the concepts of optional and time-limited marital commitments embodied in the new divorce laws have a differential effect on men and women. While they free men from the responsibilities they retained under the old system, they "free" women primarily from the security that system provided. Since the traditional system channeled men and women in different directions, most women are now ill-equipped to take advantage of the new norms. Their investments in home, family, and children have typically meant lost opportunities in the paid labor force and have made them more dependent on the long-term protection and security that the traditional law promised them. Thus it is not surprising that this research reveals that women are "suffering" more under the new laws, for these laws have removed the financial safeguards of the old law—with a decline in alimony awards and a decrease in women's share of the community property—at the same time that they have increased the financial burdens imposed on women after divorce.

For men, by contrast, the new legal assumption of time-limited commitments is likely to mean a new freedom from family financial obligations. In fact, as noted earlier, the new laws actually give men an incentive to divorce by offering them a release from the financial burdens of marriage.[50] The wealthier a man is, and the longer he has been married, the more he has to gain financially from divorce.[51]

From Protection for Housewives and Mothers to Gender-neutral Rules

The ways in which alimony, property, child custody, and child support rules are administered under the new divorce laws reflect profoundly altered assumptions about the roles of husbands and wives in marriage. These new assumptions reflect changing social reality as well as a new ideological commitment to allow both men and women more options and more latitude to define their marital roles.

If the new legal assumptions were accompanied by provisions that in fact enabled both spouses to choose the extent to which they would assume breadwinning and homemaking roles, and if they then gave each spouse "credit" for the roles they in fact assumed during marriage, then the law would accurately reflect the complexity and variety of marital roles in these years of "transition." But the present legal system seems to leave no room for such flexibility. Nor does it leave any room for individual choice.

Rather, it suggests that a woman who chooses to be a housewife or mother risks a great penalty because if she is later divorced she will pay heavily for that choice. Even if she and her husband agree to form an equal partnership in which they give priority to his career while she assumes the larger share of the housework and child care, and even if they agree that he will share his earnings and career assets with her, their agreement apparently will have no legal standing. The woman will still be expected to be self-sufficient after divorce, and the man's promise—the promise of continued support and a share of his earnings that is implied in most marriages with a traditional division of labor—will be ignored in most courts.[52]

The penalty is equally severe for the woman who works during marriage, or who works part time, but who nevertheless gives priority to her family over her work. Her claims to share her husband's income through spousal support fall on deaf ears in courts that base awards solely on her "capacity for gainful employment."[53]

Under the new legal assumptions the average divorced woman in California will be awarded no alimony,[54] a minimal amount of child support (which she is often unable to collect),[55] exactly half of the joint tangible assets (an average of less than $10,000 worth of property)[56] and an explicit directive to become immediately self-supporting. Chances are that even if she was married under the old law, and lived her life by the letter of the traditional marriage contract, and even if she is forty-five or fifty-five at the time of divorce, the court will apply the new standards of self-sufficiency to her as well.[57]

Especially disadvantaged by these new assumptions are mothers of young children and older homemakers. Today, instead of recognizing their years spent in homemaking and child care, and instead of compensating them for years of lost career opportunities and impaired earning capacities, the divorce courts accord them "equality" and presume them to be as capable as any man to support themselves after divorce.

Thus one clear implication of the present allocation of family resources at divorce is that women had better not forgo any of their own education, training, and career development to devote themselves fully or even partially to their families. The law assures that they will not be rewarded for their devotion, either in court or in the job market, and they will suffer greatly if their marriage dissolves. This is a powerful message at a time when half of all U.S. marriages are expected to end in divorce and when under the no-fault and no-consent laws in many states, a woman may have no choice about the divorce and no legal leverage to effect her financial settlement.

The concept of marital roles embodied in the new divorce laws carries an equally sobering message about motherhood. Divorcing mothers of preschool children have experienced a greater decline in alimony awards than any other group of women since the no-fault was instituted. We have seen that the vast majority of these mothers, 87 percent, are awarded no alimony: they are expected to find jobs immediately, to support themselves completely and, for the most part, to support their children as well.[58]

In addition, since the age of majority for children has dropped from twenty-one to eighteen, the divorced mother of teenage children confronts the fact that her former husband is not legally required to support their children once they reach age eighteen even if they are still in their senior year of high school, much less through college.[59] However both high school and college students in these post-child support years typically remain financially dependent on their parents. It is their mothers who are much more likely to respond to their needs and to support them, even though they are typically financially less able to do so.[60]

Finally, the woman who has raised her children to maturity and who, as a result of the priority she has given to motherhood, finds herself with no marketable skills when she is divorced at forty-five or fifty-five, typically faces the harshest deprivations after divorce.[61] The courts rarely reward her for the job she has done. Rather, the new assumptions imply that her motherhood years were wasted and worthless for she too is measured against the all-important new criterion of earning capacity.

The treatment that housewives and mothers receive under the new laws convey a clear message to the young woman who is planning her future. They tell her that divorce may send her into poverty if she invests in her family ahead of—or even alongside of—her career.

Thus the new divorce laws are institutionalizing a set of norms which may be as inappropriate in one direction as the old norms were in another direction. The old law assumed that all married women were first and foremost housewives and mothers. The new law assumes that all married women are employable and equally capable of self-sufficiency after divorce. Both views are overly simplistic, impede women's options, and exert a rigidifying influence on future possibilities.

For most women in our society, marriage and careers are no longer either/or choices. Most women do not expect to choose between work and marriage, or between a career and motherhood. The vast majority of American women want all three. But, as Vassar economist Shirley Johnson observes, when "women who have both worked full time and carried the lioness's share of the household management and child rearing responsibilities, find out that their dual role is not recognized or rewarded in divorce settlements, the effect of the new divorce laws is to encourage women to . . . shift their energies into the labor market."[62] Johnson goes on to explain why, in economic terms, it no longer pays for a woman to "invest in marriage-specific skills" since such investments have a relatively lower payoff in our society, because of the risk of marital dissolution. Rather, the economic lesson in the new divorce laws is that women should give first priority to maintaining "marketable skills over the increasingly uncertain life-time of their marriage."[63]

From Partnership to Individualism

The new divorce laws alter the traditional legal view of marriage as a partnership by rewarding individual achievement rather than investment in the family partnership. Instead of the traditional vision of a common financial future within marriage, the no-fault and no-consent standards for divorce, and the new rules for alimony, property, custody, and child support, all convey a new vision of independence for husbands and wives in marriage. In addition, the new laws confer economic advantages on spouses who invest in themselves at the expense of the marital partnership.

This focus on the individual underlies many of the changes discussed above. It reflects not only a shift in the legal relationships between the family and its adult members, but also a shift in the court's attitudes and practices in meting out rewards at divorce.

The traditional law embodied the partnership concept of marriage by rewarding sharing and mutual investments in the marital community. Implicit in the new laws, in contrast, are incentives for investing in oneself, maintaining one's separate identity, and being self-sufficient. The new stress is on individual responsibility for one's future, rather than the partnership assumption of joint or reciprocal responsibilities.

Once again, it is easy to see how these new assumptions reflect larger cultural themes: the rise of individualism, the emphasis on personal fulfillment, the belief in personal responsibility, and the importance we attach to individual "rights."[64] These trends have at once been applauded for the freedom they offer and criticized as selfish, narcissistic, and amoral.[65] Whether this change represents a decline or an advance depends on our personal values: are we more concerned with the security and stability that the old order provided, or with the misery it caused for those who were forced to remain in unhappy marriages?

Our evaluation will also depend on how we see the past. The belief that the rise of individualism has fostered a decline in the family rests on the assumption that the family was stable and harmonious in the past. But, as Dr. Arlene Skolnick notes, despite massive research in recent years, historians have not yet identified an era in which families were stable and harmonious and all family members behaved unselfishly and devoted their efforts to the collective good.[66] That "classical family of western nostalgia," to use Professor William J. Goode's term for the stereotype,[67] has been one of the major casualties of recent research in family history.[68]

But historical research does suggest a change in the psychological quality of family life. Within the family itself, relationships have become more emotionally intense. On the other hand, the ties between the family and the larger community have become more tenuous.

Historian Lawrence Stone's term "affective individualism" captures the trend.[69] Stone is referring to a growing awareness of the self as unique and a growing recognition of the individual's right to pursue his or her own goals. The rise of affective individualism has brought emotional closeness between nuclear family members, as well as a greater appreciation for the individuality of each person in the family. Historically, this trend strengthened the husband-wife unit at the expense of the larger family and the kinship network in which it was embedded.[70] More recently, as rising divorce rates demonstrate, the strength of the husband-wife unit has declined and values of "pure" individualism are emerging. The new divorce laws reflect this evolution in that they encourage notions of personal primacy for both husband and wife.

Today's individualistic norms imply that neither spouse should invest too much in marriage or place marriage above self-interest. This view supports marriage as a means of serving individual needs, reversing the traditional dictum that individuals should submerge their personal desires wherever they conflict with the "good of the family." It also challenges traditional norms of reciprocity and mutual dependence. If men are no longer solely responsible for support, and if women are no longer responsible for homemaking and child care, then neither sex can count as much on the other for support or services. By the same token, it is arguable that to the extent both spouses come to rely on themselves, both gain less from the union. Indeed, a pattern of less stable relationships when spouses are less interdependent has already been observed among both cohabiting and married couples in a recent study of American couples.[71]

Not only do the new rules for spousal responsibility undermine the marital partnership; the new property rules do so as well. In spite of the partnership principles on which they are based—that is, the idea that property accumulated during marriage is to be shared equally at divorce—the current bases for dividing property belie such principles.

If the major breadwinner is allowed to retain most of the new property or career assets he (or she) has acquired during marriage (assets such as a professional education, good will, health benefits, and enhanced earning capacity), *the law's implicit message is that one's own career is the only safe investment*. This encourages both spouses to invest in themselves before investing in each other, or their marriage, or their children.

This is one area in which the new legal assumptions are not congruent with the attitudes and assumptions of the divorced men and women we interviewed. Our interviewees rejected the limited definition of alimony as based on "need" and minimal self-sufficiency, and instead saw alimony as a means of sharing their partnership assets—the income and earning capacity they had both invested in, and the standard of living they expected to share.[72] These "sharing principles" for alimony were seen as an essential element in their implicit partnership "contract."

The legal incentive to place career before family has parallels in law professor Mary Ann Glendon's suggestion that the sources of "standing and security" in society have shifted from family to work.[73] That is, as employment relationships have moved away from concepts of termination-at-will, and have become more secure and predictable, family relationships—particularly the husband-wife relationship—have moved in the other direction and have become tenuous and insecure because they are terminable-at-will with no-fault divorce.

Thus the legal entitlements to one's job and the security of employment are being strengthened in our society at the same time that legal security in the family is being weakened.[74] In fact, Glendon has said that the only employment situation to which termination-at-will "applies more than ever is the unpaid labor force, namely to homemakers."[75] Since homemakers facing divorce are also less likely than men to have gained security in the labor force, they may be falling into a void between the family system and the work system, deprived of the protection or security of either one.

One implication of these changes is that marriage is likely to become increasingly less central to the lives of individual men and women. The privileged status of marriage in traditional family law, and the protections and restrictions placed on its inception and dissolution, reinforced its importance and encouraged husbands and wives to invest in it and to make it the center of their lives. The new laws, in contrast, discourage shared investments in marriage and thereby encourage both husbands and wives to dissociate from investments in the partnership. As more men and women follow the apparent mandate of the new laws, it seems reasonable to predict that marriage itself will lose further ground.

Indeed, sociologist William J. Goode persuasively argues that the trend is already well in progress. He observes that marriage is simply less important today than it was in the past for both men and women, and he foresees the further "decline of individual investments in family relationships over the coming decade" because investments in one's individual life and career pay off better in modern society.[76] As more women seek to follow men in the path of acquiring status, self-esteem, and a sense of individual accomplishment from their jobs, the importance of marriage will rest increasingly on its ability to provide individuals with psychic and emotional sustenance. This, Goode observes, is a difficult and fragile bond.[77] In these trends he sees profound implications for the future of intimate relationships and the bearing and rearing of children in Western nations.

The Clouded Status of Children

A final feature of the new divorce laws is the ambiguity they convey about parental responsibility for children. Under traditional law, the sustained well-being of the children of divorce was assumed to be the state's primary concern in any legal proceedings involving children. Indeed, it was from this concern that most of the traditional divorce law protections for women stemmed: women were recognized as the primary custodians of children, and in that capacity were to be accorded preferences and support to ensure the fulfillment of their responsibilities. Similarly, women who had devoted the productive years of their lives to child rearing were to be rewarded for that appropriate and honorable effort.

Under the new laws, the state's concern for the welfare of children is far less evident. Rather, it appears that in the law's practical application, at least, the children have been all but forgotten in the courts' preoccupation with parental "equality."

The same rules that facilitate divorce, facilitate the disruption of children's lives. The gender-neutral rules that encourage or force mothers to work also deprive children of the care and attention they might otherwise have. (Effectively, the fate of divorcing mothers is still the fate of the children of divorce because sex-neutral custody standards notwithstanding, mothers still remain the primary caretakers of children after divorce.) Equally important, the *de facto* effects of the current laws deprive children of both the care and the support of their fathers.

In sum, the current laws, in effect, provide that divorced fathers *may* participate more in the lives of their children if they choose to do so, but they need not so choose. The laws also decree that mothers *must* work outside the home whether they wish it or not, and thus *must* divide their energies between jobs and children. One might well ask what legal protections remain to insure parenting for children after divorce.

Before we move on to policy recommendations, it is useful to note the important role that the law can play in shaping individual options and social reality. Even as the law over time evolves to reflect social reality, it also serves as a powerful force for creating social reality.

Although the divorce law reformers knew that equality between the sexes was not yet a reality when they codified assumptions about equality in the law, they had seen trends in that direction and believed the new law would accelerate those trends. Throughout this book we have seen, however, how the law actually helped to impede any trend toward economic equality that may have been developing. The law worsened women's condition, improved men's condition, and widened the income gap between the sexes. Thus the law has moved us toward a new reality, to be sure, but it is not, in the economic sphere at least, the hoped-for reality.

So long as the laws remain in force in their present form and their present application, postdivorce equality between the sexes will remain an impossibility. For without equality in economic resources, all other "equality" is illusory.

THE NEXT STEPS

Most of the hardships occasioned by the present system are not inevitable consequences of divorce. What is required to alleviate them is a commitment to fairness, an awareness of the greater burdens that the system imposes on women and children, and a willingness to require fathers to shoulder their responsibility for their children.

Although the changes in divorce law were originally welcomed as enlightened reforms that, among other things, would support the emerging equality of men and women, this research shows that they have effected little real equality between the sexes and have brought a host of unanticipated, unintended, and unfortunate consequences for women and children.

As we embark on a discussion of new remedies, it is natural to be leary of their unanticipated consequences and to be fearful of the dislocations they may create. To minimize these risks insofar as possible, I have confined the suggestions that follow to specific cases of injustice under the present laws, and have not undertaken proposals for broad-scale societal reforms.

What are the most serious cases of injustice in the present system? Where should we direct our efforts? There are four groups that deserve our special attention.

First, there are the children of divorce. The policy recommendations for them are relatively straightforward, although they require not just legislation but also more effective administration and enforcement of the law. The children of divorce need more financial support and more effective means of securing the support they are awarded.

Child support awards should be based on the income-sharing approach because this formula is most likely to equalize the standards of living in the custodial and noncustodial household after divorce. Since it is evident that children share the economic status of their custodial parent, the goal of equalizing the standards of living in the two household should be made an explicit aim of child support awards. There should also be explicit recognition of the child's entitlement to share the standard of living of the higher-earning parent.[78] (The Wisconsin legislation that recognizes the child's entitlement to a fixed share of the father's income provides one potential model for such legislation.)

In addition, all support awards should include automatic adjustments for cost-of-living increases.[79] Children would also benefit from the use of more effective techniques to enforce these awards, including wage assignments from the inception of the award, income tax intercepts, national location services, property liens and bonds, and, where necessary, the threat and use of jail.[80]

The college-age children of divorce also need "child" support if they are financially dependent on their parents past age 18.[81] In most states legislation is needed to extend their legal minority and to require their parents to support them if they are full-time students (and financially dependent) until they complete their undergraduate education. The current rules in New York and Washington, discussed below, provide two potential models for such legislation.

Although a child's interest in family property is not recognized in the United States today, many states have special rules for the family home when there are minor children. When these rules are optional, as they are in California, their use depends on judicial discretion, and they are often ignored.[82] What is needed in California (and similar states) is a legislative directive that requires judges to maintain the family home for minor children after divorce.

The children of divorce would also benefit from a primary caretaker presumption for sole custody awards, and laws that allow joint custody only upon the agreement of both parents.[83] Such clear standards for custody awards would make it more difficult to use children as "pawns" in divorce negotiations, and would reduce both the threat and use of custody litigation in order to gain financial advantages in property or support awards. Since custody litigation and the prolonged hostility it typically generates are likely to have an adverse psychological and financial impact on the welfare of children, custody laws that designate clear priorities and minimize litigation are clearly preferable.

The second type of clear injustice involves the long-married older housewife with little or no experience in the paid labor force, who has devoted herself to her husband, home, and children in the expectation that she would share whatever income and assets the couple acquires.[84] This woman needs rules that require (rather than allow) judges to redistribute the husband's postdivorce income with the goal of equalizing the standards of living in the two households.

This recommendation rests on the same principle that underlies community property rules; it is the assumption that marriage is an equal partnership in which all the assets should be shared. This principle, as we have seen, is strongly supported by the divorced men and women we interviewed.[85] They view the sharing of income through alimony—or whatever name we choose for income transfers after divorce—as the means for providing the wife with her share of the fruits of their joint endeavors. These sharing principles are fundamental elements in the "marital contract" that most married couples agreed to and lived by during marriage.

Older women should not be measured by the new standards of equality and self-sufficiency after divorce. It is both impractical and unfair to expect women who married and lived most of their lives under a different set of social and legal rules to be forced to find employment and to support themselves. They have earned an interest in their husband's income for the rest of their lives and require a legislative presumption of permanent (i.e., continuing, open-ended) support.

Long-married older wives must also be assured of an equal share of all of their husband's career assets. While courts in most states now recognize their entitlement to share pensions and retirement benefits, few states guarantee older women the right to health and hospital insurance. Since we have seen the hardships this creates,[86] legislation should require that divorced wives be allowed to remain insured as group members (and pay group premium rates).

Women who divorce after longer marriages are also entitled to maintain their homes.[87] If the family home and the husband's pensions are the only major assets of the marriage, the older wife should be allowed to maintain her home without forfeiting her share of the pension. Similarly, if the home is the *only* major asset of the marriage, the long-married wife who has a limited earning capacity and few other resources should not be evicted from her home so that the property can be divided equally. Rather, she should be allowed to continue living in the family home.

In summary, we need "grandmother clauses" for the long-married older women who married and lived their lives under the traditional rules. *It is unfair to change the rules on them in the middle of the game. Rather, they have earned the right to an equal share of the fruits of the marital partnership.* They are entitled to one-half of the property and income it has produced and are entitled to maintain the same standard of living as their former husbands.

The third case that merits a new approach is that of the mother who retains major responsibility for the care of minor children after divorce. Whether the custody award is labeled "sole custody" or "joint legal custody" or even "joint physical custody," if this woman assumes most of the day-to-day caretaking, she requires a greater share of the family's resources. These include the continued use of the family home (which should be viewed as part of the child support award rather than as an unequal division of property) and a significant portion of her ex-husband's income so that the two households maintain, insofar as practical, equal standards of living after divorce.

Since employment will play a critical role in the postdivorce lives of younger divorced mothers, and thus in their ability to contribute to their children's and their own support, they should be awarded full support in the early years after divorce to enable them to maximize their long-range employment prospects.[88] This means generous support awards and balloon payments immediately after divorce to finance their education, training, and career counseling. Insofar as possible, every effort should be made to provide them and their children with full support in the transitional years so that forced employment does not interfere with their training and child care.

The fourth type of injustice is perhaps the most difficult because it raises most poignantly the conflict between the old rules and the new—and the special problems of the transitional generation. This is the case of the woman who is about forty years old at the time of her divorce. Although it is often asserted that the most tragic victims of the new divorce laws are the older women, from a policy perspective their situation is much easier, because the steps to rectify the injustice they suffer are clear. But this is not so for women who divorce in their middle years. Many divorcing women of forty have been employed during marriage and have also raised children who are now approaching majority or have reached it. The chances are good that although these women may have worked part or full time during marriage, they have given priority to their families and their husbands' careers, rather than their own interests. Since these women are rarely able to command a salary anywhere near their husbands', and since they have passed the point where they can recapture lost career opportunities, it is manifestly unfair to hold them to the new standards of self-sufficiency at the point of divorce, as the courts do now.[89] In addition the courts are insensitive to the triple load that many of these women have carried during marriage, managing home, work and family. They deserve some special recognition and compensation for their contributions, not harsher treatment.

On the other hand, a woman who divorces at forty is young enough to have at least twenty productive years ahead of her, and it seems inappropriate to expect her former husband to maintain her standard of living for all those years and the retirement years to follow. And yet, since her chances of remarrying are very low, her economic future rests on just this choice—her future earning capacity or his.

In these cases justice requires a complex adjustment of equities that defies easy prescription in the closing pages of this book. But at least the principles for the solution are evident, and they are the same as those enunciated above: this woman should *be awarded* an equal share of the marital partnership by fully sharing her husband's career assets, including his enhanced earning capacity, through both property and support awards; *be helped* to resume or begin paid employment with additional training, counseling, and education where necessary; and, where appropriate, *be compensated* for the detriment to her own career.

We now move on to consider the major features of the current law and more specific policy recommendations.

No-Fault, No-Consent and the Climate of Divorce

This research has shown that the no-fault reforms have generally had a positive effect on the divorce process: there is clearly less hostility and acrimony and, on the whole, all of our respondents—California men and women, and lawyers and judges—express positive feelings about the no-fault law. They strongly approve of the principles of divorce without fault, grounds, or consent, and they overwhelmingly consider this aspect of the present legal system to be appropriate and fair. Few want to return to the traditional system.[90]

These findings do not necessarily suggest that a pure no-fault system is the most desirable form of divorce law. We have seen that feelings of guilt and responsibility continue to influence men's and women's perceptions of what is fair, and that the abolition of grounds and fault has increased the power of the party who wants to terminate the marriage and typically removed the bargaining power of the economically weaker party. Since this research underscores the connection between seemingly distinct rules dealing with grounds, fault, property, and support, it would be unwise for states that do not have a pure no-fault system to read the California results of a pure no-fault system across the board. If this research has generalizable findings it is that *reforms should not be undertaken without a careful consideration of the economic consequences* of the abolition of grounds and fault and certainly not without careful consideration of the provisions necessary to provide adequate economic protection for dependent wives and children.

Thus while a pure no-fault system is not suggested for states that currently have a hybrid system, it is clear that it would be unwise and inappropriate to suggest that California return to a more traditional system. The current no-fault rules enjoy widespread support and legitimacy, and the dissatisfaction with the present regime can be dealt with through other remedies.

What concerns many laymen and professionals alike is that the abolition of fault and consent has given new leverage to the party seeking divorce, and this, coupled with the lack of financial safeguards for women and children, allows a great many men to walk away with impunity from financial responsibilities for their families. The solution, at least for California today, is not to reintroduce fault and its penalties, but rather to strengthen the economic provisions of the new laws to assure adequate protection for wives and children.

One lesson of this research is that the means to assure this economic protection cannot rely exclusively on "the law on the books." They must also include ways to mobilize the law in action—the law as it is interpreted, administered, and enforced. Here, then, are some of these means.

Property: The Equal Division Rule

There is widespread approval of the California rule that requires an equal division of all property acquired during marriage. All categories of our respondents—judges, lawyers, men and women—support the equal division rule in principle, and consider it fair and just.[91] The vast majority believe that each spouse is *entitled* to one-half of the property acquired during marriage, and almost no one prefers the old system of awarding more property to the "innocent" party while penalizing the guilty party with a lower property award.[92]

These attitudes provide strong support for retaining California's equal division rule. Further support for the present system comes from the finding that California wives are typically awarded a larger share of the marital property than wives in states with equitable distribution rules (who typically receive about a third, rather than a half, of the marital property).[93]

The only major source of dissatisfaction with the equal division rule has been with its effects on the family home.[94] But the forced sale of the family home is, as we have seen, not required by the law. Rather the law is flexible enough to permit a delay in the division of assets. What is therefore needed is not a change in the law but a change in the way judges are applying the law.

Thus the first policy recommendation of this research is for the California legislature to retain the equal division rule but to require judges to delay the sale of the family home in specific circumstances (which are discussed below).

A parallel recommendation applies to states with equitable distribution laws. It recommends the adoption of a presumption that an equal division is most equitable. That presumption would establish the important principle of each spouse's entitlement to one-half of the marital property, and yet still be flexible enough to permit special treatment for the matrimonial home as recommended below.

THE FAMILY HOME

The major complaint about the equal division rules concerns judges who have interpreted it as requiring a forced sale of the family home. This has created great hardships for families with minor children and for long-married couples whose only assets are the family home and the husband's pension.[95]

Two issues need to be considered in fashioning policy for the family home. The first concerns the use of the home, the second concerns its ownership.

The easier issue involves the use of the family home. Since there are compelling reasons for maintaining the family home for minor children, and since a delayed sale of the family home is already permissible under California law, the problem here is one of inducing judges to utilize this option.[96] Since this research has shown that most judges refuse to delay the sale of the home in most cases,[97] a legislative directive is needed *to require* judges to delay the sale of the family home in the interests of maintaining a stable home for minor children and their custodian.

One alternative is to require judges to postpone the sale and division of the family home until the youngest child reaches eighteen. Another alternative is to require a postponement for an initial period (for example, the rule in Cincinnati, Ohio, allows the custodial parent to live in the home rent free and interest free for five years after the divorce) and to allow the court to extend the period after reviewing the family circumstances after that period of time.

The more complicated issue concerns the ownership of and equity in the family home.[98] On one hand, there are sound reasons for awarding the home outright to the custodial parent, as was normally done under the old law. The parent with custody can justly assert a greater need for the family's resources which an award of the home would provide. In addition, an outright award of the family home could be seen as a form of compensation for the responsibilities of child rearing. Moreover, since women are more likely than men to be custodial parents, and are less likely to be able to buy another home, such an award would help to offset the discrepancy between the parents' standards of living after divorce. In addition, if family income is limited, an award of the home might be considered compensation for forgone spousal or child support. A final justification for awarding the home to a mother with custody is to protect her against the dismal long-range prospects that divorced women face in finding comparable housing if the family home is sold ten or fifteen years later, after the children reach majority.[99]

On the other hand, there are also sound reasons for allowing the noncustodial parent to retain his or her ownership share of the home. If the home is the only major family asset, and most of the couple's savings are invested in it, it seems inequitable to deprive the noncustodial parent of his or her interest in the investment. This consideration alone would not dissuade me from the more compelling needs of the children and custodial parent. However, an award of the entire equity in the home to one party has another practical difficulty; it creates a strong incentive to seek custody in order to acquire the home. Since wise public policy should discourage the use of children as pawns for financial gains, and should seek to minimize litigation over children,[100] lawmakers should make every effort to avoid creating financial incentives that encourage custodial claims and disputes.[101] Consequently, an outright award of the family home to the custodial parent at the time of the divorce is not recommended at this time.

Obviously, the rules for the family home must be considered in conjunction with rules for determining child custody. If, as suggested below, a primary caretaker presumption is adopted for custodial decisions, then there would be less risk of an uninterested parent seeking custody in order to get the house because his or her chances of success would be minimal. However, the risk of such suits is substantial under the "best interest" standard currently used in most states.[102]

How then should the equity in the home be apportioned? There are two solutions with considerable appeal. The first solution has already been approved by the California appellate courts: the custodial parent retains possession of the home, but the equity in the home is valued and divided at the time of divorce. The custodial parent gives the other a note for his or her share of the equity to be paid when the house is sold.[103] Although most California courts currently require the custodial parent to pay interest on the note, courts in other states use interest-free notes which they consider part of child support.

This solution has several advantages. The custodial parent is solely responsible for maintaining the home and realizes the appreciation in the value of the home. This eliminates the potential for conflict between divorced parties who are forced to remain joint owners of a house but cannot agree on expenditures for maintenance, improvements, or repairs. It also eliminates the prospect of disagreements about whether another man or woman may reside in the house. A final advantage of this solution is that the noncustodial parent's equity in the house serves as a form of collateral to ensure child support payments.[104]

The second solution is to maintain the home in joint ownership but to allow the custodial parent and children to live there "rent free" or "interest free" as part of the child support award. Joint ownership has more appeal in a fluctuating or declining real estate market where a division of equity at the time of the divorce may saddle the custodial parent with too large a note. Although the prospects of a declining real estate market appear unlikely in California at this time, a rule that requires the parties to share the risk may be considered preferable in some counties—as well as in other states.

Since the major disadvantage of joint ownership is the prospect of disagreements about maintenance and repairs, cohabitants, and the terms of the sale, an agreement about these issues could be drawn up in advance. (Such an agreement should allow the resident parent the right to manage and control the property but should provide for financial sharing of nonroutine repairs.)

In Cincinnati, Ohio, for example, courts maintain the family home in joint ownership and allow the custodial parent and children to live there for five interest-free and rent-free years after divorce. The custodial parent makes all of the decisions about the home during her or his tenancy and is responsible for its maintenance.

Similar provisions are necessary to assure an older housewife continued use and possession of the family home. Since judges may delay the sale of any asset under the current law, an explicit presumption for them to do so after a long marriage (where the home, or the home and the pension, are the only assets) should be sufficient to attain this goal within the framework of the present law. It is easy to argue, however, that an outright award of the family home would be preferable. In light of the precarious economic circumstances of most of the women divorced after long marriages, I prefer the following type of rule: if an older woman has little or no earning capacity, and has limited resources with which to buy another home at the time of the divorce, and if an equal division of family assets would require the sale of the family home, or if it would require an older housewife to "trade" her interest in her husband's pension in order to retain the family home, then the law should be amended to allow an explicit exception to the equal division rule to enable an older woman to retain the family home after divorce.[105] Such a rule could be flexible enough to accommodate a move to a smaller but comparable residence in the same neighborhood if that would enable her to maintain her standard of living, but it would preclude the unconscionable forced sale of the family home and the eviction of the older wife that we have seen under the present legal rules.[106]

Career Assets and the New Property

One of the most important policy recommendations suggested by the findings of this research concerns the recognition of career assets and other forms of new property as marital assets. Career assets are the tangible and intangible assets that are acquired in the course of a marriage as part of either spouse's career or career potential—pensions and retirement benefits, a professional education, license to practice a profession or trade, enhanced earning capacity, the goodwill value of a business or profession, medical and hospital insurance, and other benefits and entitlements.[107]

Three findings of this research underscore the ways in which these assets affect the *de facto* equality of property division.[108] First, we have seen that most couples acquire various career assets in the course of their marriage in the same way that they acquire other assets that the courts currently recognize as marital property, and that these forms of new property are typically more valuable than any of their tangible community assets at the time of divorce. Second, since these assets are commonly excluded from the division of property at divorce, the courts are not dividing the property equally or equitably. And third, since these assets are typically treated as the husband's separate property, he is thereby allowed to retain a considerably greater share of the marital assets after divorce.

These findings lead to the recommendation that all states expand the definition of marital property to include career assets such as those enumerated above, and divide these assets as part of the marital property upon divorce.

The past decade has brought a rapid increase in states that recognize pensions and retirement benefits as valuable assets to be divided at divorce.[109] This suggests that the principles for recognizing career assets have already been established in most states. Although a small but growing minority of states also allow some form of compensation for the spouse who supports the family while the other acquires a professional education, other states still reject such claims.[110] In addition, many valuable career assets, such as medical and dental insurance, are simply ignored in most states.[111]

The hardships that result from the omission of these and other yet unrecognized career assets were poignantly documented in Chapter 5. When these assets are omitted from the pool of marital property to be divided upon divorce, the husband is typically allowed to keep these assets as if they were his alone. It is, as we noted, like *promising to divide the family jewels equally but allowing the husband to keep all of the diamonds*. The omission of the career assets from the pool of marital property makes *a mockery of the equal division rule*.

Alimony

One of the ironic findings of this research is that the current alimony laws seek to protect the very same women whom we have cited as the clearest victims of injustice under the new law. In this arena the problem seems to be in the interpretation of the law and, in particular, the way in which judges balance a husband's needs against those of his former wife.

In theory, the current law guarantees support for three groups of women: mothers with custody of young children, older homemakers incapable of self-sufficiency, and women who need transitional support are theoretically exempted from the new standards.[112] Despite the guarantee, however, the new norms of self-sufficiency are in fact being applied to all of these women.

For example, under the new law alimony awards to mothers of preschool children have dropped more than for any other group of women under the new rules.[113] Judges and lawyers report that they "encourage" mothers of preschoolers to enter the labor force as soon as possible.[114]

Similarly, older women who have been housewives and mothers throughout marriages of long duration are being held to the new law's standards of self-sufficiency. Although a higher percentage of these women are awarded spousal support, still one out of three gets nothing at all.[115] In addition, even those who are awarded alimony often receive comparatively low awards and are admonished to try to get a job and become self-sufficient despite their obvious inability to do so.[116] Judges approach these cases mindful of the husband's need for "his income" and his limited capacity to support two families. Thus, despite the law's theoretical assurance of protection for long-term homemakers, in reality they are often denied that protection in court.

The findings of this research reveal a wholesale shift from permanent alimony awards, based on the premise of the wife's continued dependency, to time-limited transitional awards, based on the new assumption of self-sufficiency.[117] The median duration of these awards is twenty-five months, just about two years.[118] Thus the average award carries an expectation of a short transition to self-sufficiency.

The major impact of the no-fault's alimony reforms has fallen on middle-class and upper-middle-class women because they were the women who could (and did) count on alimony under the old law.[119] Thus, in contrast to the old law's assumption that these women would remain dependent after divorce and were therefore in need of permanent alimony, no-fault has brought an expectation that they should become both independent and self-sufficient. These women are increasingly being denied alimony altogether, especially if they have earned even minimal incomes in the past, or they are being awarded small amounts for short periods solely to "ease the transition." However, an award of $350 a month in 1984 dollars for a period of two years is not likely to be seen as a great boon to the newly divorced middle-class woman. Rather it conveys a message: find a job right away, any job, and start supporting yourself.

These observations lead to additional policy recommendations.

The inequities visited upon older women should be eliminated by support rules that aim at equalizing the standards of living of the two parties after divorce. Since this research has demonstrated that we cannot rely on judges' interpretations of the relative "needs" of the two spouses,[120] clear legislative directives are in order. They should specify that women who married and lived under a different set of social and legal rules have earned the right to share their husbands' income for the rest of their lives and to maintain a standard of living that is equal to theirs.

Clearly it is a perversion of the concept of equality to deny older homemakers alimony and expect them to be as equally capable of supporting themselves after divorce. It is also a violation of the deeper meaning of equality in marriage—that marriage is an equal partnership in which the contributions of the two spouses are of equal worth. If the husband's earning capacity is their major asset,[121] and if it is treated as his alone at divorce, the essence of the equal partnership is violated.

One lesson from this research is that a woman who is divorced after fifteen or twenty or thirty years of marriage *can not* recapture the years she has lost in the labor force.[122] But an equally important lesson is this: she should not be expected to because she was promised by both her husband and the larger society that her husband would share his income with her. That was their marriage contract, both implied and expressed, and it is simply not fair to change the rules on her in the last quarter of the game, after she has fulfilled her share of the bargain.

Thus support rules for women divorced after a marriage of long duration should specify that she will not be required to seek employment and support herself. In light of the great inequities created by the punitive treatment of these women, judicial discretion to evaluate their "needs" or to consider their earning capacities should be limited. Rather, what is required are rules that create a presumption that their needs are equal to those of their former husbands and that their marital pension, in the form of permanent alimony, is guaranteed for the rest of their lives.

Thus support awards following long marriages should be guided by four presumptions: a presumption that future earning capacity and the income it produces are assets of the marital partnership, a presumption that these assets should be shared by the two spouses after divorce, a presumption that support awards should equalize the standards of living of the two parties after divorce, and a presumption that such support shall be permanent.

In the practical application of these presumptions the courts will have to define what is a "long marriage" and an "older woman" and that definition will and should depend on the circumstances of the parties.*

A different set of support rules is required for younger women who have been housewives and mothers and have subordinated their own careers for their husbands and families. Here too, sharing principles and an effort to equalize the standards of living in the two households are essential in the early years after divorce, and for an extended period if there are minor children. But there is an additional goal for these women—the goal of helping them to maximize their earning capacities. Even if these women have been employed during marriage, it is likely that marriage has had a detrimental effect on their careers. What they need now are spousal support awards that allow them to take advantage of the benefits of counseling, education, and retraining, and enable them to fully invest in their careers.[123] Since we have seen the payoffs of high support in the early postdivorce years for long-term earning capacity, their support awards should begin with several years of balloon payments to subsidize training or retraining so that they can maximize their long-term employment potential.[124]

In both cases, the postdivorce support award should provide for cost-of-living increases so that their real values do not erode with each passing year. In addition, penalties and interest should be assessed on late payments.

Child Support

Current child support awards are too low, poorly enforced, and place a disproportionate financial burden on mothers.

Several steps could be taken to improve this situation. First, courts should establish realistic guidelines for child support awards based on the income sharing approach and the assumption that children are entitled to maintain the standard of living of the higher-income parent

---

* Some courts have adopted a twenty-year rule of thumb because of the precedent set by military and police pensions, while others have recognized the ten-year precedent set by the security system.

insofar as possible.[125] Thus each parent should contribute to child support according to his or her ability to pay—with due consideration given to the caretaking contribution of the custodial parent. (The innovative guidelines established in Delaware, Minnesota, and Wisconsin provide potential models.)[126]

A second set of child support issues concerns the support of children over age eighteen. Under the present California law they are treated as adults (even if they are still high school students), and their parents are not legally obligated to contribute to their support. The *de facto* result of this rule is that mothers' more limited resources are further strained.[127] The policy recommendation in this sphere is to require parents to support children until they complete their college education. Parental contributions for such support could be apportioned according to the parents' relative incomes, just as it is for minor children.

One model for new legislation is the New York rule that presumes support lasts until the child reaches age 21 unless the child becomes emancipated. A second model is the rule in the State of Washington which permits divorce courts to order parents to support their college age children past majority (until they complete their undergraduate education if they are full-time students).[128]

A third necessity for child support awards is that they include provisions for automatic cost of living (COLA) adjustments, as do many private and government stipends (such as social security awards). Since the purchasing power of child support awards is eroded in an inflationary economy, awards must be linked to the consumer price index or to some other basic economic indicator that will allow for automatic adjustments that maintain a steady standard of living.[129] In addition, penalties and interest should be assessed on late payments.

Fourth, to improve child support we must distinguish and emphasize the question of enforcement.[130] Since fathers who earn between $30,000 and $50,000 a year are just as likely to default on their child support as those who earn $20,000, it is evident that the father's ability to pay is not what determines compliance.[131] Rather, it is the system of enforcement—and that system clearly needs to be strengthened.[132]

One way to improve the system of enforcing child support is to shift the burden of monitoring and securing compliance from the recipient to the state. An ideal system would follow the Swedish model in which the state itself pays the full amount of the child support to the recipient and takes the full responsibility for collecting it from the donor.[133]

Short of this, however, there are other known, effective means of increasing compliance which should be adopted on a national scale: automatic wage assignments that begin with the inception of the order; channeling support payments through administrative arms of the court that monitor compliance and rapidly initiate enforcement action as soon as a single payment is overdue; intercepting state and federal income tax refunds to secure past-due support from delinquent fathers; expanding location and tracking procedures through Social Security and the Internal Revenue Service; and securing payment through the posting of bonds and obtaining liens on property.[134] While many of these enforcement procedures are incorporated into the federal legislation of 1984, they have yet to be adopted by and fully utilized by most states.[135]

Fifth, since we have seen repeated examples of judges choosing not to enforce the laws on the books—refusing to issue wage assignments, "forgiving" arrearages for past-due support, excusing flagrant offenders with no more than repeated "warnings" and refusing to require a bond or other form of security from fathers with a history of noncompliance[136]—it is evident that the system of enforcement itself requires monitoring. One solution that has been suggested follows the Michigan model of establishing an administrative division within the court to receive and monitor payments and to initiate enforcement action.[137] Since we know that a substantial increase in compliance can be achieved by the adoption of a system that includes both the threat and practice of incarceration for noncompliance, it is essential that these remedies not be left solely to the discretion of judges. Rather, sentencing guidelines and judicial monitoring are necessary to ensure that judges do not undermine the system of enforcement.

Finally, more imaginative means of securing voluntary compliance ought to be considered. For example, several counties have obtained a dramatic increase in voluntary compliance after they begin publishing the names of noncomplying fathers in local newspapers.[138]

Custody

Although the laws governing custody have changed considerably, actual custodial arrangements have not. Despite the sex-neutral laws, mothers remain the primary caretakers of children after divorce.[139] However, joint custody legislation, especially in states such as California where it is strongly favored, has significantly affected the relative bargaining positions of men and women. Women are more likely to forgo their claims to support and property if threatened with loss of custody or with custodial arrangements that they see as untenable or harmful to their children, and the new laws give men greater power to make such demands.[140] In addition, as joint legal custodians, men not only have more control over their children; they also have more control over the postdivorce lives of their ex-wives.

One problem with the current custody laws is that they treat all men and all women as if they were equally capable of caring for their children after divorce. This ignores the social reality that in most families one parent, typically the mother, has been the primary caretaking parent. Children are likely to suffer a greater loss if they are separated from the primary caretakers and primary caretakers are likely to suffer more if they lose their children.[141] Laws that ignore these social facts place a cruel and unnecessary pressure on primary caretakers to trade away financial benefits for fear of losing their children.[142]

Two alternatives are recommended in setting standards for custody awards: a primary caretaker presumption for sole custody awards, and a joint custody option only upon the agreement of both parties.

Consider first a rule that would create a presumption that custody will be awarded to the primary caretaker.[143] This would serve to maintain the child's bond to the parent more directly involved in child care during the marriage, and thus would ensure optimal continuity and stability for the child. Moreover, because it is a sex-neutral rule it accommodates cases in which the father has been the primary parent. In fact, it makes it evident that parenting during marriage, by both mothers and fathers, is to be valued and rewarded. Thus another advantage of this rule is that it encourages and rewards child caretaking during marriage. Finally, this rule provides a more clear-cut criterion than the present "best interest of the child" standard and thereby discourages the use of a custody threat as a bargaining chip.[144]

The second policy recommendation calls for laws that permit joint custody only when both parents agree.[145] We have seen that coercive joint custody laws, such as the preference for joint custody in the California law, give men equal rights without equal responsibility. Although they hold the promise of enabling men to share the responsibility of caring for children after divorce, in practice most children continue to live with their mothers. By the same token, fathers have a new justification for reducing child support and for increasing control over their former wives' decisions and lifestyle.

In addition to changing the rules for custody, it is clear that stronger social and economic supports are needed for custodial parents, whether

male or female, in the larger society. The possible range and nature
of such supports are suggested by the following statement from a Nor-
wegian social scientist who was herself recently divorced:

> Everyone [in Norway] knows that divorced [custodial] parents need more
> money and more social support because of the additional pressures in-
> volved in raising children as a single parent. As soon as I got divorced
> my income went up: both the local and national government increased
> my mother's allowance, my tax rate dropped drastically as I was now
> taxed at the lower rate of a single head of household, and my former
> husband contributed to child support. It also helped to have . . . day
> care and a husband who was willing to take some of the responsibility
> for parenting during the week.[146]

The advantages of a legal (and social) system that takes seriously
its responsibility to provide protection and support for parents and
their children after divorce is evident. For example, in another Scandi-
navian country, Sweden, the state assures custodial parents of steady
child support payments (custodial mothers receive the amount of child
support awarded to them from the state, which then collects the money
from the noncustodial parent).[147] In addition, in Sweden and Norway
all mothers are given a special mother's allowance ᵗo ensure that every
child is raised in a household with an adequate standard of living.
The state also provides universal health and hospital coverage and a
wide range of other social benefits (such as subsidized housing) that
further ensure that all children have the basic necessities of life. Finally,
both local and national tax laws give the custodial mother special
benefits so that she retains a larger portion of the income she earns.[148]
As a result of these extensive benefits and the protected legal treatment
they receive, divorced women and their children in Sweden live, on
the average, at 90 percent of their predivorce standard of living.[149]
They are spared the economic hardships that befall so many American
women and children.

The Role of Judges and Lawyers

Since all these policy recommendations focus on legislative reforms,
one might ask whether judicial education and continuing education
of the bar might not provide equally useful routes to bring about change.
One hopeful indication of the prospects for change comes from my
own experience in judicial education seminars. When I first began
presenting the data from this research, the findings were greeted with

some skepticism. Each judge insisted that he (the overwhelming majority of judges who hear family law cases are male) was not awarding
low amounts of alimony and/or child support. Further, most judges
insisted that they were not awarding a larger proportion of the family
income or property to the husband.

I soon learned to begin my talks by presenting a few hypothetical
cases and asking the judges to set awards for Ann Thompson, the
fifty-three year old housewife, and Pat Byrd, the young mother of preschool children. After collecting and tabulating their responses in front
of the audience (i.e., their awards of child and spousal support, and
their disposition of the family home when that home was the sole
asset of a family with preschool children), we proceeded to "trace
out" the implications of the awards they had just made. The results
of their awards were compared to the costs of raising children, to
state welfare and poverty levels, and to the husbands' disposable income after divorce. Women's job prospects and average wages were
examined, and the probable postdivorce income of husband and wife
were compared.

When it became clear that awards that seemed fair in the abstract—awards that would "allow" a man to keep "enough" of his
income and yet effect an "equal" division of family income and assets—
actually served in these concrete cases to severely disadvantage
women and children, the judges were more receptive to the notion
that they should reconsider the consequences of their decisions and
begin to think about what awards-setting standards might lead to more
equitable results.

While this suggests the potential benefits of judicial education, it
is clearly not a panacea. The pervasive pattern of judicial attitudes
and practices observed throughout this book—the judges' open disregard of the law requiring them to order wage attachments for fathers
who are not paying child support;[150] their willingness to forgive the
arrearage on past-due child support because it "unfairly burdens" the
father;[151] their readiness to attribute earning capacity to an older
housewife;[152] and their assumption that it is fair to divide family income
so that the wife and children share one-third, while the husband keeps
the other two-thirds for himself[153]—make one hesitate to rely on
any prescription that seeks to change judges instead of changing the
law itself.

It is also impossible to ignore the implicit sex bias in the way
many judges define what is reasonable or unreasonable. For example,
judges rarely grant a wife's request for a forced sale of the family

business so that she can obtain her share of the equity, because they see an overriding interest in preserving the "husband's" business intact.[154] However, when a husband requests an immediate sale of the family home so he can cash out his share of the equity while the wife seeks to delay the sale to ensure housing for the children, the judges tend to see the overriding interest as, again, the *husband's* need for *his* share of the equity.[155] In the first case they tell the wife that it is reasonable to make *her* wait for her share of the equity, but in the second case they say it is unreasonable to make a husband wait for his share.

Consider also what judges consider a reasonable arrangement for the management and control of a family business or closely held "family" corporation. Here the judges typically acknowledge that to compel divorced spouses to jointly manage an ongoing business would be disruptive and impractical; rather, *one* person has to be empowered to make the final decisions. They therefore award the business management and control (as well as outright ownership, in some cases) to one spouse, invariably the husband.[156] They simply overlook the *wife's right* to share equally in the control of a business or company that she partially owns.

However, when the same issues are raised about joint child custody, judges see no problem about compelling divorced spouses to cooperate in an ongoing relationship to make decisions. Nor do they see the impracticability of divided authority, or the disruption that this may cause for children. Rather, they focus on the *father's right* to share parental authority.

Finally, consider judicial attitudes towards the goodwill value of a business or a profession. Many judges frankly admit that they are reluctant to recognize the goodwill in a profession because it would be too difficult for the husband to raise the capital to "buy back his wife's share."[157] However, when an older housewife who has spent twenty or thirty years in the family home points out that it is virtually impossible for her to raise the capital to buy out her husband's share of the home, judges say her practical difficulties are irrelevant.[158]

These attitudes underscore the need for the type of explicit judicial directives that have been suggested above.

Several other recommendations on the judiciary were originally suggested by attorneys in our sample and have been reiterated at virtually every meeting I have had with attorneys and bar association groups. The first is for a specialized judiciary with an interest and expertise in the family law area. It is openly acknowledged that many

California judges are political appointees with primary experience in criminal courts: they have no interest or experience in family law; and they resent hearing divorce cases and being assigned to the domestic relations calendar.* Such judges may "endure" the assignment but make no effort to keep up with recent case law developments or to master the body of knowledge necessary to make competent judgments. Thus attorneys complain of having to educate judges in the course of presenting their cases, and of facing judges who do not want to bother to read briefs or hear case law precedents.

It is therefore recommended that judges assigned to family law cases have prior experience, knowledge and interest in family law. In addition, courts could hire special commissioners with such expertise. Since these recommendations may be at odds with the current system of judicial appointments and the structure of the courts in many counties, an alternative is to require *mandatory judicial education before* judges are assigned to hear divorce cases. In addition, once a judge is assigned to the domestic relations calendar, continuing education courses, on an annual basis, should be mandatory.

Along with the need for a specialized bench and for compulsory judicial education, there is clearly a need for more judges to be assigned to hear family law cases. These cases now comprise one-half of all the cases in most counties, yet they are typically rushed through the judicial process because they are assigned only one-tenth (or less) of judicial time. Since the judges who are assigned to domestic relations can rarely handle the entire caseload of pending divorces, it is common practice in many counties to assign divorce cases that require more than a half day or day of court time to the "master calendar" where they are given the next available superior court judge. It is, as one attorney put it, "like playing Russian roulette with my client's future because we can be assigned to a judge who doesn't have a clue about family law, hasn't heard a case in 3 years, and has never dealt with a complicated pension case in his life."

This appalling situation would also be alleviated by the establishment of a specialized family law bench with knowledgeable, experienced, and interested judges who participate in annual judicial education programs. In addition, sufficient judicial personnel should be assigned to the family court so that all of the divorce cases can be heard by those judges.

---

* The central Los Angeles court is unique in having a system of specialized commissioners with expertise in family law and the attorneys in that community rate the competence of the judiciary as high.

A final suggestion for the judiciary involves awards of attorneys fees and legal costs. Attorneys frequently cited the difficulties they face in obtaining awards for appraisers' and experts' fees when they represent the lower-earning or unemployed spouse. Although the law allows judges to award attorneys' fees and legal costs, judges typically award only a fraction of the costs requested or refuse to award any fees at all. This puts a greater burden on the attorney who represents the lower-earning spouse, or the spouse who has less access to family resources, who is usually the wife. An attorney's vigorous representation of the interests of the lower-income spouse is undermined if the attorney does not have the money to pay for depositions, investigative accountants, and independent appraisals. (These are serious handicaps when added to the initial handicaps of a spouse who typically has less knowledge of the family's finances.) Thus it is urged that judges be encouraged to award attorneys' fees and legal costs to the attorney representing the lower-earning spouse so that person is not disadvantaged in the legal process.

The prospects for change through individual attorneys are also problematic. Even those attorneys who spontaneously commented on the ways the present system of divorce disadvantages women, felt there was little they could do—as individual attorneys—to change it. In their own practices, they felt they must be "realistic" in advising their clients, and this meant giving clients reliable information about how the system operates in practice. For example, one male attorney said:

> I have to think of my reputation. I don't want to be known as a woman's lawyer. I have to be fair to my male clients and let them know what the court expects of them. No man will listen to me if I tell him to give his wife half of his income or to turn the house over to her—and he could sue me for malpractice.

Another explained his advice to female clients in this way:

> I'm not doing my client any good if I lead her to believe she can maintain her life style. I have to prepare her for the worst. . . . Then if we're lucky enough to get any alimony, she'll think I'm terrific—which I am.

The lawyer's concern with maintaining his or her reputation, avoiding malpractice claims, and establishing realistic expectations to assure satisfied clients, all discourage taking risks and trying to "buck the system." In addition, since most negotiations are done with other attorneys who also "know the system," an attorney stands little chance of persuading them to deny the best interests of their own clients. Rather, an attorney who persists in trying to obtain more alimony or property for disadvantaged female clients simply risks damaging his or her own reputation as a competent lawyer.

The structure of the legal profession links attorneys to individual clients and rewards them for representing the client's interests. One particularly poignant example of this reality involved an attorney who, at the time of our interview, was struggling with the question of a wealthy doctor's support for his college-age children. While the doctor could well afford to support his children through college and graduate school, and was ready to sign an agreement to do so, the attorney had a professional responsibility to tell the doctor that the law did not require him to support his children past age eighteen. In this case the attorney felt the doctor might later regret the agreement he was about to sign, and might then allege malpractice because his attorney had not clearly informed him of the extent to which his choice was voluntary and exceeded the norms. On the other hand, the last time this attorney had handled a similar case, he wrote a letter to the client outlining his legal options (to protect himself from a future malpractice claim) and asked the client to countersign the letter. The letter had such a negative impact that the client decided not to agree to pay for these college expenses after all.

These examples suggest, once again, that the route to divorce law reform must have a strong legislative focus.

CONCLUSION

The research reported in this book reveals that the economic consequences of the present system of divorce are unfair to women and children. Divorce today spells financial disaster for too many women and for the minor children in their custody. The data reveal a dramatic contrast in financial status of divorced men and divorced women at every income level and every level of marital duration.[159] Women of all ages and at all socioeconomic levels experience a precipitous decline in standard of living within one year after divorce, while their former husbands' standard of living improves.[160] Older women and women divorced from men in the higher-income brackets experience the most radical downward mobility.[161]

These economic changes have drastic psychosocial effects on the children of divorce. The sharp decline in mothers' standard of living forces residential moves with resulting changes of schools, teachers, neighbors, and friends.[162] Mothers pressured to earn money have little time and energy to devote to their children just when the children need them most. Moreover, when the discrepancy in standard of living between children and father is great, children feel angry and rejected and are likely to share their mother's feelings of resentment.

These findings make it clear that, for all its aims at fairness, the current no-fault system of divorce is inflicting a high economic toll upon women and children. The time has come for us to recognize that divorced women and their children need greater economic protection, and to implement the legal changes necessary to achieve that goal.

We do not have to tolerate the hardships that the present legal system inflicts in order to achieve the long-range goal of equality: true equality cannot evolve while these abuses persist. Nor do we have to return to the traditional fault-based legal system to obtain economic settlements that better protect dependent wives and children. The no-fault law took a major step forward by reducing the acrimony and hostility in the legal process of divorce, but because it did not provide economic protection for women and children, it failed to achieve its loftier goals of fairness, justice, and economically based equality.

The lesson of this experience is not that the goals of the divorce law reforms were unworthy, but rather that the means used to achieve them were not in all ways appropriate. The law requires a continuous process of correction and refinement. We should not lose sight of the fact that it is the means that need correcting—not the ends.

We now have the knowledge and experience to fashion remedies that can promote those goals and, at the same time, protect women and children from the economic devastations of divorce. As our awareness of the inequities of the present system has increased, so too has our knowledge of the changes that are necessary to correct these inequities. The paths before us are clear. It is now time for us to follow through on the road to fairness, equity, and equality in the legal process of divorce.

APPENDIX A

Research Methods

This book is based on a ten-year study of the social, economic, and legal consequences of California's no-fault divorce law. Because California was the first state in the nation to adopt a "pure" no-fault law, and because its records provided detailed information on the characteristics of divorcing couples, it offered a unique laboratory for evaluating the effects of no-fault divorce. The research involved four types of data: systematic random samples of court records; interviews with members of the matrimonial bar; interviews with superior court judges and commissioners who hear family law cases; and, perhaps most important, interviews with recently divorced men and women. Each of these samples is described in this section.

In all of the interviews that we conducted, each respondent (i.e., each judge, lawyer, divorced man and woman) was presented with a series of hypothetical divorce cases (in addition to about one hundred pages of questions). Four of these cases are discussed throughout this book: one involves a young couple with preschool children, another concerns an older corporate executive and his wife after a twenty-seven-year marriage, the third focuses on a middle-aged nurse who supported her doctor husband through medical school, and the fourth deals with noncompliance with a child support award. These cases are presented in Appendix B.

After completing the early analysis of the California interviews, I had the opportunity to conduct a similar set of interviews in England and to explore the responses of English judges and attorneys to the same four hypothetical cases. Their reactions serve to highlight the unique features of the California legal perspective.

Court Records

We analyzed about 2,500 divorce cases for the court docket samples. These cases were drawn from court records between 1968 and 1977. The first two samples were drawn from divorces granted in 1968, two years *before* the no-fault law was constituted. One systematic random sample of about 500 divorce decrees was drawn from San Francisco county court records. A second systematic sample of about 500 divorce cases was drawn from Los Angeles County, giving us a total of 1,000 divorce cases in 1968.

The same procedure was used to draw two samples of divorce cases in 1972, two years *after* the no-fault law was instituted. Again, we drew systematic random samples of about 500 cases from both San Francisco and Los Angeles County divorce decrees.

Each of these random samples of approximately 500 cases was drawn from the final divorce decrees granted in each county in 1968 and 1972. In 1968, there were 26,603 divorces granted in Los Angeles County, requiring a sampling ratio of one in 53 ($n = 507$). In San Francisco, with 2,328 divorces in 1968, the sampling ratio was about one in five ($n = 498$).

In 1972, there were 35,635 divorce decrees (which were then called decrees of dissolution) granted in Los Angeles and 3,495 in San Francisco, producing a sampling ratio of about one in 71 in Los Angeles ($n = 486$) and one in seven in San Francisco ($n = 506$).

The statistics on the number of divorces per county and the random samples of divorce decrees were obtained from the California State Department of Vital Statistics.

A final sample of divorce cases was drawn from court dockets in 1977 to examine the extent of the changes that had occurred seven years after no-fault was instituted. Having found few significant differences between the San Francisco and Los Angeles samples in 1968 and 1972, we limited the 1977 sample to Los Angeles County where close to one-third of all California dissolutions were granted. Again, 500 cases were drawn from the 15,752 decrees of disolution granted in Los Angeles between January 1 and June 1, 1977. The sampling ratio was one in 31.5 ($n = 500$). Petitions filed prior to January 1, 1975 were excluded from the sample.

Decrees granted after June 1, 1977 were not included in the 1977 sampling frame because in June 1977 the California legislature voted to abolish the collection of detailed socioeconomic and demographic information on the Certificates of Registry of Final Decrees of Dissolution, the basis for these samples.[1] Although this legislation did not officially go into effect until January 1978, we were concerned that record keeping during the second six months of 1977 would be less rigorous. As a result of this legislation, further research in this area has been effectively foreclosed for the foreseeable future.

Judges

In-depth structured interviews were conducted with the forty-four judges and commissioners who hear family law cases in San Francisco and Los Angeles counties. The ninety-page interview schedule took an average of three hours to complete. Most of these interviews were conducted over a period of two (or three) days and were supplemented by court observations. About half of the interviews were tape-recorded and transcribed. Only a fraction of the interview and observational data is covered in this book which focuses on the judges' responses to the hypothetical cases presented in Appendix B.

The San Francisco sample consisted of Superior Court judges who were assigned to the domestic relations calendar of uncontested divorces and preliminary hearings for six months or more, and/or those who were regularly assigned contested divorce cases. The Los Angeles sample included all of the Superior Court judges and commissioners who heard either contested or uncontested divorce cases in 1975. In San Francisco, eighteen of the twenty eligible judges (90 percent) were interviewed; in Los Angeles, twenty-six of the twenty-seven eligible judges (96 percent) were interviewed.

The three-hour formal interviews with 44 judges and commissioners were conducted in 1974 and 1975. In 1981, twenty-six written responses to the hypothetical cases and more informal interviews with judges were obtained at a statewide judicial education seminar for family court judges. In addition, between 1980 and 1985 I have been lecturing and participating in judicial education programs and seminars and have continued to meet with and informally interview California judges throughout this period. The judicial attitudes and practices discussed in this book are therefore, to the best of my knowledge, quite current. In fact, one anecdotal indication of the consistency of judicial responses to the hypothetical cases is instructive. In a 1985 judicial education seminar with family court judges in Hawaii the median support awards in the Byrd case (see Appendix B) were *identical* to those obtained in both the 1975 interviews and the 1981 questionnaire responses from California judges.

Attorneys

In-depth structured interviews were conducted with a total of 169 matrimonial attorneys in the San Francisco Bay area and in the greater Los Angeles area. The 115-page interview schedule took an average of four hours to complete and more than half of these were conducted over two (or more) days. (The longest interview took twelve hours and three visits.) About a third of the interviews were tape-recorded and later transcribed. Here, again, only a fraction of the interview material could be utilized in this book, which, of necessity, focuses on percentages rather than the qualitative data.

The San Francisco Bay area sampling frame consisted of all members of the American Academy of Matrimonial Lawyers, all members of the Family Law Section of the San Francisco Bar Association, and those additional attorneys identified by more than two members of the above groups as being one of the three most knowledgable or effective attorneys in family law in the Bay area. The seventy-seven attorneys who were interviewed (97 percent response rate) comprised most of the family law bar in the San Francisco-Oakland-Berkeley area.

In Los Angeles County, there were over 1,400 attorneys who identified themselves as matrimonial attorneys. We therefore restricted our requests for interviews to attorneys who met one or more of the following criteria: those who had served on the Executive Committee of the Family Law Section of the Los Angeles and Beverly Hills Bar Associations within the past ten years, the twenty members of an informal organization of self-identified (and generally recognized) elite matrimonial lawyers, and those additional attorneys who were identified by more than two attorneys in the above groups as being one of the three most knowledgeable or effective attorneys in family law in the Los Angeles area. All of the ninety-two attorneys who met these criteria were interviewed (100 percent response rate).

The structured interviews were conducted in the San Francisco Bay area in 1974 and 1975 and in the greater Los Angeles area in 1975. In the years since these formal interviews were completed, I have been a lecturer and participant at numerous meetings of state and local bar groups in both California and in other states (in addition to the national American Bar Association meetings) and have thus continued to interview, discuss and analyze these issues with attorneys through early 1985.

Divorced Men and Women

In-depth structured interviews with 228 recently divorced men and women (114 men and 114 women) were conducted in the greater Los Angeles area in 1978. These interviews took place, on the average, one year after the legal divorce. The 148-page interview schedule (with 454 questions) took between four and six hours to complete and averaged closer to six. Here again, there were a few extremely long interviews (twelve and fourteen hours). Since we anticipated having difficulty in getting respondents and in gaining their cooperation for our long interviews, we were surprised by the respondents' willingness to cooperate and to share vast amounts of personal information with us.*

The sampling procedure was as follows. First, a random sample was drawn from final decrees of dissolution granted in Los Angeles County between May and July 1977. This sample was then stratified by length of marriage and socioeconomic status. To enable us to examine systematically the effects of marital duration and income on the terms of the divorce settlement, we intentionally oversampled long-married and high-property couples since most divorced couples are young and have little property at the time of the divorce.

To this end, we first divided the sample into four groups of marital duration: marriages of four years or less, marriages of five to ten years, marriages of eleven to seventeen years and marriages of eighteen or more years. In order to obtain a sufficient number of couples of each marital duration, and in order to obtain a significant number of couples in long marriages, we sought to interview fifty respondents in each of the first three groups and seventy-five respondents in the group of couples married eighteen years or more, for a total of 225 interviews. This required oversampling couples in longer marriages and undersampling couples in shorter marriages.

Cases in each of these groups were also stratified by socioeconomic (SES) status. Here we used the husband's occupation at the time of the divorce as the major determinant of the family's status. In order to obtain a sufficient number of couples of each SES group (and in order to obtain a significant number of couples with higher incomes and more property to divide) we oversampled higher SES groups and undersampled lower SES groups.

Our final aim was to obtain a sample that was evenly divided by sex so within each of the target cells we randomly chose the husband as our respondent in half the cases, and the wife as our respondent

---

* Other researchers who have interviewed divorced men and women have been similarly surprised by their respondents' willingness to share their experiences with an interviewer.[2]

in the other half, so that we ended up with half male and half female respondents. The target sample looked like this:

Target Sample of Divorced Men and Women

LENGTH OF MARRIAGE	SOCIOECONOMIC STATUS		
	Low and Average SES	*Higher SES*	TOTAL
0–4 years	25	25	50
5–10 years	25	25	50
11–17 years	25	25	50
18 years or more	25	50	75
Total	100	125	225

Since this book seeks to provide a portrait of the entire population of divorced persons I have "corrected" for the over-representation of long-married high-income families in the interview sample in two ways. First, instead of using sample averages, I have controlled for both length of marriage and income in most of the tables and statistics reported in the text. Second, when income and marital duration are not controlled, the interview responses reported in this book are weighted to reflect the proportion of each group of respondents in a normal sample of divorced persons (e.g., the 1977 docket sample).

Other researchers have been plagued by the problems of locating divorced persons once they have been identified as part of a sample.[2] As Graham Spanier and Linda Thompson state, "locating and recruiting a sample of separated and divorced individuals is a heroic task because of their reticence and mobility."[3] In anticipation of such problems we drew an initial sample three times the size of our target sample.

These people were sent a letter describing the research and asking them to return a postcard if they were willing to be interviewed. In addition to the positive responses we received, there were responses indicating that the parties had reconciled (or, in one case, that they had never been divorced), had moved out of the state, did not speak English or Spanish, or were in a mental institution (one person) or jail (one person). These cases were eliminated from the sample and we proceeded to try to contact all of those who did not respond. Our first step was simply to send another copy of our first letter. If this did not produce a response we followed up with a different letter asking them to respond, even if they did not want to be interviewed. Whenever these letters were returned with new addresses new letters were sent to the new address. If letters were returned because the addressee was unknown we tried to locate them by phone, by using reverse directions, or to obtain a new address through the department of motor vehicles or utility companies.

We also followed up on all of those who did not respond to our letters by telephone and, where necessary, by relocating them. In addition to the above procedures we located some potential respondents by calling members of their family and in a few cases asking their attorneys to forward a letter for us. Since I had extensive experience in locating missing people (for my Ph.D. dissertation on people who disappear[4]), we were quite successful and located more people than we needed for our target quotas.

By the time we reached the date we had arbitrarily set as a cutoff for location efforts, we had located over 50 percent of the respondents. (This rate compares favorably to the 37 percent location rate reported by Spanier and Thompson.[5])

By that time we also found ourselves in the awkward situation of having more volunteers than we needed for the sample in several groups. (For example, we had an 86 percent location rate for men and women married over eighteen years.) In those cases we randomly selected respondents and sent special letters and/or called the others once our interviews were completed.

Overall, only 17 percent of the potential respondents whom we located refused to be interviewed. The other 83 percent agreed to the interview. This 83 percent also compares favorably with the 61 percent response rate reported by Spanier and Thompson.[6]*

Our initial concern about the respondents' ability to deal with the detailed financial questions we asked was similarly unfounded. Not only were the respondents extremely knowledgeable about the economic aspects of the divorce; we were amazed at their ability to recall precisely the appraised value of their house, the amount of the mortgage, the value of the pension plan, etc. Although some of them had prepared for our interviews and had file folders with letters from attorneys, appraisals, and copies of court orders, few needed to refer to this information: the figures were clearly "imprinted" in their memories.

Similarly, our concern about conflicting appraisals and being of-

---

* There was only one group where we did not have an excess of volunteers: we did not locate enough male respondents who had been married for less than four years from the lower SES group. In that case, we drew a supplementary sample which brought the *location rate for that group* down to 23 percent. The response rate for those located in *that group* was 67 percent.

fered more than one value for an asset proved unfounded. Since most items of property had to be valued in the legal process—either by the court or by agreement—in order to accomplish an equal division of property, the respondents were able to report the agreed-upon value of most assets.

Since these interviews are the only source of complete economic information—information about income, occupation, and employment as well as property ownership and value—the data reported in this book rely heavily on these interviews. (Recall that some of this information was missing from some court records.)

We did not anticipate the aura of importance that seemed to be attached to these interviews. Nor did we anticipate the positive esprit de corps that developed among the interviewers. Perhaps it began when the Los Angeles divorcees, who were potential respondents, received a personal letter from a professor from Northern California, asking them to participate in the study, or with the special all day training session that we required already experienced interviewers to attend. Or perhaps it was the freedom we gave the interviewers to spend our resources on "extras" where necessary—to pay for babysitters, to take the time to call respondents the day after the interview to thank them, and to try to respond to special requests for help.

We knew something was different when people began calling in response to our initial letter and telling us why they *wanted* to participate. As our interviewing supervisor said:

> The respondents reacted to the interviews and to the study as if we were somebody. It wasn't just the university. That was important, but they thought we were really something, the courts are something, . . . that people can really change the laws and can really do something for them. They thought a lot of the interviewers came from San Francisco to interview them, and they looked upon the study as a very very important study. It was the letter and the attitude of the interviewers. . . . Also, you said it's going to take two or three hours, and everybody reacted to that. The respondents I spoke to said "that long? what's going on?" And then I'd say well it's so important and everything you say is so important. Also the letter said this study is actually going to accomplish something . . . you know you didn't just say we are interested in finding out your opinions, attitudes, such and such but you said that other states are looking to what is happening in California. . . . and we care about your experiences and what you think about the law. . . . I think they really felt that their responses were going to do some good.
>
> The interviewers also looked upon it as an important thing. It was the way we briefed them, I think we instilled that in them. I had interviewers call me up and ask if it was okay to do a second follow up call, you know, another call to thank them, the next day, to see how they

were doing, they'd say, I'm a little bit concerned about how he's doing, is it okay if I make a second call? They were really close after the interview. It established a special bond. The interviewers felt responsible for the people. . . . They were doing this big important work together . . . they were a team and were looking after their teammates.

Many of the interviewers had trouble leaving the interview. Respondents would follow them out to their cars, or invite them to stay to dinner. You know (one male interviewer) found it so hard to have to keep turning down invitations to play tennis and bridge: he felt he was letting down a new friend.

In short, we were fortunate in obtaining enthusiastic cooperation from both respondents and interviewers and this undoubtedly contributed to the unusually high response rate.

English Solicitors, Barristers, and Judges

One way of discovering the assumptions made in our own society is to look at the way the same problems are approached in another society. In 1980 and 1981 I was fortunate to have the opportunity to interview a sample of legal experts in England who were dealing with many of the same basic issues following their divorce law reform in 1973.

The English respondents were obtained through a process of referrals from reputed experts. I made every effort to interview anyone who was identified as an expert by at least two other experts.

The final "sample" consisted of eleven solicitors (i.e., attorneys), nine barristers (i.e., specialized attorneys who present cases in court and act as consultants), four law professors, two judges, and one registrar (i.e., a local judge). The solicitors were geographically diverse, but the barristers, judges, and law professors were concentrated in London and Oxford. Although this "sample" of English judges and lawyers is admittedly unsystematic, their responses to the hypothetical divorce cases provide an illuminating contrast to the California data.

Like the California respondents, the English experts were asked to predict the outcomes of hypothetical divorce cases and to explain the rationale for their predictions. Here it is necessary to add a cautionary note about the question of comparability. When I began this research, I assumed that the same factual situation (i.e., the same case) would have the same "social meaning" in the two societies. Thus I translated the hypothetical divorce cases that I had used in California, with only minor changes, to English situations. However, I soon discovered that several structural features of English society created a different set of options for English respondents dealing with the same "factual" case:

1. The English tax structure, especially at the upper income levels, served to substantially "enlarge" the total amount of family income that was "available" to English families after divorce.
2. The English system of social welfare benefits provided more extensive benefits and a better "minimal" standard of living for lower-income families after divorce.
3. The English courts could "award" the right to remain in council housing (i.e., low-cost publically owned housing) and other "entitlements" as part of the divorce settlement. Although such entitlements were not treated as property with an established cash value, they nevertheless enlarged the pool of valuable family assets that were awarded upon divorce.
4. In England there were fewer—or, at least most people assumed there were fewer—opportunities for employment and child care for divorced women with small children, especially in contrast to the perceived availability of jobs, including part-time jobs, and child care facilities for mothers of young children in California.

These unanticipated complications led me to be more cautious in reporting the *quantitative* results of this inquiry (i.e., the precise dollar awards and the percentages of family income awarded to each spouse). Instead I have tried to adopt a more anthropological approach by reporting and analyzing the distinctly different cultural and legal perspectives from which the two sets of experts approached the financial issues of divorce.

Four Divorce Cases

A series of hypothetical cases was presented to each respondent (judges, lawyers, and divorced men and women) in California and in England.

Each of the legal experts was asked to predict the outcome of the case. Then they were asked what they themselves thought was fair. The men and women were asked what they thought was fair. In addition, all respondents were asked specific questions about alimony, child support, and the division of property. After these initial questions all respondents were asked about the reasons for their decisions and the rationale for the awards.

The questions that accompanied these cases varied slightly by the type of respondent. The lawyers were first asked to predict the outcome of each case and then asked what they themselves considered fair. Judges were first asked how they would decide the case. Then they were asked to predict other judges' responses. The divorced men and women were asked what outcome they thought would be fair.

Following are the text of four of the hypothetical cases:

The Thompsons: A senior executive and homemaker after a twenty-seven-year marriage

Victor Thompson, aged fifty-five, is a senior executive at IBM with a net (after tax) income of $72,000 per year (or $6,000 per month).

His wife, Ann, has been a housewife and mother throughout their twenty-seven-year marriage, raising three children (who are now in college). She has never been employed outside of the home.

This was the first marriage for both the husband and wife. At the time of the divorce Ann is fifty-three; Victor is fifty-five.

Victor was bored with the marriage and had recently fallen in love with a younger woman.

The couple has the following property:

> a home and furnishing with an equity value of $90,000
> a car worth $5,000
> a second car worth $2,000
> stocks with a current value of $10,000.

The Byrd Family: A young couple with two young children

In the following case the respondents were told that the parties had agreed to have the children live with their mother after the divorce.

The facts in this case varied somewhat among our four samples, although the husband's income and occupation remained the constant. The ages of the children ranged from one and three, to four and six, and the ages of the parents from twenty-three and twenty-seven, to thirty-one and thirty-two. None of these variations seem to have affected the responses, which were amazingly consistent across all samples. This is one of the Los Angeles attorneys' versions of the case.

Pat and Ted Byrd have decided to divorce after seven years of marriage. Ted is twenty-eight and Pat is twenty-seven. Ted has worked as an accountant for Xerox for the past seven years. He earns $14,000 a year gross or $1,000 a month net (income after taxes), with some expectation of upward mobility.

The Byrds have two children—John, aged 6, and Jean, aged 4. Throughout the marriage Pat has been a housewife and mother. Since their son John was born soon after her graduation from college, she has never worked outside the home. Pat does not want to take a job because she wants to be a full-time mother to her preschool daughter.

The Byrds have the following property:

> household furnishings worth about $3,000
> a new sports car

In some versions of this case the following information was included:

The Byrds live in their own home which has a market value of $40,000. Their equity is $20,000. Monthly payments on the home (including utilities) are $400 per month.

The Roses: A nurse supports her doctor husband's education

Sheila Rose, a twenty-nine-year old registered nurse, has supported the family for ten of the eleven years of this marriage while her husband, Barry, finished college, medical school, an internship, and two years of residency. Last year she earned $14,440 net (or $1,200 net per month).

Barry Rose is a thirty-year-old doctor. He is self-employed and began his practice one year before the divorce, earning $24,000 net ($2,000 net per month). His income is expected to rise steadily.

The Roses do not have any children.

Their property consists of:

> household furniture
> personal items worth $1,000
> a car worth $2,000
> a medical practice valued at $10,000, exclusive of goodwill (This includes $6,000 worth of medical equipment.)

The Roses also have debts of approximately $10,000, all of which were incurred for Barry's medical equipment.

The Stones: Past due child support

Stephen and Beverly have been divorced for three years. Beverly has custody of their three minor children. At the time of the divorce, Stephen was ordered to pay $200 a month in child support ($67 per child). He stopped paying this amount five months ago.

Beverly earns $250 *net* (income after taxes) per month as a waitress. Stephen earns $650 *net* (income after taxes) per month as a delivery truck driver. He has remarried and now has two children with his new wife. Stephen stopped paying child support to Beverly as he claims he cannot afford to support two families. His new wife is not employed.

Legal Appendix—Divorce Laws in the United States

TABLE C-1
Grounds for Divorce

	A NO-FAULT: IRRETRIEVABLE BREAKDOWN SOLE GROUND	B INCOMPATIBILITY AS GROUNDS	C BREAKDOWN ADDED TO TRADITIONAL GROUNDS	D LIVING SEPARATE & APART AS GROUNDS	E JUDICIAL SEPARATION OR MAINTENANCE AS GROUNDS	F MUTUAL CONSENT DIVORCES
Alabama		x	x		2 years	
Alaska		x	x			
Arizona	x					x
Arkansas			x	3 years		
California	x					
Colorado	x					x
Connecticut			x	1½ years*1		
Delaware		x	x	6 months		
Florida	x		x			
Georgia			x			
Hawaii	x			2 years	any period	x
Idaho			x	5 years		
Illinois			*2	*2		*2
Indiana			x			
Iowa	x					
Kansas		x				
Kentucky	x					

417

TABLE C-1

Grounds for Divorce (Continued)

	A NO-FAULT: IRRETRIEVABLE BREAKDOWN SOLE GROUND	B INCOMPATIBILITY AS GROUNDS	C BREAKDOWN ADDED TO TRADITIONAL GROUNDS	D LIVING SEPARATE & APART AS GROUNDS	E JUDICIAL SEPARATION OR MAINTENANCE AS GROUNDS	F MUTUAL CONSENT DIVORCES
Louisiana				1 year	1 year	
Maine			x		x	
Maryland			x	1 year*3		
Massachusetts			x*4			
Michigan	x					
Minnesota	x			6 months		x
Mississippi			x			
Missouri	x					
Montana	x					
Nebraska	x					
Nevada		x		5 years		
New Hampshire				2 years		
New Jersey				1½ years		
New Mexico		x				
New York					1 year	x
North Carolina					1 year*5	
North Dakota			x		4 years	x
Ohio			x*4	1 year		x*4
Oklahoma		x				

State				
Oregon	x			x
Pennsylvania		x	3 years*6		x
Rhode Island		x	3 years		
South Carolina			1 year		
South Dakota*7					x
Tennessee		x	2 years		x
Texas		x	3 years		
Utah				3 years	
Vermont				6 months	
Virginia			1 year*8	1 year	x
Washington	x				
West Virginia		x	1 year		
Wisconsin		x	1 year		x
Wyoming		x			
Washington, D.C.			6 months*10	1 year*10	

*1. 18 months living separate and apart *and* incompatability.

*2. Irretrievable breakdown *and* two years living saparated and apart required, if both parties consent the period becomes 6 months.

*3. Voluntary 12 consecutive months or 2 year uninterrupted separation.

*4. Separation agreement also required.

*5. Court must find alimony/support resolved.

*6. Plus a) irretrievable breakdown, b) consent, c) court finding as to irretrievable breakdown and living apart.

*7. Grounds are fault-based only: adultery, alcoholism, desertion, conviction of a felony, and extreme cruelty.

*8. Separate support for one year is sufficient, 6 months if there is a separation.

*9. If separation agreement, and no minor children.

*10. 6 months voluntary, 1 year involuntary.

Source: Doris Freed and Timothy Walker "Family Law in the Fifty States: an Overview" *Family Law Quarterly*, Vol. 18, Winter 1985, Table 3, pp. 380–81. Reprinted with permission.

TABLE C-2

Use of Fault in Alimony Awards

	A MARITAL FAULT NOT CONSIDERED	B MARITAL FAULT IS A BAR TO ALIMONY	C COHABITATION ENDS OR MODIFIES ALIMONY
Alabama			X
Alaska	X		
Arizona	X		
Arkansas	X		
California			*1
Colorado	X		
Connecticut			*2
Delaware	X		
Florida			
Georgia		X	X
Hawaii			
Idaho		X	
Illinois	X		*3
Indiana			
Iowa			
Kansas			
Kentucky			
Louisiana		X	X
Maine	X		
Maryland			*3
Massachusetts			
Michigan			
Minnesota	X		
Mississippi		*4	X
Missouri			
Montana	X		
Nebraska			
Nevada			
New Hampshire			*5
New Jersey			X
New Mexico			
New York			X

TABLE C-2

Use of Fault in Alimony Awards (*Continued*)

	A MARITAL FAULT NOT CONSIDERED	B MARITAL FAULT IS A BAR TO ALIMONY	C COHABITATION ENDS OR MODIFIES ALIMONY
North Carolina		x	x
North Dakota			
Ohio			x (permissive)
Oklahoma			x
Oregon	x		
Pennsylvania			x
Rhode Island			
South Carolina		x	
South Dakota			x
Tennessee			x
Texas		x	
Utah			x
Vermont			
Virginia		x	
Washington	x		
West Virginia			
Wisconsin	x		*3
Wyoming			
Washington, D.C.			

*1. Creates presumption of decreased need.
*2. Discretionary.
*3. Insofar as changes economic status.
*4. Adultery is a bar to child custody and alimony.
*5. A factor.

Source: Doris Freed and Timothy Walker, "Family Law in the Fifty States: an Overview" *Family Law Quarterly,* Vol. 18, Winter 1985, Table 8, pp. 402–403. Reprinted with permission.

TABLE C-3

Use of Fault in Property Awards

	A FAULT EXCLUDED	B FAULT OR MERITS MAY BE CONSIDERED	C STATUTES SILENT RE: FAULT
Alabama		x	
Alaska			
Arizona			x
Arkansas			
California	x		
Colorado	x		
Connecticut		x	
Delaware	x		
Florida		x	
Georgia		x	
Hawaii		x	
Idaho		x	
Illinois	x		
Indiana			
Iowa	x		
Kansas			*1
Kentucky		x	
Louisiana		x	
Maine	x		
Maryland		x	
Massachusetts		x	
Michigan		x	
Minnesota	x		
Mississippi			
Missouri			
Montana			x
Nebraska			
Nevada	x		
New Hampshire	x		
New Jersey	x		
New Mexico	x		
New York		x	

TABLE C-3

Use of Fault in Property Awards (*Continued*)

	A FAULT EXCLUDED	B FAULT OR MERITS MAY BE CONSIDERED	C STATUTES SILENT RE: FAULT
North Carolina		x	
North Dakota		x	
Ohio			
Oklahoma			x
Oregon	x		
Pennsylvania		x	x
Rhode Island		x	
South Carolina		x	
South Dakota			
Tennessee	x		
Texas		x	
Utah			x
Vermont		x	
Virginia		x	
Washington	x		
West Virginia	*2		
Wisconsin	x		
Wyoming		x	
Washington, D.C.		x	

*1. Court may consider "such other factors as court deems proper."
*2. Fault excluded for property settlement; *not* for alimony.

Source: Modified from Doris Freed and Timothy Walker "Family Law in the Fifty States: an Overview" *Family Law Quarterly,* Vol. 18, Winter 1985, Table 7, pp. 394–95.

TABLE C-4

Property Subject to Division at Divorce

	A	B	C	D	E
	COMMUNITY PROPERTY STATE	TITLE CONTROLS	ALL PROPERTY CONSIDERED	ONLY MARITAL PROPERTY CONSIDERED	GIFTS AND INHERITANCE EXCLUDED?
Alabama				x*1	yes*1
Alaska				x*2	
Arizona	x				
Arkansas				x	
California	x				
Colorado				x*3	yes*3
Connecticut			x		no
Delaware				x	no
Florida			x		
Georgia				x	no
Hawaii			x		no
Idaho	x				
Illinois				x	yes
Indiana			x		no
Iowa			x		yes*5
Kansas			x		no
Kentucky				x	yes
Louisiana	x				
Maine				x	yes
Maryland				x	yes
Massachusetts			x	*4	*4
Michigan			x		no
Minnesota				x	
Mississippi		x			
Missouri				x	no
Montana			x		
Nebraska				x	unclear
Nevada	x				
New Hampshire				x	no
New Jersey				x	yes
New Mexico	x				

TABLE C–4

Property Subject to Division at Divorce (*Continued*)

	A COMMUNITY PROPERTY STATE	B TITLE CONTROLS	C ALL PROPERTY CONSIDERED	D ONLY MARITAL PROPERTY CONSIDERED	E GIFTS AND INHERITANCE EXCLUDED?
New York				x	unclear
North Carolina				x	
North Dakota				x	no
Ohio				x	
Oklahoma				x	yes
Oregon				x	
Pennsylvania			x		yes
Rhode Island			x		
South Carolina				x	x
South Dakota			x		unclear
Tennessee				*3	*3
Texas	x				
Utah			x		
Vermont			x		
Virginia				x	yes
Washington	x				
West Virginia				unclear	
Wisconsin				x	yes
Wyoming			x		
Washington, D.C.				x	yes

*1. Unless property used for the common benefit of both parties.
*2. Court may invade separate property.
*3. Increase in value of inherited property included.
*4. Court has discretion to invade inherited property.
*5. Excluded unless there is a finding that refusal to do so would work substantial injustice.

Source: Modified with permission from Doris Freed and Timothy Walker, "Family Law in the Fifty States: an Overview" *Family Law Quarterly,* Vol. 18, Winter 1985, Table 6, pp. 390–391.

TABLE C–5

Recognition of Spousal Contribution to Professional Degrees

	STATES WITH STATUTES	STATES WITH CASE LAW DECISIONS	
	Requiring Consideration in	*Granting an Award of*	*Denying an Award of*
Alabama			
Alaska			
Arizona		equity (restitution)*1	
Arkansas			
California	support	reimbursement*2	
Colorado		support & property	
Connecticut		support	
Delaware			support
Florida	support	reimbursement*3	
Georgia	support		
Hawaii			
Idaho			
Illinois			property
Indiana	support & property		
Iowa	support & property	support, reimbursement	
Kansas			property
Kentucky		property, reimbursement	
Louisiana			
Maine			
Maryland			
Massachusetts		property	
Michigan		support, property & reimbursement	
Minnesota		reimbursement	
Mississippi			
Missouri			
Montana			
Nebraska	support & property		
Nevada			
New Hampshire			property
New Jersey		support, reimbursement	
New Mexico			

426

TABLE C–5

Recognition of Spousal Contribution to Professional Degrees (*Continued*)

| | STATES WITH STATUTES | STATES WITH CASE LAW DECISIONS | |
	Requiring Consideration in	Granting an Award of	Denying an Award of
New York	support & property	support	
North Carolina	property		
North Dakota			
Ohio		support	
Oklahoma		support & reimbursement	
Oregon			
Pennsylvania	support & property		
Rhode Island			
South Carolina			
South Dakota			
Tennessee			
Texas			property
Utah	property		
Vermont			
Virginia			
Washington		property	
West Virginia			
Wisconsin	support & property	support, property	
Wyoming			property
Washington, D.C.			

*1 = equitable relief, restitution
*2 = reimbursement if paid within last ten years
*3 = more than reimbursement in short marriage

Source: Lenore J. Weitzman's modification of Table 9 from Doris Freed and Timothy Walker, "Family Law in the Fifty States: an Overview" *Family Law Quarterly*, Vol. 18, Winter 1985, p. 412.

TABLE C–6

Statutes Providing for Conversion of Insurance at Divorce

	A STATES WITH STATUTES PROVIDING FOR CONVERSION
Alabama	
Alaska	
Arizona	
Arkansas	x
California	x
Colorado	
Connecticut	
Delaware	x
Florida	x
Georgia	x
Hawaii	x
Idaho	
Illinois	x
Indiana	
Iowa	
Kansas	
Kentucky	
Louisiana	
Maine	x
Maryland	
Massachusetts	x
Michigan	
Minnesota	x
Mississippi	
Missouri	
Montana	
Nebraska	
Nevada	
New Hampshire	
New Jersey	x
New Mexico	x
New York	x
North Carolina	

TABLE C–6

Statues Providing for Conversion of Insurance at Divorce (*Continued*)

	A
	STATES WITH STATUTES PROVIDING FOR CONVERSION
North Dakota	
Ohio	x
Oklahoma	
Oregon	x
Pennsylvania	x
Rhode Island	
South Carolina	x
South Dakota	x
Tennessee	
Texas	
Utah	x
Vermont	
Virginia	x
Washington	
West Virginia	
Wisconsin	x
Wyoming	x
Washington, D.C.	

Source: Doris Freed and Timothy Walker, "Family Law in the Fifty States: an Overview" *Family Law Quarterly,* Vol. 18, Winter 1985, Table 10, p. 427. Reprinted with permission.

TABLE C-7

Joint Custody Statutes (as of 1985)

STATE/CITE	YEAR ENACTED	TYPE OF JOINT CUSTODY STATUTE			
		Court Has Option	Parties' Agreement	One Party's Request	Presumption or Preference
Alaska § 25.20.060 − .130	1982	x*			
California C.C. § 4600, § 4600.5	1980			x	x
Colorado § 14–10–123.5	1983		x*		
Connecticut G.S.A. § 46b–56(a)	1982	x	x*		x
Florida § 61.13(2)(b)	1982	x			x*
Hawaii R.S. § 571–46, 46.1	1980	x		x	
Idaho § 32–717B	1982				x*
Illinois C. 40, § 602, 603.1	1982	x*	x		
Indiana § 31–1–11.5–21	1984	x	x*		
Iowa C.A. § 598.21.6	1977	x*			

ADDITIONAL PROVISIONS OR JOINT CUSTODY				OTHER PROVISIONS
"Friendly Parent"	Evidentiary Standard	Court Must Write Reasons for Denial	Modification at Any Time	
		x	x	* Court can order mediation within 30 days after petition for child custody filed
x	x	x	x*	* Modification/ termination of order upon request of one or both parents
			x	* Court must find the arrangement to be in the best interests of the child
	x	x	x	* Court may order joint legal custody only per parties' agreement; otherwise parties must submit to conciliation.
x	x*			* Shared custody unless finding of detriment
			x*	* Modification/ termination of joint custody order upon request of one parent or court's own motion
		x		* Absent a preponderance of evidence to the contrary, there is a presumption that joint custody is in the best interests of the child.
			x	* The court can order an investigation to determine if joint custody is appropriate.
				* Parties' agreement is primary but not determinative.
	x			* Factors considered in determining the best interests of the child do not mandate an award for joint custody.

TABLE C–7

Joint Custody Statutes (as of 1985) (*Continued*)

STATE/CITE	YEAR ENACTED	TYPE OF JOINT CUSTODY STATUTE			
		Court Has Option	*Parties' Agreement*	*One Party's Request*	*Presumption or Preference*
Kansas *S.A. § 60–1610(b)*	1979		x*	x	x
Kentucky *R.S. § 403.270(3)*	1980	x*			
Louisiana *Art. 146, 147*	1982		x*		x
Maine *R.S.A. §§ 19–214, 752*	1981	x	x		
Massachusetts *G.L. Ch. 208, § 31*	1983		x*		x
Michigan *C.L.A. § 25.95, 312*	1980	x		x	
Minnesota *§ 518.03 & .17*	1981	x*			
Mississippi *§ 93–5–24*	1983	x	x	x	
Missouri *§ 452.375*	1983	x	x*		
Montana *R.C.A. § 40–4–222–25*	1981	x*		x	

ADDITIONAL PROVISIONS OR JOINT CUSTODY				OTHER PROVISIONS
"Friendly Parent"	*Evidentiary Standard*	*Court Must Write Reasons for Denial*	*Modification at Any Time*	
		x		* Both parties acting individually or in concert may submit a plan to the court prior to the issuance of a custody decree.
				* When custody is contested, the court can order an investigation.
				* The court shall order the parties to submit a plan for implementation of the order.
		x*		* The court must write its reasons for denying an award agreed to by the parents.
	x		x	* Awards permitted in accordance with parents' agreement *unless* finding of not in best interests; shared legal custody is presumed to be in the best interests of the child.
x	x	x		Child support provisions
				"Ability of parents to cooperate" factor
			x*	Modification by parents' petition or one parent's showing a material change in circumstances.
				* Parties must set forth a written plan for joint custody.
x		x		* Court must follow specific guidelines for modification.

TABLE C-7

Joint Custody Statutes (as of 1985) (*Continued*)

STATE/CITE	YEAR ENACTED	TYPE OF JOINT CUSTODY STATUTE			
		Court Has Option	Parties' Agreement	One Party's Request	Presumption or Preference
Nevada R.S. § 125.490	1981				x*
New Hampshire R.S.A. § 458.17	1982			x	x
New Mexico S.A. § 40–4.9.1	1981				x*
North Carolina G.S. § 50–13.2(b)	1967	x*			
Ohio R.C. § 3109.04	1981	x	x*		
Oklahoma Title 10, § 21.1	1983	x			x*
Oregon R.S. § 107–105(1) & 107–137	1977	x*			
Pennsylvania P.S. 23 § 1005	1982	x*	x	x	
Texas C.A. § 14.06(a)	1979	x	x*		
Wisconsin § 767.24	1978		x*		

Source: Lenore J. Weitzman's and Jennifer King's update of Joanne Schulman's March 1982 tabulation of joint custody statutes in "Second Thoughts on Joint Custody," *Golden Gate Law Review* Vol. 12, 1982, pp. 572–573.

ADDITIONAL PROVISIONS OR JOINT CUSTODY				OTHER PROVISIONS
"Friendly Parent"	Evidentiary Standard	Court Must Write Reasons for Denial	Modification at Any Time	
x	x	x	x	* Presumption that joint custody is in the best interests of the child if the parties have agreed.
	x*	x	x	* The court can appoint a guardian ad litem to represent the interests of the child in the custody proceedings.
	x	x	x	* The court may award joint legal without joint physical custody.
				* If in the best interests of the child, the court can award custody to two or more persons.
		x		* The parties must file a plan for joint custody, care and control which must be approved by the court.
				* The preference is for a parent or both parents jointly.
				* Best interests of the child are the primary consideration.
x		x	x	* The court may require parents to attend counseling sessions and consider the recommendations of the counselor.
				* Terms of the agreement are not enforceable as contract terms unless the parties so stipulate.
				Joint custody means "equal rights and responsibilities."

TABLE C–8

Provisions for Enforcement of Child Support

	A STATES WITH DISCRETION TO HAVE PAYMENT MADE DIRECTLY TO COURT OFFICER*	B PROHIBITING MODIFICATION OF PAST DUE SUPPORT PAYMENTS†	C HEALTH INSURANCE MAY BE REQUIRED†
Alabama			
Alaska	x	x	
Arizona	x	x	
Arkansas	x		
California		x	x
Colorado	x	x	
Connecticut	x		
Delaware	x		
Florida	x		
Georgia	x		
Hawaii	x		
Idaho	x	x	
Illinois	x	x	
Indiana	x		
Iowa	x		
Kansas	x		
Kentucky	x		
Louisiana		x	
Maine			x
Maryland	x		
Massachusetts	x		
Michigan	x		
Minnesota	x		
Mississippi			
Missouri	x		
Montana	x	x	
Nebraska			
Nevada		x	
New Hampshire			
New Jersey			
New Mexico			

TABLE C–8

Provisions for Enforcement of Child Support (*Continued*)

	A STATES WITH DISCRETION TO HAVE PAYMENT MADE DIRECTLY TO COURT OFFICER*	B PROHIBITING MODIFICATION OF PAST DUE SUPPORT PAYMENTS†	C HEALTH INSURANCE MAY BE REQUIRED†
New York			x
North Carolina			
North Dakota	x		
Ohio			
Oklahoma			
Oregon		x	
Pennsylvania			
Rhode Island	x		
South Carolina	x		
South Dakota	x		
Tennessee			
Texas		x	
Utah			
Vermont			
Virginia	x		
Washington	x		
West Virginia			
Wisconsin	x		x
Wyoming			
Washington, D.C.	x		

Sources:
  * Doris Freed and Timothy Walker, "Family Law in the Fifty States: an Overview" *Family Law Quarterly,* Vol. 18, Winter 1985, Table 13, pp. 442–43. Reprinted with permission.
  † Chart of State Legislation on Child Support (as of December 1983) prepared by the National Conference of State Legislatures, Denver, Colorado.

Notes

INTRODUCTION

1. By 1981 all states but Illinois and South Dakota had some form of no-fault divorce law. Illinois instituted a new law in 1984, leaving South Dakota as the only state with its traditional law unchanged. Doris Jonas Freed and Henry H. Foster, "Family Law in the Fifty States: An Overview," *Family Law Quarterly* Vol. 17, no. 4, Winter 1984, pp. 373–74.

2. Interview with Arthur Norton, U.S. Bureau of the Census, March 1984. See also Paul Glick, "Children of Divorced Parents in Demographic Perspective," *Journal of Social Issues* Vol. 35, 1979, p. 175 (hereafter cited as Glick "Children of Divorce"). The impact of divorce on children is discussed in more detail in Chapters 8, 9, and 10. Most children of divorced parents will live with their mothers and will experience living in a fatherless home for at least five years. Thornton and Freedman, "American Family," p. 8. In addition, even if their mother remarries, one-third of the white children and one-half of the black children will experience a second marital breakup before they reach adulthood. Larry Bumpass, "Children and Marital Disruptions: A Replication and Update," Center for Demography and Ecology, *Working paper No. 82–57* (Madison, Wis.: University of Wisconsin, January 1983).

3. Kevin Gray, *Reallocation of Property on Divorce* (Abingdon, Oxon, Great Britain: Professional Books Limited, 1977) p. 1.

4. But see Chapter 10 in Lenore J. Weitzman, *The Marriage Contract: Spouses, Lovers, and the Law* (New York: The Free Press, 1983).

5. Mary Ann Glendon, "Property Rights Upon Dissolution of Marriage and Informal Unions" in *The Cambridge Lectures 1981*, Nancy E. Eastham and Boris Krivy, eds. (London: Butterworths, 1982).

6. Arland Thornton and Deborah Freedman, "The Changing American Family," *Population Bulletin* Vol. 38, no. 4, October 1983, p. 7 (hereafter cited as Thornton and Freedman, "American Family").

7. Ibid.

8. Ibid. There is no reason to believe that we will not continue to have a high divorce rate even though the number of divorces and the rate of divorce may fluctuate because of the changing age composition of the U.S. population. A dramatic increase in the number of long-term cohabitants (or a decrease in remarriage rates) could depress the divorce rate, but would not alter the social reality of a high divorce society.

9. In 1980, over 132,000 marriages were dissolved. Personal communication from Dr. Robert B. Mielke, Research Analyst, Department of Health Services, State of California (Oct. 27, 1981). California has had over 100,000 divorces every year since 1970.

10. Kingsley Davis, "The Future of Marriage," *Bulletin of the American Academy of Arts and Sciences* Vol. 36, no. 8, May 1983, p. 33.

11. Norton interview, March 1984.

12. In our 1978 interviews with recently divorced Californians, only 26 percent of the men and 31 percent of the women reported that they felt there was any stigma attached to divorce. On the other hand, a third of both sexes reported receiving more favorable treatment or having someone perceive them as more interesting, coping, or desirable because they were divorced.

13. Lenore J. Weitzman and Ruth B. Dixon, "The Alimony Myth: Does No-Fault Divorce Make a Difference," *Family Law Quarterly* Vol. 14, no. 3, Fall 1980, pp. 141–85.

14. Lenore J. Weitzman and Ruth B. Dixon, "Child Custody Awards: Legal Standards and Empirical Patterns for Child Custody, Support and Visitation After Divorce" *University of California, Davis Law Review*, Vol. 12, no. 2, Summer 1979, pp. 472–521.

15. Herma Hill Kay, "The California Background" unpublished paper written for the California Divorce Law Research Project, Center for the Study of Law and Society, University of California at Berkeley, September, 1977 (on file at the author's office at the School of Law, University of California, Berkeley).

16. William J. Goode, *After Divorce* (New York: The Free Press, 1956), also published as *Women in Divorce* (New York: The Free Press, 1965).

CHAPTER 1—THE LEGAL TRADITION

1. Homer Clark, *The Law of Domestic Relations in the United States* (St. Paul, Minn.: West Publishing Co., 1968), p. 281 (hereafter cited as Clark, *Domestic Relations*).

2. But see Lenore J. Weitzman, *The Marriage Contract: Spouses, Lovers, and the Law* (New York: The Free Press, 1983), pp. 5–134 (hereafter cited Weitzman, *The Marriage Contract*); Clark, *Domestic Relations;* and Herma Hill Kay, *Sex-Based Discrimination: Text, Cases and Materials* (especially the section on "Marriage and Family Life") (St. Paul, Minn.: West Publishing Co., 1981), pp. 163–319 (hereafter cited as Kay, *Sex-Based Discrimination*).

3. Clark, *Domestic Relations,* p. 281.

4. William Blackstone, *Commentaries on the Laws of England* Vol. I, 1765, George Sharswood, ed. (Philadelphia, Pa.: J. B. Lippincott Co., 1908), pp. 442–445.

5. See generally Clark, *Domestic Relations;* Kay, *Sex-Based Discrimination;* and Barbara Babcock, Ann E. Freedman, Eleanor Holmes Norton, and Susan Ross, *Sex Discrimination and the Law: Causes and Remedies* (Boston: Little, Brown and Co., 1975).

6. David Margolick, "For Differing Reasons, Many Join Appeal in Marital Rape Case," *New York Times,* Dec. 18, 1984, p. 23.

7. David Margolick, "Top Court in New York Rules Men Can Be Charged in Rape of Wives," *New York Times,* Dec. 21, 1984, p. 1; *New York Times* editorial, Dec. 18, 1984, p. 18.

8. Weitzman, *The Marriage Contract,* pp. 5–22.

9. Ibid.

10. Clark, *Domestic Relations,* p. 181.

11. Mary Moers Wenig, "The Uniform Marital Property Act," *Probate Notes* Vol. 9, 1983, p. 139 (hereafter cited as Wenig, "Uniform Marital Property Act").

12. L. Lewisohn, *The Vehement Flame: The Story of Stephen Escott* (1948), quoted in Wenig, "Uniform Marital Property Act," p. 140.

13. Herma Hill Kay, "A Family Court: The California Proposal," in *Divorce and After,* Paul Bohannan, ed. (Garden City, N.Y.: Doubleday, 1970), p. 221 (hereafter cited as Kay, "A Family Court"). I am referring explicitly to divorce, the legal termination of a valid marriage, as distinguished from an annulment, which is a declaration that a purported marriage was invalid from its beginning. If a marriage is annulled, "in strict legal theory it never existed at all" Kay, "A Family Court," p. 222.

14. Max Rheinstein, *Marriage, Stability, Divorce and the Law* (Chicago: University of Chicago Press, 1972), p. 24.

15. Clark, *Domestic Relations,* pp. 242–43.

16. Kay, "A Family Court," p. 221.

17. Clark, *Domestic Relations,* p. 349.

18. Raoul Lionel Felder, *Divorce: The Way Things Are, Not The Way Things Should Be* (New York: World, 1971), pp. 137–38.

19. Ibid., p. 85.

20. *Brown v. Brown,* 198 Tenn. 600, 281 S.W. 2d 492 (1955).

21. Stephanie A. Allen, "Nonadversarial Family Law Practice," in *California Marital Dissolution Practice* Vol. 1, Jon A. Rantzman and Paul I. Peyrat,

eds. (Berkeley, Calif.: California Continuing Education of the Bar, 1981), p. 4.

22. *De Burgh v. De Burgh,* 39 Cal. 2d 858, 250 P. 2d 598 (1952).

23. Michael Wheeler, *No-Fault Divorce* (Boston: Beach Press, 1974), p. 17 (hereafter cited as Wheeler, *No-Fault Divorce*).

24. Ibid., p. 16.

25. *California Civil Code,* Section 139 repealed by Stats. 1969, C. 1608, p. 3313, Section 3, operative January 1, 1970. Replaced by Sections 4380, 4801, 4811.

26. Quoted in Wheeler, *No-Fault Divorce,* p. 57.

27. *Arnold v. Arnold,* 76 Cal. App. 2d 877, 881, 882, 174 P.2d 674 (Dist. Ct. App. 1946).

28. William P. Hogoboom, "The California Family Law Act of 1970: 18 Months' Experience," *Journal of Missouri Bar* Vol. 27, no. 11, 1971, pp. 584–589.

29. Doris Jonas Freed and Henry H. Foster, "Family Law in the Fifty States: An Overview," *Family Law Quarterly* Vol. 17, no. 4, Winter 1984, pp. 379–380.

30. Wheeler, *No-Fault Divorce,* p. 17.

CHAPTER 2—THE DIVORCE LAW REVOLUTION

1. Max Rheinstein, *Marriage, Stability, Divorce and the Law* (Chicago: University of Chicago Press, 1972), p. 373.

2. This historical review is based largely on an unpublished paper by Professor Herma Hill Kay, "The California Background," written for the California Divorce Law Research Project, Center for the Study of Law and Society, University of California, Berkeley, September, 1977 (on file at the author's office at the School of Law, University of California, Berkeley) (hereafter cited as Kay, "California Background").

3. Kay, "California Background," pp. 8–22.

4. Ibid.

5. Final Report of the Assembly Interim Committee on Judiciary, 1965, pp. 50–51.

6. Kay, "California Background," p. 17.

7. Ibid., p. 18.

8. Ibid., p. 21. (Fourteen of the fifteen members of the public who testified were men, and ten identified themselves as divorced.)

9. Ibid.

10. Ibid., p. 41.

11. Ibid., p. 7.

12. Ibid.

13. Howard Krom, "California's Divorce Law Reform: An Historical Analysis," *Pacific Law Journal* Vol. 1, no. 1, 1970, p. 163 (hereafter cited as Krom, "California's Reform").

14. Kay, "California Background," p. 21.

15. Ibid.

16. Ibid.

17. Ibid., pp. 75–77. Several Catholics were prominent in the reform group and the final proposal was supported in several diocesean newspapers.

18. Ibid., p. 51.

19. Ibid.

20. Ibid., p. 52.

21. Ibid., pp. 59–66.

22. Krom, "California's Reform," p. 156.

23. Ibid.; William P. Hogoboom "The California Family Law Act of 1970: 18 Months' Experience," *Journal of the Missouri Bar* Vol. 27, no. 11, 1971, (hereafter cited as Hogoboom, "California Experience"); Herma Hill Kay, "A Family Court: The California Proposal," in *Divorce and After,* Paul Bohannan, ed. (Garden City, N.Y.: Doubleday, 1970), pp. 215–248.

24. Kay, "California Background," p. 50.

25. Riane Tennenhaus Eisler, *Dissolution: No-Fault Divorce, Marriage and the Future of Women* (New York: McGraw Hill, 1977), pp. 14–15.

26. Ibid.

27. Mutual consent divorce is possible in Alaska, Mississippi, New York, Ohio, Pennsylvania, Puerto Rico, Tennessee, and Virginia. Doris Jonas Freed and Henry H. Foster, "Family Law in the Fifty States: An Overview," *Family Law Quarterly* Vol. 17, no. 4, Winter 1984, pp. 365–447, Table 1 (hereafter cited as Freed and Foster, "Family Law 1984").

28. Frances Leonard, "The Disillusionment of Divorce for Older Women" (Washington, D.C.: Older Women's League, 1980), p. 2.

29. Krom, "California's Reform," p. 169.

30. Kay, "California Background," p. 52. They did, however, explicitly reject the suggestion of the divorced men (in United States Divorce Reform, Inc.) that alimony be abolished.

31. Ibid., p. 60.

32. *California Civil Code,* Section 4801(a) (West 1983).

33. Ignoring the fact that even full-time year-round female workers earn less than 60 percent of what men earn, one commentator declared that "it does seem somewhat anachronistic, in an era of increasing feminine [sic] equality, that the statutes providing for alimony have remained on the books for as long as they have." Stuart Brody, "California's Divorce Reform: Its Sociological Implications," *Pacific Law Journal* Vol. 1, 1970, p. 228.

34. Kay, "California Background," p. 70, citing columnist Charles McCabe, *San Francisco Chronicle,* Aug. 18, 1969, p. 39, col. 8.

35. Hogoboom, "California Experience," p. 687.

36. Ruth B. Dixon and Lenore J. Weitzman, "Evaluating the Impact of No-Fault Divorce in California," *Family Relations* Vol. 29, 1980, pp. 297–307.

37. I am indebted to Professor Bohannon for allowing me to use his interviews for this comparative review.

38. Graham B. Spanier and Linda Thompson, *Parting: The Aftermath of Separation and Divorce* (Beverly Hills, Calif.: Sage Publications, 1984), pp. 90–97.

39. Ibid., p. 91.

40. Ibid., p. 92.

41. Ibid., p. 93.

42. Ibid., p. 95.

43. Ibid., p. 95.

44. Ibid., p. 95.

45. Surprisingly, in an earlier analysis Spencer and Anderson found that satisfaction with the legal process explained only a trivial amount of variance in adjustment to marital separation, but they did not compare adjustment after a fault and no-fault process. Graham B. Spanier and E. A. Anderson, "The Impact of the Legal System on Adjustment to Marital Separation," *Journal of Marriage and the Family* Vol. 41, 1979, pp. 605–613.

46. The statistics on state laws in this review are, unless otherwise cited, based on the comprehensive analysis of family law by Doris Jonas Freed and Timothy B. Walker, "Family Law in the Fifty States: An Overview," *Family Law Quarterly* Vol. 18, no. 4, Winter 1985, pp. 369–471 (hereafter cited as Freed and Walker, "Family Law 1985"). I am especially thankful for the authors' willingness to share a prepublication copy of their article with me and for their permission to adopt their tables for Appendix C, the Legal Appendix.

47. Ibid., Table 1.

48. *California Civil Code,* Sections 4550–4556 (West 1983). This section of the Civil Code is indexed for inflation so that the statutory amount of property may be adjusted. It was originally $5,000 but was increased to $10,000 in 1978 (added by stats. 1978, c. 508, p. 1655, section 2).

49. Freed and Walker, "Family Law 1985," p. 388.

50. Freed and Foster, "Family Law 1984," p. 382.

51. *Bisig v. Bisig,* 469 A.2d 1348 (N.H. 1983); *Gayet v. Gayet,* 92 N.J. 149, 456 A.2d 102 (1983).

52. *Orr v. Orr,* 440 U.S. 268 (1979).

53. Freed and Foster, "Family Law 1984," p. 384.

54. *In re Marriage of Mirise,* 673 P.2d 803 (Colorado App. 1983).

55. Indiana Code, 31–1–11.5–9, Section 9(c), (West Supp. 1984).

56. Maryland Statute, Factor 3, cited in Freed and Foster, "Family Law 1984," p. 387.

57. See Chapters 6 and 7, pages 169–171 and 193–194.

58. See for example, recent cases in Utah and New Jersey: *Higley v. Higley,* 676 P.2d 379 (Utah 1983); *Yeiderman v. Yeiderman,* 669 P.2d 406 (Utah 1983); *Kulakowski v. Kulakowski,* 191 N.J. Supr. 609, 468 A.2d 733 (1982); *Mahoney v. Mahoney,* 91 N.J. 488, 453 A.2d 527 (1982).

59. See Chapter 6, pp. 169–171, Chapter 7, pp. 193–214.

60. See Chapter 5, especially pp. 135–139.

61. See, for example Mary Ann Glendon, "Family Law Reform in the 1980's," *Louisiana Law Review* Vol. 44, no. 6, July 1984, p. 1556.

62. Emily Jane Goodman, "With Equitable Distribution, Divorce Lawyers' Fees Soar," *New York Times*, Jan. 13, 1983 p. 17, cols. 1–2.

63. *Uniform Marital Property Act*, approved by the Uniform Law Commissioners, July 1983 (Chicago: National Conference of Commissioners on Uniform State Laws, 1983). The *Uniform Act* recognizes that each spouse has a vested ownership right in all property acquired by the personal efforts of either during marriage. The act "establishes marriage as an economic unit, in which keeping house is as valuable as bringing home the pay check." Press release, Uniform Law Commissioners, July 28, 1983, Chicago, Illinois.

64. William P. Cantwell, a Denver attorney who acted as chair of the committee that drafted the Uniform Marital Property Act, emphasized that this 50/ 50 relationship during marriage should foster a more equitable division at divorce, "since equality of ownership provides a solid base for reallocation of assets." Ibid.

65. Freed and Foster, "Family Law 1984," p. 416.

66. Ibid., p. 415.

67. Freed and Walker, "Family Law 1985," p. 434.

68. Ibid., p. 428.

69. Ibid. See also Patricia Hoff's monograph on child snatching (distributed by the American Bar Association, Chicago, Il).

CHAPTER 3—MARITAL PROPERTY

1. Judith Avner and Kim Greene, "State ERA Impact on Family Law," *Family Law Reporter* Vol. 8, 1982, p. 4023.

2. Elizabeth A. Cheadel, "The Development of Sharing Principles in Common Law Marital Property States," *UCLA Law Review* Vol. 28, no. 6, 1981, pp. 1269–1313.

3. *Community property* is defined by the California Civil Code as *all property* acquired by husband and wife, or by either, *during marriage* with the exception of property acquired by gift, bequest, devise, or descent (and their rents, issues, and profits). *California Civil Code*, Sections 687 (West, 1982), 5107–5108 (West, 1983).

    Separate property, in contrast, is defined as property owned by one spouse before marriage, or acquired during marriage by gift or inheritance, as well as the rents, issues, and profits from such property. *California Civil Code*, Sections 5107–5108 (West, 1983).

    See also Gerald E. Lichtig, "Characterization of Property," in *California Marital Dissolution Practice* Vol. 1, Jon A. Rantzman and Paul I. Peyret, eds. (Berkeley, Calif.: California Continuing Education of the Bar, 1981), pp. 188–189 (hereafter cited as Lichtig, "Property").

4. There are two exceptions to the equal division rule. The first allows an unequal division of property if the parties agree to it (either in a written agreement or by oral stipulation in court). *California Civil Code,* Section 4800(a) (West Supp. 1985). The second exception permits the court to award all of the property to one person if (a) the total value of the community property is less than $5,000 and (b) one party "cannot be located through the exercise of reasonable diligence." *California Civil Code,* Section 4800(b)(3) (West 1983).

5. Data on property (and other financial issues) were recorded from the petition, response, motions, temporary orders, and the interlocutory decree of divorce. (The final decree of divorce is pro forma.) The interlocutory decree, which sets out the court orders for property, support, and custody, typically had the most complete information and is the most common source of the data reported below. In the event of a discrepancy between the claims of the two spouses, we relied on the courts' listing of the community assets in the interlocutory decree. (If, however, property was "divided equally by private agreement" and not listed on the interlocutory, we relied on the listing of property in the petition and/or response.)

6. Among couples with substantial assets, one also finds confirmation of separate property assets in the interlocutory decree.

7. Because a divorce court may divide only community property, determining what is community property is the pivotal issue in many propertied divorces. That is why most property disputes in California are disagreements about whether an asset is separate or community property. The determining factors include the time and method by which the property was acquired, the source of funds used for acquisition, presumptions created by the form of title and evidence sufficient to rebut them, and the effect of agreements regarding ownership. Lichtig, "Property," pp. 187–188.

8. For purposes of this discussion, it is reasonable to generalize from our Los Angeles samples to the population of divorcing couples in the state of California. For a more detailed comparison of the characteristics of our sample and the statewide population, see Ruth B. Dixon and Lenore J. Weitzman, "Evaluating the Impact of No-Fault Divorce in California," *Family Relations* Vol. 29, no. 3, July 1980, pp. 297–307. Unfortunately, Karen Seal does not report any data on the amount of property owned by the divorcing couples she studied in San Diego County. However, her data on the division of property, discussed in Chapter 4, parallel those of this research and indicate that our data on property ownership are likely to hold true throughout the state. Karen Seal "A Decade of No-Fault Divorce" *Family Advocate* Vol. 1, No. 1, 1979, pp. 10, 11, 14, 15.

9. Divorcing couples have, on the average, a lower net worth than married couples in the United States. A 1984 study by the Federal Reserve Board calculated the typical family's net worth as $20,752 in 1977.

10. There are no data on the *amount of property* owned by couples divorcing in Pennsylvania in 1977 reported by Graham Spanier and Linda Thompson, *Parting: The Aftermath of Separation and Divorce* (Beverly Hills, Calif.: Sage Publications, 1984); or in Gay Kitson and Marvin Sussman's analysis

of divorce in Ohio in "Marital Complaints, Demographic Characteristics and Symptoms of Mental Distress in Divorce," *Journal of Marriage and the Family* Vol. 44, 1982, pp. 87–101; or in Robert Weiss's research in Massachusetts reported in *Marital Separation* (New York: Basic Books, 1975); or in David Chambers' analysis of Michigan divorces in *Making Fathers Pay* (Chicago: University of Chicago Press, 1979); or in Judith Cassetty's *Child Support and Public Policy* (Lexington, Mass.: D.C. Heath and Company, 1978). Cassetty observes that the proportion of divorced women "who are awarded property of any consequential size at the time of marital dissolution is probably quite small overall" and she calls for further research on the relationship between property settlements and child support (p. 83).

11. William J. Goode, *After Divorce* (New York: The Free Press, 1956), p. 217.

12. Ibid.

13. Ibid. Goode reported that about one-fifth of the families had property worth less than $1,000, about one-fifth had property between $1,000 and $4,000. Only 18 percent of the families had property worth $4,000 or more.

14. Robert E. McGraw, Gloria J. Sterin, and Joseph M. Davis, "A Case Study in Divorce Law Reform and Its Aftermath," *Journal of Family Law* Vol. 20, no. 3, 1981–82, pp. 443–487 (hereafter cited as McGraw, et al., "Case Study in Cleveland").

15. Ibid. On page 470 they report 37 percent, and on page 483 they report 38 percent.

16. Martha L. Fineman reports that most of the 228 Wisconsin attorneys she surveyed believed that the vast majority of divorce cases were those in which there was little property to divide. (Their median estimates were between $15,000 and $30,000 in 1982–83.) Martha L. Fineman, "Implementing Equality: Ideology, Contradiction and Social Change," *Wisconsin Law Review* Vol. 1983, no. 4, p. 883.

17. As law professor Mary Ann Glendon observed, "One of the problems with the existing law is that it contemplates the special case in which there is sufficient marital property to divide (to provide both spouses with a home, etc.) rather than the typical case in which there are minor children and *not enough property* to divide." Mary Ann Glendon, "Property Rights Upon Dissolution of Marriages and Informal Unions," in *The Cambridge Lectures 1981,* Nancy E. Eastham and Boris Krivy, eds. (London: Butterworths, 1982), p. 254 (hereafter cited as Glendon, "Property Rights").

18. The results are also similar to the English data reported by J. Todd and L. Jones, *Matrimonial Property* (London: Her Majesty's Printing Office, 1972), p. 9; and the Scottish data reported in A. J. Manners and I. Rauta, *Family Property in Scotland* (Edinburgh: Her Majesty's Stationery Office, 1981).

19. U.S. Bureau of the Census, "Child Support and Alimony: 1978," *Current Population Reports* Series P–23, No. 112, 1981, p. 1.

20. Ibid., p. 11, Table F.

21. Ibid.

22. The Census Bureau reports that it decided to omit the question on the value of property awards from its 1981 survey because of these difficulties. U.S. Bureau of the Census, "Child Support and Alimony, 1981," *Current Population Reports* Series P-23, No. 124, 1983, p. 5.

23. These values were obtained in the in-depth interviews. Most of the respondents relied on either the court's valuation of the asset or the value agreed upon in negotiations.

24. Glendon, "Property Rights," pp. 249–253.

25. *In re Marriage of Brown*, 15 Cal. 3d 838, 126 Cal. Rptr 633 544 P.2d 561 (1976).

26. McGraw et al. found a similar increase in home ownership reported in divorce records in Cleveland, Ohio, from 21 percent in 1965, to 37 percent in 1978. They suggest that this indicates a shift in the characteristics of divorcing couples to a higher level of rootedness in the community. McGraw et al., "Case Study in Cleveland," p. 470.

CHAPTER 4—DIVIDING THE PROPERTY

1. *California Civil Code,* Section 4800 (West 1983). The definition of community property examined in Chapter 3 was basically left unaltered by the no-fault reforms. A 1971 amendment made either spouse's *after separation* earnings and accumulations his or her separate property (*California Civil Code,* Section 5118 [West 1983]). Under the old law, the wife's after separation earnings were separate property, but the husband's continued as community property until a legal separation or dissolution was obtained. H. Freeman, W. Hogoboom, W. MacFaden, L. Olsen & R. Li, *Attorney's Guide to Family Law Act and Practice* (Berkeley, Calif.: Continuing Education of the Bar, 1972), pp. 246–47 (hereafter cited as Freeman et. al., *Attorney's Guide,* 1972).

2. *California Civil Code,* Sections 4800(a) and (b) (West Supp. 1985). Community debts may be divided unequally if there are no assets to divide or if, after the equal division of the community assets, there remain community obligations to be disposed of. See *In re Marriage of Eastis,* 47 Cal. App. 3d 459, 120 Cal. Rptr. 861 (1975).

3. Herma Hill Kay, "Background Paper on the Legislative History in California," unpublished manuscript written for the California Divorce Law Research Project, September 1977, quoting an unpublished paper by Dr. Don Jackson, a member of the Governor's Commission.

4. Ibid., p. 56.

5. Ibid., p. 77.

6. Ibid., p. 77–78.

7. Ibid., p. 78.

8. Exhibit A, Revision No. 51 in the Report of the Committee on Family Law and the Family Court Act (of the California State Bar Association) submitted

to the Senate Judiciary Committee, January 1969. Quoted in Howard A. Krom, "California's Divorce Law Reform: An Historical Analysis," *Pacific Law Journal* Vol. 1, no. 1, January 1970, pp. 156–181, 174.

9. Ibid., pp. 174, 176.

10. See generally, Herma Hill Kay, "Review of Max Rheinstein, *Marriage, Stability, Divorce and the Law,*" *California Law Review* Vol. 60, 1972; Kay, "A Family Court: The California Proposal," in *Divorce and After,* Paul Bohannon, ed. (Garden City, N.Y.: 1967), p. 215; R. Levy, *Uniform Marriage and Divorce Legislation: A Preliminary Analysis* (Chicago: National Conference of Commissioners on Uniform State Laws, 1968), pp. 168–169.

11. Doris Jonas Freed and Henry H. Foster, "Divorce in the Fifty States: An Overview," *Family Law Quarterly* Vol. 14, no. 4, Winter 1981, p. 230 (hereafter cited as Freed and Foster, "Divorce 1981"); and Martha L. Fineman, "Implementing Equality: Ideology, Contradiction and Social Change," *Wisconsin Law Review* Vol. 1983, no. 4, 1983, pp. 801–802 (hereafter cited as Fineman, "Implementing Equality").

12. As Wisconsin State Senator Katie Morrison explained the need for the 50/50 presumption, "What happens now . . . is that some courts wish to begin with the assumption that the homemaker gets one-third, and the husband two-thirds. Austin, "Divorce Reform Bill Described," *Milwaukee Sentinel,* Jan. 31, 1977, p. 6.

13. Freed and Foster, "Divorce 1981," p. 230.

14. Ibid. This is also Fineman's assertion in "Implementing Equality."

15. Mary Ann Glendon, "Property Rights Upon Dissolution of Marriages and Informal Unions," in *The Cambridge Lectures, 1981,* Nancy E. Eastham and Boris Krivy, eds. (London: Butterworths, 1982) (hereafter cited as Glendon, "Property Rights"). Glendon quotes a *New York Times* article that found the main effect one year after New York's "equitable distribution" law was adopted was that the cost of divorce had risen 20 to 50 percent because of increased lawyers' fees. Castillo, "Changed Divorce Laws in New York Brings in Higher Fees to Lawyers," *New York Times,* Feb. 2, 1981, p. 1, col. 1.) Two years later, in 1983, attorney Emily June Goodman found lawyers' fees still soaring under New York's equitable distribution law. Emily June Goodman, "With Equitable Distribution Divorce Lawyers' Fees Soar," *New York Times,* Jan. 13, 1983, p. 17, cols. 1–2.

16. Karen Seal, "A Decade of No-Fault Divorce," *Family Advocate* Vol. 1, no. 1, 1977, pp. 10, 11, 14, 15 (hereafter cited as Seal, "No-Fault Divorce").

17. Ibid., p. 11.

18. Ibid.

19. This is why most of the data reported in this book rely on the interviews with divorced men and women, which provide detailed and complete information on all aspects of the financial settlement.

20. Seal, "No-Fault Divorce," p. 12.

21. Ibid., p. 12.

22. Ibid., p. 12.

23. Tax Reform Act of 1984, H.R. 4170, Public Law No. 98–369.

24. Annuities, life insurance, and transfers in trust are also covered by the act. The recipient takes the donor spouse's basis for the purpose of computing capital gains or losses in the future.

25. See, e.g., *In re Marriage of Emmett,* 109 Cal. App. 3d 753, 760–61, 169 Cal. Rptr. 473, 477–78 (1980); *In re Marriage of Marx,* 97 Cal. App. 3d 552, 560, 159 Cal. Rptr. 215, 220 (1979).

26. Cal. Assembly Comm. on the Judiciary, Report on Assembly Bill No. 530 and Senate Bill No. 252 (The Family Act), 1 Assembly J. 785, 787 (Reg. Sess. 1970).

27. Seal, "No-Fault Divorce," p. 14.

28. Frances Leonard, "The Disillusionment of Divorce for Older Women," *Gray Paper* No. 6 (Washington, D.C.: Older Women's League, 1980), p. 9.

29. Ibid.

30. *In re Marriage of Boseman,* 31, Cal. App. 3d 372, 375, 107 Cal. Rptr. 232, 234 (1973). The appellate court remanded for clarification of the proceeds of the house sale but upheld the temporary award of the residence to the wife. *In re Marriage of Boseman,* 31 Cal. App. 3d at 378, 107 Cal. Rptr. at 237.

31. *In re Marriage of Herrmann,* 84 Cal. App. 3d 361, 148 Cal. Rptr. 550 (1978).

32. *In re Marriage of Duke,* 101 Cal. App. 3d 152 at 155–56, 161 Cal. Rptr. 444 at 446 (italics omitted) modified 102 Cal. App. 3d 619d (1980).

33. California Civil Code § 4800.7(a)–(c) (added by stats. 1984, c. 463, p. —, § 1).

34. This summary is based on Stephen Cretney's excellent discussion of the policy aims, content, and results of the English law in *Principles of Family Law* (London: Sweet & Maxwell, 1979), pp. 85–169 (hereafter cited as Cretney, *Family Law*). I was also aided by John Eekelaar's perceptive analysis of the issues in *Family Law and Public Policy* 2nd edition (London: Weidenfeld & Nicolson, 1984) (hereafter cited as Eekelaar, *Family Law*).

35. In 1977, 26 percent of the divorce petitions in England alleged adultery and 37 percent alleged unreasonable behavior. Together, these fault-based grounds accounted for close to two-thirds of the divorces. Cretney, *Family Law,* p. 166.

36. In theory, the court may deny this divorce if it will cause grave financial hardship to a dependent spouse.

37. There is also a ban on divorce within the first three years of marriage, which the 1980 Law Commission recommended be abolished.

38. Cretney, *Family Law,* p. 219.

39. The Matrimonial Proceedings and Property Act of 1970 has been incorporated into Part II of the Matrimonial Causes Act of 1973.

40. A nationwide English study reported that about half of the couples either owned or were purchasing the matrimonial home. W. Barrington Baker, John Eekelaar, Colin Gibson, Susan Raikes, *The Matrimonial Jurisdiction of Registrars* (Oxford, England: Centre for Socio-Legal Studies, 1977), p. 36. Similarly, in California, 48 percent of the 1978 divorcing couples owned or were purchasing a family home (see Table 5, Chapter 3).

41. I am indebted to Professor Mary Ann Glendon for suggesting this label for the principle the English experts were using. Personal conversation, March 1984. See also, Glendon, "Property Rights."

42. John Eekelaar, "Some Principles of Financial and Property Adjustment on Divorce," *Law Quarterly Review* Vol. 95, 1979, pp. 253–254.

43. Ibid. See also Eekelaar *Family Law* pp. 76–80, 113, 134–137.

44. The Law Commission, *The Financial Consequences of Divorce: The Basic Policy,* Law Commission No. 103 (London: Her Majesty's Stationery Office, 1980), pp. 3–4.

45. As Mary Ann Glendon states it: "One way or another, the household goods and matrimonial home, or its use for a period of time, usually will and should be awarded to the custodial spouse." Glendon, "Property Rights," p. 255.

46. Interview with Joanne Schulman, staff attorney, National Center on Women and Family Law, January 8, 1985.

47. Ibid.

48. Andree Brooks, "Changing Laws in Property," *New York Times,* Aug. 12, 1984, Section 8, p. 12.

49. This was suggested by Dr. Harry Woolf, Institute for Advanced Study, Princeton, New Jersey, January 1984.

50. In either case, the California husband would receive a note for his half of the equity in the house at the time of the divorce. The note would be paid off with interest, upon sale of the house. If the home increased in value while the wife was living in (and maintaining) it, the increment belonged to her.

51. These 1977–1978 statistics predated *McCarty v. McCarty,* 101 S.Ct. 2728 (1981) and *Hisquierdo v. Hisquierdo,* 439 U.S. 572 (1979), holding that federal pensions for military and railroad employees may not be divided as community property upon divorce. These cases were later overturned by federal legislation discussed in Chapter 5.

52. Seal, "No-Fault Divorce," p. 12.

53. Ibid.

54. Gerald E. Lichtig, "Valuation and Division of Property," in *California Marital Dissolution Practice* Vol. 1, Jon A. Rantzman and Paul I. Peyret, eds. (Berkeley, Calif.: Continuing Education of the Bar, 1981), pp. 232–234.

55. *In re Marriage of Eastis,* 47 Cal. App. 3d 459, 120 Cal. Rptr. 861 (1975).

56. *California Civil Code,* Section 4800(b)(4) (West Supp. 1985).

57. Glendon, "Property Rights", p. 254.

58. Jessica Pincus, "How Equitable is New York's Equitable Distribution Law?" *Columbia Human Rights Law Review* Vol. 14, no. 2, 1982–83, pp. 439 and 459, notes 37 and 158.

59. New Jersey Supreme Court Task Force on Women in the Courts, "Summary Report" (Parsippany, N.J.: New Jersey Judicial College, 1983), p. 8.

60. Ibid.

61. Harriet N. Cohen and Adria S. Hillman, "Analysis of Seventy Select Deci-

sions After Trial Under New York State's Equitable Distribution Law, from January 1981 through October 1984, November 1, 1984." Unpublished ms., p. 5.

62. Ibid., pp. 4–5.

63. Ibid., pp. 6–7.

64. Ibid., pp. 10–11.

65. Lester Wallman, television editorial, WNBC-TV, New York City, November 14, 1982, cited in testimony of attorney Judith Avner, N.O.W. Legal Defense and Education Fund, before the Uniform Law Commissioners, February 18, 1983, Washington, D.C.

66. Avner, ibid., p. 7.

67. This is Fineman's assertion in "Implementing Equality." She cites appellate cases in Wisconsin before the 1977 equal division rule was adopted. However, to assert that judges have the power to award more property to housewives does not mean that is what most trial court judges have actually done. In fact, those who initiated the Wisconsin equal division rule judged the situation differently and asserted that women were often awarded no more than a third of the marital assets. Neither position was supported by empirical data.

68. Henry H. Foster and Doris J. Freed, "Commentary on Equitable Distribution," *New York Law School Law Review* Vol. 26, no. 1, 1981, pp. 47–48.

69. "Marital Dissolution: The Economic Impact on Connecticut Men and Women: Report of the PCSW Family Law Task Force, State of Connecticut," November 1979.

70. Ibid., p. 3.

71. Ibid., p. 16.

CHAPTER 5—THE NEW PROPERTY

1. This concept was first introduced in Lenore J. Weitzman, "Legal Regulation of Marriage: Tradition and Change," *California Law Review* Vol. 62, 1974, p. 1169. See also Weitzman, *The Marriage Contract: Spouses, Lovers and the Law* (New York: Free Press, 1981), pp. 89–97.

2. Hannah Papaneck, "Men, Women, and Work: Reflections on the Two-Person Career," *American Journal of Sociology* Vol. 78, 1973, p. 852.

3. See Susan Prager, "Sharing Principles and the Future of Marital Property Law," *UCLA Law Review* Vol. 25, no. 1, 1977, pp. 6–11. Of necessity, if the assets built in two spouses' careers are comparable, there may not be any need for reapportionment of career assets upon divorce.

4. Barbara Strudler Wallston, Martha A. Foster, and Michael Berger, "I Will Follow Him: Myth, Reality or Forced Choice—Job Seeking Experiences of Dual Career Couples," in *Dual Career Couples,* Jeff Bryson and Rebecca Bryson, eds. (New York: Human Sciences Press, 1978). See also Lynda Holmstrom, *The Two-Career Family* (Cambridge, Mass: Schenkmann, 1972), pp. 30–32.

5. Doris Jonas Freed and Timothy B. Walker, "Family Law in the Fifty States: An Overview," *Family Law Quarterly* Vol. 18, no. 4, Winter 1985, pp. 424–426 (hereafter cited as Freed and Walker, "Family Law 1985").

6. *Janssen v. Janssen,* 331 N.W.2d 752 (Minn. Sup. Ct. 1983).

7. Saul Ross, "Pension, Retirement and Disability Benefits," in *California Marital Dissolution Practice,* Jon A. Rantzman and Paul I. Peyret, eds. (Berkeley, Calif.: Continuing Education of the Bar, 1981), pp. 286–287 (hereafter cited as Ross, "Pension Benefits").

8. *In re Marriage of Brown,* 15 Cal. 3d 838, 841, 842, 544 P.2d 561, 126 Cal. Rptr. 633 (1976).

9. *In re Marriage of Brown* 15 Cal. 3d 838, 841, 842, 544 P.2d 561, 562, 126 Cal. Rptr. 633, 634.

10. *In re Marriage of Brown,* 15 Cal. 3d 838, 847, 544 P.2d 561, 566, 126 Cal. Rptr. 633, 638 (referring to *California Civil Code,* Section 4800).

11. Freed and Walker, "Family Law 1985," p. 424.

12. *King v. King,* 9 *Family Law Reporter* 2273 (Pa. Ct. C. P. 1983).

13. *Carpenter v. Carpenter,* 657 P.2d 646 (Okla. 1983).

14. Retirement Equity Act of 1984, Public Law 98–397, enacted August 23, 1984.

15. The act specifies what is a qualified domestic relations order, and requires that specific information be included in the order to qualify. Attorneys drafting such orders are urged to "fully review the provisions of the law" to insure that the order qualifies. Freed and Walker, "Family Law 1985," p. 373.

16. Freed and Walker, "Family Law 1985," p. 373.

17. *Smith v. Lewis,* 13 Cal. 3d 349, 118 Cal. Rptr. 621 (1975).

18. Ibid.

19. *McCarty v. McCarty,* 453 U.S. 210 (1981).

20. Ibid.

21. *Hisquierdo v. Hisquierdo,* 439 U.S. 572, 99 S.Ct. 802, 59 L.Ed. 2d 1 (1979).

22. *McCarty v. McCarty,* 453 U.S. 210, 69 L.Ed. 2d 589 (1981).

23. August 15, 1982 letter from Doris Mozley, Chesapeake, Va., to author with copy of letter sent to 20,000 military wives dated May, 1982.

24. Ibid.

25. See, e.g., "Ex-Military Wives Fight Benefit Loss," *The Ledger Star,* Aug. 2, 1982; "Military Wives, Ex-Wives Picket to Protest Treatment on Pensions," *Virginia-Pilot,* Aug. 3, 1982; and D. N. Mozley "The Other Side of the Ex-Spouse Coin," *Navy Times,* July 12, 1982, p. 21.

26. This case is summarized from Kristi Turnquist, "Military Injustice: Ex-Wives Are Casualties—Divorce is a Raw Deal for Wives of Servicemen," *Willamette Week,* Jan. 18, 1983, pp. 1, 9, 17, 22.

27. Pub. L. 97–252, Title 10, 10 U.S.C. Section 1408(d)(1).

28. 10 U.S.C. Section 1408(e)(1).

29. 22 U.S.C.A. Section 4606(b) (West Supp., 1981).

30. *Your Pension Rights at Divorce: What Women Need to Know* (Washington, D.C.: Women's Legal Defense Fund, 1983), p. 10 (hereafter cited as *Your Pension Rights*).

31. Ibid., p. 10.

32. Pub. L. 95–366 Section 1(a), 92 Stat. 600, 5 U.S.C. Section 8345(j)(1) (1976 ed., Supp.III).

33. A 1983 District of Columbia case held that the Civil Service Reform Act permitted, but did not require, states to treat these pensions as marital or community property. *Barbour v. Barbour,* 464 A.2d 915 (D.C. App. 1983).

34. Robert Peer, "Study Challenges Pension Proposal: Effect Upon Women of Social Security Formula Disputed," *New York Times,* Dec. 30, 1984, pp. 1, 11.

35. Ibid.

36. Ibid. For example, if the husband had average annual earnings of $18,000, he and his wife would receive $951 in monthly benefits on retirement. If the wife earned an additional $6,300 a year, their total monthly benefits would be only $5 more a month ($956 a month).

37. Ibid.

38. Ibid.

39. Sylvia Porter, "New Older Women's League Helps That Invisible Group," syndicated column, Oct. 13, 1980 (hereafter cited as Porter, "New Older Women's League").

40. Ibid. Porter notes that only 2 percent of widows receive their husband's pension checks.

41. Frances Leonard, "Older Women and Pensions: Catch 22," *Gray Paper* No. 1, Tish Sommers and Laurie Shields, eds. (Washington, D.C.: Older Women's League, 1980), p. 8 (hereafter cited as Leonard, "Pensions"); citing Fact Sheet issued by Congresswoman Pat Schroeder's office, 1979.

42. Leonard, "Pensions," pp. 8–9. As Sylvia Porter explains, "If the husband turns down the survivor's option, rarely is the wife notified that she'll get no pension in case of his death; the news comes as an ugly shock" (Porter, "New Older Women's League").

43. Retirement Equity Act of 1984, Public Law 98–397, enacted August 23, 1984.

44. Ibid.

45. Porter, "New Older Women's League."

46. Leonard, "Pensions."

47. Ross, "Pension Benefits," p. 293.

48. *Your Pension Rights,* p. 4.

49. See generally, Projector, "Putting a Value on a Pension Plan," *Family Advocate,* Summer, 1979, Vol. 2, no. 1, pp. 37, 41.

50. *In re Marriage of Brown,* 15 Cal. 3d at 848, 544 P.2d at 567, 126 Cal. Rptr. at 639 (1976).

51. Ibid.

454

NOTES

52. Arthur H. Gold, "Small Business and Professional Practices," in *California Marital Dissolution Practice*, Jon A. Rantzman and Paul I. Peyret, eds. (Berkeley, Calif.: Continuing Education of the Bar, 1981), p. 312 (hereafter cited as Gold, "Small Business").

53. *Koelsch v. Koelsch*, __ Ariz. __, __ P.2d __ (Ct. of App. Feb., 1984).

54. *In re Marriage of Brown*, 15 Cal 3d at 848, 544 P.2d at 567, 126 Cal. Rptr. at 639 (1976).

55. Gold, "Small Business."

56. *Mueller v. Mueller*, 144 Cal. App. 2d 245, 301 P.2d 90 (1956).

57. *In re Marriage of Slater*, 100 Cal. App. 3d 241, 160 Cal. Rptr. 686 (1979); *In re Marriage of Barnert*, 85 Cal. App. 3d 413, 149 Cal. Rptr. 616 (1978); *In re Marriage of Foster*, 42 Cal. App. 3d 577, 117 Cal. Rptr. 49 (1974); *In re Marriage of Fortier*, 34 Cal. App. 3d 384, 109 Cal. Rptr. 915 (1973); *Golden v. Golden*, 270 Cal. App. 2d 401, 75 Cal. Rptr. 735 (1969).

58. *In re Marriage of Lopez*, 38 Cal. App. 3d 93, 113 Cal. Rptr. 58. (1974); *Todd v. Todd*, 272 Cal. App. 2d 786, 78 Cal. Rptr. 131 (1969).

59. *In re Marriage of Webb*, 94 Cal. App. 3d 335, 156 Cal. Rptr. 334 (1979).

60. *In re Marriage of Winn*, 98 Cal. App. 3d 363, 159 Cal. Rptr. 554 (1979).

61. See generally, Kennedy and Thomas, "Putting a Value on Education and Professional Goodwill," *Family Advocate* Vol. 2, no. 1, Summer 1979, p. 3.

62. *In re Marriage of Foster*, 42 Cal. App. 3d 577, 584, 117 Cal. Rep. 49, 54 (1974).

63. In *Fortier*, the value of the goodwill was held to be the market value at which the goodwill could be sold at the time of the dissolution of the marriage. *In re Marriage of Fortier*, 34 Cal. App. 3d at 388, 109 Cal. Rptr. at 918 (1973).

64. The *Lopez* court listed the practitioner's age, health, past demonstrated earning power, professional reputation in the community (as to his judgment, skill, and knowledge), comparative professional success, and the nature and duration of his business as a sole practitioner or as a member of a partnership or professional corporation to which his professional efforts have made a proprietary contribution *In re Marriage of Lopez*, 38 Cal. App. 3d at 109, 110, 113 Cal. Rptr. at 68 (1974). To these considerations, the *Foster* court added "the situation of the business premises, the amount of patronage, the personality of the parties engaged in the business, the length of time the business has been established, and the habit of its customers in continuing to patronize the business" *In re Marriage of Foster*, 42 Cal. App. 3d at 583, 117 Cal. Rptr. at 53 (1974).

65. *Inman v. Inman*, 578 S.W.2d 266, (Ky. Ct. App. 1979).

66. Ibid.

67. *Lynn v. Lynn*, 49 U.S.L.W. 2402 (N.J. Super. Ct. Dec. 30, 1980).

68. Freed and Walker, "Family Law 1985," p. 441.

69. Ibid.

70. *Reen v. Reen*, 8 *Family Law Reporter* 2193 (Mass. P. and Fam. Ct., Hampden Div., Dec. 23, 1981).

71. *Woodworth v. Woodworth,* 337 N.W.2d 332 (Mich. App. 1983).

72. *Moss v. Moss,* 80 Mich. App. 693, 264 N.W.2d 97 (1978).

73. *Woodworth v. Woodworth,* 337 N.W.2d 332 (Mich. App. 1983).

74. Ibid.

75. *In re Neuhaus,* 9 *Family Law Reporter* 2168 (Wash. Sup. Ct., Pierce Cty, Nov. 29, 1982).

76. Ibid.

77. *Gillette v. Gillette,* 677 P.2d 152 (Wash. Sup. Ct. 1984).

78. *In re Marriage of Goldstein,* 423 N.E.2d 1201 (Ill. App. 1981).

79. *Wilcox v. Wilcox,* 365 N.E.2d 792 (Ind. App. 1977); *In re Marriage of MacNamara* 339 N.E.2d 371 (Ind. App. 1980).

80. *Reuben v. Reuben,* 461 A.2d 733 (N.H. 1983).

81. *Frausto v. Frausto,* 611 S.W.2d 656 (Tex. Civ. App. 1981).

82. Doris Jonas Freed and Henry H. Foster, "Family Law in the Fifty States: An Overview," *Family Law Quarterly* Vol. 17, no. 4, 1984, pp. 365–447.

83. Ibid.

84. *In re Sullivan,* 134 Cal. App. 3d 634, 184 Cal. Rptr. 796 (1982).

85. Ibid.

86. *In re Sullivan,* 134 Cal. App. 3d 634, 184 Cal. Rptr. 796, 798 (1982).

87. *In re Sullivan,* 134 Cal. App. 3d 634, 184 Cal. Rptr. 796, 815 (1982). (Concurring opinion.)

88. *In re Sullivan,* 134 Cal. App. 3d 634, 184 Cal. Rptr. 796, 800 (1982).

89. *California Civil Code,* Sections 4800.3(b)(1) and (c), (c)(1), (c)(2), (c)(3) effective Jan. 1, 1985 (West Supp. 1985, added by Stats 1984, C. 1661, Section 2).

90. *California Civil Code,* Section 4801(a)(1) (West Supp. 1985).

91. *Daniels v. Daniels,* 20 Ohio App. 2d 458, 185 N.E.2d 733 (1961).

92. *Lira v. Lira,* 68 Ohio App. 2d 164, 428 N.E.2d 445 (1980).

93. *Adair v. Adair,* 670 P.2d 1002 (Okla. App. Div. 1983).

94. *Mahoney v. Mahoney,* 91 N.J. 488, 453 A.2d 527 (1982).

95. Ibid. citations omitted, emphasis added.

96. Freed and Walker "Family Law 1985," p. 411.

97. Joan Krauskopf, "Recompense for Financing Spouse's Education: Legal Protection of the Marital Investor in Human Capital," *Kansas Law Review* Vol. 28, 1980, p. 379 (hereafter cited as Krauskopf, "Spouse's Education").

98. Ibid. Gary Becker, *A Treatise on the Family* (Cambridge, Mass.: Harvard University Press, 1981); Gary Becker, *Human Capital: A Theoretical and Empirical Analysis, with Special Reference to Education* 2nd ed. (New York: Columbia University Press, 1975); *Investment in Human Capital,* B. F. Kiker, ed. (Columbia, South Carolina: Univ. of South Carolina Press, 1971).

99. *In re Marriage of Lundberg,* 107 Wis. 2d 1, 318 N.W.2d 918 (1982).

100. Krauskopf, "Spouse's Education," pp. 382–383.

101. *In re Marriage of Lundberg* 107 Wis. 2d 1, 318 N.W.2d 918 (1982).

102. *In re Marriage of Lundberg,* 107 Wis. 2d 1, 318 N.W.2d 918, 924 (1982).

103. *In re Marriage of Lundberg,* 107 Wis. 2d 1, 318 N.W.2d 918, 920 (1982).

104. *Morgan v. Morgan,* 81 Misc. 2d 616, 366 N.Y.S.2d 977 (Sup. Ct. 1975), *modified,* 52 A.D.2d 804, 383 N.Y.S.2d 343 (1976).

105. *Morgan v. Morgan,* 81 Misc. 2d 616, 360 N.Y.S.2d 977 (Sup. Ct. 1975).

106. *Morgan v. Morgan,* 81 Misc. 2d 616, 366 N.Y.S.2d 977 (Sup. Ct. 1975).

107. Ibid.

108. *Morgan v. Morgan,* 52 A.D. 2d 804, 383 N.Y.S.2d 343 (1976).

109. Charles Reich, "Individual Rights and Social Welfare: The Emerging Legal Issues," *Yale Law Journal* Vol. 74, 1964–65, pp. 1245–1257.

110. Judy Klemesrud, "New Focus on Concerns of Older Women," *New York Times,* Oct. 13, 1980, p. 15, Col. 1 (hereafter cited as Klemesrud, "Older Women").

111. Frances Leonard, "Access to Health Insurance for Mid-life Women: An Overview," memo, Older Women's League, January 1984, p. 1.

112. Klemesrud, "Older Women."

113. Interview with Frances Leonard, Legal Counsel, Older Women's League, January 1985 hereafter cited as Leonard interview, 1985.

114. August 15, 1982, letter from Doris Mozley, founder of EXPOSE (discussed on pp. 116–117).

115. Caryle Murphy, "Divorced Military Wives Seek Benefit Reforms," *Washington Post,* Oct. 22, 1984, pp. A1, A6, A7.

116. Ibid.

117. Frances Leonard interview, January 1985.

118. Kathy Bernard, "Her Day in Court: Divorcee Takes 'Benefits' Fight to High Court," *Lewiston Morning Tribune,* Oct. 11, 1984, pp. 1, 9A.

119. Marilyn Chase, "Single Trouble: The No-Fault Divorce Has a Fault of Its Own, Many Women Learn," *Wall Street Journal,* Jan. 21, 1985, p. 1, col. 1 and p. 12, cols. 1–4.

120. This account is summarized from Chase's article, ibid., p. 12.

121. Freed and Walker, "Family Law 1985," p. 426.

122. Ibid., pp. 426–427.

123. See, e.g., *Argonaut Ins. Co. v. Industrial Accident Comm.,* 57 Cal. 2d 589, 371 P.2d 281, 21 Cal. Rptr. 545 (1962); *Thrifty Drug Stores, Inc. v. Workers Comp Appeals Bd.,* 95 Cal. App. 3d 937, 157 Cal. Rptr. 459 (1979).

124. See, e.g., *Kircher v. Atchison, T., & S.F. Ry.,* 32 Cal. 2d 176, 195 P.2d 427 (1948); *Groat v. Walkup Drayage and Warehouse Co.,* 14 Cal. App. 2d 350, 58 P.2d 200 (1936).

125. See., e.g., *Gall v. Union Ice Co.,* 108 Cal. App. 2d 303, 239 P.2d 48 (1951).

126. *Rodriguez v. McDonnell Douglas,* 87 Cal. App. 3d 626, 151 Cal. Rptr. 399 (1978).

127. *Rodriguez v. McDonnell Douglas,* 87 Cal. App. 3d 626, 656, 151 Cal. Rptr.

399, 416, quoting J. Stein, *Damages and Recovery—Personal Injury and Death Actions,* Section 58 (1972), p. 94.

128. *Jeffares v. Workmen's Comp. Appeals Bd.,* 6 Cal. App. 3d 548, 552–53, 86 Cal. Rptr. 288, 290–91 (1970) (citation omitted).

CHAPTER 6—REDEFINING ALIMONY

1. An earlier version of this chapter was co-authored by Ruth Dixon and published as Lenore J. Weitzman and Ruth B. Dixon, "The Alimony Myth: Does No-Fault Divorce Make a Difference?" *Family Law Quarterly* Vol. 14, no. 3, Fall 1980, pp. 141–185.

2. Norman N. Lobsenz, "Are Divorce and Alimony Unfair to Men?" *Reader's Digest* Vol. 75, Oct. 1959, p. 194 (condensed from *Redbook,* Jan. 1959) (hereafter cited as Lobsenz, "Are Divorce and Alimony Unfair?").

3. See, for example, Maurice R. Franks, *A Lawyer Reveals: How to Avoid Alimony* (New York: Dutton, 1975); Max Gunther, "Fraternity of Crippled Men," *New York Times Magazine,* Sept. 19, 1965; Samuel H. Hofstadter, "Do Our Alimony Laws Need Reforming?" *Good Housekeeping* Vol. 165, 1967, p. 24; and Lobsenz, "Are Divorce and Alimony Unfair?"

4. In explaining why she voted against the Equal Rights Amendment, a middle-aged housewife explains that it was the alimony issue:

> The way I see it, alimony has a very important deterrent value—it keeps families together. . . . take us for example—Morris and I don't have the greatest marriage in the world. We're not proud of the fact, but we live with it. And one of the reasons we live with it is *alimony!* If Morris didn't have that threat hanging over him, he'd probably walk right out of here, without leaving me a red cent!

Garry Trudeau, "Doonesbury," *San Francisco Chronicle,* January 18, 1976.

5. Samuel H. Hofstadter and Shirley R. Levittan, "Alimony—A Reformulation," *Journal of Family Law* Vol. 7, 1967, p. 55.

6. Dr. Karen Seal reports that 66 percent of the divorced women in San Diego County were awarded alimony in 1968, but these figures include nominal awards of $1 a year (which are largely symbolic). Karen Seal, "A Decade of No-Fault Divorce," *Family Advocate* Vol. 1, no. 4, 1979, p. 12 (hereafter cited as Seal, "No-Fault Divorce").

7. National Commission on the Observance of International Women's Year, ". . . *To Form a More Perfect Union* . . . ," *Justice for American Women* (Washington, D.C.: U.S. Government Printing Office, 1976), p. 229. This is also the statistic reported in the 1978 Census Bureau survey discussed in note 39 below.

8. Max Rheinstein, *Marriage Stability, Divorce and the Law* (Chicago: University of Chicago Press, 1972), p. 23 (hereafter cited as Rheinstein, *Marriage, Divorce and the Law*); Chester G. Vernier and John B. Hurlbut, "The Historical Background of Alimony Law and its Present Statutory Structure," *Law*

and Contemporary Problems Vol. 6, 1939, pp. 197–212; Morris Ploscowe, "Alimony," *The Annals* Vol. 22, May 1969, p. 383.

9. Homer Clark, *Domestic Relations* (St. Paul, Minn.: West Publishing Co., 1968), p. 420 (hereafter cited as Clark, *Domestic Relations*).

10. The courts continued to apply these norms for permanent awards. For example, in *Edwards v. Edwards* a man who had paid alimony for eighteen years after his marriage of fifteen years ended in divorce went back to court to have his alimony payments terminated. The court refused, saying time alone was not sufficient justification for modification if there had been no change in circumstances. *Edwards v. Edwards,* 52 Cal. App. 3d 12, 124 Cal. Rptr. 742 (1975).

11. Rheinstein, *Marriage, Divorce and the Law,* pp. 32–34.

12. John Hogue, "Does No-Fault Divorce Portend No-Fault Alimony?" *University of Pittsburgh Law Review* Vol. 34, Spring 1973, p. 488.

13. For the provisions of the traditional marriage contract, see Chapter 1 in Lenore J. Weitzman, *The Marriage Contract: Spouses, Lovers and the Law* (New York: The Free Press, 1981).

14. Judith Areen, *Family Law: Cases and Materials* (Mineola, New York: The Foundation Press, 1978), p. 635.

15. Ibid., p. 635.

16. *Casper v. Casper,* 510 S.W.2d 253 (Ky 1974).

17. Herma Hill Kay, *Sex-Based Discrimination in Family Law* (St. Paul, Minn.: West Publishing Co., 1974).

18. Clark, *Domestic Relations,* pp. 441, 446.

19. Economist Elizabeth Landes attempts to demonstrate empirically that alimony has served to "compensate the wife for the opportunity costs she incurs by entering and investing in the marriage." Elizabeth M. Landes, "Economic Analysis of Alimony," *The Journal of Legal Studies* Vol. 7, no. 1, January 1978, p. 35.

20. Writing in 1974, Foster and Freed counted fifteen common law jurisdictions that still did not subject separate property to equitable distribution upon divorce. Henry Foster Jr. and Doris Jonas Freed, "Marital Property Reform in New York: Partnership of Co-Equals?" *Family Law Quarterly* Vol. 8, 1974, p. 170.

   By 1980 there were possibly only five common law jurisdictions that barred equitable or equal distribution of marital property upon divorce. Henry Foster Jr., "Equitable Distribution," *New York Law Journal,* July 24, 1980, p. 1, col. 2. However, as we noted in Chapter 4, women in these equitable distribution states were still not *guaranteed* half—or even a third—of what was regarded as "the husband's separate property" as it was divided according to judges' concepts of "justice and equity."

21. Riane Tennenhaus Eisler, *Dissolution: No-Fault Divorce, Marriage and the Future of Women* (New York: McGraw Hill, 1977), pp. 43–44 (hereafter cited as Eisler, *Dissolution*).

22. Ibid., p. 45.

23. Texas is the only state that does not allow alimony at all. Indiana limits alimony to cases of incapacity.

24. *Orr v. Orr,* 440 U.S. 268 (1979).

25. *California Civil Code,* Section 4801(a)(5) (West 1983) (emphasis added).

26. Eisler, *Dissolution,* p. 44.

27. Ibid. [emphasis added].

28. Charles W. Johnson, "The Family Law Act: A Guide to the Practitioner," *Pacific Law Journal* Vol. 1, 1970, pp. 147–155. Howard A. Krom, "California's Divorce Law Reform: An Historical Analysis," *Pacific Law Journal* Vol. 1, 1970, pp. 156–181; Timothy B. Walker, "Disarming the Litigious Man: A Glance at Fault and California's New Divorce Legislation," *Pacific Law Journal* Vol. 1, 1970, pp. 182–222.

29. Stuart A. Brody, "California's Divorce Reform: Its Sociological Implications," *Pacific Law Journal* Vol. 1, 1970, p. 228. Brody notes that "the prior alimony statutes were developed in the 1870's, a time when married women were considered helpless objects to be protected, certainly not as wage earners capable of sustaining themselves financially."

30. Clark, *Domestic Relations,* p. 441.

31. Uniform Marriage and Divorce Act, Section 308. Adopted in 1974. (Section 9A, Uniform Laws Annotated, 1973, p. 96).

32. Note that her contribution may go beyond direct and tangible assistance in his work. For example, economist Lee Benham has shown that a wife's level of education positively and significantly influences her husband's wages. Lee Benham, "Benefits of Women's Education Within Marriage," in *Economics of the Family: Marriage, Children and Human Capital,* T. W. Schultz, ed. (Chicago: University of Chicago Press, 1974), p. 375.

33. In San Francisco County, open-ended alimony awards dropped from 57 to 42 percent in the same period.

34. The mean duration was forty-one months, reflecting the impact of the 13 percent of the awards that were for more than ten years.

35. The nationwide trend toward short term rehabilitative alimony awards is discussed on pp. 45–46 and in Doris Jonas Freed and Timothy B. Walker, "Family Law in the Fifty States: An Overview," *Family Law Quarterly* Vol. 18, no. 4, Winter 1985.

36. This is statistically significant at the 0.05 level, one-tailed test.

37. This difference is statistically significant at the 0.01 level, one-tailed test.

38. Seal, "No-Fault Divorce," p. 12.

39. U.S. Bureau of the Census, "Child Support and Alimony: 1981," *Current Population Reports* Series P–23, no. 124, May 1983, Table A, p. 2, hereafter cited as "Alimony, 1981."

40. Elaine Tyler May, *The Pursuit of Domestic Perfection: Marriage and Divorce in Los Angeles,* 1880–1920. Unpublished Ph.D. dissertation, University of California, Los Angeles, 1975, p. 101 (hereafter cited as May, *Pursuit of Domestic Perfection*).

41. *In re Marriage of Rosan,* 24 Cal. App. 3d 855, 101 Cal. Rptr. 295 (1972).

42. *In re Marriage of Rosan* 24 Cal. App. 3d 855, 101 Cal. Rptr. 295, 302 (1972).

43. *In re Marriage of Rosan,* 24 Cal. App. 3d 855, 101 Cal. Rptr. 295, 303 (1972).

44. *In re Marriage of Rosan,* 24 Cal. App. 3d 855, 101 Cal. Rptr. 295, 303 (1972).

45. *In re Marriage of Rosan,* 24 Cal. App. 3d 855, 101 Cal. Rptr. 295, 304 (1972).

46. Herma Hill Kay, personal conversation, 1978.

47. Eisler, *Dissolution,* p. 46.

48. See, for example, *In re Marriage of Brantner,* 67 Cal. App. 3d 416, 419, 136 Cal. Rptr. 635 (1977); *In re Marriage of Morrison,* 20 Cal. App. 3d 437, 143 Cal. Rptr. 139 (1978); and *In re Marriage of Fenton,* 134 Cal. 3d 451, 458, 184 Cal. Rptr. 597, 599 (1982).

49. *California Civil Code,* Section 4801(a) (West Supp. 1985).

50. U.S. Bureau of the Census, "Alimony, 1981," p. 2.

51. Robert Schoen, Harry N. Greenblatt, and Robert B. Mielke, "California's Experience with Non-adversary Divorce," *Demography* Vol. 2, no. 2, May 1975, p. 233. These researchers report that 78 percent of all divorce petitions in California were filed by wives who automatically assumed the legal role of an "innocent" plaintiff against an erring husband.

52. William P. Hogoboom, "The California Family Law Act of 1970: 18 Months' Experience," *Journal of the Missouri Bar* Vol. 27, no. 11, 1971, p. 587.

53. For an explanation of the model used, see Peter H. Rossi, William A. Sampson, and Christine E. Bose, "Measuring Household Social Standing," *Social Science Research* Vol. 3, 1974, pp. 169–190. This part of the research was based on the techniques invented by Professor Rossi for measuring the various attitudinal components of a judgmental response, and we are indebted to him for helping us generate these cases.

54. Personal conversation with Professor Michael Wald, Stanford University, March 1980.

55. Paul Jacobson, *American Marriage and Divorce* (New York: Holt Rinehart, 1959), p. 126.

56. May, *Pursuit of Domestic Perfection,* p. 177.

57. Caleb Foote, Robert J. Levy, and Frank M. Sandor, *Cases and Materials on Family Law,* first edition (Boston: Little, Brown & Co., 1966).

58. Jacobus tenBroek, "California's Dual System of Family Law: Its Origin, Development, and Present Status," *Stanford Law Review* Vol. 16, 1964, pp. 257–317 and 800–831.

59. Sharon Johnson, "No-Fault Divorce: 10 Years Later, Some Virtues, Some Flaws," *New York Times,* March 30, 1979, p. A22; *Time,* Jan. 1, 1979, p. 64.

CHAPTER 7—WHERE THE LAW FAILS

1. *California Civil Code,* Section 4801(a)(5) (West 1983).

2. Elizabeth Waldman, Allyson Sherman Grossman, Howard Hayghe, and Beverly L. Johnson, "Working Mothers in the 1970's: A Look at the Statistics," *Monthly Labor Review,* Vol. 102, No. 10, October 1979, pp. 39–49, especially p. 42.

3. Marilyn Chase, "The No-Fault-Divorce Has a Fault of Its Own, Many Women Learn," *The Wall Street Journal,* Jan. 21, 1985, p. 1, col. 1 (hereafter cited as Chase, "No-Fault Divorce").

4. Tish Sommers and Laurie Shields, Personal interview, April 4, 1980, Oakland, California.

5. *In re Marriage of Brantner,* 67 Cal. App. 3d 416, 419, 136 Cal. Rptr. 635 (1977).

6. *In re Marriage of Brantner,* 67 Cal. App. 3d 416, 419, 420, 136 Cal. Rptr. 635 (1977) (emphasis added).

7. Matrimonial Proceedings and Property Act of 1970 (effective 1971), consolidated into the Matrimonial Causes Act 1973. See also John Eckelaar, *Family Law and Social Policy* 2d ed. (London: Weidenfeld and Nicolson, 1984).

8. See, for example, Hillary Land's excellent essay on taxation, social security, and housing policy in England, which documents the legal presumption of a married woman's financial dependency on her husband found in the English social security system, tax system, national insurance system, and in housing policy. Hillary Land, "Women: Supporters or Supported?" in *Sexual Divisions and Society: Process and Change,* Diana Leonard Barker and Sheila Allen, eds. (London: Tavistock, 1976), pp. 108–132; and Hillary Land and Roy Parker, "United Kingdom" in *Family and Policy: Government and Families in Fourteen Countries,* Sheila Kammerman and Alfred Kahn, eds. (New York: Columbia University Press, 1978), pp. 331–366.

   For example, only the husband can sign the couple's joint income tax return (unless the wife has opted for separate taxation). "Should too much tax be deducted from a woman's pay, the rebate may be sent to her husband because, legally, it belongs to him. Even if the marital home is jointly owned, it is assumed that he will claim the tax relief on the interest element of the mortgage payments." (Ibid., p. 343). Similarly, the National Insurance Act provides support for disabled, sick, and unemployed men, but married women in these categories are still expected to depend in the first place on their husbands.

   Along the same lines, Katherine O'Donovan observes that even if a wife works, it is assumed that she is merely supplementing her husband's wages—and, of course, it is always assumed that she nevertheless retains her full responsibility to care for her children, husband, and sick or elderly relatives. Thus the British tax system allows married men with incapacitated wives an additional personal allowance. Katherine O'Donovan, "The Male Appendage—Legal Definitions of Women," in *Fit Work for Women,* Sandra Berman, ed. (London: Croom Helm, 1979), pp. 134–152. See also, *Families in Britain,* Rona N. Rapoport, Michael P. Fogarty and Robert Rapoport, eds. (London: Routledge & Kegan Paul, 1982).

9. The Matrimonial Causes Act 1973 states: "The respondent may oppose the grant of a decree on the ground that the dissolution of the marriage will result in grave financial or other hardship to him and that it would in all the circumstances be wrong to dissolve the marriage. The act goes on to state: "for the purposes of this section hardship shall include the loss of the chance of acquiring any benefit which the respondent might acquire if the marriage were not dissolved." Section 5, Matrimonial Causes Act.

10. See, for example, The Law Commission, *The Financial Consequences of Divorce: The Basic Policy,* Law Commission No. 103 (London: Her Majesty's

Stationery Office, 1980); and Campaign for Justice in Divorce, *An Even Better Way Out* (mimeo), 1979, p. 4, note 8.

11. See, generally, National Center for Health Statistics, U.S. Department of Health, *Monthly Vital Statistics Report* (Supp. Sept. 12, 1980).

12. Arland Thornton and Deborah Freedman, "The Changing American Family," *Population Bulletin* Vol. 38, no. 4, Oct. 1983, p. 10.

13. Ralph E. Smith, "The Movement of Women into the Labor Force," in *The Subtle Revolution,* R. Smith, ed. (Washington, D.C.: The Urban Institute, 1979), p. 10.

14. Ibid.

15. Victor R. Fuchs, "His and Hers: Gender Differences in Work and Income, 1959–1979," Working Paper No. 1501, *Working Paper Series* (Cambridge, Mass.: National Bureau of Economic Research, 1984).

16. Although married women with children are more likely to work part time, divorced women with children are more likely to work full time because they cannot survive on the income of a part time job.

17. Doris Jonas Freed and Henry H. Foster, "Family Law in the Fifty States: An Overview" *Family Law Quarterly* Vol. 17, no. 4, Winter 1984, p. 381.

18. See generally Laurie Shields, *Displaced Homemakers—Organizing for a New Life* (New York: McGraw-Hill, 1981), pp. 71–112 (on "Laboratories of Hope") (hereafter cited as Shields, *Displaced Homemakers*).

19. Frank Mott, "The Socioeconomic Status of Households Headed by Women: Results from the National Longitudinal Surveys," R. & D. Monograph No. 72 for the Employment & Training Administration, U.S. Department of Labor, 1979, p. 33 (hereafter cited as Mott, "Households Headed by Women").

20. Ibid.

21. Ibid., p. 33.

22. Frances Leonard, "The Disillusionment of Divorce for Older Women" (Washington D.C.: Older Women's League, 1980), p. 5 (hereafter cited as Leonard "Divorce and Older Women").

23. Shields, *Displaced Homemakers,* p. 21.

24. Chase, "No-Fault Divorce," p. 12, col. 3; and Kathy Barnard, "Her Day in Court: Divorce Takes 'Benefits' Fight to High Court," *Lewiston Morning Tribune,* Oct. 11, 1984, p. 1.

25. Ibid.

26. Leonard, "Divorce and Older Women," and Frances Leonard, "Not Even for Dogcatcher: Employment Discrimination and Older Women" (Washington D.C.: Older Women's League, 1980), pp. 1–12.

27. Testimony of Eleanor Cutri Smeal, President, National Organization for Women. Before the Subcommittee on Retirement Income and Employment of the Select Committee on Aging, United States House of Representatives, May 7, 1979.

28. *Hayes v. Hayes,* D700 518 Superior Court, Los Angeles, California (1969 through 1975). The following summary is based on attorney Riane Eisler's account of this case, which is in turn based on the court docket, cited above, and personal interviews with Janne Hayes and her attorney. Riane

Tennenhaus Eisler, *Dissolution: No-Fault Divorce, Marriage and the Future of Women* (New York: McGraw Hill, 1977), pp. 24–31 (hereafter cited as Eisler, *No-Fault Divorce*).

29. Ibid., p. 25.

30. Assembly Committee Report on Assembly Bill No. 530 and Senate Bill No. 252 (The Family Law Act) submitted by Committee on the Judiciary, James B. Hayes, Chairman, Aug. 8, 1969, printed in the *Assembly Daily Journal* (Sacramento, California, Aug. 8, 1969).

31. Points and Authorities of Petitioner in Opposition to Opening Points and Authorities to Respondent, Order to Show Cause, *Hayes v. Hayes,* D 700 518, filed June 18, 1974.

32. Eisler, *No-Fault Divorce,* p. 30 citing "Hayes' Ex-Wife Seeks Welfare, Food Stamps," *Los Angeles Times,* June 6, 1975.

33. Eisler, p. 30 citing "Not Upset by Former Wife, Hayes Says," *Los Angeles Times,* June 10, 1975.

34. Harriet N. Cohen and Adria S. Hillman, *Analysis of Seventy Select Decisions After Trial Under New York State's Equitable Distribution Law, From January 1981 Through October 1984, Analyzed November 1, 1984* (New York: Women's Bar Association, 1984).

35. Ibid., p. 14.

36. Chase, "No-Fault Divorce," p. 12, col. 1.

37. Ibid.

CHAPTER 8—CHILD CUSTODY

1. An earlier version of the first half of this chapter was co-authored by Ruth B. Dixon, and published as "Child Custody Awards: Legal Standards and Empirical Patterns for Child Custody, Support and Visitation After Divorce," *University of California at Davis Law Review* Vol. 12, no. 2, Summer 1979, pp. 472–521. Herma Hill Kay, William J. Goode, Jerome H. Skolnick, Julie A. Fulton, and Robert Weiss provided valuable critiques of earlier drafts, and Joyce A. Bird, Carol Dixon, Susan Feller, and Cassie Leavitt provided helpful research assistance.

2. National Center for Health Statistics, *Monthly Vital Statistics Report,* Vol. 33, no. 11, supp., Feb. 28, 1985, p. 1.

3. Dr. Paul Glick, chief of the Population Division of the U.S. Census Bureau, reports that "the total number of young children [in the United States] in 1977 was about the same as in 1960, but . . . the number [of children] living with a separated parent doubled, [and] the number living with a divorced parent tripled . . . by contrast, the number of children living with two parents declined by 10 percent . . . By 1977, less than 70 percent of all children under eighteen were living with their two natural parents in a continuous first marriage." Paul C. Glick, "The Future of the American Family," *Current Population Reports,* January 1979, p. 3.

4. Ibid. and Paul C. Glick, "Children of Divorced Parents in Demographic Perspective," *Journal of Social Issues* Vol. 35, 1979, pp. 170–82.

5. Arthur J. Norton, Assistant Chief, Population Division, U.S. Bureau of the Census, interview, March 1984.

6. Sandra Hofferth, "Updating Children's Life Course," Center for Population Research, National Institute of Child Health and Human Development, Washington, D.C., 1983.

7. Ibid.

8. Doris Jonas Freed and Timothy B. Walker, "Family Law in the United States: An Overview," *Family Law Quarterly* Vol. 18, no. 4, Winter 1985, p. 434, Table XI (hereafter cited as Freed and Walker, "Family Law 1985"). See also Table C-7 in the Legal Appendix, and pp. 245–257 in Chapter 8.

9. The concern for the child's welfare as opposed to the parents' rights is considered the unifying principle of modern custody decisions. See Homer Clark, *The Law of Domestic Relations* (St. Paul, Minn.: West Publishing Co., 1968), Section 17.1 (hereafter cited as Clark, *Domestic Relations*).

10. Interview with Joanne Schulman, staff attorney, National Center on Women and Family Law, New York City, N.Y., January 8, 1985 (hereafter cited as Schulman Interview, 1985).

11. Henry Foster and Doris Jonas Freed, "Life with Father: 1978," *Family Law Quarterly* Vol. 11, 1978, pp. 321, 322. (hereafter cited as Foster and Freed, "Life with Father"). See also Henry Foster, "Dependent Children and the Law," *University of Pittsburgh Law Review* Vol. 18, 1957, p. 579.

12. Robert Mnookin, "Child Custody Adjudication: Judicial Functions in the Face of Indeterminacy," *Law and Contemporary Problems,* Summer 1975, p. 226, 233–34 (hereafter cited as Mnookin, "Child Custody").

    Foster and Freed note that the father's absolute right to the custody of his children was ordinarily conditioned upon his fitness as a parent, but "the father usually prevailed even in unlikely situations." Foster and Freed, "Life with Father," p. 326 (citing *King v. De Manneville,* 102 Eng. Rep. 1054 [K.B. 1804]).

13. William Blackstone, *Commentaries on the Law of England,* p. 493; cited in Foster and Freed, "Life with Father," p. 325.

    The married woman's inferior legal position with respect to her children provides but one example of her generally subordinate legal status under common law. See generally Herma Hill Kay, *Sex-Based Discrimination: Text, Cases and Materials* (especially the chapter on "Marriage and Family Life") (St. Paul, Minn.: West Publishing Co., 1981).

14. *King v. DeManneville,* 102 Eng. Rep. 1054, 1055 (K.B. 1804).

15. Foster and Freed, "Life with Father," p. 341.

16. Mnookin, "Child Custody," p. 234; Foster and Freed, "Life with Father," p. 326 (citing Justice Talfourd's Act, An Act to Amend the Law Relating to the Custody of Infants, 1839, 2 & 3 Vict. c. 54).

17. For an outline of the "tender years" presumption in favor of the mother, see generally Clark, *Domestic Relations*, 17.4 (a).

18. Nancy D. Polikoff, "Gender and Child Custody Determinations: Exploding the Myths," in *Families, Politics and Public Policies: A Feminist Dialogue on Women and the State*, Irene Diamond, ed. (New York: Longman, 1983), p. 186, note 18 (hereafter cited as Polikoff, "Gender and Child Custody").

19. Mnookin, "Child Custody," p. 234. The paternal preference was characterized as fiction as early as 1887. A. Lloyd, *Law of Divorce*, 242 (1887), cited in Mnookin, "Child Custody," p. 235.

20. Mnookin, "Child Custody," pp. 234–45; Foster and Freed, "Life with Father," pp. 326–27.

21. Interview with Nancy Polikoff, staff attorney, Women's Legal Defense Fund, Washington, D.C., December 28, 1984.

22. Mnookin, "Child Custody," p. 235.

23. Ibid.

24. *Washburn v. Washburn*, 49 Cal. App. 2d 581, 588, 122 P.2d 96, 100 (2d Dist. 1942).

25. Allan Roth, "The Tender Years Presumption in Child Custody Disputes," *Journal of Family Law* Vol. 15, 1976–77, pp. 423, 436.

26. *Krieger v. Krieger*, 59 Idaho 301, 81 P.2d 1081 (1938) (emphasis added).

27. *Wojnarowicz v. Wojnarowicz*, 48 N.J. Super. 349, 353, 137 A.2d 618, 260 (ch. Div. 1958). *Kirstukas v. Kirstukas*, 14 Md. App. 190, 286 A.2d 535 538 (1972).

28. Commonwealth ex. rel. *Lucas v. Kreischer*, 450 Pa. 352, 299 A.2d 243, 245 (1973) (emphasis added, citations omitted).

29. The widely cited work of John Bowlby, which supported these assertions, has recently been challenged. John Bowlby, *Child Care and the Growth of Love*, Second Edition (Baltimore, Md.: Penguin Books, 1965). A respected advocate of the psychological basis for the mother presumption is Andrew Watson, a professor of law and psychiatry at the University of Michigan. See e.g., Andrew Watson, "The Children of Armageddon: Problems of Custody Following Divorce," *Syracuse Law Review* Vol. 21, 1969, pp. 76–86, in which Watson advocates a presumption in favor of the mother for children under ten years of age, and for all female children.

30. James Levine, *Who Will Raise the Children: New Options for Fathers (and Mothers)* (Philadelphia: J. B. Lippincott Co., 1976), p. 41 (hereafter cited as Levine, *New Options*). For a critical review of the academic acceptance of the maternal role, see generally, Rochelle P. Wortis, "The Acceptance of the Concept of the Maternal Role by Behavioral Scientists: Its Effects on Women," *American Journal of Orthopsychiatry* Vol. 41, 1971, pp. 733–46.

31. Bruno Bettelheim, "Fathers Shouldn't Try to Be Mothers," *Parents Magazine*, October 1956, pp. 124–25, cited in Levine, *New Options*, p. 22. Fathers' rights advocates have adopted a similar strategy in seeking to legitimate their claims to custody, pointing to research that emphasizes the father's role in child development. See, for example, Philip E. Solomon, "The Fa-

thers' Revolution in Custody Cases," *Trial,* Oct. 1977, pp. 33–37 (hereafter cited as Solomon, "Fathers' Revolution in Custody").

32. Robert J. Levy and Phoebe Ellsworth, "Legislative Reform of Child Custody Adjudication," *Law and Society Review,* Nov. 1969, p. 4.

33. Ibid., p. 4.

34. Between 1969 and 1975, nine states passed legislation explicitly stipulating that the sex of the parent should not be a factor in determining custody. Levine, *New Options,* p. 44.

35. Foster and Freed, "Life with Father," p. 332.

36. It had "supposedly been discarded" in the other nine states with state ERAs. Foster and Freed, "Life with Father," p. 333.

37. Most of this research is summarized in Paul Jacobson, *American Marriage and Divorce* (New York: Rinehart & Company, 1959), pp. 131–32, with the following exceptions: the 1948 Michigan data was reported in William J. Goode, *After Divorce* (New York: The Free Press, 1956); page citations are to the 1965 paperback edition published under the title *Women in Divorce* (New York: The Free Press, 1965), p. 29 (hereafter cited as Goode, *Women in Divorce*); the 1960 Maine data comes from Maine Department of Health and Welfare, *Social Casework Services in a Divorce* Court (1960); and the 1956 Indiana data was reported in Harold T. Christenson and Hanna H. Meissner, "An Analysis of Divorce in Tippecanoe County, Indiana," *Sociology and Social Research* Vol. 40, 1956, p. 248. In addition, Levine cites these statewide data from Missouri: in 1960, 7.9 percent of custody awards were to fathers; in 1968, 7.6 percent; and in 1973, 6.4 percent. Levine, *New Options,* p. 47, n. 23.

38. Ibid.

39. Polikoff, "Gender and Child Custody," p. 186. See also Michael Grosbard, "Who Gets the Child? Custody, Guardianship and the Rise of a Judicial Patriarchy in Nineteenth Century America," *Feminist Studies* Vol. 9, no. 2, Summer 1983.

40. Prior to its amendment, the *California Civil Code,* Section 4600, read, "Custody should be awarded in the following order of preference: (a) To either parent according to the best interests of the child, but other things being equal, custody should be given to the mother if the child is of tender years. . . ." 1969 Cal. Stats. 3330, Ch. 1608, Section 8. (The current version is in the *California Civil Code,* Section 4600 [West Supp. 1985].)

41. Elaine Tyler May, *Great Expectations: Marriage and Divorce in Post-Victorian America* (Chicago: University of Chicago Press, 1980), Table 11, p. 173 (hereafter cited as May, *Great Expectations*). May found an increase in the percentage of mother custody awards between 1880 and 1920, from 78 percent to 84 percent of the cases. Although children "legally belonged" to the father in 1880, he was awarded sole custody in only 12 percent of the cases.

42. *California Civil Code,* Section 4509 (West 1983) (emphasis added).

43. As Ira Victor and Win Ann Winkler describe it:

". . . the parent desiring custody has to prove the unfitness of the other parent, [and] the one who will stoop the lowest in mudslinging, slander, character defamation, perjury, and vilification of the other is the one who has the best chance of gaining custody . . . or being declared the most 'fit' parent."

Ira Victor and Win Ann Winkler, *Fathers and Custody* (New York: Hawthorn Books, 1977), p. 37.

44. National Center on Women and Family Law (Laurie Woods, Vicki Been, and Joanne Schulman), "Sex and Economic Discrimination in Child Custody Awards," *Clearinghouse Review* Vol. 16, no. 11, April 1983, pp. 1133–34 (hereafter cited as Schulman et al., "Economic Discrimination in Child Custody Awards"). They state that "unless the children themselves have been battered, the court will generally not deny visitation or custody solely on the basis of violence against the other parent—even when the acts are committed in front of the children."

45. Ibid. and Schulman interview, 1985.

46. Amy Hirsch, staff attorney, Jacksonville Area Legal Aid, Florida, "New Florida Legislation Provides Protection for Battered Women and Their Children in Custody Cases," *The Women's Advocate* Vol. 5, no. 5, September 1984, p. 1.

47. Freeman, Hogoboom, MacFaden, Olson, and Li, *Attorney's Guide to Family Law Act and Practice,* 2d ed., C. Brosnahan and Colburn, eds (Berkeley, Calif.: Continuing Education of the Bar, 1972), p. 300.

48. Although few of the men or women we interviewed said that they used the legal process to embarrass or harass their ex-spouses, many of them felt that their ex-spouses (or their spouses' lawyers) undertook a variety of unnecessary legal actions to harass *them.*

49. Divorced men in California were organized and acted as a pressure group in the 1960s in the debates on the no-fault law (see Chapter 2, p. 17), but the focus on parenting flourished in the early 1970's with the establishment of Equal Rights for Fathers' groups. See, for example, Del Lane, "Group Works for Fathers' Rights," *Oakland Tribune,* Jan. 2, 1974, p. 19, col. 1 (hereafter cited as Lane, "Father's Rights"); and Levine, *New Options.*

50. The decline in fathers requesting physical custody in Los Angeles between 1968 and 1972, from 18.4 percent to 11.1 percent, is statistically significant at the 0.05 level. The increase in San Francisco is not significant.

51. Judge E. M. Porter, Los Angeles Municipal Court, address to American Academy of Matrimonial Lawyers, Northern California Chapter, Regional Family Law Symposium, April 10, 1977, p. 133. Legal custody may be awarded to one or more persons, or the child may be made a ward of the court. See *California Civil Code,* Section 4600 (West 1983, Cum. Supp. 1985).

52. Brigitte M. Bodenheimer, "Equal Rights, Visitation and the Right to Move," *Family Advocate* Vol. 1, no. 1, Summer 1978, pp. 18, 19.

53. *California Civil Code,* Section 4601 (West 1983) provides: "Reasonable

visitation rights shall be awarded to a parent unless it is shown that such visitation would be detrimental to the best interests of the child. In the discretion of the court, reasonable visitation rights may be granted to any other person having an interest in the welfare of the child."

54. Attorney Richard Johnson observes that the use of "reasonable" visitation orders has often led to more litigation between "unreasonable" parents. Richard Johnson, "Visitation: When Access Becomes Excess," *Family Advocate* Vol. 1, no. 1, Summer 1978, pp. 14, 15.

55. Goode, *Women in Divorce,* p. 313.

56. Ibid.

57. Carol Bruch, "Making Visitation Work: Dual Parenting Orders," *Family Advocate,* Vol. 1, no. 1, Summer 1978, pp. 22, 41. Bruch also argues that the child's relationship with the custodial parent will be enriched by occasionally relieving that parent of the duties of a single-parent household.

58. Alabama, Arkansas, Illinois, Iowa, Louisiana, New York, Missouri, Montana, and Nevada. Freed and Walker, "Family Law 1985," pp. 451–454.

59. Ibid., p. 452.

60. Act of Aug. 17, 1972, Stats. 1972, c. 1007, p. 1855, Section 1 [codified at *California Civil Code,* Section 4600(b) (West 1983, Cum. Supp. 1985)].

61. The "new legal era" probably began with the Supreme Court's decision in *Stanley v. Illinois* 405 U.S. 645 (1972), in which the presumption that an unwed father is an unfit parent was held to be unconstitutional as a denial of both due process and equal protection.

    In the years directly preceding the change in the California law, the national and local news media had focused considerable attention on fathers who had asked for custody of their young children. Levine observes, "Fathers' rights groups were springing up all over the country" (between 1972 and 1975). Divorced fathers in the San Francisco Bay area formed an active organization, Equal Rights for Fathers, in 1973, which aided men seeking legal help and social support for their custody claims. *Equal Rights for Fathers* leaflet, n.d. (circa 1973), P.O. Box 6367, Albany, CA 94706. Fathers United for Equal Justice, which started in Boston as a group of six divorced men meeting to share their problems, grew into a 600-member organization by 1975.

62. The negative effects of the pro-mother presumption on women are discussed in Lenore J. Weitzman, *The Marriage Contract: Spouses, Lovers, and the Law* (New York: The Free Press, 1983), pp. 115–120. See also Betty Rollin, "Motherhood: Who Needs It?" in *The Family in Transition,* Arlene and Jerome Skolnick, eds. (Boston: Little, Brown, 1971).

63. Psychotherapists Susan Gettlemen and Janet Markowitz argue that women should relinquish custody to their husbands "so that they themselves will have more time and energy to devote to education and job training and can, therefore, move more rapidly toward economic self-sufficiency." Susan Gettlemen and Janet Markowitz, *The Courage to Divorce* (New York: Ballantine Books, 1974), pp. 217–19. As these authors note, many women "have become primary caretakers not just because they are capable and

devoted to their children, but because they have grown up in a society that conditions them to be mothers, while offering them few other alternatives." They therefore argue that women (and children) would be better off if this role were not perpetuated, and if it was instead normal to award custody to fathers after divorce.

64. See generally Olaf Palme, "The Emancipation of Man," *Journal of Social Issues* Vol. 28, 1972, pp. 237–46; Warren Farrell, *The Liberated Man: Beyond Masculinity; Freeing Men and Their Relationships with Women* (New York: Random House, 1975); Joseph Pleck, "Men's Family Work Role," *The Family Coordinator* Vol. 28, no. 4, 1979, pp. 481–488; and Robert Fein, "Research on Fathering: Social Policy and an Emergent Perspective," *Journal of Social Issues* Vol. 34, 1978, pp. 122–35.

65. As did the glib empiricism of legal scholars who deduced a social trend from a single case. See, e.g., Solomon, "Fathers' Revolution in Custody"; Daniel Molinoff, "Increased Demand by Divorced Fathers for Custody," *New York Times* April 27, 1977, p. 7, col. 1; and Molinoff, "Life with Father," *New York Times Magazine,* May 22, 1977, pp. 12–17.

66. The docket data also indicate a relationship between the husbands' request and the ages of the children. Husbands were almost twice as likely to ask for custody if there was a teenage child in the family rather than a preschool child. Among those fathers who did request custody, however, the child's age made no difference in their likelihood of success.

   As expected, fathers were more likely to be awarded custody of their sons than their daughters. In the sample of divorcing couples, fathers contested in 17 percent of the families with one male child, and in 11 percent of the families with children of mixed sexes, in contrast to 0 percent of the families with only girls.

67. Sixty-one percent of the fathers who asked for custody were petitioners, in contrast to the 36 percent of husband petitioners in the overall sample.

68. In 1977, a response was filed in only 40 percent of the cases in which the father got custody, in contrast to 70 percent of the cases in which the wife received custody.

69. Data gathered by Adele Hendrickson, Attorney in Charge, Family Law Unit, Oakland, Calif., cited in Nancy Polikoff, "Gender and Child Custody," note 5.

70. Walter D. Johnson, "Divorce, Alimony, Support and Custody: A Survey of Judges' Attitudes in One State," *Family Law Reporter* Vol. 3, 1976, p. 4003.

71. This section focuses exclusively on the sample of Los Angeles attorneys (n = 92) because these interviews were conducted more recently. The responses of the San Francisco attorneys to similar questions do not contradict the results reported here.

72. Lane, "Father's Rights," p. 19, col. 1.

73. Eugenia MacGowan, "Custody," in *California Marital Dissolution Practice,* Vol. 2 (Berkeley, Calif.: Continuing Education of the Bar, 1983), p. 994 (hereafter cited as MacGowan, "Custody").

74. Polikoff, "Gender and Child Custody," p. 189.

75. Ibid., p. 188.

76. Unpublished research conducted by Professor Lois Hoffman, University of Michigan.

77. Polikoff, "Gender and Child Custody," pp. 188–189.

78. Schulman et al., "Economic Discrimination in Child Custody Awards," p. 1134.

79. Ibid.

80. Ibid.

81. Ibid.

82. Polikoff quoted in Sue Chastain, "More Women Bear Costs of Child Support," *The Philadelphia Inquirer,* Jan. 13, 1985, pp. 1–I and 6–I.

83. When the results were stratified by length of marriage, we found that among men married 1–4 years, 0 percent of those with children said that they wanted custody; among those married 5–10 years, 30 percent wanted custody; and among those married more than 17 years, 55 percent wanted custody. These data support the finding from the docket data that men are much more likely to want custody of teenage children, especially in comparison to preschool children. (These data are presented by length of marriage rather than by age of children because of the complexity of grouping families with several children of different ages.)

84. This is a slightly higher percentage than in the random sample of 1977 divorce decrees, which is a product of our stratified sample.

85. *Garska v. McCoy,* 278 S.E.2d 357, 363 (W.Va 1981).

86. *Garska v. McCoy,* 278 S.E.2d 357, 361 (W.Va 1981).

87. Although several states had optional joint-custody laws (joint custody as an option, and joint custody when parents agree), California was the first state to institute a joint custody preference for all families. *California Civil Code,* Section 4600.5 (West 1983, Cum. Supp. 1985).

88. Freed and Walker, "Family Law 1985," Table 11, p. 434.

89. This discussion is summarized from Joanne Schulman and Valerie Pitt, "Second Thoughts on Joint Custody: Analysis of Legislation and Its Impact for Women and Children," *Golden Gate University Law Review* Vol. 12, no. 3., Summer 1982, pp. 539–577 (hereafter cited as Schulman and Pitt, "Second Thoughts on Joint Custody").

90. Committee on the Family Court, New York County Lawyers' Association, Report No. 81–A (June 1981), cited in Schulman, "Second Thoughts on Joint Custody," p. 549, n. 60.

91. Schulman and Pitt, "Second Thoughts on Joint Custody," p. 550.

92. Bobette A. Levy and Carole R. Chambers, "The Folly of Joint Custody," *Family Advocate* Vol. 3 no. 4, Spring 1981, p. 8.

93. Schulman and Pitt, "Second Thoughts on Joint Custody," p. 551.

94. Ibid.

95. Ibid. p. 552.

96. Gary Skoloff, "Joint Custody: A Jaundiced View—Calling Soloman's Bluff," *Trial,* March 1984, p. 54.

97. Joseph Goldstein, Anna Freud, and Albert J. Solnit, *Beyond the Best Interests of the Child* (New York: The Free Press, 1973) (hereafter cited as Goldstein, Freud, and Solnit, *Beyond the Best Interests*).

98. Interview with psychologist Judith S. Wallerstein, Marin, California, February 10, 1985 (hereafter cited as Wallerstein Interview, 1985).

99. *California Civil Code,* Section 4600(a), (West 1983, Cum. Supp. 1985).

100. Goldstein, Freud, and Solnit, *Beyond the Best Interests.*

101. Judith S. Wallerstein and Joan Kelly, *Surviving the Breakup: How Children and Parents Cope with Divorce* (New York: Basic Books, 1980) (hereafter cited as Wallerstein and Kelly, *Surviving the Breakup*).

102. *California Civil Code,* Section 4607(a), (West Supp. 1985).

103. *California Civil Code,* Section 4600.5, (West Supp. 1985).

104. *California Civil Code,* Section 4600.5(c), (West Supp. 1985).

105. *California Civil Code,* Section 4600(a), (West Supp. 1985).

106. *California Civil Code,* Section 4600(b), (West Supp. 1985).

107. MacGowan, "Custody," p. 997.

108. Eleanor E. Maccoby and Robert Mnookin, seminar presented at the Center for Youth Development, Stanford University, May 1983 (hereafter cited as Maccoby and Mnookin).

109. Interview with Judith S. Wallerstein and Dorothy Huntington, Center for the Family in Transition, Marin, California, February 11, 1985 (hereafter cited as Wallerstein and Huntington, 1985).

110. Maccoby and Mnookin, Table 2.

111. Wallerstein and Huntington, 1985.

112. Susan Steinman, "The Experience of Children in a Joint-Custody Arrangement: A Report of a Study," *American Journal of Orthopsychiatry* Vol. 51, no. 3, July 1981.

113. Ibid., p. 410.

114. Ibid., p. 411.

115. Ibid.

116. Jessica Pearson and Nancy Thoennes, "Child Custody, Child Support Arrangements and Child Support Payment Patterns," paper presented at the Child Support Enforcement Research Workshop, August 1984, Washington, D.C., pp. 12–13 (hereafter cited as Pearson and Thoennes, "Custody and Support").

117. Lillian Kozak, Chair, N.Y. State NOW Marriage and Divorce Task Force, "Presentation Concerning N.Y. Joint Custody Legislation," March 21, 1981. Cited in Joanne Schulman "Second Thoughts on Joint Custody" Family *Advocate* Vol. 5, no. 2, p. 31.

118. Wallerstein and Kelly, "Surviving the Breakup."

119. Ibid.

120. Wallerstein Interview, 1985.

121. Ibid.

122. Pearson and Thoennes, "Custody and Support," p. 9.

123. Ibid., pp. 9–10.

124. Ibid., p. 14.

125. W. Patrick C. Pheer, James C. Beck, Barbara B. Hauser, Susan C. Clark, and Ruth A. Whitney, "An Empirical Study of Custody Agreements: Joint vs. Sole Legal Custody," *Journal of Law and Psychiatry,* forthcoming.

126. Ibid., pp. 14, 18.

127. Ibid., p. 18.

128. May, *Great Expectations,* p. 173, Table 11.

129. Interview with Barbara Hauser, Director, Family Service Clinic, Middlesex Probate Court, Cambridge, Mass., held in Princeton, New Jersey, July 20, 1984.

130. This is also the finding of William Goode's classic study of divorce, *Women in Divorce.*

131. Frank F. Furstenberg, Christine W. Nord, James L. Peterson, and Nicholas Zill, "The Life Course of Children of Divorce: Marital Disruption and Parental Contact," *American Sociological Review* Vol. 48, October 1983, pp. 656–668 (hereafter cited as Furstenberg et al., "Children of Divorce").

132. Ibid., pp. 663–664.

133. Ibid., p. 664.

134. Ibid.

135. Ibid., pp. 665–666.

136. Ibid., p. 666.

137. Wallerstein Interview, 1985.

138. Furstenberg et al., "Children of Divorce," p. 666.

139. Ibid., p. 663, Table 6.

140. This is not to deny, however, that the law plays an important role in structuring options and creating incentives.

141. This is the major finding of the research conducted by John Eekelaar and Eric Clive on the role of the courts in custody decision in Great Britain. Eekelaar and Clive found that most custodial arrangements are made by the parents. Although the British courts always completed their required review of the custodial arrangements, they almost never changed the parents' custodial arrangements. John Eekelaar and Eric Clive, *Custody After Divorce* (Oxford, England: Centre for Socio-Legal Studies, Wolfson College, 1977).

CHAPTER 9—CHILD SUPPORT

1. U.S. Bureau of the Census, "Child Support and Alimony: 1981," *Current Population Reports,* Series P–23, No. 124 (Washington, D.C.: U.S. Government Printing Office, 1983), p. 1 (hereafter cited as "Child Support 1981").

2. Statement in Hearing before the Subcommittee on Public Assistance and Unemployment Compensation of the Committee on Ways and Means,

U.S. House of Representatives, Ninety-Eighth Congress, First Session, July 14, 1983, Serial 98–41 (Washington, D.C.: U.S. Government Printing Office, 1984), pp. 34–35 (hereafter cited as "House Hearings 1983").

3. Office of Child Support Enforcement, U.S. Department of Health and Human Services, "Child Support: An Agenda for Action" (Washington, D.C.: U.S. Government Printing Office, 1984) (hereafter cited as "An Agenda").

4. Ruth E. Murphy, statement in "House Hearings 1983," p. 275.

5. Ibid.

6. "Child Support Law Passed," *The Miami Herald,* Aug. 9, 1984, p. 4A (hereafter cited as *Miami Herald,* "Child Support Law").

7. Ibid.

8. Excerpted from Presidential Proclamation, 1983, as cited in "An Agenda," p. 4.

9. Office of Child Support Enforcement, U.S. Dept. of Health and Human Services, "Child Support: New Help is Available," (August 1984), p. 1.

10. *Miami Herald,* "Child Support Law."

11. U.S. Bureau of the Census, "Child Support and Alimony: 1978," Series P–23, No. 112 (Washington, D.C.: U.S. Government Printing Office, 1981), p. 5, Table B.

12. "Child Support 1981," p. 3, Table B.

13. Ibid., p. 2.

14. Ibid., p. 3, Table B.

15. Ibid., p. 1.

16. Ibid.

17. Judith Cassetty, *Child Support and Public Policy* (Lexington, Mass.: D. C. Heath, 1978), pp. 64–65, Table 4–1.

18. Los Angeles Superior Court, Department 2, Guidelines for Temporary Support Orders, 1978.

19. George Norton, Esq. "A Proposal for Statewide Support Schedules," *Family Law News* Vol. 5, no. 5, September/October 1982, pp. 1–4.

20. Statement of Mary Ann Cook, Wisconsin Department of Health and Social Services, in "House Hearings 1983," pp. 230–240; see also Irwin Garfunkel and Elizabeth Uhr, "A New Approach to Child Support," *The Public Interest* No. 75, Spring 1984, pp. 111–122 (hereafter cited as Garfunkel and Uhr, "Approach to Child Support").

21. Summary Report of the New Jersey Supreme Court Task Force on Women in the Courts, New Jersey Judicial College, November 21, 1983, Parsippany, New Jersey, p. 8. The authors of the report state that the New Jersey data are based on testimony from attorneys from all parts of the state and are corroborated by a League of Women Voters' study of all divorces in Bergen County in April, 1978.

22. David Chambers, *Making Fathers Pay* (Chicago: University of Chicago Press, 1979), p. 40 (hereafter cited as Chambers, *Making Fathers Pay*).

23. Canadian Institute of Law Research and Reform, *Matrimonial Support*

Failures: Reasons, Profiles, and Perceptions of Individuals Involved (Edmonton, Alberta: Institute of Law Research and Reform, 1981), p. 22 (hereafter cited as Canadian Institute, *Matrimonial Support Failures*).

24. Gloria Sternin and Joseph Davis, "Divorce Awards and Outcomes: A Study of Pattern and Change in Cuyahoga County, Ohio, 1965–1978," *Journal of Family Law* Vol. 20, no. 3, 1981–82, pp. 443–487.

25. *California Civil Code,* Section 4700 (West 1983).

26. Barbara Bergmann, "Setting Appropriate Levels of Child-Support Payments" in *The Parental Child-Support Obligation,* Judith Cassetty, ed. (Lexington, Mass.: D. C. Heath, 1983), pp. 115–118 (hereafter cited as Cassetty, *Parental Child-Support*).

27. Judith Cassetty, "Emerging Issues in Child-Support Policy and Practice," in *Parental Child-Support,* pp. 5–6.

28. Portions of this discussion were first presented in Lenore J. Weitzman and Ruth B. Dixon, "Child Custody Awards," *University of California at Davis Law Review* Vol. 12, no. 2, Summer 1978, pp. 473–521; and Lenore J. Weitzman, "The Economics of Divorce," *University of California at Los Angeles Law Review* Vol. 28, no. 6, August 1981, pp. 1181–1268 (hereafter cited as Weitzman "The Economics of Divorce").

29. Thomas Espenshade, "Raising a Child Can Now Cost $85,000," *Intercom,* September 1980, pp. 10, 11 (hereafter cited as Espenshade, "Raising a Child").

30. Thomas Tilling, "Your $250,000 Baby," *Parents,* November 1980, p. 83.

31. Espenshade, "Raising a Child," pp. 9–11.

32. See *California Welfare and Institutions Code,* Sections 11450, 11453.1 (West 1980 & Supp. 1981).

33. April 1985 interview with Sue North, legislative aide to California Assemblyman Art Agnos, sponsor of A.B. 1527 citing Weitzman, "The Economics of Divorce," and *California Civil Code* § 4720 (West Supp. 1985).

34. While 42 percent of all *married* women with children under six years of age were in the labor force in 1978, 60 percent of the *divorced* women with preschool children were working. Ralph E. Smith, "The Movement of Women into the Labor Force" in *The Subtle Revolution,* Ralph E. Smith, ed. (Washington, D.C.: The Urban Institute, 1979).

35. Karen Seal, "A Decade of No-Fault Divorce," *Family Advocate* Vol. 1, no. 4, Spring 1979, pp. 10, 14.

36. The figures were compiled by Joan P. Emerson of the Bay Area Child Care Project and reported by the Children's Council of San Francisco. The figures for full-time care are generally based on a ten-hour day, but the hours of care range from eight to twelve hours per day for a five-day week.

37. When I ask judges to estimate the cost of food and the cost of clothing for children of various ages in judicial training seminars, their estimates are typically less than the poverty standards established by the U.S. government.

38. Thomas Espenshade, "The Value and Cost of Children," *Population Bulletin* Vol. 32, 1977, p. 43.

39. Gerald and Myrna Silver, *Weekend Fathers* (Los Angeles: Stratford Press, 1981).

40. Chambers, *Making Fathers Pay*, p. 47, Figure 4.2.

41. Canadian Institute, *Matrimonial Support Failures*, p. 22.

42. Bureau of Labor Statistics, U.S. Department of Labor, *Three Standards of Living for an Urban Family of Four Persons*, 1967. This budget is computed for a four-person urban family (husband and wife and two children) and kept current by frequent adjustments. See, for example, McCraw, "Medical Care Costs Lead Rise in 1976–1977 Family Budgets," *Monthly Labor Review*, November 1978, p. 33.

43. Bureau of Labor Statistics, U.S. Department of Labor, *Revised Equivalence Scale for Estimating Equivalent Incomes or Budget Costs by Family Type*, Bulletin No. 1570–2 (1968).

44. Chambers, *Making Fathers Pay*, p. 48.

45. Ibid.

46. Ibid.

47. In fact, a Louisiana court held that because the custodial parent contributes day-to-day care, it is not appropriate to divide support evenly between the two parents. *Arceneaux v. Arceneaux* 426 So.2d 745 (La. App. 1983).

48. While the court cannot ordinarily order a parent to support a child who is over eighteen unless that child is "incapable of self support" [*Levy v. Levy*, 245 Cal. App. 2d 341, 363, 53 Cal. Rptr. 790, 803 (1966)], it can incorporate a voluntary agreement for child support into the court order. Only 6 percent of the parents we interviewed with children over eighteen had signed such voluntary agreements. Similarly, less than 5 percent of the cases in the court docket samples had such an agreement.

49. Letter from H. M. Saville-Hyde to California Assemblyman R. Katz, May 3, 1983.

50. Class survey, Sociology 139, Prof. L. Weitzman, Stanford University, Winter 1983, co-authored by Mary E. Barton, Jacqueline Cashin, Merilyn Chapman, Lee Anne Cummings, Catherine Del Masso, Barbara Major, Yvette M. Palazuelos, and Christopher Rose. I am indebted to Patti Gumport for assistance with the statistical analysis of these data.

51. Most states require parents to support children over age eighteen with mental or physical disabilities (see, e.g., Alabama and Louisiana). A growing number of states also allow the courts to extend a child support obligation until age twenty-one (e.g., Colorado, Florida, New York, and New Jersey) if the child is not disabled but is still dependent by virtue of being a full-time student. The justification for post-majority support lies in the realistic concern that a child of eighteen is not emancipated and self-sufficient in terms of daily support and educational expenses.

52. Walter Wadlington and Monrad G. Paulsen, *Domestic Relations: 1980 Supplement* (Mineola, New York: Foundation Press, 1980), pp. 80–81.

53. *Childers v. Childers,* 89 Wash. 2d 592, P.2d 201 (1978).

54. Philip Eden, "How Inflation Flaunts the Court's Orders," *Family Advocate* Vol. 1, no. 4, Spring 1979, p. 2 (hereafter cited as Eden, "Inflation").

55. These calculations are based on the Consumer Price Index for 1975–1984 and a projection of the 1983–84 rate through 1984.

56. Ibid.

57. Eden, "Inflation," p. 4.

58. Ibid.

59. See, for example, *In re Marriage of Lamm,* 682 P.2d 67 (Colo. App. 1984); *Orman v. Orman,* 344 N.W.2d 415 (Minn. 1984); *In re Marriage of Edwards,* 99 Wash 2d 913, 665 P.2d 883 (1983).

60. *In re Marriage of Stamp,* 300 N.W.3d 375 (Iowa 1980).

61. April 1985 interview with Sue North, legislative aide to California Assemblyman Art Agnos who sponsored AB 1528 which became *California Civil Code* Section 4700.1.

62. "Child Support 1981." Along the same lines, a 1975 nationwide poll showed that only 44 percent of divorced mothers were awarded child support and that of those mothers, only 47 percent were able to collect the support regularly, 29 percent collected it "sometimes" or "rarely," and the remaining 21 percent had never collected even a single dollar of the child support the court had ordered. Barbara Bryant, *American Women Today and Tomorrow* (Washington, D.C.: National Commission on the Observance of International Women's Year, U.S. Govt Printing Office, 1977), p. 24.

63. Canadian Institute, *Matrimonial Support Failures,* p. 3

64. That is, they filed an order to show cause why their ex-spouse should not be found in contempt of court for failing to pay alimony or child support.

65. This is summarized from a more extensive review of the literature in Lenore J. Weitzman, *The Marriage Contract: Spouses, Lovers, and the Law* (New York: The Free Press, 1981).

66. The reported percentages for full compliance vary from a low of 22 percent of all fathers (in a 1973 study of AFDC fathers cited in Carol Adaire Jones, Nancy M. Gordon, and Isabel V. Sawhill, "Child Support Payments in the U.S.," *Urban Institute Working Paper* No. 992–03, 1976, p. 78), to a high of 38 percent (in a study covering the first year after the court order discussed in Kenneth Eckhardt, "Deviance, Visibility and Legal Action: The Duty to Support," *Social Problems* Vol. 15, 1968, pp. 470–77).

67. Fred H. Steininger, "Study of Divorce and Support Orders in Lake County, Indiana, 1956–1957," cited in Henry Foster and Doris Jonas Freed, *Law and the Family—New York* (Rochester, N.Y.: Lawyers Cooperative Publishing Co., 1966), p. xv.

68. U.S. Bureau of the Census, "Divorce, Child Custody, and Child Support," *Current Population Reports,* Series P–23, No. 84, June 1979, pp. 3–4.

69. Ibid.

70. Statement of Gail Forsythe, "House Hearings 1983," p. 105.

71. Ibid.

72. Nan Hunter, "Women and Child Support," in *Families, Politics, and the State,* Irene Diamond, ed. (New York: Longman, 1983), p. 209 (hereafter cited as Hunter, "Child Support").

73. 1984 Child Support Enforcement amendments to Title IV–D of the Social Security Act.

74. "House Hearings 1983," p. 277.

75. Sue Clarry, *Dissolution: A Handbook on Divorce for Santa Clara County Women* (San Jose, Calif.: National Organization for Women, San Jose–South Bay Chapter, 1979).

76. Statement of Alexis Kursteiner, "House Hearings 1983," p. 281.

77. Statement of Elaine Fromm, "House Hearings 1983," p. 111.

78. Statement of Secretary of Health and Human Services, Margaret Heckler, "House Hearings 1983.

79. Statement of Senator Paula Hawkins in Hearings before the Committee on Finance, United States Senate, Ninety-Eighth Congress, Second Session, January 24–26, 1984 (Washington, D.C.: U.S. Government Printing Office, 1984), p. 15.

80. Hunter, "Child Support," p. 209.

81. Cynthia and Allen Mondell, *Who Remembers Mama,* broadcast by P.B.S., April 18, 1979. This moving documentary on the plight of divorced women is available from Media Projects, Inc., 5215 Homer Street, Dallas, TX 75206.

82. Ibid., p. 19.

83. Ibid.

84. Canadian Institute, *Matrimonial Support Failures,* p. 20.

85. Ibid.

86. *Washington Post,* Jan. 16, 1984, editorial page.

87. The *California Civil Code* states that a noncustodial parent's duty to make child support payments is not affected by the custodial parent's frustration of visitation rights by refusing access to the child or by moving out of state. *California Civil Code,* Section 4382 (West 1983) Added by Stats. 1980, c. 237, p. 480, Section 1. The rationale for this rule is that the child should not be deprived of food and clothing because of the custodial parent's actions.

88. Interview with Joanne Schulman, staff attorney, National Center on Women and Family Law, New York City, New York, January 8, 1985.

89. These include liens, wage assignments, garnishment of wages, and contempt. California courts are also authorized to award reasonable attorneys' fees incurred in the enforcement of existing child support orders. It is significant to note that the chapter on child support in the attorney's guide to family law does not *even mention* the possibility of compliance problems. Max Goodman, "Spousal and Child Support," in *California Marital Dissolution Practice* Vol. 1, Jon A. Rantzman and Paul I. Peyrat, eds. (Berkeley, Calif.: Continuing Education of the Bar, 1981), pp. 143–184. But see Michael E. Barber's excellent chapter on "Enforcement of Orders" in Vol. 2, pp. 891–962.

90. Canadian Institute, *Matrimonial Support Failures*, p. 3.

91. Chambers, *Making Fathers Pay*, p. 101. Chambers' research is based on 13,000 case files along with interviews with fathers, ex-wives, court personnel, judges, and jail keepers (see generally, the Methodological Appendix, pp. 283–303).

92. "The Solution to Non-Support: Jail the Parent," report of David Chambers' research in *Marriage and Divorce Today*, Dec. 1977, p. 2.

93. Chambers, *Making Fathers Pay*, pp. 258–261.

94. Ibid.

95. Ibid.

96. *California Civil Code*, Section 4701(a) (West Supp. 1981) allows the judges to order a wage assignment in any case; there is no need to wait for arrearages.

97. Letter from the Honorable Rosemary Barkett, West Palm Beach, Florida, November 10, 1980, to the Judicial Education Project, NOW Legal Defense and Education Fund.

98. David Chandler, "A Florida Judge Has a Remedy for the Child-Support Problem—Jailing Fathers Who Welsh on Their Obligations," *People* Vol. 21, May 7, 1984, p. 138.

99. *California Civil Code*, Section 4701 (West Supp. 1985). As of July 1983 the law permits wage assignments when the payor is one month in arrears. The burden is still on the custodial parent to file a petition requesting the assignment. In addition, the payor must be served with the notice of her intent to seek a wage assignment fifteen days before the petition for a wage assignment may be filed.

100. Cited in *Matter of Farmer, New York Law Journal*, Jan. 16, 1984, p. 13, col. 2 (N.Y. City Family Court, 1984).

101. *LeClaire v. Le Claire*, 118 Cal. App. 3d 931 (1979).

102. Blanche Bernstein, "Shouldn't Low Income Fathers Support Their Children?" *Public Interest* Vol. 66, 1982.

103. Ibid.

104. "Public Attitudes Toward Child Support Enforcement," unpublished manuscript prepared by the Missouri Department of Social Services. James Eastman, Director, Research and Statistics, March 1982 (Submitted to Fred Schutzman, Deputy Director, Office of Child Support Enforcement, U.S. Dept. of Health and Human Services, Washington, D.C.).

105. "House Hearings, 1933," p. 28.

106. Ibid.

107. Child Support Enforcement Amendments of 1984.

108. Ibid. There are strong financial incentives for states to collect child support from nonwelfare cases because the state receives a federal incentive payment equal to 6 percent of their collections. Since nonwelfare cases are likely, in general, to involve higher amounts of child support, this is the first time that states stand to benefit from enforcement of these cases over (or in addition to) welfare case collections.

109. Ibid.

110. Ibid.

111. Statement of Margaret Heckler, press release, August 8, 1984.

112. Garfunkel and Uhr, "Approach to Child Support."

113. Anders Agell, "Paying of Maintenance in Sweden," in Canadian Institute of Law Research and Reform, *Conference Materials and Papers* for a conference on Matrimonial and Child Support, May 27–30, 1981 (Edmonton, Alberta, Canada: Institute of the Law Research and Reform, University of Alberta, October, 1982), pp. 1–24; and Anders Agell, *Underhall: Till Barn Och Make* (Uppsala, Sweden: Iustus Forlag, 1979). See also, Rita Liljeström, "Sweden," in *Family Policy: Government and Families in Fourteen Countries,* Sheila B. Kamerman and Alfred J. Kahn, eds. (New York: Columbia Univ. Press, 1978), pp. 17–48 (hereafter cited as Kamerman and Kahn, eds., *Family Policy*).

114. Nicole Questiaux and Jacques Fournier, "France," in Kamerman and Kahn, eds., *Family Policy*.

115. Garfinkel and Uhr, "Approach to Child Support."

116. Interview with Irwin Garfinkel, April 1985. See also Andree Brooks, "More Child Support Urged," *New York Times,* Feb. 22, 1985, p. 23.

117. Less than one out of five fathers seek sole physical custody. See pp. 225–227 and 256–257 in Chapter 8.

118. Jessica Pearson found that "husbands who contested custody wound up paying less child support than their noncontesting counterparts. In such cases, child support payments were both absolutely lower than payments made by husbands who did not contest custody and also comprised a smaller proportion of the husband's gross monthly income." Pearson concludes that her findings lend "some support to claims that one of the covert goals of custody litigation is to minimize a man's financial liability. Particularly in cases of contested child custody, child support orders were found to routinely fall below minimum standards established by social welfare agencies and the courts alike. It is sad but ironic that the most fought over children appear to face the most disadvantaged financial situation following their parents' divorce." Jessica Pearson, "Summary of Research," prepared for the Wingspread Conference Child Custody, Sponsored by the Women's Legal Defense Fund, March, 1984, p. 3.

119. Nancy Polikoff, "Gender and Child-Custody Determinations: Exploding the Myths," in *Families, Politics and Public Policies: A Feminist Dialogue on Women and the State,* Irene Diamond, ed. (New York: Longman, 1983), p. 195.

120. Henry H. Foster, Jr. and Doris Jonas Freed, "Law and the Family: Politics of Divorce Process—Bargaining Leverage, Unfair Edge," *New York Law Journal* Vol. 192, no. 7, July 11, 1984, p. 6 (hereafter cited as Foster and Freed, "Bargaining Leverage").

121. Ibid.

122. *Garska v. McCoy,* 278 S.E.2d 357, 361 (W.Va. 1981).

123. Ibid.

124. Carol Gilligan, *In a Different Voice* (Cambridge, Mass.: Harvard University Press, 1983).

125. These issues are explored in more depth in Robert Mnookin, "Divorce Bargaining: The Limits on Private Ordering," in *The Resolution of Family Conflict: Comparative Legal Perspectives,* John M. Eekelaar and Sanford N. Katz, eds. (Toronto: Butterworths, 1984) and Robert Mnookin and Lewis Kornhauser, "Bargaining in the Shadow of the Law: The Case of Divorce" *Yale Law Journal* Vol. 88, 1979, p. 88.

126. The experiences of women whose husbands refused to pay alimony are discussed in pp. 160–163, Chapter 6.

127. Foster and Freed "Bargaining Leverage," p. 6.

128. Judith S. Wallerstein and Joan Kelly, *Surviving the Breakup: How Children and Parents Cope with Divorce* (New York: Basic Books, 1980).

129. Ibid., p. 22.

130. Ibid.

131. Ibid., p. 231.

132. Ibid., p. 25.

133. Ibid.

134. Ibid.

135. Ibid., p. 183.

136. Ibid., p. 42.

137. Ibid.

138. Ibid., p. 231.

139. Ibid.

140. E. Mavis Hetherington, "Children and Divorce" in *Parent–Child Interaction: Theory, Research and Prospects,* R. W. Henderson (ed.) (New York: Academic Press, 1981).

141. Cassetty, *Parental Child-Support,* p. 3.

142. Ibid.

143. Testimony of Dan Coats, "House Hearings 1983," p. 84.

CHAPTER 10—ECONOMIC CONSEQUENCES

1. These assumptions are discussed in Chapters 6 and 7 on alimony awards, pp. 157–158, 165–166, 176–177 in Chapter 6, and pp. 184–187, 197, 204–206, in Chapter 7.

2. See Chapter 7, pp. 206, 209, and Chapter 6, 165–169.

3. The special problems that older women face at divorce are discussed in Chapter 7, pp. 187–194, 198–201, 209–212.

4. The issue of support for dependent children over eighteen is discussed in Chapter 9, pp. 278–281.

5. The study is discussed in Chapter 9, p. 279.

6. *In re Marriage of Rosan,* 24 Cal. App. 3d 855, 101 Cal. Rptr. 295 (1972); *In re Marriage of Brantner,* 67 Cal. App. 3d 416, 136 Cal. Rptr. 635 (1977);

In re Marriage of Morrison, 20 Cal. 3d 437, 143 Cal. Rptr. 139, 573 P.2d 41 (1978). See also Lillian B. Rubin, *Women of Certain Age* (New York: Harper and Row, 1979) and Janet Zollinger Giele, *Women in the Middle Years* (New York: Wiley, 1982).

7. *In re Marriage of Andreen,* 76 Cal. App. 3d 667, 143 Cal. Rptr. 94 (1978).

8. This finding is also reported by E. Mavis Hetherington, Martha Cox, and Roger Cox, "The Aftermath of Divorce," in *Mother–Child, Father–Child Relations,* J. H. Stevens, Jr. and M. Mathews, eds. (Washington, D.C.: NAEYC, 1977) (hereafter cited as Hetherington et al., "Aftermath of Divorce").

9. Prudence Brown and Hanna Fox, "Sex Differences in Divorce," in *Gender and Disordered Behavior: Sex Differences in Psychopathology,* Edith S. Gomberg and Violet Franks, eds. (New York: Brunner/Mazel, 1979), pp. 113–114.

10. Judith Wallerstein and Joan Kelly, *Surviving the Breakup: How Parents and Children Cope with Divorce* (New York: Basic Books, 1980), p. 23 (hereafter cited as Wallerstein and Kelly, *Surviving the Breakup*).

11. Robert S. Weiss, *Marital Separation* (New York: Basic Books, 1975).

12. "Report of NOW Conference on Marriage and Divorce," *New York Times,* Jan. 21, 1974, p. 232, cols. 7–8. See also Betty Friedan, *It Changed My Life* (New York: Random House, 1976).

13. Saul Hoffman and John Holmes, "Husbands, Wives, and Divorce," in *Five Thousand American Families—Patterns of Economic Progress* (Ann Arbor, Mich.: Institute for Social Research, 1976), p. 24 (hereafter cited as Hoffman and Holmes, "Divorce").

14. Ibid., p. 27 (Table 2.1), p. 31 (Table 2.2). Hoffman and Holmes are frequently cited as showing that divorced men have only a 10 percent decline in real money income. While this figure is shown in Table 2.1, it is based on the husband's total postdivorce income before alimony and/or child support is paid. Once these support payments are deducted from the husband's income, husbands experience a 19 percent decline in real income.

15. Ibid., p. 27 (Table 2.1).

16. This index, which is based on the Department of Agriculture's "Low-Cost Food Budget," adjusted for the size, age, and sex composition of the family, is described in note 19, below.

17. Hoffman and Holmes, "Divorce," p. 27 (Table 2.1). This is closer to the rate of improvement of married couples who improved their standard of living by 21 percent. (Note that their income rose 22 percent, but their income in relation to needs rose 21 percent.)

18. Ibid., p. 31 (Table 2.2).

19. We assumed that the basic needs level for each family was the Lower Standard Budget devised by the Bureau of Labor Statistics, U.S. Department of Labor, *Three Standards of Living for an Urban Family of Four Persons* (1967). This budget is computed for a four-person urban family (husband and wife and two children) and kept current by frequent adjustments. See,

e.g., McCraw, "Medical Care Costs Lead Rise in 1976–77 Family Budgets," *Monthly Labor Review,* Nov. 1978, p. 33. A Labor Department report devised a method for adjusting this standard budget to other types of families, depending on family size, age of oldest child, and age of head of household. Bureau of Labor Statistics, U.S. Department of Labor, *Revised Equivalence Scale for Estimating Equivalent Incomes or Budget Costs by Family Type,* Bulletin No. 1570–2 (1968). For example, the needs of a family of two persons (husband and wife) with the head of household of age thirty-five was calculated at 60 percent of the base figure for a Lower Standard Budget.

A Lower Standard Budget was calculated for each family in our interview sample three different ways: once for the predivorce family, once for the wife's postdivorce family, and once for the husband's postdivorce family. The income over needs for each family was then computed. Membership in postdivorce families of husbands and wives included a new spouse or cohabitor (where applicable), and any children whose custody was assigned to that spouse. I am indebted to my research assistant, David Lineweber, for programming this analysis.

20. Robert S. Weiss, "The Impact of Marital Dissolution on Income and Consumption in Single-Parent Households," *Journal of Marriage and the Family* Vol. 46, February 1984, pp. 115–127; Thomas Espenshade, "The Economic Consequences of Divorce," *Journal of Marriage and the Family,* Vol. 41, August 1979, pp. 615–625.

Similar results in California are reported by Marilyn Little, "Divorce and the Feminization of Poverty," paper presented at the meetings of Sociologists for Women in Society, American Sociological Association, August 30, 1983. See also Ruth A. Brandwein, Carole A. Brown, and E. M. Fox, "Women and Children Lost: The Social Situation of Divorced Mothers and Their Families," *Journal of Marriage and the Family* Vol. 36, 1974, pp. 498–514.

21. Bureau of the Census, U.S. Dept. of Commerce, "Money Income of Families and Persons in the United States: 1979," *Current Population Reports* Series P–60, No. 129, 1981, p. 23.

22. Bureau of the Census, U.S. Dept. of Commerce, "Families Maintained by Female Householders 1970–79," *Current Population Reports* Series P–23, No. 107, 1980, p. 36.

23. National Center on Women and Family Law, "Sex and Economic Discrimination in Child Custody Awards," *Clearinghouse Review* Vol. 16, no. 11, April 1983, p. 1132.

24. Angus Campbell, Philip E. Converse, and Willard L. Rodgers, *The Quality of American Life: Perceptions, Evaluations, and Satisfactions* (New York: Russell Sage Foundation, 1976), pp. 420 and 404, Table 12–5.

25. Ibid., p. 404, Table 12–5.

26. Ibid., p. 398, Table 12–2, pp. 420, 421.

27. Ann Goetting, "Divorce Outcome Research: Issues and Perspectives," in *The Family In Transition,* Fourth Edition, Arlene S. Skolnick and Jerome H. Skolnick, eds. (Boston: Little Brown & Co., 1983), p. 369 (reprinted from *Journal of Family Issues* Vol. 2, no. 3, Sept. 1981), pp. 350–378. (hereafter

cited as Goetting, "Divorce Outcomes," with page citations to the Skolnick volume).

28. Hetherington et al., "Aftermath of Divorce."

29. "Living Alone: Do Today's Independent Lifestyles Reflect A Trend Toward Social Isolation And A Consequent Threat to Health And Well-being?" *Institute for Social Research Newsletter* (Ann Arbor, Mich.: University of Michigan, August 1984), pp. 3–4.

30. Ibid., pp. 3–4.

31. Ibid., p. 4.

32. T. Holmes and R. Rahe, "The Social Readjustment Rating Scale," *Journal of Psychosomatic Research* Vol. 11, 1967, pp. 213–218. See generally, Bruce Dohrenwend, "Social Status and Stressful Life Events," *Journal of Personality and Social Psychology* Vol. 28, 1973.

33. D. Landbrook, "The Wealth and Survival of the Divorced," *Conciliation Courts Review* Vol. 14, 1976, pp. 21–33.

34. Bernard L. Bloom, Shirley J. Asher, and Stephen W. White, "Marital Disruption as a Stressor: A Review and Analysis," *Psychological Bulletin* Vol. 85, 1978, pp. 867–894.

35. Goetting, "Divorce Outcomes," pp. 370–72.

36. James J. Lynch, *The Broken Heart: The Medical Consequences of Loneliness in America* (New York: Basic Books, 1977).

    Ann Goetting cautions that a lot of this research does not control for social class: "Since both poor health and high mortality on the one hand, and divorce on the other, are more common among the lower than the higher socioeconomic classes, the relationship between health and divorce may be at least partly due to factors associated with social class." Goetting, "Divorce Outcomes," p. 370.

37. Bruce P. Dohrenwend and Barbara S. Dohrenwend, *Social Status and Psychological Disorder* (New York: Wiley, 1969); Jerome Myers, Jacob Lindenthal, and M. Pepper, "Social Class, Life Events, and Psychiatric Symptoms: A Longitudinal Study." Paper presented at Conference on Stressful Life Events, New York, June 1973.

38. P. Berkman, "Spouseless motherhood, psychological stress, and physical morbidity," *Journal of Health and Social Behavior* Vol. 10, 1969, p. 330.

39. Prudence Brown, "Psychological Distress and Personal Growth among Women Coping with Marital Dissolution," doctoral dissertation, University of Michigan, 1976. *Dissertation Abstracts International* Vol. 37, 1976, pp. 947–8. Gay Kitson and Marvin M. Sussman, "The Process of Marital Separation and Divorce: Male and Female Similarities and Differences," Unpublished paper, Case Western Reserve University, Cleveland, Ohio, November 1976.

40. Jane R. Chapman and Gordon Chapman, "Poverty Viewed as a Woman's Problem—the U.S. Case," in *Women and the World of Work,* Anne Hoiberg, ed. (New York: Plenum, 1982).

41. Diana Pearce, "The Feminization of Poverty: Women, Work and Welfare," *Urban and Social Change Review,* Feb. 1978; and Diana Pearce and Har-

riette McAdoo, "Women and Children: Alone and in Poverty" (Washington, D.C.: National Advisory Council on Economic Opportunity, September 1981), p. 1 (hereafter cited as Pearce and McAdoo, "Women and Children in Poverty").

42. House Hearings on Child Support Enforcement legislation before the subcommittee on Public Assistance and Unemployment Compensation of the Committee on Ways and Means of the U.S. House of Representatives on July 14, 1983, p. 13. (Washington, D.C.: U.S. Government Printing Office, 1984) (hereafter cited as House Hearings 1983).

43. Ibid.

44. Barbara Ehrenreich and Francis Fox Piven, "The Feminization of Poverty: When the Family Wage System Breaks Down," *Dissent,* 1984, p. 162 (hereafter cited as Ehrenreich and Piven, "Feminization of Poverty").

45. National Advisory Council on Economic Opportunity, *Critical Choices for the '80s,* August 1980, p. 1 (Washington, D.C.: National Advisory Council, 1980).

46. Ibid.

47. Christopher Jencks, "Divorced Mothers, Unite", *Psychology Today,* November 1982, pp. 73–75 (hereafter cited as Jencks, "Divorced Mothers").

48. Ehrenreich and Piven, "Feminization of Poverty," p. 163.

49. Ibid., p. 162; Pearce and McAdoo, "Women and Children in Poverty"; Heather L. Ross and Isabel V. Sawhill, *Time of Transition: The Growth of Families Headed by Women* (Washington, D.C.: The Urban Institute Press, 1975).

50. Pearce and McAdoo, "Women and Children in Poverty," pp. 6, 18.

51. Briefing paper prepared for California Assemblyman Thomas H. Bates for hearings on "The Feminization of Poverty," San Francisco, Calif., April 8, 1983, mimeo, p. 6 (hereafter cited as Bates brief).

52. Ibid. Pearce and McAdoo, "Women and Children in Poverty."

53. See generally, Pearce and McAdoo, "Women and Children in Poverty," and Ehrenreich and Piven, "Feminization of Poverty."

54. Child care is clearly one of the most fundamental needs of single mothers, and yet, in 1983, fully 84 percent of the working mothers were *not* able to obtain government-licensed child care for their children. California Commission on the Status of Women, Briefing Paper for hearings on the Feminization of Poverty conducted by California Assemblyman Thomas H. Bates, April 8, 1983.

55. Ehrenreich and Piven, "Feminization of Poverty."

56. Samuel H. Preston, "Children and the Elderly: Divergent Paths for American's Dependents," Presidential address to the Population Association to be published in *Demography* Vol. 21, no. 4, forthcoming, citing Bureau of the Census, U.S. Dept. of Commerce, "Money Income and Poverty Status 1982," *Current Population Reports* Series P–60, No. 140, 1983. Citations that follow are to pages in the Preston manuscript.

57. Ibid., p. 15.

58. Interview with Dr. Arthur Norton, March, 1984.

59. Sandra Hofferth, "Updating Children's Life Course," Center for Population Research, National Institute for Child Health and Development, 1983.

60. Wallerstein and Kelly, *Surviving the Breakup,* p. 231.

61. Ibid.

62. See Chapter 9, pp. 283–284, citing Bureau of the Census, "Child Support and Alimony, 1981," *Current Population Reports,* Series P–23, No. 124.

63. House Hearings 1983, p. 27.

64. Children's Defense Fund, *American Children in Poverty* (Washington, D.C.: Children's Defense Fund, 1984).

65. Ibid.

66. Goetting, "Divorce Outcomes," and Nicholas Zil and James Peterson, "Trends in the Behavior and Emotional Well-Being of U.S. Children," Paper given at the 1982 Annual Meeting of the Association for the Advancement of Science, Washington, D.C., 1982.

67. William F. Hodges, Carol W. Tierney, and Helen K. Bushbaum, "The Cumulative Effect of Stress on Preschool Children of Divorced and Intact Families," *Journal of Marriage and the Family* Vol. 46, no. 3, August 1984, pp. 611–629, 614.

68. Ibid.

69. Ibid., citing their earlier work.

70. Jencks, "Divorced Mothers."

71. Ibid.

CHAPTER 11—DIVORCE AND THE ILLUSION OF EQUALITY

1. Herma Hill Kay, "A Family Court: The California Proposal," in *Divorce and After,* Paul Bohannan, ed. (New York: Doubleday, 1970), p. 248.

2. See generally, Leo Kanowitz, *Women and the Law* (Albuquerque, New Mexico: University of New Mexico Press, 1969); Barbara A. Babcock, Ann E. Freedman, Eleanor Holmes Norton, Susan D. Ross, *Sex Discrimination and the Law: Causes and Remedies* (Boston: Little Brown & Co., 1975); Herma Hill Kay, *Sex-Based Discrimination in Family Law* (St. Paul, Minn.: West Publishing Co., 1974); and Lenore J. Weitzman, *The Marriage Contract: Spouses, Lovers, and the Law* (New York: The Free Press, 1983).

3. Custody awards are discussed in detail in Chapter 8, pp. 215–261.

4. The division of property is discussed in Chapter 4, pp. 70–109. For the effects of these awards, see also Chapter 5, on the New Property, pp. 110–142, and Chapter 10 on The Economic Consequences of Divorce, pp. 323–356.

5. The forced sale of the family home is discussed in Chapter 4, pp. 78–96.

6. The forced sale of the home after a lengthy marriage is discussed in Chapter 4, pp. 80–83, 92–96. See also Chapter 10, pp. 334–336.

7. The new property and its treatment at divorce is discussed in Chapter 5, pp. 110–142.

8. Betty Friedan, *It Changed My Life* (New York: Random House, 1976), p. 325 (hereafter cited as Friedan, *It Changed My Life*).

9. This was the assumption of the divorced men and women we interviewed. See pp. 150–163, especially 159 in Chapter 6 and pp. 190, 193 in Chapter 7.

10. Friedan, *It Changed My Life*, p. 326.

11. Women's willingness to forego support or property when threatened with the loss of custody is discussed in Chapter 9, pp. 310–318.

12. Ibid.

13. Joint custody is discussed in Chapter 8, pp. 245–258.

14. This may be true even if the award is labeled joint physical custody. See p. 250.

15. The data, however, suggested that men with joint custody are *not* more likely to pay child support. See p. 255.

16. The data on alimony awards are discussed in Chapter 6, pp. 164–180.

17. The difficulties women have collecting court-ordered support are discussed in Chapter 9 on child support, pp. 283–295.

18. The changes in men's and women's standards of living after divorce are shown in Figure 3, p. 338 and discussed on pp. 337–343 of Chapter 10.

19. The low value of community property is discussed in Chapter 3, pp. 54–61. The forced sale of the family home is discussed in Chapter 4, pp. 78–96.

20. These census data are discussed in Chapter 9 on child support, pp. 283–284.

21. The aims of the California reformers and a brief history of the no-fault law are discussed in Chapter 2, pp. 16–19.

22. Ibid. See also, Herma Hill Kay, "The California Background," unpublished paper written for the California Divorce Law Research Project, Center for the Study of Law and Society, University of California, Berkeley, September 1977 (on file at the author's office in the Boalt Hall School of Law, University of California, Berkeley) (hereafter cited as Kay "California Background").

23. Ibid.

24. The belief that the community property system protected women is discussed in Chapter 4, pp. 71–72.

25. The aims of the legal reformers are discussed in Chapter 2, pp. 17–19 and pp. 20–40.

26. See Chapter 2, p. 17 and note 10, and Kay "California Background," p. 21.

27. The reasons for the perpetration of the alimony myth are discussed in Chapter 6, pp. 180–182.

28. Under the old law, before no-fault, the wife was typically awarded the family home. See Chapter 4, pp. 78–79.

29. Women's loss of bargaining leverage under the no-fault–no-consent rules is discussed in Chapter 2, pp. 26–31.

30. This point is made by attorney Riane Eisler, who notes that the California law was changed *before* the feminist movement began to have an impact:

> It has been said, sometimes even by the men drafting these laws, that no-fault is a product of women's liberation, or of what some people call the "male backlash." But the first no-fault divorce laws in this country were passed in California early in 1969, by an almost all-male legislature, before most people had even heard of the women's liberation movement.

Dissolution: No-Fault Divorce, Marriage and the Future of Women (New York: McGraw-Hill, 1977) p. 11. I am indebted to Mary Sylvester who checked twelve sources on the legal history of the California legal reform and was unable to find any mention of feminist participation or women's issues, with the exception of the Eisler observation quoted above and Professor Kay's statement that no organized women's groups participated. Kay, "The California Background," pp. 78, 79.

31. Kay, "The California Background," p. 45.

32. Ibid., pp. 79–80.

33. Assembly Committee Report on Assembly Bill No. 530 and Senate Bill No. 252 (The Family Law Act) submitted by Committee on the Judiciary, James A. Hayes, Chairman, August 8, 1969, printed in *Assembly Daily Journal* (Sacramento, California, Aug. 8, 1969).

34. The traditional law of marriage and divorce is discussed in Chapter 1.

35. The grounds for divorce and the barriers they created are discussed in Chapter 1, pp. 7–10.

36. The major features of the no-fault reforms are discussed in Chapter 2, pp. 20–40. The trends throughout the United States are discussed on pp. 41–51.

37. This is the underlying theme of the changes discussed in Chapter 2, pp. 20–28.

38. The shift from moral to economic criteria is discussed in Chapter 2, pp. 22–26 and 28–31.

39. No-consent rules are discussed on pp. 26–28.

40. The data on the shift from permanent to short-term transitional alimony awards are discussed in Chapter 6, pp. 164–167. The trends in other states are discussed in Chapter 2, pp. 45–46.

41. See Chapter 6, pp. 165–166.

42. No-fault's impact on home sales is discussed in Chapter 4, pp. 78–84 and pp. 84–96, where the treatment of the family home in California is compared to that in England.

43. The judges' negative attitudes towards a delayed sale of the family home are discussed in Chapter 4, pp. 81, 84.

44. Noncompliance with alimony awards is discussed in Chapter 6, pp. 160–162 and Chapter 7, p. 192. Noncompliance with child support awards is

discussed on pp. 283–295 and the attitudes of judges and attorneys are reviewed on pp. 300–306 in Chapter 9.

45. The California judges' attitudes towards wage assignments are discussed on pp. 292–293 and 302–303 in Chapter 9 on child support.

46. See pp. 259–260 in Chapter 8, discussing the data from Frank F. Furstenburg, Christine W. Nord, James L. Peterson, and Nicholas Zill, "The Life Course of Children of Divorce: Marital Disruption and Parental Contact," *American Sociological Review* Vol. 48, October 1983, pp. 656–668.

47. The data on child support awards are reviewed on pp. 264–278, and the data on noncompliance are reviewed on pp. 283–285, both in Chapter 9.

48. Samuel H. Preston, "Children and the Elderly: Divergent Paths for America's Dependents," *Demography* Vol. 21, no. 4, November 1984, pp. 435–457.

49. The decline of the maternal presumption and the effects of "best interest" standards and joint custody preferences are discussed in Chapter 8. See especially pp. 239–243 and 247–248.

50. The incentives the new laws provide for men to divorce are discussed in Chapter 2, pp. 25, 27–35, in Chapter 10, p. 330 and, by implication, on pp. 330–343 where the income and standards of living of men and women after divorce are compared.

51. Chapter 10 shows that husbands are much better off than their former wives in higher-income families. See tables on pp. 326, 328, 333, and 338, and accompanying text.

52. This is most clearly reflected in alimony awards, or rather, the absence of alimony awards to housewives. See Chapter 6, pp. 176–178 and Chapter 7, pp. 187–194. The importance of sharing concepts is discussed in Chapter 6, pp. 152–156 and 158–159.

53. As we saw in Chapter 6, once a woman earns $10,000 a year she is presumed to be self-sufficient and not in need of alimony. See pp. 178–180.

54. Only 17 percent of the divorced women are awarded alimony. See Chapter 6, pp. 167–168.

55. The average child support award is the equivalent of $216 a month for one child and $337 a month for two children in 1984 dollars. See Chapter 9, pp. 265–266. Less than half of the fathers fully comply with child support orders. See Chapter 9, pp. 283–285.

56. This is in part explained by the minimal amount of property that most divorcing couples own. See Chapter 3, on the value of the marital property, especially pp. 54–61, and Chapter 4, pp. 104–106, on the results of the equal division rule.

57. The treatment of older women is discussed in Chapter 7, pp. 187–194 and 198–203; in Chapter 4, pp. 80–83; and in Chapter 10, pp. 330–336.

58. The treatment of mothers of young children is discussed in Chapter 7, pp. 184–187, 195–198 and 201–203.

59. The issue of support for dependent children over eighteen is discussed in Chapter 9, pp. 278–281.

60. College-age children are more likely to turn to their mothers for support. See Chapter 9, p. 279.

61. See, for example, the treatment of older housewives in alimony awards in Chapter 7, pp. 187–194, in property awards and the forced sale of the home in Chapter 4, pp. 80–83, and in their standard of living after divorce on pp. 330–336 in Chapter 10.

62. Shirley Johnson, "The Economic Position of Divorced Women," *Fairshare*, 1985, forthcoming.

63. Ibid.

64. Barbara Ehrenreich offers a fascinating explanation for the recent "flight from commitment": it was men, she argues, who first rebelled against their traditional sex roles and abandoned the breadwinner ethic for the individualism of the "me" generation. See Barbara Ehrenreich, *The Hearts of Men* (Garden City, New York: Anchor Press/Doubleday, 1983).

65. See, for example, Christopher Lasch, *The Culture of Narcissism* (New York: Norton, 1979).

66. Arlene S. Skolnick, *The Intimate Environment: Exploring Marriage and The Family,"* third edition (Boston: Little Brown, 1983), p. 22 (hereafter cited as Skolnick, *Intimate Environment*).

67. William J. Goode, *World Revolution in Family Patterns* (New York: The Free Press, 1963), pp. 6–7.

68. Skolnick, *Intimate Environment*, p. 22.

69. Lawrence Stone, *The Family, Sex and Marriage in England, 1500–1800* (New York: Harper and Row, 1977).

70. Ibid. For a summary of Stone's thesis, see Lawrence Stone, "The Historical Origins of the Modern Family," The O. Meredith Wilson Lecture in History published by the Dept. of History, University of Utah, Salt Lake City, Utah, 1982, pp. 11–12.

71. Pepper Schwartz, master lecture presented at the National Council on Family Relations, October 18, 1984, drawing on data from Philip Blumstein and Pepper W. Schwartz, *American Couples: Money, Work, Sex* (New York: William Morrow & Co., 1983).

72. The importance of sharing concepts in alimony is seen in the attitudes reported in Chapter 6, pp. 151–156 and 158–159.

73. Mary Ann Glendon, *The New Family and The New Property* (Toronto: Butterworths, 1981).

74. Ibid.

75. Ibid.

76. William J. Goode, "Individual Investments in the Family Collectivity," *The Tocqueville Review* Vol. 6, no. 1, Summer 1984.

77. Ibid.

78. The income-sharing approach for child support awards is discussed in Chapter 9, pp. 269, 272–276.

79. Cost of living adjustments for support awards are discussed in Chapter 9, pp. 281–283.

80. These enforcement techniques are discussed in Chapter 9, pp. 302–309.

81. Support for dependent children over 18 is discussed in Chapter 9, pp. 278–281.

82. The reluctance of California judges to delay the sale of the home in the interests of minor children is discussed in Chapter 4, pp. 78–84, especially pp. 84, and 86–92.

83. The primary caretaker standard for child custody is discussed in Chapter 8, pp. 244–245. Joint custody upon mutual consent is discussed in Chapter 8, pp. 245–246.

84. The situation of the long-married housewife is discussed in several chapters. See, for example, Chapters 6 and 7 on alimony awards, pp. 170–171, pp. 187–194 and 198–203; Chapter 4 on property, pp. 80–83; Chapter 10 on standards of living after divorce, pp. 330–336.

85. The importance of sharing concepts in alimony awards is discussed in Chapter 6, pp. 152–156 and 158–159.

86. See Chapter 5, pp. 135–139, for the problems older women face in securing medical insurance.

87. See pages 80–83 in Chapter 4 on the forced sale of the family home and the eviction of long-married housewives, and pp. 92–96 for the comparison with the English protections for older housewives.

88. Proposals for postdivorce support for young mothers are discussed in more detail in Chapter 7, pp. 207–209.

89. Their perceptions of the injustice of the new standards are discussed in Chapter 6, pp. 158–159, 173–174, and in Chapter 7, pp. 190, 210.

90. Attitudes toward the no-fault reforms are discussed in Chapter 2, pp. 20–28, 38–40.

91. Attitudes toward the equal division rule are discussed in Chapter 4, pp. 103–104.

92. Ibid.

93. The limited data on property awards in equitable distribution states is discussed in Chapter 4, pp. 106–108.

94. Dissatisfaction with the forced sale of the family home was expressed by 40 percent of the attorneys. (See Chapter 4, p. 79.)

95. These cases are discussed in Chapter 4, pp. 79–84.

96. The law and legal practice regarding delayed sale of the family home are discussed in Chapter 4, pp. 79–84 and 86–96.

97. See Chapter 4, pp. 78–84, especially p. 84, and 86–92, especially 90–91.

98. Alternative options for awards of the equity in the family home are discussed in Chapter 4, pp. 84, 88–92.

99. This problem is discussed on pp. 88–89 in Chapter 4.

100. The detrimental effects of prolonged conflict on children are discussed in Chapter 8, p. 254.

101. As we saw in Chapter 9, the current laws are open to this type of abuse. See pp. 310–318.

102. Ibid. and pp. 242–243.
103. The division of the home equity at divorce with a note to the noncustodial parent is discussed in Chapter 4, pp. 83–84, 90–91.
104. The 1984 child support enforcement legislation explicitly approves of the use of property as security to ensure child support payments.
105. This would avoid the hardships discussed on pp. 80–82 in Chapter 4.
106. This is similar to the standard the English legal experts used to assure adequate and comparable housing for the older housewife. See Chapter 4, pp. 93–94.
107. Career assets are discussed in detail in Chapter 5, pp. 110–142.
108. The impact of career assets on the division of property is reviewed in Chapter 5, pp. 110–111, 141–142.
109. Pension and retirement benefits are discussed on pp. 113–121 in Chapter 5.
110. Compensation for spousal contributions to a professional education is discussed on pp. 124–135 in Chapter 5.
111. Medical and dental insurance are discussed on pp. 135–139 in Chapter 5.
112. The current standards for alimony awards are discussed on pp. 147–150 in Chapter 6.
113. Alimony awards to mothers of preschool children are discussed on pp. 184–187 in Chapter 7.
114. Judges' attitudes towards alimony for young mothers are discussed on pp. 186–187 in Chapter 7.
115. Alimony awards to long-married wives are discussed on pp. 187–194 in Chapter 7. (See also pp. 169–171 in Chapter 6.)
116. The amount of alimony awarded is discussed on pp. 171–174 in Chapter 6.
117. The shift from permanent to short-term alimony awards is discussed on pp. 164–167 in Chapter 6.
118. See pp. 165–167.
119. See pp. 146–149.
120. See, for example, Figure 1, p. 273 and Table 28, p. 333 on the consequences of the current apportionment of postdivorce family income.
121. In Chapter 3 we saw that earning capacity and income are, in fact, worth more than the tangible assets of the marriage.
122. The dismal employment prospects of these women are discussed on pp. 209–212 in Chapter 7.
123. These proposals are discussed on pp. 207–209 in Chapter 7.
124. Ibid.
125. The income-sharing approach is discussed on pp. 269, 272–276 in Chapter 9.
126. Interview with Susan Paikin, Delaware Family Court, August 1984, and p. 310.
127. Support for dependent children over eighteen is discussed on pp. 278–281 in Chapter 9.

128. See pp. 279–280 in Chapter 9.
129. Cost-of-living adjustments for support awards are discussed on pp. 281–283 in Chapter 9.
130. The importance of enforcement is underscored by the discussion of the difficulties women reported in collecting child support on pp. 284–295 in Chapter 9.
131. See Table 25, p. 296.
132. The problems in the present system of enforcement are discussed on pp. 283–309 in Chapter 9.
133. The Swedish system is discussed on pp. 309–310 in Chapter 9. See also Anders Agell, "Paying of Maintenance in Sweden," 1981. Paper presented at the International Conference on Matrimonial and Child Support, May 27–30, 1981, The Institute of Law Research and Reform (Edmonton, Alberta, Canada: University of Alberta, 1982) (hereafter cited as Agell, "Maintenance").
134. See generally Chapter 9, pp. 283–309.
135. The 1984 child support enforcement law is discussed on pp. 307–309 in Chapter 9.
136. Judges' reluctance to order wage assignments is discussed on pp. 292–293, 302–303, the "forgiving of arrearages," on p. 293, and their use of repeated warnings instead of jail, on pp. 305–306, all in Chapter 9.
137. The Michigan system is discussed on pp. 298–299. See also, David Chambers, *Making Fathers Pay* (Chicago: University of Chicago Press, 1979).
138. Report of John Schambre, Program Specialist, Office of Child Support Enforcement, Region IX, San Francisco, at Hawaii Child Support Enforcement Judicial Education Seminar, January 18, 1985.
139. The changes in child custody laws and the patterns of custody awards are reviewed in Chapter 8, pp. 215–261. See p. 257 for summary table.
140. Women's willingness to compromise their financial claims for custody is discussed on pp. 310–318 in Chapter 9.
141. This position is asserted in Joseph Goldstein, Anna Freud, and Albert J. Solnit, *Beyond the Best Interests of the Child* (New York: The Free Press, 1973) and Nancy D. Polikoff, "Gender and Child Custody Determinations: Exploding the Myths," in *Families, Politics and Public Policy: A Feminist Dialogue on Women and the State,* Irene Diamond, ed. (New York: Longman, 1983), pp. 183–202.
142. See pp. 233–235 in Chapter 8 on custodial "agreements" and pp. 310–318 in Chapter 9 on male-female differences in negotiations on custody and support.
143. The primary caretaker presumption is discussed on pp. 244–245 in Chapter 8.
144. The best interest standard is discussed on pp. 231–243 in Chapter 8.
145. The difficulties that arise from laws that permit joint custody without both partners' agreement are discussed on pp. 246–247 in Chapter 8.
146. Personal interview on file at author's office.
147. Agell, "Maintenance."

148. Ibid.

149. Sheila B. Kamerman and Alfred J. Kahn, "Child Support: Some International Developments," in *The Parental Child-Support Obligation,* Judith Cassetty, ed. (Lexington, Mass.: D. C. Heath and Co., 1983), pp. 227–239.

150. Judges' attitudes towards wage attachments are discussed on pp. 292–293 and 302–303 in Chapter 9.

151. See p. 293 and p. 302 on forgiving arrearages.

152. See pp. 188–189 on judges' assumptions about women's earning capacities.

153. See, for example, Figure 1 on p. 273 and the responses to the Byrd case (pp. 264–267) for judges' division of a typical family's income.

154. See pp. 97–101 in Chapter 4 on the disposition of a family business.

155. See pp. 81–92 in Chapter 4 on the disposition of the family home.

156. See pp. 97–101 in Chapter 4.

157. See pp. 123–124 in Chapter 5 for judges' attitudes toward goodwill.

158. See pp. 81–84 in Chapter 4 on judges' refusal to delay the sale of the family home for older housewives.

159. See pp. 232–243, Chapter 10.

160. See Figure 3, p. 338, Chapter 10.

161. See Table 28, p. 333, Chapter 10.

162. The effects of divorce on children are discussed on pp. 318–321 in Chapter 9, and pp. 352–354 in Chapter 10.

APPENDIX A—RESEARCH METHODS

1. California Statutes, 1977, Chapter 676, Section 6.

2. See, for example, Graham B. Spanier and Linda Thompson, *Parting: The Aftermath of Separation and Divorce* (Beverly Hills, Ca: Sage Publications, 1984), p. 22 (hereafter cited as Spanier and Thompson, *Parting*); and Judith S. Wallerstein and Joan B. Kelly, *Surviving the Breakup: How Children and Parents Cope with Divorce* (New York: Basic Books, 1980), p. 321.

3. Spanier and Thompson, *Parting,* p. 22.

4. Lenore J. Weitzman, *Social Suicide: A Study of Missing Persons,* Ph.D. dissertation, Department of Sociology, Columbia University, 1970.

5. Spanier and Thompson, *Parting,* p. 22.

6. Ibid.

Index